ITIL® Service Design

London: TSO

information & publishing solutions

Published by TSO (The Stationery Office) and available from:

Online
www.tsoshop.co.uk

Mail, Telephone, Fax & E-mail
TSO
PO Box 29, Norwich, NR3 1GN
Telephone orders/General enquiries: 0870 600 5522
Fax orders: 0870 600 5533
E-mail: customer.services@tso.co.uk
Textphone: 0870 240 3701

TSO@Blackwell and other Accredited Agents
Customers can also order publications from:
TSO Ireland
16 Arthur Street, Belfast BT1 4GD
Tel: 028 9023 8451 Fax: 028 9023 5401

First edition Crown Copyright 2007
Second edition Crown Copyright 2011

First published 2011

ISBN 9780113313051

Printed in the United Kingdom for The Stationery Office

Material is FSC certified and produced using ECF pulp.
Sourced from fully sustainable forests.

P002425498   c70   07/11

Contents

List of figures

List of tables

Foreword

Back in the 1980s no one truly understood IT service management (ITSM), although it was clear that it was a concept that needed to be explored. Hence a UK government initiative was instigated and ITIL® was born. Over the years, ITIL has evolved and, arguably, is now the most widely adopted approach in ITSM.

It is globally recognized as the best-practice framework. ITIL's universal appeal is that it continues to provide a set of processes and procedures that are efficient, reliable and adaptable to organizations of all sizes, enabling them to improve their own service provision.

In the modern world the concept of having a strategy to drive the business forward with adequate planning and design transitioning into day-to-day operation is compelling. Once the business has decided the IT service strategy, it is necessary to design services that are capable of meeting the agreed requirements. Knowing the direction that you are travelling is of vital importance but meaningless unless you confirm (design) the mode of travel. This publication shows you how to ensure that the strategic vision set out in service strategy can be achieved and explains the processes and procedures that will enable you to do this.

The principles contained within *ITIL Service Design* have been proven countless times in the real world. We encourage feedback from business and the ITSM community, as well as other experts in the field, to ensure that ITIL remains relevant. This practice of continual service improvement is one of the cornerstones of the ITIL framework and the fruits of this labour are here before you in this updated edition.

There is an associated qualification scheme so that individuals can demonstrate their understanding and application of the ITIL practices. So whether you are starting out or continuing along the ITIL path, you are joining a legion of individuals and organizations who have recognized the benefits of good-quality service and have a genuine resolve to improve their service level provision.

ITIL is not a panacea to all problems. It is, however, a tried and tested approach that has been proven to work.

I wish you every success in your service management journey.

Frances Scarff

Head of Best Management Practice
Cabinet Office

Preface

'Quality in a product or service is not what the supplier puts in. It is what the customer gets out and is willing to pay for.' Peter Drucker

This is the second book in the series of five ITIL core publications containing advice and guidance around the activities and processes associated with the five stages of the service lifecycle. The primary purpose of the service design stage of the service lifecycle is to design service solutions that meet the current and future needs of the business. Therefore the accurate identification, documentation and agreement of customer and business requirements are fundamental to the production of good service solution designs.

Service design takes the outputs from service strategy, the preceding stage of the service lifecycle, and uses them to ensure that the solution designs produced are consistent with the overall IT service provider strategy. The trigger for this design activity is the production of a change proposal for a new business requirement by the activities within the service strategy stage of the lifecycle. Service design takes this new business requirement and, using the five aspects of design, creates services and their supporting practices that meet business demands for functionality, security, performance, reliability and flexibility. Service design produces a service design package (SDP) that enables the build, test and release activities of service transition, and the operation, support and improvement activities of service operation and continual service improvement to occur.

Services are assets that deliver value to the business, the customers and their assets as they are used within their business processes. How well services are designed with the customers' needs and assets in mind will predict the value that can be derived from the delivery and operation of the services. In the absence of service design, services will evolve informally, often without taking full account of the business needs and overall view.

All IT service providers, whether internal or external, are part of a value network and fill a critical role in the service lifecycle by integrating best practices for service design and the service lifecycle into innovative services for the business customer. *ITIL Service Design* provides the knowledge and skills required to assemble the best combination of service assets to produce effective, measurable, scalable and innovative services that can be used along the path towards service excellence.

Any IT service provider who is expected to deliver quality to the business customer must have the capability to design services that meet the customer's expectations, and then go on to exceed those expectations. The guidance in this publication will help organizations to do just that.

Contact information

Full details of the range of material published under the ITIL banner can be found at:

www.best-management-practice.com/IT-Service-Management-ITIL/

If you would like to inform us of any changes that may be required to this publication, please log them at:

www.best-management-practice.com/changelog/

For further information on qualifications and training accreditation, please visit

www.itil-officialsite.com

Alternatively, please contact:

APM Group – The Accreditor Service Desk
Sword House
Totteridge Road
High Wycombe
Buckinghamshire
HP13 6DG
UK

Tel: +44 (0) 1494 458948
Email: servicedesk@apmgroupltd.com

Acknowledgements

2011 EDITION

Authors and mentors

Lou Hunnebeck (Third Sky)	Author
Colin Rudd (IT Enterprise Management Services Ltd (ITEMS))	Mentor
Shirley Lacy (ConnectSphere)	Project mentor
Ashley Hanna (HP)	Technical continuity editor

Other members of the ITIL authoring team

Thanks are due to the authors and mentors who have worked on all the publications in the lifecycle suite and contributed to the content in this publication and consistency across the suite. They are:

David Cannon (HP), Vernon Lloyd (Fox IT), Anthony T. Orr (BMC Software), Stuart Rance (HP), Randy Steinberg (Migration Technologies Inc.) and David Wheeldon (David Wheeldon IT Service Management).

Project governance

Members of the project governance team included:

Jessica Barry, APM Group, project assurance (examinations); Marianna Billington, itSMFI, senior user; Emily Egle, TSO, team manager; Janine Eves, TSO, senior supplier; Phil Hearsum, Cabinet Office, project assurance (quality); Tony Jackson, TSO, project manager; Paul Martini, itSMFI, senior user; Richard Pharro, APM Group, senior supplier; Frances Scarff, Cabinet Office, project executive; Rob Stroud, itSMFI, senior user; Sharon Taylor, Aspect Group Inc., adviser to the project board (technical) and the ATO sub-group, and adviser to the project board (training).

For more information on the ATO sub-group see: www.itil-officialsite.com/News/ATOSubGroupAppointed.aspx

For a full list of acknowledgements of the ATO sub-group at the time of publication, please visit: www.itil-officialsite.com/Publications/PublicationAcknowledgements.aspx

Wider team

Change advisory board

The change advisory board (CAB) spent considerable time and effort reviewing all the comments submitted through the change control log and their hard work was essential to this project. Members of the CAB involved in this review included:

David Cannon, Emily Egle, David Favelle, Ashley Hanna, Kevin Holland, Stuart Rance, Frances Scarff and Sharon Taylor.

Once authors and mentors were selected for the 2011 update, a revised CAB was appointed and now includes:

Emily Egle, David Favelle, Phil Hearsum, Kevin Holland and Frances Scarff.

Reviewers

Claire Agutter, IT Training Zone; Nick Bakker, Getronics Consulting; Ernest R. Brewster, Independent; David M. Brink, Solutions3; Jeroen Bronkhorst, HP; Tony Brough, DHL Supply Chain; Karen Brusch, itSMF Service Level Management SIG; Alison Cartlidge, Steria; Janaki Chakravarthy, Independent; Christiane Chung Ah Pong, NCS Pte Ltd, Singapore; Federico Corradi, Cogitek; Michelle Davids, Pink Elephant South Africa; Narinder Dua; Jenny Dugmore, Service Matters; Frank Eggert, MATERNA GmbH; David Favelle, UXC Consulting/Lucid IT; Carlos Fernandez-Baladron, Independent; Thomas Fischer, Danish Agency for Governmental IT; Ryan Fraser, HP; Sandeep Gondhalekar, Quint Wellington Redwood; James R. Haustein, Cornell University; Kevin Holland, NHS Connecting for Health; Michael Imhoff, Nielsen IBM; Steve Ingall, iCore-ltd; James F. Kerrigan, Independent; Brad Laatsch, HP; Chandrika Labru, Tata Consultancy Services; Brenda Langworthy Peery, Tractare Ltd; Reginald Lo, Third Sky; Jane McNamara, Lilliard Associates Ltd; Judit Pongracz, ITeal Consulting;

Anju Saxena, Tata Consultancy Services; Noel Scott, Symantec; Arun Simha, L-3 Communications STRATIS; Helen Sussex, Logica; J.R. Tietsort, Micron Technology; Ken Turbitt, Service Management Consultancy (SMCG) Ltd; Theresa Wright, Computacenter (UK) Ltd; Rob Young, Fox IT.

2007 EDITION

Chief architect and authors

Thanks are still due to those who contributed to the 2007 edition of *Service Design*, upon which this updated edition is based.

Sharon Taylor (Aspect Group Inc)	Chief architect
Vernon Lloyd (Fox IT)	Author
Colin Rudd (IT Enterprise Management Services Ltd (ITEMS))	Author

All names and organizations were correct at publication in 2007.

For a full list of all those who contributed to the 2007 and 2011 editions of *Service Strategy, Service Design, Service Transition, Service Operation* and *Continual Service Improvement*, please go to

www.itil-officialsite.com/Publications/PublicationAcknowledgements.aspx

Introduction

1

1 Introduction

ITIL is part of a suite of best-practice publications for IT service management (ITSM).[1] ITIL provides guidance to service providers on the provision of quality IT services, and on the processes, functions and other capabilities needed to support them. ITIL is used by many hundreds of organizations around the world and offers best-practice guidance applicable to all types of organization that provide services. ITIL is not a standard that has to be followed; it is guidance that should be read and understood, and used to create value for the service provider and its customers. Organizations are encouraged to adopt ITIL best practices and to adapt them to work in their specific environments in ways that meet their needs.

ITIL is the most widely recognized framework for ITSM in the world. In the 20 years since it was created, ITIL has evolved and changed its breadth and depth as technologies and business practices have developed. ISO/IEC 20000 provides a formal and universal standard for organizations seeking to have their service management capabilities audited and certified. While ISO/IEC 20000 is a standard to be achieved and maintained, ITIL offers a body of knowledge useful for achieving the standard.

In 2007, the second major refresh of ITIL was published in response to significant advancements in technology and emerging challenges for IT service providers. New models and architectures such as outsourcing, shared services, utility computing, cloud computing, virtualization, web services and mobile commerce have become widespread within IT. The process-based approach of ITIL was augmented with the service lifecycle to address these additional service management challenges. In 2011, as part of its commitment to continual improvement, the Cabinet Office published this update to improve consistency across the core publications.

The ITIL framework is based on the five stages of the service lifecycle as shown in Figure 1.1, with a core publication providing best-practice guidance for each stage. This guidance includes key principles, required processes and activities,

organization and roles, technology, associated challenges, critical success factors and risks. The service lifecycle uses a hub-and-spoke design, with service strategy at the hub, and service design, transition and operation as the revolving lifecycle stages or 'spokes'. Continual service improvement surrounds and supports all stages of the service lifecycle. Each stage of the lifecycle exerts influence on the others and relies on them for inputs and feedback. In this way, a constant set of checks and balances throughout the service lifecycle ensures that as business demand changes with business need, the services can adapt and respond effectively.

In addition to the core publications, there is also a complementary set of ITIL publications providing guidance specific to industry sectors, organization types, operating models and technology architectures.

1.1 OVERVIEW

ITIL Service Design provides best-practice guidance for the service design stage of the ITIL service lifecycle. Although this publication can be read

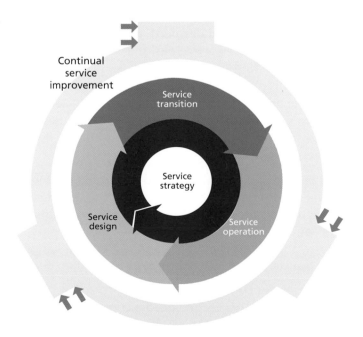

Figure 1.1 The ITIL service lifecycle

---

1 ITSM and other concepts from this chapter are described in more detail in Chapter 2.

in isolation, it is recommended that it is used in conjunction with the other core ITIL publications.

1.1.1 Purpose and objective of service design

The purpose of the service design stage of the lifecycle is to design IT services, together with the governing IT practices, processes and policies, to realize the service provider's strategy and to facilitate the introduction of these services into supported environments ensuring quality service delivery, customer satisfaction and cost-effective service provision.

The objective of service design is to design IT services so effectively that minimal improvement during their lifecycle will be required. However, continual improvement should be embedded in all service design activities to ensure that the solutions and designs become even more effective over time, and to identify changing trends in the business that may offer improvement opportunities. Service design activities can be periodic or exception-based when they may be triggered by a specific business need or event.

1.1.2 Scope

ITIL Service Design provides guidance for the design of appropriate and innovative IT services to meet current and future agreed business requirements. It describes the principles of service design and looks at identifying, defining and aligning the IT solution with the business requirement. It also introduces the concept of the service design package and looks at selecting the appropriate service design model. This publication covers the methods, practices and tools to achieve excellence in service design. It discusses the fundamentals of the design processes and attends to what are called the 'five aspects of service design' (see Chapter 3).

ITIL Service Design enforces the principle that the initial service design should be driven by a number of factors, including the functional requirements, the requirements within service level agreements (SLAs), the business benefits and the overall design constraints.

The processes considered important to successful service design are design coordination, service catalogue management, service level management, availability management, capacity management, IT service continuity management, information

security management and supplier management. They are described in detail in Chapter 4, although it should be noted that almost all of these processes are also active throughout the other stages of the service lifecycle. All processes within the service lifecycle must be linked closely together for managing, designing, supporting and maintaining the services, the IT infrastructure, the environment, the applications and the data. Other processes are described in detail in the other core ITIL publications. The interfaces between processes need to be clearly defined when designing a service or improving or implementing a process.

The appendices described at the end of this chapter give examples of important service design documents and templates such as the service design package and SLAs.

1.1.3 Usage

ITIL Service Design provides access to proven best practice based on the skill and knowledge of experienced industry practitioners in adopting a standardized and controlled approach to service management. Although this publication can be used and applied in isolation, it is recommended that it is used in conjunction with the other core ITIL publications. All of the core publications need to be read to fully appreciate and understand the overall lifecycle of services and IT service management.

1.1.4 Value to business

Selecting and adopting the best practice as recommended in this publication will assist organizations in delivering significant benefits. With good service design, it is possible to deliver quality, cost-effective services and to ensure that the business requirements are being met consistently.

Adopting and implementing standard and consistent approaches for service design will:

- **Reduce total cost of ownership (TCO)** Cost of ownership can only be minimized if all aspects of services, processes and technology are designed properly and implemented against the design.
- **Improve quality of service** Both service and operational quality will be enhanced through services that are better designed to meet the required outcomes of the customer.

- **Improve consistency of service** This will be achieved by designing services within the corporate strategy, architectures and constraints.
- **Ease the implementation of new or changed services** Integrated and full service designs and the production of comprehensive service design packages will support effective and efficient transitions.
- **Improve service alignment** Involvement of service design from the conception of the service will ensure that new or changed services match business needs, with services designed to meet service level requirements.
- **Improve service performance** Performance will be enhanced if services are designed to meet specific performance criteria and if capacity, availability, IT service continuity and financial plans are recognized and incorporated.
- **Improve IT governance** By building controls into designs, service design can contribute towards the effective governance of IT.
- **Improve effectiveness of service management and IT processes** Processes will be designed with optimal quality and cost effectiveness.
- **Improve information and decision-making** Comprehensive and effective measurements and metrics will enable better decision-making and continual improvement of services and service management practices throughout the service lifecycle.
- **Improve alignment with customer values and strategies** For organizations with commitments to concepts such as green IT or that establish strategies such as the use of cloud technologies, service design will ensure that all areas of services and service management are aligned with these values and strategies.

1.1.5 Target audience

ITIL Service Design is relevant to organizations involved in the development, delivery or support of services, including:

- Service providers, both internal and external
- Organizations that aim to improve services through the effective application of service management principles and a service lifecycle approach

- Organizations that require a consistent managed approach across all service providers in a supply chain or value network
- Organizations that are going out to tender for their services.

The publication is also relevant to any professional involved in the management of services, particularly:

- IT architects
- IT managers and practitioners
- IT service owners
- Business relationship managers.

1.2 CONTEXT

The context of this publication is the ITIL service lifecycle as shown in Figure 1.1.

The ITIL core consists of five lifecycle publications. Each provides part of the guidance necessary for an integrated approach as required by the ISO/IEC 20000 standard specification. The five publications are:

- *ITIL Service Strategy*
- *ITIL Service Design*
- *ITIL Service Transition*
- *ITIL Service Operation*
- *ITIL Continual Service Improvement*

Each one addresses capabilities having direct impact on a service provider's performance. The core is expected to provide structure, stability and strength to service management capabilities, with durable principles, methods and tools. This serves to protect investments and provide the necessary basis for measurement, learning and improvement. The introductory guide, *Introduction to the ITIL Service Lifecycle*, provides an overview of the lifecycle stages described in the ITIL core.

ITIL guidance can be adapted to support various business environments and organizational strategies. Complementary ITIL publications provide flexibility to implement the core in a diverse range of environments. Practitioners can select complementary publications as needed to provide traction for the ITIL core in a given context, in much the same way as tyres are selected based on the type of vehicle, purpose and road conditions. This is to increase the durability and portability of knowledge assets and to protect investments in service management capabilities.

1.2.1 Service strategy

At the centre of the service lifecycle is service strategy. Value creation begins here with understanding organizational objectives and customer needs. Every organizational asset including people, processes and products should support the strategy.

ITIL Service Strategy provides guidance on how to view service management not only as an organizational capability but as a strategic asset. It describes the principles underpinning the practice of service management which are useful for developing service management policies, guidelines and processes across the ITIL service lifecycle.

Topics covered in *ITIL Service Strategy* include the development of market spaces, characteristics of internal and external provider types, service assets, the service portfolio and implementation of strategy through the service lifecycle. Business relationship management, demand management, financial management, organizational development and strategic risks are among the other major topics.

Organizations should use *ITIL Service Strategy* to set objectives and expectations of performance towards serving customers and market spaces, and to identify, select and prioritize opportunities. Service strategy is about ensuring that organizations are in a position to handle the costs and risks associated with their service portfolios, and are set up not just for operational effectiveness but for distinctive performance.

Organizations already practising ITIL can use *ITIL Service Strategy* to guide a strategic review of their ITIL-based service management capabilities and to improve the alignment between those capabilities and their business strategies. *ITIL Service Strategy* will encourage readers to stop and think about why something is to be done before thinking of how.

1.2.2 Service design

For services to provide true value to the business, they must be designed with the business objectives in mind. Design encompasses the whole IT organization, for it is the organization as a whole that delivers and supports the services. Service design is the stage in the lifecycle that turns a service strategy into a plan for delivering the business objectives.

ITIL Service Design (this publication) provides guidance for the design and development of services and service management practices. It covers design principles and methods for converting strategic objectives into portfolios of services and service assets. The scope of *ITIL Service Design* is not limited to new services. It includes the changes and improvements necessary to increase or maintain value to customers over the lifecycle of services, the continuity of services, achievement of service levels, and conformance to standards and regulations. It guides organizations on how to develop design capabilities for service management.

Other topics in *ITIL Service Design* include design coordination, service catalogue management, service level management, availability management, capacity management, IT service continuity management, information security management and supplier management.

1.2.3 Service transition

ITIL Service Transition provides guidance for the development and improvement of capabilities for introducing new and changed services into supported environments. It describes how to transition an organization from one state to another while controlling risk and supporting organizational knowledge for decision support. It ensures that the value(s) identified in the service strategy, and encoded in service design, are effectively transitioned so that they can be realized in service operation.

ITIL Service Transition describes best practice in transition planning and support, change management, service asset and configuration management, release and deployment management, service validation and testing, change evaluation and knowledge management. It provides guidance on managing the complexity related to changes to services and service management processes, preventing undesired consequences while allowing for innovation.

ITIL Service Transition also introduces the service knowledge management system, which can support organizational learning and help to improve the overall efficiency and effectiveness of all stages of the service lifecycle. This will enable people to benefit from the knowledge and experience of others, support informed decision-making, and improve the management of services.

1.2.4 Service operation

ITIL Service Operation describes best practice for managing services in supported environments. It includes guidance on achieving effectiveness and efficiency in the delivery and support of services to ensure value for the customer, the users and the service provider.

Strategic objectives are ultimately realized through service operation, therefore making it a critical capability. *ITIL Service Operation* provides guidance on how to maintain stability in service operation, allowing for changes in design, scale, scope and service levels. Organizations are provided with detailed process guidelines, methods and tools for use in two major control perspectives: reactive and proactive. Managers and practitioners are provided with knowledge allowing them to make better decisions in areas such as managing the availability of services, controlling demand, optimizing capacity utilization, scheduling of operations, and avoiding or resolving service incidents and managing problems. New models and architectures such as shared services, utility computing, web services and mobile commerce to support service operation are described.

Other topics in *ITIL Service Operation* include event management, incident management, request fulfilment, problem management and access management processes; as well as the service desk, technical management, IT operations management and application management functions.

1.2.5 Continual service improvement

ITIL Continual Service Improvement provides guidance on creating and maintaining value for customers through better strategy, design, transition and operation of services. It combines principles, practices and methods from quality management, change management and capability improvement.

ITIL Continual Service Improvement describes best practice for achieving incremental and large-scale improvements in service quality, operational efficiency and business continuity, and for ensuring that the service portfolio continues to be aligned to business needs. Guidance is provided for linking

improvement efforts and outcomes with service strategy, design, transition and operation. A closed loop feedback system, based on the Plan-Do-Check-Act (PDCA) cycle, is established. Feedback from any stage of the service lifecycle can be used to identify improvement opportunities for any other stage of the lifecycle.

Other topics in *ITIL Continual Service Improvement* include service measurement, demonstrating value with metrics, developing baselines and maturity assessments.

1.3 ITIL IN RELATION TO OTHER PUBLICATIONS IN THE BEST MANAGEMENT PRACTICE PORTFOLIO

ITIL is part of a portfolio of best-practice publications (known collectively as Best Management Practice or BMP) aimed at helping organizations and individuals manage projects, programmes and services consistently and effectively (see Figure 1.2). ITIL can be used in harmony with other BMP products, and international or internal organization standards. Where appropriate, BMP guidance is supported by a qualification scheme and accredited training and consultancy services. All BMP guidance is intended to be tailored for use by individual organizations.

BMP publications include:

- *Management of Portfolios* (MoP)™ Portfolio management concerns the twin issues of how to do the 'right' projects and programmes in the context of the organization's strategic objectives, and how to do them 'correctly' in terms of achieving delivery and benefits at a collective level. MoP encompasses consideration of the principles upon which effective portfolio management is based; the key practices in the portfolio definition and delivery cycles, including examples of how they have been applied in real life; and guidance on how to implement portfolio management and sustain progress in a wide variety of organizations. Office of Government Commerce (2011). *Management of Portfolios*. TSO, London.

- *Management of Risk* (M_o_R®) M_o_R offers an effective framework for taking informed decisions about the risks that affect performance objectives. The framework allows organizations to assess risk accurately

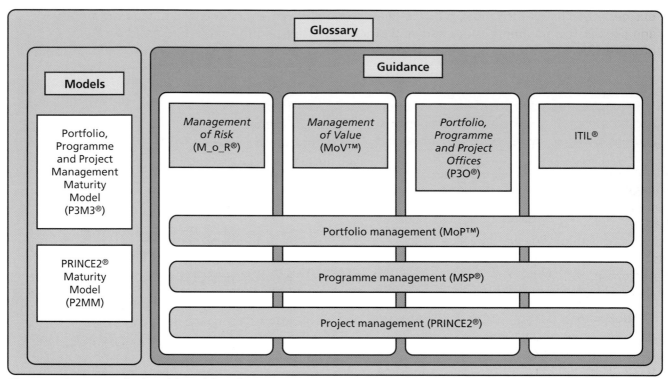

Figure 1.2 ITIL's relationship with other Best Management Practice guides

(selecting the correct responses to threats and opportunities created by uncertainty) and thereby improve their service delivery. Office of Government Commerce (2010). *Management of Risk: Guidance for Practitioners*. TSO, London.

■ *Management of Value* **(MoV™)** MoV provides a cross-sector and universally applicable guide on how to maximize value in a way that takes account of organizations' priorities, differing stakeholders' needs and, at the same time, uses resources as efficiently and effectively as possible. It will help organizations to put in place effective methods to deliver enhanced value across their portfolio, programmes, projects and operational activities to meet the challenges of ever-more competitive and resource-constrained environments. Office of Government Commerce (2010). *Management of Value*. TSO, London.

■ *Managing Successful Programmes* **(MSP®)** MSP provides a framework to enable the achievement of high-quality change outcomes and benefits that fundamentally affect the way in which organizations work. One of the core

themes in MSP is that a programme must add more value than that provided by the sum of its constituent project and major activities. Cabinet Office (2011). *Managing Successful Programmes*. TSO, London.

■ *Managing Successful Projects with PRINCE2®* PRINCE2 (PRojects IN Controlled Environments, V2) is a structured method to help effective project management via clearly defined products. Key themes that feature throughout PRINCE2 are the dependence on a viable business case confirming the delivery of measurable benefits that are aligned to an organization's objectives and strategy, while ensuring the management of risks, costs and quality. Office of Government Commerce (2009). *Managing Successful Projects with PRINCE2*. TSO, London.

■ *Portfolio, Programme and Project Offices* **(P3O®)** P3O provides universally applicable guidance, including principles, processes and techniques, to successfully establish, develop and maintain appropriate support structures. These structures will facilitate delivery of

business objectives (portfolios), programmes and projects within time, cost, quality and other organizational constraints.
Office of Government Commerce (2008). *Portfolio, Programme and Project Offices*. TSO, London.

1.4 WHY IS ITIL SO SUCCESSFUL?

ITIL embraces a practical approach to service management – do what works. And what works is adapting a common framework of practices that unite all areas of IT service provision towards a single aim – that of delivering value to the business. The following list defines the key characteristics of ITIL that contribute to its global success:

- **Vendor-neutral** ITIL service management practices are applicable in any IT organization because they are not based on any particular technology platform or industry type. ITIL is owned by the UK government and is not tied to any commercial proprietary practice or solution.
- **Non-prescriptive** ITIL offers robust, mature and time-tested practices that have applicability to all types of service organization. It continues to be useful and relevant in public and private sectors, internal and external service providers, small, medium and large enterprises, and within any technical environment. Organizations should adopt ITIL and adapt it to meet the needs of the IT organization and their customers.
- **Best practice** ITIL represents the learning experiences and thought leadership of the world's best-in-class service providers.

ITIL is successful because it describes practices that enable organizations to deliver benefits, return on investment and sustained success. ITIL is adopted by organizations to enable them to:

- Deliver value for customers through services
- Integrate the strategy for services with the business strategy and customer needs
- Measure, monitor and optimize IT services and service provider performance
- Manage the IT investment and budget
- Manage risk
- Manage knowledge
- Manage capabilities and resources to deliver services effectively and efficiently

- Enable adoption of a standard approach to service management across the enterprise
- Change the organizational culture to support the achievement of sustained success
- Improve the interaction and relationship with customers
- Coordinate the delivery of goods and services across the value network
- Optimize and reduce costs.

1.5 CHAPTER SUMMARY

ITIL Service Design comprises:

- Chapter 2 Service management as a practice
This chapter explains the concepts of service management and services, and describes how these can be used to create value. It also summarizes a number of generic ITIL concepts that the rest of the publication depends on.

- Chapter 3 Service design principles
This chapter describes some of the key principles of service design that will enable service providers to plan and implement best practice in service design. These principles are the same irrespective of the organization; however, the approach may need to be tailored to circumstances, including the size of the organization, geographic distribution, culture and available resources. It concludes with a table showing the major inputs and outputs for the service design lifecycle stage.

- Chapter 4 Service design processes
Chapter 4 sets out the processes and activities on which effective service design depends and how they integrate with the other stages of the lifecycle.

- Chapter 5 Service design technology-related activities
Chapter 5 considers the technology-related activities of requirement engineering and the development of technology architectures.

- Chapter 6 Organizing for service design
This chapter identifies the organizational roles and responsibilities that should be considered to manage the service design lifecycle stage and processes. These roles are provided as guidelines and can be combined to fit into a variety of organizational structures. Examples of organizational structures are also provided.

■ Chapter 7 Technology considerations
ITIL service management practices gain momentum when the right type of technical automation is applied. This chapter provides recommendations for the use of technology in service design and the basic requirements a service provider will need to consider when choosing service management tools.

■ Chapter 8 Implementing service design
For organizations new to ITIL, or those wishing to improve their maturity and service capability, this chapter outlines effective ways to implement the service design lifecycle stage.

■ Chapter 9 Challenges, risks and critical success factors
It is important for any organization to understand the challenges, risks and critical success factors that could influence their success. This chapter discusses typical examples of these for the service design lifecycle stage.

■ Appendices A–K
These appendices provide working templates and examples of how the practices can be applied. They are provided to help organizations capitalize on industry experience and expertise already in use. Each can be adapted within any organizational context.

● Appendix A The service design package
● Appendix B Service acceptance criteria
● Appendix C Process documentation template
Appendix D Design and planning documents and their contents
● Appendix E Environmental architectures and standards
● Appendix F Sample service level agreement and operational level agreement
● Appendix G Service catalogue example
● Appendix H The service management process maturity framework
● Appendix I Example of the contents of a statement of requirements and/or invitation to tender
● Appendix J Typical contents of a capacity plan
● Appendix K Typical contents of a recovery plan

■ Appendix L Procurement documents
This appendix lists and briefly describes types of document that are frequently utilized in the process of procuring services from an external supplier.

■ Appendix M Risk assessment and management
This appendix contains basic information about several commonly used approaches to the assessment and management of risk.

■ Appendix N Related guidance
This contains a list of some of the many external methods, practices and frameworks that align well with ITIL best practice. Notes are provided on how they integrate into the ITIL service lifecycle, and when and how they are useful.

■ Appendix O Examples of inputs and outputs across the service lifecycle
This appendix identifies some of the major inputs and outputs between each stage of the service lifecycle.

■ Abbreviations and glossary
This contains a list of abbreviations and a selected glossary of terms.

Service management as a practice 2

2   Service management as a practice

2.1   SERVICES AND SERVICE MANAGEMENT

2.1.1   Services

Services are a means of delivering value to customers by facilitating the outcomes customers want to achieve without the ownership of specific costs and risks. Services facilitate outcomes by enhancing the performance of associated tasks and reducing the effect of constraints. These constraints may include regulation, lack of funding or capacity, or technology limitations. The end result is an increase in the probability of desired outcomes. While some services enhance performance of tasks, others have a more direct impact – they perform the task itself.

The preceding paragraph is not just a definition, as it is a recurring pattern found in a wide range of services. Patterns are useful for managing complexity, costs, flexibility and variety. They are generic structures useful to make an idea applicable in a wide range of environments and situations. In each instance the pattern is applied with variations that make the idea effective, economical or simply useful in that particular case.

> **Definition: outcome**
>
> The result of carrying out an activity, following a process, or delivering an IT service etc. The term is used to refer to intended results, as well as to actual results.

An outcome-based definition of service moves IT organizations beyond business–IT alignment towards business–IT integration. Internal dialogue and discussion on the meaning of services is an elementary step towards alignment and integration with a customer's business (Figure 2.1). Customer outcomes become the ultimate concern of business relationship managers instead of the gathering of requirements, which is necessary but not sufficient. Requirements are generated for internal coordination and control only after customer outcomes are well understood.

Customers seek outcomes but do not wish to have accountability or ownership of all the associated costs and risks. All services must have a budget

when they go live and this must be managed. The service cost is reflected in financial terms such as return on investment (ROI) and total cost of ownership (TCO). The customer will only be exposed to the overall cost or price of a service, which will include all the provider's costs and risk mitigation measures (and any profit margin if appropriate). The customer can then judge the value of a service based on a comparison of cost or price and reliability with the desired outcome.

> **Definitions**
>
> *Service*: A means of delivering value to customers by facilitating outcomes customers want to achieve without the ownership of specific costs and risks.
>
> *IT service*: A service provided by an IT service provider. An IT service is made up of a combination of information technology, people and processes. A customer-facing IT service directly supports the business processes of one or more customers and its service level targets should be defined in a service level agreement. Other IT services, called supporting services, are not directly used by the business but are required by the service provider to deliver customer-facing services.

Customer satisfaction is also important. Customers need to be satisfied with the level of service and feel confident in the ability of the service provider to continue providing that level of service – or even improving it over time. The difficulty is that customer expectations keep shifting, and a service provider that does not track this will soon find itself losing business. *ITIL Service Strategy* is helpful in understanding how this happens, and how a service provider can adapt its services to meet the changing customer environment.

Services can be discussed in terms of how they relate to one another and their customers, and can be classified as core, enabling or enhancing.

Core services deliver the basic outcomes desired by one or more customers. They represent the value that the customer wants and for which they are willing to pay. Core services anchor the value proposition for the customer and provide the basis for their continued utilization and satisfaction.

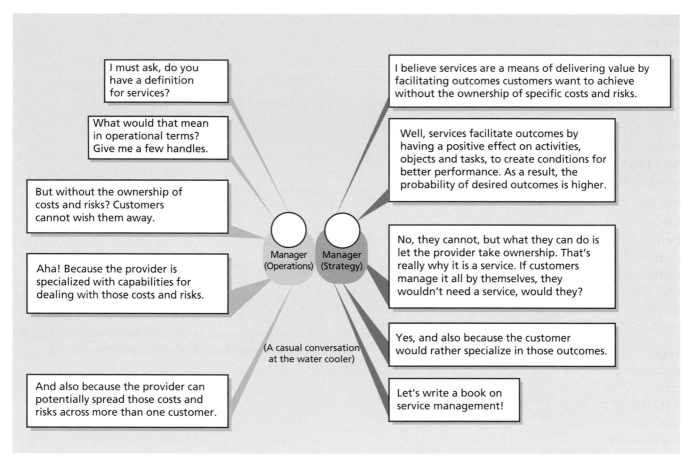

Figure 2.1 Conversation about the definition and meaning of services

Enabling services are services that are needed in order for a core service to be delivered. Enabling services may or may not be visible to the customer, but the customer does not perceive them as services in their own right. They are 'basic factors' which enable the customer to receive the 'real' (core) service.

Enhancing services are services that are added to a core service to make it more exciting or enticing to the customer. Enhancing services are not essential to the delivery of a core service, and are added to a core service as 'excitement' factors, which will encourage customers to use the core service more (or to choose the core service provided by one company over those of its competitors).

Services may be as simple as allowing a user to complete a single transaction, but most services are complex. They consist of a range of deliverables and functionality. If each individual aspect of these complex services were defined independently, the service provider would soon find it impossible to track and record all services.

Most service providers will follow a strategy where they can deliver a set of more generic services to a broad range of customers, thus achieving economies of scale and competing on the basis of price and a certain amount of flexibility. One way of achieving this is by using service packages. A service package is a collection of two or more services that have been combined to offer a solution to a specific type of customer need or to underpin specific business outcomes. A service package can consist of a combination of core services, enabling services and enhancing services.

Where a service or service package needs to be differentiated for different types of customer, one or more components of the package can be changed, or offered at different levels of utility and warranty, to create service options. These different service options can then be offered to customers and are sometimes called service level packages.

2.1.2 Service management

When we turn on a water tap, we expect to see water flow from it. When we turn on a light switch, we expect to see light fill the room. Not so many years ago, these very basic things were not as reliable as they are today. We know instinctively that the advances in technology have made them reliable enough to be considered a utility. But it isn't just the technology that makes the services reliable. It is how they are managed.

The use of IT today has become the utility of business. Business today wants IT services that behave like other utilities such as water, electricity or the telephone. Simply having the best technology will not ensure that IT provides utility-like reliability. Professional, responsive, value-driven service management is what brings this quality of service to the business.

Service management is a set of specialized organizational capabilities for providing value to customers in the form of services. The more mature a service provider's capabilities are, the greater is their ability to consistently produce quality services that meet the needs of the customer in a timely and cost-effective manner. The act of transforming capabilities and resources into valuable services is at the core of service management. Without these capabilities, a service organization is merely a bundle of resources that by itself has relatively low intrinsic value for customers.

> **Definitions**
>
> *Service management:* A set of specialized organizational capabilities for providing value to customers in the form of services.
>
> *Service provider:* An organization supplying services to one or more internal or external customers.

Organizational capabilities are shaped by the challenges they are expected to overcome. An example of this is provided by Toyota in the 1950s when it developed unique capabilities to overcome the challenge of smaller scale and financial capital compared to its American rivals. Toyota developed new capabilities in production engineering, operations management and managing suppliers to compensate for its inability to afford large inventories, make components, produce raw materials or own the companies that produced them (Magretta, 2002).[2]

Service management capabilities are similarly influenced by the following challenges that distinguish services from other systems of value creation, such as manufacturing, mining and agriculture:

- Intangible nature of the output and intermediate products of service processes: they are difficult to measure, control and validate (or prove)
- Demand is tightly coupled with the customer's assets: users and other customer assets such as processes, applications, documents and transactions arrive with demand and stimulate service production
- High level of contact for producers and consumers of services: there is little or no buffer between the service provider's creation of the service and the customer's consumption of that service
- The perishable nature of service output and service capacity: there is value for the customer from assurance on the continued supply of consistent quality. Providers need to secure a steady supply of demand from customers.

Service management is more than just a set of capabilities. It is also a professional practice supported by an extensive body of knowledge, experience and skills. A global community of individuals and organizations in the public and private sectors fosters its growth and maturity. Formal schemes exist for the education, training and certification of practising organizations, and individuals influence its quality. Industry best practices, academic research and formal standards contribute to and draw from its intellectual capital.

The origins of service management are in traditional service businesses such as airlines, banks, hotels and phone companies. Its practice has grown with the adoption by IT organizations of a service-oriented approach to managing IT applications, infrastructure and processes. Solutions to business problems and support for business models, strategies and operations are increasingly in the form of services. The popularity of shared services and outsourcing has contributed to the increase in the number of organizations that behave as service providers, including internal IT

---

2 Magretta, J. (2002). *What Management Is: How it Works and Why it's Everyone's Business.* The Free Press, New York.

organizations. This in turn has strengthened the practice of service management while at the same time imposed greater challenges.

2.1.3 IT service management

Information technology (IT) is a commonly used term that changes meaning depending on the different perspectives that a business organization or people may have of it. A key challenge is to recognize and balance these perspectives when communicating the value of IT service management (ITSM) and understanding the context for how the business sees the IT organization. Some of these meanings are:

■ IT is a collection of systems, applications and infrastructures which are components or sub-assemblies of a larger product. They enable or are embedded in processes and services.

■ IT is an organization with its own set of capabilities and resources. IT organizations can be of various types such as business functions, shared services units and enterprise-level core units.

■ IT is a category of services utilized by business. The services are typically IT applications and infrastructure that are packaged and offered by internal IT organizations or external service providers. IT costs are treated as business expenses.

■ IT is a category of business assets that provide a stream of benefits for their owners, including, but not limited to, revenue, income and profit. IT costs are treated as investments.

Every IT organization should act as a service provider, using the principles of service management to ensure that they deliver the outcomes required by their customers.

> **Definitions**
>
> *IT service management (ITSM)*: The implementation and management of quality IT services that meet the needs of the business. IT service management is performed by IT service providers through an appropriate mix of people, process and information technology.
>
> *IT service provider*: A service provider that provides IT services to internal or external customers.

ITSM must be carried out effectively and efficiently. Managing IT from the business perspective enables organizational high performance and value creation.

A good relationship between an IT service provider and its customers relies on the customer receiving an IT service that meets its needs, at an acceptable level of performance and at a cost that the customer can afford. The IT service provider needs to work out how to achieve a balance between these three areas, and communicate with the customer if there is anything which prevents it from being able to deliver the required IT service at the agreed level of performance or price.

A service level agreement (SLA) is used to document agreements between an IT service provider and a customer. An SLA describes the IT service, documents service level targets, and specifies the responsibilities of the IT service provider and the customer. A single agreement may cover multiple IT services or multiple customers.

2.1.4 Service providers

There are three main types of service provider. While most aspects of service management apply equally to all types of service provider, other aspects such as customers, contracts, competition, market spaces, revenue and strategy take on different meanings depending on the specific type. The three types are:

■ **Type I – internal service provider** An internal service provider that is embedded within a business unit. There may be several Type I service providers within an organization.

■ **Type II – shared services unit** An internal service provider that provides shared IT services to more than one business unit.

■ **Type III – external service provider** A service provider that provides IT services to external customers.

ITSM concepts are often described in the context of only one of these types and as if only one type of IT service provider exists or is used by a given organization. In reality most organizations have a combination of IT service providers. In a single organization it is possible that some IT units are dedicated to a single business unit, others provide shared services, and yet others have been outsourced or depend on external service providers.

Many IT organizations who traditionally provide services to internal customers find that they are dealing directly with external users because of the online services that they provide. *ITIL Service Strategy* provides guidance on how the IT organization interacts with these users, and who owns and manages the relationship with them.

2.1.5 Stakeholders in service management

Stakeholders have an interest in an organization, project or service etc. and may be interested in the activities, targets, resources or deliverables from service management. Examples include organizations, service providers, customers, consumers, users, partners, employees, shareholders, owners and suppliers. The term 'organization' is used to define a company, legal entity or other institution. It is also used to refer to any entity that has people, resources and budgets – for example, a project or business.

Within the service provider organization there are many different stakeholders including the functions, groups and teams that deliver the services. There are also many stakeholders external to the service provider organization, for example:

- **Customers** Those who buy goods or services. The customer of an IT service provider is the person or group who defines and agrees the service level targets. This term is also sometimes used informally to mean user – for example, 'This is a customer-focused organization.'
- **Users** Those who use the service on a day-to-day basis. Users are distinct from customers, as some customers do not use the IT service directly.
- **Suppliers** Third parties responsible for supplying goods or services that are required to deliver IT services. Examples of suppliers include commodity hardware and software vendors, network and telecom providers, and outsourcing organizations.

There is a difference between customers who work in the same organization as the IT service provider, and customers who work for other organizations. They are distinguished as follows:

- **Internal customers** These are customers who work for the same business as the IT service provider. For example, the marketing department is an internal customer of the IT organization because it uses IT services. The head of marketing and the chief information officer both report to the chief executive officer. If IT charges for its services, the money paid is an internal transaction in the organization's accounting system, not real revenue.
- **External customers** These are customers who work for a different business from the IT service provider. External customers typically purchase services from the service provider by means of a legally binding contract or agreement.

2.1.6 Utility and warranty

The value of a service can be considered to be the level to which that service meets a customer's expectations. It is often measured by how much the customer is willing to pay for the service, rather than the cost to the service provider of providing the service or any other intrinsic attribute of the service itself.

Unlike products, services do not have much intrinsic value. The value of a service comes from what it enables someone to do. The value of a service is not determined by the provider, but by the person who receives it – because they decide what they will do with the service, and what type of return they will achieve by using the service. Services contribute value to an organization only when their value is perceived to be higher than the cost of obtaining the service.

From the customer's perspective, value consists of achieving business objectives. The value of a service is created by combining two primary elements: utility (fitness for purpose) and warranty (fitness for use). These two elements work together to achieve the desired outcomes upon which the customer and the business base their perceptions of a service.

Utility is the functionality offered by a product or service to meet a particular need. Utility can be summarized as 'what the service does', and can be used to determine whether a service is able to meet its required outcomes, or is 'fit for purpose'. Utility refers to those aspects of a service that contribute to tasks associated with achieving outcomes. For example, a service that enables a business unit to process orders should allow sales people to access customer details, stock availability, shipping information etc. Any aspect of the service that improves the ability of sales people to improve the performance of the task of processing sales orders would be considered utility. Utility can therefore represent any attribute of a service that removes, or reduces the effect of, constraints on the performance of a task.

Warranty is an assurance that a product or service will meet its agreed requirements. This may be a formal agreement such as a service level agreement or contract, or a marketing message or brand image. Warranty refers to the ability of a service to be available when needed, to provide the required capacity, and to provide the required reliability in terms of continuity and security. Warranty can be summarized as 'how the service is delivered', and can be used to determine whether a service is 'fit for use'. For example, any aspect of the service that increases the availability or speed of the service would be considered warranty. Warranty can therefore represent any attribute of a service that increases the potential of the business to be able to perform a task. Warranty refers to any means by which utility is made available to the users.

Utility is *what* the service does, and warranty is *how* it is delivered.

Customers cannot benefit from something that is fit for purpose but not fit for use, and vice versa. The value of a service is therefore only delivered when both utility and warranty are designed and delivered. Figure 2.2 illustrates the logic that a service has to have both utility and warranty to create value. Utility is used to improve the performance of the tasks required to achieve an outcome, or to remove constraints that prevent the task from being performed adequately (or both). Warranty requires the service to be available, continuous and secure and to have sufficient capacity for the service to perform at the required level. If the service is both fit for purpose and fit for use, it will create value.

It should be noted that the elements of warranty in Figure 2.2 are not exclusive. It is possible to define other components of warranty, such as usability, which refers to how easy it is for the user to access and use the features of the service to achieve the desired outcomes.

The warranty aspect of the service needs to be designed at the same time as the utility aspect in order to deliver the required value to the business. Attempts to design warranty aspects after a service has been deployed can be expensive and disruptive.

Information about the desired business outcomes, opportunities, customers, utility and warranty of the service is used to develop the definition of a service. Using an outcome-based definition helps to ensure that managers plan and execute all aspects of service management from the perspective of what is valuable to the customer.

2.1.7 Best practices in the public domain
Organizations benchmark themselves against peers and seek to close gaps in capabilities. This enables them to become more competitive by improving their ability to deliver quality services

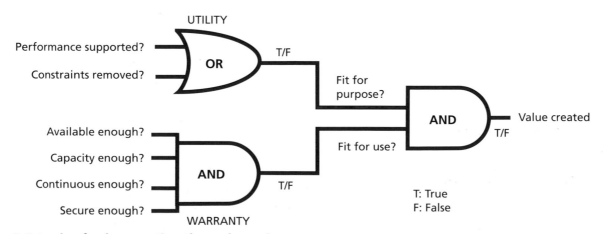

Figure 2.2 Logic of value creation through services

that meet the needs of their customers at a price their customers can afford. One way to close such gaps is the adoption of best practices in wide industry use. There are several sources for best practice including public frameworks, standards and the proprietary knowledge of organizations and individuals (Figure 2.3). ITIL is the most widely recognized and trusted source of best-practice guidance in the area of ITSM.

Public frameworks and standards are attractive when compared with proprietary knowledge for the following reasons:

■ Proprietary knowledge is deeply embedded in organizations and therefore difficult to adopt, replicate or even transfer with the cooperation of the owners. Such knowledge is often in the form of tacit knowledge which is inextricable and poorly documented.

■ Proprietary knowledge is customized for the local context and the specific needs of the business to the point of being idiosyncratic.

Unless the recipients of such knowledge have matching circumstances, the knowledge may not be as effective in use.

■ Owners of proprietary knowledge expect to be rewarded for their investments. They may make such knowledge available only under commercial terms through purchases and licensing agreements.

■ Publicly available frameworks and standards such as ITIL, LEAN, Six Sigma, COBIT, CMMI, PRINCE2, PMBOK®, ISO 9000, ISO/IEC 20000 and ISO/IEC 27001 are validated across a diverse set of environments and situations rather than the limited experience of a single organization. They are subject to broad review across multiple organizations and disciplines, and vetted by diverse sets of partners, suppliers and competitors.

■ The knowledge of public frameworks is more likely to be widely distributed among a large community of professionals through publicly

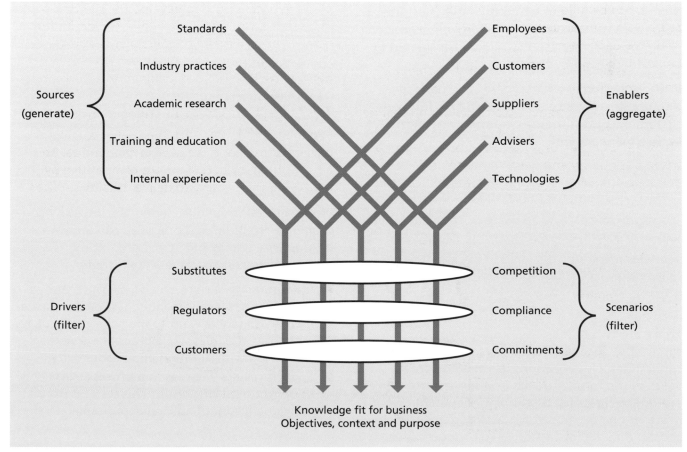

Figure 2.3 Sources of service management best practice

available training and certification. It is easier for organizations to acquire such knowledge through the labour market.

Ignoring public frameworks and standards can needlessly place an organization at a disadvantage. Organizations should cultivate their own proprietary knowledge on top of a body of knowledge based on public frameworks and standards. Collaboration and coordination across organizations become easier on the basis of shared practices and standards. Further information on best practice in the public domain is provided in Appendix N.

2.2 BASIC CONCEPTS

2.2.1 Assets, resources and capabilities

The service relationship between service providers and their customers revolves around the use of assets – both those of the service provider and those of the customer. Each relationship involves an interaction between the assets of each party.

Many customers use the service they receive to build and deliver services or products of their own and then deliver them on to their own customers. In these cases, what the service provider considers to be the customer asset would be considered to be a service asset by their customer.

Without customer assets, there is no basis for defining the value of a service. The performance of customer assets is therefore a primary concern for service management.

> **Definitions**
>
> *Asset*: Any resource or capability.
>
> *Customer asset*: Any resource or capability used by a customer to achieve a business outcome.
>
> *Service asset*: Any resource or capability used by a service provider to deliver services to a customer.

There are two types of asset used by both service providers and customers – resources and capabilities. Organizations use them to create value in the form of goods and services. Resources are direct inputs for production. Capabilities represent an organization's ability to coordinate, control and deploy resources to produce value. Capabilities are typically experience-driven, knowledge-intensive, information-based and firmly embedded within an organization's people, systems, processes and technologies. It is relatively easy to acquire resources compared to capabilities (see Figure 2.4 for examples of capabilities and resources).

Service providers need to develop distinctive capabilities to retain customers with value propositions that are hard for competitors to duplicate. For example, two service providers may have similar resources such as applications, infrastructure and access to finance. Their capabilities, however, differ in terms of management systems, organization structure, processes and knowledge assets. This difference is reflected in actual performance.

Capabilities by themselves cannot produce value without adequate and appropriate resources. The productive capacity of a service provider is dependent on the resources under its control. Capabilities are used to develop, deploy and coordinate this productive capacity. For example, capabilities such as capacity management and availability management are used to manage the performance and utilization of processes, applications and infrastructure, ensuring service levels are effectively delivered.

2.2.2 Processes

> **Definition: process**
>
> A process is a structured set of activities designed to accomplish a specific objective. A process takes one or more defined inputs and turns them into defined outputs.

Processes define actions, dependencies and sequence. Well-defined processes can improve productivity within and across organizations and functions. Process characteristics include:

- **Measurability** We are able to measure the process in a relevant manner. It is performance-driven. Managers want to measure cost, quality and other variables while practitioners are concerned with duration and productivity.
- **Specific results** The reason a process exists is to deliver a specific result. This result must be individually identifiable and countable.

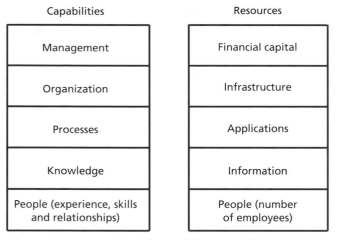

Capabilities

Capabilities
Management
Organization
Processes
Knowledge
People (experience, skills and relationships)

Resources

Resources
Financial capital
Infrastructure
Applications
Information
People (number of employees)

Figure 2.4 Examples of capabilities and resources

- **Customers** Every process delivers its primary results to a customer or stakeholder. Customers may be internal or external to the organization, but the process must meet their expectations.
- **Responsiveness to specific triggers** While a process may be ongoing or iterative, it should be traceable to a specific trigger.

A process is organized around a set of objectives. The main outputs from the process should be driven by the objectives and should include process measurements (metrics), reports and process improvement.

The output produced by a process has to conform to operational norms that are derived from business objectives. If products conform to the set norm, the process can be considered effective (because it can be repeated, measured and managed, and achieves the required outcome). If the activities of the process are carried out with a minimum use of resources, the process can also be considered efficient.

Inputs are data or information used by the process and may be the output from another process.

A process, or an activity within a process, is initiated by a trigger. A trigger may be the arrival of an input or other event. For example, the failure of a server may trigger the event management and incident management processes.

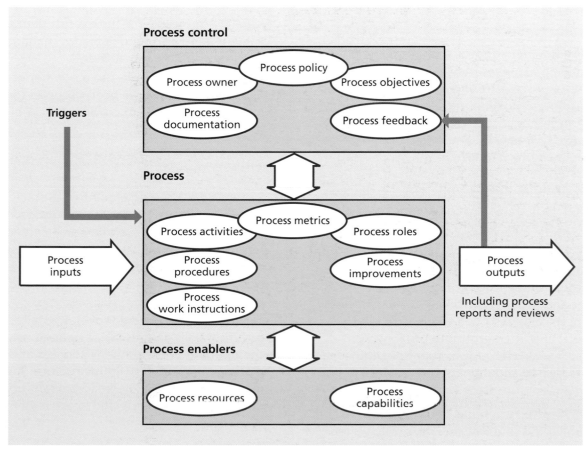

Figure 2.5 Process model

A process may include any of the roles, responsibilities, tools and management controls required to deliver the outputs reliably. A process may define policies, standards, guidelines, activities and work instructions if they are needed.

Processes, once defined, should be documented and controlled. Once under control, they can be repeated and managed. Process measurement and metrics can be built into the process to control and improve the process as illustrated in Figure 2.5. Process analysis, results and metrics should be incorporated in regular management reports and process improvements.

2.2.3 Organizing for service management

There is no single best way to organize, and best practices described in ITIL need to be tailored to suit individual organizations and situations. Any changes made will need to take into account resource constraints and the size, nature and needs of the business and customers. The starting point for organizational design is strategy. Organizational development for service management is described in more detail in *ITIL Service Strategy* Chapter 6.

2.2.3.1 Functions

A function is a team or group of people and the tools or other resources they use to carry out one or more processes or activities. In larger organizations, a function may be broken out and performed by several departments, teams and groups, or it may be embodied within a single organizational unit (e.g. the service desk). In smaller organizations, one person or group can perform multiple functions – for example, a technical management department could also incorporate the service desk function.

For the service lifecycle to be successful, an organization will need to clearly define the roles and responsibilities required to undertake the processes and activities involved in each lifecycle stage. These roles will need to be assigned to individuals, and an appropriate organization structure of teams, groups or functions will need to be established and managed. These are defined as follows:

- **Group** A group is a number of people who are similar in some way. In ITIL, groups refer to people who perform similar activities –

even though they may work on different technologies or report into different organizational structures or even different companies. Groups are usually not formal organizational structures, but are very useful in defining common processes across the organization – for example, ensuring that all people who resolve incidents complete the incident record in the same way.

- **Team** A team is a more formal type of group. These are people who work together to achieve a common objective, but not necessarily in the same organizational structure. Team members can be co-located, or work in multiple locations and operate virtually. Teams are useful for collaboration, or for dealing with a situation of a temporary or transitional nature. Examples of teams include project teams, application development teams (often consisting of people from several different business units) and incident or problem resolution teams.

- **Department** Departments are formal organizational structures which exist to perform a specific set of defined activities on an ongoing basis. Departments have a hierarchical reporting structure with managers who are usually responsible for the execution of the activities and also for day-to-day management of the staff in the department.

- **Division** A division refers to a number of departments that have been grouped together, often by geography or product line. A division is normally self-contained.

ITIL Service Operation describes the following functions in detail:

- **Service desk** The single point of contact for users when there is a service disruption, for service requests, or even for some categories of request for change. The service desk provides a point of communication to users and a point of coordination for several IT groups and processes.

- **Technical management** Provides detailed technical skills and resources needed to support the ongoing operation of IT services and the management of the IT infrastructure. Technical management also plays an important role in the design, testing, release and improvement of IT services.

- **IT operations management** Executes the daily operational activities needed to manage IT services and the supporting IT infrastructure. This is done according to the performance standards defined during service design. IT operations management has two sub-functions that are generally organizationally distinct. These are IT operations control and facilities management.
- **Application management** Is responsible for managing applications throughout their lifecycle. The application management function supports and maintains operational applications and also plays an important role in the design, testing and improvement of applications that form part of IT services.

The other core ITIL publications do not define any functions in detail, but they do rely on the technical and application management functions described in *ITIL Service Operation*. Technical and application management provide the technical resources and expertise to manage the whole service lifecycle, and practitioner roles within a particular lifecycle stage may be performed by members of these functions.

2.2.3.2 Roles

A number of roles need to be performed during the service lifecycle. The core ITIL publications provide guidelines and examples of role descriptions. These are not exhaustive or prescriptive, and in many cases roles will need to be combined or separated. Organizations should take care to apply this guidance in a way that suits their own structure and objectives.

> **Definition: role**
>
> A role is a set of responsibilities, activities and authorities granted to a person or team. A role is defined in a process or function. One person or team may have multiple roles – for example, the roles of configuration manager and change manager may be carried out by a single person.

Roles are often confused with job titles but it is important to realize that they are not the same. Each organization will define appropriate job titles and job descriptions which suit their needs, and individuals holding these job titles can perform one or more of the required roles.

It should also be recognized that a person may, as part of their job assignment, perform a single task that represents participation in more than one process. For example, a technical analyst who submits a request for change (RFC) to add memory to a server to resolve a performance problem is participating in activities of the change management process at the same time as taking part in activities of the capacity management and problem management processes.

See Chapter 6 for more details about the roles and responsibilities described in *ITIL Service Design*.

2.2.3.3 Organizational culture and behaviour

Organizational culture is the set of shared values and norms that control the service provider's interactions with all stakeholders, including customers, users, suppliers, internal staff etc. An organization's values are desired modes of behaviour that affect its culture. Examples of organizational values include high standards, customer care, respecting tradition and authority, acting cautiously and conservatively, and being frugal.

High-performing service providers continually align the value network for efficiency and effectiveness. Culture through the value network is transmitted to staff through socialization, training programmes, stories, ceremonies and language.

Constraints such as governance, capabilities, standards, resources, values and ethics play a significant role in organizational culture and behaviour. Organizational culture can also be affected by structure or management styles resulting in a positive or negative impact on performance. Organizational structures and management styles contribute to the behaviour of people, process, technology and partners. These are important aspects in adopting service management practices and ITIL.

Change related to service management programmes will affect organizational culture and it is important to prepare people with effective communication plans, training, policies and procedures to achieve the desired performance outcomes. Establishing cultural change is also an important factor for collaborative working between the many different people involved in service management. Managing people through service transitions is discussed at more length in Chapter 5 of *ITIL Service Transition*.

2.2.4 The service portfolio

The service portfolio is the complete set of services that is managed by a service provider and it represents the service provider's commitments and investments across all customers and market spaces. It also represents present contractual commitments, new service development, and ongoing service improvement plans initiated by continual service improvement. The portfolio may include third-party services, which are an integral part of service offerings to customers.

The service portfolio represents all the resources presently engaged or being released in various stages of the service lifecycle. It is a database or structured document in three parts:

- **Service pipeline** All services that are under consideration or development, but are not yet available to customers. It includes major investment opportunities that have to be traced to the delivery of services, and the value that will be realized. The service pipeline provides a business view of possible future services and is part of the service portfolio that is not normally published to customers.
- **Service catalogue** All live IT services, including those available for deployment. It is the only part of the service portfolio published to customers, and is used to support the sale and delivery of IT services. It includes a customer-facing view (or views) of the IT services in use, how they are intended to be used, the business processes they enable, and the levels and quality of service the customer can expect for each service. The service catalogue also includes information about supporting services required by the service provider to deliver customer-facing services. Information about services can only enter the service catalogue after due diligence has been performed on related costs and risks.
- **Retired services** All services that have been phased out or retired. Retired services are not available to new customers or contracts unless a special business case is made.

Service providers often find it useful to distinguish customer-facing services from supporting services:

- **Customer-facing services** IT services that are visible to the customer. These are normally services that support the customer's business processes and facilitate one or more outcomes desired by the customer.
- **Supporting services** IT services that support or 'underpin' the customer-facing services. These are typically invisible to the customer, but are essential to the delivery of customer-facing IT services.

Figure 2.6 illustrates the components of the service portfolio, which are discussed in detail in *ITIL Service Strategy*. These are important components of the service knowledge management system (SKMS) described in section 2.2.5.

2.2.5 Knowledge management and the SKMS

Quality knowledge and information enable people to perform process activities and support the flow of information between service lifecycle stages and processes. Understanding, defining, establishing and maintaining information is a responsibility of the knowledge management process.

Implementing an SKMS enables effective decision support and reduces the risks that arise from a lack of proper mechanisms. However, implementing an SKMS can involve a large investment in tools to store and manage data, information and knowledge. Every organization will start this work in a different place, and have their own vision of where they want to be, so there is no simple answer to the question 'What tools and systems are needed to support knowledge management?' Data, information and knowledge need to be interrelated across the organization. A document management system and/or a configuration management system (CMS) can be used as a foundation for implementation of the SKMS.

Figure 2.7 illustrates an architecture for service knowledge management that has four layers including examples of possible content at each layer. These are:

- **Presentation layer** Enables searching, browsing, retrieving, updating, subscribing and collaboration. The different views onto the other layers are suitable for different audiences. Each view should be protected to ensure that only authorized people can see or modify the underlying knowledge, information and data.

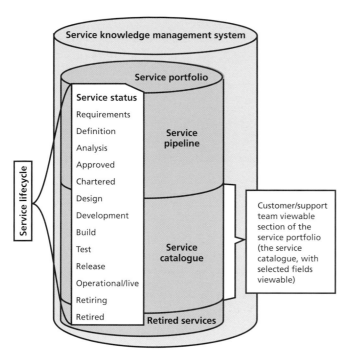

Figure 2.6 The service portfolio and its contents

- **Knowledge processing layer** Is where the information is converted into useful knowledge which enables decision-making.
- **Information integration layer** Provides integrated information that may be gathered from data in multiple sources in the data layer.
- **Data layer** Includes tools for data discovery and data collection, and data items in unstructured and structured forms.

In practice, an SKMS is likely to consist of multiple tools and repositories. For example, there may be a tool that provides all four layers for the support of different processes or combinations of processes. Various tools providing a range of perspectives will be used by different stakeholders to access this common repository for collaborative decision support.

This architecture is applicable for many of the management information systems in ITIL. A primary component of the SKMS is the service portfolio, covered in section 2.2.4. Other examples include the CMS, the availability management information system (AMIS) and the capacity management information system (CMIS).

2.3 GOVERNANCE AND MANAGEMENT SYSTEMS

2.3.1 Governance

Governance is the single overarching area that ties IT and the business together, and services are one way of ensuring that the organization is able to execute that governance. Governance is what defines the common directions, policies and rules that both the business and IT use to conduct business.

Many ITSM strategies fail because they try to build a structure or processes according to how they would like the organization to work instead of working within the existing governance structures.

> **Definition: governance**
>
> Ensures that policies and strategy are actually implemented, and that required processes are correctly followed. Governance includes defining roles and responsibilities, measuring and reporting, and taking actions to resolve any issues identified.

Governance works to apply a consistently managed approach at all levels of the organization – first by ensuring a clear strategy is set, then by defining the policies whereby the strategy will be achieved. The policies also define boundaries, or what the organization may not do as part of its operations.

Governance needs to be able to evaluate, direct and monitor the strategy, policies and plans. Further information on governance and service management is provided in Chapter 5 of *ITIL Service Strategy*. The international standard for corporate governance of IT is ISO/IEC 38500, described in Appendix N.

2.3.2 Management systems

A system is a number of related things that work together to achieve an overall objective. Systems should be self-regulating for agility and timeliness. In order to accomplish this, the relationships within the system must influence one another for the sake of the whole. Key components of the system are the structure and processes that work together.

A systems approach to service management ensures learning and improvement through a big-picture view of services and service management.

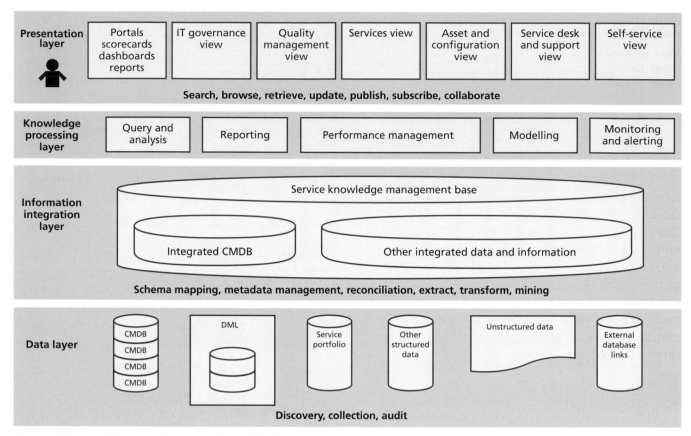

Figure 2.7 Architectural layers of an SKMS

It extends the management horizon and provides a sustainable long-term approach.

By understanding the system structure, the interconnections between all the assets and service components, and how changes in any area will affect the whole system and its constituent parts over time, a service provider can deliver benefits such as:

- Ability to adapt to the changing needs of customers and markets
- Sustainable performance
- Better approach to managing services, risks, costs and value delivery
- Effective and efficient service management
- Simplified approach that is easier for people to use
- Less conflict between processes
- Reduced duplication and bureaucracy.

Many businesses have adopted management system standards for competitive advantage and to ensure a consistent approach in implementing service management across their value network.

Implementation of a management system also provides support for governance (see section 2.3.1).

Definition: management system (ISO 9001)

The framework of policy, processes, functions, standards, guidelines and tools that ensures an organization or part of an organization can achieve its objectives.

A management system of an organization can adopt multiple management system standards, such as:

- A quality management system (ISO 9001)
- An environmental management system (ISO 14000)
- A service management system (ISO/IEC 20000)
- An information security management system (ISO/IEC 27001)
- A management system for software asset management (ISO/IEC 19770).

Service providers are increasingly adopting these standards to be able to demonstrate their service management capability. As there are common elements between such management systems, they should be managed in an integrated way rather than having separate management systems. To meet the requirements of a specific management system standard, an organization needs to analyse the requirements of the relevant standard in detail and compare them with those that have already been incorporated in the existing integrated management system. Appendix N provides further information on these standards.

ISO management system standards use the Plan-Do-Check-Act (PDCA) cycle shown in Figure 2.8. The ITIL service lifecycle approach embraces and enhances the interpretation of the PDCA cycle. You will see the PDCA cycle used in the structure of the guidance provided in each of the core ITIL publications. This guidance recognizes the need to drive governance, organizational design and management systems from the business strategy, service strategy and service requirements.

> **Definition: ISO/IEC 20000**
>
> An international standard for IT service management.

ISO/IEC 20000 is an internationally recognized standard that allows organizations to demonstrate excellence and prove best practice in ITSM.

Part 1 specifies requirements for the service provider to plan, establish, implement, operate, monitor, review, maintain and improve a service management system (SMS). Coordinated integration and implementation of an SMS, to meet the Part 1 requirements, provides ongoing control, greater effectiveness, efficiency and opportunities for continual improvement. It ensures that the service provider:

- Understands and fulfils the service requirements to achieve customer satisfaction
- Establishes the policy and objectives for service management
- Designs and delivers changes and services that add value for the customer
- Monitors, measures and reviews performance of the SMS and the services
- Continually improves the SMS and the services based on objective measurements.

Service providers across the world have successfully established an SMS to direct and control their service management activities. The adoption of an SMS should be a strategic decision for an organization.

One of the most common routes for an organization to achieve the requirements of ISO/IEC 20000 is by adopting ITIL service management

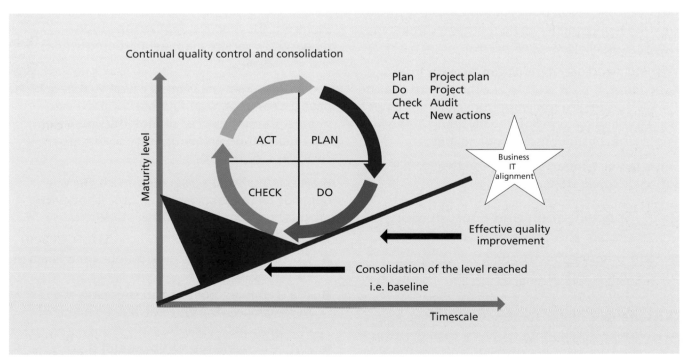

Figure 2.8 Plan-Do-Check-Act cycle

best practices and using the ITIL qualification scheme for professional development.

Certification to ISO/IEC 20000-1 by an accredited certification body shows that a service provider is committed to delivering value to its customers and continual service improvement. It demonstrates the existence of an effective SMS that satisfies the requirements of an independent external audit. Certification gives a service provider a competitive edge in marketing. Many organizations specify a requirement to comply with ISO/IEC 20000 in their contracts and agreements.

2.4 THE SERVICE LIFECYCLE

Services and processes describe how things change, whereas structure describes how they are connected. Structure helps to determine the correct behaviours required for service management.

Structure describes how process, people, technology and partners are connected. Structure is essential for organizing information. Without structure, our service management knowledge is merely a collection of observations, practices and conflicting goals. The structure of the service lifecycle is an organizing framework, supported by the organizational structure, service portfolio and service models within an organization. Structure can influence or determine the behaviour of the organization and people. Altering the structure of service management can be more effective than simply controlling discrete events.

Without structure, it is difficult to learn from experience. It is difficult to use the past to educate for the future. We can learn from experience but we also need to confront directly many of the most important consequences of our actions.

See Chapter 1 for an introduction to each ITIL service lifecycle stage.

2.4.1 Specialization and coordination across the lifecycle

Organizations need a collaborative approach for the management of assets which are used to deliver and support services for their customers.

Organizations should function in the same manner as a high-performing sports team. Each player in a team and each member of the team's organization who are not players position themselves to support the goal of the team. Each player and team member has a different specialization that contributes to the whole. The team matures over time taking into account feedback from experience, best practice, current process and procedures to become an agile high-performing team.

Specialization and coordination are necessary in the lifecycle approach. Specialization allows for expert focus on components of the service but components of the service also need to work together for value. Specialization combined with coordination helps to manage expertise, improve focus and reduce overlaps and gaps in processes. Specialization and coordination together help to create a collaborative and agile organizational architecture that maximizes utilization of assets.

Coordination across the lifecycle creates an environment focused on business and customer outcomes instead of just IT objectives and projects. Coordination is also essential between functional groups, across the value network, and between processes and technology.

Feedback and control between organizational assets helps to enable operational efficiency, organizational effectiveness and economies of scale.

2.4.2 Processes through the service lifecycle

Each core ITIL lifecycle publication includes guidance on service management processes as shown in Table 2.1.

Service management is more effective if people have a clear understanding of how processes interact throughout the service lifecycle, within the organization and with other parties (users, customers, suppliers).

Process integration across the service lifecycle depends on the service owner, process owners, process practitioners and other stakeholders understanding:

- The context of use, scope, purpose and limits of each process
- The strategies, policies and standards that apply to the processes and to the management of interfaces between processes
- Authorities and responsibilities of those involved in each process

■ The information provided by each process that flows from one process to another; who produces it; and how it is used by integrated processes.

Integrating service management processes depends on the flow of information across process and organizational boundaries. This in turn depends on implementing supporting technology and management information systems across organizational boundaries, rather than in silos. If service management processes are implemented, followed or changed in isolation, they can become a bureaucratic overhead that does not deliver value for money. They could also damage or negate the operation or value of other processes and services.

Table 2.1 The processes described in each core ITIL publication

Core ITIL lifecycle publication	Processes described in the publication
ITIL Service Strategy	Strategy management for IT services
	Service portfolio management
	Financial management for IT services
	Demand management
	Business relationship management
ITIL Service Design	Design coordination
	Service catalogue management
	Service level management
	Availability management
	Capacity management
	IT service continuity management
	Information security management
	Supplier management
ITIL Service Transition	Transition planning and support
	Change management
	Service asset and configuration management
	Release and deployment management
	Service validation and testing
	Change evaluation
	Knowledge management
ITIL Service Operation	Event management
	Incident management
	Request fulfilment
	Problem management
	Access management
ITIL Continual Service Improvement	Seven-step improvement process

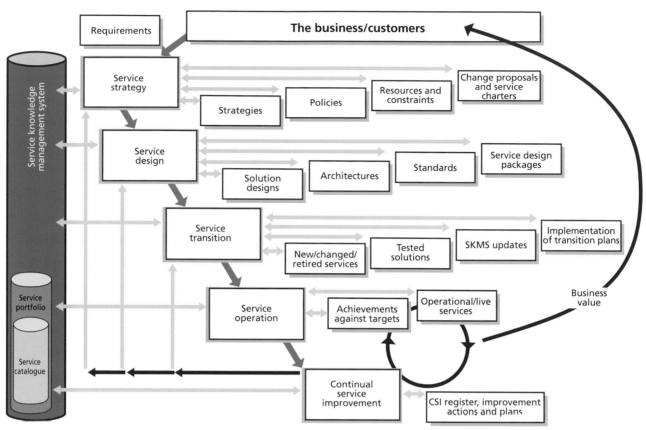

Figure 2.9 Integration across the service lifecycle

As discussed in section 2.2.2, each process has a clear scope with a structured set of activities that transform inputs to deliver the outputs reliably. A process interface is the boundary of the process. Process integration is the linking of processes by ensuring that information flows from one process to another effectively and efficiently. If there is management commitment to process integration, processes are generally easier to implement and there will be fewer conflicts between processes.

Stages of the lifecycle work together as an integrated system to support the ultimate objective of service management for business value realization. Every stage is interdependent as shown in Figure 2.9. See Appendix O for examples of inputs and outputs across the service lifecycle.

The SKMS, described in section 2.2.5, enables integration across the service lifecycle stages. It provides secure and controlled access to the knowledge, information and data that are needed to manage and deliver services. The service portfolio represents all the assets presently

engaged or being released in various stages of the lifecycle.

Chapter 1 provides a summary of each stage in the service lifecycle but it is also important to understand how the lifecycle stages work together.

Service strategy establishes policies and principles that provide guidance for the whole service lifecycle. The service portfolio is defined in this lifecycle stage, and new or changed services are chartered.

During the service design stage of the lifecycle, everything needed to transition and operate the new or changed service is documented in a service design package. This lifecycle stage also designs everything needed to create, transition and operate the services, including management information systems and tools, architectures, processes, measurement methods and metrics.

The activities of the service transition and service operation stages of the lifecycle are defined during service design. Service transition ensures that the

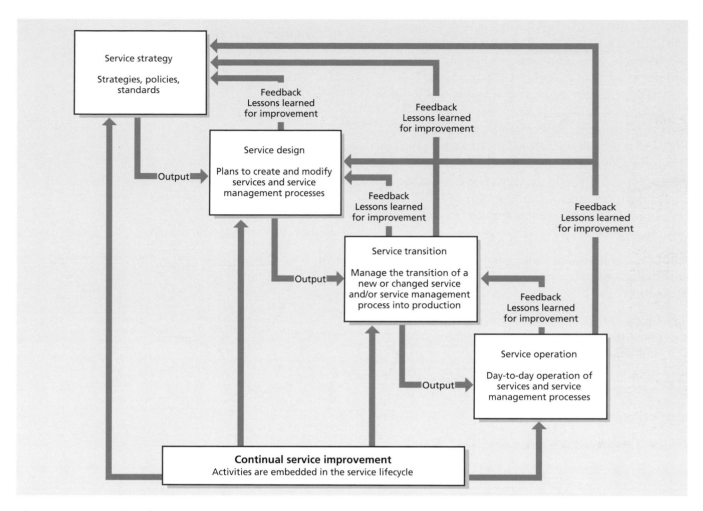

Figure 2.10 Continual service improvement and the service lifecycle

requirements of the service strategy, developed in service design, are effectively realized in service operation while controlling the risks of failure and disruption.

The service operation stage of the service lifecycle carries out the activities and processes required to deliver the agreed services. During this stage of the lifecycle, the value defined in the service strategy is realized.

Continual service improvement acts in tandem with all the other lifecycle stages. All processes, activities, roles, services and technology should be measured and subjected to continual improvement.

Most ITIL processes and functions have activities that take place across multiple stages of the service lifecycle. For example:

■ The service validation and testing process may design tests during the service design stage and perform these tests during service transition.
■ The technical management function may provide input to strategic decisions about technology, as well as assisting in the design and transition of infrastructure components.
■ Business relationship managers may assist in gathering detailed requirements during the service design stage of the lifecycle, or take part in the management of major incidents during the service operation stage.
■ All service lifecycle stages contribute to the seven-step improvement process.

Appendix O identifies some of the major inputs and outputs between each stage of the service lifecycle. Chapter 3 of each core ITIL publication provides more detail on the inputs and outputs of the specific lifecycle stage it describes.

The strength of the service lifecycle rests upon continual feedback throughout each stage of the lifecycle. This feedback ensures that service optimization is managed from a business perspective and is measured in terms of the value the business derives from services at any point in time during the service lifecycle. The service lifecycle is non-linear in design. At every point in the service lifecycle, the process of monitoring, assessment and feedback between each stage drives decisions about the need for minor course corrections or major service improvement initiatives.

Figure 2.10 illustrates some examples of the continual feedback system built into the service lifecycle.

Adopting appropriate technology to automate the processes and provide management with the information that supports the processes is also important for effective and efficient service management.

Service design
principles

3

3 Service design principles

'See first that the design is wise and just: that ascertained, pursue it resolutely; do not for one repulse forgo the purpose that you resolved to effect.' William Shakespeare (1564–1616)

'The common mistake that people make when trying to design something completely foolproof is to underestimate the ingenuity of complete fools.' Douglas Adams (1952–2001)

The main purpose of the service design stage of the lifecycle is the design of new or changed services for introduction into the live environment. In this context, the retirement of a service also constitutes a 'change' and must be carefully designed. This stage of the lifecycle is also responsible for the design of the service provider's overall service management system and the many aspects required to deliver services effectively such as processes, architectures and tools.

3.1 SERVICE DESIGN BASICS

If services or processes are not designed they will evolve organically. If they evolve without proper controls, the tendency is simply to react to environmental conditions that have occurred rather than to understand clearly the overall vision and needs of the business. Designing to match the anticipated environment is much more effective and efficient, but often impossible – hence the need to consider iterative and incremental approaches to service design. Iterative and incremental approaches are essential to ensure that services introduced to the live environment continually adapt in alignment with evolving business needs. In the absence of formalized service design, services will often be unduly expensive to run, prone to failure, resources will be wasted and services will not be fully aligned to business needs. It is unlikely that any improvement programme will ever be able to achieve what proper design should achieve in the first place. Without service design, cost-effective service is not possible.

Adopting and implementing standardized and consistent approaches for service design will:

- Enable projects to estimate the cost, timing, resource requirement and risks associated with the service design stage more accurately

- Result in higher volumes of successful change
- Make design methods easier for people to adopt and follow
- Enable service design assets to be shared and reused across projects and services
- Reduce delays from the need to redesign prior to completion of service transition
- Improve management of expectations for all stakeholders involved in service design including customers, users, suppliers, partners and projects
- Increase confidence that the new or changed service can be delivered to specification without unexpectedly affecting other services or stakeholders
- Ensure that new or changed services will be maintainable and cost-effective.

All designs and design activities need to be driven principally by the business needs and requirements of the organization. Within this context they must also reflect the needs of the strategies, plans and policies produced by service strategy processes, as illustrated in Figure 2.9.

Figure 2.9 gives a good overview of some of the key links, inputs and outputs involved at each stage of the service lifecycle. It illustrates key outputs produced by each stage, which are used as inputs by the subsequent stages. The service portfolio acts as 'the spine' of the service lifecycle. It is the single integrated source of information on the status of each service, together with other service details and the interfaces and dependencies between services. The information within the service portfolio is used by the activities within each stage of the service lifecycle.

The key output of the service design stage is the design of service solutions to meet the changing requirements of the business. When designing these solutions, input from many different areas needs to be considered within the various activities involved in designing the service solution, from identifying and analysing requirements, through to building a solution and service design package (SDP – see Appendix A) to hand over to service transition.

3.1.1 Holistic service design

There are five individual aspects of service design, and these are discussed in much greater detail later in this chapter. These aspects are the design of:

■ Service solutions for new or changed services
■ Management information systems and tools, (especially the service portfolio, including the service catalogue)
■ Technology architectures and management architectures
■ The processes required
■ Measurement methods and metrics.

It is important that a holistic, results-driven approach to all aspects of design is adopted, and that when changing or amending any of the individual elements of design all other aspects are considered. When designing and developing a new application, this should not be done in isolation, but should also consider the impact on the overall service, the management information systems and tools (e.g. service portfolio and service catalogue), the architectures, the technology, the service management processes, and the necessary measurements and metrics. This will ensure not only that the functional elements are addressed by the design, but also that all of the management and operational requirements are addressed as a fundamental part of the design and are not added as an afterthought.

This holistic approach and the five aspects of design identified above are important parts of the service provider's overall service management system. For more on establishing a service management system, see section 2.3.2.

This approach should also be used when the change to the service is its retirement. Unless the retirement of a service or any aspect of a service is carefully planned, the retirement could cause unexpected negative effects on the customer or business which might otherwise have been avoided.

> **Key message**
>
> A holistic approach should be adopted for all service design aspects and areas to ensure consistency and integration within all activities and processes across the entire IT technology, providing end-to-end business-related functionality and quality.

Not every change within an IT service will require the instigation of the same level of service design activity. It can be argued that every change, no matter how small, needs to be designed, but the scale of the activity necessary to ensure success will vary greatly from one change type to another. Every organization must define what categories of change require what level of design activity and ensure that everyone within the organization is clear on these requirements. In other words, all changes should be assessed for their service design requirements to determine the correct service design activities to undertake in each circumstance. This should be part of the change management process impact assessment described within *ITIL Service Transition*.

3.1.2 IT service design and overall business change

IT service design is a part of the overall business change process. This business change process and the role of IT are illustrated in Figure 3.1. The diagram shows the overall flow of the process used to manage change on the business side – the 'business change process'. The individual steps of the change process reflect that when it is invoked,

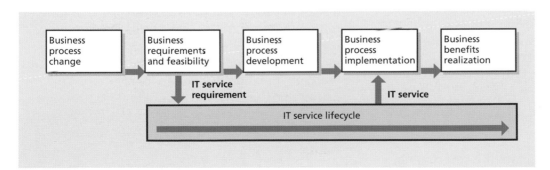

Figure 3.1 The business change process

the element changing on the business side is most often a business process (a 'business process change'), resulting in the need for a supporting change in IT service.

Once accurate information on what is required has been obtained and signed off with regard to the changed needs of the business, the plan for the delivery of a service to meet the agreed need can be developed. The role of the service design stage within this overall business change process can be described as the design of appropriate and innovative IT services, including their architectures, processes, policies and documentation, to meet current and future agreed business requirements.

3.1.3 Scope and flow of service design

The service design stage of the lifecycle starts with a set of new or changed business requirements and ends with the development of a service solution designed to meet the documented needs of the business. This service solution, together with its SDP, is then passed to service transition to evaluate, build, test and deploy the new or changed service, or to retire the service, if this is the change required. On completion of these transition activities, control is transferred to the service operation stage of the service lifecycle. The overall scope of service design and the five aspects of design are illustrated in Figure 3.2 within the context of the IT service provider's relationship to the business. Figure 3.2 shows how IT and the business interact through the provision of service

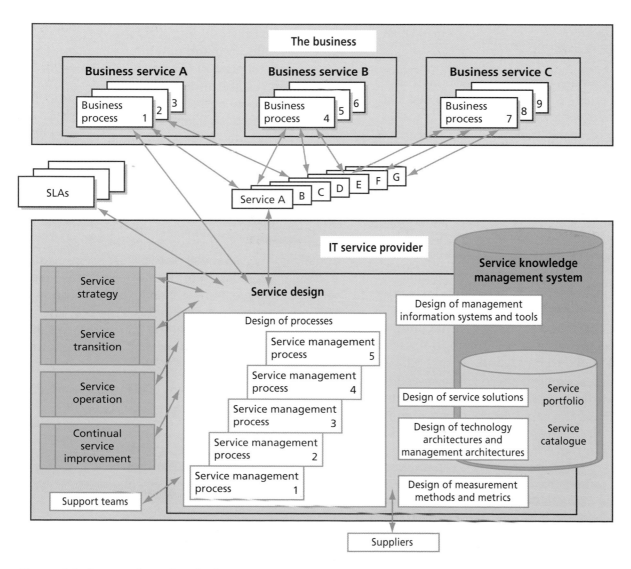

Figure 3.2 Scope of service design

and how the work of service design is part of the complete service lifecycle.

There are five individual aspects of service design:

■ **Service solutions for new or changed services** The requirements for new or changed services are extracted from the service portfolio. Each requirement is analysed, documented and agreed, and a solution design is produced that is then compared with the strategies and constraints from service strategy to ensure that it conforms to corporate and IT policies. The design must ensure that this new or changed service is consistent with all other services, and that all other services that interface with, underpin or depend on the new or changed service are consistent with the new service. If not, either the design of the new service or the other existing services will need to be adapted.

Each individual service solution design is also considered in conjunction with each of the other four aspects of service design.

■ **The management information systems and tools, especially the service portfolio** The management information systems and tools should be reviewed to ensure they are capable of supporting the new or changed service. (Examples of several of the key management information systems and tools to be addressed are shown in Figure 3.2.)

■ **The technology architectures and management architectures** These are reviewed to ensure that all the technology architectures and management architectures are consistent with the new or changed service and have the capability to operate and maintain the new service. If not, then either the architectures will need to be amended or the design of the new service will need to be revised.

■ **The processes required** These are reviewed to ensure that the processes, roles, responsibilities and skills have the capability to operate, support and maintain the new or changed service. If not, the design of the new service will need to be revised or the existing process capabilities will need to be enhanced. This includes all IT and service management processes, not just the processes involved in the service design stage itself.

■ **The measurement methods and metrics** These are reviewed to ensure that the existing measurement methods can provide the required metrics on the new or changed service. If not, then the measurement methods will need to be enhanced or the service metrics will need to be revised.

Completion of all of the above activities during the service design stage will ensure minimal issues arising during the subsequent stages of the service lifecycle. Therefore service design must consolidate the key design issues and activities of all IT and service management processes within its own design activities, to ensure that all aspects are considered and included within all designs for new or changed services as part of everyday process operation.

3.1.4 Value to the business

In ITIL it is understood that the focus on business processes supported and business value provided is a fundamental principle of IT service management. With this focus, the impact of technology on the business and how business change may impact technology can both be predicted. The creation of a totally integrated service catalogue – including business units, processes and services, and their relationships and dependencies on IT services, technology and components – is crucial to increasing the IT service provider's capability to meet the business's needs. All aspects of service design are vital elements in supporting and enhancing the capability of the IT service provider, particularly the design of the service portfolio, the service catalogue and the individual IT services. All of these activities will also improve the alignment of IT service provision with the business's goals and its evolving needs.

The business focus in ITIL service management (ITSM) enables an IT service provider organization to:

■ Align IT service provision with business goals and objectives

■ Prioritize all IT activities based on business impact and urgency, ensuring critical business processes and services receive the most attention

■ Increase business productivity and profitability through the increased efficiency and effectiveness of IT processes

- Support the requirements for corporate governance with appropriate IT governance and controls
- Create competitive advantage through the exploitation and innovation of IT infrastructure as a whole
- Improve service quality, customer satisfaction and user perception
- Ensure regulatory and legislative compliance
- Ensure appropriate levels of protection on all IT and information assets
- Ensure that IT services continue to be aligned with changing business needs over time.

3.1.4.1 Demonstrating business value

The ability to measure and demonstrate value to the business requires the capability to link business outcomes, objectives and their underpinning processes and functions to the IT services and their underpinning assets, processes and functions. The service provider can ensure that service provision is linked to business value by:

- Agreeing services, service level agreements (SLAs) and targets across the whole enterprise, ensuring critical business processes receive most attention
- Measuring IT quality in business/user terms, reporting what is relevant to users (e.g. customer satisfaction, business value)
- Mapping business processes to IT services and IT infrastructure, to ensure that dependencies between the relationships are well understood, and to reduce the possibility of disruptions caused by loss of focus on business services and processes
- Mapping business processes to business and service measurements, to ensure focus on IT service measurements related to business performance measurements and desired business outcomes
- Mapping infrastructure resources to services in order to take full advantage of critical IT components that are linked to critical business processes. This mapping is done within the configuration management system (CMS), and may also use information within the complete service knowledge management system (SKMS). (More information on the CMS can be found within *ITIL Service Transition*.)

- Providing end-to-end performance monitoring and measurement of IT services supporting business processes, regularly reported against SLA targets.

3.1.5 Comprehensive and integrated service design

It is essential that IT systems and services are designed, planned, implemented and managed appropriately for the business as a whole. The requirement then is to provide IT services that:

- Are business- and customer-oriented, focused and driven
- Are cost-effective
- Meet the customer's security requirements
- Are flexible and adaptable, yet fit for purpose at the point of delivery
- Can absorb an ever-increasing demand in the volume and speed of change
- Meet increasing business demands for continuous operation
- Are managed and operated to an acceptable level of risk
- Are responsive, with appropriate availability and capacity matched to business needs.

With all these pressures on both IT and the business, the temptation – and unfortunately the reality in some cases – is to 'cut corners' on the design and planning processes or to ignore them completely. However, in these situations the design and planning activities are even more essential to the overall delivery of quality services. Therefore, more time rather than less should be devoted to the design processes and their implementation.

In order that effective, quality design can be achieved, even when timescales are short and pressure to deliver services is high, organizations should ensure that the importance of the service design stage is fully understood and that support is provided to maintain and mature service design as a fundamental element of service management. Organizations should strive continually to review and improve their service design capability, in order that service design can become a consistent and repeatable practice, enabling organizations to deliver quality services against challenging timescales. Having a mature service design practice will also enable organizations to reduce risk in the transition and operational stages of service.

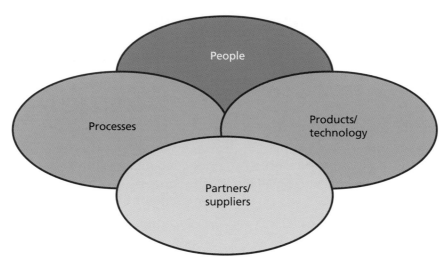

Figure 3.3 The four Ps

In general, the key to the successful provision of IT services is an appropriate level of design and planning to determine which projects, processes and services will have the greatest impact or benefit to the business. With the appropriate level of thought, design, preparation and planning, effort can be targeted at those areas that will yield the greatest return. Risk assessment and management are key requirements within all design activities. Therefore, risk assessment and management must be included as an integrated part of addressing all five aspects of service design. This will ensure that the risks involved in the provision of services and the operation of processes, technology and measurement methods are aligned with business risk and impact, because risk assessment and management are embedded within all design processes and activities.

Many designs, plans and projects fail through a lack of preparation and management. The implementation of ITSM as a practice is about preparing and planning the effective and efficient use of the four Ps: the people, the processes, the products (services, technology and tools) and the partners (suppliers, manufacturers and vendors), as illustrated in Figure 3.3.

However, there is no benefit in producing designs, plans, architectures and policies and keeping them to yourself. They must be published, agreed, circulated and actively used.

It is important that the right interfaces and links to the design activities exist. When designing new or changed services, it is vital that the entire service lifecycle and ITSM processes are involved from

the outset. Often difficulties occur in operations when a newly designed service is handed over for live running at the last minute. The following are actions that need to be undertaken from the outset of a service design to ensure that the solution meets the requirements of the business:

■ The new service solution should be added to the overall service portfolio from the concept phase, and the service portfolio should be updated to reflect the current status through any incremental or iterative development. This will be beneficial not only from the financial perspective, but also from all other areas during design.

■ As part of the initial service/system analysis, there will be a need to understand the service level requirements (SLRs) for the service when it goes live.

■ From the SLRs, the various processes and functions must ascertain if customer's requirements can be met with current resources and capabilities. For example, the capacity management team can model this within the current infrastructure to ascertain if it will be able to support the new service. If organizational policies require it, the results from the modelling activities can be built into the capacity plan.

■ If new infrastructure is required for the new service, or extended support, financial management for IT services will need to be involved to set the budget.

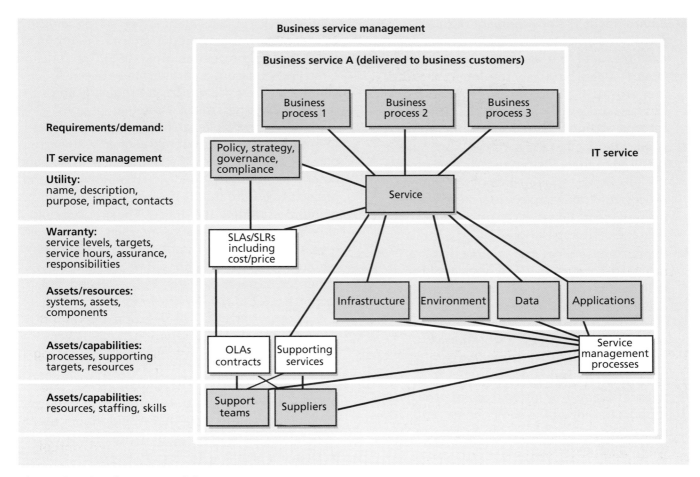

Figure 3.4 Service composition

- An initial business impact analysis and risk assessment should be conducted on services well before implementation as invaluable input into IT service continuity strategy, availability design, security design and capacity planning.
- The service desk will need to be made aware of new services well in advance of live operation to prepare and train service desk staff and potentially IT customer staff.
- The technical management, application management and IT operations management functions (see *ITIL Service Operation*) also need to be made aware of new services to allow them to plan for effective operational support of the services.
- Service transition can start planning the implementation and build into the change schedule.
- Supplier management will need to be involved if procurement is required for the new service.

The composition of a service and its constituent parts is illustrated in Figure 3.4.

Service design must consider all these aspects when designing service solutions to meet new and evolving business needs:

- **Business process** To define the functional needs of the service being provided – for example, telesales, invoicing, orders, credit checking
- **Service** The service itself that is being delivered to the customers and business by the service provider – for example, email, billing
- **Policy, strategy, governance, compliance** The elements defined by the organization to direct activity and thereby ensure adherence to organizational goals and objectives
- **SLAs/SLRs** The documents agreed with the customers that specify the level, scope and quality of service to be provided, either now for an existing service (SLAs) or in the future for a new service (SLRs)
- **Infrastructure** All of the IT equipment necessary to deliver the service to the customers and users, including servers, network circuits, switches, personal computers (PCs), telephones

- **Environment** The environment required to secure and operate the infrastructure – for example, data centres, power, air conditioning
- **Data** The data necessary to support the service and provide the information required by the business processes – for example, customer records, accounts ledger
- **Applications** All of the software applications required to manipulate the data and provide the functional requirements of the business processes – for example, enterprise resource management, financial or customer relationship management applications
- **Supporting services** Any services that are necessary to support the operation of the delivered service – for example, a shared service, a managed network service
- **Operational level agreements (OLAs) and underpinning contracts** Any underpinning agreements necessary to deliver the quality of service agreed within the SLA
- **Support teams** Any internal teams providing support for any of the components required to provide the service – for example, Unix, mainframe, networks
- **Suppliers** Any external third parties necessary to provide support for any of the components required to provide the service – for example, networks, hardware, software
- **Service management processes** Any processes needed by the service provider to ensure the successful provision of the service.

The design activities must not just consider each of the components above in isolation, but also must consider the relationships between each of the components and their interactions and dependencies on any other components and services, in order to provide an effective and comprehensive solution that meets the business needs.

3.1.6 Setting direction, policy and strategy for IT services

In order to ensure that business and IT services remain synchronized, many companies have a committee consisting of senior management roles from the business and IT organizations. This committee has the overall accountability for setting governance, direction, policy and strategy for IT services which form a critical element of the

overall service management system of the service provider. Many organizations refer to this group as the IT strategy or steering group (ISG). The function of an ISG is to act as a partnership between IT and the business. It should meet regularly and review the business and IT strategies, designs, plans, service portfolio, architectures and policies to ensure that they are closely aligned with each other. It should provide the vision, set direction and determine priorities of individual programmes and projects to ensure that IT is aligned and focused on business targets and drivers. The group should also ensure that unrealistic timescales, which could jeopardize quality or disrupt normal operational requirements, are not imposed or attempted by either the business or IT (see Figure 3.5 and also section 6.8.6.2 of *ITIL Service Strategy*).

The ISG will include discussions on all aspects of the business that involve IT service, as well as proposed or possible change at a strategic level. Subjects for the ISG to discuss may include:

- **Reviewing business and IT plans** To identify any changes in either area that would trigger the need to create, enhance or improve services
- **Demand planning** To identify any changes in demand for both short- and long-term planning horizons; such changes may be increases or decreases in demand, and concern both business-as-usual and projects
- **Project authorization and prioritization** To ensure that projects are authorized and prioritized to the mutual satisfaction of both the business and IT
- **Review of projects** To ensure that the expected business benefits are being realized in accordance with project business cases, and to identify whether the projects are on schedule
- **Potential outsourcing** To identify the need and content of sourcing strategies for the IT service provision
- **Business/IT strategy review** To discuss major changes to business strategy and major proposed changes to IT strategy and technology, to ensure continued alignment
- **Business continuity and IT service continuity** The group, or a working party from the group, is responsible for aligning business continuity and IT service continuity strategies

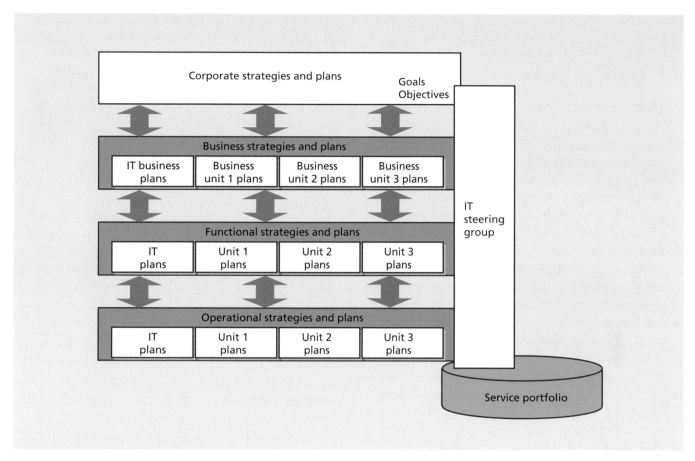

Figure 3.5 The IT steering/strategy group

- **Policies and standards** The ISG is responsible for ensuring that IT policies and standards, particularly in relation to financial strategy and performance management, are in place and aligned with the overall corporate vision and objectives.

The IT steering group sets the direction for policies and plans from corporate to operational levels of IT organization and ensures that they are consistent with corporate level strategies (see Figure 3.5).

The ISG has an important role to play in the alignment of business and IT strategies and plans, as illustrated in Figure 3.5. As a key source of input to the ISG in its decision-making role, the service portfolio enables the ISG to:

- Direct and steer the selection of investment in those areas that yield the greatest business value and return on investment (ROI)
- Perform effective programme and project selection, prioritization and planning

- Exercise effective ongoing governance and active management of the 'pipeline' of business requirements
- Ensure that the projected business benefits of programmes and projects are realized.

3.1.7 Optimizing design performance

The optimizing of design activities requires the implementation of documented processes, together with an overriding quality management system (such as ISO 9001) for their continual measurement and improvement. It is important that when considering the improvement and optimization of service design activities, the impact of the activities on all stages of the lifecycle should be measured and not just the impact on the design stage. Therefore service design measurements and metrics should look at the amount of rework activity and improvement activity that is needed on transition, operation and improvement activities as a result of inadequacies within the design of new and changed service solutions. More information on measurement of service design can be found in section 8.5.

3.2 SERVICE DESIGN GOALS

The main goals and objectives of service design are to:

- Design services to satisfy business objectives and align with business needs, based on the quality, compliance, risk and security requirements, delivering more effective and efficient IT and business solutions by coordinating all design activities for IT services to ensure consistency and business focus
- Design services that can be easily and efficiently developed and enhanced within appropriate timescales and costs, and, wherever possible, reduce, minimize or constrain the long-term costs of service provision
- Design an efficient and effective service management system, including processes for the design, transition, operation and improvement of high-quality IT services, together with the supporting tools, systems and information, especially the service portfolio, to manage services through their lifecycle
- Identify and manage risks so that they can be removed or mitigated before services go live
- Design secure and resilient IT infrastructures, environments, applications and data/ information resources and capability that meet the current and future needs of the business and customers
- Design measurement methods and metrics for assessing the effectiveness and efficiency of the design processes and their deliverables
- Produce and maintain IT plans, processes, policies, architectures, frameworks and documents for the design of quality IT solutions, to meet current and future agreed business needs
- Assist in the development of policies and standards in all areas of design and planning of IT services and processes, receiving and acting on feedback on design processes from all other areas and incorporating the actions into a continual process of improvement
- Develop the skills and capability within IT by moving strategy and design activities into operational tasks, making effective and efficient use of all IT service resources

- Contribute to the improvement of the overall quality of IT service within the imposed design constraints, especially by reducing the need for reworking and enhancing services once they have been implemented in the live environment.

3.3 BALANCED DESIGN

For any new business requirements, the design of services is a delicate balancing act, ensuring that not only the functional requirements but also the performance targets are met. In other words, ensuring that all required utility and warranty can be delivered by the service being designed. All of this needs to be balanced with regard to the resources available within the required timescale and the costs for the new services. Jim McCarthy, author of *Dynamics of Software Development*,[3] states that as a development manager, you are working with only three things (see Figure 3.6):

- **Functionality** The service or product and everything that is part of the service and its provision
- **Resources** The people, technology and money available for the effort
- **Schedule** The timescales for completion.

Note that throughout this publication, the word 'functionality' typically refers primarily to the utility of a service – what it does for the customer. In this context, however, McCarthy was using the term to refer to both utility and warranty (what the service will do and how it will do it) – this is what is being designed. We use resources to deliver this functionality to the customer within the schedule required.

Another way of putting this is that the service provider must always remember that the customer's business requirements include not only the details of the service itself, but also cost (associated with the investment in the resources) and schedule.

This concept is extremely important to service design activities and to the balance between the effort that is spent in the design, development and delivery of services in response to business requirements. Service design is a delicate balancing

---

3 McCarthy, Jim (2005). *Dynamics of Software Development*. Microsoft Press, Washington.

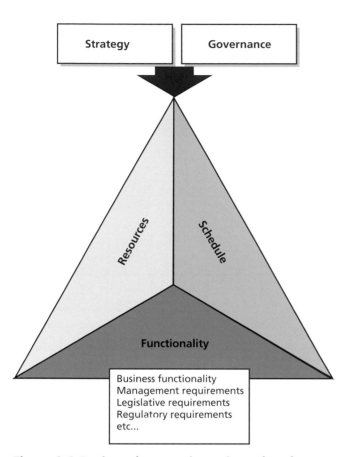

Figure 3.6 Project elements in a triangulated relationship

the live environment. A holistic approach to the design of IT services should be adopted to ensure that a comprehensive and integrated solution is designed to meet the agreed requirements of the business. This approach should also ensure that all of the necessary mechanisms and functionality are implemented within the new service so it can be effectively managed and improved throughout its operational life to achieve all of its agreed service targets. A formal, structured approach should be adopted to ensure all aspects of the service are addressed as well as ensure its smooth introduction and operation within the live environment.

3.4 IDENTIFYING SERVICE REQUIREMENTS

Service design must consider all elements of the service by taking a holistic approach to the design of a new service. This approach should consider the service and its constituent components and their inter-relationships, ensuring that the services delivered meet the requirements of the business in all of the following areas:

■ The scalability of the service to meet future requirements, in support of the long-term business objectives
■ The business processes and business units supported by the service
■ The IT service and the agreed business requirements for functionality (i.e. utility)
■ The service itself and its SLR or SLA (addressing warranty)
■ The technology components used to deploy and deliver the service, including the infrastructure, the environment, the data and the applications
■ The internally delivered supporting services and components and their associated OLAs
■ The externally supplied supporting services and components and their associated underpinning contracts, which will often have their own related agreements and/or schedules
■ The performance measurements and metrics required
■ The legislated or required security levels
■ Sustainability requirements (see section N.7 in Appendix N).

act of all three elements and the constant dynamic adjustment of all three to meet changing business needs. Changing one side of the triangle invariably has an impact on at least one of the other sides if not both of them. A comprehensive understanding of business drivers and needs is therefore vital in order that the most effective business solutions are designed and delivered, using the most appropriate balance of these three elements.

It is likely that business drivers and needs will change during design and delivery, due to market pressures. The functionality and resources should be considered for all stages of the service lifecycle, so that services are not only designed and developed effectively and efficiently, but that the effectiveness and efficiency of the service are maintained throughout all stages of its lifecycle.

Due consideration should be given within service design to all subsequent stages within the service lifecycle. Often designers and architects only consider the development of a new service up to the time of implementation of the service into

The relationships and dependencies between these elements are illustrated in Figure 3.7.

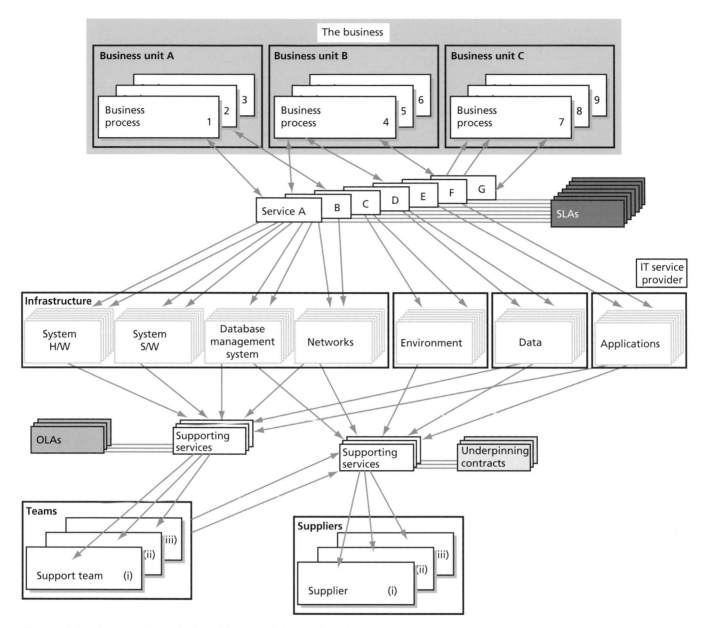

Figure 3.7 The service relationships and dependencies

No service can be designed, transitioned and operated in isolation. The relationship of each service to its supporting components and services must be clearly understood and recognized by all people within the service provider organization. It is also essential that all targets contained within supporting agreements, such as OLAs and contracts, underpin those agreed between the service provider and its customers. Some of these concepts are discussed in more detail in later sections with respect to the individual aspects of service design. However, when an individual aspect of a service is changed, all other areas of the service should also be considered to ensure that

any amendments necessary to support the change are included in the overall design. Increasingly, services are complex and are delivered by a number of partner or supplier organizations. Where multiple service providers are involved in delivery of a service, it is vital that a central service design authority is established, to ensure services and processes are fully integrated across all parties.

Within the specific area of technology there are four separate technology domains that will need to be addressed, as they are the supporting components of every service and contribute to its overall performance:

- **Infrastructure** The management and control of all infrastructure elements, including mainframes, servers, network equipment, database systems, mass storage systems, systems software, utilities, backup systems, firewalls, development and test environments, management tools etc.
- **Environmental** The management and control of all environmental aspects of all major equipment rooms, including the physical space and layout, power, air conditioning, cabling, physical security etc.
- **Data/information** The management and control of all data and information and its associated access, including test data where applicable
- **Applications** The management and control of all applications software, including both bought-in applications and in-house developed applications software.

3.5 IDENTIFYING AND DOCUMENTING BUSINESS REQUIREMENTS AND DRIVERS

IT must retain accurate information on business requirements and drivers if it is to provide the most appropriate catalogue of services with an acceptable level of service quality that is aligned to business needs. Business drivers are the people, information and tasks that support the fulfilment of business objectives. This requires that IT develops and maintains close, regular and appropriate relationships and exchange of information in order to understand the operational, tactical and strategic requirements of the business. The business relationship management process as detailed in *ITIL Service Strategy* plays a vital role in this work. The business information needs to be obtained and agreed in three main areas to maintain service alignment:

- **Information on the requirements of existing services** What changes will be required to existing services with regard to:
  - New facilities/features and functionality requirements (utility)
  - Changes in business processes, dependencies, priorities, criticality and impact
  - Changes in volumes of service transactions
  - Increased service levels and service level targets due to new business drivers, or

reduced for old services, lowering priority for those due for replacement (warranty)
  - Business justification, including the financial and strategic aspects
  - Requirements for additional service management information
- **Information on the requirements of new services:**
  - Facilities/features and functionality required (utility)
  - Management information required and management needs
  - Business processes supported, dependencies, priorities, criticality and impact
  - Business cycles and seasonal variations
  - SLRs and service level targets (warranty)
  - Business transaction levels, service transaction levels, numbers and types of users and anticipated future growth
  - Business justification, including the financial and strategic aspects
  - Predicted level of change – for example, known future business requirements or enhancements
  - Level of business capability or support to be provided – for example, local business-based support
- **Information on the requirements for retiring services:**
  - Exact scope of retirement: what facilities/features and functionality are to be retired
  - Business justification, including financial and strategic aspects
  - What, if anything, will replace the retiring service
  - Interfaces and dependencies with other services, components or configurations
  - Disposal and/or reuse requirements for the service assets and configuration items associated with the retiring service
  - Business requirements related to the retirement strategy and plan, such as timing of the retirement and the retirement approach to be used (i.e. phased retirement)
  - Archiving strategy for any business data and any potential access requirements for archived data related to the retiring service.

This collection of information is the first and most important stage for designing and delivering new services or major changes to existing services. The need for accurate and representative information from the business is paramount. This must be agreed and signed off with senior representatives within the business. If incorrect or misleading information is obtained and used at this stage, then all subsequent stages will be delivering services that do not match the needs of the business. Also, there must be some formal process for the agreement and acceptance of changes to the business requirements, as these will often evolve during the service lifecycle. The requirements and the design must evolve with the changing business environment to ensure that the business expectations are met. However, this must be a carefully managed process to ensure that the rate of change is kept at an agreed and manageable level, and does not 'swamp' and excessively delay the project or its implementation.

In order to design and deliver IT services that meet the needs of the customers and the business, clear, concise, unambiguous specifications of the requirements must be documented and agreed. Time spent in these activities will prevent issues and discussion from arising later with regard to variances from customer and business expectation. This business requirements stage should consist of:

- Appointment of a project manager, the creation of a project team and the agreement of project governance by the application of a formal, structured project methodology
- Identification of all stakeholders, including the documentation of all requirements from all stakeholders and the stakeholder benefits they will obtain from the implementation
- Requirements analysis, prioritization, agreement and documentation
- Determination and agreement of outline budgets and business benefits. The budget must be committed by management because it is normal practice to decide next year's budget in the last quarter of the previous year, so any plans must be submitted within this cycle
- Resolution of the potential conflict between business units and agreement on corporate requirements
- Sign-off processes for the agreed requirements and a method for agreeing and accepting changes to the agreed requirements. Often

the process of developing requirements is an iterative or incremental approach that needs to be carefully controlled to manage 'scope creep'
- Development of a customer engagement plan, outlining the main relationships between IT and the business and how these relationships and necessary communication to wider stakeholders will be managed. The development of this plan is typically led by the business relationship management process (see *ITIL Service Strategy*) and done in cooperation with the design coordination process (see section 4.1).

Where service requirements are concerned, they frequently come with a price tag (which might not be entirely known at this stage), so there always needs to be a balance between the service achievable and the cost. This may mean that some requirements may be too costly to include and may have to be dropped during the financial assessment involved within the design process. If this is necessary, all decisions to omit any service requirements from the design of the service must be documented and agreed with the representatives of the business. There is often difficulty when the business requirements and the budget allocated for the solution do not take into account the full service costs, including the ongoing costs throughout its lifecycle.

3.6 DESIGN ACTIVITIES

All design activities are triggered by changes in business needs or service improvements. A structured and holistic approach to the design activities should be adopted to ensure consistency and integration is achieved throughout the IT service provider organization, within all design activities. Too often organizations focus on the functional requirements, almost to the exclusion of other important areas such as manageability and operational requirements. A design or architecture by definition needs to consider all design aspects. It is not a smaller organization that combines these aspects, it is a sensible one.

Key message

Architectures and designs should be kept clear, concise, simple and relevant. All too often, designs and architectures are complex and theoretical and do not relate to the 'real world'.

The key inputs and outputs of the overall service design stage are described in section 3.12. The following shows more detail regarding these, taking into consideration the range of activity in the stage.

The inputs to the various design activities are:

- Corporate visions, strategies, objectives, policies and plans, business visions, including business continuity plans
- Service management visions, strategies, policies, objectives and plans
- Constraints and requirements for compliance with legislated standards and regulations
- All IT strategies, policies and strategic plans
- Details of business requirements
- All constraints, financial budgets and plans
- The service portfolio
- ITSM processes, risks and issues registers
- Service transition plans (change, configuration and release, and deployment management plans)
- Security policies, handbooks and plans
- The procurement and contract policy and supplier strategy
- The current staff knowledge, skills and capability
- IT business plans, business and IT quality plans and policies
- Service management plans, including service level management plans, SLAs and SLRs, service improvement plan(s) (SIPs), capacity plans, availability plans, IT service continuity plans
- Relevant improvement opportunities from the continual service improvement (CSI) register
- Measurement tools and techniques.

The deliverables from the design activities are:

- Suggested revisions to IT strategies and policies
- Revised designs, plans and technology and management architectures, including:
  - The IT infrastructure and infrastructure management and environmental strategy, designs, plans, architectures and policies
  - The applications and data strategies, designs, plans, architectures and policies
- Designs for new or changed services, processes and technologies, including sourcing strategy (buy or build, or a combination), documented in service design packages

- Process review and analysis reports, with designs for revised and improved processes and procedures
- Designs for revised measurement methods and processes
- Managed levels of risk, and risk assessment and management reports
- Business cases and feasibility studies, together with statements of requirements (SoRs) and invitations to tender (ITTs) (for a description of different types of procurement documents, see Appendix L)
- Revised budgets and service costing
- Comments and feedback on all other plans
- Business benefit and realization reviews and reports.

3.7 DESIGN ASPECTS

An overall, integrated approach should be adopted for the design activities documented in the previous section and should cover the five aspects of service design as listed in section 3.1.1 and further explained in section 3.1.3. As a reminder, these five aspects are:

- Service solutions for new or changed services
- Management information systems and tools
- Technology architectures and management architectures
- The processes required
- Measurement methods and metrics.

In addressing the five aspects, the desired business outcomes and planned results should be clearly defined so that what is delivered meets the expectations of the customers and users. This focus on results should be adopted within each of the five aspects to deliver quality, repeatable consistency and continual improvement throughout the organization.

The key aspect is the design of new or changed service solutions to meet changing business needs. Every time a new service solution is produced, it needs to be checked against each of the other aspects to ensure that it will integrate and interface with all of the other services already in existence. These five aspects of service design are covered in more detail in the following sections. The plans produced by service design for the design, transition and subsequent operation of these five different aspects should include:

- The approach taken and the associated timescales
- The organizational impact of the new or changed solution on both the business and IT
- The commercial impact of the solution on the organization, including the funding, costs and budgets required
- The technical impact of the solution and the staff and their roles, responsibilities, skills, knowledge, training and competences required to deploy, operate, maintain and optimize the new solution to the business

- The commercial justification assessment of the impact of the solution on existing business – this impact must be assessed from the point of view of IT and service management processes, including both their capacity and performance
- The assessment and mitigation of risks to services, processes and service management activities
- Communication planning and all aspects of communication with all interested parties
- The impact of the solution on new or existing contracts or agreements

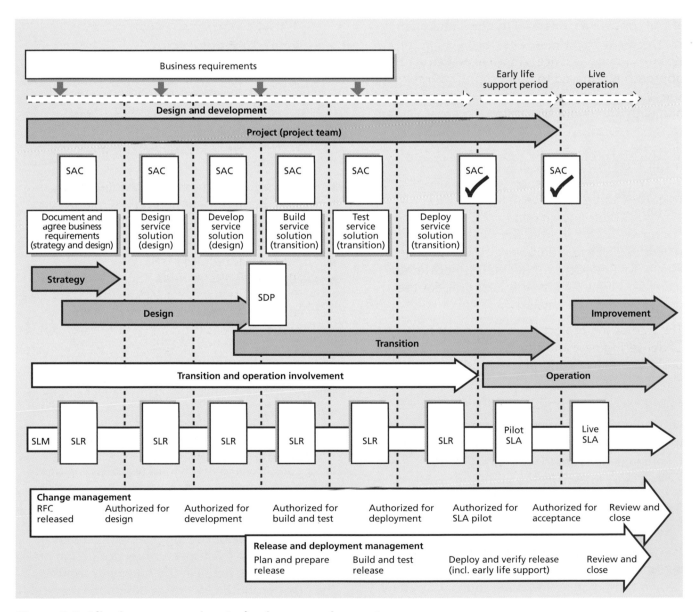

Figure 3.8 Aligning new services to business requirements

- The expected outcomes from the operation of the new or changed service in measurable terms, generally expressed within new or existing SLAs, service levels and customer satisfaction
- The production of a service design package (see Appendix A) containing everything necessary for the subsequent testing, introduction and operation of the solution or service
- The production of a set of service acceptance criteria (SAC) (see Appendix B) that will be used to ensure that the service provider is ready to deliver and support the new or changed service in the live environment.

3.7.1 Designing service solutions

There are many activities that have to be completed within the service design stage for a new or changed service. A formal and structured approach is required to produce the new service at the right cost, utility (functionality) and warranty and within the right timeframe. An example of such an approach and its constituent stages are illustrated in Figure 3.8, together with the other major areas that will need to be involved along the way. This approach must be iterative/incremental to ensure that the service delivered meets the evolving and changing needs of the business during the business process development and the IT service lifecycle. Additional project managers and project teams may need to be allocated to manage the stages within the lifecycle for the deployment of the new service.

The role of the project team within this activity of delivering new and changing IT services to the business and its relationship to design activities is also illustrated in Figure 3.8.

Figure 3.8 shows the lifecycle of a service from the initial or changed business requirement through the design, transition and operation stages of the lifecycle. It is important that there is effective transfer of knowledge at all stages between the operational staff and the project staff to ensure smooth progression through each of the stages illustrated.

The areas that need to be considered within the design of the service solution should include:

- Analysing the agreed business requirements
- Reviewing the existing IT services and infrastructure and producing alternative service solutions, with a view to reusing or exploiting existing components and services wherever possible
- Designing the service solutions to the new requirements, including their constituent components, in terms of the following, and documenting this design:
  - The facilities/features and functionality required (utility), and information required for the monitoring of the performance of the service or process
  - The business processes supported, dependencies, priorities, criticality and impact of the service, together with the business benefits that will be delivered by the service
  - Business cycles and seasonal variations, and the related business transaction levels, service transaction levels, the numbers and types of users and anticipated future growth, and the business continuity requirements
  - SLRs and service level targets (warranty) and the necessary service measuring, reporting and reviewing activities
  - The timescales involved and the planned outcomes from the new service and the impact on any existing services
  - The requirements for testing, including any user acceptance testing (UAT) and responsibilities for managing the test results
  - Requirements for integration into the overall service management system
- Ensuring that the contents of the SAC are incorporated and the required achievements planned into the initial design
- Evaluating and costing alternative designs, highlighting advantages as well as disadvantages of the alternatives (for detailed information about service economics and service costing, see *ITIL Service Strategy*, sections 3.6 and 4.3)
- Agreeing the expenditure and budgets

- Agreeing the required timelines to complete design, develop, build, test and deploy the service
- Re-evaluating and confirming the business benefits, including the ROI from the service, which further includes identification and quantification of all service costs and all business benefits and increased revenues. The costs should cover the total cost of ownership (TCO) of the service and include start-up costs such as design costs, transition costs, project budget, and all ongoing operational costs including management, support and maintenance
- Agreeing the preferred solution and its planned outcomes and targets (utility and warranty)
- Checking the solution is in balance with all corporate and IT strategies, policies, plans and architectural documents; and if not, revising either the solution or the strategic documentation (taking into account the effect on other strategic documents, services and components) wherever possible reusing or exploiting existing components (e.g. software objects, 'corporate' data, hardware), unless the strategy dictates otherwise. The changing of strategy will involve a significant amount of work and would be done in conjunction with service strategy
- Ensuring that all of the appropriate corporate and IT governance and security controls are included with the solution
- Completing an 'organizational readiness assessment' to ensure that the service can be effectively operated to meet its agreed targets and that the organization has the appropriate capability to deliver to the agreed level. This will include:
    - The commercial impact on the organization from both a business and IT perspective, including all of the business benefits and all of the costs (both one-off project costs and the ongoing annual operation costs) involved in the design, development and ongoing operation and support of the service
    - Assessment and mitigation of the risks associated with the new or changed service, particularly with regard to the operation, security, availability and continuity of the service

- The business capability and maturity. This activity should be performed by the business itself to ensure that all of the right processes, structure, people, roles, responsibilities and facilities are in place to operate the new service
- The IT capability and maturity. This should include:
    - The environment and all areas of technology, having considered the impact on existing components of the infrastructure and existing services
    - The IT organizational structure and the roles and responsibilities
    - The IT processes and their documentation
    - The skills, knowledge and competence of the staff
    - The IT management processes and supporting tools
- The supplier and supporting agreements necessary to maintain and deliver the service
- The assembly of an SDP for the subsequent transition, operation and improvement of the new or changed service solution.

3.7.2 Designing management information systems and tools

The most effective way of managing all aspects of services through their lifecycle is by using appropriate management information systems and tools to support and automate efficient processes. Management information systems themselves are typically part of a larger system or framework of policies, processes, functions, standards, guidelines and tools that are planned and managed together and are used to ensure that the desired objectives are achieved. This larger system or framework is known as a management system and examples include a quality management system, an information security management system, or even the overall service management system.

3.7.2.1 Designing the service portfolio

The service portfolio is the most critical management information system used to support all processes and describes a provider's services in terms of business value. It articulates business needs and the provider's response to those needs. By definition, business value terms correspond to market terms, providing a means for comparing service competitiveness across alternative providers. By acting as the basis of a decision framework, a service portfolio either clarifies or helps to clarify the following strategic questions:

- Why should a customer buy these services?
- Why should they buy these services from us?
- What are the pricing or chargeback models?
- What are our strengths and weaknesses, priorities and risks?
- How should our resources and capabilities be allocated?

Ideally the service portfolio should form part of a comprehensive SKMS and be registered as a document in the CMS. Further information on both the CMS and the SKMS is provided within *ITIL Service Transition.*

Once a strategic decision to charter a service is made, this is the stage in the service lifecycle when service design begins architecting the service, which will eventually become part of the service catalogue. The service portfolio should contain information relating to every service and its current status within the organization. It is recommended that the options of status within the service portfolio should include:

- **Requirements** A set of outline requirements have been received from the business or IT for a new or changed service
- **Definition** The set of requirements for the new service are being assessed, defined and documented and the SLR is being produced
- **Analysis** The set of requirements for the new service is being analysed and prioritized
- **Approved** The set of requirements for the new service has been finalized and authorized
- **Chartered** The new service requirements are being communicated and resources and budgets allocated
- **Design** The new service and its constituent components are being designed – and procured, if required
- **Development** The service and its constituent components are being developed or harvested, if applicable
- **Build** The service and its constituent components are being built

- **Test** The service and its constituent components are being tested
- **Release** The service and its constituent components are being released
- **Operational/live** The service and its constituent components are operational within the live environment
- **Retiring** The service is still being delivered in the live environment to legacy customers, but will not be sold to or activated for new customers
- **Retired** The service and its constituent components have been retired.

The service portfolio would therefore contain details of all services and their status with respect to the current stage within the service lifecycle, as illustrated in Figure 2.6.

As part of the design of its service portfolio, each organization should define clear policies regarding the service lifecycle and the relationship between each service status and the service's progression through the sections of the service portfolio. The relationship between service status and portfolio shown in Figure 2.6 illustrates one possible approach. In this example those services within the service portfolio that are of a status between 'chartered' and 'retiring' appear in the service catalogue and are therefore accessible to customers and users.

The design of the service portfolio and its ongoing management should take into consideration these practices:

- Each version of a service should be assigned a number or other unique identifier to assist in clearly monitoring the progress of that version of the service throughout its lifecycle.
- It is preferable that each particular version of a service should only exist in one section of the portfolio at a time, be it service pipeline, service catalogue or retired services.
- Newer versions of a service may be in the pipeline while the current version is in the catalogue, or in the catalogue while an older version is in the retired services.
- If an organization identifies any circumstances in which two different service versions might appropriately exist in the same section of the

portfolio simultaneously, the organization should carefully define the rules governing such circumstances (see example).

- Organizations should define clear and unambiguous policies regarding what conditions are required for each defined service status to be achieved.

- From the 'requirements' status to the 'chartered' status, a service should appear in the service pipeline.

- Once a service achieves the 'operational' status in the live environment, it should appear in the service catalogue.

- Between 'chartered' and 'operational' each organization should make clear and unambiguous policies regarding when a service will move from pipeline to catalogue, based on the organization's desired goals, objectives and uses for the pipeline and catalogue. Many factors may influence these policies, such as the type of service provider, the role of the pipeline and catalogue in customer communications, ease of support by toolsets etc.

- Between 'operational' and 'retired', each organization should have clear and unambiguous policies regarding when a service will move from catalogue to retired services, based on the organization's desired goals, objectives and uses for the catalogue and retired services.

- There should be clear designation of responsibility and accountability for all aspects of a service as it progresses through its lifecycle. It should be clearly defined which person or role has accountability for each version of a service during each status in its lifecycle.

Service strategy and service design personnel, as well as personnel in other important areas such as change management, will need access to all records within the service portfolio. Other members of the service provider organization will have access to a permitted subset of the records within the service portfolio. Although the service portfolio is designed during service design, it is managed during service strategy and beyond through the service portfolio management process. Full details on service portfolio management are discussed in *ITIL Service Strategy*.

Example of multiple versions

A large business is migrating from one operating system (OS) to another. Because of the size of the organization and the consequential scope of the migration, the work has to be completed in a phased deployment. The current version of the 'ABC' service in the operational environment cannot function on the new operating system and therefore a new version has been designed and has been transitioned onto the workstations that are part of the first phase of the OS deployment.

As a result, there are now legitimately two different versions of the ABC service in the operational environment, and therefore in the service catalogue, at the same time. The older version may have a different status, such as 'retiring', to reflect the fact that it is gradually being withdrawn from use, but both versions will continue to be valid until the OS deployment is complete.

The service pipeline is a subset of the overall service portfolio, organized into a database or structured document listing all services that are under consideration or development, but are not yet available to customers. The service pipeline provides a business view of possible future services and is part of the service portfolio that is not normally published to customers. The service pipeline contains details of all of the business requirements that have not yet been addressed via services released to the live environment. It is used as a basis for the definition, analysis, prioritization and approval by the ISG and service strategy, of all requests for new or changed services, to ensure that new and changed services are aligned to business requirements. It will principally be used as input to the activities of the service strategy and service design stages of the service lifecycle. It also provides valuable input to the activities of the service transition stage of the lifecycle in determining the services to be released.

The service catalogue is a subset of the overall service portfolio, organized into a database or structured document with information about all live IT services, including those available for deployment. The service catalogue is the only part of the service portfolio published to customers, and is used to support the sale and delivery of IT services. The service catalogue includes information about deliverables, prices, contact points, ordering and request processes. Details regarding the service catalogue and its management may be found in section 4.2. The service catalogue management process must ensure that all of the details within the overall service portfolio are accurate and up-to-date as the requirement and its new or changed service is migrated into the live environment. This will involve close liaison with all service transition activities.

Retired services are a subset of the overall service portfolio representing those services that are phased out or retired. The retirement of a service must be carefully planned during service design and is managed through service transition. When services are retired, the related knowledge and information is stored in a knowledge base for future use. Retired services are not available to new customers or contracts unless a special business case is made. Such services may be reactivated into operation under special conditions and SLAs that are to be approved by senior management. This is necessary because such services may cost a lot more to support and may disrupt economies of scale and scope. The policies governing the reactivation of a service must be clearly defined and carefully adhered to.

Various elements of the same service can have different statuses at the same time. Otherwise the service portfolio would be unable to support 'incremental and iterative' development. Each organization should carefully design its service portfolio, the content and the access allowed to the content. The content should include:

- Service name
- Service version
- Service description
- Service status
- Service classification and criticality
- Applications used
- Data and/or data schema used
- Business processes supported
- Business owners
- Business users
- IT owners
- Warranty level, SLA and SLR references
- Supporting services
- Supporting resources
- Dependent services

- Supporting OLAs, contracts and agreements
- Service costs
- Service charges (if applicable)
- Service revenue (if applicable)
- Service metrics.

The service portfolio is the main source of information on the requirements and services and needs to be very carefully designed to meet all the needs of all its users. The design of the service portfolio needs to be considered in the same way as the design of IT services themselves to ensure that it meets all of these needs. This approach should also be used for all of the other service management information systems, including the:

- SKMS
- CMS
- Capacity management information system (CMIS)
- Availability management information system (AMIS)
- Security management information system (SMIS)
- Supplier and contract management information system (SCMIS).

3.7.3 Designing technology architectures and management architectures

The architectural design activities within an IT organization are concerned with providing the overall strategic blueprints for the development and deployment of an IT infrastructure that will satisfy the current and future needs of the business. Although these aspects underpin the delivery of quality IT services, they alone cannot deliver quality IT services, and it is essential that the people, process and partner/supplier aspects surrounding these technological components (products) are also considered.

'Architecture' is a term used in many different contexts. In this context it can be described as the fundamental organization of a system, embodied in its components, their relationships to each other and to the environment, and the principles guiding its design and evolution. 'System' is used in the most general, not necessarily IT, sense to mean a collection of components organized to accomplish a specific function or set of functions.

So the system could be, for example, a whole organization, a business function, a product line or an information system. Each of these

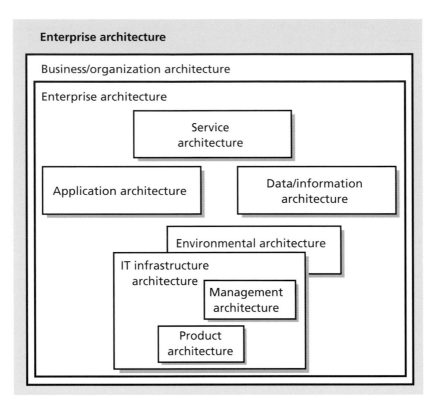

Figure 3.9 Enterprise architecture

systems will have an 'architecture' made up of the components of the system, the relationships between them (such as control interfaces and data exchanges), the relationships between the system and its environment (political, organizational, technological etc.) and the design principles that inform, guide and constrain its structure and operation, as well as its future development.

In essence, 'architectural design' can be described as the development and maintenance of IT policies, strategies, architectures, designs, documents, plans and processes for the deployment and subsequent operation and improvement of appropriate IT services and solutions throughout an organization.

The work of architectural design needs to assess and reconcile many types of needs, some of which may be in conflict with one another. The work should ensure that:

- The IT infrastructures, environments, data, applications and external services serve the needs of the business, its products and services. This activity not only includes the technology components but also their management.
- The right balance is struck between innovation, risk and cost while seeking a competitive edge, where desired by the business.

- There is compliance with relevant architectural frameworks, strategies, policies, regulations and standards.
- A coordinated interface is provided between IT designers and planners, strategists, business designers and planners.

The architectural design activities should use input from the business, service strategy, its plans, designers and planners to develop appropriate designs, plans, architectures and policies for all areas of IT. These designs, plans, architectures and policies should cover all aspects of IT, including roles and responsibilities, services, technology, architecture and frameworks, processes and procedures, partners and suppliers, and management methods. The work of architectural design must also cover all areas of technology, including the infrastructure, environment, applications and data, and it should be closely linked to the overall business planning and design processes.

Any enterprise is a complex system, with many types of component, such as its staff, business functions and processes, organizational structure and physical distribution, information resources and information systems, financial

Table 3.1 Enterprise architecture frameworks

Full framework name	Framework abbreviation
Architecture of integrated information systems framework	ARIS
Bredemeyer framework	Bredemeyer
Business transformation enablement programme transformation framework	BTEP
Department of Defense architecture framework	DODAF
CSC catalyst	Catalyst
Computer integrated manufacturing open systems architecture	CIMOSA
Enterprise architecture framework	Gartner
Enterprise architecture planning	EAP
Extended enterprise architecture framework	E2AF
Federal Enterprise Architecture (FEA) reference models	FEA
Generalized enterprise reference architecture and methodology	GERAM
Integrated architecture framework	IAF
Pillars of Enterprise Architecture (EA)	Forrester
Reference model for open distributed processing	RM-ODP
Technical architectural framework for information management	TAFIM
Treasury enterprise architecture framework	TEAF
The Open Group Architecture Framework (TOGAF®) technical reference model	TOGAF
Zachman framework	Zachman

and other resources including technology, and the strategies, plans, management, policies and governance structures that drive the enterprise. An enterprise architecture should show how all these components (and others) are integrated in order to achieve the business objectives, both now and in the future.

The complete enterprise architecture can be large and complex. Here we are interested in those architectures concerned with the business of the organization and the information systems that support it. Each of these architectures calls on distinct architectural disciplines and areas of expertise, as illustrated in Figure 3.9.

Enterprise architecture is defined by Gartner[4] as:

'The process of translating the business's vision and strategy into effective enterprise change by creating, communicating and improving key requirements, principles and models that describe the enterprise's future state and enable its evolution toward it.'

There are many proprietary and non-proprietary frameworks for the development of an enterprise architecture, as illustrated in Table 3.1.

These frameworks include descriptions of the organizational structure, business processes, planning and control systems, management and governance mechanisms, policies and procedures of the enterprise. They show how these components interoperate and contribute to the achievement of business goals and objectives, and provide the basis for identifying the requirements for information systems that support these business processes.

4 Basualdo, Militza (2010). Business value through enterprise architecture. Executive Programs Road Notes, Gartner.

The enterprise architecture should be an integrated element of the business architecture and should include the following major areas (Figure 3.10):

- **Service architecture** This translates applications, infrastructure, organization and support activities into a set of services. The service architecture provides the independent, business integrated approach to delivering services to the business. It provides the model for making a distinction between the service architecture, the application architecture, the data architecture and the infrastructure architecture. It also provides fault tolerance, future proofing and security controls. This means that, potentially, changes occurring within any technology architectures will be transparent to the users of the service – for example, web-based self-service delivery mechanisms. It should include

not just the services themselves and their overall integration, but also the management of those services.

- **Application architecture** This provides a blueprint for the development and deployment of individual applications, maps business and functional requirements onto applications, and shows the inter-relationships between applications. Emerging application architectures are likely to be component-based. Such an approach maximizes reuse and helps to maintain flexibility in accommodating changes in sourcing policy.

- **Data/information architecture** This describes the logical and physical data assets of the enterprise and the data management resources. It shows how the information resources are managed and shared for the benefit of the enterprise. A strategy on centralized versus distributed data

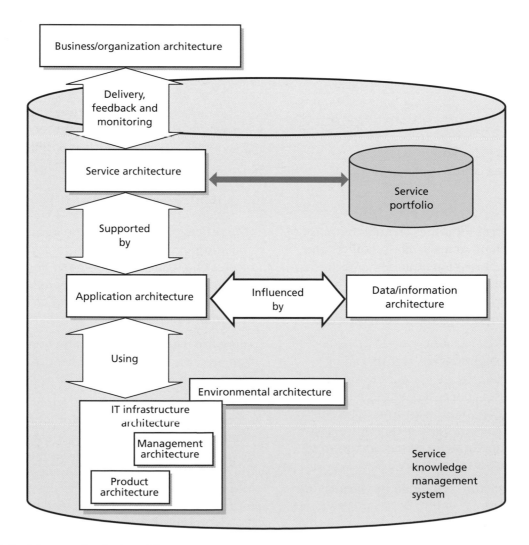

Figure 3.10 Architectural relationships

will almost certainly have been devised as part of such an architecture. The data/information architecture will include consideration of data warehousing technologies that facilitate the exploitation of corporate information assets. It will increasingly cover content management and the facilities for delivery of information over multiple channels.

- **IT infrastructure architecture** This describes the structure, functionality and geographical distribution of the hardware, software and communications components that underpin and support the overall architecture, together with the technical standards applying to them. This should also include:
  - A 'product architecture' that describes the particular proprietary products and industry standards that the enterprise uses to implement the infrastructure in conformance with the IT infrastructure architecture principles
  - A 'management architecture' consisting of the management tools used to manage the products, processes, environments etc.
- **Environmental architecture** This describes all aspects, types and levels of environment controls and their management. An illustration of the type of environmental information required is included in Appendix E (see also section N.7 in Appendix N).

The relationships between these architectural perspectives can be seen in Figure 3.10. The development, documentation and maintenance of business and IT architectures will typically form part of the processes of strategic thinking and strategy development in the organization.

Within the framework described earlier, it is possible to identify (at least) three architectural roles. These could all report to a senior 'enterprise architect' in the organization:

- **Business/organizational architect** Concerned with business models, business processes and organizational design – the structural and functional components of the organization and their relationship, and how the business functions and activities of the organization are distributed among them; also the governance of the organization and the roles and responsibilities required

- **Service architect** (often separate roles of applications architect and information/data architect) Concerned with the service, data and application architectures – the logical architectures supporting the business and the relationships between them
- **IT infrastructure architect** Concerned with the physical technology model, the infrastructure components and their relationships, including choices of technologies, interfaces and protocols, and the selection of products to implement the infrastructure.

In some organizations, the roles of business/organizational architect, information systems architect (or possibly separate roles of applications architect and data architect) and IT infrastructure architect will be separate functions. In others, some or all of the roles may be combined. The roles may reside in separate parts of the organization or even outside it. For example:

- The business/organizational architect role may reside within the business strategy and planning function in the corporate headquarters.
- The service architect role may form part of an internal function with responsibility for handling relationships between the business, external suppliers and IT partners relating to service issues. A key responsibility of such a function is the maintenance of the service architecture. This function may be within an IT function or within the business side of an organization.
- The IT infrastructure architect role may reside with the service provider/partner who is responsible for producing the IT infrastructure architecture used for the delivery of IT services to the organization.

If the necessary architectures are in place, then the role of service design is affected in the following ways:

- It must work within the agreed architectural framework and standards
- It will be able to reuse many of the assets created as part of the architecture
- It should work closely with all three architectural roles to ensure maximum benefit from the work done in creating the architecture.

If architecture design is to be accomplished effectively and economically, the documents, processes and activities of the business and architectural design should be closely coordinated and synchronized. A list of these design documents and their content is contained in Appendices C and D. The individual details of technology included within architectural design are considered in the following sections.

> **Key message**
>
> The real benefit and return on investment of the enterprise architecture comes not from the architecture itself, but from the ability of an organization to design and successfully implement projects and solutions in a rapid and consistent manner.

3.7.3.1 Technology management

A strategic approach should be adopted with regard to the planning of an information technology and its management. This implies creating 'architectures' or 'blueprints' for the long-term framework of the technology used and planned. IT planners, designers and architects need to understand the business, the requirements and the current technology in order to develop appropriate IT architectures for the short, medium and long term. Technology design also needs to take account of the likely IT services that it will underpin, or at least the types of service from an understanding of the business and its future direction, because the business will demand IT services and it will need an appropriate technology to provide and deliver those services. If it is possible to provide a longer-term technology, which can underpin a number of IT services, then taking a strategic approach will provide benefit in the longer term.

Architectures need to be developed within the major areas of technology.

Technology architectures

Architectures are needed in all areas of information technology. Where relevant they need to be developed in the following areas:

- Applications and systems software
- Information, data and database, including information security and confidentiality, data warehousing and data mining
- Infrastructure design and architecture:
  - Central server, mainframe architectures, distributed regional servers, including local file and print servers
  - Data networks (LANs, MANs, WANs, VPNs, protocols etc.), internet, intranet and extranet systems
  - Converged network technologies, including voice networks (PABXs, Centrex, handsets, mobiles, faxes etc.)
  - Client systems (desktop PCs, laptop PCs, mobile access devices (hand-held devices, mobile phones, palmtops, PDAs, scanners etc.)
  - Storage devices, storage area networks (SANs), network-attached storage (NAS) including backup and recovery systems and services (servers, robots etc.)
  - Document storage, handling and management
  - Specialist areas of technology such as EPOS, ATMs, scanning devices, GPS systems etc.
- Environmental systems and equipment, including their monitoring and management.

This will result in a hierarchy of architectures, which will need to be dovetailed to construct an integrated set of technology architectures for the organization. The infrastructure architecture should aim to provide relatively few standardized platforms for hosting applications. It must also lay down standards for application architectures that are to be hosted in controlled data centres so that these fit in with the standardized operating, monitoring and security requirements.

Management architectures

IT must manage costs, deliver the right services at the right time, secure information assets, provide dependable service and lead the business in leveraging technologies. This requires automated procedures and management tools in order to achieve this effectively and efficiently. The selection of an appropriate management architecture is key to establishing the required level of control and automation. There are two separate approaches to developing a management architecture.

- **Selecting a proprietary management architecture** This is based on selecting a single set of management products and tools from a single proprietary management solutions supplier. This approach will normally require less effort, will support and integrate within an overall tool architecture, but will often mean that compromises will have to be made with management functionality and facilities, which may result in gaps.

■ **Selecting a 'best of breed' architecture** This approach involves the selection of a set of 'best of breed' management tools and products from a number of management solutions suppliers and then integrating them to provide a comprehensive management solution. Although this will generally require more effort in the integration of the tools into a single comprehensive management solution, it will often provide greater management functionality and facilities, leading to long-term cost savings.

The challenges for IT management are to coordinate and work in partnership with the business in the building of these management solutions, supporting the appropriate processes and providing the required measurements and metrics. This has to be achieved while reducing or optimizing the costs involved, particularly the annual, ongoing costs. The best way of minimizing costs is to design cleverly and carefully – for example, making best use of capacity so that additional capacity is not unnecessarily bought (with its associated ongoing costs) – or designing a backup/recovery solution that does not require a complete additional set of infrastructure. Considerable costs can be saved by intelligent and careful design, using technology that is supportable and causes few problems in the operational environment.

The main method of realizing these goals is to design solutions that give a reduction in the overall network management and support costs, while maintaining or even improving the quality of service delivered to the business.

To gain the greatest benefit from the use of the four Ps, organizations should determine the roles of processes and people, and then implement the tools to automate the processes, facilitating people's roles and tasks. The best way of achieving this is to develop a model or architecture based on these principles. This architecture should facilitate the implementation of a set of integrated tools and processes that support 'end-to-end' management of all areas of the technology used, ensuring that there are no gaps and no 'technical silos'.

However, IT faces a big challenge in developing and maintaining the soft skills required to perform these management roles and processes effectively. In truly efficient organizations, these roles and processes are aligned to those of the business. This ensures that the business and IT management processes and information have similar targets and goals. However, all too often, organizations devote insufficient time and effort to the development of the soft skills (for example, interpersonal skills, communication skills, meeting skills) necessary for the processes and the business alignment to be effectively achieved.

There are five areas that need to be considered with regard to the design of a management architecture. The relationships between these architectural perspectives is illustrated in Figure 3.11. The development, documentation and maintenance of business and IT architectures will typically form part of the processes of strategic thinking and strategy development in the organization.

These five management areas to be considered can be briefly defined as:

■ **Business** The needs, requirements, processes, objectives and goals of the business units and managers within the organization

■ **People** The scope, tasks and activities of the managers and staff involved in the management of the provision of IT services

■ **Processes** The processes and procedures used to manage IT services to the business and its customers

■ **Tools** The management and support tools required to effectively manage the IT infrastructure

■ **Technology** The IT products and technology used to deliver the service and information to the right person, in the right place at the right time.

Such an architecture can be used to design and implement efficient, effective and integrated management solutions that are aligned to the business requirements of the organization and its business managers. This management architecture can be applied within an organization to (see also Figure 3.11):

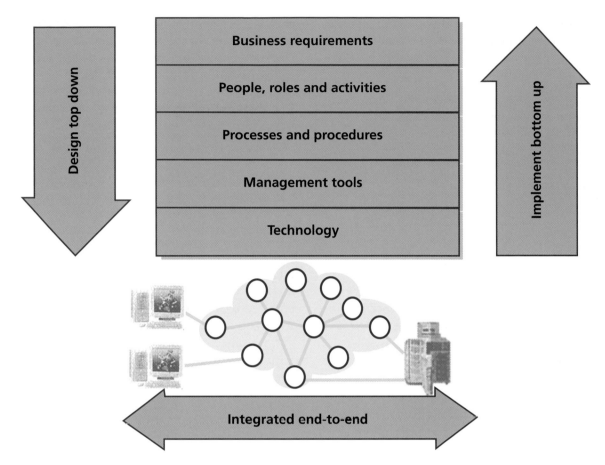

Figure 3.11   Integrated business-driven technology management

- Design from the top down, ensuring that the service management and technology management processes, tools and information are aligned with the business needs and goals
- Implement from the bottom up, ensuring that efficient and effective service management and technology management processes are fully integrated with the tools and technology in use within the organization
- Integrate processes and tools, ensuring greater exploitation of tools in the management and support of technology and end-to-end processes.

The key to the development of a management architecture is to ensure that it is driven by business needs and not developed for IT needs in isolation.

Key message

Management architectures need to be business-aligned, not technology-driven.

Within this overall structure, a management architecture is needed that can be applied to all areas of IT management and not just to individual isolated areas. This can then be implemented in a coordinated programme of inter-working, to provide overall end-to-end enterprise management so essential to the effective management of today's IT infrastructure. If only individual areas buy into the architecture, individual 'islands of excellence' will develop, and it will be impossible to provide the complete end-to-end solutions required to support today's e-business solutions.

As well as ensuring that all areas of the IT are integrated, it is vital that the management architecture is developed from the business and service perspectives (i.e. 'top down'). Therefore, the key elements to agree and define before developing the management architecture are:

- Management of the business processes: What are the business processes and how do they relate to network and IT services and components?

■ Management of service quality: What is service quality? How and where will it be measured?

These are the key elements that need to be determined by senior level management and IT management. They provide crucial input to the development of business-focused management architectures. All too often management tools and processes have been focused on components and component management rather than services and business processes. This needs to be changed, with emphasis clearly on the design of management systems, processes and tools that are driven by business needs and are focused on the management of business processes and IT services. Appropriate design and implementation of management architecture will allow service management processes to focus on managing services and service quality and operate from end to end across the entire IT enterprise, providing true enterprise service management. This will truly facilitate the management of services to ensure that services and service quality are closely aligned to the needs of the business.

The architectures described suggest that the future of network and systems management will be less focused on the technology and become more integrated with the overall requirements of the business and IT management. These new systems and processes are already starting to evolve as the management standards for the exchange of management information between tools become more fully defined by organizations such as the Distributed Management Task Force (DMTF). In essence, management systems will become:

■ More focused on business needs
■ More closely aligned to business processes
■ Less dependent on specific technology and more 'service-centric'
■ More integrated with other management tools and processes as the management standards evolve. This will involve the integration of systems management, operational management and service management tools and processes, with fewer 'technology silos' and 'islands of excellence'
■ Part of end-to-end management systems and processes, more focused on provision of quality and customer services

■ More flexible. There will be a move away from some of the more rigid, single-supplier frameworks to a more open 'best-of-breed' approach.

3.7.4 Designing processes

This section provides a general introduction to process theory and practice, which is the basis for the design of ITIL processes that are used in the service lifecycle. A process model enables understanding and helps to articulate the distinctive features of a process.

A process is a structured set of activities designed to accomplish a specific objective. A process takes one or more inputs and turns them into defined outputs. A process includes all of the roles, responsibilities, tools and management controls required to reliably deliver the outputs. A process may also define or revise policies, standards, guidelines, activities, processes, procedures and work instructions if they are needed.

Process control is the activity of planning and regulating a process, with the objective of performing a process in an effective, efficient and consistent manner. As mentioned in Chapter 2, processes, once defined, should be documented and controlled. Once under control, they can be repeated and become manageable. Degrees of control over processes can be defined, and then process measurement and metrics can be built into the process to control and improve the process, as illustrated in Figure 2.5.

The generic process elements show data enters the process, is processed, is output and the outcome is measured and reviewed. This very basic description underpins any process description. A process is always organized around a set of objectives. The main outputs from the process should be driven by the objectives and should always include process measurements (metrics), reports and process improvement.

Each process should be owned by a process owner, who should be accountable for the process and its improvement and for ensuring that a process meets its objectives. The objectives of any IT process should be defined in measurable terms and should be expressed in terms of business benefits and underpinning business strategy and goals. Service design should assist each process owner with the design of processes, in order to ensure that all processes use standard terms and templates, are consistent and integrate with each other to provide end-to-end integration across all areas.

The output produced by a process has to conform to operational norms that are derived from business objectives. If products conform to the set norm, the process can be considered effective (because it achieves its objectives and can be repeated, measured and managed). If the activities are carried out with a minimum use of resources, the process can also be considered efficient. Process analysis, results and metrics should be incorporated in regular management reports and process improvements.

All these areas should be included within the design of any process. The ITIL publications have been written around 'sets of processes' that reflect the stages in the lifecycle of a service. The service design set of processes detailed in this publication covers the processes closely related to all aspects of design, although in most cases these processes are not limited to service design work only.

Working with defined processes has been the foundation of ITIL from its beginning. By defining what the organization's activities are, which inputs are necessary and which outputs will result from the process, it is possible to work in a more efficient and effective manner. Measuring and steering the activities increases this effectiveness. Finally, by adding norms to the process, it is possible to add quality measures to the output.

This approach underpins the Plan-Do-Check-Act cycle of continual improvement for any quality management system. Plan the purpose of the process in such a way that process actions can be reviewed, assessed or audited for successful achievement and improved.

Norms define certain conditions that the results should meet. Defining norms introduces quality aspects to the process. Even before starting, it is important to think about what the process outcomes should look like. To discover whether or not process activities are contributing optimally to the business goal and the objectives of the process, aligned to business goals, the effectiveness should be measured on a regular basis. Measuring allows comparison of what has actually been done with what the organization set out to do, and to

identify and implement improvements within the process.

Each organization should adopt a formalized approach to the design and implementation of service management processes. The objective should not be to design 'perfect processes', but to design practical and appropriate processes with 'in-built' improvement mechanisms, so that the effectiveness and efficiency of the processes are improved in the most suitable manner for the organization. Documentation standards, processes and templates should be used to ensure that the processes are easily adopted throughout the organization. Some example process documentation templates are included in Appendix C.

The goal for now and in the future is to design processes and support these with tools that can provide integration between organizations. This has now become possible because management tools are providing support of open standards, such as the DMTF, which support the exchange of information based on ITIL concepts, such as incidents, problems and changes with standard formats and contents. This allows service providers to support efficient and effective process interfaces with their main suppliers with automated exchange of key operational information in real time.

3.7.4.1 Designing roles – the RACI model

When designing a service or a process, it is imperative that all the roles are clearly defined. A trademark of high-performing organizations is the ability to make the right decisions quickly and execute them effectively. Whether the decision involves a strategic choice or a critical operation, being clear on who has input, who decides and who takes action will enable the organization to move forward rapidly.

A key characteristic of a process is that all related activities need not necessarily be limited to one specific organizational unit. Service asset and configuration management process activities, for example, can be conducted in departments such as computer operations, system programming, application management, network management, systems development and even non-IT departments such as procurement, warehouse or accounting. Since services, processes and their component activities run through an entire organization, the individual activities should be clearly mapped to well-defined roles. The roles and activities are coordinated by process managers. Once detailed procedures and work instructions have been developed, an organization must map the defined roles and the activities of the process to its existing staff. Clear definitions of accountability and responsibility are critical success factors (CSFs) for any improvement activity. Without this, roles and responsibilities within the new process can be confusing, and individuals will revert to 'the way we've always done it' before the new procedures were put in place.

To help with this task the RACI model or 'authority matrix' is often used within organizations to define the roles and responsibilities in relation to processes and activities. The RACI model provides a compact, concise, easy method of tracking who does what in each process and it enables decisions to be made with pace and confidence.

RACI is an acronym for the four main roles of being:

- **Responsible** The person or people responsible for correct execution – for getting the job done
- **Accountable** The person who has ownership of quality and the end result. Only one person can be accountable for each task
- **Consulted** The people who are consulted and whose opinions are sought. They have involvement through input of knowledge and information

- **Informed** The people who are kept up to date on progress. They receive information about process execution and quality.

Some use the RACI definitions, but switch the order to Accountable, Responsible, Consulted and Informed or ARCI, but the meanings and usage remain unaltered.

Occasionally an expanded version of RACI is used, called RACI-VS, with two further roles as follows:

- **Verifies** The person or group that checks whether the acceptance criteria have been met
- **Signs off** The person who approves the V decision and authorizes the product handover. This could be the 'A' person.

A third variation of the RACI model is RASCI, where the S represents Supportive. This role provides additional resources to conduct the work, or plays a supportive role in implementation, for example. This could be beneficial for IT service implementation.

Applying the RACI model to a process, only one person should hold end-to-end accountability for the process, typically the process owner. Similarly, there is only one person accountable for any individual activity, although several people may be responsible for executing parts of the activity.

The RACI chart in Table 3.2 shows the structure and power of RACI modelling. The rows represent a number of required activities and the columns identify the people who make the decisions, carry out the activities or provide input.

Table 3.2 An example of a simple RACI matrix

	Director service management	Service level manager	Problem manager	Security manager	Procurement manager
Activity 1	AR	C	I	I	C
Activity 2	A	R	C	C	C
Activity 3	I	A	R	I	C
Activity 4	I	A	R	I	
Activity 5	I	R	A	C	I

Whether RACI or some other tool or model is used, the important thing is to not just leave the assignment of responsibilities to chance or leave it to the last minute to decide. Conflicts can be avoided and decisions can be made quickly if the roles are allocated in advance.

To build a RACI chart, the following steps are required:

- Identify the processes/activities
- Identify and define the roles
- Conduct meetings and assign the RACI codes
- Identify any gaps or overlaps – for example, where there are multiple Rs or no Rs (see analysis below)
- Distribute the chart and incorporate feedback
- Ensure that the allocations are being followed.

Analysis of a RACI chart to identify weaknesses or areas for improvement should include considering both the role and activity perspectives.

Role analysis

Role analysis involves asking:

- Many As: Are duties segregated properly? Should someone else be accountable for some of these activities? Is this causing a bottleneck in some areas that will delay decisions?
- Many Rs: Is this too much for one function?
- No empty spaces: Does this role need to be involved in so many tasks?
- Also, does the type or degree of participation fit this role's qualifications?

Activity analysis

Activity analysis can indicate:

- More than one A: only one role can be accountable
- No As: at least one A must be assigned to each activity
- More than one R: too many roles responsible often means that no one takes responsibility. Responsibility may be shared, but only if roles are clear
- No Rs: at least one role must be responsible
- Many Cs: Is there a requirement to consult with so many roles? What are the benefits and can the extra time be justified?

- No Cs and Is: Are the communication channels open to enable people and departments to talk to each other and keep each other up to date?

It is important to understand the distinction between a formal function within an organization and the process roles that the individuals in that function are expected to carry out. Persons within a formal function may fulfil more than one specific service management role and carry out activities relating to more than one process. For example, an individual with the job title of 'network administrator' is responsible for carrying out incident management as well as capacity management activities. Although the network administrator may report to a different functional line manager, they are also responsible for carrying out activities for the service desk function and capacity management process owners.

Developing an authority matrix can be a tedious and time-consuming exercise but it is a crucially important one. The authority matrix clarifies to all involved which activities they are expected to fulfil, as well as identifying any gaps in service delivery and responsibilities. It is especially helpful in clarifying the staffing model necessary for improvement.

Experience teaches us that using an authority matrix helps with two major activities that are often overlooked or hard to identify. One is that all the 'Rs' on a RACI matrix typically represent potential OLA opportunities. The second is that identifying roles that must be kept informed aids in exposing communication and workflow paths. This can be very helpful when defining the communication procedures within CSI activities.

Potential problems with the RACI model include:

- Having more than one person accountable for a process means that in practice no one is accountable
- Delegation of responsibility or accountability without necessary authority
- Focus on matching processes and activities with departments
- Incorrect division/combination of functions; conflicting agendas or goals
- Combination of responsibility for closely related processes, such as incident management, problem management, service asset and

configuration management, change management and release and deployment management. Combining responsibilities can in some cases reduce the checks and balances that support good governance or could overload some persons filling a combined role.

3.7.4.2 Processes and RACI

In order to fully understand an authority matrix we must first begin with an example of a process. In this case, we will use the change management process. (For the complete change management process, see section 4.2, *ITIL Service Transition*.) Each of the major activities of the process is then expanded into a detailed flow of specific procedures, tasks and work instructions. As an example, the fifth activity of the change management process – authorize change build and test – is expanded into an authorization model

(Figure 3.12). In this example, different levels of change require different change authorization levels, thus the need for assignment of authority to different roles.

Utilizing the change authorization model shown in Figure 3.12, the authorization activity can be expanded into the detailed procedural steps necessary to determine the level at which the change authorization must be granted. Then an example authority matrix is created based on the RACI model to illustrate the linkage between many of the roles we have discussed, the detailed procedures, and the level of responsibility assigned to each role in the successful execution of the procedure and, moving up, the process (see Table 3.3).

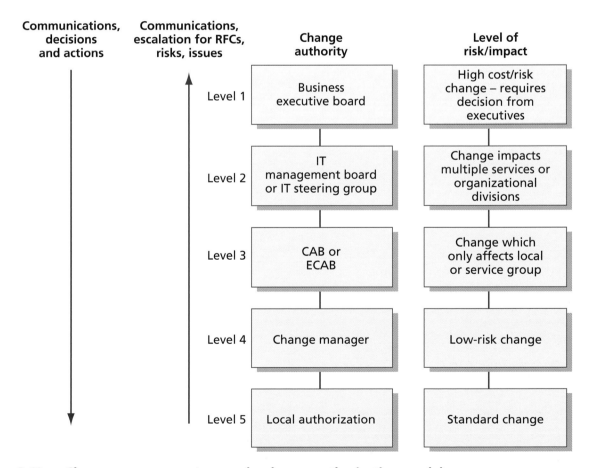

Figure 3.12   Change management example: change authorization model

Table 3.3 RACI matrix – sample change management authority matrix based on authorization procedure

No.	Process roles — Activity within procedure:	Customer	Change initiator	Service desk	Change manager	Change practitioner	CAB	ECAB	Release and deployment manager	IT management board	Business executive board
1.0	Determine level of risk:	RC	C	C	AR	C					
1.1	Level 5 – standard change Local authorization		C		AR	RI					
1.2	Level 4 – low-risk change Change manager authorization		C		AR	RI					
1.3	Level 3 – affects only local or service groups RFC to CAB for assessment		C		AR		CI				
1.4	Level 2 – affects multiple services or organizational divisions RFC to IT management board for assessment		C		AR		C			CI	
1.5	Level 1 – high-cost/high-risk change RFC to business executive board for assessment		C		AR						CI
2.0	Endorsed? Yes – go to 2.1 No – go to 3.1				ARI		I				
2.1	CAB members estimate impact and resources, confirm priority, schedule changes				A		R		C		
3.0	Authorized? Not authorized – go to 3.1 Authorized – go to 3.2	I	I	I	A	I	R				
3.1	RFC rejected and closed (initiator informed with a brief explanation of why it was rejected)	I	I		A	R	I	I			
3.2	Change is scheduled for action through release and deployment	CI	I		AR	RC			C		

Key: R = responsible; A = accountable; C = consulted; I = informed; RFC = request for change; CAB = change advisory board; ECAB = emergency change advisory board

3.7.5 Designing measurement methods and metrics

'If you can't measure it then you can't manage it.'
Peter Drucker

In order to manage and control processes and services, they have to be monitored and measured. The design of the measurement methods and metrics is one of the five aspects of service design, including designing metrics to manage and control design activities themselves. Measurements and metrics are covered in detail in *ITIL Continual Service Improvement*. This section covers those aspects that are particularly relevant and appropriate to designing the measurement of the quality of processes and their deliverables.

Care should be exercised when selecting measurements and metrics and the methods used to produce them. This is because the metrics and measurements chosen will actually affect and change the behaviour of people working within the activities and processes being measured, particularly where this relates to objectives, personal and team performance and performance-related pay schemes. Therefore only measurements that encourage progression towards meeting business objectives or desired behavioural change should be selected.

In all the design activities, the requirement should be to:

■ Design solutions that are 'fit for purpose'
■ Design for the appropriate level of quality/warranty – not over-engineered or under-engineered (fit for use)
■ Design solutions that are 'right first time' and meet their expected targets
■ Design solutions that minimize the amount of 'rework' or 'add-ons' that have to be rapidly developed after solutions have been deployed
■ Design solutions that are effective and efficient from the perspective of the business and the customers. The emphasis should be on the solutions that are effective above all and that are efficient within the constraint of remaining effective.

Measurement methods and metrics should reflect these requirements and be designed to measure the ability of processes to match these requirements. All of the measurements and metrics used should reflect the quality and success of the organization's processes from the perspective of the business, customers and users. They need to reflect the ability of the delivered solutions to meet the identified and agreed requirements of the business.

The process measurements selected need to be appropriate for the capability and maturity of the processes being measured. Immature processes are not capable of supporting sophisticated measurements, metrics and measurement methods. There are four types of metrics that can be used to measure the capability and performance of processes:

■ **Progress** Milestones and deliverables in the capability of the process
■ **Compliance** Compliance of the process to governance requirements, regulatory requirements and compliance of people to the use of the process
■ **Effectiveness** The accuracy and correctness of the process and its ability to deliver the 'right result'
■ **Efficiency** The productivity of the process, its speed, throughput and resource utilization.

Measurements and metrics should develop and change as the maturity and capability of a process develops. Initially, with immature processes the first two levels of metrics should be used to measure the progress and compliance of the process as it develops in maturity. As the process maturity develops, greater use should be made of effectiveness and efficiency metrics, but not to the detriment of compromising the progress or compliance of the process.

The selection of the metrics, the point of measurement and the methods of measuring, calculating and reporting on the metrics must be carefully designed and planned. The primary metrics should always focus on determining the effectiveness and the quality of the solutions provided. Secondary metrics can then measure the efficiency of the processes used to produce and manage the solution. The priority should always be to ensure that the processes provide the correct results for the business. Therefore the measurement methods and metrics should always provide this business-focused measurement above all.

Too many organizations collect measurements in individual areas, but fail to aggregate them

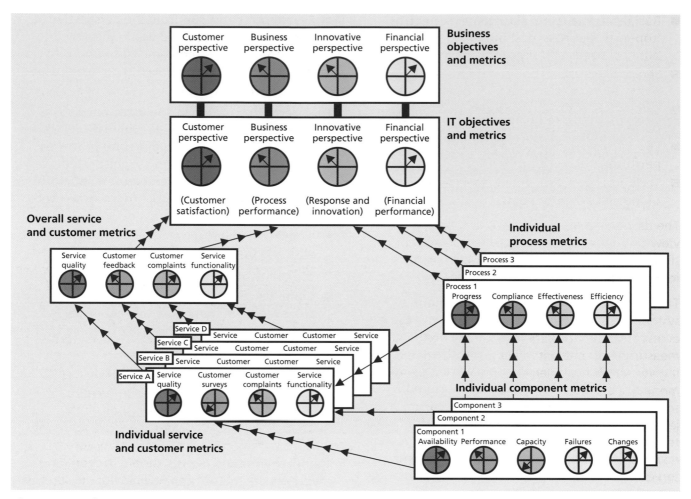

Figure 3.13 The metrics tree

together and gain the full benefit of the measurements, and therefore suffer because:

- Measurements are not aligned with business objectives and needs
- There is no overall visibility of the 'top-level' picture
- There are gaps in areas where measurements are not recorded
- Individual areas are well measured and others are poorly measured or are not measured
- There is no consistency in the method, presentation and calculation of the measurements
- Decisions and improvement actions are based on incomplete or inaccurate information.

The most effective method of measurement is to establish a 'metrics tree' or 'key performance indicator (KPI) tree', an approach which employs a hierarchy of metrics to create a comprehensive view at multiple, interconnected levels. Organizations should attempt to develop automated 'metrics tree' measurement systems, such as that illustrated in Figure 3.13.

The tree in Figure 3.13, based on a typical balanced scorecard, uses dials to represent metrics results for each level shown. It is important to note the linkage from the lowest level of the tree of individual component metrics all the way up to objectives and metrics of the business itself. Balanced scorecards represent a management system that enables increasing numbers of organizations to clarify their vision and strategy into action. They provide feedback regarding the internal business processes and external outcomes in order continually to improve strategic performance and results. This enables everybody within the organization to get a picture of the performance of the organization at the appropriate level. The advantages include:

- Business managers and customers can get a 'top-level' business 'dashboard', aligned with business needs and processes.
- Senior IT managers and customers can focus on the top-level IT management dashboard.
- Service owners and customers can focus on the performance of particular services.
- Process owners and managers can view the performance of their processes.
- Technical specialists can look at the performance of individual components.

The dashboard also presents an opportunity to view trends over time, rather than static data, so that potential performance degradation can be identified and rectified at an early stage.

This means that within a hierarchical metrics system, each person in the organization can get access to an appropriate level of information and measurement that suits their particular need. It gives senior management the opportunity to monitor a top-level dashboard to ensure that services continue to be delivered to their agreed levels, and it also provides the capability for technical specialists and process owners to drill down to the detail to analyse variance from agreed service, component or process performance.

Obviously the collection, analysis and presentation of this data can be a very labour-intensive activity and therefore should be automated wherever possible. This can be achieved using analysis tools based on macros, scripts, spreadsheets or preferably on specific web-based solutions. The measurements at each of the levels should be specifically defined to meet the needs of the business, customers and users of the information.

More detailed information on measurements, metrics and measurement methods are contained in *ITIL Continual Service Improvement*.

3.8 THE SUBSEQUENT DESIGN ACTIVITIES

Once the desired service solution has been designed, then the subsequent activities must also be completed in the service design stage before the solution passes into the service transition stage.

3.8.1 Evaluation of alternative solutions

An additional evaluation stage may be necessary if external supplier services and solutions are involved. This consists of the following:

- Selecting a set of suppliers and completing a tendering process. This will require the production and completion of:
  - Documentation of the scope of the service and production of an SoR and/or a terms of reference document
  - Issuing a request for information, request for proposal, request for quotation and ITT documents as appropriate
  - Producing and agreeing a set of solution and supplier evaluation criteria and a scoring process.
- Evaluation and review of supplier responses and selection of the preferred supplier(s) and their proposed solution(s). This may also involve running trials or even prototyping or proof of concept activities if significant new concepts or technology are involved in the new service in order to ensure that new components meet their expectations.
- Evaluation and costing of the alternative designs, possibly including identification of potential suppliers and evaluation of their alternative proposals, technologies, solutions and contracts. There is a need to ensure that costing covers one-off costs and ongoing costs of operation and ownership, including support and maintenance (for detailed information about service economics and service costing, see *ITIL Service Strategy*, sections 3.6 and 4.3).

3.8.2 Procurement of the preferred solution

It is possible that no external elements will be required for the solution. However, this is unusual as suppliers of software are highly likely to be involved. Where external suppliers are involved in the preferred solution, the activities consist of:

- Completing all necessary checks on the preferred supplier
- Finalizing the terms and conditions of any new contracts, ensuring that all corporate policies are enforced
- The procurement of the selected solution.

3.8.3 Developing the service solution

The development phase consists of translating the service design into a plan for the development, reuse or redevelopment of the components required to deliver the service and the subsequent implementation of the developed service. It may need to be developed into a programme of plans if this is a major service change. Each plan or project within the programme will be responsible for delivering one or more components of the service and will include:

- The needs of the business
- The strategy to be adopted for the development and/or purchase of the solution
- The timescales involved
- The resources required, taking into consideration facilities, IT infrastructure and the right personnel skills in order to ensure the delivery service meets the customer's needs
- The development of the service and its constituent components, including the management and other operational mechanisms, such as measurement, monitoring and reporting
- Service and component test plans.

Careful project management will need to be used to ensure that conflict is avoided and that the compatible components are developed from the various development activities.

3.9 DESIGN CONSTRAINTS

All design activities operate within many constraints. These constraints come from the business and service strategy and cover many different areas, as illustrated in Figure 3.14.

This means that designers are not always 'free' to design the most desirable solution for the business because it does not fall within the imposed constraints, as illustrated in Figure 3.14. The primary constraints that determine the boundaries of a service solution design are the utility and warranty desired by the customer. The service provider will attempt to fulfil everything requested by the customer in these areas, but other constraints may result in carefully considered compromises. The most obvious additional constraint is the financial one. There may be insufficient budget available for the most appropriate or the preferred solution; therefore a cheaper alternative service would have to be identified and agreed with the business. The designer can only provide the solution that fits within all of the currently known constraints, or else try lifting or renegotiating some of the

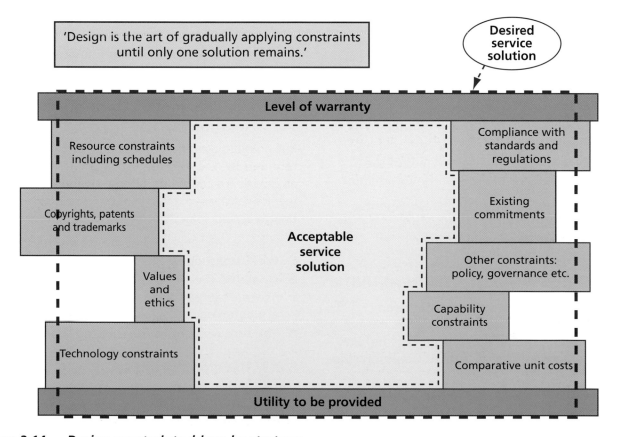

Figure 3.14   Design constraints driven by strategy

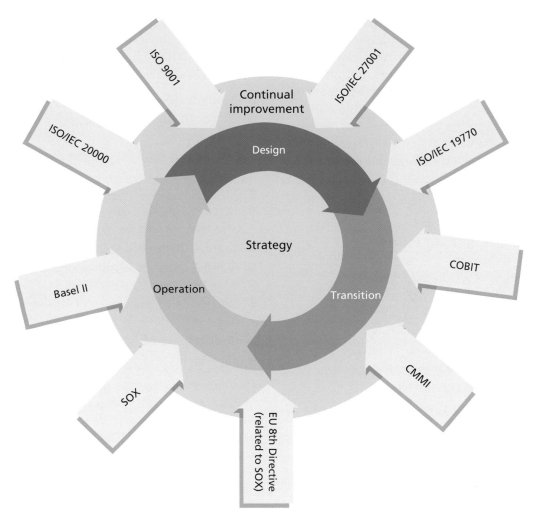

Figure 3.15 External influences on solution design

constraints – for instance, by obtaining a bigger budget. The service provider and the customer must both recognize the fact that they are free to design solutions but that they are working in an environment where many external factors can influence the design.

Many of these external influences arise from the need for good corporate and IT governance, and others are from the requirement for compliance with regulations, legislation and international standards, as illustrated in Figure 3.15. It is essential, therefore, that all designers recognize these and ensure that the designs and solutions they produce have all of the necessary controls and capability within them. For more information on some of these external influences see Appendix N.

3.10 SERVICE-ORIENTED ARCHITECTURE

It is strongly recommended that business processes and solutions should be designed and developed using a service-oriented architecture (SOA) approach. The SOA approach is considered best practice and is used by many organizations to improve their effectiveness and efficiency in the provision of IT services.

SOA is defined by OASIS (Organization for the Advancement of Structured Information Standards; www.oasis-open.org) as:

'A paradigm for organizing and utilizing distributed capabilities that may be under the control of different ownership domains. It provides a uniform means to offer, discover, interact with and use capabilities to produce desired effects consistent with measurable preconditions and expectations.'

OASIS is a not-for-profit, international consortium that drives the development, convergence and adoption of e-business standards. SOA brings value and agility to an organization by encouraging the development of 'self-contained' services that are reusable. This, in turn, promotes a flexible and modular approach to the development of 'shared services' that can be used in many different areas of the business. More and more organizations are converting business processes to common 'packaged services' that can be used and shared by many areas of the business.

Wherever possible, IT service provider organizations should use the SOA approach and principles to develop flexible, reusable IT services that are common and can be shared and exploited across many different areas of the business. When this approach is used, it is essential that IT:

- Defines and determines what a service is
- Understands and clearly identifies interfaces and dependencies between services
- Utilizes standards for the development and definition of services
- Uses common technology and toolsets
- Investigates and understands the impact of changes to 'shared services'
- Ensures that SOA-related training has been planned and achieved for IT staff members in order to establish a common language and improve the implementation and support of the new or changed services.

When SOA principles are used by the IT service provider organization, it is critical that an accurate service catalogue is maintained as part of an overall service portfolio and CMS. Adopting this approach can significantly reduce the time taken to deliver new solutions to the business and to move towards a focus on business outcomes instead of technology. The service catalogue will also show the relationship between services and applications. A single application could be part of more than one service, and a single service could utilize more than one application.

3.11 SERVICE DESIGN MODELS

The model selected for the design of IT services will depend mainly on the model selected for the delivery of IT services. Before adopting a design model for a major new service, a review of the current capability and provisions with respect to all aspects of the delivery of IT services should be conducted. This review should consider all aspects of the new service, including the:

- Business drivers and requirements
- Demands, targets and requirements of the new service
- Scope and capability of the existing service provider unit
- Scope and capability of external suppliers
- Maturity of the organizations currently involved and their processes
- Culture of the organizations involved
- IT infrastructure, applications, data, services and other components involved
- Degree of corporate and IT governance and the level of ownership and control required
- Budgets and other resources available
- Staff levels and skills.

This review/assessment provides a structured mechanism for determining an organization's capabilities and state of readiness for delivering new or revised services in support of defined business drivers and requirements. The information obtained from such an assessment can be used in determining the delivery strategy for a particular IT service or IT system. The delivery strategy is the approach taken to move an organization from a known state, based on the readiness assessment, to a desired state, determined by the business drivers and needs. There are many ways to prepare an organization for deploying a new service. The method and strategy selected should be based on the solution the organization chooses for fulfilling its key business drivers, as well as the capabilities of the IT organization and its partners. The scale of options available is quite large, and not every option needs be considered in every case. However, keeping all the options available for consideration is key for designing and operating innovative solutions to the most difficult business challenges. In the end, this may be the difference between a failed project – or even a failed company – and a successful one.

These two models, for the design and delivery of IT services, are closely related and are considered in the following two sections.

Table 3.4   Main sourcing structures (delivery strategies)

Sourcing structure	Description
Insourcing	This approach relies on utilizing internal organizational resources in the design, development, transition, maintenance, operation and/or support of new, changed or revised services.
Outsourcing	This approach utilizes the resources of an external organization or organizations in a formal arrangement to provide a well-defined portion of a service's design, development, maintenance, operations and/or support. This includes the consumption of services from application service providers (ASPs) described below.
Co-sourcing or multi-sourcing	Often a combination of insourcing and outsourcing, using a number of organizations working together to co-source key elements within the lifecycle. This generally involves using a number of external organizations working together to design, develop, transition, maintain, operate and/or support a portion of a service.
Partnership	Formal arrangements between two or more organizations to work together to design, develop, transition, maintain, operate and/or support IT service(s). The focus here tends to be on strategic partnerships that leverage critical expertise or market opportunities.
Business process outsourcing (BPO)	The increasing trend of relocating entire business functions using formal arrangements between organizations where one organization provides and manages the other organization's entire business process(es) or function(s) in a low-cost location. Common examples are accounting, payroll and call centre operations.
Application service provision	Involves formal arrangements with an application service provider (ASP) organization that will provide shared computer-based services to customer organizations over a network from the service provider's premises. Applications offered in this way are also sometimes referred to as on-demand software/applications. Through ASPs, the complexities and costs of such shared software can be reduced and provided to organizations that could otherwise not justify the investment.
Knowledge process outsourcing (KPO)	KPO is a step ahead of BPO in one respect. KPO organizations provide domain-based processes and business expertise rather than just process expertise. In other words the organization is not only required to execute a process, but also to make certain low-level decisions based on knowledge of local conditions or industry-specific information. One example is the outsourcing of credit risk assessment, where the outsourcing organization has historical information that they have analysed to create knowledge which in turn enables them to provide a service. For every credit card company to collect and analyse this data for themselves would not be as cost-effective as using KPO.
'Cloud'	Cloud service providers offer specific pre-defined services, usually on demand. Services are usually standard, but can be customized to a specific organization if there is enough demand for the service. Cloud services can be offered internally, but generally refer to outsourced service provision.
Multi-vendor sourcing	This type of sourcing involves sourcing different sources from different vendors, often representing different sourcing options from the above.

3.11.1   Delivery model options

Although the readiness assessment determines the gap between the current and desired capabilities, an IT organization should not necessarily try to bridge that gap by itself. There are many different delivery strategies or models that can be used, reflecting how and to what degree the service provider will rely on suppliers. Each strategy has its own set of advantages and disadvantages, but all require some level of adaptation and customization for the situation at hand. Table 3.4 lists the main categories of sourcing structure (delivery strategy) with a short abstract for each. Delivery practices tend to fall into one of these categories or some variant of them.

Table 3.4 highlights a key point: the set of sourcing structures/delivery strategies varies widely and ranges from a relatively straightforward situation, solely managed within the boundaries of a company, all the way to a full KPO situation, or even a multi-vendor approach. This broad range of alternatives provides significant flexibility, but often with added complexity, and in some cases additional risk. Key advantages and disadvantages of each type of strategy are listed in Table 3.5.

All of the above arrangements can be provided in both an offshore or onshore situation. In the onshore case, both organizations are based within the same country/continent, whereas in the offshore situation the organizations are in different countries/continents. Very complex sourcing arrangements exist within the IT industry and it is impossible to cover all combinations and their implications here. Complementary publications in the ITIL series will provide additional guidance on sourcing strategies.

Mergers and acquisitions can also complicate the issues. These situations occur when one company acquires or merges with another company for cash and/or equity swaps of the company's stock. Again, this occurs generally in response to industry consolidations, market expansion, or in direct response to competitive pressures. If companies that have different service delivery strategies are acquired or merge, a period of review and consolidation is often required to determine the most appropriate sourcing strategy for the newly merged organization. However, mergers and acquisitions can often provide organizations with the opportunity to consolidate the best practice from each organization, thereby improving the overall service capability and achieving synergies across the organization. Opportunities will also exist to provide improved career development options to service management personnel and to consolidate supplier contracts for services.

3.11.2 Selecting service delivery strategies

The delivery strategies are relevant to both the design and transition stages of the service lifecycle as well as the operation stage. Extreme care must be taken when selecting different strategies for different stages of the lifecycle to ensure that all organizations involved clearly understand their individual roles and responsibilities, and also every other organization's role and responsibility. This must be done to ensure acceptance and handover processes are clearly defined, agreed and accepted.

Example of response to a merger

A medium-sized bank merged with another bank that had a complementary product portfolio. The integration of applications, therefore, was simple. However, the two banks felt that consolidation of operations would be beneficial, but could not leverage the economies of scale to a sufficient extent. Outsourcing was also an option, but instead the two banks chose to partner with an outsourcing company. The banks provided the bank-specific knowledge to make their IT services organization an attractive data centre for smaller banks. The outsourcing partner provided the necessary technology expertise and new clients to benefit from the economies of scale.

So how does an organization determine the optimum delivery strategy? There is no single or simple answer to this question. It is too dependent on the unique and specific situation under consideration. For this reason, the most appropriate guidance that can be provided is to describe key advantages and disadvantages of each delivery strategy. This, in turn, can be used as a checklist to determine which delivery approach should be evaluated further and most benefit the specific project or business initiative. Table 3.5 lists each strategy and its key advantages and disadvantages for the delivery of an application or IT service.

A potential disadvantage of any solution using one or more partners is the difficulty and cost of managing an external contributor to service provision. The cost and effort of identifying, establishing, managing and terminating suppliers and contracts should not be overlooked or discounted when determining a strategy.

Table 3.5 Advantages and disadvantages of sourcing structures (delivery strategies)

Sourcing structure	Advantages	Disadvantages
Insourcing	Direct control Freedom of choice Rapid prototyping of leading-edge services Familiar policies and processes Company-specific knowledge	Scale limitations Cost and time to market for services readily available outside Dependent on internal resources and their skills and competencies
Outsourcing	Economies of scale Purchased expertise Supports focus on company core competencies Support for transient needs Test drive/trial of new services	Less direct control Exit barriers Solvency risk of suppliers Unknown supplier skills and competencies More challenging business process integration Increased governance and verification
Co-sourcing or multi-sourcing	Time to market Leveraged expertise Control Use of specialized providers	Project complexity Intellectual property and copyright protection Culture clash between companies
Partnership	Time to market Market expansion/entrance Competitive response Leveraged expertise Trust, alignment and mutual benefit 'Risk and reward' agreements	Project complexity Intellectual property and copyright protection Culture clash between companies
BPO	Single point of responsibility 'One-stop shop' Access to specialist skills Risk transferred to the outsourcer Low-cost location	Culture clash between companies Loss of business knowledge Loss of relationship with the business
ASP	Access to expensive and complex solutions Low-cost location Support and upgrades included Security and ITSCM options included	Culture clash between companies Access to facilities only, not knowledge Often usage-based charging models
KPO	Access to specialist skills, knowledge and expertise Low-cost location Significant cost savings	Culture clash between companies Loss of internal expertise Loss of relationship with the business
'Cloud'	Services are easily defined Sourcing is straightforward Mapping between the service and business outcome is relatively straightforward Greater customer control of the service	Internal clouds are still complex Focus on the technology could mask the relationship between IT activities and the business outcome Difficulty coordinating insourced offerings with external cloud services Security of information and assurance of business continuity for services hosted externally
Multi-vendor sourcing	Less risk in that the organization is not tied to a single vendor Leverage of specialized skills in different organizations ensures a more complete support model	Could be difficult to coordinate the different vendors' activities and services Requires a very clear understanding of the overall value chain and each vendor's role

Ultimately, the strategy selected will depend on the capability and needs of the specific organization, its business and people – culture and capabilities. Whichever strategy is selected, its success and operation should be measured and regularly reviewed for effectiveness and efficiency and adapted to fit the changing business needs. The selection adopted with regard to IT service provision can often be influenced by the overall business culture and its approach to outsourcing and partnering.

3.11.3 Design and development approaches

It is also important to understand the current generic lifecycle types, methods and approaches to IT service development, in order to decide on standards for the service design stage of the lifecycle. To achieve this, a good understanding is needed of the following aspects of the various service development lifecycle (SDLC) approaches:

- The structure (e.g. milestones/stages/phases)
- The activities (e.g. the workflows or detailed steps/tasks described within an approach)
- The primary models associated with the chosen method, typically giving a process perspective, a data perspective, an event perspective and, often, a user perspective. Examples include use case diagrams, class diagrams and state chart diagrams from the unified modelling language (UML).

For more detail on SDLC, see Chapter 5.

3.11.3.1 Rapid application development

It is necessary to understand the differences between object-oriented and structured systems development, the basic principles of the 'agile' movement, and to recognize how a commitment to a software package solution changes the structure of the approach. Some of the most well-known terms in this area include 'rapid application development' (RAD), 'agile software development' and 'accelerated development'. While representing different approaches, they share a focus on the rapid, frequent delivery of working software produced in a highly collaborative environment.

These approaches, which by default address a single system (and related services) only, can be supplemented by architectural approaches, such as those based on component-based reuse (see section 3.10 for further discussion of architecture).

The application lifecycle model described in the section on management of applications (section 5.3) can be viewed as an example of a linear or 'waterfall' (or 'V' model)-based approach, and will not be discussed in further detail here, other than for comparison purposes with other approaches.

The 'agile' approach can feature development where requirements and solutions can evolve as different teams work together. It uses continuous feedback, planning, testing, integration and continuous evolution.

The main feature of RAD is the introduction of increments and iterations in the development process for the management of the risks associated with uncertainty and changing requirements. Traditional approaches have assumed that a complete set of requirements could be defined early in the lifecycle and that development costs could be controlled by managing change. However, discouraging change can mean being unresponsive to business conditions. RAD approaches accept that change is inevitable and attempt to minimize the costs of responding to them while still retaining the required quality.

The use of increments implies that a service is developed piece by piece, where every piece could support one of the business functions that the entire service needs. Incremental delivery could result in shorter time to market for specific business functions. The development of every increment requires traversal of all lifecycle stages.

Iterative development implies that the lifecycle will be traversed more than once, by design. Techniques such as prototyping are used to get a better understanding of the requirements (by testing functional, management and operational activities and through communication with users).

> **Key message**
>
> In RAD, combinations of iterative and incremental approaches are possible. It is possible to start with the specification of requirements for the entire service, followed by the design and development of the application incrementally.

RAD development methods, including the unified process and dynamic systems development method

(DSDM), are seen as a response to business expectations, with the goal of reducing the cost of change throughout a development project. DSDM utilizes continuous user involvement in an iterative development and incremental approach, which is responsive to changing requirements, to develop a software system that satisfies the business requirements on time and on budget.

Another example, Extreme Programming (XP), calls for developers to:

■ Produce a first service delivery in weeks, to achieve an early win and rapid feedback
■ Invent simple solutions, so there is less to modify and also facilitating change
■ Improve design quality continually
■ Test early for less expensive fault-finding
■ Use basic disciplines such as reviews, configuration and change management to keep control.

To make good use of an incremental approach, the design process needs to be based on a separation of concerns (SoC), by grouping functions within increments in such a way that their interdependence is minimized (see section 5.3.8 for more information on SoC).

In general terms, accelerated application development methods adopt a three-stage lifecycle model: accelerated analysis and design, time-boxed development, and production and implementation. The methods are usually underpinned by software engineering technology, and rely on joint (IT–user) working and prototyping to quickly define requirements and create a working prototype.

From a business perspective, the use of incremental development and delivery by developers means that a valid, distinct part of the overall service can be delivered before the development team is in a position to complete the whole project. This approach offers early benefits to the business, and provides an opportunity for both the business and development team to discover emergent service properties and learn from their experience. However, it is often difficult to find a sufficiently small first increment that can provide a meaningful service to business.

RAD methods embodying iteration and incremental delivery can be used to reduce both development and implementation risks. The actual projects may not necessarily be easier to

manage, but they can facilitate implementation and acceptance. They offer more options for contingency and enable developers to deal with changing business requirements and environmental conditions. They also provide both milestones and decision points for project control purposes. These methods can additionally be used to:

■ Reach or converge on a design acceptable to the customer and feasible to the development team
■ Limit the project's exposure to the unpredictable elements of both business and environmental change
■ Save development time, although for a successful RAD project, something other than schedule must be negotiable. (RAD has the best chance for success if the business is willing to negotiate on both functionality and quality.)

Important RAD constraints or CSFs include:

■ 'Fitness for business purpose' as the criterion for acceptance of deliverables
■ Representation of all parties that can impact application requirements throughout the development process
■ Customers, developers and management accepting informal deliverables – for example, notes from user workshops rather than formal requirements documents
■ Creation of the minimum documentation necessary to facilitate future development and maintenance
■ Empowerment of development teams to make decisions traditionally left to management
■ Iteration being used in such a manner as to converge towards an acceptable business solution
■ Prototypes that can incorporate evolving requirements quickly, to gain consensus early in the lifecycle.

The use of RAD approaches requires skilled, multidisciplinary teams who are able to advise on when to apply such approaches. Table 3.6 compares and contrasts aspects of the conventional or 'waterfall' approach with RAD approaches.

3.11.3.2 Off-the-shelf solutions
Many organizations now choose to fulfil their IT service requirements through purchasing and implementing commercial off-the-shelf (COTS) software package solutions. A framework for

Table 3.6 Comparison between conventional ('waterfall') and RAD approaches

Category	Conventional development	Accelerated development
General approach	Sequential phases	Evolutionary
User resource commitment	±15% throughout the project	100% throughout project for project sponsor, ±30% for selected others
Risk	Higher – longer-term project problems may not emerge until well into the development project	Lower – problems surface early in the development process, requiring quick resolution
Executive sponsorship	Has approval authority, but not actively involved	High participation – sets scope, reviews progress and resolves issues
Use of joint session, iteration and prototyping techniques	Optional	Required
Developer skills	Specialists, some with limited experience acceptable	Highly experienced, multi-skilled professionals required
Use of process support technology, e.g. CASE tools	Optional	Required
Team structure	Usually large with specialized skill sets	Usually small with general skill sets, supplemented by specialists as needed
Rigorous scope management	Necessary	Critical
Phase structure	Four to five phases	Three phases
Individual accountability	Difficult to assess	Precise accountability

CASE = computer-aided software engineering.

selecting, customizing and implementing these off-the-shelf packaged solutions is required and includes the need to:

- Fully understand the advantages and disadvantages of the package approach
- Define a framework for effective software package selection
- Define a framework for effective customization and integration
- Define functional requirements at the appropriate level
- Develop a checklist of management and operational requirements
- Define product and supplier requirements
- Define service integration requirements
- Identify and investigate potential off-the-shelf software package solutions
- Present recommendations about the fit of a selected off-the-shelf software package against agreed requirements, and define the implications of this.

Detailed standards will be needed on:

- Packages and prototyping
- Defining the structure of weighted evaluation matrices
- Iteration in package selection.

Additionally, procedures for evaluating and comparing competing packages in terms of customization/integration requirements are needed and should include:

- Evaluating the functional match
- Scripted demonstrations and user-driven evaluation
- Evaluating the management and operational match
- Evaluating the implementation requirements match.

Standards for documenting requirements prior to package market investigation should include those that specifically show:

Table 3.7 Service design inputs and outputs by lifecycle stage

Lifecycle stage	Service design inputs (from the lifecycle stage in the first column)	Service design outputs (to the lifecycle stage in the first column)
Service strategy	Vision and mission Service portfolio Policies Strategies and strategic plans Priorities Service charters including service packages and details of utility and warranty Financial information and budgets Documented patterns of business activity and user profiles Service models	Input to business cases and the service portfolio Service design packages Updated service models Service portfolio updates including the service catalogue Financial estimates and reports Design-related knowledge and information in the SKMS Designs for service strategy processes and procedures
Service transition	Service catalogue updates Feedback on all aspects of service design and service design packages Input and feedback to transition plans Response to requests for change (RFCs) Knowledge and information in the SKMS (including the CMS) Design errors identified in transition for re-design Evaluation reports	Service catalogue Service design packages, including: ■ Details of utility and warranty ■ Acceptance criteria ■ Service models ■ Designs and interface specifications ■ Transition plans ■ Operation plans and procedures RFCs to transition or deploy new or changed services Input to change evaluation and CAB meetings Designs for service transition processes and procedures SLAs, OLAs and underpinning contracts
Service operation	Operational requirements Actual performance information RFCs to resolve operational issues Historical incident and problem records	Service catalogue Service design package, including: ■ Details of utility and warranty ■ Operations plans and procedures ■ Recovery procedures Knowledge and information in the SKMS Vital business functions HW/SW maintenance requirements Designs for service operation processes and procedures SLAs, OLAs and underpinning contracts Security policies

Table continues

Table 3.7 continued

Lifecycle stage	Service design inputs (from the lifecycle stage in the first column)	Service design outputs (to the lifecycle stage in the first column)
Continual service improvement	Results of customer and user satisfaction surveys	Service catalogue
	Input to design requirements	Service design packages including details of utility and warranty
	Data required for metrics, KPIs and CSFs	Knowledge and information in the SKMS
	Service reports	Achievements against metrics, KPIs and CSFs
	Feedback on service design packages	Design of services; measurements; processes; infrastructure; systems
	RFCs for implementing improvements	Design for the seven-step improvement process and procedures
		Improvement opportunities logged in the CSI register

- High-level functions (for scoping purposes)
- Business functions and significant events
- Significant input and output requirements
- Data (static) structures
- Identifying relationships between those structures, functions and events
- Service-wide management and operational requirements
- Non-functional requirements such as performance, throughput, disaster recovery capabilities, infrastructure and security standards.

When evaluating COTS solutions, consider the following three ways in which a requirement can be fulfilled:

- Available off the shelf
- Can be configured. Estimate the effort to perform the configuration. This only needs to be done once and will be preserved over upgrades of the product
- Must be customized. Estimate the effort to perform the customization initially and to repeat it on each upgrade of the product, bearing in mind that the customization concept might not be applicable to future releases.

Also investigate the strategy and release plan of the package supplier and ascertain whether it is aligned to yours, and to what extent you can expect your future requirements to be met by the package.

3.12 SERVICE DESIGN INPUTS AND OUTPUTS

The main inputs to service design are requirements for new or changed services. The main output of service design is the service design package, which includes all of the information needed to manage the entire lifecycle of a new or changed service. Table 3.7 shows the major service design inputs and outputs, by lifecycle stage. Appendix O provides a summary of the major inputs and outputs between each stage of the service lifecycle.

Service design
processes

4

4 Service design processes

This chapter describes and explains the fundamentals of the key processes supporting service design. These processes are principally responsible for providing key information for the design of new or changed service solutions. The processes described in this chapter are:

- Design coordination
- Service catalogue management
- Service level management
- Availability management
- Capacity management
- IT service continuity management (ITSCM)
- Information security management
- Supplier management.

There are no situations within IT service provision with either internal or external service providers where there are no processes in the service design

area. All IT service provider organizations already have some elements of their approach to the five aspects of service design in place, no matter how basic. Before starting on the implementation or the improvement of activities and processes, a review should be conducted of what elements are in place and working successfully. Many service provider organizations already have mature processes in place for designing IT services and solutions.

In order to develop effective and efficient service solutions that meet the current and evolving requirements of the business as well as the needs of IT, it is essential that the inputs and needs of all other areas and processes are considered and reviewed within each of the service design activities, as illustrated in Figure 4.1. This will ensure that all service solutions are consistent and compatible with existing solutions and will

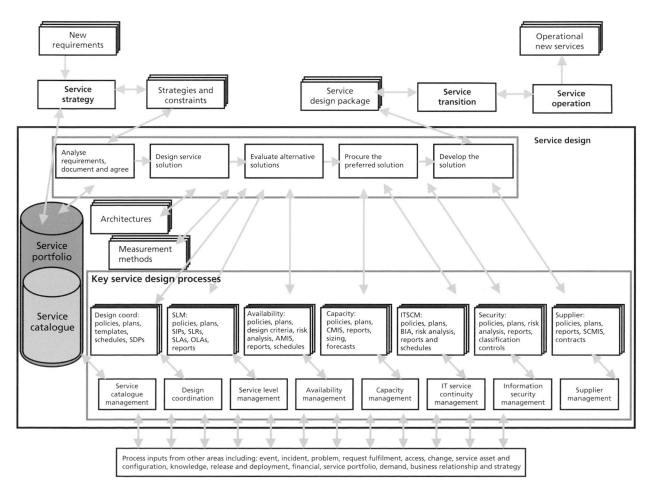

Figure 4.1 Service design – the big picture

meet the expectations of the customers and users. Critical facets of the key processes should be consolidated into all of the service design activities, so that all inputs are automatically referenced every time a new or changed service solution is produced.

4.1 DESIGN COORDINATION

The activities of the service design stage are detailed and complex. Only through well-coordinated action can a service provider hope to create comprehensive and appropriate designs that will support the achievement of the required business outcomes.

4.1.1 Purpose and objectives

The purpose of the design coordination process is to ensure the goals and objectives of the service design stage are met by providing and maintaining a single point of coordination and control for all activities and processes within this stage of the service lifecycle.

The objectives of the design coordination process are to:

- Ensure the consistent design of appropriate services, service management information systems, architectures, technology, processes, information and metrics to meet current and evolving business outcomes and requirements
- Coordinate all design activities across projects, changes, suppliers and support teams, and manage schedules, resources and conflicts where required
- Plan and coordinate the resources and capabilities required to design new or changed services
- Produce service design packages (SDPs) based on service charters and change requests
- Ensure that appropriate service designs and/or SDPs are produced and that they are handed over to service transition as agreed
- Manage the quality criteria, requirements and handover points between the service design stage and service strategy and service transition
- Ensure that all service models and service solution designs conform to strategic, architectural, governance and other corporate requirements

- Improve the effectiveness and efficiency of service design activities and processes
- Ensure that all parties adopt a common framework of standard, reusable design practices in the form of activities, processes and supporting systems, whenever appropriate
- Monitor and improve the performance of the service design lifecycle stage.

4.1.2 Scope

The scope of the design coordination process includes all design activity, particularly all new or changed service solutions that are being designed for transition into (or out of, in the case of a service retirement) the live environment.

Some design efforts will be part of a project, whereas others will be managed through the change process alone without a formally defined project. Some design efforts will be extensive and complex while others will be simple and swift. Not every design activity requires the same level of rigor to ensure success, so a significant number of design efforts will require little or no individual attention from the design coordination process. Most design coordination process activity focuses around those design efforts that are part of a project, as well as those that are associated with changes of defined types. Typically, the changes that require the most attention from design coordination are major changes, but any change that an organization believes could benefit from design coordination may be included.

Each organization should define the criteria that will be used to determine the level of rigour or attention to be applied in design coordination for each design. Some organizations take the perspective that all changes, regardless of how small in scope, have a 'design' stage, as it is important that all changes have clear and correct plans for how to implement them. In this perspective, the lifecycle stage of service design still occurs, even if the designs for simple or standard changes are usually pre-built and are reused frequently and quickly. Sometimes the stage is quite complex and long and sometimes it is simply a rapid check that the right 'design' (procedure) is being used. Other organizations take the perspective that only changes that fit certain criteria, such as those associated with a project or major change, have a formal service design stage. In this perspective, changes that fail to meet the agreed criteria may be considered out of the scope of this process.

Whichever perspective is adopted by an organization, the end result should be more successful changes that deliver the required business outcomes with minimal disruption or other negative impacts on business operations. If an organization's approach produces that result, then the organization is performing design coordination correctly.

The design coordination process includes:

- Assisting and supporting each project or other change through all the service design activities and processes
- Maintaining policies, guidelines, standards, budgets, models, resources and capabilities for service design activities and processes
- Coordinating, prioritizing and scheduling of all service design resources to satisfy conflicting demands from all projects and changes
- Planning and forecasting the resources needed for the future demand for service design activities
- Reviewing, measuring and improving the performance of all service design activities and processes
- Ensuring that all requirements are appropriately addressed in service designs, particularly utility and warranty requirements
- Ensuring the production of service designs and/ or SDPs and their handover to service transition.

The design coordination process does not include:

- Responsibility for any activities or processes outside of the design stage of the service lifecycle
- Responsibility for designing the detailed service solutions themselves or the production of the individual parts of the SDPs. These are the responsibility of the individual projects or service management processes.

4.1.3 Value to the business

The main value of the design coordination process to the business is the production of a set of consistent quality solution designs and SDPs that will provide the desired business outcomes.

Through the work of design coordination organizations can:

- Achieve the intended business value of services through design at acceptable risk and cost levels
- Minimize rework and unplanned labour costs associated with reworking design issues during later service lifecycle stages
- Support the achievement of higher customer and user satisfaction and improved confidence in IT and in the services received
- Ensure that all services conform to a consistent architecture, allowing integration and data exchange between services and systems
- Provide improved focus on service value as well as business and customer outcomes
- Develop improved efficiency and effectiveness of all service design activities and processes, thereby supporting higher volumes of successful change delivered in a timely and cost-effective manner
- Achieve greater agility and better quality in the design of service solutions, within projects and major changes.

4.1.4 Policies, principles and basic concepts

A structured and holistic approach to design activities should be adopted, so that all available information is considered and to ensure that consistency and integration are achieved throughout the IT organization, within all design activities. The design coordination process provides guidelines and policies to allow for this holistic approach and the coordination to ensure the practices are followed.

4.1.4.1 Policies

The service provider should define policies for which service design efforts require which type of attention from design coordination. For example, the policy might specify that the design portion of all projects, as well as for all changes that meet specific criteria (such as major changes) should receive individual coordination, while other changes must simply adhere to predefined design standards for that change type. These design standards are likely to be embedded in the change model and/or associated documented procedures for executing changes of that type.

The level of required documentation should also be established by policy. For design efforts that are part of a project or are associated with changes that meet specific criteria (such as major changes), a full service SDP will be required. For other changes, if in scope, the 'service design' may be documented very simply, and may even be pre-built if the change has been done before.

The design coordination policies should include:

- Adherence to corporate standards and conventions
- Explicit attention to governance and regulatory compliance in all design activities
- Standards for elements of a comprehensive design for new or changed services such as:
  - Document templates
  - Documentation plans
  - Training plans
  - Communications and marketing plans
  - Measurement and metrics plans
  - Testing plans
  - Deployment plans
- Criteria for resolving conflicting demands for service design resources
- Standard cost models.

Design coordination policies are likely to provide for appropriate variations within acceptable parameters for designs of different types and scopes. For example, since the user community will likely start with a sound basis of practical knowledge, the acceptable content of a training plan for a change to a well-established existing service might differ from the requirements for a training plan for an entirely new service. Regardless, the policies and standards established should result in the most appropriate SDPs while expending the least possible time and effort to produce them.

Table 4.1 CSI approach for design coordination implementation

CSI approach step	Guidance
What is the vision?	Consider how, in a perfect world, service design should work at your organization. Come to consensus among the key stakeholders regarding what you would like to create and what the critical success factors for service design should be.
Where are we now?	As objectively as possible, assess the current state of service design activities. How are they performed now? By whom are they performed and under what circumstances? What are the challenges and weaknesses in the current approach? What is working well? Where do the greatest pain points exist in the current approach? What capabilities do we have or will we need to have? What risks exist? To the extent possible, collect baseline measurements of the performance of current practices.
Where do we want to be?	Based on the overall vision for service design and the current state of these activities, agree on priorities for improvement. Improvement opportunities will exist in many processes that are active during service design, but the implementation of the design coordination process should provide for reliable, repeatable and consistent overall practices for service design. Based on the agreed priorities, select the specific design coordination practices to implement, defining them clearly with SMART objectives. (See the glossary and *ITIL Continual Service Improvement* for more information about SMART objectives.)
How do we get there?	Devise a detailed plan for how to move from the current state to the achievement of the agreed improvements and then execute the plan.
Did we get there?	Use the metrics associated with the SMART objectives to determine whether the improvement(s) to service design practices have been successfully implemented. If a gap still remains between the new current state and the desired state, additional work may be necessary.
How do we keep the momentum going?	Use ongoing monitoring of the performance of service design practices to ensure that new or revised practices become institutionalized. Encourage feedback and suggestions for improvement from all other stages in the lifecycle.

4.1.4.2 Principles – balance and prioritization

Perhaps the single most important guideline to be followed in design coordination is balance. A comprehensive design that addresses all aspects of utility and warranty, as well as the needs of the service throughout its lifecycle, is certainly the goal. Care must be taken, however, not to set up standards or documentation requirements that create excessive bureaucracy without consistently returning better services to the business and/or customer. The goal should be to put just enough definition, measurement and control of design activities in place to successfully manage the work and improve results, but no more.

When implementing a formal design coordination process, a service provider should build on their current practices and leverage the steps of the continual service improvement (CSI) approach as a guide. See Chapter 3 of *ITIL Continual Service Improvement* for details of this approach.

Table 4.1 shows how the CSI approach may be applied to the implementation of design coordination. Key to success will be prioritization. Do not attempt to implement more new practices than the organization can absorb at any one time. To do so may result in undesirable disruption to design activities already under way or in a failure of the organization to successfully adopt the new or revised practices.

4.1.4.3 Principles – integration with project management

In most organizations many design efforts are managed as part of a project utilizing formal project management methods. Many organizations have historically relied heavily on the experience of the project manager to ensure successful design, but not all project managers have the requisite detailed knowledge of what makes for good design. Furthermore, under the pressure of project deadlines and other constraints, many project managers struggle to consistently manage customer expectations and prevent excessive or unmanaged change to the scope of the project.

As part of design coordination, it is important that practices, documents, procedures or deliverables deemed to be needed for design success should be integrated into the overall project management methodology and all project managers trained to contribute appropriately. Agreement to these

improvements should be reached away from the pressures of any individual project. Once agreed and in place, project managers will all work in the same way to enforce the methods and each individual project will benefit from the improvements.

4.1.5 Process activities, methods and techniques

The following work occurs during the service design stage and should be coordinated by the design coordination process:

- Requirements collection, analysis and engineering to ensure that business requirements are clearly documented and agreed
- Requirements collection, analysis and engineering to ensure that service provider and technical requirements are clearly documented and agreed, and that they support the business requirements correctly
- Design of appropriate service solutions, technology, processes, information and metrics to meet business requirements
- Review and revision of the design of all processes and the maintenance of processes and process documents involved in service design, including designs, plans, architectures and policies
- Production and maintenance of IT policies and design documents, including designs, plans, architectures and policies
- Review and revision of all design documents for completeness and adherence to standards
- Planning for the deployment and implementation of IT strategies using 'roadmaps', programmes and project plans
- Risk assessment and management of all design processes and deliverables
- Ensuring alignment with all corporate and IT strategies and policies
- Production of service designs and/or SDPs for new or changed services.

Design coordination activities themselves fall into two categories:

- **Activities relating to the overall service design lifecycle stage** These activities include the development, deployment and continual improvement of appropriate service design

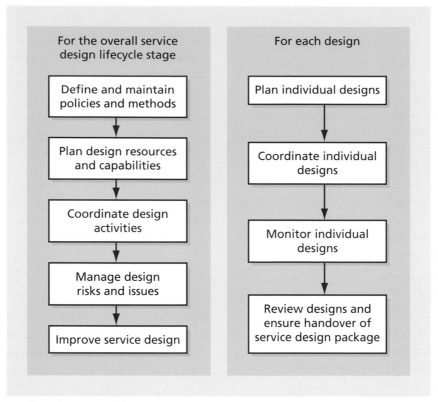

Figure 4.2 Design coordination activities

practices, as well as the coordination of actual design activity across projects and changes. These activities may be performed by design coordination process manager(s).

■ **Activities relating to each individual design**
These activities focus on ensuring that each individual design effort and SDP, whether part of a project or simply associated with a change, conforms with defined practices, and that they produce a design that will support the required business outcomes. These activities may be performed by a project manager or other individual with direct responsibility for the project or change, with the assistance and guidance of the design coordination process manager(s).

The activities within the design coordination process are shown in Figure 4.2.

Overall lifecycle stage activities should include:

■ Define and maintain policies and methods
■ Plan design resources and capabilities
■ Coordinate design activities
■ Manage design risks and issues
■ Improve service design.

Individual design activities should include:

■ Plan individual designs
■ Coordinate individual designs
■ Monitor individual designs
■ Review designs and ensure handover of SDPs.

4.1.5.1 Define and maintain policies and methods (overall activity)

This activity is used to define the overall holistic approach to service design. This is to ensure that consistent and accurate designs are produced to ultimately provide services in the operational environment which deliver and continue to deliver their required business outcomes.

Design coordination should work collaboratively with all processes engaged in any part of the service design stage to ensure that a common framework of standard reusable processes, procedures and systems are used to improve the effectiveness and efficiency of overall service design. This includes agreeing, using and managing the quality criteria, requirements, interfaces and hand-off points between the service design stage and other stages, particularly service strategy and service transition.

Of particular importance will be defining the level of design coordination needed for different types of project and change. Design coordination, project management and change management should collaborate to define policies and consistent practices for the design work associated with projects and changes. This may involve predefining design requirements for different project types or change models and predefining actual designs for standard changes. For the latter, this would mean that the service design stage for standard changes would effectively be completed in advance, streamlining the processing of such changes, while still ensuring proper control.

Design coordination should maintain a set of architectural documents and principles for the design of service solutions and the production of SDPs. As circumstances change, design coordination may need to handle the revision of any architectural documents necessitated by changes in IT strategy or new or changed service solutions. All policies and methods should be regularly reviewed for relevance and performance as part of the 'improve service design' activity.

4.1.5.2 Plan design resources and capabilities (overall activity)

Design coordination is responsible for planning and coordination of the resources and capabilities required for new or changed services and producing the appropriate SDPs. Completely new services or changes to services, service packages and associated service options that come through service strategy may require significant resources for service design. But even changes that do not require explicit attention during service strategy may impact resource planning for overall service design as the same resources required for changes that do come through service strategy may also be required for those that do not. Managing competing demand for shared resources is an important part of this activity.

To successfully plan and coordinate both resources and capabilities, design coordination needs to be well informed regarding activity in the service portfolio (particularly the service pipeline) as well as the change management process. Maintaining regular communication with business relationship

managers and service owners will help to ensure that this process is informed of changes (including those requiring a project) that will require design resources.

It is not enough, however, for this process to consider design resources. The required capabilities must also be identified and maintained. As design coordination works to define consistent, reliable and repeatable methods for service design, required capabilities will be identified. As part of this planning activity, design coordination should identify gaps in current capabilities and work with management and the leaders of the various functional units to plan to fill those gaps. This may be done through such actions as:

- Providing training to existing personnel
- Hiring new staff
- Identifying and implementing technologies to automate design activities, enforce requirements and enforce standards
- Creating new processes and/or procedures to enhance organizational capabilities
- Identifying and implementing improvements to existing processes and/or procedures
- Developing new knowledge and making it readily accessible (via the knowledge management process).

4.1.5.3 Coordinate design activities (overall activity)

Coordinating design activity on a project-by-project basis is not enough. Ensuring that all designs are moving forward in the most effective and efficient manner requires oversight of all design activity, regardless of whether it is being conducted as part of a formal project or being managed through change management without a project. This activity is concerned with coordination of all design activities across projects and changes, managing schedules, resources and conflicts, and suppliers and support teams where required.

Design coordination must be closely integrated with the other service design processes as well as the change management process, where appropriate, to ensure that schedules are clear and design milestones are communicated and met. It must also ensure that all designs cover both functional (utility) and operational (warranty) requirements, including management systems, architectures, measurement and metrics systems, and processes.

The most effective IT service providers integrate all five aspects of design (see section 3.7 for a detailed discussion of these aspects), rather than design them in isolation. This ensures that an integrated enterprise architecture is produced, consisting of a set of standards, designs and architectures that satisfy all of the management and operational requirements of services, as well as the functionality required by the business. This integrated design ensures that when a new or changed service is implemented, it not only provides the functionality required by the business, but also meets and continues to meet all its service levels and targets in all areas. This ensures that no weaknesses (or an absolute minimum) will need to be addressed retrospectively. Consequently, design coordination should provide advice and guidance on design principles and criteria and the service acceptance criteria for differing levels of utility and warranty.

In order to achieve integrated design, the overall coordination of design activities needs to ensure:

- Good communication between the various design activities and all concerned parties, including the business and IT planners, designers, architects and strategists
- The latest versions of all appropriate business and IT plans and strategies are available to all designers
- All architectural documents, service models, service solution designs and SDPs conform to strategic, architectural, governance and other corporate requirements, as well as IT policies and plans
- Good communication and coordination with service transition processes to ensure proper handover to this stage
- The architectures and designs:
  - Are flexible and enable IT to respond quickly to new business needs
  - Integrate with all strategies and policies
  - Support the needs of other stages of the service lifecycle
  - Facilitate new or changed services and solutions, appropriately aligned with the needs and timescales of the business.

4.1.5.4 Manage design risks and issues (overall activity)

Design coordination should use formal risk assessment and management techniques to manage risks associated with design activities and reduce the number of issues that can subsequently be traced to poor design. Attention should be paid to both risks that are common to all design efforts as well as those associated with individual projects and changes.

Policies and procedures should be established for documenting and responding to issues during the design stage and these procedures should be integrated into design processes and the organization's project management methodology, wherever appropriate.

4.1.5.5 Improve service design (overall activity)

The design coordination process can ensure that the goals and objectives of the service design stage are consistently achieved by continually working to improve the effectiveness and efficiency of service design activities and processes. In order to accomplish this, design coordination must monitor and measure the performance of the service design stage of the lifecycle. This will allow the identification of improvement opportunities based on objective data and information instead of relying on anecdotal information or who complains the loudest.

The CSI approach described earlier for use in implementing design coordination should be used for continual process improvement as well. All improvement ideas are logged in the CSI register for consideration. Those improvements selected for action will typically be added to appropriate service improvement plans (SIPs).

4.1.5.6 Plan individual designs (individual activity)

The design activity for each individual project or change needs to be carefully planned. As the maturity of design practices grows, this planning should be easier and easier to execute as it will draw upon standards and templates already built and tested. Simple changes will have planning already completed, while projects and more complex changes will leverage previous work and modify existing materials to meet their specific needs.

Design activities should focus on ensuring that the resulting design can deliver the required business outcomes. It is important for the service provider to remember that the desired business outcomes include not only the utility of the service, but also such things as cost and schedule. This means that the design activities must consider functionality (utility), warranty, requirements to establish the service in effective use in the organization, and requirements to operate, maintain and support the service on an ongoing basis – in other words, the full SDP. Furthermore, if the service charter calls for more than one service option, designs must be able to support all required options. To establish the service in effective use, it must not only be working as designed, but users must also know that it exists and how to use it and the service provider must know how to care for the service. Service designs should include designs for monitoring, maintenance and support. For the service provider to operate and support the service, proper measurements need to be in place to routinely monitor, manage and improve the service.

4.1.5.7 Coordinate individual designs (individual activity)

This work, like that of individual design planning, will most frequently be performed by a project manager or other individual with direct responsibility for the particular project or change. As they execute this activity of the design coordination process, they will draw upon the body of experience developed by the process from other designs. It is during this activity that close attention must be paid to scheduling of both the service provider and customer resources to ensure involvement of the right people at the right time to create an accurate and complete design.

The work of the design stage is likely to be highly iterative as requirements are gathered, documented, agreed, translated into designs, validated with the customer and adjustments made. It is even possible that as the service design stage progresses, information will come to light that requires re-visiting the strategic decisions previously made about the service. In this case, the service portfolio management process and other processes may be re-engaged as appropriate.

As methods mature, the service provider should improve its capabilities around drawing out requirements from the customer that truly reflect their required business outcomes, allowing fewer iterations and therefore more efficient design. Some iteration, however, will almost always be needed in projects or changes of all but the smallest scope. Where service providers adopt the use of rapid or 'agile' design and development methods, they should improve their capabilities in executing each iteration so that the overall service design is achieved effectively and efficiently.

Throughout design activities it is important that all requirements of service, business and project change management be carefully adhered to, as well as ensuring that requirements for documentation of changes to service assets via the service asset and configuration management process also be met.

4.1.5.8 Monitor individual designs (individual activity)

The design coordination process should monitor each ongoing design effort to ensure that there is adherence to agreed methods; that there are no conflicts with other ongoing design efforts; that design milestones are being met; and that the development of a comprehensive design that will support the achievement of the required business outcomes is taking place. It is better to identify early on that a design effort is struggling and to correct the situation than to continue and suffer from the weaknesses that will almost certainly result later in the project or change.

4.1.5.9 Review designs and ensure handover of SDP (individual activity)

The last step in any individual design effort is to perform a final review of the designs for compliance with standards and conventions, and to ensure that all agreed requirements for the SDP have been completed correctly. Any issues should be documented and it should be determined whether they require revisiting any part of service design, or whether they can be addressed as part of the plan for service transition.

Once all required criteria for an SDP have been met, the SDP can be officially handed over for service transition, typically via the activity of the transition planning and support process. This may involve the use of formal checklists and there may be a corresponding authorization from change management required at this stage. The people involved in the service transition work are likely to be many of the same people who were involved in service design, so this step is likely to be performed by a change of status on the record for the service in the service portfolio and the documentation of this milestone having been completed.

4.1.6 Triggers, inputs, outputs and interfaces

4.1.6.1 Triggers

The triggers for the design coordination process are changes in the business requirements and services, and therefore the main triggers are requests for change (RFCs) and the creation of new programmes and projects. Another major trigger for the review of design coordination activities would be the revision of the overall IT strategy.

4.1.6.2 Inputs

A number of sources of information are relevant to the design coordination process. These include:

- Service charters for new or significantly changed services
- Change requests from any stages of the service lifecycle
- Change records and authorized changes
- Business information from the organization's business and IT strategy, plans and financial plans, and information on their current and future requirements
- Business impact analysis, providing information on the impact, priority and risk associated with each service or changes to service requirements
- The service portfolio, including the service catalogue and the business requirements for new or changed services in terms of service packages and service options
- The IT strategy and any associated constraints and resource limitations
- Governance requirements
- Corporate, legal and regulatory policies and requirements
- The programme and project schedule
- The schedule of change
- The configuration management system (CMS)
- Feedback from all other processes

- The enterprise architecture
- Management systems
- Measurement and metrics methods
- Processes.

4.1.6.3 Outputs

The process outputs of design coordination are potentially:

- A comprehensive and consistent set of service designs and SDPs
- A revised enterprise architecture
- Revised management systems
- Revised measurement and metrics methods
- Revised processes
- Service portfolio updates
- Updates to change records.

4.1.6.4 Interfaces

The principal interfaces to the adjacent stages of the lifecycle are:

- Service strategy: using information contained within the IT strategy and service portfolio
- Service transition: with the handover of the design of service solutions within the SDP.

The design coordination process also interfaces with all the processes that include service design activity, especially the processes described in this publication. Key process interfaces include:

- **Service portfolio management** This process provides design coordination with the service charter and all associated documentation such as business requirements, requirements for service utility and warranty (including service options), risks and priorities.
- **Change management** This process produces change requests (formal communications requesting the addition, modification or removal of something in our live environment that we have chosen to control with change management). Design coordination and change management should have collaboratively defined policies and consistent practices for the design work associated with changes. Some changes will be of a scope that they will go through the service strategy stage and service portfolio management process, while others may come to design coordination directly from change management. Design coordination provides status information on design

milestones that relate to changes. Change management provides details of authorized changes from which detailed service design activity can proceed. Change management also provides authorization at defined points in the service lifecycle, to ensure that required actions have taken place and that quality criteria have been met. Finally, the post-implementation reviews (PIRs) from change management can provide valuable feedback on areas for improvement for design coordination.

- **Financial management for IT services** This process provides details of the value proposition for the new or changed service as well as budgets available.

- **Business relationship management** This process provides design coordination with intelligence and information regarding the business's required outcomes, customer needs and priorities and serves as the interface with the customer at a strategic level.

- **Transition planning and support** Design coordination provides the SDP to the service transition stage via this process. Transition planning and support carries out the overall planning and coordination for the service transition stage of the service lifecycle, in the same way that design coordination does for the service design stage. These two processes need to be carefully interfaced to ensure consistent overall plans and resource schedules for current and future projects and changes.

- **Strategy management for IT services** This process provides information about the current and evolving service strategy to enable design coordination to ensure that design guidelines and documentation remain aligned with the strategy over time.

- **Release and deployment management** This process manages the planning and execution of individual authorized changes, releases and deployments. Planning and design for release and deployment is carried out during the service design stage of the service lifecycle. Design coordination should ensure that this is integrated with other service design activities and forms part of the overall SDP.

- **Service validation and testing** This process plans and executes tests to ensure that the service matches its design specification and will meet the needs of the business. Planning and designing tests is carried out during the service design stage of the service lifecycle and design coordination should ensure that this is integrated with other service design activities and forms part of the overall SDP.

- **Change evaluation** This process determines the performance of a service change. This includes evaluation of the service design to ensure it is able to meet the intended requirements. Design coordination should be properly interfaced with change evaluation to ensure that the required resources are available to assist in evaluation of changes.

- **Service level management** Adherence to the standards and practices developed by design coordination for successful service design is critical for this process. Service level management is responsible for defining and agreeing the service level requirements for new or changed services, which must be done in a consistent manner according to practices developed cooperatively with design coordination. Activities of these two processes should be carefully integrated with service level management activity, focusing primarily on the warranty levels that are required in the solution design and design coordination activities. This should ensure that all parts of the service solution design and SDP are appropriately addressed.

- **Availability, capacity, IT service continuity and information security management processes** Each of these processes is actively involved in service design and must perform these design activities consistently, according to practices developed cooperatively with design coordination.

- **Supplier management** In order to ensure that the contributions of suppliers to design activities are properly managed, this process must collaborate with design coordination to develop consistent and reliable practices in this area. Supplier management will then take the lead in building these practices into supplier contracts and agreements as appropriate and then managing the suppliers and their performance during service design, with the assistance of design coordination.

4.1.7 Information management

The key information generated by the design coordination process is included in the SDP, which contains everything necessary to take the service through all other stages of the service lifecycle. The SDP may consist of multiple documents which should be included in the overall service knowledge management system (SKMS), and be described by information in the CMS.

4.1.8 Critical success factors and key performance indicators

The following list includes some sample critical success factors (CSFs) for design coordination. Each organization should identify appropriate CSFs based on its objectives for the process. Each sample CSF is followed by a small number of typical key performance indicators (KPIs) that support the CSF. These KPIs should not be adopted without careful consideration. Each organization should develop KPIs that are appropriate for its level of maturity, its CSFs and its particular circumstances. Achievement against KPIs should be monitored and used to identify opportunities for improvement, which should be logged in the CSI register for evaluation and possible implementation. Thus:

- **CSF** Accurate and consistent SDPs
  - **KPI** Reduction in the number of subsequent revisions of the content of SDPs
  - **KPI** Percentage reduction in the re-work required for new or changed service solutions in subsequent lifecycle stages
- **CSF** Managing conflicting demands for shared resources
  - **KPI** Increased satisfaction with the service design activities, within project and change staff
  - **KPI** Reduced number of issues caused by conflict for service design resources
  - **KPI** Percentage increase in the number of successful new and changed services in terms of outcomes, quality, cost and timeliness
  - **KPI** Improved effectiveness and efficiency in the service design processes, activities and supporting systems
  - **KPI** Reduced number and percentage of emergency change requests submitted by projects
- **CSF** New and changed services meet customer expectations

- **KPI** Customer satisfaction score for each new or changed service meets or exceeds a designated rating
- **KPI** Percentage increase in the number of transitioned services that consistently achieve the agreed service level targets.

4.1.9 Challenges and risks

4.1.9.1 Challenges

The major challenge facing design coordination is that of maintaining high-quality designs and SDPs consistently across all areas of the business, services and infrastructure. This requires multi-talented and multi-skilled designers and architects. It also requires integration of standards and practices developed by design coordination into the organization's project management methodology, wherever appropriate.

A related challenge is ensuring that sufficient time and resources are devoted to design coordination activities and that the roles and responsibilities of the process are assigned to the appropriate individuals and/or groups to ensure completion. In most organizations many of the design coordination activities for an individual design may be assigned to a project manager. Overall lifecycle stage activities may be assigned to the process managers, but key contributions are likely to be made by the service design manager, if one exists. See Chapter 6 for more on roles.

Another significant challenge is developing common design practices that produce the desired high-quality designs without introducing unnecessary bureaucracy. It is important that the level of control around design activities be appropriate to the need. Too little control and designs will be inconsistent and fail to meet true required business outcomes. Too much control and creativity may be stifled and inefficiencies may be introduced. If the processes are too difficult to follow, resistance and non-compliance will result.

4.1.9.2 Risks

The main risks associated with the provision of the design coordination process are:

- Potential lack of skills and knowledge
- Reluctance of the business to be involved
- Poor direction and strategy

- Lack of information on business priorities and impacts
- Poorly defined requirements and desired outcomes
- Reluctance of project managers to communicate and get involved
- Poor communication
- Lack of involvement from all relevant stakeholders including customers, users, and support and other operations staff
- Insufficient interaction with and input from other lifecycle stages
- Trying to save time and money during the design stage which will result in poorer designs requiring more changes after the new or changed service goes live.

4.2 SERVICE CATALOGUE MANAGEMENT

The service catalogue is one of the most valuable elements of a comprehensive approach to service provision and, as such, it should be given proper care and attention. The service catalogue management process provides the means of devoting that care and attention in a consistent fashion, ensuring that the organization accrues all of the potential benefits of a service catalogue in the most efficient manner possible.

4.2.1 Purpose and objectives

The purpose of the service catalogue management process is to provide and maintain a single source of consistent information on all operational services and those being prepared to be run operationally, and to ensure that it is widely available to those who are authorized to access it.

The objectives of the service catalogue management process are to:

- Manage the information contained within the service catalogue
- Ensure that the service catalogue is accurate and reflects the current details, status, interfaces and dependencies of all services that are being run, or being prepared to run, in the live environment, according to the defined policies
- Ensure that the service catalogue is made available to those approved to access it in a manner that supports their effective and efficient use of service catalogue information

- Ensure that the service catalogue supports the evolving needs of all other service management processes for service catalogue information, including all interface and dependency information.

4.2.2 Scope

The scope of the service catalogue management process is to provide and maintain accurate information on all services that are being transitioned or have been transitioned to the live environment. The services presented in the service catalogue may be listed individually or, more typically, some or all of the services may be presented in the form of service packages (see *ITIL Service Strategy* for information about service packages).

The service catalogue management process covers:

- Contribution to the definition of services and service packages
- Development and maintenance of service and service package descriptions appropriate for the service catalogue
- Production and maintenance of an accurate service catalogue
- Interfaces, dependencies and consistency between the service catalogue and the overall service portfolio
- Interfaces and dependencies between all services and supporting services within the service catalogue and the CMS
- Interfaces and dependencies between all services, and supporting components and configuration items (CIs) within the service catalogue and the CMS.

The service catalogue management process does not include:

- Detailed attention to the capturing, maintenance and use of service asset and configuration data as performed through the service asset and configuration management process (see *ITIL Service Transition*)
- Detailed attention to the capturing, maintenance and fulfilment of service requests as performed through request fulfilment (see *ITIL Service Operation*).

4.2.3 Value to the business

The service catalogue provides a central source of information on the IT services delivered by the service provider organization. This ensures that all areas of the business can view an accurate, consistent picture of the IT services, their details and their status. It includes a customer-facing view (or views) of the IT services in use, how they are intended to be used, the business processes they enable, and the levels and quality of service the customer can expect for each service.

Through the work of service catalogue management, organizations can:

- Ensure a common understanding of IT services and improved relationships between the customer and service provider by utilizing the service catalogue as a marketing and communication tool
- Improve service provider focus on customer outcomes by correlating internal service provider activities and service assets to business processes and outcomes
- Improve efficiency and effectiveness of other service management processes by leveraging the information contained in or connected to the service catalogue
- Improve knowledge, alignment and focus on the 'business value' of each service throughout the service provider organization and its activities.

4.2.4 Policies, principles and basic concepts

Over the years, the IT infrastructures of organizations have grown and developed, and there may not be a clear picture of all the services currently being provided and the customers of each service. In order to establish an accurate picture, it is recommended that a service portfolio containing a service catalogue is produced and maintained to provide a central, accurate set of information on all services and to develop a service-focused culture.

> **Definition: service catalogue**
>
> The service catalogue is a database or structured document with information about all live IT services, including those available for deployment. The service catalogue is the only part of the service portfolio published to customers and is used to support the sale and delivery of IT services. The service catalogue includes information about deliverables, prices, contact points, ordering and request processes.

The service catalogue should contain details of all services currently being provided as well as those being prepared for transition to the live environment, a summary of their characteristics, and details of the customers and maintainers of each. A degree of 'detective work' may be needed to compile this list and agree it with the customers (sifting through old documentation, searching program libraries, talking with IT staff and customers, looking at procurement records, talking with suppliers and contractors etc.). If a CMS or any sort of asset database exists, these may provide valuable sources of information, although they should be verified before inclusion within either the overall service portfolio or the service catalogue.

During the service strategy stage as part of the service portfolio management process, a proposed new or significantly changed service will enter the service pipeline and due diligence will be undertaken to decide if the service will indeed move forward. This work should include participation by those involved in service design, transition, operation and improvement to ensure an informed decision. Once a service has been 'chartered' (see section 4.2 in *ITIL Service Strategy*, as well as section 3.7.2 in this publication), and it is being developed for use by customers, service design produces the detailed specifications for the service. It is at this point that a listing for the service should begin to be developed for inclusion in the service catalogue (at the appropriate time as per policy).

4.2.4.1 Policies

Each organization should develop and maintain a policy with regard to both the overall service portfolio and the constituent service catalogue, relating to the services recorded within them and what details are recorded (including what statuses are recorded for each of the services). The policy should also contain details of responsibilities for each section of the overall service portfolio and the scope of each of the constituent sections. This will include policies regarding when a service is published in the service catalogue as well as when it will be removed from the service catalogue and appear only in the retired services section of the service portfolio. For more information regarding the design of the service portfolio and recommendations regarding its constituent sections, see section 3.7.2.

The service catalogue management process produces and maintains the service catalogue, ensuring that a central, accurate and consistent source of data is provided, recording the status of all operational services or services being transitioned to the live environment, together with appropriate details of each service. The services that should be included in the catalogue will be based on the organization's predefined policies.

4.2.4.2 Defining services

What is a service? This question is not as easy to answer as it may first appear, and many organizations have failed to come up with a clear definition in an IT context. IT staff often confuse a 'service' as perceived by the customer with an IT system. In many cases, one 'service' can be made up of other 'services' (and so on), which are themselves made up of one or more IT systems within an overall infrastructure including hardware, software and networks, together with environments, data and applications. When two or more services are combined, this is called a service package.

Each organization needs to develop a policy of what a service is and how it is to be defined and agreed. A good starting point is often to ask customers what IT services they use and how those services map onto and support their business processes. Customers often have a greater clarity of what they believe a service to be.

The details of this policy will be influenced by many factors, including:

- Anticipated uses for the service catalogue, i.e.:
  - Marketing services to customers
  - Communication with customers about services on an ongoing basis

  - Reference by service provider staff regarding services and their dependencies and interfaces
  - Reference for users regarding services offered and their terms
  - Information source on how and where to place requests in relation to the services in the catalogue
- Target audiences of the service catalogue
- Current organizational culture, practices and maturity levels.

Over time an organization's policy regarding defining and naming services may evolve significantly. The key test of success is the degree to which the policy supports more effective and efficient service provisioning. (Note that this discussion refers to the definition of services, not service requests. For information on service requests and the request fulfilment process, see section 4.3 in *ITIL Service Operation*.)

4.2.4.3 Different types of service

To avoid confusion, it may be useful to define a hierarchy of services within the service catalogue, by qualifying exactly what type of service is recorded. The most valuable distinction is between:

- **Customer-facing services** IT services that are seen by the customer. These are typically services that support the customer's business units/business processes, directly facilitating some outcome or outcomes desired by the customer.
- **Supporting services** IT services that support or 'underpin' the customer-facing services. These are typically invisible to the customer, but essential to the delivery of customer-facing IT services.

Supporting services may be of many different types or go by many different names, such as infrastructure services, network services, application services or technical services. Whatever terms are used by a service provider to describe the different types of supporting service they may choose to recognize, the use and scope of each term should be clearly defined and agreed within the organization to avoid confusion. (In this context, the type of service has to do with relevance of a service to a particular group or audience or its role in the service chain. For a discussion of the different types of service relating

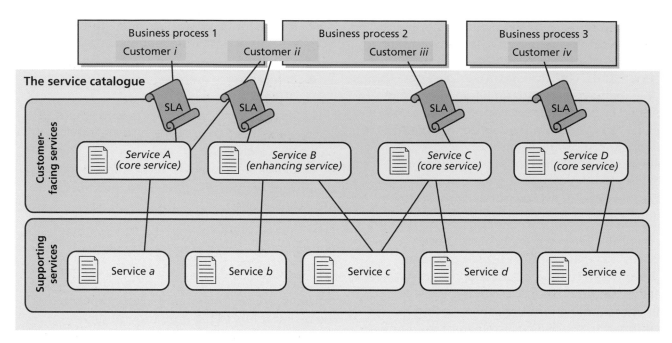

Figure 4.3 Types of service in a service catalogue

to service packaging and value creation, see *ITIL Service Strategy*, section 3.2.2.)

Figure 4.3 shows the two key types of service and an example of how they can be linked to each other and to the business customers and business processes they support. (The customer-facing services shown also reflect concepts from *ITIL Service Strategy* regarding service classifications for service packaging. Two of the three service classifications are highlighted in this particular example: core services and enhancing services.) The figure also shows one simple service package consisting of one core service and one enhancing service, with a single service level agreement (SLA) covering the package. The remaining services are all covered by their own SLAs. (While the SLA documents themselves are not part of the service catalogue, many pieces of information from the SLAs may be included in the service catalogue listings and the actual SLA documents may be accessible via the service catalogue.)

4.2.4.4 Service catalogue uses

The catalogue is useful in developing solutions for customers from one or more services. Items in the catalogue can be configured and suitably priced to fulfil a particular need. The service catalogue is an important tool for service strategy because it is the virtual projection of the service provider's actual and present capabilities. Many customers are only interested in what the provider can commit now, rather than in the future.

The service catalogue can be used by many different groups for many different purposes. Customers can use the service catalogue to understand what the service provider can do for them and to interact with the service provider regarding the services. Staff members of the service provider can use the service catalogue to understand how supporting services and service provider resources and capabilities support business activity. Users or individual consumers of a service can use the service catalogue to understand the scope of services available and to learn how to place service requests and/or report incidents associated with the provided services.

The service catalogue details each service and provides links to the service components that make up each one. By linking to the detailed information in the CMS, the service catalogue also provides an overview of the assets, processes and systems involved in each service. In order to define, document and maintain these links, the service catalogue management process should have appropriate interfaces with the service asset and configuration management process. Through their coordinated efforts these two processes provide a wealth of detailed information that is critical to long-term service management maturity and excellence in service provisioning.

The service catalogue acts as the acquisition portal for customers, including pricing and service-level commitments, and the terms and conditions for service provisioning. The service catalogue frequently also contains links to details about standard service requests, enabling users to request those services using the appropriate channels. In automated service catalogues, access to these service requests may be initiated in the service catalogue tool and then routed to the appropriate request fulfilment procedure.

The service catalogue can be used for other service management purposes (e.g. for performing a business impact analysis [BIA] as part of IT service continuity planning, or as a starting place for re-distributing workloads, as part of capacity management). The cost and effort of producing and maintaining the catalogue, with its relationships to the supporting technology components, is therefore easily justifiable. If done in conjunction with prioritization of the BIA, it is then possible to ensure that the most important services are covered first.

4.2.4.5 Service catalogue structure

The structure and presentation of the service catalogue should support the uses to which it will be put, taking into consideration the different, sometimes conflicting needs of different audiences. Not every service is of interest to every person or group. Not every piece of information about a service is of interest to every person or group. When service providers have many customers or serve many businesses, there may be multiple service catalogue views projected from the service portfolio.

When initially completed, the service catalogue may consist of a matrix, table or spreadsheet. (An example of a simple service catalogue matrix that can be used as a starting point is given in Appendix G.) Many organizations integrate and maintain their service portfolio and service catalogue as part of their CMS. By defining each service as a CI and, where appropriate, relating these to form a service hierarchy, the organization is able to relate such things as incidents and requests for change to the services affected, thus providing the basis for service monitoring and reporting using an integrated tool (e.g. 'list or give the number of incidents affecting this particular service'). It is therefore essential that changes within the service

portfolio and its constituent service catalogue are subject to the change management process.

It is advisable to present more than one view of the information in the service catalogue to accommodate the different needs of those who will use it. In order to ensure that both the customer and IT have a clear understanding of the relationship between the outcome-based, customer-facing services (see section 2.1.1 as well as section 3.4.3 in *ITIL Service Strategy*) and the business processes they support, it is recommended that a service provider, at the minimum, defines two different views, each one focusing on one type of service: a view for customers that shows the customer-facing services, and a second view for the IT service provider showing all the supporting services. The data stored in the service catalogue regarding relationships and dependencies between items would allow information in one view to be accessed from another, when deemed appropriate.

Sample service catalogue presentations

Figure 4.4 shows a service catalogue with two views:

- **The business/customer service catalogue view** This contains details of all the IT services delivered to the customers (customer-facing services), together with relationships to the business units and the business processes that rely on the IT services. This is the customer view of the service catalogue. In other words, this is the service catalogue for the business to see and use.
- **The technical/supporting service catalogue view** This contains details of all the supporting IT services, together with relationships to the customer-facing services they underpin and the components, CIs and other supporting services necessary to support the provision of the service to the customers.

Some organizations maintain a service catalogue that includes only the customer-facing services, while others maintain information only on the supporting services. The preferred situation adopted by the more mature organizations maintains both types of service within a single service catalogue, which is in turn part of a totally integrated service portfolio. (More information on the design and contents of a service catalogue is contained in Appendix G.) Some organizations project more than two views. There is no correct or

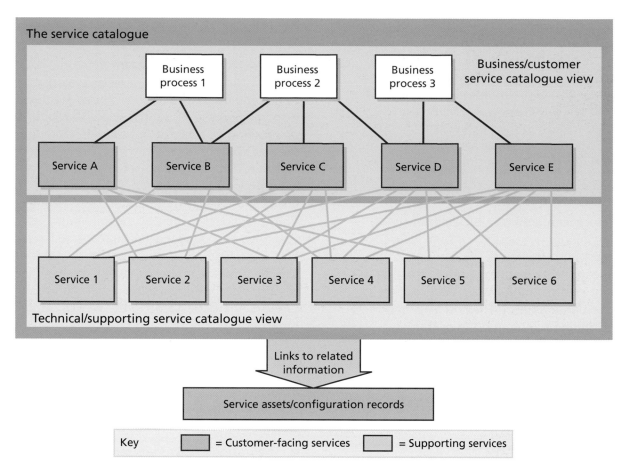

Figure 4.4 A two-view service catalogue

suggested number of views an organization should project. The number of views projected will depend upon the audiences to be addressed and the uses to which the catalogue will be put.

Figure 4.5 shows a service catalogue with three views:

- **Wholesale customer view** This contains details of all the IT services delivered to wholesale customers (customer-facing services), together with relationships to the customers they support.
- **Retail customer view** This contains details of all the IT services delivered to retail customers (customer-facing services), together with relationships to the customers they support.
- **Supporting services view** This contains details of all the supporting IT services, together with relationships to the customer-facing services they underpin and the components, CIs and other supporting services necessary to support the provision of the service to the customers.

Note in this example how customer-facing service C appears in both the wholesale view and the retail view. It is also possible that the different views might reflect hierarchical relationships beyond one level of customer and one level of supporting service. Services are also likely to be packaged and then service packages will be shown in the appropriate service catalogue view(s).

The customer-facing service catalogue view facilitates the development of a much more proactive or even pre-emptive service level management (SLM) process and supports close business alignment with clearly defined relationships between services and SLAs. The supporting service catalogue view is extremely beneficial when constructing the relationship between services, SLAs, operational level agreements (OLAs) and other underpinning agreements and components, as it will identify the technology required to support a service and the support group(s) that support the components. The combination of all views is invaluable for quickly

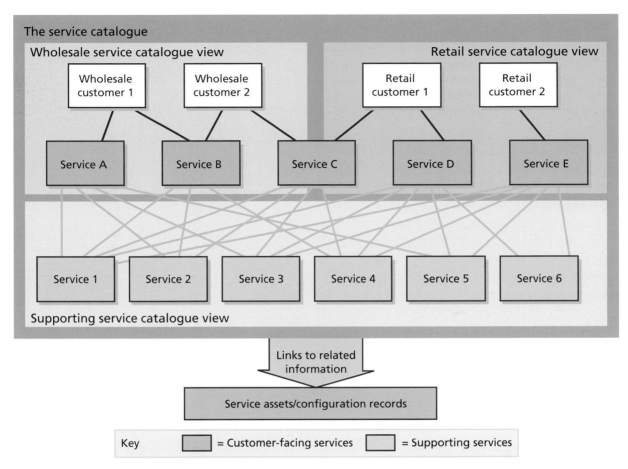

Figure 4.5 A three-view service catalogue

assessing the impact of incidents and changes on the business.

There is no single correct way to structure and deploy a service catalogue. Each service provider organization will consider its goals, objectives and uses for the service catalogue and create a structure that will meet its current and evolving needs appropriately.

4.2.5 Process activities, methods and techniques

The key activities within the service catalogue management process should include:

- Agreeing and documenting a service definition and description for each service with all relevant parties
- Interfacing with service portfolio management to agree the contents of the service portfolio and service catalogue
- Producing and maintaining an accurate service catalogue and its contents, in conjunction with the overall service portfolio

- Interfacing with the business and ITSCM on the dependencies of business units and their business processes with the customer-facing IT services contained within the service catalogue
- Interfacing with support teams, suppliers and service asset and configuration management on interfaces and dependencies between IT services and the supporting services, components and CIs contained within the service catalogue
- Interfacing with business relationship management and SLM to ensure that the information is aligned to the business and business process.

4.2.6 Triggers, inputs, outputs and interfaces

4.2.6.1 Triggers

The triggers for the service catalogue management process are changes in the business requirements and services, and therefore one of the main triggers is RFCs and the change management process. This will include new services, changes to existing services or services being retired.

4.2.6.2 Inputs

A number of sources of information are relevant to the service catalogue management process. These include:

- Business information from the organization's business and IT strategy, plans and financial plans, and information on their current and future requirements from the service portfolio
- BIA, providing information on the impact, priority and risk associated with each service or changes to service requirements
- Business requirements: details of any agreed, new or changed business requirements from the service portfolio
- The service portfolio and all related data and documents
- The CMS
- RFCs
- Feedback from all other processes.

4.2.6.3 Outputs

The process outputs of the service catalogue management process are:

- The documentation and agreement of a 'definition of the service'
- Updates to the service portfolio: should contain the current status of all services and requirements for services
- Updates to RFCs
- The service catalogue: should contain the details and the current status of every live service provided by the service provider or service being transitioned into the live environment, together with the interfaces and dependencies.

4.2.6.4 Interfaces

Every service provider process uses the service catalogue, so it could be said that the service catalogue management process interfaces with all processes, but some of the most prominent interfaces include:

- **Service portfolio management** This process determines which services will be chartered and therefore move forward for eventual inclusion in the service catalogue, as well as defining

critical information regarding each service or potential service, including any agreed service packages and service options.

- **Business relationship management** This process ensures that the relationship between the service and the customer(s) who require it is clearly defined in terms of how the service supports the customer(s) needs.
- **Service asset and configuration management** This process works collaboratively with service catalogue management to ensure that information in the CMS and information in the service catalogue are appropriately linked together to provide a consistent, accurate and comprehensive view of the interfaces and dependencies between services, customers, business processes and service assets, and CIs.
- **SLM** This process negotiates specific levels of service warranty to be delivered which will be reflected in the service catalogue.
- **Demand management** In conjunction with service portfolio management, this process determines how services will be composed into service packages for provisioning and assists service catalogue management in ensuring that these packages are appropriately represented in the service catalogue.

4.2.7 Information management

The key information within the service catalogue management process is that which is contained within the service catalogue. The main input for this information comes from the service portfolio and the business via either the business relationship management or SLM processes. This information needs to be verified for accuracy before being recorded within the service catalogue. The information and the service catalogue itself need to be maintained using the change management process.

There are many different approaches to managing service catalogue information including:

- Intranet solutions built by the service provider organization leveraging technology already in place
- Commercially available solutions designed for service catalogue management
- Solutions that are part of a more comprehensive service management suite.

The service catalogue data may be held in a single repository, or multiple repositories. Some service providers may maintain the data that supports different views of the service catalogue in different locations or toolsets. For example, detailed data for supporting services may be stored in the CMS and presented via the same interface used to access other service asset and configuration data, while data on customer-facing services may be in a browser-based application and presented to customers via the corporate intranet.

When constructing different views of the service catalogue, the service provider should consider which services (rows of data) and which data elements or fields (columns of data) should be included in each view. For example, while details of relationships of supporting services may be important to include in a view intended for staff members of the service provider, these details are typically of no interest to customers and would be excluded from a customer-facing view.

Integration with the service portfolio is critical here, as is the ability to access other closely related functionality, such as customers being able to view their service level agreement monitoring reports or to access a self-help portal for service requests. Some commercially available 'service catalogue' tools are maturing to offer management of the full service portfolio, from proposal through to retirement.

Each organization should consider carefully what solution will best serve its current and future needs. It is important, however, not to confuse the toolset used to present the service catalogue with the catalogue itself. An organization with a paper catalogue and an organization with a robust technical solution both still have a service catalogue.

4.2.8 Critical success factors and key performance indicators

The following list includes some sample CSFs for service catalogue management. Each organization should identify appropriate CSFs based on its objectives for the process. Each sample CSF is followed by a small number of typical KPIs that support the CSF. These KPIs should not be adopted without careful consideration. Each organization should develop KPIs that are appropriate for its level of maturity, its CSFs and its particular circumstances. Achievement against KPIs should be monitored and used to identify opportunities for improvement, which should be logged in the CSI register for evaluation and possible implementation. Thus we have:

- **CSF** An accurate service catalogue
  - **KPI** Increase in the number of services recorded and managed within the service catalogue as a percentage of those being delivered and transitioned in the live environment
  - **KPI** Percentage reduction in the number of variances detected between the information contained within the service catalogue and the 'real-world' situation
- **CSF** Business users' awareness of the services being provided
  - **KPI** Percentage increase in completeness of the customer-facing views of the service catalogue against operational services
  - **KPI** Percentage increase in business user survey responses showing knowledge of services listed in service catalogue
  - **KPI** Increase in measured business user access to intranet-based service catalogue
- **CSF** IT staff awareness of the technology supporting the services
  - **KPI** Percentage increase in completeness of supporting services against the IT components that make up those services
  - **KPI** Increase in service desk and other IT staff having access to information to support all live services, measured by the percentage of incidents with the appropriate service-related information.

4.2.9 Challenges and risks

4.2.9.1 Challenges

The major challenge facing service catalogue management is that of maintaining an accurate service catalogue as part of a service portfolio, incorporating all catalogue views as part of an overall CMS and SKMS. One approach may be to develop stand-alone spreadsheets or databases before trying to integrate the service catalogue and service portfolio within the CMS or SKMS. In order to achieve this, the culture of the organization needs to accept that the catalogue and portfolio are essential sources of information that everyone within the IT organization needs to use and help maintain. This will often assist in the standardization of the service catalogue and the service portfolio and enable an improvement in cost performance through economies of scale.

4.2.9.2 Risks

The risks associated with the provision of an accurate service catalogue are:

- Inaccuracy of the data in the catalogue and it not being under rigorous change control
- Poor acceptance of the service catalogue and its usage in all operational processes. The more active the catalogue is, the more likely it is to be accurate in its content
- Inaccuracy of information received from the business, IT and the service portfolio, with regard to service information
- Insufficient tools and resources required to maintain the information
- Poor access to accurate change management information and processes
- Poor access to and support of appropriate and up-to-date CMS and SKMS for integration with the service catalogue
- Circumvention of the use of the service portfolio and service catalogue
- The information is either too detailed to maintain accurately or at too high a level to be of any value. It should be consistent with the level of detail within the CMS and the SKMS.

4.3 SERVICE LEVEL MANAGEMENT

SLM is a vital process for every IT service provider organization in that it is responsible for agreeing and documenting service level targets and responsibilities within SLAs and service level requirements (SLRs) for every service and related activity within IT. If these targets are appropriate and accurately reflect the requirements of the business, then the service delivered by the service providers will align with business requirements and meet the expectations of the customers and users in terms of service quality. If the targets are not aligned with business needs, then service provider activities and service levels will not be aligned with business expectations and problems will develop. The SLA is effectively a level of assurance or warranty with regard to the level of service quality delivered by the service provider for each of the services delivered to the business. The success of SLM is very dependent on the quality of the service portfolio and the service catalogue and their contents because they provide the necessary information on the services to be managed within the SLM process.

4.3.1 Purpose and objectives

The purpose of the SLM process is to ensure that all current and planned IT services are delivered to agreed achievable targets. This is accomplished through a constant cycle of negotiating, agreeing, monitoring, reporting on and reviewing IT service targets and achievements, and through instigation of actions to correct or improve the level of service delivered.

The objectives of SLM are to:

- Define, document, agree, monitor, measure, report and review the level of IT services provided and instigate corrective measures whenever appropriate
- Provide and improve the relationship and communication with the business and customers in conjunction with business relationship management
- Ensure that specific and measurable targets are developed for all IT services
- Monitor and improve customer satisfaction with the quality of service delivered
- Ensure that IT and the customers have a clear and unambiguous expectation of the level of service to be delivered
- Ensure that even when all agreed targets are met, the levels of service delivered are subject to proactive, cost-effective continual improvement.

4.3.2 Scope

SLM should provide a point of regular contact and communication to the customers and business managers of an organization in relation to service levels. In this context, it should represent the IT service provider to the business, and the business to the IT service provider. This activity should encompass both the use of existing services and the potential future requirements for new or changed services. SLM needs to manage the expectation and perception of the business, customers and users and ensure that the quality (warranty) of service delivered by the service provider is matched to those expectations and needs. In order to do this effectively, SLM should establish and maintain SLAs for all current live services and manage the level of service provided to meet the targets and quality measurements contained within the SLAs. SLM should also produce and agree SLRs for all planned new or changed services that document warranty requirements.

This will enable SLM to ensure that all the services and components are designed and delivered to meet their targets in terms of business needs. The SLM process should include:

■ Cooperation with the business relationship management process: this includes development of relationships with the business as needed to achieve the SLM process objectives

■ Negotiation and agreement of future service level requirements and targets, and the documentation and management of SLRs for all proposed new or changed services

■ Negotiation and agreement of current service level requirements and targets, and the documentation and management of SLAs for all operational services

■ Development and management of appropriate OLAs to ensure that targets are aligned with SLA targets

■ Review of all supplier agreements and underpinning contracts with supplier management to ensure that targets are aligned with SLA targets

■ Proactive prevention of service failures, reduction of service risks and improvement in the quality of service, in conjunction with all other processes

■ Reporting and management of all service level achievements and review of all SLA breaches

■ Periodic review, renewal and/or revision of SLAs, service scope and OLAs as appropriate

■ Identifying improvement opportunities for inclusion in the CSI register

■ Reviewing and prioritizing improvements in the CSI register

■ Instigating and coordinating SIPs for the management, planning and implementation of service and process improvements.

The SLM process does not include:

■ Negotiation and agreement of requirements for service functionality (utility), except to the degree functionality influences a service level requirement or target. SLAs typically describe key elements of the service's utility as part of the service description, but SLM activity does not include agreeing what the utility will be.

■ Detailed attention to the activities necessary to deliver service levels that are accounted for in other processes such as availability management and capacity management.

■ Negotiation of underpinning supplier contracts and agreements. This is part of the supplier management process to which SLM provides critical input and consultation.

4.3.2.1 Business relationship management and service level management

While the SLM process exists to ensure that agreed achievable levels of service are provided to the customer and users, the business relationship management process is focused on a more strategic perspective. Business relationship management takes as its mission the identification of customer needs and ensuring that the service provider is able to meet the customers' needs. This process focuses on the overall relationship between the service provider and their customer, working to determine which services the service provider will deliver. See section 4.5 of *ITIL Service Strategy* for a detailed discussion of business relationship management and the relationship between it and the SLM process.

4.3.3 Value to the business

SLM provides a consistent interface to the business for all service-level-related issues. It provides the business with the agreed service targets and the required management information to ensure that those targets have been met. Where targets are breached, SLM provides feedback on the cause of the breach and details of the actions taken to prevent the breach from recurring. Thus SLM provides a reliable communication channel and a trusted relationship with the appropriate customers and business representatives at a tactical level.

4.3.4 Policies, principles and basic concepts

SLM is the name given to the process of ensuring that the required and cost-justifiable service quality is maintained and gradually improved by planning, coordinating, drafting, agreeing, monitoring and reporting of SLAs, and the ongoing review of service achievements. SLM is not only concerned with ensuring that current services and SLAs are managed, but it is also involved in ensuring that new service level requirements are captured and that new or changed services and SLAs are developed to match the business needs and expectations. SLAs provide the basis for managing the relationship between the service provider and the customer, and SLM provides that central point of focus for a group of customers, business units or lines of business.

An SLA is a written agreement between an IT service provider and the IT customer(s), defining the key service targets and responsibilities of both parties. The emphasis must be on agreement, and SLAs should not be used as a way of holding one side or the other to ransom. A true partnership should be developed between the IT service provider and the customer, so that a mutually beneficial agreement is reached – otherwise the SLA could quickly fall into disrepute and a 'blame culture' could develop that would prevent any true service quality improvements from taking place. An SLA will typically define the warranty a service is to deliver and describe the utility of the service.

An OLA is an agreement between an IT service provider and another part of the same organization that assists with the provision of services – for instance, a facilities department that maintains the air conditioning, or network support team that supports the network service. An OLA should contain targets that underpin those within an SLA to ensure that targets will not be breached by failure of the supporting activity.

SLM is responsible for ensuring that all targets and measures agreed with the business in SLAs are supported by appropriate OLAs with internal support units and underpinning contracts with external partners and suppliers. In the case of the latter, this is the contribution that SLM makes to supplier management, which has primary responsibility for the relationship between the IT service provider and its suppliers. This SLM hierarchy is illustrated in Figure 3.7 in Chapter 3.

Figure 3.7 shows the relationship between the business and its processes and the services, and the associated technology, supporting services, teams and suppliers required to meet their needs. It demonstrates how important the SLAs, OLAs and underpinning contracts are in defining and achieving the level of service required by the business.

4.3.4.1 Policies

The service provider should establish clear policies for the conduct of the SLM process. Policies typically will define such things as the minimum required content of SLAs and OLAs, when and how agreements are to be reviewed, renewed, revised and/or renegotiated, and how frequently and using what methods service level reporting will be provided.

Of particular importance will be agreeing policies between SLM and supplier management, as the performance of suppliers can be the critical element in the achievement of end-to-end service level commitments.

4.3.4.2 Contracts and agreements

The terminology used in this publication is expressed from the point of view of the IT service provider, particularly as it relates to underpinning contracts and agreements. When an IT service provider engages a third-party supplier to provide goods and/or services that are needed for the provision of service to the IT customer(s), it is important that both parties have clear and unambiguous expectations of how the supplier will meet the IT service provider's requirements. This is accomplished by documenting the terms of engagement in an agreement of some sort and this agreement supports or 'underpins' the service level targets in the SLA with the customer. If the agreement is legally binding, it is referred to as a 'contract', or more precisely an 'underpinning contract'. When the document in question simply describes the formal understanding between the two parties, but is not legally binding, the more generic term 'agreement' may be used.

It should be noted that, while not referred to here as an SLA, the contract or agreement with a supplier will typically include specified service levels to be delivered by the supplier in relation to the services contracted and may be considered by the supplier to be or include an SLA.

It should also be noted that the SLA itself between the IT service provider and the customer(s) will vary in nature, depending on the type of service provider. For example, if the IT service provider is Type I or Type II, the SLA is likely to be an internal document and not legally binding; however, if the IT service provider is Type III, then the SLA is more likely to be included as a schedule or specification in a legally binding contract with the customer (see glossary for definitions of Types I, II and III service providers).

In addition to the formal relationship between IT service provider and supplier, it is also important that internal contributors to IT service provision have clear expectations of their responsibilities and commitments. These responsibilities may be documented in OLAs which are defined as agreements between an IT service provider and another part of the same organization. They support the IT service provider's delivery of IT services to customers and define the goods or services to be provided and the responsibilities of both parties.

For purposes of simplicity, the term 'underpinning contract' is used here to refer to any kind of agreement or contract between an IT service provider and a supplier that supports the delivery of service to the customer. The term SLA is used to refer to an agreement between the IT service provider and the customer(s) only. 'Underpinning agreements' is a more generic term used to refer to all OLAs, and contracts or other agreements that underpin the customer SLAs.

4.3.5 Process activities, methods and techniques

The key activities within the SLM process should include:

- Determining, negotiating, documenting and agreeing requirements for new or changed services in SLRs, and managing and reviewing them through the service lifecycle into SLAs for operational services
- Monitoring and measuring service performance achievements of all operational services against targets within SLAs
- Producing service reports
- Conducting service reviews, identifying improvement opportunities for inclusion in the CSI register, and managing appropriate SIPs
- Collating, measuring and improving customer satisfaction, in cooperation with business relationship management
- Reviewing and revising SLAs, service scope, and OLAs

- Assisting supplier management to review and revise underpinning contracts or agreements
- Developing and documenting contacts and relationships with the business, customers and other stakeholders, in cooperation with the business relationship management process
- Logging and managing complaints and compliments, in cooperation with business relationship management
- Providing appropriate management information to aid performance management and demonstrating service achievement.

These other activities within the SLM process support the successful execution of the key activities:

- Designing SLA frameworks
- Developing, maintaining and operating SLM procedures, including procedures for logging, actioning and resolving all complaints, and for logging and distributing compliments
- Making available and maintaining up-to-date SLM document templates and standards
- Assisting with the design and maintenance of the service catalogue.

Figure 4.6 illustrates many of the interfaces between the main activities and interfaces with two other service management processes. (Note: the arrows in this diagram are not intended to define all interfaces exactly, but rather to illustrate how highly dependent on and interactive with each other all the activities of SLM are.)

Although Figure 4.6 illustrates all the main activities of SLM as separate activities, they should be implemented as one integrated SLM process that can be consistently applied to all areas of the business and to all customers. The main activities, as well as several of the other SLM activities, are described in the following sections.

The activity of 'designing SLA frameworks' is presented first, as an organization needs to determine the frameworks before it can begin negotiating agreements.

4.3.5.1 Designing SLA frameworks

Using the service catalogue as an aid, SLM must design the most appropriate SLA structure to ensure that all services and all customers are covered in a manner best suited to the

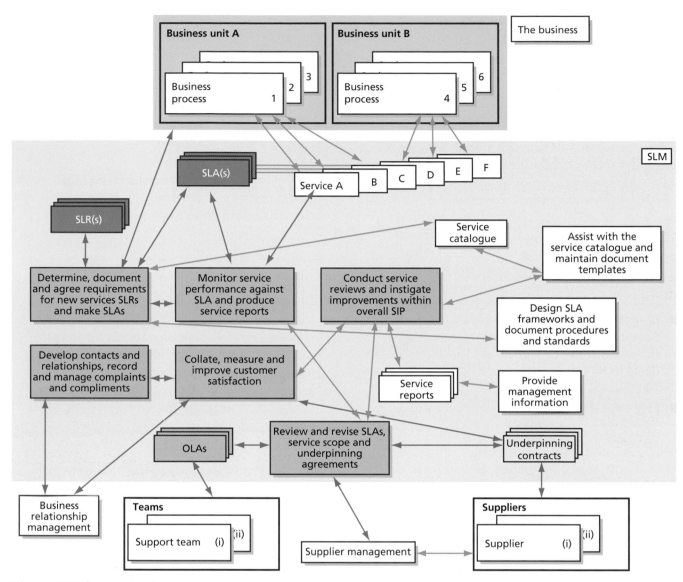

Figure 4.6 The service level management process

organization's needs. There are a number of potential options, including the following.

Service-based SLA

This is where an SLA covers one service, for all the customers of that service – for example, an SLA may be established for an organization's email service, covering all the customers of that service. This may appear fairly straightforward. However, difficulties may arise if the specific requirements of different customers vary for the same service, or if characteristics of the infrastructure mean that different service levels are inevitable (e.g. head office staff may be connected via a high-speed LAN, while local offices may have to use a lower-speed WAN line). In such cases, separate targets may be needed within the one agreement.

Difficulties may also arise in determining who should be the signatories to such an agreement. However, where common levels of service are provided across all areas of the business (for example, email or telephony), the service-based SLA can be an efficient approach to use. Multiple classes of service (for example, gold, silver and bronze) can also be used to increase the effectiveness of service-based SLAs.

Customer-based SLA

This is an agreement with an individual customer group, covering all the services they use. For example, agreements may be reached with an organization's finance department covering, say, the finance system, the accounting system, the payroll system, the billing system, the procurement system, and any other IT systems that they use. Customers often prefer such an agreement, as all of their requirements are covered in a single document. Only one signatory is normally required, which simplifies this issue.

Multi-level SLAs

Some organizations have chosen to adopt a multi-level SLA structure. For example, a three-layer structure might look as follows:

- **Corporate level** This will cover all the generic SLM issues appropriate to every customer throughout the organization. These issues are likely to be less volatile, so updates are less frequently required.
- **Customer level** This will cover all SLM issues relevant to the particular customer group or business unit, regardless of the service being used.
- **Service level** This will cover all SLM issues relevant to the specific service, in relation to a specific customer group (one for each service covered by the SLA).

As shown in Figure 4.7, such a structure allows SLAs to be kept to a manageable size, avoids unnecessary duplication, and reduces the need for frequent updates. However, it does mean that extra effort is required to maintain the necessary relationships and links within the service catalogue and the CMS.

Many organizations have found it valuable to produce standards and a set of pro-formas or templates that can be used as a starting point for all SLAs, SLRs and OLAs. The pro-forma can often be developed alongside the draft SLA. Developing standards and templates will ensure that all agreements are developed in a consistent manner, and this will ease their subsequent use, operation and management. Guidance on the items to be included in an SLA is given in Appendix F.

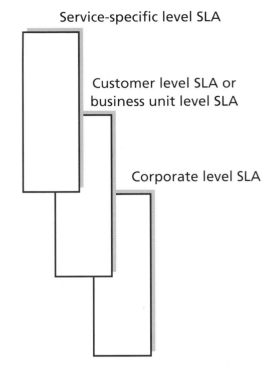

Figure 4.7 Multi-level SLAs

The wording of SLAs should be clear and concise and leave no room for ambiguity. There is usually no need for agreements to be written in legal terminology, and plain language aids a common understanding. It is often helpful to have an independent person, who has not been involved with the drafting, to do a final read-through. This often identifies potential ambiguities and difficulties that can then be addressed and clarified. For this reason alone, it is recommended that all SLAs contain a glossary, defining any terms and providing clarity for any areas of ambiguity.

It is also worth remembering that SLAs may have to cover services offered internationally. In such cases the SLA may have to be translated into several languages. Remember also that an SLA drafted in a single language may have to be reviewed for suitability in several different parts of the world (i.e. a version drafted in Australia may have to be reviewed for suitability in the USA or the UK), so differences in terminology, style and culture must be taken into account.

Where the IT services are provided to another organization by an external service provider, sometimes the service targets are contained within a contract and at other times they are contained within an SLA or schedule attached to the contract. Whatever document is used, it is essential that the targets documented and agreed are clear, specific and unambiguous, as they will provide the basis of the relationship and the quality of service delivered.

4.3.5.2 Determining, documenting and agreeing requirements for new services and producing SLRs

This is one of the earliest activities within the service design stage of the service lifecycle. Once the service catalogue has been produced and the SLA structure has been agreed, the first SLRs must be drafted. An SLR is a customer requirement for an aspect of an IT service. SLRs are based on business objectives and are used to negotiate agreed service level targets. SLRs relate primarily to the warranty of the service: What levels of service are required by the customer in order for them to be able to receive the value of the utility of the service? How available does the service need to be? How secure? How quickly must it be restored if it should fail?

While many organizations have to give initial priority to introducing SLAs for existing services, it is also important to establish procedures for agreeing service level requirements for new services being developed or procured. The SLRs should be an integral part of the overall service design criteria which also include the functional or 'utility' specifications. SLRs should, from the very start, form part of the testing/trialling criteria as the service progresses through the stages of design and development or procurement.

It is advisable to involve customers from the outset, but rather than approaching customers with a 'blank page', it may be better to produce an outline SLR draft with potential performance targets and management and operational requirements, as a starting point for more detailed and in-depth discussion. Be careful, though, not to go too far and appear to be presenting the customer with a 'fait accompli' as this may unnecessarily limit open and productive dialogue. In order to ensure a focus on required business outcomes, it is important to maintain clarity in the

difference between the SLR and the specific service level target(s) associated with the achievement of the SLR. For example, an SLR relating to performance might be expressed by the customer as 'fast enough to support the anticipated volume of orders to be placed during peak activity periods without failures or delays', while the service level target negotiated to support this requirement will define specific, measurable response times and the conditions under which the target will be deemed to have been breached.

> **Key message**
> Determining the high-level, business objective-oriented SLRs will typically begin during the service strategy stage as part of defining the information needed to make the strategic decision to charter and fund the service. The service portfolio management and business relationship management processes are very involved in this high-level warranty determination. Once the service charter has been issued, the SLM process continues the work of determining any additional SLRs and refining all SLRs to the detailed, measurable level needed for design of the service solution.

It cannot be over-stressed how difficult this activity of determining the initial targets for association with an SLR (or eventual inclusion in an SLA) is. Representatives of all of the other processes need to be consulted for their opinion on what targets can be realistically achieved, such as consulting incident management on incident targets. The capacity and availability management processes will be of particular value in determining appropriate service availability and performance targets. If there is any doubt, provisional targets should be included within a pilot SLA that is monitored and adjusted through an early life support period, as illustrated in Figure 3.8.

In developing SLRs, it can be difficult to draw out true business requirements, as the business may not know what it wants – especially if not asked previously. The business may need help in understanding and defining its needs, particularly in terms of capacity, security, availability and IT service continuity. Be aware that the requirements initially expressed may not be those ultimately agreed. The customer may describe what is wanted/needed, after which the service provider must investigate what is possible, along with the associated costs and risks of available options, presenting this information to the customer to revisit the originally stated requirement. Several iterations of negotiations may be required before an affordable balance is struck between what is sought and what is achievable and affordable. This process may involve a redesign of the service solution each time an SLR and associated service level targets are revised.

If new services are to be introduced in a seamless way into the live environment, another area that requires attention is the planning and formalization of the support arrangements for the service and its components. Advice should be sought from change management and service asset and configuration management to ensure the planning is comprehensive and covers the implementation, deployment and support of the service and its components. Specific responsibilities need to be defined and added to existing underpinning contracts/OLAs, or new ones need to be agreed. The support arrangements and all escalation routes also need adding to the CMS, including the service catalogue where appropriate, so that the service desk and other support staff are aware of them. Where appropriate, initial training and familiarization for the service desk and other support groups and knowledge transfer should be completed before live support is needed.

The definition and agreement of OLAs are likely to be highly iterative, particularly in an organization with immature SLM. Many different groups or functions may need to commit to OLAs. Proposed requirements must be compared with what can actually be delivered by each group so that commitments are realistic. The individual requirements for each group, along with the contributions from suppliers as documented in underpinning contracts, must result in an integrated, well-coordinated service delivery that appropriately supports the overall SLR targets.

Once clearly defined SLRs have been determined, associated initial service level targets will gradually be refined as the service progresses through the stages of its lifecycle, until they eventually become part of a pilot SLA during the early life support period. See section 4.3.5.3 for a discussion of pilot SLAs.

4.3.5.3 Negotiating, documenting and agreeing SLAs for operational services

Before a new or changed service is accepted into live operation, an SLA should be agreed, detailing the service level targets to be achieved and specifying the responsibilities of both the IT service provider and the customer. For a new service, the targets in the SLA are likely to originate from SLRs developed early in the service design stage. For changes to existing services, targets may also be defined in this way – as part of SLR development, particularly if the change to the service is significant, or the new targets may simply be refinements to targets in an existing SLA.

If an organization is just beginning to establish SLM and does not yet have SLAs in place for existing services, the process of defining them may require monitoring, measuring and reporting on the current levels of service being delivered and using this information to inform negotiations with customers to establish acceptable targets.

> **Key message: Only use measurable targets**
>
> There may be a temptation to agree to targets that cannot be adequately measured, but only measurable targets should be included in the SLA.

Using the SLRs or other information from the customer about the required service levels, a pilot or draft SLA should be developed. The SLA should be developed alongside the development of the service itself and gradually refined, formalized and signed before the service is introduced into live use. The development and finalization of the SLA is an iterative process necessitating the alignment of many contributions and dependencies. As SLA targets are drafted, SLM must work with all those involved in service provision, ensuring that the targets are achievable and that both internal support teams and external suppliers have clear and unambiguous expectations of what will be required of them to support the achievement of the SLA targets. OLAs and underpinning contracts or other agreements should be updated or created to ensure clarity and to identify how supporting efforts will be measured and managed.

After the new or changed service has been deployed, the pilot SLA with supporting OLAs and underpinning contracts should be ready and reporting mechanisms in place. During the early life support period, achievements against the targets should be measured, confirming either that the targets can be met, or that adjustment is required. Preference, of course, is given to revising the service provision to meet the targets rather than revising the targets themselves, but regardless of which adjustment is undertaken, it must be mutually agreed by the customer and service provider prior to signing of the final SLA.

At the end of the drafting, negotiating and piloting process, it is important to ensure that the SLA is actually signed by the appropriate managers on the customer and IT service provider sides. This gives a firm commitment by both parties that every attempt will be made to meet the agreement. Generally speaking, the more senior the signatories are within their respective organizations, the stronger the message of commitment. Once an SLA is agreed, wide publicity needs to be used to ensure that customers, users and IT staff alike are aware of its existence and of the key targets.

Steps must be taken to advertise the existence of the new SLAs and OLAs among the service desk and other support groups, with details of when they become operational. It may be helpful to extract key targets from these agreements into tables that can be on display in support areas, so that staff are always aware of the targets to which they are working. If support tools allow, these targets should be recorded within the tools, such as within a service catalogue or CMS, so that their content can be made widely available to all personnel. They should also be included as thresholds and automatically alerted against when a target is threatened or actually breached. SLAs, OLAs and the targets they contain must also be publicized amongst the user community, so that users are aware of what they can expect from the services they use, and know at what point to start expressing dissatisfaction.

It is important that the service desk staff are committed to the SLM process and become proactive ambassadors for SLAs, embracing the necessary service culture, as they are the first contact point for customers' incidents, complaints and queries. If the service desk staff are not fully aware of the SLAs in place, and do not act on their contents, customers very quickly lose faith in SLAs.

It should be noted that additional support resources (i.e. more staff) may be needed to support new or significantly changed services. There is often an expectation that an already overworked support group can magically cope with the additional effort imposed by a new service. If this expectation is unrealistic, service level targets relating to support may be endangered or even breached.

4.3.5.4 Monitoring service performance against SLA

Nothing should be included in an SLA unless it can be effectively monitored and measured at a commonly agreed point. The importance of this cannot be overstressed, as inclusion of items that cannot be effectively monitored almost always results in disputes and eventual loss of faith in the SLM process. Many organizations have discovered this the hard way and as a result have absorbed heavy costs, both in a financial sense as well as in terms of negative impacts on their credibility.

> **Anecdote: Mismatched measurements**
>
> A global network provider agreed availability targets for the provision of a managed network service. These availability targets were agreed at the point where the service entered the customer's premises. However, the global network provider could only monitor and measure availability at the point the connection left its premises. The network links were provided by a number of different national telecommunications service providers, with widely varying availability levels. The result was a complete mismatch between the availability figures produced by the network provider and the customer experience, with correspondingly prolonged and heated debate and argument.

Existing monitoring capabilities should be reviewed and upgraded as necessary. Ideally this should be done ahead of, or in parallel with, the drafting of SLAs, so that monitoring can be in place to assist with the validation of proposed targets during the service transition stage.

It is essential that monitoring matches the customer's true perception of the service. Unfortunately this is often very difficult to achieve. For example, monitoring of individual components, such as the network or server, does not guarantee that the service will be available so far as the customer is concerned. Customer perception is often that, although a failure may affect more than one service, their only concern is the service they cannot access at the time of the reported incident. Because customers and their perspectives vary, caution is needed. Without monitoring all components in the end-to-end service (which may be very difficult and costly to achieve) a true picture cannot be gained. Similarly, users must be aware that they should report incidents immediately to aid diagnostics, especially if they are performance-related, so that the service provider is aware that service targets are being breached.

A considerable number of organizations use their service desk, linked to a comprehensive CMS, to monitor the customer's perception of availability. This may involve making specific changes to incident/problem logging screens and may require stringent compliance with incident logging procedures. All of this needs discussion and agreement with the availability management process.

The service desk is also used to monitor incident response times and resolution times, but once again the logging screens may need amendment to accommodate data capture, and call-logging procedures may need tightening and must be strictly followed. If support is being provided by a third party, this monitoring may also underpin supplier management.

It is essential to ensure that any incident/problem-handling targets included in SLAs are the same as those included in service desk tools and those used for escalation and monitoring purposes. Where an organization has failed to recognize this, and perhaps used defaults provided by the tool supplier, it has ended up in a situation where it is monitoring something different from that which has been agreed in the SLAs, and is therefore unable to say whether SLA targets have been met, without considerable effort to manipulate the data. Some amendments may be needed to support tools, to include the necessary fields so that relevant data can be captured.

A notoriously difficult area to monitor is transaction response times (the time between sending a screen and receiving a response). Often end-to-end response times are technically very difficult to monitor. In such cases it may be appropriate to deal with this as follows:

- Include a statement in the SLA along the following lines: 'The services covered by the SLA are designed for high-speed response and no significant delays should be encountered. If a response time delay of more than x seconds is experienced for more than y minutes, this should be reported immediately to the service desk.'
- Agree and include in the SLA an acceptable target for the number of such incidents that can be tolerated in the reporting period.
- Create an incident category of 'poor response' (or similar) and ensure that any such incidents are logged accurately and that they are related to the appropriate service.
- Produce regular reports of occasions where SLA transaction response time targets have been breached, and instigate investigations via problem management to correct the situation.

This approach not only overcomes the technical difficulties of monitoring, but also ensures that incidents of poor response are reported at the time they occur. This is very important, as poor response is often caused by a number of transient interacting events that can only be detected if they are investigated immediately.

The preferred method, however, is to implement some form of automated client/server response time monitoring in close consultation with the service operation. Wherever possible, implement sampling or 'robot' tools and techniques to give indications of slow or poor performance. These tools provide the ability to measure or sample actual or very similar response times to those being experienced by a variety of users, and are becoming increasingly available and increasingly more cost-effective to use.

Hints and tips

In reality, some organizations have found that 'poor response' is sometimes a problem of user perception. The user, having become used to a particular level of response over a period of time, starts complaining as soon as this is slower. Take the view that 'if the user thinks the service is slow, then it is'.

If the SLA includes targets for assessing and implementing RFCs, the monitoring of targets relating to change management should ideally be carried out using whatever change management tool is in use (preferably part of an integrated service management support tool) and change logging screens and escalation processes should support this.

4.3.5.5 Producing service reports

Immediately after the SLA is agreed and accepted, monitoring must be instigated, and service achievement reports must be produced. Operational reports must be produced frequently (weekly or perhaps even more frequently) and, where possible, exception reports should be produced whenever an SLA has been broken (or threatened, if appropriate thresholds have been set to give an 'early warning'). Sometimes difficulties are encountered in meeting the targets of new services during the early life support period because of the high volume of RFCs. Limiting the number of RFCs processed during the early life support period can limit the impact of changes.

The SLA reporting mechanisms, intervals and report formats must be defined and agreed with the customers. The frequency and format of service review meetings must also be agreed with the customers. Regular intervals are recommended, with periodic reports synchronized with the reviewing cycle.

Periodic reports must be produced and circulated to customers (or their representatives) and appropriate IT managers a few days in advance of service level reviews, so that any queries or disagreements can be resolved ahead of the review meeting. The meeting is then not diverted by such issues.

The periodic reports should incorporate details of performance against all SLA targets, together with details of any trends or specific actions being undertaken to improve service quality. A useful technique is to include an SLA monitoring (SLAM) chart at the front of a service report to give an 'at-a-glance' overview of how achievements have measured up against targets. These are most effective if colour coded (red, amber, green, and sometimes referred to as RAG charts as a result). Other interim reports may be required by IT management for OLA or internal performance

reviews and/or supplier management. This is likely to be an evolving process – a first effort is unlikely to be the final outcome.

The resources required to produce and verify reports should not be underestimated. It can be extremely time-consuming, and if reports do not reflect the customer's own perception of service quality accurately, they can make the situation worse. It is essential that accurate information from all areas and all processes (e.g. incident management, problem management, availability management, capacity management, change management, and service asset and configuration management) is analysed and collated into a concise and comprehensive report on service performance, as measured against agreed business targets.

SLM should identify the specific reporting needs and automate production of these reports, as far as possible. The extent, accuracy and ease with which automated reports can be produced should form part of the selection criteria for integrated support tools. These service reports should not only include details of current performance against targets, but should also provide historic information on past performance and trends, so that the impact of improvement actions can be measured and predicted.

4.3.5.6 Conducting service reviews and instigating improvements within an overall service improvement plan

Review meetings must be held on a regular basis with customers (or their representatives) to review the service achievement in the last period and to preview any issues for the coming period. It is normal to hold such meetings monthly or, as a minimum, quarterly.

Actions should be assigned to the customer and provider as appropriate to improve weak areas where targets are not being met. All actions must be minuted, and progress should be reviewed at the next meeting to ensure that action items are being followed up and properly implemented.

Particular attention should be focused on each breach of service level to determine exactly what caused the loss of service and what can be done to prevent any recurrence. If it is decided that the service level was, or has become, unachievable, it may be necessary to review, renegotiate, review and agree different service targets. If the service break has been caused by a failure of a third party or internal support group, it may also be necessary to review the underpinning contract or OLA. Analysis of the cost and impact of service breaches provides valuable input and justification of SIP activities and actions. The constant need for improvement needs to be balanced and focused on those areas most likely to give the greatest business benefit. SIP activity is essentially part of the CSI stage of the lifecycle (see *ITIL Continual Service Improvement* for information on specific measurement and improvement techniques).

Reports should also be produced on the progress and success of the SIP, such as the number of SIP actions that were completed and the number of actions that delivered their expected benefit.

> **Hints and tips**
>
> 'A spy in both camps' – service level managers can be viewed with a certain amount of suspicion by both the IT service provider staff and the customer representatives. This is due to the dual nature of the job, where they are acting as an unofficial customer representative when talking to IT staff, and as an IT provider representative when talking to customers. This is usually aggravated when they have to represent the 'opposition's' point of view in any meeting etc. To avoid this, the service level manager should be as open and helpful as possible (within the bounds of any commercial propriety) when dealing with both sides, although colleagues should never be openly criticized.

4.3.5.7 Collating, measuring and improving customer satisfaction

There are a number of important 'soft' issues that cannot be monitored by mechanistic or procedural means, such as customers' overall feelings (these need not necessarily match the 'hard' monitoring). For example, even when there have been a number of reported service failures, customers may still have a positive feeling because they are satisfied that appropriate actions are being taken to improve things. Of course, the opposite may apply, and customers may feel dissatisfied with some issues (e.g. the manner of some staff on the service desk) when few or no SLA targets have been broken. The business relationship management process is concerned with overall customer satisfaction with all aspects of service provision. Service level management activity is focused around customer satisfaction relating specifically to the levels of service provided – essentially the warranty aspect of the service.

From the outset, it is wise to try to manage customers' expectations. This means setting proper expectations and appropriate targets in the first place, and putting a systematic process in place to manage expectations going forward, as satisfaction = perception – expectation (where a zero or positive score indicates a satisfied customer). SLAs are just documents, and in themselves do not materially alter the quality of service being provided (though they may affect behaviour and help engender an appropriate service culture, which can have an immediate beneficial effect, and make longer-term improvements possible). A degree of patience is therefore needed and should be built into expectations.

Where charges are being made for the services provided, this should modify customer demands. (Customers can have whatever they can cost-justify – provided it fits within agreed corporate strategy – and have an authorized budget for it, but no more.) Where direct charges are not made, the support of senior business managers should be enlisted to ensure that excessive or unrealistic demands are not placed on the IT provider by any individual customer group.

It is therefore recommended that attempts be made to monitor customer perception on these soft issues. Methods of doing this include:

- Periodic questionnaires and customer surveys
- Customer feedback from service review meetings
- Feedback from PIRs conducted as part of the change management process on major changes, releases, new or changed services etc.
- Telephone perception surveys (perhaps at random on the service desk, or using regular customer liaison representatives)
- Satisfaction survey handouts (left with customers following installations, service visits etc.)
- User group or forum meetings
- Analysis of complaints and compliments.

Where possible, targets should be set for these and monitored as part of the SLA (e.g. an average score of 3.5 should be achieved by the service provider on results given, based on a scoring system of 1 to 5, where 1 is poor performance and 5 is excellent). Ensure that if users provide feedback they receive some return, and demonstrate to them that their comments have been incorporated in an action plan, perhaps a SIP. All customer satisfaction measurements should be reviewed and, where variations are identified, they should be analysed with action taken to rectify the variation.

4.3.5.8 Reviewing and revising SLAs, service scope and underpinning agreements

All SLAs and the agreements that underpin them, including OLAs, and underpinning contracts, must be kept up to date. They should be brought under the control of change management and service asset and configuration management. They should also be reviewed periodically, at least annually, to ensure that they are still current and comprehensive, and are still aligned to business needs and strategy. If the agreement in question is valid for a specified period, such as a contract with a specified termination date, sufficient lead time should be given for the review to be conducted in an orderly manner and the agreement renewed or terminated as appropriate in a timely manner. This is important to ensure no interruptions to service or periods of ambiguity in regard to service target commitments. In the case of contracts or agreements with suppliers, the supplier management process is responsible for this activity with the active consultation of SLM (see section 4.3.5.9 for more detail on OLA and underpinning contract maintenance).

Reviews should ensure that the services covered and the targets for each are still relevant – and that nothing significant has changed that invalidates the agreement in any way (this should include infrastructure changes, business changes, supplier changes etc.). Where changes are made, the agreements must be updated under change management control to reflect the new situation. If all agreements are recorded as CIs within the CMS, it is easier to assess the impact and implement the changes in a controlled manner.

These reviews should also include the overall strategy documents, to ensure that all services and service agreements are kept in line with business and IT strategies and policies. Because of the dependency of SLAs on the OLAs and underpinning contracts that support them, revised SLAs cannot be finalized without careful attention to alignment between targets.

4.3.5.9 Reviewing and revising OLAs, underpinning agreements and service scope

IT service providers are dependent on their own internal support teams as well as on external partners or suppliers. The service provider cannot commit to meeting SLA targets unless their own support teams' and suppliers' performances underpin these targets. Underpinning contracts with external suppliers are mandatory, but many organizations have also identified the benefits of having simple agreements with internal support groups, usually referred to as OLAs. 'Underpinning agreements' is a term used to refer to all OLAs, and contracts or other agreements that underpin the customer SLAs.

Often these agreements are referred to as 'back-to-back' agreements. This is to reflect the need to ensure that all targets within underpinning or 'back-to-back' agreements are aligned with, and support, targets agreed with the business in SLAs or OLAs. There may be several layers of these underpinning or 'back-to-back' agreements with aligned targets. It is essential that the targets at each layer are aligned with, and support, the targets contained within the higher levels (i.e. those closest to the business targets).

OLAs need not be very complicated, but should set out specific back-to-back targets for support groups that underpin the targets included in SLAs. For example, if the SLA includes overall time to respond and fix targets for incidents (varying on the priority levels), then the OLAs should include targets for each of the elements in the support chain. The incident resolution targets included in SLAs should not normally match the same targets included in contracts or OLAs with suppliers because the SLA targets must include an element for all stages in the support cycle (e.g. detection time, service desk logging time, escalation time, referral time between group, service desk review and closure time – as well as the actual time fixing the failure). The SLA target should cover the time taken to answer calls, escalate incidents to technical support staff, and the time taken to start to investigate and to resolve incidents assigned to them. In addition, overall support hours should be stipulated for all groups that underpin the required service availability times in the SLA. If special procedures exist for contacted staff (e.g. out-of-hours telephone support), these must also be documented.

OLAs should be monitored against OLA and SLA targets, and reports on achievements provided as feedback to the appropriate managers of each support team. This highlights potential problem areas, which may need to be addressed internally or by a further review of the SLA or OLA. Serious consideration should be given to introducing formal OLAs for all internal support teams which contribute to the support of operational services.

It is also important that before committing to new or revised SLAs, existing contractual arrangements with suppliers are investigated and, where necessary, upgraded. This is likely to incur additional costs, which must either be absorbed by IT or passed on to the customer. In the latter case, the customer must agree to this, or the more relaxed targets in existing contracts should be agreed for inclusion in SLAs. This activity needs to be completed collaboratively with the supplier management process, to ensure not only that SLM requirements are met, but also that all other process requirements are considered, particularly supplier and contractual policies and standards.

4.3.5.10 Developing contacts and relationships

It is very important that the service provider develops trust and respect with the business, especially with the key business contacts. The SLM process contributes to this trust and respect by working closely with key business contacts throughout SLM activity to ensure that service levels are agreed and delivered. As customers experience the results of successful SLM, their trust in and respect for the service provider increase. This in turn improves the ability of the customer and service provider to work together efficiently and effectively. The business relationship management process ensures that the right customer representatives participate in SLM and contributes extensively to the understanding of business needs and priorities that must inform all SLM activity.

Using the service catalogue, especially the business/customer view of the service catalogue, enables SLM to be much more proactive. The service catalogue provides the information that enables SLM to understand the relationships between the services and the business units and business processes that depend on those services. It should also provide the information on all the key business and IT contacts relating to the services, their use and their importance. In order to ensure that this is done in a consistent manner, SLM should perform the following activities:

- Confirm stakeholders with business relationship management, including customers and key business managers and service users
- Assist with maintaining accurate information within the service portfolio and service catalogue
- Be flexible and responsive to the needs of the business, customers and users, and understand current and planned new business processes and their requirements for new or changed services, documenting and communicating these requirements to all other processes as well as facilitating and innovating change wherever there is business benefit
- Develop a full understanding of business, customer and user strategies, plans, business needs and objectives, ensuring that IT are working in partnership with the business, customers and users, developing long-term relationships. This should be done in conjunction with the business relationship management process
- Regularly take the customer journey and sample the customer experience, providing feedback on customer issues to IT (This applies to both IT customers and also the external business customers in their use of IT services.)
- Ensure that the correct relationship processes are in place to achieve objectives and that they are subjected to continual improvement
- Conduct and complete customer surveys, assist with the analysis of the completed surveys and ensure that actions are taken on the results (This can be done in collaboration with business relationship management.)
- Act as an IT representative in organizing and attending user groups
- Proactively market and exploit the service portfolio and service catalogue and the use of the services within all areas of the business
- Work with the business, customers and users to ensure that IT provides the most appropriate levels of service to meet business needs currently and in the future

- Promote service awareness and understanding
- Raise the awareness of the business benefits to be gained from the exploitation of new technology
- Facilitate the development and negotiation of appropriate, achievable and realistic warranty requirements, documented in SLRs and SLAs between the business and IT
- Ensure the business, customers and users understand their responsibilities/commitments to IT (i.e. IT dependencies)
- Assist with the maintenance of a register of all outstanding improvements and enhancements.

4.3.5.11 Handling complaints and compliments

The SLM process should also include activities and procedures for the logging and management of complaints and compliments that relate to service levels. This work represents a significant contribution to the overall customer satisfaction work being done in the business relationship management process. SLM may also be actively involved in the management of service level complaints and compliments originating from users, as well as from customers, as user perceptions will add an important perspective.

The logging procedures for compliments and complaints may be performed by the service desk as they are similar to those of incident management and request fulfilment. The definition of a complaint and a compliment should be agreed with the customers, together with agreed contact points and procedures for their management and analysis. All complaints and compliments should be recorded and communicated to the relevant parties. All complaints should also be actioned and resolved to the satisfaction of the originator. If not, there should be an escalation contact and procedure for all complaints that are not actioned and resolved within an appropriate timescale. All outstanding complaints should be reviewed and escalated to senior management where appropriate. Reports should also be produced on the numbers and types of complaints, the trends identified and actions taken to reduce the numbers received. Similar reports should also be produced for compliments.

4.3.6 Triggers, inputs, outputs and interfaces

SLM is a process that has many highly active connections throughout the organization and its processes. It is important that the triggers, inputs, outputs and interfaces be clearly defined to avoid duplicated effort or gaps in workflow.

4.3.6.1 Triggers

There are many triggers that instigate SLM activity. These include:

- Changes in the service portfolio, such as new or changed business requirements or new or changed services
- New or changed agreements, SLRs, SLAs, OLAs or contracts
- Service review meetings and actions
- Service breaches or threatened breaches
- Compliments and complaints
- Periodic activities such as reviewing, reporting and customer satisfaction surveys
- Changes in strategy or policy.

4.3.6.2 Inputs

A number of sources of information are relevant to the SLM process. These include:

- Business information: from the organization's business strategy, plans and financial plans, and information on its current and future requirements
- BIA: providing information on the impact, priority, risk and number of users associated with each service
- Business requirements: details of any agreed, new or changed business requirements
- The strategies, policies and constraints from service strategy
- The service portfolio and service catalogue
- Change information, including RFCs: from the change management process with a change schedule and a need to assess all changes for their impact on all services
- CMS: containing information on the relationships between the business services, the supporting services and the technology
- Customer and user feedback, complaints and compliments
- Improvement opportunities from the CSI register

■ Other inputs: including advice, information and input from any of the other processes (e.g. incident management, capacity management and availability management), together with the existing SLAs, SLRs and OLAs and past service reports on the quality of service delivered.

4.3.6.3 Outputs

The outputs of SLM should include:

■ Service reports: providing details of the service levels achieved in relation to the targets contained within SLAs. These reports should contain details of all aspects of the service and its delivery, including current and historical performance, breaches and weaknesses, major events, changes planned, current and predicted workloads, customer feedback, and improvement plans and activities

■ Service improvement opportunities for inclusion in the CSI register and for later review and prioritization in conjunction with the CSI manager

■ SIP: an overall programme or plan of prioritized improvement actions, encompassing appropriate services and processes, together with associated impacts and risks

■ The service quality plan: documenting and planning the overall improvement of service quality

■ Document templates: standard document templates, format and content for SLAs, SLRs and OLAs, aligned with corporate standards:
  ● SLAs: a set of targets and responsibilities should be documented and agreed within an SLA for each operational service
  ● SLRs: a set of targets and responsibilities should be documented and agreed within an SLR for each proposed new or changed service
  ● OLAs: a set of targets and responsibilities should be documented and agreed within an OLA for each internal support team

■ Reports on OLAs and underpinning contracts

■ Service review meeting minutes and actions: all meetings should be scheduled on a regular basis, with planned agendas and their discussions and actions recorded and progressed

■ SLA review and service scope review meeting minutes: summarizing agreed actions and revisions to SLAs and service scope

■ Updated change information, including updates to RFCs

■ Revised requirements for underpinning contracts: changes to SLAs or new SLRs may require existing underpinning contracts to be changed, or new contracts to be negotiated and agreed.

4.3.6.4 Interfaces

The most critical interfaces for the SLM process include:

■ **Business relationship management** This process ensures that the service provider has a full understanding of the needs and priorities of the business and that customers are appropriately involved/represented in the work of service level management.

■ **Service catalogue management** This process provides accurate information about services and their interfaces and dependencies to support determining the SLA framework, identifying customers/business units that need to be engaged by SLM and to assist SLM in communicating with customers regarding services provided.

■ **Incident management** This process provides critical data to SLM to demonstrate performance against many SLA targets, as well as operating with the fulfilment of SLA targets as a CSF. SLM negotiates support-related targets such as target restoration times and then the fulfilment of those targets is embedded into the operation of the incident management process.

■ **Supplier management** This process works collaboratively with SLM to define, negotiate, document and agree terms of service with suppliers to support the achievement of commitments made by the service provider in SLAs. Supplier management also manages the performance of suppliers and contracts against these terms of service to ensure related SLA targets are met.

■ **Availability, capacity, IT service continuity and information security management** These processes contribute to SLM by helping to define service level targets that relate to their area of responsibility and to validate that the targets are realistic. Once targets are agreed, the day-to-day operation of each process ensures achievements match targets.

- **Financial management for IT services** This process works with SLM to validate the predicted cost of delivering the service levels required by the customer to inform their decision-making process and to ensure that actual costs are compared with predicted costs as part of the overall management of the cost effectiveness of the service.

- **Design coordination** During the service design stage, this process is responsible for ensuring that the overall service design activities are completed successfully. SLM plays a critical role in this through the development of agreed SLRs and the associated service targets which the new or changed service must be designed to achieve.

4.3.7 Information management

SLM provides key information on all operational services, their expected targets and the service achievements and breaches for all operational services. It assists service catalogue management with the management of the service catalogue and also provides the information and trends on customer satisfaction, including complaints and compliments.

SLM is crucial in providing information on the quality of IT service provided to the customer, and information on the customer's expectation and perception of that quality of service. This information should be widely available to all areas of the service provider organization.

4.3.8 Critical success factors and key performance indicators

The following list includes some sample CSFs for SLM. Each organization should identify appropriate CSFs based on its objectives for the process. Each sample CSF is followed by a small number of typical KPIs that support the CSF. These KPIs should not be adopted without careful consideration. Each organization should develop KPIs that are appropriate for its level of maturity, its CSFs and its particular circumstances. Achievement against KPIs should be monitored and used to identify opportunities for improvement, which should be logged in the CSI register for evaluation and possible implementation.

- **CSF** Managing the overall quality of IT services required both in the number and level of services provided and managed
  - **KPI** Percentage reduction in SLA targets threatened
  - **KPI** Percentage increase in customer perception and satisfaction of SLA achievements, via service reviews and customer satisfaction survey responses
  - **KPI** Percentage reduction in SLA breaches caused because of third-party support contracts (underpinning contracts)
  - **KPI** Percentage reduction in SLA breaches caused because of internal OLAs
- **CSF** Deliver the service as previously agreed at affordable costs
  - **KPI** Total number and percentage increase in fully documented SLAs in place
  - **KPI** Percentage increase in SLAs agreed against operational services being run
  - **KPI** Percentage reduction in the costs associated with service provision
  - **KPI** Percentage reduction in the cost of monitoring and reporting of SLAs
  - **KPI** Percentage increase in the speed and of developing and agreeing appropriate SLAs
  - **KPI** Frequency of service review meetings
- **CSF** Manage the interface with the business and users
  - **KPI** Increased percentage of services covered by SLAs
  - **KPI** Documented and agreed SLM processes and procedures are in place
  - **KPI** Reduction in the time taken to respond to and implement SLA requests
  - **KPI** Increased percentage of SLA reviews completed on time
  - **KPI** Reduction in the percentage of outstanding SLAs for annual renegotiation
  - **KPI** Reduction in the percentage of SLAs requiring corrective changes (for example, targets not attainable; changes in usage levels)
  - **KPI** Percentage increase in the coverage of OLAs and third-party contracts in place, while possibly reducing the actual number of agreements (consolidation and centralization)

- KPI Documentary evidence that issues raised at service and SLA reviews are being followed up and resolved
- KPI Reduction in the number and severity of SLA breaches
- KPI Effective review and follow-up of all SLA, OLA and underpinning contract breaches.

KPIs and metrics can be used to judge the efficiency and effectiveness of SLM activities and the progress of the SIP. These metrics should be developed from the service, customer and business perspectives and should cover both subjective and objective measurements such as the following:

- Objective:
  - Number or percentage of service targets being met
  - Number and severity of service breaches
  - Number of services with up-to-date SLAs
  - Number of services with timely reports and active service reviews
- Subjective:
  - Improvements in customer satisfaction.

More information on KPIs, measurements and improvements can be found in the following section and in *ITIL Continual Service Improvement*.

> **Hints and tips**
>
> Don't fall into the trap of using percentages as the only metric. It is easy to get caught out when there is a small system with limited measurement points (i.e. a single failure in a population of 100 is only 1%; a single failure in a population of 50 is 2% – if the target is 98.5%, then the SLA is already breached). Always go for number of incidents rather than a percentage on populations of less than 100, and be careful when targets are accepted. This is another thing organizations have learned the hard way.

SLM often generates a good starting point for a SIP – and the service review process may drive this, but all processes and all areas of the service provider organization should be involved in the SIP.

Where an underlying difficulty that is adversely impacting on service quality has been identified, SLM must, in conjunction with problem management and availability management, instigate a SIP to identify and implement whatever actions are necessary to overcome the difficulties

and restore service quality. SIP initiatives may also focus on such issues as user training, service and system testing, and documentation. In these cases, the relevant people need to be involved and adequate feedback given to make improvements for the future. At any time, a number of separate initiatives that form part of the SIP may be running in parallel to address difficulties with a number of services.

Some organizations have established an up-front annual budget held by SLM from which SIP initiatives can be funded. This means that action can be undertaken quickly and that SLM is demonstrably effective. This practice should be encouraged and expanded to enable SLM to become increasingly proactive and predictive. The SIP needs to be owned and managed, with all improvement actions being assessed for risk and impact on services, customers and the business, and then prioritized, scheduled and implemented. Improvements identified by SLM are part of the overall continual service improvement approach and should be logged in the CSI register for review and prioritization. Once selected for action they are managed as part of a SIP.

If an organization is outsourcing its service delivery to a third party, the issue of service improvement should be discussed at the outset and covered (and budgeted for) in the contract, otherwise there is no incentive during the lifetime of the contract for supplier to improve service targets if they are already meeting contractual obligations and additional expenditure is needed to make the improvements.

4.3.9 Challenges and risks

4.3.9.1 Challenges

One challenge faced by SLM is that of identifying suitable customer representatives with whom to negotiate. Who 'owns' the service on the customer side? In some cases, this may be obvious, and a single customer manager is willing to act as the signatory to the agreement. In other cases, it may take quite a bit of negotiating or cajoling to find a representative 'volunteer' (beware that volunteers often want to express their own personal view rather than represent a general consensus), or it may be necessary to get all customers to sign.

If customer representatives exist who are able genuinely to represent the views of the customer community, because they frequently meet with a wide selection of customers, this is ideal. Unfortunately, all too often representatives are head-office based and seldom come into contact with genuine service customers. In the worst case, the service level manager may have to perform their own programme of discussions and meetings with customers to ensure true requirements are identified.

Anecdote: Conflict management and SLM

On negotiating the current and support hours for a large service, an organization found a discrepancy in the required time of usage between the head office and the field office's customers. The head office (with a limited user population) wanted service hours covering 8.00 to 18.00, whereas the field office (with at least 20 times the user population) stated that starting an hour earlier would be better – but all offices closed to the public by 16.00 at the latest, and so would not require a service much beyond this. The head office won the 'political' argument, and so the 8.00 to 18.00 band was set. When the service came to be used (and hence monitored) it was found that service extensions were usually asked for by the field office to cover the extra hour in the morning, and actual usage figures showed that the service had not been accessed after 17.00, except on very rare occasions. The service level manager was blamed by the IT staff for having to cover a late shift, and by the customer representative for charging for a service that was not used (i.e. staff and running costs).

Hints and tips

Care should be taken when opening discussions on service levels for the first time, as it is likely that 'current issues' (the failure that occurred yesterday) or long-standing grievances (that old printer that we have been trying to get replaced for ages) are likely to be aired at the outset. Important though these may be, they must not be allowed to get in the way of establishing the longer-term requirements. Be aware, however, that it may be necessary to address any issues raised at the outset before gaining any credibility to progress further.

Another challenge may arise if there has been no previous experience of SLM. In these cases, it is advisable to start with a draft SLA. A decision should be made on which service or customers are to be used for the draft. It is helpful if the selected customer is enthusiastic and wishes to participate – perhaps because they are anxious to see improvements in service quality. The results of an initial customer perception survey may give pointers to a suitable initial draft SLA.

Hints and tips

Do not pick an area where large problems exist as the first SLA. Try to pick an area that is likely to show some quick benefits and develop the SLM process. Nothing encourages acceptance of a new idea quicker than success.

One difficulty sometimes encountered is that staff at different levels within the customer community may have different objectives and perceptions. For example, a senior manager may rarely use a service and may be more interested in issues such as value for money and output, whereas a junior member of staff may use the service throughout the day, and may be more interested in issues such as responsiveness, usability and reliability. It is important that all of the appropriate and relevant business requirements, at all levels, are identified and incorporated in SLAs.

Some organizations use focus groups from different levels from within the customer community to help ensure that all issues have been correctly addressed. This takes additional resources, but can be well worth the effort.

The other group of people that has to be consulted during the whole of this process is the appropriate representatives from within the IT provider side (whether internal or from an external supplier or partner). They need to agree that targets are realistic, achievable and affordable. If they are not, further negotiations are needed until a compromise acceptable to all parties is agreed. The views of suppliers should also be sought, and any contractual implications should be taken into account during the negotiation stages.

Where no past monitored data is available, it is advisable to leave the agreement in draft format for an initial period, until monitoring can confirm that initial targets are achievable. Targets may have to be re-negotiated in some cases. Many organizations negotiate an agreed timeframe for IT to negotiate and create a baseline for establishing realistic service targets. When targets and timeframes have been confirmed, the SLAs must be signed.

Once the initial SLA has been completed, and any early difficulties overcome, then move on and gradually introduce SLAs for other services/customers. If it is decided from the outset to go for a multi-level structure, it is likely that the corporate-level issues have to be covered for all customers at the time of the initial SLA. It is also worth trialling the corporate issues during this initial phase.

> **Hints and tips**
>
> Don't go for easy targets at the corporate level. They may be easy to achieve, but have no value in improving service quality or credibility. Also, if the targets are set at a sufficiently high level, the corporate SLA can be used as the standard that all new services should reach.

4.3.9.2 Risks

Some of the risks associated with service level management are:

- A lack of accurate input, involvement and commitment from the business and customers
- Lack of appropriate tools and resources required to agree, document, monitor, report and review agreements and service levels
- The process becomes a bureaucratic, administrative process, rather than an active and proactive process delivering measurable benefit to the business
- Access to and support of appropriate and up-to-date CMS and SKMS
- Bypassing the use of the SLM processes
- Business and customer measurements are too difficult to measure and improve, so are not recorded
- Inappropriate business and customer contacts and relationships are developed
- High customer expectations and low perception
- Poor and inappropriate communication is achieved with the business and customers.

4.4 AVAILABILITY MANAGEMENT

Availability is one of the most critical parts of the warranty of a service. If a service does not deliver the levels of availability required, then the business will not experience the value that has been promised. Without availability the utility of the service cannot be accessed. Availability management process activity extends across the service lifecycle.

4.4.1 Purpose and objectives

The purpose of the availability management process is to ensure that the level of availability delivered in all IT services meets the agreed availability needs and/or service level targets in a cost-effective and timely manner. Availability management is concerned with meeting both the current and future availability needs of the business.

Availability management defines, analyses, plans, measures and improves all aspects of the availability of IT services, ensuring that all IT infrastructure, processes, tools, roles etc. are appropriate for the agreed availability service level targets. It provides a point of focus and management for all availability-related issues, relating to both services and resources, ensuring that availability targets in all areas are measured and achieved.

The objectives of availability management are to:

- Produce and maintain an appropriate and up-to-date availability plan that reflects the current and future needs of the business
- Provide advice and guidance to all other areas of the business and IT on all availability-related issues
- Ensure that service availability achievements meet all their agreed targets by managing services and resources-related availability performance
- Assist with the diagnosis and resolution of availability-related incidents and problems
- Assess the impact of all changes on the availability plan and the availability of all services and resources
- Ensure that proactive measures to improve the availability of services are implemented wherever it is cost-justifiable to do so.

Availability management should ensure the agreed level of availability is provided. The measurement and monitoring of IT availability is a key activity to ensure availability levels are being met consistently.

Availability management should look to continually optimize and proactively improve the availability of the IT infrastructure, the services and the supporting organization, in order to provide cost-effective availability improvements that can deliver business and customer benefits.

4.4.2 Scope

The scope of the availability management process covers the design, implementation, measurement, management and improvement of IT service and component availability. Availability management commences as soon as the availability requirements for an IT service are clear enough to be articulated. It is an ongoing process, finishing only when the IT service is decommissioned or retired.

The availability management process includes two key elements:

- **Reactive activities** These involve the monitoring, measuring, analysis and management of all events, incidents and problems involving unavailability. These activities are principally performed as part of the operational roles.
- **Proactive activities** These involve the proactive planning, design and improvement of availability. These activities are principally performed as part of the design and planning roles.

These activities are described in detail in section 4.4.5.

Availability management needs to understand the service and component availability requirements from the business perspective in terms of the:

- Current business processes, their operation and requirements
- Future business plans and requirements
- Service targets and the current IT service operation and delivery
- IT infrastructure, data, applications and environment and their performance
- Business impacts and priorities in relation to the services and their usage.

Understanding all of this will enable availability management to ensure that all the services and components are designed and delivered to meet their targets in terms of agreed business needs. The availability management process:

- Should be applied to all operational services and technology, particularly those covered by SLAs. It can also be applied to those IT services deemed to be business-critical, regardless of whether formal SLAs exist
- Should be applied to all new IT services and for existing services where SLRs or SLAs have been established
- Should be applied to all supporting services and the partners and suppliers (both internal and external) that form the IT support organization as a precursor to the creation of formal agreements
- Should consider all aspects of the IT services and components and supporting organizations that may impact availability, including training, skills, process effectiveness, procedures and tools.

The availability management process should include:

- Monitoring of all aspects of availability, reliability and maintainability of IT services and the supporting components, with appropriate events, alarms and escalation, with automated scripts for recovery
- Maintaining a set of methods, techniques and calculations for all availability measurements, metrics and reporting
- Actively participating in risk assessment and management activities
- Collecting measurements and the analysis and production of regular and ad hoc reports on service and component availability
- Understanding the agreed current and future demands of the business for IT services and their availability
- Influencing the design of services and components to align with business availability needs
- Producing an availability plan that enables the service provider to continue to provide and improve services in line with availability targets defined in SLAs, and to plan and forecast future availability levels required, as defined in SLRs
- Maintaining a schedule of tests for all resilience and fail-over components and mechanisms
- Assisting with the identification and resolution of any incidents and problems associated with service or component unavailability

■ Proactively improving service or component availability wherever it is cost-justifiable and meets the needs of the business.

The availability management process does not include business continuity management (BCM) and the resumption of business processing after a major disaster. The support of BCM is included within ITSCM. However, availability management does provide key inputs to ITSCM, and the two processes have a close relationship, particularly in the assessment and management of risks and in the implementation of risk reduction and resilience measures.

4.4.3 Value to the business

The availability management process ensures that the availability of systems and services matches the evolving agreed needs of the business. The role of IT within the business is now pivotal. The availability and reliability of IT services can directly influence customer satisfaction and the reputation of the business. This is why availability management is essential in ensuring IT delivers the levels of service availability required by the business to satisfy its business objectives and deliver the quality of service demanded by its customers.

In today's competitive marketplace, customer satisfaction with service(s) provided is paramount. Customer loyalty can no longer be relied on, and dissatisfaction with the availability and reliability of IT service can be a key factor in customers taking their business to a competitor. Availability can also improve the ability of the business to follow an environmentally responsible strategy by using green technologies and techniques in availability management.

4.4.4 Policies, principles and basic concepts

The availability management process is continually trying to ensure that all operational services meet their agreed availability targets, and that new or changed services are designed appropriately to meet their intended targets, without compromising the performance of existing services.

4.4.4.1 Policies

As a matter of policy, the availability management process, just like capacity management, must be involved in all stages of the service lifecycle, from strategy and design, through transition and operation to improvement. The appropriate availability and resilience should be designed into services and components from the initial design stages. This will ensure not only that the availability of any new or changed service meets its expected targets, but also that all existing services and components continue to meet all of their targets. This is the basis of stable service provision.

The service provider organization should establish policies defining when and how availability management must be engaged throughout each lifecycle stage. Policies should also be established regarding the criteria to be used to define availability and unavailability of a service or component and how each will be measured.

4.4.4.2 Guiding principles of availability

An effective availability management process, consisting of both the reactive and proactive activities, can 'make a big difference' and will be recognized as such by the business, if the deployment of availability management within an IT organization has a strong emphasis on the needs of the business and customers. To reinforce this emphasis, there are several guiding principles that should underpin the availability management process and its focus:

■ Service availability is at the core of customer satisfaction and business success: there is a direct correlation in most organizations between service availability and customer and user satisfaction, where poor service performance is defined as being unavailable.
■ Recognizing that when services fail, it is still possible to achieve business, customer and user satisfaction and recognition: the way a service provider reacts in a failure situation has a major influence on customer and user perception and expectation.
■ Improving availability can only begin after understanding how the IT services support the operation of the business.
■ Service availability is only as good as the weakest link in the chain: it can be greatly increased by the elimination of single points of failure or an unreliable or weak component.
■ Availability is not just a reactive process. The more proactive the process, the better service availability will be. Availability should not purely react to service and component failure. The

more often events and failures are predicted, pre-empted and prevented, the higher the level of service availability.

■ It is cheaper to design the right level of service availability into a service from the start, rather than try and 'bolt it on' subsequently. Adding resilience into a service or component is invariably more expensive than designing it in from the start. Also, once a service gets a bad name for unreliability, it becomes very difficult to change the image. Resilience is also a key consideration of ITSCM, and this should be considered at the same time.

Availability management is completed at two interconnected levels:

■ **Service availability** This involves all aspects of service availability and unavailability and the impact of component availability, or the potential impact of component unavailability on service availability.

■ **Component availability** This involves all aspects of component availability and unavailability.

4.4.4.3 Aspects of availability

Availability management relies on the monitoring, measurement, analysis and reporting of the following aspects.

Availability

Availability is the ability of a service, component or CI to perform its agreed function when required. It is often measured and reported as a percentage. Note that downtime should only be included in the following calculation when it occurs within the agreed service time (AST). However, total down time should also be recorded and reported.

$$\text{Availability (\%)} = \frac{\text{Agreed service time (AST)} - \text{downtime}}{\text{AST}} \times 100$$

Reliability

Reliability is a measure of how long a service, component or CI can perform its agreed function without interruption. The reliability of the service can be improved by increasing the reliability of individual components or by increasing the resilience of the service to individual component failure (i.e. increasing the component redundancy, for example by using load-balancing techniques). It is often measured and reported as the mean time between service incidents (MTBSI) or mean time between failures (MTBF):

$$\text{Reliability (MTBSI in hours)} = \frac{\text{Available time in hours}}{\text{Number of breaks}}$$

$$\text{Reliability (MTBF in hours)} = \frac{\text{Available time in hours} - \text{Total downtime in hours}}{\text{Number of breaks}}$$

Maintainability

Maintainability is a measure of how quickly and effectively a service, component or CI can be restored to normal working after a failure. It is measured and reported as the mean time to restore service (MTRS) and should be calculated using the following formula:

$$\text{Maintainability (MTRS in hours)} = \frac{\text{Total downtime in hours}}{\text{Number of service breaks}}$$

MTRS should be used to avoid the ambiguity of the more common industry term mean time to repair (MTTR), which in some definitions includes only repair time, but in others includes recovery time. The downtime in MTRS covers all the contributory factors that make the service, component or CI unavailable:

Example: measuring availability, reliability and maintainability

A situation where a 24 × 7 service has been running for a period of 5,020 hours with only two breaks, one of six hours and one of 14 hours, would give the following figures:

Availability	= (5,020–(6+14))/5,020 × 100	= 99.60%
Reliability (MTBSI)	= 5,020/2	= 2,510 hours
Reliability (MTBF)	= 5,020–(6+14)/2	= 2,500 hours
Maintainability (MTRS)	= (6+14)/2	= 10 hours

- Time to record
- Time to respond
- Time to resolve
- Time to physically repair or replace
- Time to recover.

Serviceability

Serviceability is the ability of a third-party supplier to meet the terms of its contract. This contract will include agreed levels of availability, reliability and/or maintainability for a supporting service or component. These aspects and their inter-relationships are illustrated in Figure 4.8.

Although the principal service target contained within SLAs for customers and the business is availability, as illustrated in Figure 4.8, some customers also require reliability and maintainability targets to be included in the SLA as well. Where these are included they should relate to end-to-end service reliability and maintainability, whereas the reliability and maintainability targets contained in OLAs and contracts relate to component and supporting service targets and can often include availability targets relating to the relevant components or supporting services.

Vital business function

The term vital business function (VBF) is used to reflect the part of a business process that is critical to the success of the business. An IT service may support a number of business functions that are less critical. For example, an automated teller machine (ATM) or cash dispenser service VBF would be the dispensing of cash. However, the ability to obtain a statement from an ATM may not be considered as vital. This distinction is important and should influence availability design and associated costs. The more vital the business function generally, the greater the level of resilience and availability that needs to be incorporated into the design required in the supporting IT services. For all services, whether VBFs or not, the availability requirements should be determined by the business and not by IT. The initial availability targets are often set at too high a level, and this leads to either over-priced services or an iterative discussion between the service provider and the business to agree an appropriate compromise between the service availability and the cost of the service and its supporting technology.

Certain VBFs may need special designs, which are now being used as a matter of course within service design plans, incorporating:

- **High availability** A characteristic of the IT service that minimizes or masks the effects of IT component failure to the users of a service.
- **Fault tolerance** The ability of an IT service, component or CI to continue to operate correctly after failure of a component part.
- **Continuous operation** An approach or design to eliminate planned downtime of an IT service. Note that individual components or CIs may be down even though the IT service remains available.
- **Continuous availability** An approach or design to achieve 100% availability. A continuously available IT service has no planned or unplanned downtime.

Industry view

Many suppliers commit to high availability or continuous availability solutions only if stringent environmental standards and resilient processes are used. They often agree to such contracts only after a site survey has been completed and additional, sometimes costly, improvements have been made.

4.4.4.4 Role of measurement

The availability management process depends heavily on the measurement of service and component achievements with regard to availability.

Key messages

'If you don't measure it, you can't manage it.'

'If you don't measure it, you can't improve it.'

'If you don't measure it, you probably don't care.'

'If you can't influence or control it, then don't measure it.'

What to measure and how to report it inevitably depends on which activity is being supported, who the recipients are and how the information is to be utilized. It is important to recognize the differing perspectives of availability to ensure measurement and reporting satisfies these varied needs:

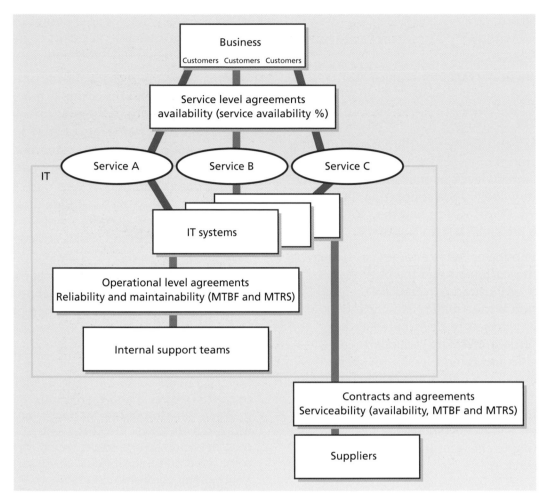

Figure 4.8 Availability terms and measurements

- The business perspective considers IT service availability in terms of its contribution or impact on the VBFs that drive the business operation.
- The user perspective considers IT service availability as a combination of three factors, namely the frequency, the duration and the scope of impact, i.e. all users, some users, all business functions or certain business functions – the user also considers IT service availability in terms of response times. For many performance-centric applications, poor response times are considered equal in impact to failures of technology.
- The IT service provider perspective considers IT service and component availability with regard to availability, reliability and maintainability.

In order to satisfy the differing perspectives of availability, availability management needs to consider the spectrum of measures needed to report the 'same' level of availability in different ways. Measurements need to be meaningful and add value if availability measurement and reporting are ultimately to deliver benefit to the IT and business organizations. This is influenced strongly by the combination of 'what you measure' and 'how you report it'.

4.4.5 Process activities, methods and techniques

Availability management should perform the reactive and proactive activities illustrated in Figure 4.9.

4.4.5.1 Reactive activities

The reactive aspect of availability management involves work to ensure that current operational services and components deliver the agreed levels of availability and to respond appropriately when they do not. The reactive activities include:

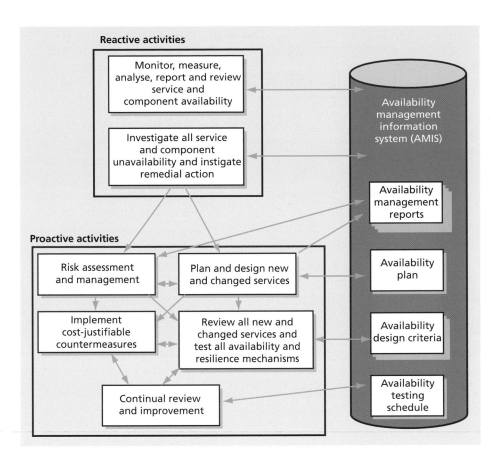

Figure 4.9 The availability management process

- Monitoring, measuring, analysing, reporting and reviewing service and component availability
- Investigating all service and component unavailability and instigating remedial action. This includes looking at events, incidents and problems involving unavailability.

These activities are primarily conducted within the service operation stage of the service lifecycle and are linked into the monitoring and control activities and incident management processes (see *ITIL Service Operation*).

4.4.5.2 Proactive activities

The proactive activities of availability management involve the work necessary to ensure that new or changed services can and will deliver the agreed levels of availability and that appropriate measurements are in place to support this work. They include producing recommendations, plans and documents on design guidelines and criteria for new and changed services, and the continual improvement of service and reduction of risk in

existing services wherever it can be cost-justified. These are key aspects to be considered within service design activities.

Proactive activities include:

- Planning and designing new or changed services:
  - Determining the VBFs, in conjunction with the business and ITSCM
  - Determining the availability requirements from the business for a new or enhanced IT service and formulating the availability and recovery design criteria for the supporting IT components
  - Defining the targets for availability, reliability and maintainability for the IT infrastructure components that underpin the IT service to enable these to be documented and agreed within SLAs, OLAs and contracts
  - Performing risk assessment and management activities to ensure the prevention and/or recovery from service and component unavailability

- Designing the IT services to meet the availability and recovery design criteria and associated agreed service levels
- Establishing measures and reporting of availability, reliability and maintainability that reflect the business, user and IT support organization perspectives

- Risk assessment and management:
  - Determining the impact arising from IT service and component failure in conjunction with ITSCM and, where appropriate, reviewing the availability design criteria to provide additional resilience to prevent or minimize impact to the business
- Implementing cost-justifiable counter-measures, including risk reduction and recovery mechanisms
- Reviewing all new and changed services and testing all availability and resilience mechanisms
- Continual reviewing and improvement:
  - Producing and maintaining an availability plan that prioritizes and plans IT availability improvements.

4.4.5.3 Reactive availability management

Monitoring, measuring, analysing and reporting service and component availability

A key output from the availability management process is the measurement and reporting of IT availability. Availability measures should be incorporated into SLAs, OLAs and any underpinning contracts. These should be reviewed regularly at service level review meetings. Measurement and reporting provide the basis for:

- Monitoring the actual availability delivered versus agreed targets
- Establishing measures of availability and agreeing availability targets with the business
- Identifying unacceptable levels of availability that impact the business and users
- Reviewing availability with the IT support organization
- Continual improvement activities to optimize availability.

IT service provider organizations have, for many years, measured and reported on their perspective of availability. Traditionally these measures have concentrated on component availability and have been somewhat divorced from the business and user views. Typically these traditional measures are based on a combination of an availability percentage (%), time lost and the frequency of failure. Some examples of these traditional measures are as follows:

- **Per cent available** The truly 'traditional' measure that represents availability as a percentage and, as such, much more useful as a component availability measure than a service availability measure. It is typically used to track and report achievement against a service level target. It tends to emphasize the 'big number' such that if the service level target was 98.5% and the achievement was 98.3%, then it does not seem that bad. This can encourage complacent behaviour within the IT support organization.
- **Per cent unavailable** The inverse of the above. This representation, however, has the benefit of focusing on non-availability. Based on the above example, if the target for non-availability is 1.5% and the achievement was 1.7%, then this is a much larger relative difference. This method of reporting is more likely to create awareness of the shortfall in delivering the level of availability required.
- **Duration** This is achieved by converting the percentage unavailable into hours and minutes. This provides a more 'human' measure that people can relate to. If the weekly downtime target is two hours, but in one week the actual downtime was four hours, this would represent a trend leading to an additional four days of non-availability to the business over a full year. This type of measure and reporting is more likely to encourage focus on service improvement.
- **Frequency of failure** This is used to record the number of interruptions to the IT service. It helps provide a good indication of reliability from a user perspective. It is best used in combination with 'duration' to take a balanced view of the level of service interruptions and the duration of time lost to the business.
- **Impact of failure** This is the true measure of service unavailability. It depends on mature incident recording where the inability of users to perform their business tasks is the most important piece of information captured. All other measures suffer from a potential to mask the real effects of service failure and are often converted to a financial impact.

A business may have, for many years, accepted that the IT availability that it experiences is represented in terms of component availability rather than overall service or business availability. However, this is no longer being viewed as acceptable and businesses are keen to better represent availability in measure(s) that demonstrate the positive and negative consequences of IT availability on their business and users.

Key messages

The most important availability measurements are those that reflect and measure availability from the business and user perspective.

Availability management needs to consider availability from both a business/IT service provider perspective and from an IT component perspective. These are entirely different aspects, and while the underlying concept is similar, the measurement, focus and impact are entirely different.

The sole purpose of producing these availability measurements and reports, including those from the business perspective, is to improve the quality and availability of IT service provided to the business and users. All measures, reports and activities should reflect this purpose.

Availability, when measured and reported to reflect the experience of the user, provides a more representative view on overall IT service quality. The user view of availability is influenced by three factors:

- Frequency of downtime
- Duration of downtime
- Scope of impact.

Measurements and reporting of user availability should therefore embrace these factors. The methodology employed to reflect user availability could consider two approaches:

- **Impact by user minutes lost** This is to base calculations on the duration of downtime multiplied by the number of users impacted. This can be the basis to report availability as lost user productivity, or to calculate the availability percentage from a user perspective, and can also include the costs of recovery for lost productivity (e.g. increased overtime payments).

- **Impact by business transaction** This is to base calculations on the number of business transactions that could not be processed during the period of downtime. This provides a better indication of business impact reflecting differing transaction processing profiles across the time of day, week etc. In many instances it may be the case that the user impact correlates to a VBF – for example, if the user takes customer purchase orders and a VBF is customer sales. This single measure is the basis to reflect impact to the business operation and user.

The method employed should be influenced by the nature of the business operation. A business operation supporting data entry activity is well suited to reporting that reflects user productivity loss. Business operations that are more customer-facing, for example ATM services, benefit from reporting transaction impact. It should also be noted that not all business impact is user-related. With increasing automation and electronic processing, the ability to process automated transactions or meet market cut-off times can also have a large financial impact that may be greater than the ability of users to work.

The IT support organization needs to have a keen awareness of the user experience of availability. However, the real benefits come from aggregating the user view into the overall business view. A guiding principle of the availability management process is that: 'Improving availability can only begin when the way technology supports the business is understood'. Therefore availability management is not just about understanding the availability of each IT component, but is also about understanding the impact of component failure on service and user availability. From the business perspective, an IT service can only be considered available when the business is able to perform all vital business functions required to drive the business operation. For the IT service to be available, it therefore relies on all components on which the service depends being available, i.e. systems, key components, network, data and applications.

The traditional IT approach would be to measure individually the availability of each of these components. However, the true measure of availability has to be based on the positive and negative impacts on the VBFs on which the business operation is dependent. This approach ensures that SLAs and IT availability reporting are based on measures that are understood by both the business and IT. By measuring the VBFs that rely on IT services, measurement and reporting becomes business-driven, with the impact of failure reflecting the consequences to the business. It is also important that the availability of the services is defined and agreed with the business and reflected within SLAs. This definition of availability should include:

- What is the minimum available level of functionality of the service?
- At what level of service response is the service considered unavailable?
- Where will this level of functionality and response be measured?
- What are the relative weightings for partial service unavailability?
- If one location or office is impacted, is the whole service considered unavailable, or is this considered to be 'partial unavailability'? This needs to be agreed with the customers.

Hints and tips

When defining 'available' and 'unavailable' for a particular service it is not only important that the agreed levels are measurable, but also that any acceptable 'partial availability' is clearly defined. If it is possible for the scope of service unavailability to be limited, the IT service provider and customer may wish to identify the most likely of these situations and agree to terms for associated service levels. For example, if a vital business function remains available even though less critical features are down, this might be defined as 'partial unavailability' and the agreed service restoration targets might be more lenient. Or if the primary work location remains available, and only satellite offices are affected, this might be considered to be 'partial unavailability'. The key is to be sure that the customer's true business needs are reflected and that the balance of cost and availability are appropriately managed.

Reporting and analysis tools are required for the manipulation of data stored in the various databases utilized by availability management. These tools can either be platform- or PC-based and are often a combination of the two. This will be influenced by the database repository technologies selected and the complexity of data processing and reporting required. Availability management, once implemented and deployed, will be required to produce regular reports on an agreed basis – for example, monthly availability reports, availability plan and service failure analysis (SFA) status reports. These reporting activities can require much manual effort and the only solution is to automate as much of the report generation activity as possible. For reporting purposes, organizational reporting standards should be used wherever possible. If these do not exist, IT standards should be developed so that IT reports can be developed using standard tools and techniques. This means that the integration and consolidation of reports will subsequently be much easier to achieve.

Investigating all service and component unavailability and instigating remedial action

When a service or component becomes unavailable based on the agreed terms, the situation must be investigated and the appropriate corrective action undertaken.

UNAVAILABILITY ANALYSIS

All events and incidents causing unavailability of services and components should be investigated, with remedial actions being implemented within either the availability plan or the overall SIP. Trends should be produced from this analysis to direct and focus activities such as SFA to those areas causing the most impact or disruption to the business and the users.

The overall costs of an IT service are influenced by the levels of availability required and the investments required in technology and services provided by the IT support organization to meet this requirement. Availability certainly does not come for free. However, it is important to reflect that the unavailability of IT also has a cost, and therefore unavailability is not free either. For highly critical business processes and VBFs, it is necessary to consider not only the cost of providing the service, but also the costs that are incurred from failure. The optimum balance to strike is the cost of the availability solution weighed against the costs of unavailability.

Before any SLR is accepted, and ultimately the SLR or SLA negotiated and agreed between the business and the IT organization, it is essential that the availability requirements of the business are analysed to assess if/how the IT service can deliver the required levels of availability. This applies not only to new IT services that are being introduced, but also to any requested changes to the availability requirements of existing IT services.

The cost of an IT failure could simply be expressed as the number of business or IT transactions impacted, either as an actual figure (derived from instrumentation) or based on an estimation. When measured against the VBFs that support the business operation, this can provide an obvious indication of the consequence of failure. The advantage of this approach is the relative ease of obtaining the impact data and the lack of any complex calculations. It also becomes a 'value' that is understood by both the business and IT organization. This can be the stimulus for identifying improvement opportunities and can become a key metric in monitoring the availability of IT services.

The major disadvantage of this approach is that it offers no obvious monetary value that would be needed to justify any significant financial investment decisions for improving availability. Where significant financial investment decisions are required, it is better to express the cost of failure arising from service, system, application or function loss to the business as a monetary 'value'.

The monetary value can be calculated as a combination of the tangible costs associated with failure, but can also include a number of intangible costs. The monetary value should also reflect the cost impact to the whole organization, i.e. the business and IT organization.

Tangible costs can include:

- Lost user productivity
- Lost IT staff productivity
- Lost revenue
- Overtime payments
- Wasted goods and material
- Litigation, imposed fines or penalty payments.

These costs are often well understood by the finance area of the business and IT organization, and in relative terms are easier to obtain and aggregate than the intangible costs associated with an IT failure.

Intangible costs can include:

- Loss of customers

- Loss of customer goodwill (customer dissatisfaction)
- Loss of business opportunity (to sell, gain new customers or revenue etc.)
- Damage to business reputation
- Loss of confidence in IT service provider
- Damage to staff morale.

It is important not simply to dismiss the intangible costs (and the potential consequences) on the grounds that they may be difficult to measure. The overall unavailability of service, the total tangible cost and the total intangible costs arising from service unavailability are all key metrics in the measurement of the effectiveness of the availability management process.

THE EXPANDED INCIDENT LIFECYCLE

A guiding principle of availability management is to recognize that it is still possible to gain customer satisfaction even when things go wrong. One approach to help achieve this requires availability management to ensure that the duration of any incident is minimized to enable normal business operations to resume as quickly as possible. An aim of availability management is to ensure the duration and impact from incidents impacting IT services are minimized, to enable business operations to resume as quickly as possible. The analysis of the 'expanded incident lifecycle' enables the total IT service downtime for any given incident to be broken down and mapped against the major stages through which all incidents progress (the lifecycle). Availability management should work closely with incident management and problem management in the analysis of all incidents causing unavailability.

A good technique to help with the technical analysis of incidents affecting the availability of components and IT services is to take an incident 'lifecycle' view. Every incident passes through several major stages. The time elapsed in these stages may vary considerably. For availability management purposes, the standard incident 'lifecycle', as described within incident management, has been expanded to provide additional help and guidance particularly in the area of 'designing for recovery'. Figure 4.10 illustrates the expanded incident lifecycle.

From the above it can be seen that an incident can be broken down into individual stages within

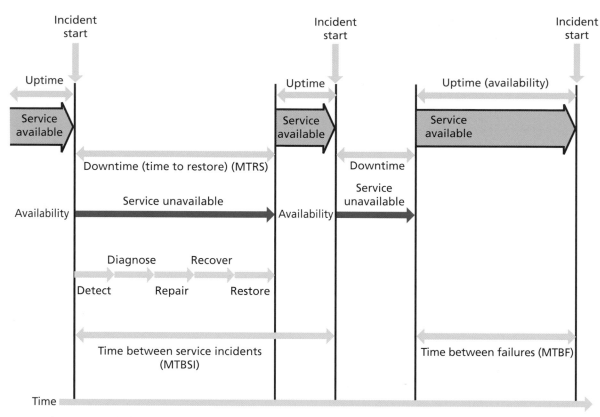

Figure 4.10 The expanded incident lifecycle

a lifecycle that can be timed and measured. This lifecycle view provides an important framework in determining, among others, systems management requirements for event and incident detection, diagnostic data capture requirements and tools for diagnosis, recovery plans to aid speedy recovery and how to verify that IT service has been restored. The individual stages of the lifecycle are considered in more detail as follows:

1 **Incident detection** This is the time at which the IT service provider organization is made aware of an incident. Systems management tools positively influence the ability to detect events and incidents and therefore to improve levels of availability that can be delivered. Implementation and exploitation should have a strong focus on achieving high availability and enhanced recovery objectives. In the context of recovery, such tools should be exploited to provide automated failure detection, assist failure diagnosis and support automated error recovery, with scripted responses. Tools are very important in reducing all stages of the incident lifecycle, but principally the detection of events and incidents. Ideally the event is automatically

detected and resolved, before the users have noticed it or have been impacted in any way.

2 **Incident diagnosis** This is the time at which diagnosis to determine the underlying cause has been completed. When IT components fail, it is important that the required level of diagnostics is captured, to enable problem determination to identify the root cause and resolve the issue. The use and capability of diagnostic tools and skills is critical to the speedy resolution of service issues. For certain failures, the capture of diagnostics may extend service downtime. However, the non-capture of the appropriate diagnostics creates and exposes the service to repeat failures. Where the time required to take diagnostics is considered excessive, or varies from the target, a review should be instigated to identify if techniques and/or procedures can be streamlined to reduce the time required. Equally the scope of the diagnostic data available for capture can be assessed to ensure only the diagnostic data considered essential is taken. The additional downtime required to capture diagnostics

should be included in the recovery metrics documented for each IT component.

3 **Incident repair** This is the time at which the failure has been repaired/fixed. Repair times for incidents should be continuously monitored and compared against the targets agreed within OLAs, underpinning contracts and other agreements. This is particularly important with respect to externally provided services and supplier performance. Wherever breaches are observed, techniques should be used to reduce or remove the breaches from similar incidents in the future.

4 **Incident recovery** This is the time at which component recovery has been completed. The backup and recovery requirements for the components underpinning a new IT service should be identified as early as possible within the design cycle. These requirements should cover hardware, software and data and recovery targets. The outcome from this activity should be a documented set of recovery requirements that enables the development of appropriate recovery plans. To anticipate and prepare for performing recovery such that reinstatement of service is effective and efficient requires the development and testing of appropriate recovery plans based on the documented recovery requirements. Wherever possible, the operational activities within the recovery plan should be automated. The testing of the recovery plans also delivers approximate timings for recovery. These recovery metrics can be used to support the communication of estimated recovery of service and validate or enhance the component failure impact analysis documentation. Availability management must continuously seek and promote faster methods of recovery for all potential incidents. This can be achieved via a range of methods, including automated failure detection, automated recovery, more stringent escalation procedures, and exploitation of new and faster recovery tools and techniques. Availability requirements should also contribute to determining what spare parts are kept within the Definitive Spares to facilitate quick and effective repairs, as described within *ITIL Service Transition*.

5 **Incident restoration** This is the time at which normal business service is resumed. An incident can only be considered 'closed' once service has been restored and normal business operation has resumed. It is important that the restored IT service is verified as working correctly as soon as service restoration is completed and before any technical staff involved in the incident are stood down. In the majority of cases, this is simply a case of getting confirmation from the affected users. However, the users for some services may be customers of the business, i.e. ATM services, internet-based services. For these types of services, it is recommended that IT service verification procedures are developed to enable the IT service provider organization to verify that a restored IT service is now working as expected. These could simply be visual checks of transaction throughput or user simulation scripts that validate the end-to-end service.

Each stage, and the associated time taken, influences the total downtime perceived by the user. By taking this approach it is possible to see where time is being 'lost' for the duration of an incident. For example, the service was unavailable to the business for 60 minutes, yet it only took five minutes to apply a fix – where did the other 55 minutes go?

Using this approach identifies possible areas of inefficiency that combine to make the loss of service experienced by the business greater than it need be. These could cover areas such as poor automation (alerts, automated recovery etc.), poor diagnostic tools and scripts, unclear escalation procedures (which delay the escalation to the appropriate technical support group or supplier), or lack of comprehensive operational documentation. Availability management needs to work in close association with incident and problem management to ensure repeat occurrences are eliminated. It is recommended that these measures are established and captured for all availability incidents. This provides availability management with metrics for both specific incidents and trending information. This information can be used as input to SFA assignments, SIP activities and regular availability management reporting and to provide an impetus for continual improvement activity to pursue cost-effective improvements. It can also enable targets to be set for specific stages of the incident lifecycle. While accepting that each incident may have a wide range of technical complexity, the targets can be used to reflect the consistency of how the IT service provider organization responds to incidents.

An output from the availability management process is the real-time monitoring requirements for IT services and components. To achieve the levels of availability required and/or ensure the rapid restoration of service following an IT failure requires investment and exploitation of a systems management toolset. Systems management tools are an essential building block for IT services that require a high level of availability and can provide an invaluable role in reducing the amount of downtime incurred. Availability management requirements cover the detection and alerting of IT service and component exceptions, automated escalation and notification of IT failures, and the automated recovery and restoration of components from known IT failure situations. This makes it possible to identify where 'time is being lost' and provides the basis for the identification of factors that can improve recovery and restoration times. These activities are performed on a regular basis within service operation.

SERVICE FAILURE ANALYSIS

SFA is a technique designed to provide a structured approach to identifying the underlying causes of service interruptions to the user. SFA utilizes a range of data sources to assess where and why shortfalls in availability are occurring. SFA enables a holistic view to be taken to drive not just technology improvements, but also improvements to the IT support organization, processes, procedures and tools. SFA is run as an assignment or project, and may utilize other availability management methods and techniques to formulate the recommendations for improvement. The detailed analysis of service interruptions can identify opportunities to enhance levels of availability. SFA is a structured technique to identify improvement opportunities in end-to-end service availability that can deliver benefits to the user. Many of the activities involved in SFA are closely aligned with those of problem management, and in a number of organizations these activities are performed jointly by problem and availability management.

The high-level objectives of SFA are to:

- Improve the overall availability of IT services by producing a set of improvements for implementation or input to the availability plan
- Identify the underlying causes of service interruption to users

- Assess the effectiveness of the IT support organization and key processes
- Produce reports detailing the major findings and recommendations
- Ensure that availability improvements derived from SFA-driven activities are measured.

SFA initiatives should use input from all areas and all processes including, most importantly, the business and users. Each SFA assignment should have a recognized sponsor(s) (ideally, joint sponsorship from the IT and business) and involve resources from many technical and process areas. The use of the SFA approach:

- Provides the ability to deliver enhanced levels of availability without major cost
- Provides the business with visible commitment from the IT support organization
- Develops in-house skills and competencies to avoid expensive consultancy assignments related to availability improvement
- Encourages cross-functional team work and breaks barriers between teams, and is an enabler to lateral thinking, challenging traditional thoughts and providing innovative, and often inexpensive, solutions
- Provides a programme of improvement opportunities that can make a real difference to service quality and user perception
- Provides opportunities that are focused on delivering benefit to the user
- Provides an independent 'health check' of IT service management processes and is the stimulus for process improvements.

To maximize both the time of individuals allocated to the SFA assignment and the quality of the delivered report, a structured approach is required. This structure is illustrated in Figure 4.11. This approach is similar to many consultancy models utilized within the industry, and in many ways availability management can be considered as providing via SFA a form of internal consultancy.

The high-level structure in Figure 4.11 is described briefly as follows.

1 **Select opportunity** Prior to scheduling an SFA assignment, there needs to be agreement as to which IT service or technology is to be selected. It is recommended that an agreed number of assignments are scheduled per year within the availability plan and, if possible, the IT services

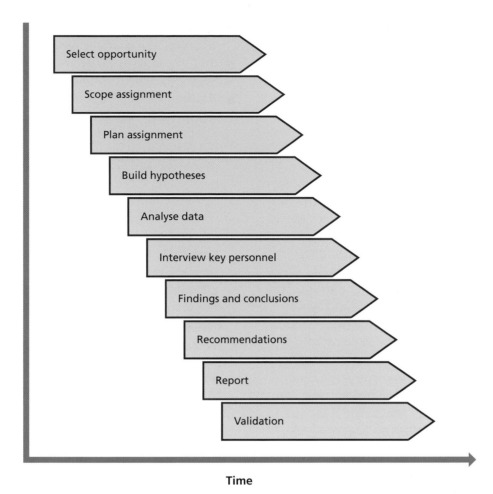

Figure 4.11 The structured approach to SFA

are selected in advance as part of the proactive approach to availability management. Before commencing with the SFA, it is important that the assignment has a recognized sponsor from within the IT organization and/or the business and that they are involved and regularly updated with progress of the SFA activity. This ensures organizational visibility to the SFA and ensures recommendations are endorsed at a senior level within the organization.

2 **Scope assignment** This is to state explicitly what areas are and are not covered within the assignment. This is normally documented in terms of reference issued prior to the assignment.

3 **Plan assignment** The SFA assignment needs to be planned a number of weeks in advance of the assignment commencing, with an agreed project plan and a committed set of resources. The project should look at identifying improvement opportunities that benefit the user. It is therefore important that an end-

to-end view of the data and management information system (MIS) requirements is taken. The data and documentation should be collected from all areas and analysed from the user and business perspective. A 'virtual' SFA team should be formed from all relevant areas to ensure that all aspects and perspectives are considered. The size of the team should reflect the scope and complexity of the SFA assignment.

4 **Build hypotheses** This is a useful method of building likely scenarios, which can help the study team draw early conclusions within the analysis period. These scenarios can be built from discussing the forthcoming assignment with key roles (for example, senior management and users) or by using the planning session to brainstorm the list from the assembled team. The completed hypotheses list should be documented and input to the analysis period to provide some early focus on the data and MIS that match the individual

scenarios. It should be noted that this approach also eliminates perceived issues, i.e. no data or MIS substantiates what is perceived to be a service issue.

5 **Analyse data** The number of individuals who form the SFA team dictates how to allocate specific analysis responsibilities. During this analysis period the hypotheses list should be used to help draw some early conclusions.

6 **Interview key personnel** It is essential that key business representatives and users are interviewed to ensure the business and user perspectives are captured. It is surprising how this dialogue can identify quick win opportunities, as often what the business views as a big issue can be addressed by a simple IT solution. Therefore these interviews should be initiated as soon as possible within the SFA assignment. The study team should also seek input from key individuals within the IT service provider organization to identify additional problem areas and possible solutions that can be fed back to the study team. The dialogue also helps capture those issues that are not easily visible from the assembled data and MIS reports.

7 **Findings and conclusions** After analysis of the data and MIS provided, interviews and continual revision of the hypotheses list, the study team should be in a position to start documenting initial findings and conclusions. It is recommended that the team meet immediately after the analysis period to share their individual findings and then take an aggregate view to form the draft findings and conclusions. It is important that all findings can be evidenced by facts gathered during the analysis. During this phase of the assignment, it may be necessary to validate finding(s) by additional analysis to ensure the SFA team can back up all findings with clear documented evidence.

8 **Recommendations** After all findings and conclusions have been validated, the SFA team should be in a position to formulate recommendations. In many cases, the recommendations to support a particular finding are straightforward and obvious. However, the benefit of bringing a cross-functional team together for the SFA assignment is to create an environment for innovative lateral-thinking approaches. The SFA assignment leader should facilitate this session with the aim of identifying recommendations that are practical and sustainable once implemented.

9 **Report** The final report should be issued to the sponsor with a management summary. Reporting styles are normally determined by the individual organizations. It is important that the report clearly shows where loss of availability is being incurred and how the recommendations address this. If the report contains many recommendations, an attempt should be made to quantify the availability benefit of each recommendation, together with the estimated effort to implement. This enables informed choices to be made on how to take the recommendations forward and how these should be prioritized and resourced.

10 **Validation** It is recommended that for each SFA, key measures that reflect the business and user perspectives prior to the assignment are captured and recorded as the 'before' view. As SFA recommendations are progressed, the positive impacts on availability should be captured to provide the 'after' view for comparative purposes. Where anticipated benefits have not been delivered, this should be investigated and remedial action taken. Having invested time and effort in completing the SFA assignment, it is important that the recommendations, once agreed by the sponsor, are then taken forward for implementation. The best mechanism for achieving this is by incorporating the recommendations as activities to be completed within the availability plan or the overall SIP. The success of the SFA assignment as a whole should be monitored and measured to ensure its continued effectiveness.

4.4.5.4 Proactive availability management

The capability of the availability management process is positively influenced by the range and quality of proactive techniques utilized by the process. This activity and those that follow include descriptions of the proactive techniques of the availability management process. All of the proactive activities described interact with each other and the boundaries between them are rarely sharp. Organizations should seek to ensure that all proactive activities consider both the component and the end-to-end service perspectives.

Planning and designing new or changed services

The availability management process ensures that new or changed services are designed appropriately to meet the customer's availability-related requirements, defined in service level targets. The design must be developed not only to ensure that the new or changed service will meet its availability specifications, but also to ensure that performance of existing services is not negatively impacted. The work involves producing recommendations, plans and documents on design guidelines and criteria for new and changed services. The availability requirements of the business must be clearly defined and understood so that appropriate availability and recovery design criteria can be developed.

REQUIREMENTS DEFINITION

Where new IT services are being developed, it is essential that availability management takes an early and participative design role in determining the availability requirements. This enables availability management to influence positively the IT infrastructure design to ensure that it can deliver the level of availability required. The importance of this participation early in the design of the IT infrastructure cannot be underestimated. There needs to be a dialogue between IT and the business to determine the balance between the business perception of the cost of unavailability and the exponential cost of delivering higher levels of availability.

It is important that the level of availability designed into the service is appropriate to the business needs, the criticality of the business processes being supported and the available budget. The business should be consulted early in the service design lifecycle so that the business availability needs of a new or enhanced IT service can be costed and agreed. This is particularly important where stringent availability requirements may require additional investment in service management processes, IT service and system management tools, high-availability design and special solutions with full redundancy.

It is likely that the business need for IT availability cannot be expressed in technical terms. Availability management therefore provides an important role in being able to translate the business and user requirements into quantifiable availability targets and conditions. This is an important input into the IT service design and provides the basis for assessing the capability of the IT design and IT support organization in meeting the availability requirements of the business.

The business requirements for IT availability should contain at least:

- A definition of the VBFs supported by the IT service
- A definition of IT service downtime, i.e. the conditions under which the business considers the IT service to be unavailable
- The business impact caused by loss of service, together with the associated risk
- Quantitative availability requirements, i.e. the extent to which the business tolerates IT service downtime or degraded service
- The required service hours, i.e. when the service is to be provided
- An assessment of the relative importance of different working periods
- Specific security requirements
- The service backup and recovery capability.

Once the IT technology design and IT support organization are determined, the service provider organization is then in a position to confirm if the availability requirements can be met. Where shortfalls are identified, dialogue with the business is required to present the cost options that exist to enhance the proposed design to meet the availability requirements. This enables the business to reassess if lower or higher levels of availability are required, and to understand the appropriate impact and costs associated with its decision.

Determining the availability requirements is likely to be an iterative process, particularly where there is a need to balance the business availability requirement against the associated costs. The necessary steps are:

■ Determining the business impact caused by loss of service
■ From the business requirements, specifying the availability, reliability and maintainability requirements for the IT service and components supported by the IT support organization
■ For IT services and components provided externally, identifying the serviceability requirements
■ Estimating the costs involved in meeting the availability, reliability, maintainability and serviceability requirements
■ Determining, with the business, if the costs identified in meeting the availability requirements are justified
■ Determining, from the business, the costs likely to be incurred from loss or degradation of service

■ Where these are seen as cost-justified, defining the availability, reliability, maintainability and serviceability requirements in agreements and negotiating them into contracts.

IDENTIFYING VITAL BUSINESS FUNCTIONS

VBF refers to the part of a business process that is critical to the success of the business. An IT service may also support less critical business functions and processes, and it is important that the VBFs are recognized and documented to provide the appropriate business alignment and focus. It is the business which determines and validates the VBFs.

DESIGNING FOR AVAILABILITY

The level of availability required by the business influences the overall cost of the IT service provided. In general, the higher the level of availability required by the business, the higher the cost. These costs are not just the procurement of the base IT technology and services required to underpin the IT infrastructure. Additional costs are incurred in providing the appropriate service management processes, systems management tools and high-availability solutions required to meet the more stringent availability requirements. The greatest level of availability should be included in

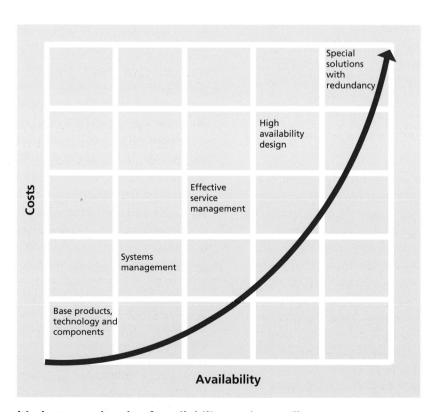

Figure 4.12 Relationship between levels of availability and overall costs

the design of those services supporting the most critical of the VBFs.

When considering how the availability requirements of the business are to be met, it is important to ensure that the level of availability to be provided for an IT service is at the level actually required, and is affordable and cost-justifiable to the business. Figure 4.12 indicates the products and processes required to provide varying levels of availability and the cost implications.

BASE PRODUCTS AND COMPONENTS

The procurement or development of the base products, technology and components should be based on their capability to meet stringent availability and reliability requirements. These should be considered as the cornerstone of the availability design. The additional investment required to achieve even higher levels of availability will be wasted and availability levels not met if these base products and components are unreliable and prone to failure.

SYSTEMS MANAGEMENT

Systems management should provide monitoring, diagnostic and automated error recovery to enable fast detection and speedy resolution of potential and actual IT failure.

SERVICE MANAGEMENT PROCESSES

Effective service management processes contribute to higher levels of availability. Processes such as availability management, incident management, problem management, change management, service asset and configuration management play a crucial role in the overall management of the IT service.

HIGH-AVAILABILITY DESIGN

The design for high availability needs to consider the elimination of SPOFs and/or the provision of alternative components to provide minimal disruption to the business operation should an IT component failure occur. The design also needs to eliminate or minimize the effects of planned downtime to the business operation normally required to accommodate maintenance activity, the implementation of changes to the IT infrastructure or business application. Recovery criteria should define rapid recovery and IT service reinstatement as a key objective within the designing for recovery phase of design.

SPECIAL SOLUTIONS WITH FULL REDUNDANCY

To approach continuous availability in the range of 100% requires expensive solutions that incorporate full mirroring or redundancy. Redundancy is the technique of improving availability by using duplicate components. For stringent availability requirements to be met, these need to be working autonomously in parallel. These solutions are not just restricted to the IT components, but also to the IT environments, i.e. data centres, power supplies, air conditioning and telecommunications.

As illustrated in Figure 4.12, there is a significant increase in costs when the business requirement is higher than the optimum level of availability that the IT infrastructure can deliver. These increased costs are driven by major redesign of the technology and the changing of requirements for the IT support organization.

> **Hints and tips**
>
> If costs are seen as prohibitive, either:
>
> ■ Reassess the IT infrastructure design and provide options for reducing costs and assess the consequences on availability; or
> ■ Reassess the business use and reliance on the IT service and renegotiate the availability targets within the SLA.

SERVICE AVAILABILITY DESIGN

The SLM process is normally responsible for communicating with the business on how its availability requirements for IT services are to be met and negotiating the SLR/SLA for the IT service design stage. Availability management therefore provides important support and input to both SLM and design processes during this period. While higher levels of availability can often be provided by investment in tools and technology, there is no justification for providing a higher level of availability than that needed and afforded by the business. The reality is that satisfying availability requirements is always a balance between cost and quality. This is where availability management can play a key role in optimizing availability of the IT service design to meet increasing availability demands while deferring an increase in costs.

Designing service for availability is a key activity driven by availability management. This ensures that the required level of availability for an IT service can be met. Availability management needs to ensure that the design activity for availability looks at the task from two related, but distinct, perspectives:

- **Designing for availability** This activity relates to the technical design of the IT service and the alignment of the internal and external suppliers required to meet the availability requirements of the business. It needs to cover all aspects of technology, including infrastructure, environment, data and applications.
- **Designing for recovery** This activity relates to the design points required to ensure that in the event of an IT service failure, the service and its supporting components can be reinstated to enable normal business operations to resume as quickly as possible. This again needs to cover all aspects of technology.

Additionally, the ability to recover quickly may be a crucial factor. In simple terms, it may not be possible or cost-justified to build a design that is highly resilient to failure(s). The ability to meet the availability requirements within the cost parameters may rely on the ability consistently to recover in a timely and effective manner. Design for recovery should take into consideration the business needs identified through the BIA, such as specific recovery time objectives and recovery point objectives. All aspects of availability should be considered in the service design activity and should consider all stages within the service lifecycle.

The contribution of availability management within the design activities is to provide:

- The specification of the availability requirements for all components of the service
- The requirements for availability measurement points (instrumentation)
- The requirements for new/enhanced systems and service management
- Assistance with the IT infrastructure design
- The specification of the reliability, maintainability and serviceability requirements for components supplied by internal support teams and external suppliers
- Validation of the final design to meet the minimum levels of availability required by the business for the IT service.

If the availability requirements cannot be met, the next task is to re-evaluate the service design and identify cost-justified design changes. Improvements in design to meet the availability

requirements can be achieved by reviewing the capability of the technology to be deployed in the proposed IT design. For example:

- The exploitation of fault-tolerant technology to mask the impact of planned or unplanned component downtime
- Duplexing, or the provision of alternative IT infrastructure components to allow one component to take over the work of another component
- Improving component reliability by enhancing testing regimes
- Improved software design and development
- Improved processes and procedures
- Systems management enhancements/ exploitation
- Improved externally supplied services, contracts or agreements
- Developing the capability of people with more training.

Hints and tips

Consider documenting the availability design requirements and considerations for new IT services and making them available to the design and implementation functions. Longer term seek to mandate these requirements and integrate within the appropriate governance mechanisms that cover the introduction of new IT services.

Part of the activity of designing for availability must ensure that all business, data and information security requirements are incorporated within the service design. The overall aim of IT security is 'balanced security in depth', with justifiable controls implemented to ensure that the information security policy is enforced and that continued IT services within secure parameters (i.e. confidentiality, integrity and availability) continue to operate. During the gathering of availability requirements for new IT services, it is important that requirements that cover IT security are defined. These requirements need to be applied within the design stage for the supporting technology. For many organizations, the approach taken to IT security is covered by an information security policy owned and maintained by information security management. In the execution of the security policy, availability management plays an important role in its operation for new IT services.

Where the business operation has a high dependency on IT service availability, and the cost of failure or loss of business reputation is considered to be unacceptable, the business may define stringent availability requirements. These factors may be sufficient for the business to justify the additional costs required to meet these more demanding levels of availability. Achieving agreed levels of availability begins with the design, procurement and/or development of good-quality products and components. However, in isolation, these are unlikely to deliver the sustained levels of availability required. Achieving a consistent and sustained level of availability will require investment in and deployment of effective service management processes, systems management tools, high-availability design and ultimately special solutions with full mirroring or redundancy.

Designing for availability is a key activity, driven by availability management, which ensures that the stated availability requirements for an IT service can be met. However, availability management should also ensure that within this design activity there is focus on the design elements required to ensure that when IT services fail, the service can be reinstated to enable normal business operations to resume as quickly as is possible. 'Designing for recovery' may at first sound negative. Clearly good availability design is about avoiding failures and delivering, where possible, a fault-tolerant IT infrastructure. However, with this focus is too much reliance placed on technology, and has as much emphasis been placed on the fault-tolerance aspects of the IT infrastructure? The reality is that failures will occur. The way the IT organization manages failure situations can have a positive effect on the perception of the business, customers and users of the IT services.

Key message

Every failure is an important 'moment of truth' – an opportunity to make or break your reputation with the business.

By providing focus on the 'designing for recovery' aspects of the overall availability, design can ensure that every failure is an opportunity to maintain and even enhance business and user satisfaction. To provide an effective 'design for recovery' and

to enable an effective recovery from IT failure, it is important to recognize that both the business and the IT organization have needs that must be satisfied. The service provider has informational needs that will help it manage the impact of failure on its business and set expectations within the business, user community and its business customers. The needs include the skills, knowledge, processes, procedures and tools required to enable the technical recovery to be completed in an optimal time.

A key aim is to prevent minor incidents from becoming major incidents by ensuring the right people are involved early enough to avoid mistakes being made and to ensure the appropriate business and technical recovery procedures are invoked at the earliest opportunity. The instigation of these activities is the responsibility of the incident management process and is typically initiated by the service desk. To ensure business needs are met during major IT service failures, and to ensure the most optimal recovery, the incident management process and service desk need to have defined procedures for assessing and managing all incidents and to execute them effectively.

Key message

Ensuring the right people are involved in a recovery early enough is not the responsibility of availability management. However, the effectiveness of the incident management process and service desk can strongly influence the overall recovery period. The use of availability management methods and techniques to further optimize IT recovery may be the stimulus for subsequent continual improvement activities to the incident management process and the service desk.

In order to remain effective, the maintainability of IT services and components should be monitored, and their impact on the 'expanded incident lifecycle' understood, managed and improved.

COMPONENT FAILURE IMPACT ANALYSIS

Component failure impact analysis (CFIA) can be used to predict and evaluate the impact on IT services arising from component failures within the technology. The output from a CFIA can be used to identify where additional resilience should be considered to prevent or minimize the impact of component failure to the business operation and users. This is particularly important during the service design stage, where it is necessary to predict and evaluate the impact on IT service availability arising from component failures within the proposed IT service design. However, the technique can also be applied to existing services and infrastructure.

CFIA is a relatively simple technique that can be used to provide this information. IBM devised CFIA in the early 1970s, with its origins based on hardware design and configuration. However, it is recommended that CFIA be used in a much wider context to reflect the full scope of the IT infrastructure and applications, i.e. hardware, network, software, applications, data centres and support staff. Additionally, the technique can also be applied to identify impact and dependencies on IT support organization skills and competencies among staff supporting the new IT service. This activity is often completed in conjunction with ITSCM and possibly capacity management.

The output from a CFIA provides vital information to ensure that the availability and recovery design criteria for the new IT service is influenced to

prevent or minimize the impact of failure to the business operation and users. CFIA achieves this by providing and indicating:

- SPOFs that can impact availability
- The impact of component failure on the business operation and users
- Component and people dependencies
- Component recovery timings
- The need to identify and document recovery options
- The need to identify and implement risk reduction measures.

The above can also provide the stimulus for input to ITSCM to consider the balance between recovery options and risk reduction measures, i.e. where the potential business impact is high there is a need to concentrate on high-availability risk reduction measures, i.e. increased resilience or standby systems.

Having determined the IT infrastructure configuration to be assessed, the first step is to create a grid with CIs on one axis and the IT

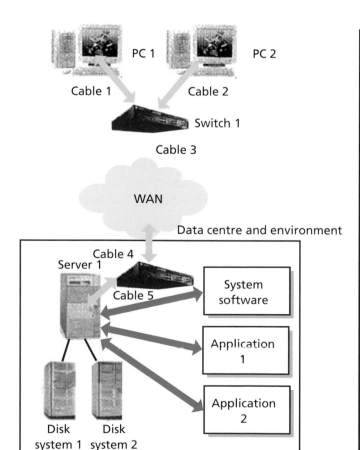

CI	Service 1	Service 2
PC 1	M	M
PC 2	M	M
Cable 1	M	M
Cable 2	M	M
Switch 1	X	X
Cable 3	X	X
WAN	X	X
Cable 4	X	X
Switch 2	X	X
Cable 5	X	X
Data centre	X	X
Server 1	X	X
Disk 1	A	A
Disk 2	A	A
System S/W	X	X
Application 1	X	
Application 2		X

Figure 4.13 Component failure impact analysis

services that have a dependency on the CI on the other, as illustrated in Figure 4.13. This information should be available from the CMS, or alternatively it can be built using documented configuration charts and SLAs.

The next step is to perform the CFIA and populate the grid as follows:

- Leave a blank when a failure of the CI does not impact the service in any way
- Insert an 'X' when the failure of the CI causes the IT service to be inoperative
- Insert an 'A' when there is an alternative CI to provide the service
- Insert an 'M' when there is an alternative CI, but the service requires manual intervention to be recovered.

Having built the grid, CIs that have a large number of Xs are critical to many services and can result in high impact should they fail. Equally, IT services having high counts of Xs are complex and vulnerable to failure. This basic approach to CFIA can provide valuable information in quickly identifying SPOFs, IT services at risk from CI failure and what alternatives are available should CIs fail. It should also be used to assess the existence and validity of recovery procedures for the selected CIs. The above example assumes common infrastructure supporting multiple IT services. The same approach can be used for a single IT service by mapping the component CIs against the VBFs and users supported by each component, thus understanding the impact of a component failure on the business and user. The approach can also be further refined and developed to include and develop 'component availability weighting' factors that can be used to assess and calculate the overall effect of the component failure on the total service availability.

To undertake an advanced CFIA requires the CFIA matrix to be expanded to provide additional fields required for the more detailed analysis. This could include fields such as:

- **Component availability weighting** A weighting factor appropriate to the impact of failure of the component on the total service availability. For example, if the failure of a switch can cause 2,000 users to lose service out of a total service user base of 10,000, then the weighting factor should be 0.2, or 20%.

- **Probability of failure** This can be based on the reliability of the component as measured by the MTBF information if available or on the current trends. This can be expressed as a low/medium/high indicator or as a numeric representation.
- **Recovery time** This is the estimated recovery time to recover the CI. This can be based on recent recovery timings, recovery information from disaster recovery testing or a scheduled test recovery.
- **Recovery procedures** This is to verify that up-to-date recovery procedures are available for the CI.
- **Device independence** Where software CIs have duplex files to provide resilience, this is to ensure that file placements have been verified as being on separate hardware disk configurations. This also applies to power supplies – it should be verified that alternative power supplies are connected correctly.
- **Dependency** This is to show any dependencies between CIs. If one CI failed, there could be an impact on other CIs – for example, if the security CI failed, the operating system might prevent backup processing.

Single point of failure analysis

A SPOF is any configuration item that can cause an incident when it fails, and for which a countermeasure has not been implemented. A single point of failure may be a person or a step in a process or activity, as well as a component of the IT infrastructure. It is important that no unrecognized SPOFs exist within the IT infrastructure design or the actual technology, and that they are avoided wherever possible.

The use of SPOF analysis or CFIA as techniques to identify SPOFs is recommended. SPOF and CFIA analysis exercises should be conducted on a regular basis, and wherever SPOFs are identified, CFIA can be used to identify the potential business, customer or user impact and help determine what alternatives can or should be considered to cater for this weakness in the design or the actual infrastructure. Countermeasures should then be implemented wherever they are cost-justifiable. The impact and disruption caused by the potential failure of the SPOF should be used to cost-justify its implementation.

FAULT TREE ANALYSIS

Fault tree analysis (FTA) is a technique that can be used to determine a chain of events that has caused an incident or may cause an incident in the future. FTA, in conjunction with calculation methods, can offer detailed models of availability. This can be used to assess the availability improvement that can be achieved by individual technology component design options. Using FTA:

- Information can be provided that can be used for availability calculations
- Operations can be performed on the resulting fault tree; these operations correspond with design options
- The desired level of detail in the analysis can be chosen.

FTA makes a representation of a chain of events using Boolean notation. Figure 4.14 gives an example of a fault tree.

Essentially FTA distinguishes the following events:

- **Basic events** These are terminal points for the fault tree – for example, power failure, operator error. Basic events are not investigated in great depth. If basic events are investigated in further depth, they automatically become resulting events.

- **Resulting events** These are intermediate nodes in the fault tree, resulting from a combination of events. The highest point in the fault tree is usually a failure of the IT service.
- **Conditional events** These are events that only occur under certain conditions – for example, failure of the air-conditioning equipment only affects the IT service if equipment temperature exceeds the serviceable values.
- **Trigger events** These are events that trigger other events – for example, power failure detection equipment can trigger automatic shutdown of IT services.

These events can be combined using logic operators, i.e.:

- **AND-gate** The resulting event only occurs when all input events occur simultaneously
- **OR-gate** The resulting event occurs when one or more of the input events occurs
- **Exclusive OR-gate** The resulting event occurs when one and only one of the input events occurs
- **Inhibit gate** The resulting event only occurs when the input condition is not met.

Based on these definitions, Figure 4.14 depicts an analysis in which there is one 'AND' gate on the lower right side. Both the primary and fail-over lines must be down for the network to be down. There is also an 'OR' gate on the left of the diagram; if any one of the three listed events occurs, the system will be down. Finally, the 'Inhibit' gate shows that only if the failure occurs during service hours will the service itself be considered to be down.

This is the basic FTA technique. This technique can also be refined, but complex FTA and the mathematical evaluation of fault trees are beyond the scope of this publication.

MODELLING

To assess if new components within a design can match the stated requirements, it is important that the testing regime instigated ensures that the availability expected can be delivered. Simulation, modelling or load testing tools to generate the expected user demand for the new IT service should be seriously considered to ensure components continue to operate under anticipated volume and stress conditions.

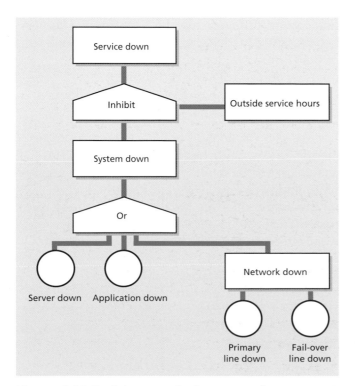

Figure 4.14 Fault tree analysis – example

Modelling tools are also required to forecast availability and to assess the impact of changes to the IT infrastructure. Inputs to the modelling process include descriptive data of the component reliability, maintainability and serviceability. A spreadsheet package to perform calculations is usually sufficient. If more detailed and accurate data is required, a more complex modelling tool may need to be developed or acquired. The lack of readily available availability modelling tools in the marketplace may require such a tool to be developed and maintained 'in-house', but this is a very expensive and time-consuming activity that should only be considered where the investment can be justified. Unless there is a clearly perceived benefit from such a development and the ongoing maintenance costs, the use of existing tools and spreadsheets should be sufficient. However, some system management tools do provide modelling capability and can provide useful information on trending and forecasting availability needs.

Risk assessment and management

To assess the vulnerability of failure within the configuration and capability of the IT service and support organization it is recommended that existing or proposed IT infrastructure, service configurations, service design and supporting organization (internal and external suppliers) are subject to formal risk assessment and management exercises. Risk assessment and management is a technique that can be used to identify and quantify risks and justifiable countermeasures that can be implemented to protect the availability of IT systems.

The identification of risks and the provision of justified countermeasures to reduce or eliminate the threats posed by such risks can play an important role in achieving the required levels of availability for a new or enhanced IT service. Risk assessment should be undertaken during the design stage for the IT technology and service to identify:

- Risks that may incur unavailability for IT components within the technology and service design
- Risks that may incur confidentiality and/or integrity exposures within the IT technology and service design.

Most risk assessment and management methodologies involve the use of a formal approach to the assessment of risk and the subsequent mitigation of risk with the implementation of cost-justifiable countermeasures (Figure 4.15). Appendix M describes several broadly known and used approaches to the assessment and management of risk.

As illustrated in Figure 4.15, risk assessment involves the identification and assessment of the level (measure) of the risks calculated from the assessed values of assets and the assessed levels of threats to, and vulnerabilities of, those assets. Risk is also determined to a certain extent by its acceptance. Some organizations and businesses may be more willing to accept risk whereas others are not.

Risk management involves the identification, selection and adoption of countermeasures justified by the identified risks to assets in terms of

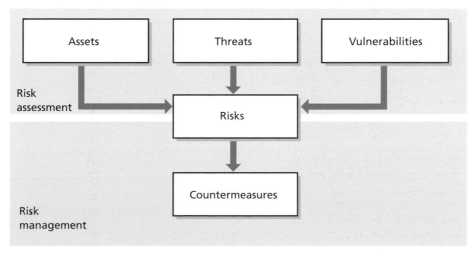

Figure 4.15 Risk assessment and management

their potential impact on services if failure occurs, and the reduction of those risks to an acceptable level. Risk management is an activity that is associated with many other activities, especially the IT service continuity management and information security management processes and the service transition lifecycle stage. All of these risk assessment exercises should be coordinated rather than being separate activities.

This approach, when applied via a formal method, ensures coverage is complete, together with sufficient confidence that:

- All possible risks and countermeasures have been identified
- All vulnerabilities have been identified and their levels accurately assessed
- All threats have been identified and their levels accurately assessed
- All results are consistent across the broad spectrum of the technology reviewed
- All expenditure on selected countermeasures can be justified.

Formal risk assessment and management methods are now an important element in the overall design and provision of IT services. The assessment of risk is often based on the probability and potential impact of an event occurring. Countermeasures are implemented wherever they are cost-justifiable, to reduce the impact of an event, or the probability of an event occurring, or both.

It should be noted that the risk assessment and management described here aligns in its essentials with an asset-focused approach required in ISO/IEC 27001. Management of risk (M_o_R) provides an alternative generic framework for the management of risk across all parts of an organization – strategic, programme, project and operational (see Appendix N for more details).

Implementing cost-justifiable countermeasures

The risks identified to service and component availability should be addressed through appropriate risk reduction measures and the development of effective recovery mechanisms. These countermeasures may be implemented as part of the overall design of the new or changed service, as well as through the implementation

of best practice in the areas of maintenance and continual review and improvement.

PLANNED AND PREVENTIVE MAINTENANCE

All IT components should be subject to a planned maintenance strategy. This can be considered part of the risk reduction strategy for services and components. The frequency and levels of maintenance required varies from component to component, taking into account the technologies involved, criticality and the potential business benefits that may be introduced. Planned maintenance activities enable the IT support organization to provide:

- Preventive maintenance to avoid failures
- Planned software or hardware upgrades to provide new functionality or additional capacity
- Business requested changes to the business applications
- Implementation of new technology and functionality for exploitation by the business.

The requirement for planned downtime clearly influences the level of availability that can be delivered for an IT service, particularly those that have stringent availability requirements. In determining the availability requirements for a new or enhanced IT service, the amount of downtime and the resultant loss of income required for planned maintenance may not be acceptable to the business. This is becoming a growing issue in the area of 24 × 7 service operation. In these instances, it is essential that continuous operation is a core design feature to enable maintenance activity to be performed without impacting the availability of IT services.

Where the required service hours for IT services are less than 24 hours per day and/or seven days per week, it is likely that the majority of planned maintenance can be accommodated without impacting IT service availability. However, where the business needs IT services available on a 24-hour and seven-day basis, availability management needs to determine the most effective approach in balancing the requirements for planned maintenance against the loss of service to the business. Unless mechanisms exist to allow continuous operation, scheduled downtime for planned maintenance is essential if high levels of availability are to be achieved and sustained. For all IT services, there should logically be a 'low-impact' period for the implementation of maintenance. Once the requirements for managing scheduled maintenance have been defined and agreed, these should be documented as a minimum in:

- SLAs
- OLAs
- Underpinning contracts
- Change management schedules
- Release and deployment management schedules.

> **Hints and tips**
>
> Availability management should ensure that building in preventive maintenance is one of the prime design considerations for a '24 × 7' IT service.

The most appropriate time to schedule planned downtime is clearly when the impact on the business and its customers is least. This information should be provided initially by the business when determining the availability requirements. For an existing IT service, or once the new service has been established, monitoring of business and customer transactions helps establish the hours when IT service usage is at its lowest. This should determine the most appropriate time for the component(s) to be removed for planned maintenance activity.

To accommodate the individual component requirements for planned downtime while balancing the IT service availability requirements of the business provides an opportunity to consider scheduling planned maintenance to multiple components concurrently. The benefit of this approach is that the number of service disruptions required to meet the maintenance requirements is reduced. While this approach has benefits, there are potential risks that need to be assessed. For example:

- The capability of the IT support organization to coordinate the concurrent implementation of a high number of changes
- The ability to perform effective problem determination where the IT service is impacted after the completion of multiple changes
- The impact of change dependency across multiple components where back-out of a failed change requires multiple changes to be removed.

The effective management of planned downtime is an important contribution in meeting the required levels of availability for an IT service. Where planned downtime is required on a cyclic basis to an IT component(s), the time that the component is unavailable to enable the planned maintenance activity to be undertaken should be defined and agreed with the internal or external supplier. This becomes a stated objective that can be formalized, measured and reported. All planned maintenance should be scheduled, managed and controlled to ensure that the individual objectives are achieved, time slots are not exceeded, and that activities are coordinated with all other schedules of activity to minimize clashes and conflict (e.g. change and release schedules, testing schedules). In addition they provide an early warning during the maintenance activity of the time allocated to the planned outage duration being breached. This can enable an early decision to be made on whether the activity is allowed to complete with the potential to further impact service or to abort the activity and instigate the back-out or other remediation plan. Planned downtime and performance against the stated objectives for each component should be recorded and used in service reporting.

Reviewing all new and changed services and testing all availability and resilience mechanisms

During the service transition stage all the elements designed to contribute to service and component availability need to be reviewed and tested. Availability review and testing procedures and policies should be embedded into overall transition methods, processes and practices to ensure that the promised levels of availability will be delivered.

In addition to the reviews and tests that occur during service transition, regularly scheduled reviews and tests are required for the most comprehensive approach.

Availability testing schedule

A key deliverable from the availability management process is the 'availability testing schedule'. This is a schedule for the regular testing of all availability mechanisms. Some availability mechanisms, such as 'load balancing', 'mirroring' and 'grid computing', are used in the provision of normal service on a day-by-day basis; others are used on a fail-over or manual reconfiguration basis. It is essential, therefore, that all availability mechanisms are tested in a regular and scheduled manner to ensure that when they are actually needed for real they work. This schedule needs to be maintained and widely circulated so that all areas are aware of its content and so that all other proposed activities can be synchronized with its content, such as:

■ The change schedule
■ Release plans and the release schedule
■ All transition plans, projects and programmes
■ Planned and preventive maintenance schedules
■ The schedule for testing IT service continuity plans and recovery mechanisms
■ Business plans and schedules
■ Capacity plans.

Continual review and improvement

Changing business needs and customer demand may require the levels of availability provided for an IT service to be reviewed. Such reviews should form part of the regular service reviews with the business undertaken by SLM. Other inputs should also be considered on a regular basis from ITSCM, particularly from the updated BIA and risk assessment exercises. The criticality of services will often change and it is important that the design and the technology supporting such services is regularly reviewed and improved by availability management to ensure that the change of importance in the service is reflected within a revised design and supporting technology and documentation. Where the required levels of availability are already being delivered, it may take considerable effort and incur significant cost to achieve a small incremental improvement within the level of availability.

A key activity for availability management is to look continually at opportunities to optimize the availability of the IT infrastructure in conjunction with overall CSI activities. The benefits of this regular review approach are that, sometimes, enhanced levels of availability may be achievable, but with much lower costs. The optimization approach is a sensible first step to delivering better value for money. A number of availability management techniques can be applied to identify optimization opportunities. It is recommended that the scope should not be restricted to the technology, but also include a review of both the business process and other end-to-end business-owned responsibilities. To help achieve these aims, availability management needs to be recognized as a leading influence over the IT service provider organization to ensure continued focus on availability and stability of the technology.

Availability management can provide the IT support organization with a real business and user perspective on how deficiencies within the technology and the underpinning process and procedure impact on the business operation and ultimately their customers. The use of business-driven metrics can demonstrate this impact in real terms and, importantly, also help quantify the benefits of improvement opportunities. Availability management can play an important role in helping the IT service provider organization recognize where it can add value by exploiting its technical skills and competencies in an availability context. The continual improvement technique can be used by availability management to harness this technical capability. This can be used with either small groups of technical staff or a wider group within a workshop or SFA environment.

The impetus to improve availability comes from one or more of the following:

■ The inability of existing or new IT services to meet SLA targets on a consistent basis
■ Period(s) of IT service instability resulting in unacceptable levels of availability
■ Availability measurement trends indicating a gradual deterioration in availability
■ Unacceptable IT service recovery and restoration times
■ Requests from the business to increase the level of availability provided

- Increasing impact on the business and its customers of IT service failures as a result of growth and/or increased business priorities or functionality
- A request from SLM to improve availability as part of an overall SIP
- Availability management monitoring and trend analysis.

Availability management should take a proactive role in identifying and progressing cost-justified availability improvement opportunities within the availability plan. The ability to do this places reliance on having appropriate and meaningful availability measurement and reporting. To ensure availability improvements deliver benefits to the business and users, it is important that measurement and reporting reflect not just IT component availability but also availability from a business operation and user perspective – that is, end-to-end service availability.

Where the business has a requirement to improve availability, the process and techniques to reassess the technology and IT service provider organization capability to meet these enhanced requirements should be followed. An output of this activity is enhanced availability and recovery design criteria. To satisfy the business requirement for increased levels of availability, additional financial investment may be required to enhance the underpinning technology and/or extend the services provided by the IT service provider organization. It is important that any additional investment to improve the levels of availability delivered can be cost-justified. Determining the cost of unavailability as a result of IT failure(s) can help support any financial investment decision in improving availability.

CONTRIBUTE TO PRODUCTION OF THE PROJECTED SERVICE OUTAGE DOCUMENT

Availability management should work closely with change management, the process which produces and maintains the projected service outage (PSO) document. This document describes any variations from the service availability agreed within SLAs. This should be produced based on input from:

- The change schedule
- The release schedules
- Planned and preventive maintenance schedules
- Availability testing schedules

- ITSCM and BCM testing schedules.

The PSO contains details of all scheduled and planned service downtime within the agreed service hours for all services. These documents should be agreed with all the appropriate areas and representatives of both the business and IT. Once the PSO has been agreed, the service desk should ensure that it is communicated to all relevant parties so that everyone is made aware of any additional, planned service downtime.

4.4.6 Triggers, inputs, outputs and interfaces

4.4.6.1 Triggers

Many events may trigger availability management activity. These include:

- New or changed business needs or new or changed services
- New or changed targets within agreements, such as SLRs, SLAs, OLAs or contracts
- Service or component breaches, availability events and alerts, including threshold events, exception reports
- Periodic activities such as reviewing, revising or reporting
- Review of availability management forecasts, reports and plans
- Review and revision of business and IT plans and strategies
- Review and revision of designs and strategies
- Recognition or notification of a change of risk or impact of a business process or VBF, an IT service or component
- Request from SLM for assistance with availability targets and explanation of achievements.

4.4.6.2 Inputs

A number of sources of information are relevant to the availability management process. Some of these are as follows:

- **Business information** From the organization's business strategy, plans and financial plans, and information on their current and future requirements, including the availability requirements for new or enhanced IT services
- **Business impact information** From BIAs and assessment of VBFs underpinned by IT services

- **Reports and registers** Previous risk assessment reports and a risk register
- **Service information** From the service portfolio and the service catalogue
- **Service information** From the SLM process, with details of the services from the service portfolio and the service catalogue, service level targets within SLAs and SLRs, and possibly from the monitoring of SLAs, service reviews and breaches of the SLAs
- **Financial information** From financial management for IT services, the cost of service provision, the cost of resources and components
- **Change and release information** From the change management process with a change schedule, the release schedule from release and deployment management and a need to assess all changes for their impact on service availability
- **Service asset and configuration management** Containing information on the relationships between the business, the services, the supporting services and the technology
- **Service targets** From SLAs, SLRs, OLAs and contracts
- **Component information** On the availability, reliability and maintainability requirements for the technology components that underpin IT service(s)
- **Technology information** From the CMS on the topology and the relationships between the components and the assessment of the capabilities of new technology
- **Past performance** From previous measurements, achievements and reports and the availability management information system (AMIS)
- **Unavailability and failure information** From incidents and problems
- **Planning information** From other processes such as the capacity plan from capacity management.

4.4.6.3 Outputs

The outputs produced by availability management should include:

- The availability MIS (AMIS)
- The availability plan for the proactive improvement of IT services and technology
- Availability and recovery design criteria and proposed service targets for new or changed services

- Service availability, reliability and maintainability reports of achievements against targets, including input for all service reports
- Component availability, reliability and maintainability reports of achievements against targets
- Revised risk assessment reviews and reports and an updated risk register
- Monitoring, management and reporting requirements for IT services and components to ensure that deviations in availability, reliability and maintainability are detected, actioned, recorded and reported
- An availability management test schedule for testing all availability, resilience and recovery mechanisms
- The planned and preventive maintenance schedules
- Contributions for the PSO to be created by change in collaboration with release and deployment management
- Details of the proactive availability techniques and measures that will be deployed to provide additional resilience to prevent or minimize the impact of component failures on the IT service availability
- Improvement actions for inclusion within the SIP.

4.4.6.4 Interfaces

The key interfaces that availability management has with other processes are:

- **SLM** This process relies on availability management to determine and validate availability targets and to investigate and resolve service and component breaches.
- **Incident and problem management** These are assisted by availability management in the resolution and subsequent justification and correction of availability incidents and problems.
- **Capacity management** This provides appropriate capacity to support resilience and overall service availability. The process also uses information from demand management about patterns of business activity and user profiles to understand business demand for IT services and provides this information to availability management for business-aligned availability planning.

- **Change management** This leads to the creation of the PSO with contributions from availability management. When changes are proposed to a service, availability must assess the change for availability-related issues including any potential impact on achievement of availability service levels.
- **IT service continuity management (ITSCM)** Availability management works collaboratively with this process on the assessment of business impact and risk and the provision of resilience, fail-over and recovery mechanisms. Availability focuses on normal business operation and ITSCM focuses on the extraordinary interruption of service.
- **Information security management (ISM)** If the data becomes unavailable, the service becomes unavailable. ISM defines the security measures and policies that must be included in the service design for availability and design for recovery.
- **Access management** Availability management provides the methods for appropriately granting and revoking access to services as needed.

4.4.7 Information management

The availability management process should maintain an AMIS that contains all of the measurements and information required to complete the availability management process and provide the appropriate information to the business on the level of IT service provided. This information, covering services, components and supporting services, provides the basis for regular, ad hoc and exception availability reporting and the identification of trends within the data for the instigation of improvement activities. These activities and the information contained within the AMIS provide the basis for developing the content of the availability plan.

In order to provide structure and focus to a wide range of initiatives that may need to be undertaken to improve availability, an availability plan should be formulated and maintained. The availability plan should have aims, objectives and deliverables and should consider the wider issues of people, processes, tools and techniques as well as having a technology focus. In the initial stages it may be aligned with an implementation plan for availability management, but the two are different and should not be confused. As the availability

management process matures, the plan should evolve to cover the following:

- Actual levels of availability versus agreed levels of availability for key IT services. Availability measurements should always be business- and customer-focused and report availability as experienced by the business and users.
- Activities being progressed to address shortfalls in availability for existing IT services. Where investment decisions are required, options with associated costs and benefits should be included.
- Details of changing availability requirements for existing IT services. The plan should document the options available to meet these changed requirements. Where investment decisions are required, the associated costs of each option should be included.
- Details of the availability requirements for forthcoming new IT services. The plan should document the options available to meet these new requirements. Where investment decisions are required, the associated costs of each option should be included.
- A forward-looking schedule for the planned SFA assignments.
- Regular reviews of SFA assignments should be completed to ensure that the availability of technology is being proactively improved in conjunction with the SIP.
- A technology futures section to provide an indication of the potential benefits and exploitation opportunities that exist for planned technology upgrades. Anticipated availability benefits should be detailed, where possible based on business-focused measures, in conjunction with capacity management. The effort required to realize these benefits where possible should also be quantified.

During the production of the availability plan, it is recommended that liaison with all functional, technical and process areas is undertaken. The availability plan should cover a period of one to two years, with a more detailed view and information for the first six months. The plan should be reviewed regularly, with minor revisions every quarter and major revisions every half year. Where the technology is only subject to a low level of change, this may be extended as appropriate.

It is recommended that the availability plan is considered complementary to the capacity plan and financial plan, and that publication is aligned with the capacity and business budgeting cycle. If a demand is foreseen for high levels of availability that cannot be met due to the constraints of the existing IT infrastructure or budget, then exception reports may be required for the attention of both senior IT and business management.

In order to facilitate the production of the availability plan, availability management may wish to consider having its own database repository. The AMIS can be utilized to record and store selected data and information required to support key activities such as report generation, statistical analysis and availability forecasting and planning. The AMIS should be the main repository for the recording of IT availability metrics, measurements, targets and documents, including the availability plan, availability measurements, achievement reports, SFA assignment reports, design criteria, action plans and testing schedules.

Hints and tips

Be pragmatic, define the initial tool requirements and identify what is already deployed that can be used and shared to get started as quickly as possible. Where basic tools are not already available, work with the other IT service and systems management processes to identify common requirements with the aim of selecting shared tools and minimizing costs. The AMIS should address the specific reporting needs of availability management not currently provided by existing repositories and integrate with them and their contents.

4.4.8 Critical success factors and key performance indicators

The following list includes some sample CSFs for availability management. Each organization should identify appropriate CSFs based on its objectives for the process. Each sample CSF is followed by a small number of typical KPIs that support the CSF. These KPIs should not be adopted without careful consideration. Each organization should develop KPIs that are appropriate for its level of maturity, its CSFs and its particular circumstances. Achievement against KPIs should be monitored and used to identify opportunities for improvement,

which should be logged in the CSI register for evaluation and possible implementation.

- **CSF** Manage availability and reliability of IT service
  - **KPI** Percentage reduction in the unavailability of services and components
  - **KPI** Percentage increase in the reliability of services and components
  - **KPI** Effective review and follow-up of all SLA, OLA and underpinning contract breaches relating to availability and reliability
  - **KPI** Percentage improvement in overall end-to-end availability of service
  - **KPI** Percentage reduction in the number and impact of service breaks
  - **KPI** Improvement in the MTBF
  - **KPI** Improvement in the MTBSI
  - **KPI** Reduction in the MTRS
- **CSF** Satisfy business needs for access to IT services
  - **KPI** Percentage reduction in the unavailability of services
  - **KPI** Percentage reduction of the cost of business overtime due to unavailable IT
  - **KPI** Percentage reduction in critical time failures – for example, specific business peak and priority availability needs are planned for
  - **KPI** Percentage improvement in business and users satisfied with service (by customer satisfaction survey results)
- **CSF** Availability of IT infrastructure and applications, as documented in SLAs, provided at optimum costs:
  - **KPI** Percentage reduction in the cost of unavailability
  - **KPI** Percentage improvement in the service delivery costs
  - **KPI** Timely completion of regular risk assessment and system review
  - **KPI** Timely completion of regular cost-benefit analysis established for infrastructure CFIA
  - **KPI** Percentage reduction in failures of third-party performance on MTRS/MTBF against contract targets
  - **KPI** Reduced time taken to complete (or update) a risk assessment

- **KPI** Reduced time taken to review system resilience
- **KPI** Reduced time taken to complete an availability plan
- **KPI** Timely production of management reports
- **KPI** Percentage reduction in the incidence of operational reviews uncovering security and reliability exposures in application designs.

4.4.9 Challenges and risks

4.4.9.1 Challenges

Availability management faces many challenges, but the main challenge is to actually meet and manage the expectations of the customers, the business and senior management. These expectations are frequently that services will always be available not just during their agreed service hours, but that all services will be available on a 24-hour, 365-day basis. When they are not, it is assumed that they will be recovered within minutes. This is only the case when the appropriate level of investment and design has been applied to the service, and this should only be made where the business impact justifies that level of investment. However, the message needs to be publicized to all customers and areas of the business, so that when services do fail they have the right level of expectation on their recovery. It also means that availability management must have access to the right level of quality information on the current business need for IT services and its plans for the future. This is another challenge faced by many availability management processes.

Another challenge facing availability management is the integration of all of the availability data into an integrated set of information (AMIS) that can be analysed in a consistent manner to provide details on the availability of all services and components. This is particularly challenging when the information from the different technologies is often provided by different tools in differing formats.

Yet another challenge facing availability management is convincing the business and senior management of the investment needed in proactive availability measures. Investment is always recognized once failures have occurred, but by then it is really too late. Persuading businesses and customers to invest in resilience to avoid the possibility of failures that may happen is a difficult challenge. Availability management should work closely with ITSCM, information security management and capacity management in producing the justifications necessary to secure the appropriate investment.

4.4.9.2 Risks

Some of the major risks associated with availability management include:

- A lack of commitment from the business to the availability management process
- A lack of commitment from the business and a lack of appropriate information on future plans and strategies
- A lack of senior management commitment or a lack of resources and/or budget to the availability management process
- Labour-intensive reporting processes
- The processes focus too much on the technology and not enough on the services and the needs of the business
- The AMIS is maintained in isolation and is not shared or consistent with other process areas, especially ITSCM, information security management and capacity management. This investment is particularly important when considering the necessary service and component backup and recovery tools, technology and processes to meet the agreed needs.

4.5 CAPACITY MANAGEMENT

Capacity management is a process that extends across the service lifecycle. A key success factor in managing capacity is ensuring it is considered during the design stage. It is for this reason that the capacity management process is included here. Capacity management is supported initially in service strategy where the decisions and analysis of business requirements and customer outcomes influence the development of patterns of business activity, lines of service (LOS) and service options. This provides the predictive and ongoing capacity indicators needed to align capacity to demand. Capacity management provides a point of focus and management for all capacity- and performance-related issues, relating to both services and resources.

Like availability, capacity is an important part of the warranty of a service. If a service does not deliver the levels of capacity and performance required, then the business will not experience the value that has been promised. Without capacity and performance the utility of the service cannot be accessed.

4.5.1 Purpose and objectives

The purpose of the capacity management process is to ensure that the capacity of IT services and the IT infrastructure meets the agreed capacity- and performance-related requirements in a cost-effective and timely manner. Capacity management is concerned with meeting both the current and future capacity and performance needs of the business.

The objectives of capacity management are to:

- Produce and maintain an appropriate and up-to-date capacity plan, which reflects the current and future needs of the business
- Provide advice and guidance to all other areas of the business and IT on all capacity- and performance-related issues
- Ensure that service performance achievements meet all of their agreed targets by managing the performance and capacity of both services and resources
- Assist with the diagnosis and resolution of performance- and capacity-related incidents and problems
- Assess the impact of all changes on the capacity plan, and the performance and capacity of all services and resources
- Ensure that proactive measures to improve the performance of services are implemented wherever it is cost-justifiable to do so.

4.5.2 Scope

The capacity management process should be the focal point for all IT performance and capacity issues. Capacity management considers all resources required to deliver the IT service, and plans for short-, medium- and long-term business requirements.

The process should encompass all areas of technology, both hardware and software, for all IT technology components and environments. Capacity management should also consider space planning and environmental systems

capacity. Capacity management could consider human resource capacity where a lack of human resources could result in a breach of SLA or OLA targets, a delay in the end-to-end performance or service response time, or an inability to meet future commitments and plans (e.g. overnight data backups not completed in time because no operators were present to load required media).

In general, human resource management is a line management responsibility, although the staffing of a service desk should use identical capacity management techniques. The scheduling of human resources, staffing levels, skill levels and capability levels should therefore be included within the scope of capacity management.

The capacity management process should include:

- Monitoring patterns of business activity through performance, utilization and throughput of IT services and the supporting infrastructure, environmental, data and applications components and the production of regular and ad hoc reports on service and component capacity and performance
- Undertaking tuning activities to make the most efficient use of existing IT resources
- Understanding the agreed current and future demands being made by the customer for IT resources, and producing forecasts for future requirements
- Influencing demand in conjunction with the financial management for IT services and demand management processes
- Producing a capacity plan that enables the service provider to continue to provide services of the quality defined in SLAs and that covers a sufficient planning timeframe to meet future service levels required as defined in the service portfolio and SLRs
- Assisting with the identification and resolution of any incidents and problems associated with service or component capacity or performance
- The proactive improvement of service or component performance, wherever it is cost-justifiable and meets the needs of the business.

Capacity management also includes understanding the potential for the delivery of new services. New technology needs to be understood and, if appropriate, used to innovate and deliver the services required by the customer. Capacity management should recognize that the rate of technological change will probably increase and that new technology should be harnessed to ensure that the IT services continue to satisfy changing business expectations. A direct link to the service strategy and service portfolio is needed to ensure that emerging technologies are considered in future service planning.

Capacity management has a close, two-way relationship with the service strategy and planning processes within an organization. On a regular basis, the long-term strategy of an organization is encapsulated in an update of the business plans. The service strategy will reflect the business plans and strategy, which are developed from the organization's understanding of the external factors such as the competitive marketplace, economic outlook and legislation, and its internal capability in terms of manpower, delivery capability etc. Often a shorter-term tactical plan or business change plan is developed to implement the changes necessary in the short to medium term to progress the overall business plan and service strategy. Capacity management needs to understand the short-, medium- and long-term plans of the business and IT while providing information on the latest ideas, trends and technologies being developed by the suppliers of computing hardware and software.

The organization's business plans drive the specific IT service strategy, the contents of which capacity management needs to be familiar with, and to which capacity management needs to have had significant and ongoing input. The right level of capacity at the right time is critical. Service strategy plans will be helpful to capacity planning by identifying the timing for acquiring and implementing new technologies, hardware and software.

Capacity management is responsible for ensuring that IT resources are planned and scheduled to provide a consistent level of service that is matched to the current and future needs of the business, as agreed and documented within SLAs and OLAs. In conjunction with the business and its plans, capacity management provides a capacity plan that outlines the IT resources and funding needed to support the business plan, together with a cost justification of that expenditure.

4.5.3 Value to the business

A well-executed capacity management process will benefit the business by:

- Improving the performance and availability of IT services the business needs by helping to reduce capacity- and performance-related incidents and problems
- Ensuring required capacity and performance are provided in the most cost-effective manner
- Contributing to improved customer satisfaction and user productivity by ensuring that all capacity- and performance- related service levels are met
- Supporting the efficient and effective design and transition of new or changed services through proactive capacity management activities
- Improving the reliability of capacity-related budgeting through the use of a forward-looking capacity plan based on a sound understanding of business needs and plans
- Improving the ability of the business to follow an environmentally responsible strategy by using green technologies and techniques in capacity management.

4.5.4 Policies, principles and basic concepts

Capacity management ensures that the capacity and performance of the IT services and systems match the evolving agreed demands of the business in the most cost-effective and timely manner. Capacity management is essentially a balancing act:

- **Balancing costs against resources needed** The need to ensure that processing capacity that is purchased is cost-justifiable in terms of business need, and the need to make the most efficient use of those resources.
- **Balancing supply against demand** The need to ensure that the available supply of IT processing power matches the demands made on it by the business, both now and in the future. It may also be necessary to manage or influence the demand for a particular resource.

4.5.4.1 Policies

The driving force for capacity management should be the business requirements of the organization and to plan the resources needed to provide service levels in line with SLAs and OLAs. Policies should be established defining the required points of interface between the capacity management and SLM processes to ensure this connection to business requirements is appropriately established and maintained. Capacity management needs to understand the total IT and business environments, including:

■ The current business operation and its requirements, through the patterns of business activity (as provided by the demand management process)
■ The future business plans and requirements via the service portfolio
■ The service targets and the current IT service operation though SLAs and standard operating procedures
■ All areas of IT technology and its capacity and performance, including infrastructure, data, environment and applications.

Understanding all of this will enable capacity management to ensure that all the current and future capacity and performance aspects of services are provided cost-effectively.

It should be the service provider's policy that capacity management processes and planning must be involved in all stages of the service lifecycle from strategy and design, through transition and operation to improvement. From a strategic perspective, the service portfolio contains the IT resources and capabilities. The advent of service-oriented architecture, virtualization and the use of value networks in IT service provision are important factors in the management of capacity. The appropriate capacity and performance should be designed into services and components from the initial design stages. This will ensure not only that the performance of any new or changed service meets its expected targets, but also that all existing services continue to meet all of their targets. This is the basis of stable service provision.

4.5.4.2 Planning and managing complexity

Managing the capacity of large distributed IT infrastructures is a complex and demanding task, especially when the IT capacity and the financial investment required is ever-increasing. Therefore it makes even more sense to plan for growth. While the cost of the upgrade to an individual component in a distributed environment is usually less than the upgrade to a component in

a mainframe environment, there are often many more components in the distributed environment that need to be upgraded. Also, there could now be economies of scale because the cost per individual component could be reduced when many components need to be purchased. Capacity management should have input to the service portfolio and procurement process to ensure that the best deals with suppliers are negotiated.

Capacity management provides the necessary information on current and planned resource utilization of individual components to enable organizations to decide, with confidence:

■ Which components to upgrade (i.e. more memory, faster storage devices, faster processors, greater bandwidth)
■ When to upgrade – ideally this is not too early, resulting in expensive over-capacity, nor too late, failing to take advantage of advances in new technology, resulting in bottle-necks, inconsistent performance and, ultimately, customer dissatisfaction and lost business opportunities
■ How much the upgrade will cost – the forecasting and planning elements of capacity management feed into budgetary lifecycles, ensuring planned investment.

Many of the other processes are less effective if there is no input to them from the capacity management process. For example:

■ Can the change management process properly assess the effect of any change on the available capacity?
■ When a new service is implemented, can the SLM process be assured that the SLRs of the new service are achievable, and that the SLAs of existing services will not be affected?
■ Can the problem management process properly diagnose the underlying cause of incidents caused by poor performance?
■ Can the IT service continuity process accurately determine the capacity requirements of the key business processes?

Capacity management is one of the forward-looking processes that, when properly carried out, can forecast business events and impacts often before they happen. Good capacity management ensures that there are no surprises with regard to service and component design and performance.

The overall capacity management process is continually trying to match IT resources and capacity cost-effectively to the ever-changing needs and requirements of the business. This requires the tuning (or 'optimization') of the current resources and the effective estimation and planning of the future resources.

One of the key activities of capacity management is to produce a plan that documents the current levels of resource utilization and service performance and, after consideration of the service strategy and plans, forecasts the future requirements for new IT resources to support the IT services that underpin the business activities. The plan should indicate clearly any assumptions made. It should also include any recommendations quantified in terms of resource required, cost, benefits, impact etc.

The service provider should establish pre-defined intervals for the production and maintenance of a capacity plan. It is, essentially, an investment plan and should therefore be published annually, in line with the business or budget lifecycle, and completed before the start of negotiations on future budgets. A quarterly reissue of the updated plan may be necessary to take into account changes in service plans, to report on the accuracy of forecasts and to make or refine recommendations. This takes extra effort but, if it is regularly updated, the capacity plan is more likely to be accurate and to reflect the changing business need.

The typical contents of a capacity plan are described in Appendix J.

4.5.4.3 Capacity management sub-processes

Capacity management is an extremely technical, complex and demanding process, and in order to achieve results, it requires three supporting sub-processes: business capacity management, service capacity management and component capacity management. These sub-processes are described briefly in this section and in more detail in section 4.5.5.

Business capacity management

The business capacity management sub-process translates business needs and plans into requirements for service and IT infrastructure, ensuring that the future business requirements for IT services are quantified, designed, planned and implemented in a timely fashion. This can be achieved by using the existing data on the current resource utilization by the various services and resources to trend, forecast, model or predict future requirements. These future requirements come from the service strategy and service portfolio detailing new processes and service requirements, changes, improvements, and also the growth in the existing services.

Service capacity management

The service capacity management sub-process focuses on the management, control and prediction of the end-to-end performance and capacity of the live, operational IT services usage and workloads. It ensures that the performance of all services, as detailed in service targets within SLAs and SLRs, is monitored and measured, and that the collected data is recorded, analysed and reported. Wherever necessary, proactive and reactive action should be instigated, to ensure that the performance of all services meets their agreed business targets. This is performed by staff with knowledge of all the areas of technology used in the delivery of end-to-end service, and often involves seeking advice from the specialists involved in component capacity management. Wherever possible, automated thresholds should be used to manage all operational services, to ensure that situations where service targets are breached or threatened are rapidly identified and cost-effective actions to reduce or avoid their potential impact are implemented.

Component capacity management

The component capacity management sub-process focuses on the management, control and prediction of the performance, utilization and capacity of individual IT technology components. It ensures that all components within the IT infrastructure that have finite resource are monitored and measured, and that the collected data is recorded, analysed and reported. Again, wherever possible, automated thresholds should be implemented to manage all components, to ensure that situations where service targets are breached or threatened by component usage or performance are rapidly identified, and cost-effective actions to reduce or avoid their potential impact are implemented.

There are many similar activities that are performed by each of the above sub-processes,

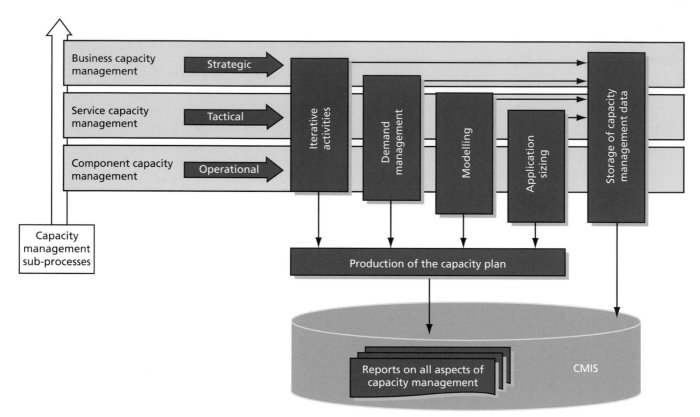

Figure 4.16 Capacity management sub-processes

but each sub-process has a very different focus. Business capacity management is focused on the current and future business requirements, while service capacity management is focused on the delivery of the existing services that support the business, and component capacity management is focused on the IT infrastructure that underpins service provision. The role that each of these sub-processes plays in the overall process, the production of the capacity plan and the storage of capacity-related data is illustrated in Figure 4.16.

The tools used by capacity management need to conform to the organization's management architecture and integrate with other tools used for the management of IT systems and automating IT processes. The monitoring and control activities within service operation will provide a good basis for the tools to support and analyse information for capacity management. The IT operations management function and the technical management departments such as network management and server management may carry out the bulk of the day-to-day operational duties, participating in the capacity management process by providing performance information to the process.

4.5.5 Process activities, methods and techniques

Some activities in the capacity management process are reactive, while others are proactive. The proactive activities of capacity management should include:

- Pre-empting performance issues by taking the necessary actions before they occur
- Producing trends of the current component utilization and estimating the future requirements, using trends and thresholds for planning upgrades and enhancements
- Modelling and trending the predicted changes in IT services (including service retirements), and identifying the changes that need to be made to services and components of the IT infrastructure and applications to ensure that appropriate resource is available
- Ensuring that upgrades are budgeted, planned and implemented before SLAs and service targets are breached or performance issues occur
- Actively seeking to improve service performance wherever it is cost-justifiable

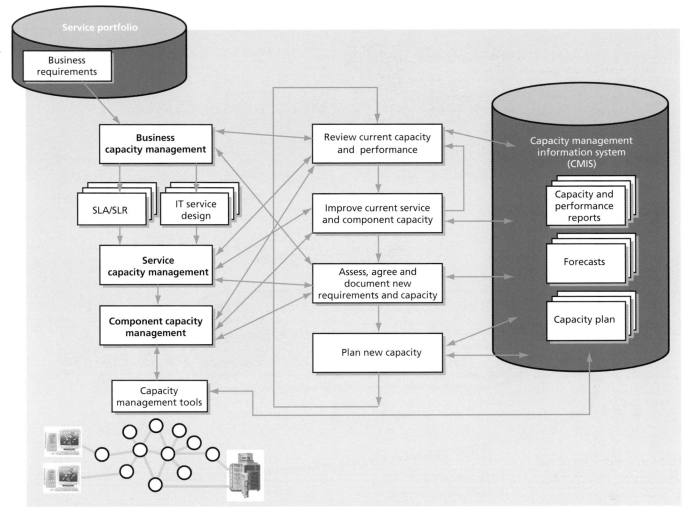

Figure 4.17 Capacity management overview with sub-processes

- Producing and maintaining a capacity plan that reflects all trends, predicted changes, future requirements and plans for meeting them
- Tuning (optimizing) the performance of services and components.

The reactive activities of capacity management should include:

- Monitoring, measuring, reporting and reviewing the current performance of both services and components
- Responding to all capacity-related 'threshold' events and instigating corrective action
- Reacting to and assisting with specific performance issues. For example, the service desk may refer incidents of poor performance to technology management, which will employ capacity management techniques to resolve them.

These individual activities together allow an organization to:

- Assess, agree and document new requirements and capacity
- Plan new capacity
- Review current capacity and performance
- Improve current service and component capacity.

Figure 4.17 provides a high-level overview of the capacity management process with its sub-processes, related documents and data, as well as the relationships to capacity management tools.

Key message

The more successful the proactive and predictive activities of capacity management, the less need there will be for the reactive activities of capacity management.

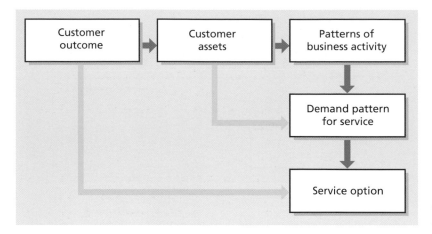

Figure 4.18 Capacity must support business requirements

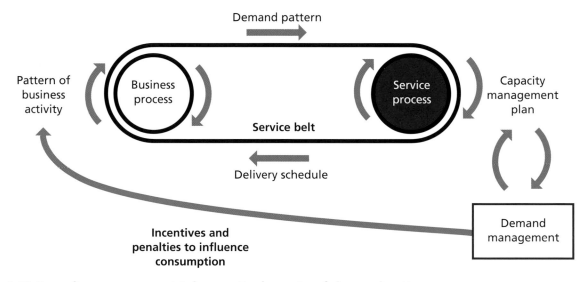

Figure 4.19 Capacity management takes particular note of demand pattern

4.5.5.1 Business capacity management

The main objective of the business capacity management sub-process is to ensure that the future business requirements (customer outcomes) for IT services are considered and understood, and that sufficient IT capacity to support any new or changed services is planned and implemented within an appropriate timescale. Figure 4.18 illustrates that business capacity management is influenced by the patterns of business activity and how services are used.

The capacity management process must be responsive to changing requirements for capacity demand. New services or changed services will be required to underpin the changing business. Existing services will require modification to provide extra functionality. Old services will become obsolete, freeing up spare capacity. As

a result, the ability to satisfy the customers' SLRs and SLAs will be affected. It is the responsibility of capacity management to predict the demand for capacity for such changes and manage the demand at a tactical level.

These new requirements may come to the attention of capacity management from many different sources and for many different reasons, but the principal sources of supply should be the patterns of business activity from demand management. The demand management process will analyse patterns of business activity to find out how these patterns generate demand patterns for IT service and, together with service portfolio management, will create service packages and service options at the right level of utility and warranty to efficiently support these patterns (see section 4.4 in *ITIL Service Strategy* for more information on demand management). This information will inform all the work of capacity management and allow for more successful and more proactive capacity management. Examples of resulting actions could be a recommendation to upgrade to take advantage of new technology, or the implementation of a tuning activity to resolve a performance problem. Figure 4.19 shows the cycle of demand management.

Capacity management needs to be included in all strategic, planning and design activities, being involved as early as possible within each activity, such as:

- Assisting and supporting the development of service strategy
- Involvement in the review and improvement of IT strategies and policies
- Involvement in the review and improvement of technology architectures.

Key message

Capacity management should not be a last-minute 'tick in the box' just prior to customer acceptance and operational acceptance.

If early involvement can be achieved from capacity management within these activities, then the planning and design of IT capacity can be closely aligned with business requirements and can ensure that service targets can be achieved and maintained.

Assist with agreeing service level requirements

Capacity management should assist SLM in understanding the customers' capacity and performance requirements, in terms of required service/system response times, expected throughput, patterns of usage and volume of users. Capacity management should help in the negotiation process by providing possible solutions to a number of scenarios. For example, if the number of users is fewer than 2,000, then response times can be guaranteed to be less than two seconds. If more than 2,000 users connect concurrently, then extra network bandwidth is needed to guarantee the required response time, or a slower response time will have to be accepted. Modelling, trending or application sizing techniques are often employed here to ensure that predictions accurately reflect the real situation.

Design, procure or amend service configuration

Capacity management should be involved in the design of new or changing services and make recommendations for the procurement of hardware and software, where performance and/or capacity are factors. In some instances capacity management instigates the implementation of the new requirement through change management, where it is also represented on the change advisory board. In the interest of balancing cost and capacity, the capacity management process obtains the costs of alternative proposed solutions and recommends the most appropriate cost-effective solution.

Verify service level agreements

The SLA should include details of the anticipated service throughputs and the performance requirements. Capacity management advises SLM on achievable targets that can be monitored and on which the service design has been based. Confidence that the service design will meet the SLRs and provide the ability for future growth can be gained by using modelling, trending or sizing techniques.

Support service level agreement negotiation

The results of the predictive techniques provide the verification of service performance capabilities. There may be a need for SLM to renegotiate SLAs based on these findings. Capacity management provides support to SLM should renegotiations be necessary, by recommending potential solutions and associated cost information. Once assured that the requirements are achievable, it is the responsibility of SLM to agree the service levels and sign the SLA.

Control and implementation

All changes to service and resource capacity must follow all IT processes such as change, release, configuration and project management to ensure that the right degree of control and coordination is in place for all changes and that any new or change components are recorded and tracked through their lifecycle.

4.5.5.2 Service capacity management

The main objective of the service capacity management sub-process is to identify and understand the IT services, their use of resource, working patterns, peaks and troughs, and to ensure that the services meet their SLA targets, i.e. to ensure that the IT services perform as required. In this sub-process, the focus is on managing service performance, as determined by the targets contained in the agreed SLAs or SLRs.

The service capacity management sub-process ensures that the services meet the agreed capacity service targets. The monitored service provides data that can identify trends from which normal service levels can be established. By regular monitoring and comparison with these levels, exception conditions can be defined, identified and reported on. Therefore capacity management informs SLM of any service breaches or near misses.

There will be occasions when incidents and problems are referred to capacity management from other processes, or it is identified that a service could fail to meet its SLA targets. On some of these occasions, the cause of the potential failure may not be resolved by component capacity management. For example, when the failure is analysed it may be found that there is no lack of capacity, or no individual component is over-utilized. However, if the design or coding of an application is inefficient, then the service performance may need to be managed, as well as individual hardware or software resources. Service capacity management should also be monitoring service workloads and transactions to ensure that they remain within agreed limitations and thresholds.

The key to successful service capacity management is to forecast issues, wherever possible, by monitoring changes in performance and monitoring the impact of changes. So this is another sub-process that, whenever possible, has to be proactive and predictive, even pre-emptive, rather than reactive. However, there are times when it has to react to specific performance problems. From a knowledge and understanding of the performance requirements of each of the services being used, the effects of changes in the use of services can be estimated, and actions taken to ensure that the required service performance can be achieved.

4.5.5.3 Component capacity management

The main objective of component capacity management is to identify and understand the performance, capacity and utilization of each of the individual components within the technology used to support the IT services, including the infrastructure, environment, data and applications. This ensures the optimum use of the current hardware and software resources in order to achieve and maintain the agreed service levels. All hardware components and many software components in the IT infrastructure have a finite capacity that, when approached or exceeded, has the potential to cause performance problems.

This sub-process is concerned with components such as processors, memory, disks, network bandwidth, network connections etc. So information on resource utilization needs to be collected on a continuous basis. Monitors should be installed on the individual hardware and software components, and then configured to collect the necessary data, which is accumulated and stored over a period of time. This is an activity generally carried out through monitoring and control within service operation. A direct feedback to component capacity management should be applied within this sub-process.

As in service capacity management, the key to successful component capacity management is to forecast issues, wherever possible, and it therefore has to be proactive and predictive as well. However, there are times when component capacity management has to react to specific problems that are caused by a lack of capacity, or the inefficient use of the component. From a knowledge and understanding of the use of resource by each of the services being run, the effects of changes in the use of services can be estimated and hardware or software upgrades can be budgeted and planned. Alternatively, services can be balanced across the existing resources to make most effective use of the current resources.

4.5.5.4 Design-related activities

The three sub-processes of capacity management can all benefit from attention to the exploitation of new technology and to designing resilience into our services and infrastructure. While both of these activities may be seen as associating most directly with component capacity management, they may also be applied to service capacity management and business capacity management. Organizations should aspire to be as proactive as possible in the performance of these activities.

Exploitation of new technology

This involves understanding new techniques and new technology and how they can be used to support the business and innovate improvements. It may be appropriate to introduce new technology to improve the provision and support of the IT services on which the organization is dependent. This information can be gathered by studying professional literature (magazine and press articles) and by attending:

- Promotional seminars by hardware and software suppliers
- User group meetings of suppliers of potential hardware and software
- User group meetings for other IT professionals involved in capacity management.

Each of these provides sources of information relating to potential techniques, technology, hardware and software, which might be advantageous for IT to implement to realize business benefits. However, at all times capacity management should recognize that the introduction and use of this new technology must be cost-justified and deliver real benefit to the business. It is not just the new technology itself that is important, but capacity management should also keep aware of the advantages to be obtained from the use of new technologies, using techniques such as 'grid computing', 'virtualization' and 'on-demand computing'.

Designing resilience

Capacity management assists with the identification and improvement of the resilience within the IT infrastructure or any subset of it, wherever it is cost-justified. In conjunction with availability management, capacity management should use techniques such as CFIA (as described in section 4.4 on availability management) to identify how susceptible the current configuration is to the failure or overload of individual components and make recommendations on any cost-effective solutions.

Capacity management should be able to identify the impact on the available resources of particular failures, and the potential for running the most important services on the remaining resources. So the provision of spare capacity can act as resilience or fail-over in failure situations.

The requirements for resilience in the IT infrastructure should always be considered at the time of the service or system design. However, for many services, the resilience of the service is only considered after it is in live operational use. Incorporating resilience into service design is much more effective and efficient than trying to add it at a later date, once a service has become operational.

4.5.5.5 The ongoing iterative activities of capacity management

The activities described in this section are necessary to support the sub-processes of capacity management, and these activities can be done both reactively and proactively.

The major differences between the sub-processes are in the data that is being monitored and collected, and the perspective from which the data is analysed. For example, the level of utilization of individual components in the infrastructure – such as processors, disks, and network links – is of interest in component capacity management, while the transaction throughput rates and response times of the entire service are of interest in service capacity management. For business capacity management, the transaction throughput rates for the online service need to be translated into business volumes – for example, in terms of sales invoices raised or orders taken. The biggest challenge facing capacity management is to understand the relationship between the demands and requirements of the business and the business workload, and to be able to translate these in terms of the impact and effect of these on the service and resource workloads and utilizations, so that appropriate thresholds can be set at each level.

A number of the activities need to be carried out iteratively and form a natural cycle, as illustrated in Figure 4.20.

These activities provide the basic historical information and triggers necessary for all of the other activities and processes within capacity management. Monitors should be established on all the components and for each of the services. The data should be analysed using, wherever possible, expert systems to compare usage levels against thresholds. The results of the analysis should be included in reports, and

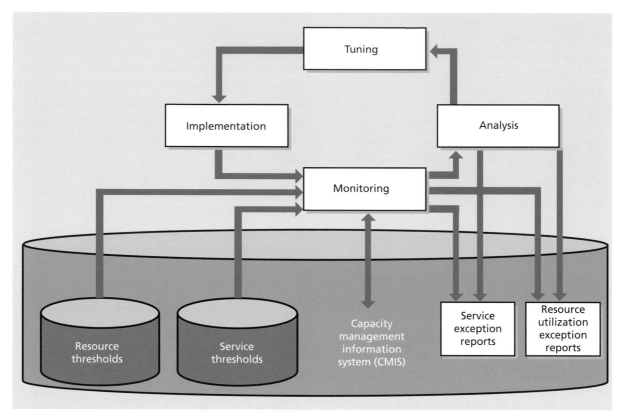

Figure 4.20 Ongoing iterative activities of capacity management

recommendations made as appropriate. Some form of control mechanism may then be put in place to act on the recommendations. This may take the form of balancing services, balancing workloads, changing concurrency levels and adding or removing resources. All of the information accumulated during these activities should be stored in the capacity management information system (CMIS) and the cycle then begins again, monitoring any changes made to ensure they have had a beneficial effect and collecting more data for future actions. These iterative activities are primarily performed as part of the service operation stage of the service lifecycle.

Monitoring

The monitors should be specific to particular operating systems, hardware configurations, applications etc. It is important that the monitors can collect all the data required by the capacity management process, for a specific component or service. Typical monitored data includes:

- Processor utilization
- Memory utilization
- Per cent processor per transaction type

- I/O rates (physical and buffer) and device utilization
- Queue lengths
- Disk utilization
- Transaction rates
- Response times
- Batch duration
- Database usage
- Index usage
- Hit rates
- Concurrent user numbers
- Network traffic rates.

In considering the data that needs to be included, a distinction needs to be drawn between the data collected to monitor capacity (e.g. throughput) and the data to monitor performance (e.g. response times). Data of both types is required by the service and component capacity management sub-processes. This monitoring and collection needs to incorporate all components in the service, thus monitoring the 'end-to-end' customer experience. The data should be gathered at total resource utilization level and at a more detailed profile for the load that each service places on each particular component. This needs to be carried out across the whole technology, host or server, the network, local server and client or workstation. Similarly the data needs to be collected for each service.

THRESHOLD MANAGEMENT AND CONTROL

Part of the monitoring activity should be of thresholds and baselines or profiles of the normal operating levels. If these are exceeded, alarms should be raised and exception reports produced. These thresholds and baselines should have been determined from the analysis of previously recorded data, and can be set at both the component and service levels. The technical limits and constraints on the individual services and components can be used by the monitoring activities to set the thresholds at which warnings and alarms are raised and exception reports are produced. However, care must be exercised when setting thresholds, because many thresholds are dependent on the work being run on the particular component.

All thresholds should be set below the level at which the component or service is over-utilized, or below the targets in the SLAs. When the threshold is reached or threatened, there is still an opportunity to take corrective action before the SLA has been breached, or the resource has become over-utilized and there has been a period of poor performance. The monitoring and management of these events, thresholds and alarms is covered in detail in *ITIL Service Operation*.

Often it is more difficult to get the data on the current business volumes as required by the business capacity management sub-process. These statistics may need to be derived from the data available to the service and component capacity management sub-processes.

The management and control of service and component thresholds is fundamental to the effective delivery of services to meet their agreed service levels. It ensures that all service and component thresholds are maintained at the appropriate levels and are continuously, automatically monitored, and alerts and warnings generated when breaches occur. Once defined, thresholds and how they are to be implemented and used should be documented as part of the service design package.

Whenever monitored thresholds are breached or threatened, alarms are raised and breaches, warnings and exception reports are produced. Analysis of the situation should then be completed and remedial action taken whenever justified, ensuring that the situation does not recur. The same data items can be used to identify when SLAs are breached or likely to be breached or when component performance degrades or is likely to be degraded. By setting thresholds below or above the actual targets, action can be taken and a breach of the SLA targets avoided.

Threshold monitoring should not only alarm on exceeding a threshold, but should also monitor the rate of change and predict when the threshold will be reached. For example, a disk-space monitor should monitor the rate of growth and raise an alarm when the current rate will cause the disk to be full within the next N days. If a 1GB disk has reached 90% capacity, and is growing at 100KB per day, it will be 1,000 days before it is full. If it is growing at 10MB per day, it will only be 10 days before it is full. The monitoring and management of these events and alarms is covered in detail in *ITIL Service Operation*.

There may be occasions when optimization of infrastructure components and resources is needed to maintain or improve performance or throughput. This can often be done through workload management, which is a generic term to cover such actions as:

- Rescheduling a particular service or workload to run at a different time of day or day of the week etc. (usually away from peak times to off-peak windows) – which will often mean having to make adjustments to job-scheduling software
- Moving a service or workload from one location or set of CIs to another – often to balance utilization or traffic
- Technical 'virtualization': setting up and using virtualization techniques and systems to allow the movement of processing around the infrastructure to give better performance/resilience in a dynamic fashion
- Limiting or moving demand for components or resources through demand management techniques, in conjunction with financial management for IT services (see section 4.5.5.6).

It will only be possible to manage workloads effectively if a good understanding exists of which workloads will run at what time and how much resource utilization each workload places on the IT infrastructure. Diligent monitoring and analysis of workloads, together with a comprehensive CMIS, are therefore needed on an ongoing operational basis.

RESPONSE TIME MONITORING

Many SLAs have user response times as one of the targets to be measured, but equally many organizations have great difficulty in supporting this requirement. User response times of IT and network services can be monitored and measured in the following ways:

- **Incorporating specific code within client and server applications software** This can be used to provide complete 'end-to-end' service response times or intermediate timing points to break down the overall response into its constituent components. The figures obtained from these tools give the actual response times as perceived by the users of a service.

- **Using 'robotic scripted systems' with terminal emulation software** These systems consist of client systems with terminal emulation software (e.g. browser or Telnet systems) and specialized scripted software for generating and measuring transactions and responses. These systems generally provide sample 'end-to-end' service response times and are useful for providing representative response times, particularly for multi-phase transactions or complex interactions. These only give sample response times, not the actual response times as perceived by the real users of the service.

- **Using distributed agent monitoring software** Useful information on service response times can be obtained by distributing agent systems with monitoring software at different points of a network (e.g. within different countries on the internet). These systems can then be used to generate transactions from a number of locations and give periodic measurements of an internet site as perceived by international users of an internet website. However, again the times received are only indications of the response times and are not the real user response times.

- **Using specific passive monitoring systems** Tracking a representative sample number of client systems. This method relies on the connection of specific network monitoring systems, often referred to as 'sniffers', which are inserted at appropriate points within the network. These can then monitor, record and time all traffic passing a particular point within the network. Once recorded, this traffic can then be analysed to give detailed information on the service response times. Once again, however, these systems can only be used to give an approximation to the actual user response times. These times are often very close to the real-world situation, although this depends on the position of the monitor itself within the IT infrastructure.

In some cases, a combination of a number of systems may be used. The monitoring of response times is a complex process even if it is an in-house service running on a private network. If this is an external internet service, the process is much more complex because of the sheer number of different organizations and technologies involved.

Anecdote

A private company with a major website implemented a website monitoring service from an external supplier that would provide automatic alarms on the availability and responsiveness of its website. The availability and speed of the monitoring points were lower than those of the website being monitored. Therefore the figures produced by the service were of the availability and responsiveness of the monitoring service itself, rather than those of the monitored website.

Hints and tips

When implementing external monitoring services, ensure that the service levels and performance commitments of the monitoring service are in excess of those of the service(s) being monitored.

Analysis

The data collected from the monitoring should be analysed to identify trends from which the normal utilization and service levels, or baselines, can be established. By regular monitoring and comparison with this baseline, exception conditions in the utilization of individual components or service thresholds can be defined, and breaches or near misses in the SLAs can be reported and actioned.

Also the data can be used to predict future resource usage, or to monitor actual business growth against predicted growth.

Analysis of the data may identify issues such as:

- 'Bottlenecks' or 'hot spots' within the infrastructure
- Inappropriate distribution of workload across available resources
- Inappropriate database indexing
- Inefficiencies in the application design
- Unexpected increase in workloads or transaction rates
- Inefficient scheduling or memory usage.

The use of each component and service needs to be considered over the short, medium and long term, and the minimum, maximum and average utilization for these periods recorded. Typically, the short-term pattern covers the utilization over a 24-hour period, while the medium term may cover a one- to four-week period, and the long term a year-long period. Over time, the trend in the use of the resource by the various IT services will become apparent. The usefulness of this information is further enhanced by recording any observed contributing factors to peaks or valleys in utilization – for example, if a change of business process or staffing coincides with any deviations from normal utilization.

It is important to understand the utilization in each of these periods, so that changes in the use of any service can be related to predicted changes in the level of utilization of individual components. The ability to identify the specific hardware or software components on which a particular IT service depends is improved greatly by an accurate, up-to-date and comprehensive CMS.

When the utilization of a particular resource is considered, it is important to understand both the total level of utilization and the utilization by individual services of the resource.

Understanding both the individual pieces and the whole

If a processor that is 75% loaded during the peak hour is being used by two different services, A and B, it is important to know how much of the total 75% is being used by each service. Assuming the system overhead on the processor is 5%, the remaining 70% load could be split evenly between the two services. If a change in either service A or service B is estimated to double its loading on the processor, then the processor would be overloaded.

However, if service A uses 60% and service B uses 10% of the processor, then the processor would be overloaded if service A doubled its loading on the processor. But if service B doubled its loading on the processor, then the processor would not necessarily be overloaded.

Tuning

The analysis of the monitored data may identify areas of the configuration that could be tuned to better utilize the service, system and component resources or improve the performance of the particular service.

Tuning techniques that are of assistance include:

- **Balancing workloads and traffic** Transactions may arrive at the host or server at a particular gateway, depending on where the transaction was initiated; balancing the ratio of initiation points to gateways can provide tuning benefits.
- **Balancing disk traffic** Storing data on disk efficiently and strategically – for example, striping data across many spindles may reduce data contention.
- **Definition of an accepted locking strategy** This specifies when locks are necessary and the appropriate level – for example, database, page, file, record and row. Delaying the lock until an update is necessary may provide benefits.
- **Efficient use of memory** This may include looking to utilize more or less memory, depending on the circumstances.

Before implementing any of the recommendations arising from the tuning techniques, it may be appropriate to consider testing the validity of the recommendation. For example, 'Can demand management be used to avoid the need to carry out any tuning?' or 'Can the proposed change be modelled to show its effectiveness before it is implemented?'

Implementation

The objective of this activity is to introduce to the live operation services any changes that have been identified by the monitoring, analysis and tuning activities. The implementation of any changes arising from these activities must be undertaken through a strict, formal change management process. The impact of system tuning changes can have major implications on the customers of the service. The impact and risk associated with these types of change are likely to be greater than that of other types of change.

It is important that further monitoring takes place, so that the effects of the change can be assessed. It may be necessary to make further changes or to regress some of the original changes.

4.5.5.6 Demand management in capacity management

The prime objective of demand management at the tactical level is to influence user and customer demand for IT services and manage the impact on IT resources. Information provided by the strategic demand management process (see *ITIL Service Strategy*) is an important input to the type of demand management occurring as part of the capacity management process.

This tactical demand management activity can be carried out as a short-term requirement because there is insufficient current capacity to support the work being run, or, as a deliberate policy of IT management, to limit the required capacity in the long term.

Short-term demand management may occur when there has been a partial failure of a critical resource in the IT infrastructure. For example, if there has been a failure of a processor within a multi-processor server, it may not be possible to run the full range of services. However, a limited subset of the services could be run. Capacity management should be aware of the business priority of each of the services, know the resource requirements of each service (in this case, the amount of processor power required to run the service) and then be able to identify which services can be run while there is a limited amount of processor power available.

Long-term demand management may be required when it is difficult to cost-justify an expensive upgrade. For example, many processors are heavily utilized for only a few hours each day, typically 10.00–12.00 and 14.00–16.00. Within these periods, the processor may be overloaded for only one or two hours. For the hours between 18.00 and 08.00, these processors are only very lightly loaded and the components are under-utilized. Is it possible to justify the cost of an upgrade to provide additional capacity for only a few hours in 24 hours? Or is it possible to influence the demand and spread the requirement for resource across 24 hours, thereby delaying or avoiding altogether the need for a costly upgrade?

Demand management needs to understand which services are utilizing the resource, to what level, and the schedule for its use. Then a decision can be made on whether it will be possible to influence the use of resource and, if so, which option is appropriate.

The influence on the services that are running could be exercised by:

- **Physical constraints** For example, it may be possible to stop some services from being available at certain times, or to limit the number of customers who can use a particular service by limiting the number of concurrent users; or the constraint could be implemented on a specific resource or component, for example, by limiting the number of physical connections to a network router or switch.
- **Financial constraints** If charging for IT services is in place, reduced rates could be offered for running work at times of the day when there is currently less demand for the resource. This is known as differential charging.

4.5.5.7 Modelling and trending

A prime objective of capacity management is to predict the behaviour of IT services under a given volume and variety of work. Modelling is an activity that can be used to accomplish this to beneficial effect in any of the sub-processes of capacity management.

The different types of modelling range from making estimates based on experience and current resource utilization information, to pilot studies, prototypes and full-scale benchmarks. The former is a cheap and reasonable approach for day-to-day small decisions, while the latter is expensive, but may be advisable when implementing a large new project or service. With all types of modelling, similar levels of accuracy can be obtained, but all are totally dependent on the skill of the person constructing the model and the information used to create it.

Baselining

The first stage in modelling is to create a baseline model that reflects accurately the performance that is currently being achieved. When this baseline model has been created, predictive modelling can be done, i.e. ask the 'What if?' questions that reflect failures, planned changes to the hardware and/or the volume/variety of workloads. If the baseline model is accurate, then the accuracy of the result of the potential failures and changes can be trusted.

Effective capacity management, together with modelling techniques, enables capacity management to answer the 'What if?' questions. What if the throughput of service A doubles? What if service B is moved from the current server onto a new server – what will be the effect on the response times of the two services?

Trend analysis

Trend analysis can be done on the resource utilization and service performance information that has been collected by the capacity management process. The data can be analysed in a spreadsheet, and the graphical and trending and forecasting facilities used to show the utilization of a particular resource over a previous period of time, and how it can be expected to change in the future.

Typically, trend analysis only provides estimates of future resource utilization information. Trend analysis is less effective in producing an accurate estimate of response times, in which case either analytical or simulation modelling should be used. Trend analysis is most effective when there is a linear relationship between a small number of variables, and less effective when there are non-linear relationships between variables or when there are many variables.

Analytical modelling

Analytical models are representations of the behaviour of computer systems using mathematical techniques – for example, multi-class network queuing theory. Typically, a model is built using a software package on a PC by specifying within the package the components and structure of the configuration that need to be modelled, and the utilization of the components – for example, processor, memory and disks – by the various workloads or applications. When the model is run, the queuing theory is used to calculate the response times in the computer system. If the response times predicted by the model are sufficiently close to the response times recorded in real life, the model can be regarded as an accurate representation of the computer system.

The technique of analytical modelling requires less time and effort than simulation modelling, but typically it gives less accurate results. Also, the model must be kept up-to-date. However, if the results are within 5% accuracy for utilization, and 15–20% for online application response times, the results are usually satisfactory.

Simulation modelling

Simulation involves the modelling of discrete events (for example, transaction arrival rates) against a given hardware configuration. This type of modelling can be very accurate in sizing new applications or predicting the effects of changes on existing applications, but can also be very time-consuming and therefore costly.

When simulating transaction arrival rates, have a number of staff enter a series of transactions from prepared scripts, or use software to input the same scripted transactions with a random arrival rate. Either of these approaches takes time and effort to prepare and run. However, it can be cost-justified for organizations with very large services and systems where the major cost and the associated performance implications assume great importance.

4.5.5.8 Application sizing

The primary objective of application sizing is to estimate the resource requirements to support a proposed change to an existing service or the implementation of a new service, to ensure that it meets its required service levels. To achieve this, application sizing has to be an integral part of the service lifecycle.

Application sizing has a finite lifespan. It is initiated at the design stage for a new service, or when there is a major change to an existing service, and is completed when the application is accepted into the live operational environment. Sizing activities should include all areas of technology related to the applications, and not just the applications themselves. This should include the infrastructure, environment and data, and will often use modelling and trending techniques.

During the initial requirements and design, the required service levels must be specified in an SLR. This enables the service design and development to employ the pertinent technologies and products to achieve a design that meets the desired levels of service. It is much easier and less expensive to achieve the required service levels if service design considers the required service levels at the very beginning of the service lifecycle, rather than at some later stage.

Other considerations in application sizing are the resilience aspects that it may be necessary to build into the design of new services. Capacity management is able to provide advice and guidance to the availability management process on the resources required to provide the required level of performance and resilience.

The sizing of the application should be refined as design and development progress. Modelling can be used during application sizing.

The SLRs of the planned application developments should not be considered in isolation. The resources to be utilized by the application are likely to be shared with other services, and potential threats to existing SLA targets must be recognized and managed.

When purchasing software packages from external suppliers, it is just as important to understand the resource requirements needed to support the service. Often it can be difficult to obtain this information from the suppliers and it may vary, depending on throughput. Therefore, it is beneficial to identify similar customers of the product and to gain an understanding of the resource implications from them. It may be pertinent to benchmark, evaluate or trial the product prior to purchase.

Key message

Quality must be built in.

Some aspects of service quality can be improved after implementation (additional hardware can be added to improve performance, for example). Others – particularly aspects such as reliability and maintainability of applications software – rely on quality being 'built in', since to attempt to add it at a later stage is, in effect, redesign and redevelopment, normally at a much higher cost than the original development. Even in the hardware example quoted above, it is likely to cost more to add additional capacity after service implementation rather than as part of the original project.

4.5.6 Triggers, inputs, outputs and interfaces

4.5.6.1 Triggers

There are many triggers that will initiate capacity management activities. These include:

- New and changed services requiring additional capacity
- Service breaches, capacity or performance events and alerts, including threshold events
- Exception reports
- Periodic revision of current capacity and performance and the review of forecasts, reports and plans
- Periodic trending and modelling
- Review and revision of business and IT plans and strategies
- Review and revision of designs and strategies
- Review and revision of SLAs, OLAs, contracts or any other agreements
- Request from SLM for assistance with capacity and/or performance targets and explanation of achievements.

4.5.6.2 Inputs

A number of sources of information are relevant to the capacity management process. Some of these are as follows.

- **Business information** From the organization's business strategy, plans and financial plans, and information on their current and future requirements
- **Service and IT information** From service strategy, the IT strategy and plans and current budgets, covering all areas of technology and technology plans, including the infrastructure,

environment, data and applications, and the way in which they relate to business strategy and plans

- **Component performance and capacity information** Of both existing and new technology, from manufacturers and suppliers
- **Service performance issue information** The incident and problem management processes, with incidents and problems relating to poor performance
- **Service information** From the SLM process, with details of the services from the service portfolio and the service catalogue and service level targets within SLAs and SLRs, and possibly from the monitoring of SLAs, service reviews and breaches of the SLAs
- **Financial information** From financial management for IT services, the cost of service provision, the cost of resources, components and upgrades, the resultant business benefit and the financial plans and budgets, together with the costs associated with service and component failure. Some of the costs of components and upgrades to components will be obtained from procurement, suppliers and manufacturers
- **Change information** From the change management process, with a change schedule and a need to assess all changes for their impact on the capacity of the technology
- **Performance information** From the CMIS on the current performance of both all existing services and IT infrastructure components
- **CMS** Containing information on the relationships between the business, the services, the supporting services and the technology
- **Workload information** From the IT operations team, with schedules of all the work that needs to be run, and information on the dependencies between different services and information, and the interdependencies within a service.

4.5.6.3 Outputs

The outputs of capacity management are used within all other parts of the process, by many other processes and by other parts of the organization. Often this information is supplied as electronic reports or displays on shared areas, or as pages on intranet servers, to ensure the most up-to-date information is always used. The information provided is as follows:

- **CMIS** This holds the information needed by all sub-processes within capacity management. For example, the data monitored and collected as part of component and service capacity management is used in business capacity management to determine what infrastructure components or upgrades to components are needed, and when.
- **Capacity plan** This is used by all areas of the business and IT management, and is acted on by the IT service provider and senior management of the organization to plan the capacity of the IT infrastructure. It also provides planning input to many other areas of IT and the business. It contains information on the current usage of service and components, and plans for the development of IT capacity to meet the needs in the growth of both existing service and any agreed new services. The capacity plan should be actively used as a basis for decision-making. Too often, capacity plans are created and never referred to or used.
- **Service performance information and reports** This is used by many other processes. For example, the capacity management process assists SLM with the reporting and reviewing of service performance and the development of new SLRs or changes to existing SLAs. It also assists the financial management for IT services process by identifying when money needs to be budgeted for IT infrastructure upgrades, or the purchase of new components.
- **Workload analysis and reports** This is used by IT operations to assess and implement changes in conjunction with capacity management to schedule or reschedule when services or workloads are run, to ensure that the most effective and efficient use is made of the available resources.
- **Ad hoc capacity and performance reports** These are used by all areas of capacity management, IT and the business to analyse and resolve service and performance issues.
- **Forecasts and predictive reports** These are used by all areas to analyse, predict and forecast particular business and IT scenarios and their potential solutions.
- **Thresholds, alerts and events**
- **Improvement actions** For inclusion in a SIP.

4.5.6.4 Interfaces

The key interfaces that capacity management has with other processes are:

- **Availability management** This process works with capacity management to determine the resources needed to ensure the required availability of services and components.
- **Service level management** This process provides assistance with the determining capacity targets and the investigation and resolution of service and component capacity-related breaches.
- **ITSCM** Capacity management assists with the assessment of business impact and risk and determining the capacity needed to support risk reduction measures and recovery options.
- **Incident and problem management** Capacity management provides assistance with the resolution and subsequent justification and correction of capacity-related incidents and problems.
- **Demand management** By anticipating the demand for services based on user profiles and patterns of business activity, and identifying the means to influence that demand, this process provides strategic decision-making and critical related data on which capacity management can act.

4.5.7 Information management

The aim of the CMIS is to provide the relevant capacity and performance information to produce reports and support the capacity management process. These reports provide valuable information to many IT and service management processes. These reports should include the following:

- **Component-based reports** For each component there should be a team of technical staff responsible for its control and management. Reports must be produced to illustrate how components are performing and how much of their maximum capacity is being used.
- **Service-based reports** Reports and information must also be produced to illustrate how the service and its constituent components are performing with respect to their overall service targets and constraints. These reports will provide the basis of SLM and customer service reports.
- **Exception reports** Reports that show management and technical staff when the capacity and performance of a particular component or service becomes unacceptable are required from analysis of capacity data. Thresholds can be set for any component, service or measurement within the CMIS. An example threshold may be that processor percentage utilization for a particular server has breached 70% for three consecutive hours, or that the concurrent number of logged-in users exceeds the agreed limit.

In particular, exception reports are of interest to the SLM process in determining whether the targets in SLAs have been breached. Also the incident and problem management processes may be able to use the exception reports in the resolution of incidents and problems.

While the focus of exception reporting usually focuses on indications of insufficient capacity, excess capacity should also be identified. Unused capacity may represent an opportunity for cost savings.

- **Predictive and forecast reports** To ensure the IT service provider continues to provide the required service levels, the capacity management process must predict future workloads and growth. To do this, future component and service capacity and performance must be forecast. This can be done in a variety of ways, depending on the techniques and the technology used. Changes to workloads by the development and implementation of new functionality and services must be considered alongside growth in the current functionality and services driven by business growth. A simple example of a capacity forecast is a correlation between a business driver and component utilization – for example, processor utilization against the number of customer accounts. This data can be correlated to find the effect that an increase in the number of customer accounts will have on processor utilization. If the forecasts on future capacity requirements identify a requirement for increased resource, this requirement needs to be input into the capacity plan and included within the IT budget cycle.

Often capacity reports are consolidated together and stored on an intranet site so that anyone can access and refer to them.

4.5.7.1 Capacity management information system data

Often capacity data is stored in technology-specific tools and databases, and full value of the data, the information and its analysis is not obtained. The true value of the data can only be obtained when the data is combined into a single set of integrated, information repositories or set of databases.

The CMIS is a set of tools, data and information that is used to support capacity management and is the cornerstone of a successful capacity management process. Information contained within the CMIS is stored and analysed by all the sub-processes of capacity management because it is a repository that holds a number of different types of data, including business, service, resource or utilization and financial data, from all areas of technology.

However, the CMIS is unlikely to be a single database, and probably exists in several physical locations. Data from all areas of technology, and all components that make up the IT services, can then be combined for analysis and provision of technical and management reporting. Only when all of the information is integrated can 'end-to-end' service reports be produced. The integrity and accuracy of the data within the CMIS need to be carefully managed. If the CMIS is not part of an overall CMS or SKMS, then links between these systems need to be implemented to ensure consistency and accuracy of the information recorded within them.

The information in the CMIS is used to form the basis of performance and capacity management reports and views that are to be delivered to customers, IT management and technical personnel. Also, the data is utilized to generate future capacity forecasts and allow capacity management to plan for future capacity requirements. Often a web interface is provided to the CMIS to provide the different access and views required outside of the capacity management process itself.

The full range of data types stored within the CMIS is as follows:

- **Business data** It is essential to have quality information on the current and future needs of the business. The future business plans of the organization need to be considered and the effects on the IT services understood. The business data is used to forecast and validate how changes in business drivers affect the capacity and performance of the IT infrastructure. Business data should include business transactions or measurements such as the number of accounts, the number of invoices generated, the number of product lines.

- **Service data** To achieve a service-orientated approach to capacity management, service data should be stored within the CMIS. Typical service data are transaction response times, transaction rates, workload volumes etc. In general, the SLAs and SLRs provide the service targets for which the capacity management process needs to record and monitor data. To ensure that the targets in the SLAs are achieved, SLM thresholds should be included, so that the monitoring activity can measure against these service thresholds and raise exception warnings and reports before service targets are breached.

- **Component data** The CMIS also needs to record resource data consisting of utilization, threshold and limit information on all of the technological components supporting the services. Most of the IT components have limitations on the level to which they should be utilized. Beyond this level of utilization, the resource will be over-utilized and the performance of the services using the resource will be impaired. For example, the maximum recommended level of utilization on a processor could be 80%, or the utilization of a shared Ethernet LAN segment should not exceed 40%.

  Also, components have various physical limitations beyond which greater connectivity or use is impossible. For example, the maximum number of connections through an application or a network gateway is 100, or a particular type of disk has a physical capacity of 15 Gb. The CMIS should therefore contain, for each component and the maximum performance and capacity limits, current and past utilization rates and the associated component thresholds. Over time this can mean accumulation of vast amounts of data, so there need to be good techniques for analysing, aggregating and archiving this data.

- **Financial data** The capacity management process requires financial data. For evaluating alternative upgrade options, when proposing various scenarios in the capacity plan, the financial cost of the upgrades to the components of the IT infrastructure, together with information about the current IT hardware budget, must be known and included in the considerations. Most of this data may be available from the financial management for IT services process, but capacity management needs to consider this information when managing the future business requirements.

4.5.8 Critical success factors and key performance indicators

The following list includes some sample CSFs for capacity management. Each organization should identify appropriate CSFs based on its objectives for the process. Each sample CSF is followed by a small number of typical KPIs that support the CSF. These KPIs should not be adopted without careful consideration. Each organization should develop KPIs that are appropriate for its level of maturity, its CSFs and its particular circumstances. Achievement against KPIs should be monitored and used to identify opportunities for improvement, which should be logged in the CSI register for evaluation and possible implementation.

- **CSF** Accurate business forecasts
  - **KPI** Production of workload forecasts on time
  - **KPI** Percentage accuracy of forecasts of business trends
  - **KPI** Timely incorporation of business plans into the capacity plan
  - **KPI** Reduction in the number of variances from the business plans and capacity plans
- **CSF** Knowledge of current and future technologies
  - **KPI** Increased ability to monitor performance and throughput of all services and components
  - **KPI** Timely justification and implementation of new technology in line with business requirements (time, cost and functionality)
  - **KPI** Reduction in the use of old technology, causing breached SLAs due to problems with support or performance
- **CSF** Ability to demonstrate cost effectiveness
  - **KPI** Reduction in last-minute buying to address urgent performance issues
  - **KPI** Reduction in the over-capacity of IT

- **KPI** Accurate forecasts of planned expenditure
- **KPI** Reduction in the business disruption caused by a lack of adequate IT capacity
- **KPI** Relative reduction in the cost of production of the capacity plan
- **CSF** Ability to plan and implement the appropriate IT capacity to match business need
  - **KPI** Percentage reduction in the number of incidents due to poor performance
  - **KPI** Percentage reduction in lost business due to inadequate capacity
  - **KPI** All new services implemented match SLRs
  - **KPI** Increased percentage of recommendations made by capacity management are acted on
  - **KPI** Reduction in the number of SLA breaches due to either poor service performance or poor component performance.

4.5.9 Challenges and risks

4.5.9.1 Challenges

One of the major challenges facing capacity management is persuading the business to provide information on its strategic business plans, to enable the IT service provider organization to provide effective business capacity management. This is particularly true in outsourced situations where there may be commercial or confidential reasons why this data cannot be shared. Even if the data on the strategic business is available there may be issues with regard to the quality or accuracy of the data contained within the business plans with regard to business capacity management.

Another challenge is the combination of all of the component capacity management data into an integrated set of information that can be analysed in a consistent manner to provide details of the usage of all components of the services. This is particularly challenging when the information from the different technologies is provided by different tools in differing formats. Often the quality of component information on the performance of the technology is variable in both its quality and accuracy.

The amounts of information produced by business capacity management, and especially service capacity management and component capacity management, are huge and the analysis of this information is difficult to achieve. The people and the processes need to focus on the key resources and their usage, while not ignoring other areas. In order to do this, appropriate thresholds must be used, and reliance placed on the tools and technology to automatically manage the technology and provide warnings and alerts when things deviate significantly from the 'norm'.

4.5.9.2 Risks

Some of the major risks associated with capacity management include:

- A lack of commitment from the business to the capacity management process
- A lack of appropriate information from the business on future plans and strategies
- A lack of senior management commitment or a lack of resources and/or budget for the capacity management process
- Service capacity management and component capacity management performed in isolation because business capacity management is difficult, or there is a lack of appropriate and accurate business information
- The processes become too bureaucratic or manually intensive
- The processes focus too much on the technology (component capacity management) and not enough on the services (service capacity management) and the business (business capacity management)
- The reports and information provided are too bulky or too technical and do not give the information required or appropriate to the customers and the business.

4.6 IT SERVICE CONTINUITY MANAGEMENT

As technology is a core component of most business processes, continued or high availability of IT is critical to the survival of the business as a whole. This is achieved by introducing risk reduction measures and recovery options. Like all elements of IT service management, successful implementation of the ITSCM process can only be achieved with senior management commitment and the support of all members of the organization. Ongoing maintenance of the

recovery capability is essential if it is to remain effective.

Service continuity is an essential part of the warranty of a service. If a service's continuity cannot be maintained and/or restored in accordance with the requirements of the business, then the business will not experience the value that has been promised. Without continuity the utility of the service cannot be accessed.

> **Recovery is understood**
>
> Since effecting recovery when required is a fundamental element of ITSCM, the concept of continuity in this context encompasses risk reduction and recovery. When the word 'continuity' is used in this section, recovery should be understood to be included.

4.6.1 Purpose and objectives

The purpose of the IT service continuity management process is to support the overall business continuity management (BCM) process by ensuring that, by managing the risks that could seriously affect IT services, the IT service provider can always provide minimum agreed business continuity-related service levels.

In support of and alignment with the BCM process, ITSCM uses formal risk assessment and management techniques to:

- Reduce risks to IT services to agreed acceptable levels
- Plan and prepare for the recovery of IT services.

For a definition of BCM, please see the glossary at the end of this publication.

The objectives of ITSCM are to:

- Produce and maintain a set of IT service continuity plans that support the overall business continuity plans of the organization
- Complete regular BIA exercises to ensure that all continuity plans are maintained in line with changing business impacts and requirements
- Conduct regular risk assessment and management exercises to manage IT services within an agreed level of business risk in conjunction with the business and the availability management and information security management processes

- Provide advice and guidance to all other areas of the business and IT on all continuity-related issues
- Ensure that appropriate continuity mechanisms are put in place to meet or exceed the agreed business continuity targets
- Assess the impact of all changes on the IT service continuity plans and supporting methods and procedures
- Ensure that proactive measures to improve the availability of services are implemented wherever it is cost-justifiable to do so
- Negotiate and agree contracts with suppliers for the provision of the necessary recovery capability to support all continuity plans in conjunction with the supplier management process.

4.6.2 Scope

ITSCM focuses on those events that the business considers significant enough to be treated as a 'disaster'. Less significant events will be dealt with as part of the incident management process. What constitutes a disaster will vary from organization to organization. The impact of a loss of a business process, such as financial loss, damage to reputation or regulatory breach, is measured through a BIA exercise, which determines the minimum critical requirements. The specific IT technical and service requirements are supported by ITSCM. The scope of ITSCM within an organization is determined by the organizational structure, culture and strategic direction (both business and technology) in terms of the services provided and how these develop and change over time.

ITSCM primarily considers the IT assets and configurations that support the business processes. If (following a disaster) it is necessary to relocate to an alternative working location, provision will also be required for items such as office and personnel accommodation, copies of critical paper records, courier services and telephone facilities to communicate with customers and third parties.

The scope will need to take into account the number and location of the organization's offices and the services performed in each.

ITSCM does not usually directly cover longer-term risks such as those from changes in business direction, diversification, restructuring, major

competitor failure, and so on. While these risks can have a significant impact on IT service elements and their continuity mechanisms, there is usually time to identify and evaluate the risk and include risk mitigation through changes or shifts in business and IT strategies, thereby becoming part of the overall business and IT change management programme.

Similarly, ITSCM does not usually cover minor technical faults (for example, non-critical disk failure), unless there is a possibility that the impact could have a major impact on the business. These risks would be expected to be covered mainly through the service desk and the incident management process, or resolved through the planning associated with the processes of availability management, problem management, change management, service asset and configuration management and 'business as usual' operational management.

The ITSCM process includes:

- The agreement of the scope of the ITSCM process and the policies adopted
- BIA to quantify the impact loss of IT service would have on the business
- Risk assessment and management – the risk identification and risk assessment to identify potential threats to continuity and the likelihood of the threats becoming reality. This also includes taking measures to manage the identified threats where this can be cost-justified. The approach to managing these threats will form the core of the ITSCM strategy and plans
- Production of an overall ITSCM strategy that must be integrated into the BCM strategy. This can be produced following the BIA and the development of the risk assessment, and is likely to include elements of risk reduction as well as selection of appropriate and comprehensive recovery options
- Production of an ITSCM plan, which again must be integrated with the overall BCM plans
- Testing of the plans
- Ongoing operation and maintenance of the plans.

4.6.3 Value to the business

ITSCM provides an invaluable role in supporting the BCM process. In many organizations, ITSCM is

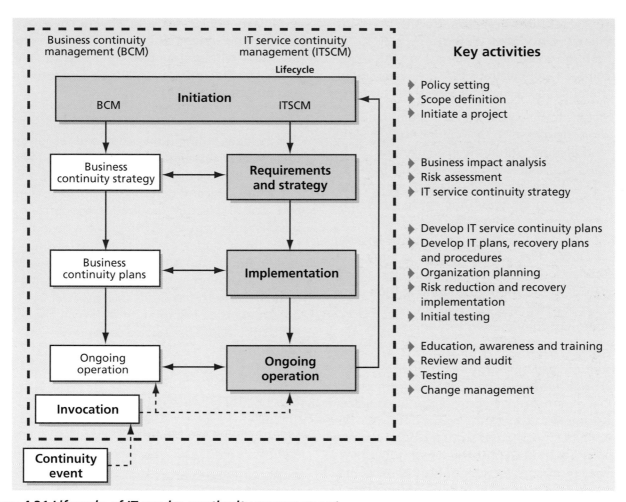

Figure 4.21 Lifecycle of IT service continuity management

used to raise awareness of continuity requirements and is often used to justify and implement a BCM process and business continuity plans. ITSCM should be driven by business risk as identified by BCM, and ensure that the recovery arrangements for IT services are aligned to identified business impacts, risks and needs.

4.6.4 Policies, principles and basic concepts

A lifecycle approach should be adopted to the setting up and operation of an ITSCM process. Figure 4.21 shows the lifecycle of ITSCM, from initiation through to continual assurance that the protection provided by the plan is current and reflects all changes to services and service levels. ITSCM is a cyclic process through the lifecycle to ensure that once service continuity plans have been developed they are kept aligned with business continuity plans and business priorities. Figure

4.21 also shows the role played within the ITSCM process of BCM.

Initiation and, to a significant extent, the requirements stages are principally BCM activities. ITSCM should only be involved in these stages to support the BCM activities and to understand the relationship between the business processes and the impacts caused on them by loss of IT service. As a result of these initial BIA and risk assessment activities, BCM should produce a business continuity strategy, and the first real ITSCM task is to produce an ITSCM strategy that underpins the BCM strategy and its needs.

The business continuity strategy should principally focus on business processes and associated issues (e.g. business process continuity, staff continuity, buildings continuity). Once the business continuity strategy has been produced, and the role that IT services has to fulfil within the strategy has been determined, an ITSCM strategy can be produced that supports and enables the business continuity strategy. This ensures that cost-effective decisions can be made, considering all the 'resources' to deliver a business process. Failure to do this tends to encourage ITSCM options that are faster, more elaborate and more expensive than actually needed.

The activities to be considered during initiation depend on the extent to which continuity facilities have been applied within the organization. Some parts of the business may have established individual business continuity plans based around manual workarounds, and IT may have developed continuity plans for systems perceived to be critical. This is good input to the process. However, effective ITSCM depends on supporting vital business functions. The only way of implementing effective ITSCM is through the identification of critical business processes and the analysis and coordination of the required technology and supporting IT services.

This situation may be even more complicated in outsourcing situations where an ITSCM process within an external service provider or outsourcer organization has to meet the needs not only of the customer BCM process and strategy, but also of the outsourcer's own BCM process and strategy. These needs may be in conflict with one another, or may conflict with the BCM needs of one of the other outsourcing organization's customers.

However, in many organizations BCM is absent or has very little focus, and often ITSCM is required to fulfil many of the requirements and activities of BCM. The rest of this section has assumed that ITSCM has had to perform many of the activities required by BCM. Where a BCM process is established with business continuity strategies and plans in place, these documents should provide the focus and drive for establishing ITSCM.

4.6.5 Process activities, methods and techniques

The following sections contain details of each of the stages within the ITSCM lifecycle.

4.6.5.1 Stage 1 – Initiation

The initiation process covers the whole of the organization and consists of the following activities.

Policy setting

This should be established and communicated as soon as possible so that all members of the organization involved in, or affected by, business continuity issues are aware of their responsibilities to comply with and support ITSCM. As a minimum, the policy should set out management intention and objectives.

Define scope and specify terms of reference

This includes defining the scope and responsibilities of all staff in the organization. It covers such tasks as undertaking a risk assessment and business impact analysis and determination of the command and control structure required to support a business interruption. There is also a need to take into account such issues as outstanding audit points, regulatory or client requirements and insurance organization stipulations, and compliance with standards such as ISO/IEC 27001, the standard on information security management, which also addresses service continuity requirements.

Initiate a project

The initiation of formal IT service continuity management is best organized into a project. The project can be used to bring ITSCM to the 'ongoing operation' stage. Setting up the project includes:

- **Allocating resources** The establishment of an effective business continuity environment requires considerable resource in terms of both money and personnel. Depending on the maturity of the organization with respect to ITSCM, there may be a requirement to familiarize and/or train staff to accomplish stage 2 tasks. Alternatively, the use of experienced external consultants may assist in completing the analysis more quickly. However, it is important that the organization can then maintain the process going forward without the need to rely totally on external support.
- **Defining the project organization and control structure** ITSCM and BCM projects are potentially complex and need to be well organized and controlled. It is strongly advisable to use a recognized standard project planning methodology such as PRojects IN Controlled Environments (PRINCE2) or Project Management Body of Knowledge (PMBOK).
- **Agreeing project and quality plans** Plans enable the project to be controlled and variances addressed. Quality plans ensure that the deliverables are achieved and to an acceptable level of quality. They also provide

a mechanism for communicating project resource requirements and deliverables, thereby obtaining 'buy-in' from all necessary parties.

4.6.5.2 Stage 2 – Requirements and strategy

Ascertaining the business requirements for IT service continuity is a critical component in order to determine how well an organization will survive a business interruption or disaster and the costs that will be incurred. If the requirements analysis is incorrect, or key information has been missed, this could have serious consequences on the effectiveness of ITSCM mechanisms. This stage can effectively be split into two sections:

■ **Requirements** Perform BIA and risk assessment
■ **Strategy** Following the requirements analysis, the strategy should document how the risks will be managed through risk reduction measures and recovery options required to support the business.

Requirements – business impact analysis

The purpose of a BIA is to quantify the impact to the business that loss of service would have. This impact could be a 'hard' impact that can be precisely identified – such as financial loss – or 'soft' impact – such as public relations, moral, health and safety or loss of competitive advantage. The BIA will identify the most important services to the organization and will therefore be a key input to the strategy.

The BIA identifies:

■ The form that the damage or loss may take – for example:
  ● Lost income
  ● Additional costs
  ● Damaged reputation
  ● Loss of goodwill
  ● Loss of competitive advantage
  ● Breach of law, health and safety regulations
  ● Risk to personal safety
  ● Immediate and long-term loss of market share
  ● Political, corporate or personal embarrassment
  ● Loss of operational capability, for example, in a command and control environment

■ How the degree of damage or loss is likely to escalate after a service disruption, and the times of the day, week, month or year when disruption will be most severe
■ The staffing, skills, facilities and services (including the IT services) necessary to enable critical and essential business processes to continue operating at a minimum acceptable level
■ The time within which minimum levels of staffing, facilities and services should be recovered
■ The time within which all required business processes and supporting staff, facilities and services should be fully recovered
■ The relative business recovery priority for each of the IT services.

One of the key outputs from a BIA exercise is a graph of the anticipated business impact caused by the loss of a business process or the loss of an IT service over time, as illustrated in Figure 4.22.

This graph can then be used to drive the business and IT continuity strategies and plans. More preventive measures need to be adopted with regard to those processes and services with earlier and higher impacts, whereas greater emphasis should be placed on continuity and recovery measures for those where the impact is lower and takes longer to develop. A balanced approach of both measures should be adopted to those in between.

These items provide the drivers for the level of ITSCM mechanisms that need to be considered or deployed. Once presented with these options, the business may decide that lower levels of service or increased delays are more acceptable, based on a cost-benefit analysis, or it may be that comprehensive disaster prevention measures will need to be implemented.

These assessments enable the mapping of critical service, application and technology components to critical business processes, thus helping to identify the ITSCM elements that need to be provided. The business requirements are ranked and the associated ITSCM elements confirmed and prioritized in terms of risk reduction and recovery planning. The results of the BIA, discussed earlier, are invaluable input to several areas of process design including SLM to understand the required service levels.

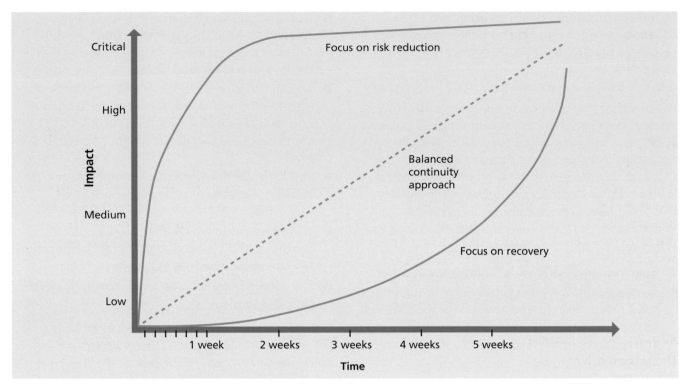

Figure 4.22 Graphical representation of business impacts

Impacts should be measured against particular scenarios for each business process, such as an inability to settle trades in a money market dealing process, or an inability to invoice for a period of days.

Example of business impact

An example is a money market dealing environment where loss of market data information could mean that the organization starts to lose money immediately as trading cannot continue. In addition, customers may go to another organization, which would mean potential loss of core business. Loss of the settlement system does not prevent trading from taking place, but if trades already conducted cannot be settled within a specified period of time, the organization may be in breach of regulatory rules or settlement periods and suffer fines and damaged reputation. This may actually be a more significant impact than the inability to trade because of an inability to satisfy customer expectations.

It is also important to understand how impacts may change over time. For instance, it may be possible for a business to function without a

particular process for a short period of time. In a balanced scenario, impacts to the business will occur and become greater over time. However, not all organizations are affected in this way. In some organizations, impacts are not apparent immediately. At some point, however, for any organization, the impacts will accrue to such a level that the business can no longer operate. ITSCM ensures that contingency options are identified so that the appropriate measure can be applied at the appropriate time to keep business impacts from service disruption to a minimum level.

When conducting a BIA, it is important that senior business area representatives' views are sought on the impact following loss of service. It is also equally important that the views of supervisory staff and more junior staff are sought to ensure all aspects of the impact following loss of service are ascertained. Often different levels of staff will have different views on the impact, and all will have to be taken into account when producing the overall strategy.

In many organizations it will be impossible, or it will not be cost-justifiable, to recover the total service in a very short timescale. In many cases, business processes can be re-established without a full complement of staff, systems and other facilities, and still maintain an acceptable level of service to clients and customers. The business recovery objectives should therefore be stated in terms of:

■ The time within which a pre-defined team of core staff and stated minimum facilities must be recovered

■ The timetable for recovery of remaining staff and facilities.

It may not always be possible to provide the recovery requirements to a detailed level. There is a need to balance the potential impact against the cost of recovery to ensure that the costs are acceptable. The recovery objectives do, however, provide a starting point from which different business recovery and ITSCM options can be evaluated.

Requirements – risk assessment

The second driver in determining ITSCM requirements is the likelihood that a disaster or other serious service disruption will actually occur. This is an assessment of the level of threat and the extent to which an organization is vulnerable to that threat. Risk assessment can also be used in assessing and reducing the chance of normal operational incidents and is a technique used by availability management to ensure the required availability and reliability levels can be maintained. Risk assessment is also a key aspect of information security management. A diagram on risk assessment and management (Figure 4.15) is contained within the availability management process in section 4.4.

A number of risk assessment and management methods are available for both the commercial and government sectors. Risk assessment is the assessment of the risks that may give rise to service disruption or security violation. Risk management is concerned with identifying appropriate risk responses or cost-justifiable countermeasures to combat those risks.

A standard methodology, such as the Management of Risk (M_o_R), should be used to assess and manage risks within an organization. The M_o_R framework is described in greater detail in Appendix M.

Conducting a formal risk assessment using M_o_R or another structured method will typically result in a risk profile, containing many risks

that are outside the defined level of 'acceptable risk'. Following the risk assessment it is possible to determine appropriate risk responses or risk reduction measures (ITSCM mechanisms) to manage the risks, i.e. reduce the risk to an acceptable level or mitigate the risk. Wherever possible, appropriate risk responses should be implemented to reduce either the impact or the likelihood, or both, of these risks from manifesting themselves. In the context of ITSCM, there are a number of risks that need to be taken into consideration. Table 4.2 is not a comprehensive list but does give some examples of risks and threats that need to be addressed by the ITSCM process.

IT service continuity strategy

The results of the BIA and the risk assessment will enable appropriate business and IT service continuity strategies to be produced in line with the business needs. The strategy will be an optimum balance of risk reduction and recovery or continuity options. This includes consideration of the relative service recovery priorities and the changes in relative service priority for the time of day, day of the week, and monthly and annual variations. Those services that have been identified as high impacts in the short term within the BIA will want to concentrate efforts on preventive risk reduction methods – for example, through full resilience and fault tolerance – while an organization that has low short-term impacts would be better suited to comprehensive recovery options, as described in the following sections. Similar advice and guidance can be found in the Business Continuity Institute's *BCI Good Practice Guidelines*.

RISK RESPONSE MEASURES

Most organizations will have to adopt a balanced approach where risk reduction and recovery are complementary and both are required. This entails reducing, as far as possible, the risks to the continued provision of the IT service and is usually achieved through availability management. However well planned, it is impossible to completely eliminate all risks – for example, a fire in a nearby building will probably result in damage, or at least denial of access, as a result of the implementation of a cordon. As a general rule, the invocation of a recovery capability should only be taken as a last resort. Ideally, an organization should assess all of the risks to reduce the potential

Table 4.2 Examples of risks and threats

Risk	Threat
Loss of internal IT systems/ networks, PABXs, ACDs etc.	Fire
	Power failure
	Arson and vandalism
	Flood
	Aircraft impact
	Weather damage, e.g. hurricane
	Environmental disaster
	Terrorist attack
	Sabotage
	Catastrophic failure
	Electrical damage, e.g. lightning
	Accidental damage
	Poor-quality software
Loss of external IT systems/ networks, e.g. e-commerce servers, cryptographic systems	All of the above
	Excessive demand for services
	Denial of service attack, e.g. against an internet firewall
	Technology failure, e.g. cryptographic system
Loss of data	Technology failure
	Human error
	Viruses, malicious software, e.g. attack applets
Loss of network services	Damage or denial of access to network service provider's premises
	Loss of service provider's IT systems/networks
	Loss of service provider's data
	Failure of the service provider
Unavailability of key technical and support staff	Industrial action
	Denial of access to premises
	Resignation
	Sickness/injury
	Transport difficulties
Failure of service providers, e.g. outsourced IT	Commercial failure, e.g. insolvency
	Denial of access to premises
	Unavailability of service provider's staff
	Failure to meet contractual service levels

requirement to recover the business, which is likely to include the IT services.

The risk reduction measures need to be implemented and should be instigated in conjunction with availability management, as many of these reduce the probability of failure affecting the availability of service. Typical risk reduction measures include:

■ Installation of uninterruptible power supply and backup power to the computer

- Fault-tolerant systems for critical applications where even minimal downtime is unacceptable – for example, a banking system
- RAID arrays and disk mirroring for LAN servers to prevent data loss and to ensure continued availability of data
- Spare equipment/components to be used in the event of equipment or component failure – for example, a spare LAN server already configured with the standard configuration and available to replace a faulty server with minimum build and configuration time
- The elimination of SPOFs, such as single access network points or a single power supply into a building
- Resilient IT systems and networks
- Outsourcing services to more than one provider
- Greater physical and IT-based security controls
- Better controls to detect service disruptions, such as fire detection systems, coupled with suppression systems
- A comprehensive backup and recovery strategy, including off-site storage.

The above measures will not necessarily solve an ITSCM issue and remove the risk totally, but all or a combination of them may significantly reduce the risks associated with the way in which services are provided to the business. The detailed IT service continuity strategy will be developed to meet the agreed business needs, reflected in such specifications as recovery point objectives and recovery time objectives.

OFF-SITE STORAGE

One risk response method is to ensure all vital data is backed up and stored off-site. Once the recovery strategy has been defined, an appropriate backup strategy should be adopted and implemented to support it. The backup strategy must include regular (probably daily) removal of data (including the CMS to ease recovery) from the main data centres to a suitable off-site storage location. This will ensure retrieval of data following relatively minor operational failure as well as total and complete disasters. As well as the electronic data, all other important information and documents should be stored off-site, with the main example being the ITSCM plans.

ITSCM RECOVERY OPTIONS

An organization's ITSCM strategy is a balance between the cost of risk reduction measures and recovery options to support the recovery of critical business processes within agreed timescales. The following is a list of the potential IT recovery options that need to be considered when developing the strategy.

MANUAL WORKAROUNDS

For certain types of service, manual workarounds can be an effective interim measure for a limited timeframe until the IT service is resumed. For instance, a service desk call-logging service could survive for a limited time using paper forms linked to a laptop computer with a spreadsheet.

RECIPROCAL ARRANGEMENTS

In the past, reciprocal arrangements were typical contingency measures where agreements were put in place with another organization using similar technology. This is no longer effective or possible for most types of IT system, but can still be used in specific cases – for example, setting up an agreement to share high-speed printing facilities. Reciprocal arrangements can also be used for the off-site storage of backups and other critical information.

GRADUAL RECOVERY

This option (sometimes referred to as 'cold standby') includes the provision of empty accommodation, fully equipped with power, environmental controls and local network cabling infrastructure, telecommunications connections, and available in a disaster situation for an organization to install its own computer equipment. It does not include the actual computing equipment, so is not applicable for services requiring speedy recovery, as setup time is required before recovery of services can begin. This recovery option is only recommended for services that can bear a delay of recovery time in days or weeks, not hours. Any non-critical service that can bear this type of delay should take into account the cost of this option versus the benefit to the business before determining if a gradual recovery option should be included in the ITSCM options for the organization.

The accommodation may be provided commercially by a third party (for a fee) or may be private (established by the organization itself) and provided as either a fixed or portable facility.

A portable facility is typically a prefabricated building provided by a third party and located, when needed, at a predetermined site agreed with the organization. This may be in another location some distance from the home site, perhaps another owned building. The replacement computer equipment will need to be planned, but suppliers of computing equipment do not always guarantee replacement equipment within a fixed deadline, though they would normally do so under their best efforts.

INTERMEDIATE RECOVERY

This option (sometimes referred to as 'warm standby') is selected by organizations that need to recover IT facilities within a predetermined time or recovery time objective to prevent impacts to the business process. The predetermined time will have been agreed with the business during the BIA.

Most common is the use of commercial facilities, which are offered by third-party recovery organizations to a number of subscribers, spreading the cost across those subscribers. Commercial facilities often include operation, system management and technical support. The cost varies depending on the facilities requested, such as processors, peripherals, communications, and how quickly the services must be restored.

The advantage of this service is that the customer can have virtually instantaneous access to a site, housed in a secure building, in the event of a disaster. It must be understood, however, that the restoration of services at the site may take some time, as delays may be encountered while the site is reconfigured for the organization that invokes the service, and the organization's applications and data will need to be restored from backups.

One potentially major disadvantage is the security implications of running IT services at a third party's data centre. This must be taken into account when planning to use this type of facility. For some organizations, the external intermediate recovery option may not be appropriate for this reason. If the site is invoked, there is often a daily fee for use of the service in an emergency, although this may be offset against additional cost of working insurance.

Commercial recovery services can be provided in self-contained, portable or mobile form where an agreed system is delivered to a customer's site, within an agreed time.

FAST RECOVERY

This option (sometimes referred to as 'hot standby') provides for fast recovery and restoration of services and is sometimes provided as an extension to the intermediate recovery provided by a third-party recovery provider. Some organizations will provide their own facilities within the organization, but not on an alternative site to the one used for the normal operations. Others implement their own internal second locations on an alternative site to provide more resilient recovery.

Where there is a need for a fast restoration of a service, it is possible to 'rent' floor space at the recovery site and install servers or systems with application systems and communications already available, and data mirrored from the operational servers. In the event of a system failure, the customers can then recover and switch over to the backup facility with little loss of service. This typically involves the re-establishment of the critical systems and services within a 24-hour period.

IMMEDIATE RECOVERY

This option (also often referred to as 'hot standby', 'mirroring', 'load balancing' or 'split site') provides for immediate restoration of services, with no significant loss of service to the customer. For business critical services, organizations requiring continuous operation will provide their own facilities within the organization, but not on the same site as the normal operations. Sufficient IT equipment will be 'dual located' in either an owned or hosted location to run the compete service from either location in the event of loss of one facility, with no loss of service to the customer. The second site can then be recovered while the service is provided from the single operable location. This is an expensive option, but may be justified for critical business processes or VBFs where non-availability for a short period could result in a significant impact, or where it would not be appropriate to be running IT services on a third party's premises for security or other reasons. The facility needs to be located separately and far enough away from the home site so that it will not

Table 4.3 Example set of recovery options

	Manual	Immediate	Fast	Intermediate	Gradual
Service desk	Yes		Yes	Yes	Yes
Mainframe payroll	Yes			Yes	Yes
Financial system			Yes		Yes
Dealer system		Yes		Yes	Yes

be affected by a disaster affecting that location. However, these mirrored servers and sites options should be implemented in close liaison with availability management as they support services with high levels of availability.

The strategy is likely to include a combination of risk response measures and a combination of the above recovery options, as illustrated in Table 4.3.

Table 4.3 shows that a number of options may be used to provide continuity of service and that, initially, continuity of the service desk is provided using manual processes such as a set of forms, and maybe a spreadsheet operating from a laptop computer, while recovery plans for the service are completed on an alternative 'fast recovery' site. Once the alternative site has become operational, the service desk can switch back to using the IT service. However, use of the external 'fast recovery' alternative site is probably limited in duration, so while running temporarily from this site, the 'intermediate site' can be made operational and long-term operations can be transferred there.

Different services within an organization require different in-built resilience and different recovery options. Whatever option is chosen, the solution will need to be cost-justified. As a general rule, the longer the business can survive without a service, the cheaper the solution will be. For example, a critical healthcare system that requires continuous operation will be very costly, as potential loss of service will need to be eliminated by the use of immediate recovery, whereas a service whose absence does not severely affect the business for a week or so could be supported by a much cheaper solution, such as intermediate recovery.

As well as the recovery of the computing equipment, planning needs to include the recovery of accommodation and infrastructure for both IT and user staff. Other areas to be taken into

account include critical services such as power, telecommunications, water, couriers, post, paper records and reference material.

4.6.5.3 Stage 3 – Implementation

Once the strategy has been approved, the detailed IT service continuity plans need to be produced in line with the business continuity plans and the measures to implement the strategy need to be put in place. The measures to implement the strategy will include putting in place both the defined risk reduction and recovery option arrangements and performing initial testing to ensure that what was planned has been achieved.

Develop IT service continuity plans and procedures

ITSCM plans need to be developed to enable the necessary information for critical systems, services and facilities to either continue to be provided or to be reinstated within an acceptable period to the business. An example of an ITSCM recovery plan, a key part of the overall IT service continuity plan, is given in Appendix K. Generally the business continuity plans rely on the availability of IT services, facilities and resources. As a consequence of this, ITSCM plans need to address all activities to ensure that the required services, facilities and resources are delivered in an acceptable operational state and are 'fit for purpose' when accepted by the business. This entails not only the restoration of services and facilities, but also the understanding of dependencies between them, the testing required prior to delivery (performance, functional, operational and acceptance testing) and the validation of data integrity and consistency.

It should be noted that the continuity plans are more than just recovery plans, and should include documentation of the resilience measures and the measures that have been put into place to enable recovery, together with explanations of why a particular approach has been taken (this facilitates decisions should invocation determine that the particular situation requires a modification to the plan). However, the format of the plan should enable rapid access to the recovery information itself, perhaps as an appendix that can be accessed directly. All key staff should have access to copies of all the necessary recovery documentation.

Management of the distribution of the plans is important to ensure that copies are available to key staff at all times. The plans should be controlled documents (with formalized documents maintained under the control of change management and service asset and configuration management) to ensure that only the latest versions are in circulation and each recipient should ensure that a personal copy is maintained off-site.

The plan should ensure that all details regarding recovery of the IT services following a disaster are fully documented. It should have sufficient details to enable a technical person unfamiliar with the systems to be able to follow the procedures. The recovery plans include key details such as the data recovery point, a list of dependent systems, the nature of the dependency and their data recovery points, system hardware and software requirements, configuration details and references to other relevant or essential information about the service and systems.

It is a good idea to include a checklist that covers specific actions required during all stages of recovery for the service and system. For example, after the system has been restored to an operational state, connectivity checks, functionality checks or data consistency and integrity checks should be carried out prior to handing the service over to the business.

There are a number of technical plans that may already exist within an organization, documenting recovery procedures from a normal operational failure. The development and maintenance of these plans will be the responsibility of the specialist teams, but will be coordinated by the BCM team. These will be useful additions or appendices to the main plan. Additionally, plans that will need to be integrated with the main business continuity plan are:

- **Emergency response plan** To interface to all emergency services and activities
- **Damage assessment plan** Containing details of damage assessment contacts, processes and plans
- **Salvage plan** Containing information on salvage contacts, activities and processes
- **Vital records plan** Details of all vital records and information, together with their location, that are critical to the continued operation of the business
- **Crisis management and public relations plan** The plans on the command and control of different crisis situations and management of the media and public relations
- **Accommodation and services plan** Detailing the management of accommodation, facilities and the services necessary for their continued operation
- **Security plan** Showing how all aspects of security will be managed on all home sites and recovery sites
- **Personnel plan** Containing details of how all personnel issues will be managed during a major incident
- **Communication plan** Showing how all aspects of communication will be handled and managed with all relevant areas and parties involved during a major incident
- **Finance and administration plan** Containing details of alternative methods and processes for obtaining possible emergency authorization and access to essential funds during a major incident.

Finally, each critical business area is responsible for the development of a plan detailing the individuals who will be in the recovery teams and the tasks to be undertaken on invocation of recovery arrangements.

The ITSCM plan must contain all the information needed to recover the IT systems, networks and telecommunications in a disaster situation once a decision to invoke has been made, and then to manage the business return to normal operation once the service disruption has been resolved. One of the most important inputs into the plan development is the results of the BIA. Additionally, other areas will need to be analysed, such as SLA, security requirements, operating instructions and procedures, and external contracts. It is likely that a separate SLA with alternative targets will have been agreed if running at a recovery site following a disaster.

Other areas that will need to be implemented following the approval of the strategy are as follows.

Organization planning

During the disaster recovery process, the organizational structure will inevitably be different from normal operation and will be based around:

■ **Executive** This will include senior management/ executive board, with overall authority and control within the organization and responsible for crisis management and liaison with other departments, divisions, organizations, the media, regulators, emergency services etc.

■ **Coordination** Typically one level below the executive group, this is responsible for coordinating the overall recovery effort within the organization

■ **Recovery** A series of business and service recovery teams should represent the vital business functions and the services that need to be established to support these functions. Each team is responsible for executing the plans within its own areas and for liaison with staff, customers and third parties. Within IT, the recovery teams should be grouped by IT service and application. For example, the infrastructure team may have one or more people responsible for recovering external connections, voice services, local area networks etc. and the support teams may be split by platform, operating system or application. In addition, the recovery priorities for the service, application or its components identified during the BIA should be documented within the recovery plans and applied during their execution.

Risk reduction/recovery arrangement implementation

The specific actions necessary to enable the strategy must be implemented. Risk reduction arrangements are usually undertaken in conjunction with availability management. Specific examples include those described in the 'risk response measures' section above.

It is important to remember that the recovery is also based around a series of standby arrangements including accommodation,

procedures and people, as well as systems and telecommunications. Certain actions are necessary to implement the standby arrangements, as called for in the strategy. For example:

■ Negotiating for third-party recovery facilities and entering into a contractual arrangement

■ Preparing and equipping the standby accommodation

■ Purchasing and installing standby computer systems.

Initial testing

Experience has shown that recovery plans that have not been fully tested do not work as intended, if at all. Testing is therefore a critical part of the overall ITSCM process and the only way of ensuring that the selected strategy, standby arrangements, logistics, business recovery plans and procedures will actually work in practice.

The IT service provider is responsible for ensuring that the IT services can be recovered in the required timescales with the required functionality and the required performance following a disaster.

Four basic types of tests can be undertaken:

■ **Walk-through tests** These can be conducted when the plan has been produced simply by getting the relevant people together to see if the plan(s) at least work in a simulated way.

■ **Full tests** These should be conducted as soon as possible after the plan production and at regular intervals of at least annually thereafter. They should involve the business units to assist in proving the capability to recover the services appropriately. They should, as far as possible, replicate an actual invocation of all standby arrangements and should involve external parties if they are planned to be involved in an actual invocation. The tests must not only prove recovery of the IT services but also the recovery of the business processes. It is recommended that an independent observer records all the activities of the tests and the timings of the service recovery. The observer's documentation of the tests will be vital input into the subsequent post-mortem review. The full tests may be announced or unannounced. The first test of the plan is likely to be announced and carefully planned, but subsequent tests may be 'sprung' on key players without warning. It is also essential that many different people get involved, including those not very familiar with the IT service and systems, as the people with the most knowledge may not be available when a disaster actually occurs.

- **Partial tests** These can also be undertaken where recovery of certain elements of the overall plan is tested, such as single services or servers. These types of test should be in addition to the full test not instead of the full test. The full test is the best way of testing that all services can be recovered in required timescales and can run together on the recovery systems.

- **Scenario tests** These can be used to test reactions and plans to specific conditions, events and scenarios. They can include testing that business continuity plans and IT service continuity plans interface with each other, as well as interfacing with all other plans involved in the handling and management of a major incident.

All tests need to be undertaken against defined test scenarios, which are described as realistically as possible. It should be noted, however, that even the most comprehensive test does not cover everything. For example, in a service disruption where there has been injury to, or even death of, colleagues, the reaction of staff to a crisis cannot be tested and the plans need to make allowance for this. In addition, tests must have clearly defined objectives and CSFs, which will be used to determine the success or otherwise of the exercise.

4.6.5.4 Stage 4 – Ongoing operation

This stage consists of the activities necessary to firmly establish the ITSCM capabilities and maintain them in an accurate and reliable state as time goes on. It should be noted that maintaining the relevance of ITSCM will require ongoing participation in regular business impact analysis and risk assessment and management activities in cooperation with BCM, and action to implement any needed changes based on any resulting strategy revisions. The activities of ongoing operation are set out below.

Education, awareness and training

Education, awareness and training should cover the organization and, in particular, the IT organization, for service continuity-specific items. This ensures that all staff are aware of the implications of business continuity and of service continuity and

consider these as part of their normal working, and that everyone involved in the plan has been trained in how to implement their actions.

Review and audit

Regular review of all of the deliverables from the ITSCM process needs to be undertaken to ensure that they remain current. With service providers struggling to do everything they must to serve their customers, it may be difficult to set aside the time needed for reviews and audits, but the work is necessary. The time when the plans need to be invoked in response to a real continuity event is not the time to discover it has become obsolete.

Testing

Following the initial testing, it is necessary to establish a programme of regular testing to ensure that the critical components of the strategy are tested, preferably at least annually, although testing of IT service continuity plans should be arranged in line with business needs and the needs of the business continuity plans.

All plans should also be tested after every major business change. It is important that any changes to the IT technology are also included in the strategy, implemented in an appropriate fashion and tested to ensure that they function correctly within the overall provision of IT following a disaster. The backup and recovery of IT service should also be monitored and tested to ensure that when they are needed during a major incident, they will operate as needed. This aspect is covered more fully in *ITIL Service Operation*.

Change management

The change management process should ensure that all changes are assessed for their potential impact on the ITSCM plans. If the planned change will invalidate the plans, then the plan must be updated before the change is implemented, and it should be tested as part of the change testing.

The plans themselves must be under very strict change management and service asset and configuration management control. Inaccurate plans and inadequate recovery capabilities may result in the failure of business continuity plans. Also, on an ongoing basis, whenever there are new services or where services have major changes, it is essential that a BIA and a risk assessment is conducted on the new or changed service and the strategy and plans updated accordingly.

4.6.5.5 Invocation

Invocation is the ultimate test of the business continuity and ITSCM plans. If all the preparatory work has been successfully completed, and plans developed and tested, then an invocation of the business continuity plans should be a straightforward process, but if the plans have not been tested, failures can be expected. It is important that due consideration is given to the design of all invocation processes, to ensure that they are fit for purpose and interface with all other relevant invocation processes.

Invocation is a key component of the plans, which must include the invocation process and guidance. It should be remembered that the decision to invoke, especially if a third-party recovery facility is to be used, should not be taken lightly. Costs will be involved and the process will involve disruption to the business. This decision is typically made by a 'crisis management' team, comprising senior managers from the business and support departments (including IT), using information gathered through damage assessment and other sources.

A disruption could occur at any time of the day or night, so it is essential that guidance on the invocation process is readily available. Plans must be available to key staff in the office and away from the office.

The decision to invoke must be made quickly, as there may be a lead-time involved in establishing facilities at a recovery site. In the case of a serious building fire, the decision may be fairly easy to make. However, in the case of power failure or hardware fault, where a resolution is expected within a short period, a deadline should be set by which time if the incident has not been resolved, invocation will take place. If using external services providers, they should be warned immediately if there is a chance that invocation might take place.

The decision to invoke needs to take into account the:

- Extent of the damage and scope of the potential invocation
- Likely length of the disruption and unavailability of premises and/or services

- Time of day/month/year and the potential business impact. At year-end, the need to invoke may be more pressing to ensure that year-end processing is completed on time.

Therefore the design of the invocation process must provide guidance on how all of these areas and circumstances should be assessed to assist the person invoking the continuity plan.

The ITSCM plan should include details of activities that need to be undertaken, including:

- Retrieval of backup media or use of data vaulting to retrieve data
- Retrieval of essential documentation, procedures, workstation images etc. stored off-site
- Mobilization of the appropriate technical personnel to go to the recovery site to commence the recovery of required systems and services
- Contacting and putting on alert telecommunications suppliers, support services, application vendors etc. who may be required to undertake actions or provide assistance in the recovery process.

The invocation and initial recovery is likely to be a time of high activity, involving long hours for many individuals. This must be recognized and managed by the recovery team leaders to ensure that breaks are provided and prevent 'burn-out'. Planning for shifts and handovers must be undertaken to ensure that the best use is made of the facilities available. It is also vitally important to ensure that the usual business and technology controls remain in place during invocation, recovery and return to normal to ensure that information security is maintained at the correct level and that data protection is preserved.

Once the recovery has been completed, the business should be able to operate from the recovery site at the level determined and agreed in the strategy and relevant SLA. The objective, however, will be to build up the business to normal levels, maintain operation from the recovery site in the short term and vacate the recovery site in the shortest possible time. Details of all these activities need to be contained within the plans. If using external services, there will be a finite contractual period for using the facility. Whatever the period, a return to normal must be carefully planned and undertaken in a controlled fashion.

Typically this will be over a weekend and may include some necessary downtime in business hours. It is important that this is managed well and that all personnel involved are aware of their responsibilities to ensure a smooth transition.

4.6.6 Triggers, inputs, outputs and interfaces

4.6.6.1 Triggers

Many events may trigger ITSCM activity, including:

- New or changed business needs, or new or changed services
- New or changed targets within agreements, such as SLRs, SLAs, OLAs or contracts
- The occurrence of a major incident that requires assessment for potential invocation of either business or IT continuity plans
- Periodic activities such as the BIA or risk assessment activities, maintenance of continuity plans or other reviewing, revising or reporting activities
- Assessment of changes and attendance at change advisory board meetings
- Review and revision of business and IT plans and strategies
- Review and revision of designs and strategies
- Recognition or notification of a change of risk or impact of a business process or VBF, an IT service or component
- Initiation of tests of continuity and recovery plans
- Lessons learned from previous continuity events and associated recovery activities.

4.6.6.2 Inputs

There are many sources of input required by the ITSCM process:

- Business information: from the organization's business strategy, plans and financial plans, and information on their current and future requirements
- IT information: from the IT strategy and plans and current budgets
- A business continuity strategy and a set of business continuity plans: from all areas of the business

- Service information: from the SLM process, with details of the services from the service portfolio and the service catalogue and service level targets within SLAs and SLRs
- Financial information: from financial management for IT services, the cost of service provision, the cost of resources and components
- Change information: from the change management process, with a change schedule and a need to assess all changes for their impact on all ITSCM plans
- CMS: containing information on the relationships between the business, the services, the supporting services and the technology
- Business continuity management and availability management testing schedules
- Capacity management information identifying the resources required to run the critical services in the event of a continuity event
- IT service continuity plans and test reports from supplier and partners, where appropriate.

4.6.6.3 Outputs

The outputs from the ITSCM process include:

- A revised ITSCM policy and strategy
- A set of ITSCM plans, including all crisis management plans, emergency response plans and disaster recovery plans, together with a set of supporting plans and contracts with recovery service providers
- BIA exercises and reports, in conjunction with BCM and the business
- Risk assessment and management reviews and reports, in conjunction with the business, availability management and information security management
- An ITSCM testing schedule
- ITSCM test scenarios
- ITSCM test reports and reviews.

Forecasts and predictive reports are used by all areas to analyse, predict and forecast particular business and IT scenarios and their potential solutions.

4.6.6.4 Interfaces

Integration and interfaces exist from ITSCM to all other processes. Important examples are as follows:

- **Change management** All changes need to be considered for their impact on the continuity plans, and if amendments are required to the plan, updates to the plan need to be part of the change. The plan itself must be under change management control.
- **Incident and problem management** Incidents can easily evolve into major incidents or disasters. Clear criteria need to be agreed and documented for the invocation of the ITSCM plans.
- **Availability management** Undertaking risk assessment and implementing risk responses should be closely coordinated with the availability process to optimize risk mitigation.
- **Service level management** Recovery requirements will be agreed and documented in the SLAs. Different service levels could be agreed and documented that could be acceptable in a disaster situation.
- **Capacity management** Ensuring that there are sufficient resources to enable recovery onto replacement computers following a disaster.
- **Service asset and configuration management** The CMS documents the components that make up the infrastructure and the relationship between the components. This information is invaluable for all the stages of the ITSCM lifecycle, the maintenance of plans and recovery facilities.
- **Information security management** A very close relationship exists between ITSCM and information security management. A major security breach could be considered a disaster, so when conducting BIA and risk assessment, security will be a very important consideration.

4.6.7 Information management

ITSCM needs to record all of the information necessary to maintain a comprehensive set of ITSCM plans. This information base should include:

- Information from the latest version of the BIA
- Comprehensive information on risk within a risk register, including risk assessment and risk responses
- The latest version of the BCM strategy and business continuity plans
- Details relating to all completed tests and a schedule of all planned tests
- Details of all ITSCM plans and their contents

- Details of all other plans associated with ITSCM plans
- Details of all existing recovery facilities, recovery suppliers and partners, recovery agreements and contracts, spare and alternative equipment
- Details of all backup and recovery processes, schedules, systems and media and their respective locations.

All the above information needs to be integrated and aligned with all BCM information and all the other information required by ITSCM. Interfaces to many other processes are required to ensure that this alignment is maintained.

4.6.8 Critical success factors and key performance indicators

The following list includes some sample CSFs for ITSCM. Each organization should identify appropriate CSFs based on its objectives for the process. Each sample CSF is followed by a small number of typical KPIs that support the CSF. These KPIs should not be adopted without careful consideration. Each organization should develop KPIs that are appropriate for its level of maturity, its CSFs and its particular circumstances. Achievement against KPIs should be monitored and used to identify opportunities for improvement, which should be logged in the CSI register for evaluation and possible implementation.

- **CSF** IT services are delivered and can be recovered to meet business objectives
  - **KPI** Increase in success of regular audits of the ITSCM plans to ensure that, at all times, the agreed recovery requirements of the business can be achieved
  - **KPI** Regular successful validation that all service recovery targets are agreed and documented in SLAs and are achievable within the ITSCM plans
  - **KPI** Regular and comprehensive testing of ITSCM plans achieved consistently
  - **KPI** Regular reviews are undertaken, at least annually, of the business and IT continuity plans with the business areas
  - **KPI** Regular successful validation that IT negotiates and manages all necessary ITSCM contracts with third parties
  - **KPI** Overall reduction in the risk and impact of possible failure of IT services

- **CSF** Awareness throughout the organization of the business and IT service continuity plans
  - **KPI** Increase in validated awareness of business impact, needs and requirements throughout IT
  - **KPI** Increase in successful test results ensuring that all IT service areas and staff are prepared and able to respond to an invocation of the ITSCM plans
  - **KPI** Validated regular communication of the ITSCM objectives and responsibilities within the appropriate business and IT service areas.

4.6.9 Challenges and risks

4.6.9.1 Challenges

One of the major challenges facing ITSCM is to provide appropriate plans when there is no BCM process. If there is no BCM process, then IT is likely to make incorrect assumptions about business criticality of business processes and therefore adopt the wrong continuity strategies and options. Without BCM, expensive ITSCM solutions and plans will be rendered useless by the absence of corresponding plans and arrangements within the business. Also, if BCM is absent, then the business may fail to identify inexpensive non-IT solutions and waste money on ineffective, expensive IT solutions.

In some organizations, the business perception is that continuity is an IT responsibility, and therefore the business assumes that IT will be responsible for disaster recovery and that IT services will continue to run under any circumstances. This is especially true in some outsourced situations where the business may be reluctant to share its BCM information with an external service provider.

If there is a BCM process established, then the challenge becomes one of alignment and integration. ITSCM must ensure that accurate information is obtained from the BCM process on the needs, impact and priorities of the business, and that the ITSCM information and plans are aligned and integrated with those of the business. Having achieved that alignment, the challenge becomes one of keeping them aligned by management and control of business and IT change. It is essential, therefore, that all documents and plans are maintained under the strict control of change management and service asset and configuration management.

4.6.9.2 Risks

Some of the major risks associated with ITSCM include:

- Lack of a BCM process
- Lack of commitment from the business to the ITSCM processes and procedures
- Lack of appropriate information on future business plans and strategies
- Lack of senior management commitment or a lack of resources and/or budget for the ITSCM process
- The processes focus too much on the technology issues and not enough on the IT services and the needs and priorities of the business
- Risk assessment and management are conducted in isolation and not in conjunction with availability management and information security management
- ITSCM plans and information become out of date and lose alignment with the information and plans of the business and BCM.

4.7 INFORMATION SECURITY MANAGEMENT

Information security is a management process within the corporate governance framework, which provides the strategic direction for security activities and ensures objectives are achieved. It further ensures that the information security risks are appropriately managed and that enterprise information resources are used responsibly. Information security management provides a focus for all aspects of IT security and manages all IT security activities.

In this context, the term 'information' is used as a general term and includes data stores, databases and metadata.

Information security is a critical part of the warranty of a service. If the security of a service's information and information processing cannot be maintained at the levels required by the business, then the business will not experience the value that has been promised. Without information security the utility of the service cannot be accessed.

Information security management needs to be considered within the overall corporate governance framework. Corporate governance is the set of responsibilities and practices exercised by the board and executive management with the goal of providing strategic direction, ensuring the objectives are achieved, ascertaining the risks are being managed appropriately and verifying that the enterprise's resources are used effectively.

4.7.1 Purpose and objectives

The purpose of the information security management process is to align IT security with business security and ensure that the confidentiality, integrity and availability of the organization's assets, information, data and IT services always matches the agreed needs of the business.

The objective of information security management is to protect the interests of those relying on information, and the systems and communications that deliver the information, from harm resulting from failures of confidentiality, integrity and availability.

For most organizations, the security objective is met when:

- Information is observed by or disclosed to only those who have a right to know (confidentiality)
- Information is complete, accurate and protected against unauthorized modification (integrity)
- Information is available and usable when required, and the systems that provide it can appropriately resist attacks and recover from or prevent failures (availability)
- Business transactions, as well as information exchanges between enterprises, or with partners, can be trusted (authenticity and non-repudiation).

4.7.2 Scope

The information security management process should be the focal point for all IT security issues, and must ensure that an information security policy is produced, maintained and enforced that covers the use and misuse of all IT systems and services. Information security management needs to understand the total IT and business security environment, including the:

- Business security policy and plans
- Current business operation and its security requirements
- Future business plans and requirements
- Legislative and regulatory requirements

- Obligations and responsibilities with regard to security contained within SLAs
- The business and IT risks and their management.

Understanding all of this will enable information security management to ensure that all the current and future security aspects and risks of the business are cost-effectively managed.

Prioritization of confidentiality, integrity and availability must be considered in the context of business and business processes. The primary guide to defining what must be protected and the level of protection has to come from the business. To be effective, security must address entire business processes from end to end and cover the physical and technical aspects. Only within the context of business needs and risks can management define security.

The information security management process should include:

- The production, maintenance, distribution and enforcement of an information security policy and supporting security policies
- Understanding the agreed current and future security requirements of the business and the existing business security policy and plans
- Implementation of a set of security controls that support the information security policy and manage risks associated with access to services, information and systems
- Documentation of all security controls, together with the operation and maintenance of the controls and their associated risks
- Management of suppliers and contracts regarding access to systems and services, in conjunction with supplier management
- Management of all security breaches, incidents and problems associated with all systems and services
- The proactive improvement of security controls, and security risk management and the reduction of security risks
- Integration of security aspects within all other ITSM processes.

To achieve effective information security governance, management must establish and maintain an information security management system (ISMS) to guide the development and management of a comprehensive information security programme that supports the business objectives.

4.7.3 Value to the business

Information security management ensures that an information security policy is maintained and enforced that fulfils the needs of the business security policy and the requirements of corporate governance. It raises awareness of the need for security within all IT services and assets throughout the organization, ensuring that the policy is appropriate for the needs of the organization. It manages all aspects of IT and information security within all areas of IT and service management activity.

Information security management provides assurance of business processes by enforcing appropriate security controls in all areas of IT and by managing IT risk in line with business and corporate risk management processes and guidelines.

4.7.4 Policies, principles and basic concepts

Prudent business practices require that IT processes and initiatives align with business processes and objectives. This is critical when it comes to information security, which must be closely aligned with business security and business needs. Additionally, all processes within the IT organization must include security considerations.

Executive management is ultimately responsible for the organization's information and is tasked with responding to issues that affect its protection. In addition, boards of directors are expected to make information security an integral part of corporate governance. All IT service provider organizations must therefore ensure that they have a comprehensive information security management policy(s) and the necessary security controls in place to monitor and enforce the policies.

4.7.4.1 Policies

Information security management activities should be focused on and driven by an overall information security policy and a set of underpinning specific security policies. The information security policy should have the full support of top executive IT management and ideally the support and commitment of top executive business

management. The policy should cover all areas of security, be appropriate, meet the needs of the business and should include:

- An overall information security policy
- Use and misuse of IT assets policy
- An access control policy
- A password control policy
- An email policy
- An internet policy
- An anti-virus policy
- An information classification policy
- A document classification policy
- A remote access policy
- A policy with regard to supplier access to IT service, information and components
- A copyright infringement policy for electronic material
- An asset disposal policy
- A records retention policy.

In most cases, these policies should be widely available to all customers and users, and their compliance should be referred to in all SLRs, SLAs, OLAs, underpinning contracts and agreements.

> **Exception**
>
> The only exception to this approach is in the case of Type III service providers where the information security policies related to one external customer should be confidential from other customers, and the provider's own detailed policies are likely to be confidential from the customers for intellectual property rights reasons. The only sharing of security policies in this case should be the aspects that relate directly to the provision of service to that specific customer.

The policies should be authorized by top executive management within the business and IT, and compliance with them should be endorsed on a regular basis. All security policies should be reviewed – and, where necessary, revised – on at least an annual basis.

4.7.4.2 Risk assessment and management in information security management

To achieve the objectives of information security management, formal risk assessment and management relating to security of information and information processing is fundamental. Indeed, it is difficult to identify any part of this process that does not relate to risk management in some way. The information security management process frequently collaborates not only with the business but also with the ITSCM and availability management processes to conduct risk assessments at various levels. See Appendix M for more detail on risk assessment and management methods. Performing accurate assessment of risk and active management of risk to acceptable levels is a core competency that every organization should develop and maintain.

4.7.4.3 Information security management system

The information security management process will have a formal system to establish policy and objectives and to achieve those objectives. This system will generally consist of:

- An information security policy and specific security policies that address each aspect of strategy, controls and regulation
- A security management information system (SMIS), containing the standards, management procedures and guidelines supporting the information security policies
- A comprehensive security strategy, closely linked to the business objectives, strategies and plans

- An effective security organizational structure
- A set of security controls to support the policy
- The management of security risks
- Monitoring processes to ensure compliance and provide feedback on effectiveness
- Communications strategy and plan for security
- Training and awareness strategy and plan.

Elements of the information security management system

The information security management system (ISMS) provides a basis for the development of a cost-effective information security programme that supports the business objectives. It will involve the four Ps of people, process, products (technology) and partners (suppliers) to ensure high levels of security are in place wherever it is appropriate.

ISO/IEC 27001 is the formal standard against which organizations may seek independent certification of their ISMS (meaning their frameworks to design, implement, manage, maintain and enforce information security processes and controls systematically and consistently throughout the organizations). The ISMS shown in Figure 4.23 shows an approach that is widely used and is based on the advice and guidance described in many sources, including ISO/IEC 27001.

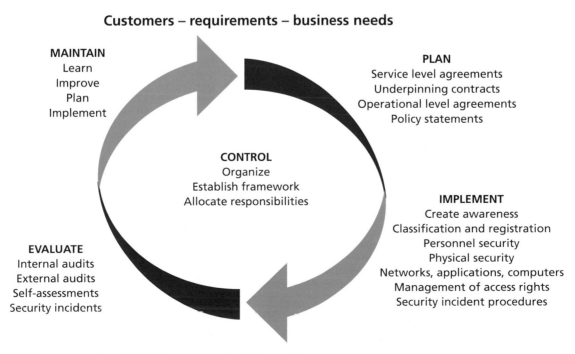

Figure 4.23 Elements of an ISMS for managing IT security

The five elements within this structure are as follows.

CONTROL

The objectives of the control element of the ISMS are to:

- Establish a management framework to initiate and manage information security in the organization
- Establish an organizational structure to prepare, approve and implement the information security policy
- Allocate responsibilities
- Establish and control documentation.

PLAN

The objective of the plan element of the ISMS is to devise and recommend the appropriate security measures, based on an understanding of the requirements of the organization.

The requirements will be gathered from such sources as business and service risk, plans and strategies, SLAs and OLAs and the legal, moral and ethical responsibilities for information security. Other factors such as the amount of funding available and the prevailing organization culture and attitudes to security must be considered.

The information security policy defines the organization's attitude and stance on security matters. This should be an organization-wide document, not just applicable to the IT service provider. Responsibility for the upkeep of the document rests with the information security manager.

IMPLEMENT

The objective of the implementation element of the ISMS is to ensure that appropriate procedures, tools and controls are in place to underpin the information security policy. Measures include:

- Accountability for assets – service asset and configuration management and the CMS are invaluable here
- Information classification – information and repositories should be classified according to the sensitivity and the impact of disclosure.

The successful implementation of the security controls and measures is dependent on a number of factors:

- The determination of a clear and agreed policy, integrated with the needs of the business
- Security procedures that are justified, appropriate and supported by senior management
- Effective marketing and education in security requirements
- A mechanism for improvement.

EVALUATE

The objectives of the evaluate element of the ISMS are to:

- Supervise and check compliance with the security policy and security requirements in SLAs and OLAs, and in underpinning contracts in conjunction with supplier management
- Carry out regular audits of the technical security of IT systems
- Provide information to external auditors and regulators, if required.

MAINTAIN

The objectives of this maintain element of the ISMS are to:

- Improve security agreements as specified in, for example, SLAs and OLAs
- Improve the implementation of security measures and controls.

This should be achieved using a PDCA (Plan-Do-Check-Act) cycle, which is a formal approach suggested by ISO/IEC 27001 for the establishment of the ISMS. This cycle is described in more detail in *ITIL Continual Service Improvement*.

Security governance

Information security governance, when properly implemented, should provide six basic outcomes:

- Strategic alignment:
  - Security requirements should be driven by enterprise requirements
  - Security solutions need to fit enterprise processes
  - Investment in information security should be aligned with the enterprise strategy and agreed-on risk profile
- Value delivery:
  - A standard set of security practices, i.e. baseline security requirements following best practices

- Properly prioritized and distributed effort to areas with greatest impact and business benefit
- Institutionalized and commoditized solutions
- Complete solutions, covering organization and process as well as technology
- A culture of continual improvement
- Risk management:
  - Agreed-on risk profile
  - Understanding of risk exposure
  - Awareness of risk management priorities
  - Risk mitigation
  - Risk acceptance/deference
- Performance management:
  - Defined, agreed and meaningful set of metrics
  - Measurement process that will help identify shortcomings and provide feedback on progress made resolving issues
  - Independent assurance
- Resource management:
  - Knowledge is captured and available
  - Documented security processes and practices, including explicitly defined the interfaces between ISM and other processes
  - Developed security architecture(s) to efficiently utilize infrastructure resources
- Business process assurance.

4.7.5 Process activities, methods and techniques

The information security management process ensures that the security aspects with regard to services and all service management activities are appropriately managed and controlled in line with business needs and risks.

The key activities within the information security management process are:

- Production and maintenance of an overall information security policy and a set of supporting specific policies
- Communication, implementation and enforcement of the security policies, including:
  - Provision of advice and guidance to all other areas of the business and IT on all information security-related issues
- Assessment and classification of all information assets and documentation

- Implementation, review, revision and improvement of a set of security controls and risk assessment and responses, including:
  - Assessment of the impact of all changes on information security policies, controls and measures
  - Implementation of proactive measures to improve information security wherever it is in the business interest and cost-justifiable to do so
- Monitoring and management of all security breaches and major security incidents
- Analysis, reporting and reduction of the volumes and impact of security breaches and incidents
- Schedule and completion of security reviews, audits and penetration tests.

The interactions between these key activities are illustrated in Figure 4.24.

The developed information security management process, together with the procedures, methods, tools and techniques, constitute the security strategy. The security manager should ensure that technologies, products and services are in place and that the overall policy is developed and well published. The security manager is also responsible for security architecture, authentication, authorization, administration and recovery.

The security strategy also needs to consider how it will embed good security practices into every area of the business. Training and awareness are vital in the overall strategy, as security is often weakest at the end-user stage. It is here, as well, that there is a need to develop methods and processes that enable the policies and standards to be more easily followed and implemented.

Resources need to be assigned to track developments in these enabling technologies and the products they support. For example, privacy continues to be important and, increasingly, the focus of government regulation, making privacy compliance technologies an important enabling technology.

4.7.5.1 Security controls

All parties involved must understand that security is not a step in the lifecycle of services and systems and that security cannot be solved through technology. Rather, information security must be

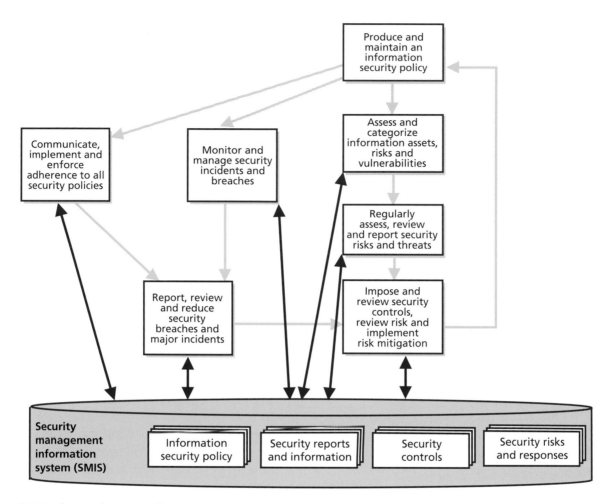

Figure 4.24 Information security management process

an integral part of all services and systems and is an ongoing process that needs to be continuously managed using a set of security controls.

The set of security controls should be designed to support and enforce the information security policy and to minimize all recognized and identified threats. The controls will be considerably more cost-effective if included within the design of all services. This will ensure the continued protection of all existing services and that new services and access to them are in line with the policy. The security controls and associated procedures for granting and preventing access to services by individuals will typically be executed on a day-to-day basis through the access management process.

Security measures can be used at a specific stage in the prevention and handling of security incidents, as illustrated in Figure 4.25. Security incidents are not solely caused by technical threats – statistics show that, for example, the large majority stem from human errors (intended or not) or procedural errors, and often have implications in other fields such as safety, legality or health.

The following stages can be identified. At the start there is a risk that a threat will materialize. A threat can be anything that disrupts the business process or has negative impact on the business. When a threat materializes, we speak of a security incident. This security incident may result in damage (to information or to assets) that has to be repaired or otherwise corrected. Suitable measures can be selected for each of these stages. The choice of measures will depend on the importance attached to the information.

■ **Preventive** Security measures are used to prevent a security incident from occurring. The best-known example of preventive measures is the allocation of access rights to a limited group of authorized people. The further requirements associated with this measure include the control of access rights (granting, maintenance and withdrawal of rights), authorization (identifying

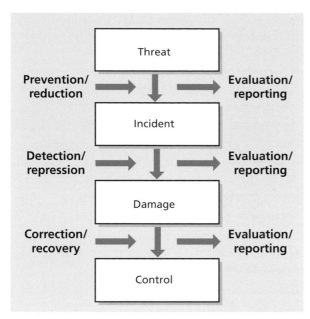

Figure 4.25 Security controls for threats and incidents

who is allowed access to which information and using which tools), identification and authentication (confirming who is seeking access) and access control (ensuring that only authorized personnel can gain access).

■ **Reductive** Further measures can be taken in advance to minimize any possible damage that may occur. These are 'reductive' measures. Familiar examples of reductive measures are making regular backups and the development, testing and maintenance of contingency plans.

■ **Detective** If a security incident occurs, it is important to discover it as soon as possible – detection. A familiar example of this is monitoring, linked to an alert procedure. Another example is virus-checking software.

■ **Repressive** Measures are then used to counteract any continuation or repetition of the security incident. For example, an account or network address is temporarily blocked after numerous failed attempts to log on or the retention of a card when multiple attempts are made with a wrong PIN number.

■ **Corrective** The damage is repaired as far as possible using corrective measures. For example, corrective measures include restoring the backup, or returning to a previous stable situation (roll-back, back-out). Fallback can also been seen as a corrective measure.

The documentation of all controls should be maintained to reflect accurately their operation, maintenance and method of operation.

4.7.5.2 Management of security breaches and incidents

In the case of serious security breaches or incidents, an evaluation is necessary in due course, to determine what went wrong, what caused it and how it can be prevented in the future. However, this process should not be limited to serious security incidents. All breaches of security and security incidents need to be studied in order to gain a full picture of the effectiveness of the security measures as a whole. A reporting procedure for security incidents is required to be able to evaluate the effectiveness and efficiency of the present security measures based on an insight into all security incidents. This is facilitated by the maintenance of log files and audit files and, of course, the incident records from the incident management process. The analysis of these statistics on security issues should lead to improvement actions focused on the reduction of the impact and volume of all security breaches and incidents, in conjunction with problem management.

4.7.6 Triggers, inputs, outputs and interfaces

4.7.6.1 Triggers

Information security management activity can be triggered by many events, including:

■ New or changed corporate governance guidelines
■ New or changed business security policy
■ New or changed corporate risk management processes and guidelines
■ New or changed business needs or new or changed services
■ New or changed requirements within agreements, such as SLRs, SLAs, OLAs or contracts
■ Review and revision of business and IT plans and strategies
■ Review and revision of designs and strategies
■ Service or component security breaches or warnings, events and alerts, including threshold events, exception reports

- Periodic activities, such as reviewing, revising or reporting, including review and revision of information security management policies, reports and plans
- Recognition or notification of a change of risk or impact of a business process or VBF, an IT service or component
- Requests from other areas, particularly SLM for assistance with security issues.

4.7.6.2 Inputs

Information security management will need to obtain input from many areas, including:

- **Business information** From the organization's business strategy, plans and financial plans, and information on its current and future requirements
- **Governance and security** From corporate governance and business security policies and guidelines, security plans, risk assessment and responses
- **IT information** From the IT strategy and plans and current budgets
- **Service information** From the SLM process with details of the services from the service portfolio and the service catalogue and service level targets within SLAs and SLRs, and possibly from the monitoring of SLAs, service reviews and breaches of the SLAs
- **Risk assessment processes and reports** From ISM, availability management and ITSCM
- **Details of all security events and breaches** From all areas of IT and ITSM, especially incident management and problem management
- **Change information** From the change management process with a change schedule and a need to assess all changes for their impact on all security policies, plans and controls
- **CMS** Containing information on the relationships between the business, the services, supporting services and the technology
- **Details of partner and supplier access** From supplier management and availability management on external access to services and systems.

4.7.6.3 Outputs

The outputs produced by the information security management process are used in all areas and should include:

- An overall information security management policy, together with a set of specific security policies
- A security management information system (SMIS), containing all the information relating to information security management
- Revised security risk assessment processes and reports
- A set of security controls, together with details of the operation and maintenance and their associated risks
- Security audits and audit reports
- Security test schedules and plans, including security penetration tests and other security tests and reports
- A set of security classifications and a set of classified information assets
- Reviews and reports of security breaches and major incidents
- Policies, processes and procedures for managing partners and suppliers and their access to services and information.

4.7.6.4 Interfaces

The effective and efficient implementation of an information security policy within an organization will, to a large extent, be dependent on good service management processes. Indeed, the effective implementation of some processes can be seen as a pre-requisite for effective security control. The key interfaces that information security management has with other processes are as follows:

- **Service level management** Information security management provides assistance with the determining of security requirements and responsibilities and their inclusion within SLRs and SLAs, together with the investigation and resolution of service and component security breaches.
- **Access management** This process performs the actions to grant and revoke access and applies the policies defined by information security management and included in the service design by availability management.
- **Change management** Information security management should assist with the assessment of every change for impact on security

and security controls. Also ISM can provide information on unauthorized changes that resulted from security breaches.

■ **Incident and problem management** Information security management provides assistance with the resolution and subsequent justification and correction of security incidents and problems. The incident management process must include the ability to identify and deal with security incidents. Service desk and service operations staff must 'recognize' a security incident.

■ **IT service continuity management** Information security management works collaboratively with ITSCM on the assessment of business impact and risk, and the provision of resilience, fail-over and recovery mechanisms. Security is a major issue when continuity plans are tested or invoked. A working ITSCM plan is a mandatory requirement for ISO/IEC 27001.

■ **Service asset and configuration management** This will give the ability to provide accurate asset information to assist with security classifications. Having an accurate CMS is therefore an extremely useful information security management input.

■ **Availability management** If data is unavailable or lacks integrity, then the ability of the service to perform its agreed function is compromised. This makes ISM a critical enabler of availability management. ISM is the process that is accountable for ensuring compliance with security policies in all services. Availability management is responsible for ensuring security requirements are defined and incorporated within the overall availability design. ISM operates collaboratively with both availability management and ITSCM to conduct integrated risk assessment and management exercises.

■ **Capacity management** This must consider security implications when selecting and introducing new technology. Security is an important consideration when procuring any new technology or software.

■ **Financial management for IT services** This should provide adequate funds to finance security requirements.

■ **Supplier management** This should assist with the joint management of suppliers and their access to services and systems, and the terms and conditions to be included within contracts concerning supplier security responsibilities.

■ **Legal and human resources issues** These must be considered when investigating security issues. Accordingly, ISM activity should be integrated with these corporate processes and functions.

4.7.7 Information management

All the information required by information security management should be contained within the SMIS. This should include all security controls, risks, breaches, processes and reports necessary to support and maintain the information security policy and the SMIS. This information should cover all IT services and components, and needs to be integrated and maintained in alignment with all other management information systems, particularly the service portfolio and the CMS. The SMIS will also provide the input to security audits and reviews and to the continual improvement activities so important to all SMISs. The SMIS will also provide invaluable input to the design of new systems and services.

4.7.8 Critical success factors and key performance indicators

The following list includes some sample CSFs for information security management. Each organization should identify appropriate CSFs based on its objectives for the process. Each sample CSF is followed by a small number of typical KPIs that support the CSF. These KPIs should not be adopted without careful consideration. Each organization should develop KPIs that are appropriate for its level of maturity, its CSFs and its particular circumstances. Achievement against KPIs should be monitored and used to identify opportunities for improvement, which should be logged in the CSI register for evaluation and possible implementation.

■ **CSF** Business is protected against security violations
  ● **KPI** Percentage decrease in security breaches reported to the service desk
  ● **KPI** Percentage decrease in the impact of security breaches and incidents
  ● **KPI** Percentage increase in SLA conformance to security clauses

■ **CSF** The determination of a clear and agreed policy, integrated with the needs of the business

- **KPI** Decrease in the number of non-conformances of the information security management process with the business security policy and process
- **CSF** Security procedures that are justified, appropriate and supported by senior management
    - **KPI** Increase in the acceptance and conformance of security procedures
    - **KPI** Increased support and commitment of senior management
- **CSF** Effective marketing and education in security requirements, and IT staff awareness of the technology supporting the services
    - **KPI** Increased awareness of the security policy and its contents, throughout the organization
    - **KPI** Percentage increase in completeness of supporting services against the IT components that make up those services
    - **KPI** Service desk supporting all services
- **CSF** A mechanism for improvement
    - **KPI** The number of suggested improvements to security procedures and controls
    - **KPI** Decrease in the number of security non-conformance detected during audits and security testing.
- **CSF** Information security is an integral part of all IT services and all ITSM processes
    - **KPI** Increase in the number of services and processes conformant with security procedures and controls
- **CSF** The availability of services is not compromised by security incidents
    - **KPI** Percentage decrease in the impact of security breaches and incidents
    - **KPI** Percentage reduction in the number of incidents of service unavailability linked to security breaches
- **CSF** Clear ownership and awareness of the security policies among the customer community
    - **KPI** Percentage increase in acceptable scores on security awareness questionnaires completed by customers and users.

4.7.9 Challenges and risks

4.7.9.1 Challenges

Information security management faces many challenges in establishing an appropriate information security policy with an effective supporting process and controls. One of the biggest challenges is to ensure that there is adequate support from the business, business security and senior management. If these are not available, it will be impossible to establish an effective information security management process. If there is senior IT management support, but there is no support from the business, IT security controls and risk assessment and management will be severely limited in what they can achieve. It is pointless implementing security policies, procedures and controls in IT if these cannot be enforced throughout the business. The major use of IT services and assets is outside of IT, and so are the majority of security threats and risks.

In some organizations the business perception is that security is an IT responsibility, and therefore the business assumes that IT will be responsible for all aspects of IT security and that IT services will be adequately protected. However, without the commitment and support of the business and business personnel, money invested in expensive security controls and procedures will be largely wasted and they will mostly be ineffective.

If there is a business security process established, then the challenge becomes one of alignment and integration. Information security management must ensure that accurate information is obtained from the business security process on the needs, risks, impact and priorities of the business and that the information security management policies, information and plans are aligned and integrated with those of the business. Having achieved that alignment, the challenge becomes one of keeping them aligned by management and control of business and IT change using strict change management and service asset and configuration management control. Again, this requires support and commitment from the business and senior management.

4.7.9.2 Risks

Information systems can generate many direct and indirect benefits, and as many direct and indirect risks. These risks have led to a gap between the need to protect systems and services and the degree of protection applied. The gap is caused by internal and external factors, including the widespread use of technology, increasing dependence of the business on IT, increasing complexity and interconnectivity of systems, disappearance of the traditional organizational boundaries, and increasingly onerous regulatory requirements.

This means that there are new risk areas that could have a significant impact on critical business operations, such as:

- Increasing requirements for availability and robustness
- Growing potential for misuse and abuse of information systems affecting privacy and ethical values
- External dangers from hackers, leading to denial-of-service and virus attacks, extortion, industrial espionage and leakage of organizational information or private data.

Because new technology provides the potential for dramatically enhanced business performance, improved and demonstrated information security can add real value to the organization by contributing to interaction with trading partners, closer customer relationships, improved competitive advantage and protected reputation. It can also enable new and easier ways to process electronic transactions and generate trust. In today's competitive global economy, if an organization wants to do business, it may well be asked to present details of its security posture and results of its past performance in terms of tests conducted to ensure security of its information resources.

Other areas of major risks associated with information security management include:

- A lack of commitment from the business to the information security management process and procedures
- Lack of commitment from the business and a lack of appropriate information on future plans and strategies
- A lack of senior management commitment or a lack of resources and/or budget for the information security management process
- The processes focusing too much on technology issues and not enough on the IT services and the needs and priorities of the business
- Risk assessment and management being conducted in isolation and not in conjunction with availability management and ITSCM

- Information security management policies, plans, risks and information becoming out of date and losing alignment with the corresponding relevant information and plans of the business and business security
- Security policies becoming bureaucratic and/ or excessively difficult to follow, discouraging compliance
- Security policies adding no value to business.

4.8 SUPPLIER MANAGEMENT

The supplier management process ensures that suppliers and the services they provide are managed to support IT service targets and business expectations. The aim of this section is to raise awareness of the business context of working with partners and suppliers, and how this work can best be directed toward realising business benefit for the organization.

It is essential that supplier management processes and planning are involved in all stages of the service lifecycle, from strategy and design, through transition and operation, to improvement. Complex business demands require the complete breadth of skills and capability to support provision of a comprehensive set of IT services to a business; therefore the use of value networks and the suppliers and the services they provide are an integral part of any end-to-end solution. Suppliers and the management of suppliers and partners are essential to the provision of quality IT services.

4.8.1 Purpose and objectives

The purpose of the supplier management process is to obtain value for money from suppliers and to provide seamless quality of IT service to the business by ensuring that all contracts and agreements with suppliers support the needs of the business and that all suppliers meet their contractual commitments.

The main objectives of the supplier management process are to:

- Obtain value for money from suppliers and contracts
- Ensure that contracts with suppliers are aligned to business needs, and support and align with agreed targets in SLRs and SLAs, in conjunction with SLM
- Manage relationships with suppliers

- Manage supplier performance
- Negotiate and agree contracts with suppliers and manage them through their lifecycle
- Maintain a supplier policy and a supporting supplier and contract management information system (SCMIS).

> **Note on terminology**
>
> The terms 'contract', 'underpinning contract' and 'agreement' can be confusing. For specific details, see section 4.3.4.2 in service level management which describes how these terms are used in this document. In this section specifically, because it focuses on the relationship with suppliers whose work naturally 'underpins' the delivery of IT services to the customer, the word 'contract', wherever it is used, should be understood to mean 'underpinning contracts and/or agreements'.

4.8.2 Scope

The supplier management process should include the management of all suppliers and contracts needed to support the provision of IT services to the business. Each service provider should have formal processes for the management of all suppliers and contracts. However, the processes should adapt to cater for the importance of the supplier and/or the contract and the potential business impact on the provision of services. Many suppliers provide support services and products that independently have a relatively minor, and fairly indirect, role in value generation, but collectively make a direct and important contribution to value generation and the implementation of the overall business strategy. The greater the contribution the supplier makes to business value, the more effort the service provider should put into the management of the supplier and the more that supplier should be involved in the development and realization of the business strategy. The smaller the supplier's value contribution, the more likely it is that the relationship will be managed mainly at an operational level, with limited interaction with the business. It may be appropriate in some organizations, particularly large ones, to manage internal teams and suppliers, where different business units may provide support of key elements.

The supplier management process should include:

- Implementation and enforcement of the supplier policy
- Maintenance of an SCMIS
- Supplier and contract categorization and risk assessment
- Supplier and contract evaluation and selection
- Development, negotiation and agreement of contracts
- Contract review, renewal and termination
- Management of suppliers and supplier performance
- Identification of improvement opportunities for inclusion in the CSI register, and the implementation of service and supplier improvement plans
- Maintenance of standard contracts, terms and conditions
- Management of contractual dispute resolution
- Management of sub-contracted suppliers.

IT supplier management often has to comply with organizational or corporate standards, guidelines and requirements, particularly those of corporate legal, finance and purchasing, as illustrated in Figure 4.26.

In order to ensure that suppliers provide value for money and meet their service targets, the relationship between each supplier should be owned by an individual within the service provider organization. However, a single individual may own the relationship for one or many suppliers, as illustrated in Figure 4.26. To ensure that relationships are developed in a consistent manner and that suppliers' performance is appropriately reviewed and managed, roles need to be established for a supplier management process owner and a contracts manager. In smaller organizations, these separate roles may be combined into a single responsibility.

4.8.3 Value to the business

The main objectives of the supplier management process are to provide value for money from suppliers and contracts and to ensure that all targets in underpinning supplier contracts and agreements are aligned to business needs and agreed targets within SLAs. This is to ensure the delivery to the business of end-to-end, seamless, quality IT services that are aligned to the business's

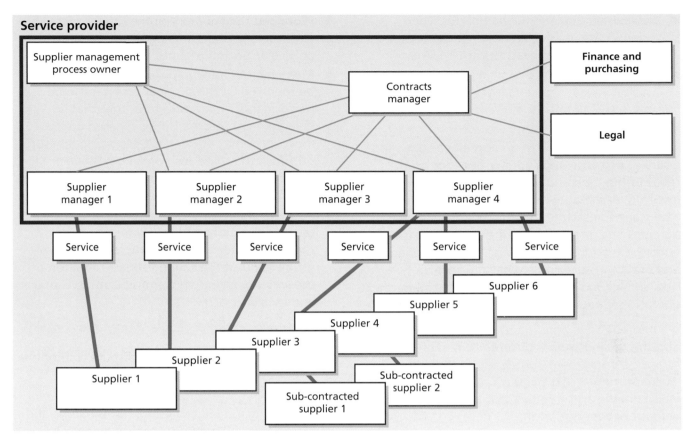

Figure 4.26 Supplier management – roles and interfaces

expectation. The supplier management process should align with all corporate requirements and the requirements of all other IT and service management processes, particularly ISM and ITSCM. This ensures that the business obtains value from supporting supplier services and that they are aligned with business needs.

4.8.4 Policies, principles and basic concepts

The supplier management process attempts to ensure that suppliers meet the terms, conditions and targets of their contracts, while trying to increase the value for money obtained from suppliers and the services they provide. All supplier management process activity should be driven by a supplier strategy and policy from service strategy. The supplier strategy, sometimes called the sourcing strategy, defines the service provider's plan for how it will leverage the contribution of suppliers in the achievement of the overall service strategy. Some organizations might adopt a strategy that dictates the use of suppliers only in very specific and limited circumstances, while

another organization might choose to make extensive use of suppliers in IT service provision.

4.8.4.1 Policies

The supplier policies adopted by an organization are the documented management directions that will guide supplier-related decisions and ensure the correct execution of the defined strategy. Supplier policies may cover such areas as:

- The acceptable methods for communication with potential suppliers before and during the solicitation, bidding and procurement processes
- Allocation of roles and responsibilities – who is authorized to interact with suppliers and who is not
- Rules regarding accepting gifts or promotional items from suppliers
- Supplier standards – for example, all suppliers for a hospital in the US must be compliant with the Health Insurance Portability and Accountability Act
- Standards and guidelines for various supplier contract types and/or agreement types

- Data ownership and access policies when suppliers are involved. These policies are developed in collaboration with Information security management.

4.8.4.2 Underpinning contracts and agreements

The nature and extent of an agreement between a service provider and supplier depends on the relationship type and an assessment of the risks involved. A pre-agreement risk assessment is a vital stage in establishing any external supplier agreement. For each party, it exposes the risks that need to be addressed and must be comprehensive and practical, covering a wide variety of risks, including financial, business reputation, operational, regulatory and legal.

A comprehensive agreement minimizes the risk of disputes arising from a difference of expectations. A flexible agreement, which adequately caters for its adaptation across the term of the agreement, is maintainable and supports change with a minimum amount of renegotiation.

The contents of a basic underpinning contract or service agreement are:

- **Basic terms and conditions** The term (duration) of the contract, the parties, locations, scope, definitions and commercial basis.
- **Service description and scope** The functionality of the services being provided and its extent, along with constraints on the service delivery, such as performance, availability, capacity, technical interface and security. Service functionality may be explicitly defined, or in the case of well-established services, included by reference to other established documents, such as the service portfolio and the service catalogue.
- **Service standards** The service measures and the minimum levels that constitute acceptable performance and quality – for example, IT may have a performance requirement to respond to a request for a new desktop system in 24 hours, with acceptable service deemed to have occurred where this performance requirement is met in 95% of cases. Service levels must be realistic, measurable and aligned with the organization's business priorities and underpin the agreed targets within SLRs and SLAs.

- **Workload ranges** The volume ranges within which service standards apply, or for which particular pricing regimes apply.
- **Management information** The data that must be reported by the supplier on operational performance – take care to ensure that management information is focused on the most important or headline reporting measures on which the relationship will be assessed. KPIs related to supplier CSFs and balanced scorecards may form the core of reported performance data.
- **Responsibilities and dependencies** Description of the obligations of the organization (in supporting the supplier in the service delivery efforts) and of the supplier (in its provision of the service), including communication, contacts and escalation.

An extended service agreement may also contain:

- Service debit and credit regime (incentives and penalties)
- Additional performance criteria.

The following is a limited sample of the legal and commercial topics typically covered by a service or contractual agreement:

- Scope of services to be provided
- Service performance requirements
- Division and agreement of responsibilities
- Contact points, communication and reporting frequency and content
- Contract review and dispute resolution processes
- Price structure
- Payment terms
- Commitments to change and investment
- Agreement change process
- Confidentiality and announcements
- Intellectual property rights and copyright
- Liability limitations
- Termination rights of each party
- Obligations at termination and beyond.

The final form of an agreement, and some of the terminology, may be dictated by the views and preferences of the procurement and legal departments, or by specialist legal firms.

Hints and tips

Seek legal advice when formalizing external supplier agreements.

Formal contracts

Formal contracts are appropriate for external supply arrangements that make a significant contribution to the delivery and development of the business. Contracts provide for binding legal commitments between IT service provider and supplier, and cover the obligations each organization has to the other from the first day of the contract, often extending beyond its termination. A contract is used as the basis for external supplier agreements where an enforceable commitment is required. High-value and/or strategic relationships are underpinned by a formal contract. The formality and binding nature of a contract are not at odds with the culture of a partnering agreement, but rather form the basis on which trust in the relationship may be founded.

A contract is likely to be structured with a main body containing the commercial and legal clauses, and with the elements of a service agreement, as described earlier, attached as schedules. Contracts may also include a number of other related documents as schedules, for example:

- Security requirements
- Business continuity requirements
- Mandated technical standards
- Migration plans (agreed pre-scheduled change)
- Disclosure agreements.

Most large organizations have procurement and legal departments specializing in sourcing contracts. Specialist legal firms may be employed to support the internal procurement and legal function when establishing significant formal contracts.

Underpinning agreements

In ITIL an SLA is defined as an agreement between an IT service provider and a customer. A service level agreement describes the IT service, documents service level targets, and specifies the responsibilities of the IT service provider and the customer. Service providers should be aware that SLAs are widely used to formalize service-based relationships, both internally and externally, and that while conforming to the definition above, these agreements vary considerably in the detail covered.

Key messages

The views of some organizations, such as the Chartered Institute of Purchase and Supply and various specialist lawyers, are that SLAs ought not to be used to manage external relationships unless they form part of an underlying contract. *The Complete Guide to Preparing and Implementing Service Level Agreements*[5] emphasizes that a stand-alone SLA may not be legally enforceable but instead 'represents the goodwill and faith of the parties signing it'. This is important in the context of an SLA between a Type III IT service provider and its external customer.

Although in this publication the term SLA is not applied to the IT service provider–supplier relationship, the same principle applies to the service level targets agreed between these two parties. It is in service providers' and suppliers' interests to ensure that agreed service levels are incorporated into an appropriate contractual framework to ensure that these commitments are legally binding.

SLAs between the IT service provider and their customer(s) and the agreements that underpin them, including formal contracts, should be reviewed on a regular basis to ensure performance conforms to the service levels that have been agreed.

The organization is likely to be dependent on its own internal support groups to some extent. To be able to achieve SLA targets, it is advisable to have formal arrangements in place called operational level agreements (OLAs) with these groups. (For more on OLAs and their negotiation, see section 4.3 on the SLM process.) It is important in supplier management that the contributions of suppliers towards service provision are coordinated and aligned with the contributions of internal support groups to ensure that the combined efforts of these groups will ensure achievement of SLA targets and that there are no gaps or duplicated efforts. The activities of the SLM and supplier management processes need to be interfaced appropriately to achieve this.

5 Pantry, S. and Griffiths, P. (2001). *The Complete Guide to Preparing and Implementing Service Level Agreements*. Library Association Publishing.

4.8.4.3 Supplier and contract management information system

In order to achieve consistency and effectiveness in the implementation of the supplier policy, an SCMIS should be established, together with clearly defined roles and responsibilities.

Ideally the SCMIS should form an integrated element of a comprehensive CMS or SKMS, recording all supplier and contract details, together with details of the type of service(s) or product(s) provided by each supplier, and all other information and relationships with other associated CIs. The services provided by suppliers will also form a key part of the service portfolio and the service catalogue. The relationship between the supporting services and the IT and business services they support are key to providing quality IT services.

This information within the SCMIS will provide a complete set of reference information for all supplier management procedures and activities:

- Definition of new supplier and contract requirements
- Evaluation and set up of new suppliers and contracts
- Supplier categorization and maintenance of the SCMIS
- Establishing new suppliers
- Management of suppliers and their performance and of the associated contracts
- Contract renewal or termination.

The first three elements within the above list are covered within the service design stage. The fourth element is part of service transition, and the last two are part of the service operation stage and are covered in more detail in *ITIL Service Transition* and *ITIL Service Operation*, respectively.

4.8.5 Process activities, methods and techniques

When dealing with external suppliers, it is strongly recommended that a formal contract with clearly defined, agreed and documented responsibilities and targets is established and managed through the stages of its lifecycle, from the identification of the business need to the operation and cessation of the contract. This activity is performed in line with the established supplier strategy and supplier policies. For a more detailed discussion of supplier strategy (otherwise called sourcing strategy), see *ITIL Service Strategy*, section 3.7.

The activities of supplier management can be summarized in this way:

- Definition of new supplier and contract requirements:
  - Identify business need and prepare of the business case, including options (internal and external), costs, timescales, targets, benefits, risk assessment
  - Produce a statement of requirement (SoR) and/or invitation to tender (ITT)
  - Ensure conformance to strategy/policy
- Evaluation of new suppliers and contracts:
  - Identify method of purchase or procurement
  - Establish evaluation criteria – for example, services, capability (both personnel and organization), quality and cost
  - Evaluate alternative options
  - Select
  - Negotiate contracts, targets and the terms and conditions, including responsibilities, closure, renewal, extension, dispute, transfer
  - Agree and award the contract
- Supplier and contract categorization and maintenance of the SCMIS:
  - Assess or reassess the supplier and contract
  - Ensure changes progressed through service transition
  - Categorize the supplier
  - Update SCMIS
  - Ongoing maintenance of the SCMIS
- Establishment of new suppliers and contracts:
  - Set up the supplier service and contract, within the SCMIS and any other associated corporate systems
  - Transition the service
  - Establish contacts and relationships
- Supplier, contract and performance management:
  - Manage and control the operation and delivery of service/products
  - Monitor and report (service, quality and costs)
  - Review and improve (service, quality and costs)

- Manage the supplier and the relationship (communication, risks, changes, failures, improvements, contacts, interfaces)
- Review, at least annually, service scope against business need, targets and agreements
- Plan for possible closure/renewal/extension

■ Contract renewal or termination:
- Review (determine benefits delivered, ongoing requirement)
- Renegotiate and renew or terminate and/or transfer
- Transition to new supplier(s) or to internal resources.

The business, IT, finance, purchasing and procurement need to work together to ensure that all stages of the contract lifecycle are managed effectively. All areas need to be jointly involved in selecting the solution and managing the ongoing performance of the supplier, with each area taking responsibility for the interests of their own area, while being aware of the implications on the organization as a whole.

The activities involved in the stages of the contract lifecycle are explained in detail in the following sections and illustrated in Figure 4.27, along with a representation of the SCMIS.

4.8.5.1 Definition of new supplier and contract requirements

The activities associated with the identification of business needs and the subsequent evaluation of new suppliers and contracts are part of the service design stage. As part of the design of a new or changed service, the IT service provider will determine if and to what extent the contribution of suppliers will be required for a sound design and subsequent successful service provision. Once this decision has been made, the detailed requirements for new suppliers or new contracts with existing suppliers can be developed.

The outputs from service design provide the inputs to all other stages of the contract lifecycle. It is vital to the ongoing success of the contract and the relationship that the business is closely involved in all aspects of these activities. Every organization should have templates and a formal method for the production of business cases and their approval and sign-off. The detailing of the business's needs and the content of the business case should be

agreed, approved and signed off by both the business and IT.

Both the original decision and the subsequent requirements should be developed to fulfil the defined supplier strategy and to ensure compliance with supplier policies.

4.8.5.2 Evaluation of new suppliers and contracts

When selecting a new supplier or contract, a number of factors need to be taken into consideration, including track record, capability, references, credit rating and size relative to the business being placed. In addition, depending on the type of supplier relationship, there may be personnel issues that need to be considered. Each organization should have processes and procedures for establishing new suppliers and contracts.

While it is recognized that factors may exist that influence the decision on type of relationship or choice of supplier (e.g. politics within the organization, existing relationships), it is essential that in such cases the reasoning is identified and the impact fully assessed to ensure costly mistakes are avoided.

Services may be sourced from a single supplier or multi-sourced. Services are most likely to be sourced from two or more competing suppliers where the requirement is for standard services or products that are readily available 'off-the-shelf'. Multi-sourcing is most likely to be used where cost is the prime determinant, and requirements for developing variants of the services are low, but may also be undertaken to spread risk. Suppliers on a multi-source list may be designated with 'preferred supplier' status within the organization, limiting or removing scope for use of other suppliers.

Partnering relationships are established at an executive level and are dependent on a willingness to exchange strategic information to align business strategies. Many strategically important supplier relationships are now positioned as partnering relationships. This reflects a move away from traditionally hierarchical relationships, where the supplier acts subordinately to the customer organization, to one characterized by:

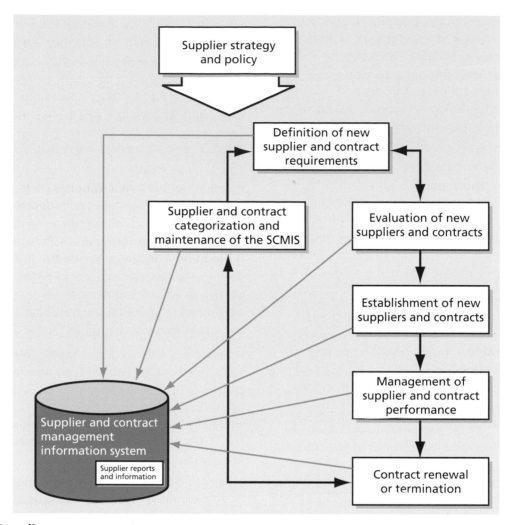

Figure 4.27 Supplier management process

- **Strategic alignment** Good alignment of culture, values and objectives, leading to an alignment of business strategies
- **Integration** A close integration of the processes of the two organizations
- **Information flow** Good communication and information exchange at all levels, especially at the strategic level, leading to close understanding
- **Mutual trust** A relationship built on mutual trust between the organizations and their staff
- **Openness** When reporting on service performance, costs and risk assessment
- **Collective responsibility** Joint partnership teams taking collective responsibility for current performance and future development of the relationship

- **Shared risk and reward** For example, agreeing how investment costs and resultant efficiency benefits are shared, or how risks and rewards from fluctuations in material costs are shared.

Both parties derive benefits from partnering. An organization derives progressively more value from a supplier relationship as the supplier's understanding of the organization as a whole increases, from its IT inventory architectures through to its corporate culture, values and business objectives. With time, the supplier is able to respond more quickly and more appropriately to the organization's needs. The supplier benefits from a longer-term commitment from the organization, providing it with greater financial stability and enabling it to finance longer-term investments, which benefit its customers.

A partnership makes it possible for the parties to align their IT infrastructures. Joint architecture and risk control agreements allow the partners to implement a range of compatible solutions from security, networking, data/information interchange, to workflow and application processing systems. This integration can provide service improvements and lowered costs. Such moves also reduce risks and costs associated with one-off tactical solutions, put in place to bridge a supplier's IT with that of the organization.

The key to a successful partnering relationship is being absolutely clear about the benefits and costs such a relationship will deliver before entering into it. Both parties then know what is expected of them at the outset. The success of the partnership may involve agreeing the transfer of staff to the partner or outsourcing organization as part of the agreement and relationship.

Service provider organizations should have documented and formal processes for evaluating and selecting suppliers based on:

- **Importance and impact** The importance of the service to the business, provided by the supplier
- **Risk** The risks associated with using the service
- **Costs** The cost of the service and its provision.

Often other areas of the service provider organization, such as legal, finance and purchasing, will get involved with this aspect of the process. Service provider organizations should have processes covering:

- Production of business case documents
- Production of SoR and ITT or proposal documents
- Formal evaluation and selection of suppliers and contracts
- The inclusion of standard clauses, terms and conditions within contracts, including early termination, benchmarking, exit or transfer of contracts, dispute resolution, management of sub-contracted suppliers and normal termination
- Transitioning of new contracts and suppliers.

These processes may, and should be, different, based on the type, size and category of the supplier and the contract.

4.8.5.3 Supplier categorization and maintenance of the supplier and contract management information system

The supplier management process should be adaptive and managers should spend more time and effort managing key suppliers than less important suppliers. This means that some form of categorization scheme should exist within the supplier management process to categorize the supplier and their importance to the service provider and the services provided to the business. Suppliers can be categorized in many ways, but one of the best methods for categorizing suppliers is based on assessing the risk and impact associated with using the supplier, and the value and importance of the supplier and its services to the business, as illustrated in Figure 4.28.

The amount of time and effort spent managing the supplier and the relationship can then be appropriate to its categorization:

- **Strategic** For significant 'partnering' relationships that involve senior managers sharing confidential strategic information to facilitate long-term plans. These relationships would normally be managed and owned at a senior management level within the service provider organization, and would involve regular and frequent contact and performance reviews. These relationships would probably require involvement of service strategy and service design resources, and would include ongoing specific improvement programmes (e.g. a network service provider supplying worldwide networks service and their support).
- **Tactical** For relationships involving significant commercial activity and business interaction. These relationships would normally be managed by middle management and would involve regular contact and performance reviews, often including ongoing improvement programmes (e.g. a hardware maintenance organization providing resolution of server hardware failures).
- **Operational** For suppliers of operational products or services. These relationships would normally be managed by junior operational management and would involve infrequent but regular contact and performance reviews (e.g.

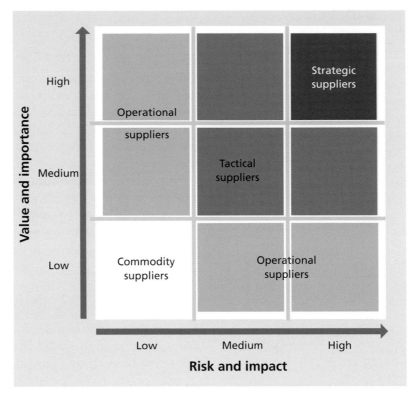

Figure 4.28 Supplier categorization

an internet hosting service provider, supplying hosting space for a low-usage, low-impact website or internally used IT service).
■ **Commodity** For suppliers providing low-value and/or readily available products and services, which could be alternatively sourced relatively easily (e.g. paper or printer cartridge suppliers).

Strategically important supplier relationships are given the greatest focus. It is in these cases that supplier managers have to ensure that the culture of the service provider organization is extended into the supplier domain so that the relationship works beyond the initial contract. The rise in popularity of outsourcing, and the increase in the scope and complexity of some sourcing arrangements, has resulted in a diversification of types of supplier relationship. At a strategic level, it is important to understand the options that are available so that the most suitable type of supplier relationship can be established to gain maximum business benefit and evolves in line with business needs.

Hints and tips

To successfully select the most appropriate type of supplier relationship, there needs to be a clear understanding of the business objectives that are to be achieved.

A number of factors, from the nature of the service to the overall cost, determine the importance of a supplier from a business perspective. As shown later, the greater the business significance of a supplier relationship, the more the business needs to be involved in the management and development of a relationship. A formal categorization approach can help to establish this importance.

Standardized versus customized services

The business value, measured as the contribution made to the business value chain, provides a more business-aligned assessment than pure contract price. Also, the more standard the services being procured, the lower the dependence the organization has on the supplier, and the more readily the supplier could be replaced (if necessary). Standardized services support the business through minimal time to market when deploying new or changed business services, and in pursuing cost-reduction strategies. More information on this subject can be found in *ITIL Service Strategy*.

The more customized those services are, the greater the difficulty in moving to an alternative supplier. Customization may benefit the business, contributing to competitive advantage through differentiated service, or may be the result of operational evolution.

Tailored services increase the dependence on the supplier, increase risk and can result in increased cost. From a supplier perspective, tailored services may decrease their ability to achieve economies of scale through common operations, resulting in narrowed margins, and reduced capital available for future investment.

Standard products and services are the preferred approach unless a clear business advantage exists, in which case a strategic supplier delivers the tailored service.

> **Hints and tips**
>
> High-value or high-dependence relationships involve greater risks for the organization. These relationships need comprehensive contracts and active relationship management.

Having established the type of supplier, the relationship then needs to be formalized. In the discussion below, the term 'agreement' is used generically to refer to any formalization of a relationship between customer and supplier organizations, and may range from the informal to comprehensive legally binding contracts. Simple, low-value relationships may be covered by a supplier's standard terms and conditions, and be managed wholly by IT. A relationship of strategic importance to the business, on the other hand, requires a comprehensive contract that ensures that the supplier supports evolving business needs throughout the life of the contract. A contract needs to be managed and developed in conjunction with procurement and legal departments and business stakeholders.

> **Hints and tips**
>
> The agreement is the foundation for the relationship. The more suitable and complete the agreement, the more likely it is that the relationship will deliver business benefit to both parties.
>
> The quality of the relationship between the service provider and its supplier(s) is often dependent on the individuals involved from both sides. It is therefore vital that individuals with the right attributes, skills, competencies and personalities are selected to be involved in these relationships.

Supplier relationships

A business service may depend on a number of internal and/or external suppliers for its delivery. These may include a mixture of strategic suppliers and commodity suppliers. Some suppliers supply directly to the organization; others are indirect or sub-contracted suppliers working via another supplier. Direct suppliers are directly managed by the service provider; indirect or sub-contracted suppliers are managed by the leading supplier. Any one supplier may provide products or services used to support a number of different business services.

Supply chain analysis shows the mapping between business services and supplier services. Analysis of business processes will reveal the suppliers involved in each process and the points of hand-off between them. Management of the supply chain ensures that functional boundaries and performance requirements are clearly established for each supplier to ensure that overall business service levels are achieved. Business services are most likely to meet their targets consistently where there are a small number of suppliers in the supply chain, and where the interfaces between the suppliers in the chain are limited, simple and well defined.

Reducing the number of direct suppliers reduces the number of relationships that need to be managed, the number of peer-to-peer supplier issues that need to be resolved, and the complexity of the supplier management activities. Some organizations may successfully reduce or collapse the whole supply chain around a single service provider, often referred to as a 'prime' supplier. Facilities management is often outsourced to a single specialist partner or supplier, who may in turn sub-contract restaurant services, vending machine maintenance and cleaning.

Outsourcing entire business services to a single 'prime supplier' may run additional risks. For these reasons, organizations need to consider carefully their supply chain strategies ahead of major outsourcing activity. The scope of outsourced services needs to be considered to reduce the number of suppliers, while ensuring that risk is managed and fits with typical competencies in the supply market.

The supplier and contract management information system

The SCMIS is a set of tools, data and information that is used to support supplier management. The SCMIS contains details of the organization's suppliers, together with details of the products and services that they provide to the business (e.g. email service, PC supply and installation, service desk), together with details of the contracts. The SCMIS contains supplier details, a summary of each product/service (including support arrangements), information on the ordering process and, where applicable, contract details. Ideally the SCMIS should be contained within the overall CMS. In most organizations, the SCMIS is owned by the supplier management process or the procurement or purchasing department.

An SCMIS is beneficial because it can be used to promote preferred suppliers and to prevent purchasing of unapproved or incompatible items. By coordinating and controlling the buying activity, the organization is more likely to be able to negotiate preferential rates.

4.8.5.4 Establishment of new suppliers and contracts

The SCMIS provides a single, central focal set of information for the management of all suppliers and contracts. When establishing new suppliers and contracts, adding them to the SCMIS needs to be handled via the change management process, to ensure that any impact is assessed and understood.

Risk management, in relation to working with suppliers, centres on assessing vulnerabilities in each supplier arrangement or contract that pose threats to any aspect of the business, including business impact, probability, customer satisfaction, brand image, market share, profitability, share

price or regulatory impacts or penalties (in some industries).

The nature of the relationship affects the degree of risk to the business. Risks associated with an outsourced or strategic supplier are likely to be greater in number, and more complex to manage, than with internal supply. It is rarely possible to 'outsource' risk, although sometimes some of the risk may be transferred to the outsourcing organization. Blaming a supplier does not impress customers or internal users affected by a security incident or a lengthy system failure. New risks arising from the relationship need to be identified and managed, with communication and escalation as appropriate.

A substantial risk assessment should have been undertaken pre-contract, but this needs to be maintained in the light of changing business needs, changes to the contract scope, or changes in the operational environment.

The service provider organization and the supplier must consider the threats posed by the relationship to their own assets, and have their own risk profile. Each must identify their respective risk owners. In a well-functioning relationship, it is possible for much or all of the assessment to be openly shared with the other party. By involving supplier experts in risk assessments, especially in operational risk assessments, the organization may gain valuable insights into how best to mitigate risks, as well as improving the coverage of the assessment.

When evaluating risks of disruption to business services or functions, the business may have different priorities for service/function restoration. BIA is a method used to assess the impacts on different areas of the business, resulting from a loss of service. Risk assessment and BIA activities relating to suppliers and contracts should be performed in close conjunction with ITSCM, availability management and information security management, with a view to reducing the impact and probability of service failure as a result of supplier or supplier service failure.

Once these activities have been completed and the supplier and contract information has been input into the SCMIS, including the nominated individuals responsible for managing the new supplier and/or contracts, frequency of service/ supplier review meetings and contractual review meetings needs to be established, with appropriate break points, automated thresholds and warnings in place. The introduction of new suppliers and contracts should be handled as major changes through transition and into operation. This will ensure that appropriate contacts and communication points are established.

4.8.5.5 Supplier, contract and performance management

At an operational level, integrated processes need to be in place between an organization and its suppliers to ensure efficient day-to-day working practices. For example:

- Is the supplier expected to conform to the organization's change management process or any other processes?
- How does the service desk notify the supplier of incidents?
- How is CMS information updated when CIs change as a result of supplier actions? Who is responsible?

There may be a conflict of interest between the service provider organization and its supplier, especially with regard to the change management, incident management, problem management, and service asset and configuration management processes. The supplier may want to use its processes and systems, whereas the service provider organization will want to use its own processes and systems. If this is the case, clear responsibilities and interfaces will need to be defined and agreed.

These and many other areas need to be addressed to ensure smooth and effective working at an operational level. To do so, all touch points and contacts need to be identified and procedures put in place so that everyone understands their roles and responsibilities. This should include identification of the single, nominated individual responsible for ownership of each supplier and contract. However, an organization should take care not to automatically impose its own processes, but to take the opportunity to learn from its suppliers.

In addition to process interfaces, it is essential to identify how issues are handled at an operational level. By having clearly defined and communicated escalation routes, issues are likely to be identified and resolved earlier, minimizing the impact. Both the organization and the supplier benefit from the early capture and resolution of issues.

Example of learning from a supplier

A contract had been awarded for a customized stores control system for which the IT organization had developed processes to support the live service once it was installed. This included procedures for recording and documenting work done on the service by field engineers (e.g. changes, repairs, enhancement and reconfigurations). At a project progress meeting, the supplier confirmed that they had looked at the procedures and could follow them if required. However, having been in this situation many times before, they had already developed a set of procedures to deal with such events. These procedures were considerably more elegant, effective and easier to follow than those developed and proposed by the IT organization.

Both sides should strive to establish good communication links. The supplier learns more about the organization's business, its requirements and its plans, helping the supplier to understand and meet the organization's needs. In turn, the organization benefits from a more responsive supplier who is aware of the business drivers and any issues, and is therefore more able to provide appropriate solutions. Close day-to-day links can help each party to be aware of the other's culture and ways of working, resulting in fewer misunderstandings and leading to a more successful and long-lasting relationship.

Formal reviews

Two levels of formal review need to take place throughout the contract lifecycle to minimize risk and ensure the business realizes maximum benefit from the contract:

- **Service/supplier performance reviews** Reports on performance should be produced on a regular basis, based on the category of supplier, and should form the basis of service review meetings. The more important the supplier, the more frequent and extensive the reports and reviews should be.
- **Service, service scope and contract reviews** These should also be conducted on a regular basis, at least annually for all major suppliers. The objective of these should be to review the service, overall performance, service scope and

targets and the contract, together with any associated agreements. This should be compared with the original business needs and the current business needs to ensure that supplier and contracts remain aligned to business needs and continue to deliver value for money.

Formal performance review meetings must be held on a regular basis to review the supplier's performance against service levels, at a detailed operational level. These meetings provide an opportunity to check that the ongoing service performance management remains focused on supporting business needs. When appropriate, the SLM process may also be represented in supplier performance review meetings. Typical topics include:

- Service performance against targets
- Incident and problem reviews, including any escalated issues
- Business and customer feedback
- Expected major changes that will (or may) affect service during the next service period, as well as failed changes and changes that caused incidents
- Key business events over the next service period that need particular attention from the supplier (e.g. quarter-end processing)
- Best practice
- Opportunities for improvement
- Progression of SIPs.

Major service improvement initiatives and actions are controlled through SIPs with each supplier, including any actions for dealing with any failures or weaknesses. Progress of existing SIPs, or the need for a new initiative, is reviewed at service review meetings. Proactive or forward-thinking organizations use SIPs not only to deal with failures but also to improve a consistently achieved service. It is important that a contract provides suitable incentives to both parties to invest in service improvement. These aspects are covered in more detail in *ITIL Continual Service Improvement*.

The governance mechanisms for suppliers and contracts are drawn from the needs of appropriate stakeholders at different levels within each organization, and are structured so that the organization's representatives face-off to their counterparts in the supplier's organization. Defining the responsibilities for each representative, meeting forums and processes ensure that each person is involved at the right time in influencing or directing the right activities.

The scale and importance of the service and/or supplier influence the governance arrangements needed. The more significant the dependency, the greater the commitment and effort involved in managing the relationship. The effort needed on the service provider side to govern an outsourcing contract should not be underestimated, especially in closely regulated industries, such as the finance and pharmaceutical sectors.

A key objective for supplier management is to ensure that the value of a supplier to the organization is fully realized. Value is realized through all aspects of the relationship, from operational performance assurance, responsiveness to change requests and demand fluctuations, through to contribution of knowledge and experience to the organization's capability. The service provider must also ensure that the supplier's priorities match the business's priorities. The supplier must understand which of its service levels are most significant to the business.

Example of supplier value

A large multinational company had software agreements in place with the same supplier in no fewer than 24 countries. By arranging a single global licensing deal with the supplier, the company made annual savings of £5 million.

Satisfaction surveys and benefits assessments
Satisfaction surveys also play an important role in revealing how well supplier service levels are aligned to business needs. If the customer does not have visibility into what is being delivered by the supplier versus what is being done by internal support groups, the service provider will need to structure satisfaction surveys carefully to be able to differentiate between the two contributions. A survey may reveal instances where there is dissatisfaction with the service, yet the supplier is apparently performing well against its targets (and vice versa). This may happen where service levels are inappropriately defined and should result in a review of the contracts, agreements and targets. Some service providers publish supplier league tables based on their survey results, stimulating competition between suppliers.

For those significant supplier relationships in which the business has a direct interest, both the business (in conjunction with the procurement department) and IT will have established their objectives for the relationship, and defined the benefits they expect to realize. This forms a major part of the business case for entering into the relationship.

These benefits must be linked and complementary, and must be measured and managed. Where the business is seeking improvements in customer service, IT supplier relationships contributing to those customer services must be able to demonstrate improved service in their own domain, and how much this has contributed to improved customer service.

For benefits assessments to remain valid during the life of the contract, changes in circumstances that have occurred since the original benefits case was prepared must be taken into account. A supplier may have been selected on its ability to deliver a 5% saving of annual operational cost compared with other options, but after two years has delivered no savings. However, where this is due to changes to contract, or general industry costs that would have also affected the other options, it is likely that a relative cost saving is still being realized. A maintained benefits case shows that saving.

Benefits assessments often receive lower priority than cost-saving initiatives, and are given less priority in performance reports than issues and problem summaries, but it is important to the long-term relationship that achievements are recognized. A benefits report must make objective assessments against the original objectives, but may also include morale-boosting anecdotal evidence of achievements and added value.

Hints and tips

It is important for both organizations, and for the longevity of the relationship, that the benefits being derived from the relationship are regularly reviewed and reported.

Balanced, managed relationships

To ensure that all activities and contacts for a supplier are consistent and coordinated, each supplier relationship should have a single nominated individual accountable for all aspects of the relationship.

Example of consistent supplier relationship management

A nationwide retail organization had an individual owning the overall management of its major network services supplier. However, services, contracts and billing were managed by several individuals spread throughout the organization. The individual owner put forward a business case for single ownership of the supplier and all the various contracts, together with consolidation of all the individual invoices into a single quarterly bill. The estimated cost savings to the organization were in excess of £600,000 per annum.

An assessment of the success of a supplier relationship, from a business perspective, is likely to be substantially based on financial performance. Even where a service is performing well, it may not be meeting one or both parties' financial targets. It is important that both parties continue to benefit financially from the relationship. A contract that squeezes the margins of a supplier too tightly may lead to under-investment by the supplier, resulting in a gradual degradation of service, or even threaten the viability of the supplier. In either case this may result in adverse business impacts to the organization.

The key to the successful long-term financial management of the contract is a joint effort directed towards maintaining the financial equilibrium, rather than a confrontational relationship delivering short-term benefits to only one party.

Building relationships takes time and effort. As a result, the organization may only be able to build long-term relationships with a few key suppliers. The experience, culture and commitment of those involved in running a supplier relationship are at least as important as having a good contract and governance regime. The right people with the right attitudes in the relationship team can make a poor contract work, but a good contract does not ensure that a team with poor relationships will deliver.

A considerable amount of time and money is normally invested in negotiating major supplier deals, with more again at risk for both parties if the relationship is not successful. Both organizations must ensure that they invest suitably in the human resources allocated to managing the relationship. The personality, behaviours and culture of the relationship representatives all influence the relationship. For a partnering relationship, all those involved need to be able to respect and work closely and productively with their opposite numbers.

4.8.5.6 Contract renewal or termination

Contract reviews must be undertaken on a regular basis to ensure each contract is continuing to meet business needs. Contract reviews assess the contract operation holistically and at a more senior level than the service reviews that are undertaken at an operational level. These reviews should consider:

- How well the contract is working and its relevance for the future
- Whether changes are needed: services, products, contracts, agreements, targets
- What is the future outlook for the relationship – growth, shrinkage, change, termination, transfer etc.?
- Commercial performance of the contract, reviews against benchmarks or market assessments, suitability of the pricing structure and charging arrangements
- Guidance on future contract direction and ensuring best-practice management processes are established
- Supplier and contract governance.

For high-value, lengthy or complex supply arrangements, the period of contract negotiation and agreement can be lengthy, costly and may involve a protracted period of negotiation. It can be a natural inclination to wish to avoid further changes to a contract for as long as possible. However, for the business to derive full value from the supplier relationship, the contract must be able to be regularly and quickly amended to allow the business to benefit from service developments.

Benchmarking provides an assessment against the marketplace. The supplier may be committed by the contract to maintaining charges against a market price. To maintain the same margin, the supplier is obliged to improve its operational efficiency in line with its competitors. Collectively, these methods help provide an assessment of an improving or deteriorating efficiency.

The point of responsibility within the organization for deciding to change a supplier relationship is likely to depend on the type of relationship. The service provider may have identified a need to change the supplier, based on the existing supplier's performance, but for a contractual relationship the decision needs to be taken in conjunction with the organization's procurement and legal departments.

The organization should take careful steps to:

- Perform a thorough impact and risk assessment of a change of supplier on the organization and its business, especially during a period of transition. This could be particularly significant in the case of a strategic relationship.
- Make a commercial assessment of the exit costs. This may include contractual termination costs if supplier liability is not clear, but the largest costs are likely to be associated with a transition project. For any significant-sized relationship, this typically includes a period of dual-supply as services are migrated. Any change associated with a change in supplier will increase costs, either immediately as fixed costs or over time where borne by the supplier and reflected back in service charges.
- Take legal advice on termination terms, applicable notice period and mechanisms, and any other consequences, particularly if the contract is to be terminated early.
- Reassess the market to identify potential benefits in changing supplier.

A prudent organization undertakes most of these steps at the time the original contract is established, to ensure the right provisions and clauses are included, but this review activity needs to be reassessed when a change of supplier is being considered.

4.8.6 Triggers, inputs, outputs and interfaces

4.8.6.1 Triggers

There are many events that could trigger supplier management activity. These include:

- New or changed corporate governance guidelines
- New or changed business and IT strategies, policies or plans
- New or changed business needs or new or changed services

- New or changed requirements within agreements, such as SLRs, SLAs, OLAs or contracts
- Review and revision of designs and strategies
- Periodic activities such as reviewing, revising or reporting, including review and revision of supplier management policies, reports and plans
- Requests from other areas, particularly SLM and information security management, for assistance with supplier issues
- Requirements for new contracts, contract renewal or contract termination
- Re-categorization of suppliers and/or contracts.

4.8.6.2 Inputs

Inputs comprise:

- **Business information** From the organization's business strategy, plans and financial plans, and information on its current and future requirements
- **Supplier and contracts strategy** This covers the sourcing policy of the service provider and the types of supplier and contract used. It is produced by the service strategy processes
- **Supplier plans and strategies** Details of the business plans and strategies of suppliers, together with details of their technology developments, plans and statements and information on their current financial status and projected business viability
- **Supplier contracts, agreements and targets** Of both existing and new contracts and agreements from suppliers
- **Supplier and contract performance information** Of both existing and new contracts and suppliers
- **IT information** From the IT strategy and plans and current budgets
- **Performance issues** The incident and problem management processes, with incidents and problems relating to poor contract or supplier performance
- **Financial information** From financial management for IT services, the cost of supplier service(s) and service provision, the cost of contracts and the resultant business benefit; and the financial plans and budgets, together with the costs associated with service and supplier failure

- **Service information** From the SLM process, with details of the services from the service portfolio and the service catalogue, service level targets within SLAs and SLRs, and possibly from the monitoring of SLAs, service reviews and breaches of the SLAs. Also customer satisfaction data on service quality
- **CMS** Containing information on the relationships between the business, the services, the supporting services and the technology.

4.8.6.3 Outputs

The outputs of supplier management are used within all other parts of the process, by many other processes and by other parts of the organization. Often this information is supplied as electronic reports or displays on shared areas or as pages on intranet servers to ensure the most up-to-date information is always used. The information provided is as follows:

- **SCMIS** This holds the information needed to execute the activities within supplier management – for example, the data monitored and collected as part of supplier management. This is then invariably used as an input to all other parts of the supplier management process.
- **Supplier and contract performance information and reports** These are used as input to supplier and contract review meetings to manage the quality of service provided by suppliers and partners. This should include information on shared risk where appropriate.
- **Supplier and contract review meeting minutes** These are produced to record the minutes and actions of all review meetings with suppliers.
- **Supplier SIPs** These are used to record all improvement actions and plans agreed between service providers and their suppliers, wherever they are needed, and should be used to manage the progress of agreed improvement actions, including risk reduction measures.
- **Supplier survey reports** Often many people within a service provider organization have dealings with suppliers. Feedback from these individuals should be collated to ensure consistency in the quality of service provided by suppliers in all areas. These can be published as league tables to encourage competition between suppliers.

4.8.6.4 Interfaces

The key interfaces that supplier management has with other processes are:

- **SLM** Supplier management provides assistance with the determining of targets, requirements and responsibilities for suppliers. It then sees to their inclusion within underpinning agreements and contracts to ensure that they support all SLR and SLA targets. SLM assists supplier management in the investigation of SLA and SLR breaches caused by poor supplier performance. SLM also provides invaluable input into the supplier management review process.
- **Change management** Supplier contracts and agreements are controlled documents and therefore subject to appropriate change management procedures. When changes are proposed, the involvement of suppliers should be assessed and reflected in planning.
- **ISM** ISM relies on supplier management for the management of suppliers and their access to services and systems, and their responsibilities with regard to conformance to the service provider's ISM policies and requirements.
- **Financial management for IT services** This process provides adequate funds to finance supplier management requirements and contracts and provides financial advice and guidance on purchase and procurement matters.
- **Service portfolio management** This process looks to supplier management input to ensure that all supporting services and their details and relationships are accurately reflected within the service portfolio.
- **ITSCM** This process works with supplier management with regard to the management of continuity service suppliers.

4.8.7 Information management

All the information required by supplier management should be contained within the SCMIS. This should include all information relating to suppliers and contracts, as well as all the information relating to the operation of the supporting services provided by suppliers. Information relating to these supporting services should also be contained within the service portfolio, together with the relationships to all other services and components. This information should be integrated and maintained in alignment with all other IT management information systems, particularly the service portfolio and the CMS.

4.8.8 Critical success factors and key performance indicators

The following list includes some sample CSFs for supplier management. Each organization should identify appropriate CSFs based on its objectives for the process. Each sample CSF is followed by a small number of typical KPIs that support the CSF. These KPIs should not be adopted without careful consideration. Each organization should develop KPIs that are appropriate for its level of maturity, its CSFs and its particular circumstances. Achievement against KPIs should be monitored and used to identify opportunities for improvement, which should be logged in the CSI register for evaluation and possible implementation.

- **CSF** Business protected from poor supplier performance or disruption
  - **KPI** Increase in the number of suppliers meeting the targets within the contract
  - **KPI** Reduction in the number of breaches of contractual targets
- **CSF** Supporting services and their targets align with business needs and targets
  - **KPI** Increase in the number of service and contractual reviews held with suppliers
  - **KPI** Increase in the number of supplier and contractual targets aligned with SLA and SLR targets
- **CSF** Availability of services is not compromised by supplier performance
  - **KPI** Reduction in the number of service breaches caused by suppliers
  - **KPI** Reduction in the number of threatened service breaches caused by suppliers
- **CSF** Clear ownership and awareness of supplier and contractual issues
  - **KPI** Increase in the number of suppliers with nominated supplier managers
  - **KPI** Increase in the number of contracts with nominated contract managers.

4.8.9 Challenges and risks

4.8.9.1 Challenges

Supplier management faces many challenges, which could include:

- Continually changing business and IT needs and managing significant change in parallel with delivering existing service
- Working with an imposed non-ideal contract, a contract that has poor targets or terms and conditions, or poor or non-existent definition of service or supplier performance targets
- Legacy issues, especially with services recently outsourced
- Insufficient expertise retained within the organization
- Being tied into long-term contracts, with no possibility of improvement, which have punitive penalty charges for early exit
- Situations where the supplier depends on the organization in fulfilling the service delivery (e.g. for a data feed) can lead to issues over accountability for poor service performance
- Disputes over charges
- Interference by either party in the running of the other's operation
- Being caught in a daily fire-fighting mode, losing the proactive approach
- Poor communication – not interacting often enough or quickly enough or not focusing on the right issues
- Personality conflicts and/or cultural conflicts
- One party using the contract to the detriment of the other party, resulting in win–lose changes rather than joint win–win changes
- Losing the strategic perspective, focusing on operational issues, causing a lack of focus on strategic relationship objectives and issues.

Key elements that can help to avoid the above issues are:

- A clearly written, well-defined and well-managed contract
- A mutually beneficial relationship
- Clearly defined (and communicated) roles and responsibilities on both sides
- Good interfaces and communications between the parties
- Well-defined service management processes on both sides
- Selecting suppliers who have achieved certification against internationally recognized certifications, such as ISO 9001 and ISO/IEC 20000.

4.8.9.2 Risks

The major areas of risk associated with supplier management include:

- Lack of commitment from the business and senior management to the supplier management process and procedures
- Lack of appropriate information on future business and IT policies, plans and strategies
- Lack of resources and/or budget for the supplier management process
- Legacy of badly written and agreed contracts that do not underpin or support business needs or SLA and SLR targets
- Suppliers agree to targets and service levels within contracts that are impossible to meet, or suppliers fail or are incapable of meeting the terms and conditions of the contract
- Supplier personnel or organizational culture are not aligned with that of the service provider or the business
- Lack of clarity and integration by supplier with service management processes, policies and procedures of the service provider
- Suppliers are not cooperative and are not willing to partake in and support the required supplier management process
- Suppliers are taken over and relationships, personnel and contracts are changed
- The demands of corporate supplier and contract procedures are excessive and bureaucratic
- Poor corporate financial processes, such as procurement and purchasing, do not support good supplier management.

Service design technology-related activities 5

5 Service design technology-related activities

This chapter considers the technology-related activities of requirement engineering and the development of technology architectures for management of data and information and for management of applications.

5.1 REQUIREMENTS ENGINEERING

Requirements engineering is the approach by which sufficient rigour is introduced into the process of understanding and documenting the requirements of the business, users and all other stakeholders, and ensuring traceability of changes to each requirement. This process comprises the stages of elicitation, analysis (which feeds back into the elicitation) and validation. All these contribute to the production of a rigorous, complete requirements document. The core of this document is a repository of individual requirements that is developed and managed. Often these requirements are instigated by IT but ultimately they need to be documented and agreed with the business.

There are many guidelines on requirements engineering, including the Recommended Practice for Software Requirements Specifications (IEEE 830), the Software Engineering Body of Knowledge (SWEBOK), capability maturity model integration (CMMI) and the V-Model, which is described in detail in *ITIL Service Transition*. Information about several international standards that may also be of use may be found in Appendix N.

It is important to remember that the guidance in this chapter focuses on the requirements for the technology related to a service. There many other areas around which an organization will need to define requirements to ensure successful design, transition and operation of a complete service, such as requirements for:

■ User training
■ Support staff training
■ Marketing and communication related to the service and its deployment

■ Service documentation
■ Organizational and cultural readiness.

The standards and methods for defining requirements of this sort will be developed as part of the design coordination process, which will also ensure ongoing adherence during the service design stage.

5.1.1 Different requirement types

A fundamental assumption here is that the analysis of the current and required business processes results in functional requirements met through IT services (comprising applications, data, infrastructure, environment and support skills).

There are commonly said to be three major types of requirements for any system. These are:

■ **Functional requirements** For a service these requirements are those necessary to support a particular business function, business process or to remove a customer or user constraint. These requirements describe the utility aspects of a service.
■ **Management and operational requirements** (sometimes referred to as non-functional requirements) These define the requirements and constraints on the service and address the need for a responsive, available and secure service, and deal with such issues as ease of deployment, operability, management needs and security. These requirements describe the warranty aspects of a service.
■ **Usability requirements** These requirements are those that relate to how easy it is for the user to access and use the service to achieve the desired outcomes, including addressing the 'look and feel' needs of the user. This requirement type is often seen as part of management and operational requirements, but for the purposes of this section it will be addressed separately. Depending on the context, these requirements enable utility, support warranty and influence user perceptions of a service.

5.1.1.1 Functional requirements

Functional requirements describe the things a service is intended to do – in other words, the utility it will provide – and can be expressed as tasks or functions that the component is required to perform. One approach for specifying functional requirements is through such methods as a system context diagram or a use case model. Other approaches show how the inputs are to be transformed into the outputs (data flow or object diagrams) and textual descriptions.

A system context diagram, for instance, captures all information exchanges between, on the one hand, the IT service and its environment and, on the other, sources or destinations of data used by the service. These information exchanges and data sources represent constraints on the service under development.

A use case model defines a goal-oriented set of interactions between external actors and the service under consideration. Actors are parties outside the service that interact with the service. An actor may represent a class of user, roles that users can play, or other services and their requirements. The main purpose of use case modelling is to establish the boundary of the proposed system and fully state the functional capabilities to be delivered to the users. Use cases are also helpful for establishing communication between business and application developers. They provide a basis for sizing and feed the definition of usability requirements. Use cases define all scenarios that an application has to support and can therefore easily be expanded into test cases. Since use cases describe a service's functionality on a level that is understandable for both business and IT, they can serve as a vehicle to specify the functional elements of a service level agreement (SLA), such as the actual business deliverables from the service.

One level 'below' the use case and the context diagram, many other modelling techniques can be applied. These models depict the static and dynamic characteristics of the services under development. A conceptual data model (whether called object or data) describes the different 'objects' in the service, their mutual relationships and their internal structure. Dynamics of the service can be described using state models (e.g. state transition diagrams) that show the various states

of the entities or objects, together with events that may cause state changes. Interactions between the different application components can be described using interaction diagrams (e.g. object interaction diagrams).

> **Hints and tips**
>
> Alongside a mature requirements modelling process, computer-aided software engineering (CASE) tools can help in getting and keeping these models consistent, correct and complete.

5.1.1.2 Management and operational requirements

Management and operational requirements (or non-functional requirements) are used to define requirements and constraints on the IT service. The requirements serve as a basis for early systems and service sizing and estimates of cost, and can support the assessment of the viability of the proposed IT service. Management and operational requirements should also encourage developers to take a broader view of project goals.

Categories of management and operational requirements include:

- **Manageability** Does it run? Does it fail? How does it fail?
- **Efficiency** How many resources does it consume?
- **Availability and reliability** How reliable does it need to be?
- **Capacity and performance** What level of capacity do we need to support storage and throughput requirements?
- **Security** What classification of security is required?
- **Installation** How much effort does it take to install the application? Is it using automated installation procedures?
- **Continuity** What level of resilience and recovery is required?
- **Controllability** Can it be monitored, managed and adjusted?
- **Maintainability** How well can the application be adjusted, corrected, maintained and changed for future requirements?
- **Operability** Do the applications disturb other applications in their functionalities?
- **Measurability and reportability** Can we measure and report on all of the required aspects of the application?

The management and operational requirements can be used to prescribe the quality or warranty attributes of the application or service being built. These quality attributes can be used to design test plans for testing the applications on their compliance with management and operational requirements.

5.1.1.3 Usability requirements

The primary purpose of usability requirements is to ensure that the service meets the expectations of its users with regard to its ease of use. To achieve this:

- Establish performance standards for usability evaluations
- Define test scenarios for usability test plans and usability testing.

Like the management and operational requirements, usability requirements can also be used as the quality attributes of the application or service being built. These quality attributes can be used to design test plans for testing the applications on their compliance to usability requirements.

In order to establish usability requirements, care must be taken to establish the types of likely users and to understand their varied needs. For example, users who are colour-blind would not find a service that relied heavily on colour differentiation easy to use, or users working in a second language may have difficulty with screen terminology that does not translate well.

5.1.2 Requirements for support – the user view

Users have formally defined roles and activities as user representatives in requirements definition and acceptance testing. They should be actively involved in identifying all aspects of service requirements, including the three categories in section 5.1.1 above, and also in:

- User training procedures and facilities
- Support activities and service desk procedures.

5.1.3 Requirements investigation techniques

A range of techniques may be used to investigate business situations and elicit service requirements. Sometimes the customers and the business are not completely sure of what their requirements actually are and will need some assistance and prompting from the designer or requirements gatherer. This must be completed in a sensitive way to ensure that it is not seen as IT dictating business requirements. The two most commonly used techniques are interviewing and workshops, but these are usually supplemented by other techniques, such as observation and scenarios.

5.1.3.1 Interviews

The interview is a key tool and can be vital in achieving a number of objectives, such as:

- Making initial contact with key stakeholders and establishing a basis for progress
- Building and developing rapport with different users and managers
- Acquiring information about the business situation, including issues and problems.

There are three areas that are considered during interviews:

- Current business processes that need to be fulfilled in any new business systems and services
- Problems with the current operations that need to be addressed
- New features required from the new business system or service and any supporting IT service.

The interviewing process is improved when the interviewer has prepared thoroughly as this saves time by avoiding unnecessary explanations and demonstrates interest and professionalism. The classic questioning structure of 'Why, What, Who, When, Where, How' provides an excellent framework for preparing for interviews.

It is equally important to formally close the interview by:

- Summarizing the points covered and the actions agreed
- Explaining what happens next, both following the interview and beyond
- Asking the interviewee how any further contact should be made.

It is always a good idea to write up the notes of the interview as soon as possible – ideally straight away and usually by the next day. The advantages of interviewing are:

- Builds a relationship with the users

- Can yield important information
- Opportunity to understand different viewpoints and attitudes across the user group
- Opportunity to investigate new areas that arise
- Collection of examples of documents and reports
- Appreciation of political factors
- Study of the environment in which the new service will operate.

The disadvantages of interviewing are:

- Expensive in elapsed time
- No opportunity for conflict resolution
- No opportunity for consensus building.

5.1.3.2 Workshops

Workshops provide a forum in which issues can be discussed, conflicts resolved and requirements elicited. Workshops are especially valuable when time and budgets are tightly constrained, several viewpoints need to be canvassed and an iterative and incremental view of service development is being taken.

The advantages of the workshop are:

- Gain a broad view of the area under investigation – having a group of stakeholders in one room will allow a more complete understanding of the issues and problems
- Increase speed and productivity – it is much quicker to have one meeting with a group of people than interviewing them one by one
- Obtain buy-in and acceptance for the IT service
- Gain a consensus view – if all the stakeholders are involved, the chance of them taking ownership of the results is improved.

There are some disadvantages, including:

- It can be time-consuming to organize – for example, it is not always easy to get all the necessary people together at the same time
- It can be difficult to get all of the participants with the required level of authority
- It can be difficult to get a mix of business and operational people to understand the different requirements.

The success or failure of a workshop session depends, in large part, on the preparatory work by the facilitator and the business sponsor for the workshop. They should spend time before the event planning the following areas:

- The objective of the workshop – this has to be an objective that can be achieved within the time constraints of the workshop.
- Who will be invited to participate in the workshop – it is important that all stakeholders interested in the objective should be invited to attend or be represented.
- The structure of the workshop and the techniques to be used. These need to be geared towards achieving the defined objective (for example, requirements gathering or prioritization) and should take the needs of the participants into account.
- Arranging a suitable venue – this may be within the organization, but it is better to use a 'neutral' venue out of the office.

During the workshop, a facilitator needs to ensure that the issues are discussed, views are aired and progress is made towards achieving the stated objective. A record needs to be kept of the key points emerging from the discussion. At the end of

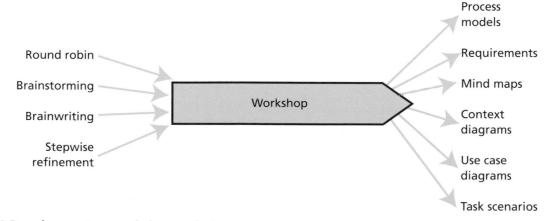

Figure 5.1 Requirements – workshop techniques

the workshop, the facilitator needs to summarize the key points and actions. Each action should be assigned to an owner.

There are two main categories of technique required for a requirements workshop – techniques for discovery and techniques for documentation, as shown in Figure 5.1.

5.1.3.3 Observation

Observing the workplace is very useful in obtaining information about the business environment and the work practices. This has two advantages:

■ A much better understanding of the problems and difficulties faced by the business users

■ It will help devise workable solutions that are more likely to be acceptable to the business.

Conversely, being observed can be rather unnerving, and the old saying 'you change when being observed' needs to be factored into your approach and findings.

Formal observation involves watching a specific task being performed. There is a danger of being shown just the 'front-story' without any of the everyday variances, but it is still a useful tool.

5.1.3.4 Protocol analysis

Protocol analysis is simply getting the users to perform a task, and for them to describe each step as they perform it.

5.1.3.5 Shadowing

Shadowing involves following a user for a period such as a day to find out about a particular job. It is a powerful way to understand a particular user role. Asking for explanations of how the work is done, or the workflow, clarifies some of the already assumed aspects.

5.1.3.6 Scenario analysis

Scenario analysis is essentially telling the story of a task or transaction. Its value is that it helps a user who is uncertain what is needed from a new service to realize it more clearly. Scenarios are also useful when analysing or redesigning business processes. A scenario will trace the course of a transaction from an initial business trigger through each of the steps needed to achieve a successful outcome.

Scenarios provide a framework for discovering alternative paths that may be followed to complete the transaction. This is extremely useful in requirements elicitation and analysis because real-life situations, including the exceptional circumstances, are debated.

Scenarios offer significant advantages:

■ They force the user to include every step, so there are no taken-for-granted elements and the problem of tacit knowledge is addressed.

■ By helping the user to visualize all contingencies, they help to cope with the uncertainty about future systems and services.

■ A workshop group refining a scenario will identify those paths that do not suit the corporate culture.

■ They provide a tool for preparing test scripts.

The disadvantages of scenarios are that they can be time-consuming to develop, and some scenarios can become very complex. Where this is the case, it is easier to analyse if each of the main alternative paths is considered as a separate scenario.

A popular approach to documenting scenario descriptions is to develop use case descriptions to support use case diagrams. However, there are also a number of graphical methods of documenting a scenario, such as storyboards, activity diagrams, task models and decision tree diagrams.

5.1.3.7 Prototyping

Prototyping is an important technique for eliciting, analysing, demonstrating and validating requirements. It is difficult for users to envisage the new service before it is actually built. Prototypes offer a way of showing the user how the new service might work and the ways in which it can be used. If a user is unclear what they need the service to do for them, utilizing a prototype often releases blocks to thinking and can produce a new wave of requirements. Incremental and iterative approaches to service development, such as the dynamic systems development method (DSDM), use evolutionary prototyping as an integral part of their development lifecycle.

There is a range of approaches to building prototypes. They may be built using an application development environment so that they mirror the service; images of the screens and navigations may be built using presentation software; or they may simply be 'mock-ups' on paper.

There are two basic methods of prototyping:

- The throw-away mock-up, which is only used to demonstrate the look and feel
- The incremental implementation, where the prototype is developed into the final system.

It is important to select consciously which is to be used, otherwise there is a danger that a poor-quality mock-up becomes the basis for the real system, causing problems later on.

There is a strong link between scenarios and prototyping because scenarios can be used as the basis for developing prototypes. In addition to confirming the users' requirements, prototyping can often help the users to identify new requirements. Prototypes are successfully used to:

- Clarify any uncertainty on the part of the service developers and confirm to the user that what they have asked for has been understood
- Open the user up to new requirements as they understand what the service will be able to do to support them
- Show users the 'look and feel' of the proposed service and elicit usability requirements
- Validate the requirements and identify any errors.

Potential problems include:

- Endless iteration
- A view that if the prototype works, the full service can be ready tomorrow.

5.1.3.8 Other techniques

Other techniques that could be used include:

- **Questionnaires** These can be useful to get a limited amount of information from a lot of people when interviewing them all would not be practical or cost-effective.
- **Special-purpose records** This technique involves the users in keeping a record about a specific issue or task. For example, they could keep a simple five-bar gate record about how often they need to transfer telephone calls – this could provide information about the problems with this business process.
- **Activity sampling** This is a rather more quantitative form of observation and can be used when it is necessary to know how people

spend their time. For example: How much time is spent on invoicing? How much time is spent on reconciling payments? How much time is spent on sorting out queries?

5.1.4 Problems with requirements engineering

Requirements, seen by users as the uncomplicated bit of a new service development, are actually the most problematic aspect, and yet the time allocated is far less than for the other phases.

Tight timescales and tight budgets – both the result of constraints on the business – place pressures on the development team to deliver a service. The trouble is that without the due time to understand and define the requirements properly, the service that is delivered on time may not be the service that the business thought it was asking for.

Studies carried out into IT project failures tell a common story. Many of the projects and unsatisfactory IT services suggest the following conclusions:

- A large proportion of errors (over 80%) are introduced at the requirements phase.
- Very few faults (fewer than 10%) are introduced at design and development – developers are developing things right, but frequently not developing the right things.
- Most of the project time is allocated to the development and testing phases of the project.
- Less than 12% of the project time is allocated to requirements.

These findings are particularly significant because the cost of correcting errors in requirements increases dramatically the later into the development lifecycle they are found.

One of the main problems with requirements engineering is the lack of detailed skill and overall understanding of the area where people use it. If accurately performed, the work can integrate requirements from numerous areas in a few questions.

Other typical problems with requirements have been identified as:

- Lack of relevance to the objectives of the service
- Lack of clarity in the wording
- Ambiguity
- Duplication between requirements

- Conflicts between requirements
- Requirements expressed in such a way that it is difficult to assess whether or not they have been achieved
- Requirements that assume a solution rather than stating what is to be delivered by the service
- Uncertainty among users about what they need from the new service
- Users omitting to identify requirements
- Inconsistent levels of detail
- Failure to include requirements from service provider stakeholders such as service operations and support staff
- An assumption that user and IT staff have knowledge that they do not possess and therefore a failure to ensure that there is a common understanding
- Failure to include non-technical requirements critical to success of the service such as requirements for training, documentation, communications and marketing
- Requirements creep – the gradual addition of seemingly small requirements without taking the extra effort into account in the project plan.

Another problem is an apparent inability on the part of the users to articulate clearly what it is they wish the service to do for them. Very often they are deterred from doing so because the nature of the requirement under discussion is explained in a straightforward statement rather than in an open-ended manner that encourages a detailed exchange.

5.1.4.1 Resolving requirements engineering problems

Defining actors

There are some participants that must take part in the requirements engineering process. They represent three broad stakeholder groups:

- The business
- The user community
- The service development/management team.

The user community should be represented by the domain expert (or subject-matter expert) and end-users.

Dealing with tacit knowledge

When developing a new service, the users will pass on to IT their explicit knowledge, i.e. knowledge of procedures and data that is at the front of their minds and that they can easily articulate. A major problem when eliciting requirements is that of tacit knowledge, i.e. those other aspects of the work that a user is unable to articulate or explain.

Some common elements that cause problems and misunderstandings are:

- **Skills** Explaining how to carry out actions using words alone is extremely difficult.
- **Taken-for-granted information** Even experienced and expert business users may fail to mention information or clarify terminology, and the analyst may not realize that further questioning is required.
- **Front-story/back-story** This issue concerns a tendency to frame a description of current working practices, or a workplace, in order to give a more positive view than is actually the case.
- **Future systems knowledge** If the study is for a new service development, with no existing expertise or knowledge in the organization, how can the prospective users know what they want?
- **Common language** The difficulty of an outsider assuming a common language for discourse, and common norms of communication. (If they do not have this, then the potential for misrepresentation of the situation can grow considerably.)
- **Intuitive understanding** This is usually born of considerable experience. Decision makers are often thought to follow a logical, linear path of enquiry while making their decisions. In reality though, as improved decision-making skills and knowledge are acquired, the linear path is often abandoned in favour of intuitive pattern recognition.
- **Organizational culture** Without an understanding of the culture of an organization, the requirements exercise may be flawed.

Communities of practice are discrete groups of workers – maybe related by task, by department, by geographical location or some other factor – that have their own sets of norms and practices,

Table 5.1 Requirements engineering – tacit and explicit knowledge

	Tacit	Explicit
Individual	Skills, values, taken-for-granted, intuitiveness	Tasks, job descriptions, targets, volumes and frequencies
Corporate	Norms, back-story, culture, communities of practice	Procedures, style guides, processes, knowledge sharing

Table 5.2 Requirements engineering: examples of explicit and tacit knowledge[6]

Technique	Explicit knowledge	Tacit knowledge	Skills	Future requirements
Interviewing	✓✓	✓	X	✓
Shadowing	✓✓	✓✓	✓✓	X
Workshops	✓✓	✓✓	X	✓✓
Prototyping	✓✓	✓✓	✓✓	✓✓
Scenario analysis	✓✓	✓✓	X	✓✓
Protocol analysis	✓✓	✓✓	✓✓	X

Key: ✓✓ = suitable technique to discover this kind of knowledge; ✓ = less suitable technique to discover this kind of knowledge; X = unsuitable technique to discover this kind of knowledge.

[6] Rugg, G. and Maiden, N.A.M. (1995). Knowledge acquisition techniques for requirements engineering. Conference paper: 1994 workshop on requirements elicitation for software systems, Keele, Staffordshire.

distinct from other groups within the organization and the organization as a whole.

Table 5.1 provides some examples of tacit versus explicit knowledge that might be expected to come from both individuals and the corporation.

Table 5.2 shows the relationship between various techniques of requirements gathering and the kinds of knowledge they are most likely to develop. For example, the technique of shadowing is suitable for uncovering both explicit and tacit knowledge, as well as observing skills (how to carry something out); however, this technique is not likely to uncover future requirements.

5.1.5 Documenting requirements

The requirements document is at the heart of the process and can take a number of forms. Typically the document will include a catalogue of requirements, with each individual requirement documented using a standard template. One or more models showing specific aspects, such as the processing or data requirements, may supplement this catalogue.

Before they are formally entered into the catalogue, requirements are subject to careful scrutiny. This scrutiny may involve organizing the requirements into groupings and checking that each requirement is 'well-formed'.

Once the document is considered to be complete, it must be reviewed by business representatives and confirmed to be a true statement of the requirements at that point in time. During this stage the reviewers examine the requirements and question whether they are well-defined, clear and complete.

As we uncover the requirements from our various users, we need to document them. This is best done in two distinct phases – building the requirements list and, later, developing an organized requirements catalogue. The requirements list tends to be an informal document and can be presented in a table as four columns:

- Requirements
- Source
- Comment
- Detail level.

Each requirement in the list must be checked to see whether or not it is well formed and SMART (specific, measurable, achievable, relevant and time-bound).

When checking the individual and totality of requirements, the following checklist can be used:

■ Are the requirements, as captured, unambiguous?
■ Is the meaning clear?
■ Is the requirement aligned to the service development and business objectives, or is it irrelevant?
■ Is the requirement reasonable, or would it be expensive and time-consuming to satisfy?
■ Do any requirements conflict with one another such that only one may be implemented?
■ Do they imply a solution rather than state a requirement?
■ Is each requirement entered separately, or are they really several requirements grouped into one entry?
■ Do several requirements overlap or duplicate each other?

There are several potential outcomes from the exercise:

■ Accept the requirement as it stands
■ Re-word the requirement to remove jargon and ambiguity
■ Merge duplicated/overlapping requirements
■ Take unclear and ambiguous requirements back to the users for clarification.

5.1.5.1 The requirements catalogue

The requirements catalogue is the central repository of the users' requirements, and all the requirements should be documented here, following the analysis as described above. The requirements catalogue should form part of the service pipeline within the overall service portfolio. As the requirements take shape, requirements from all stakeholders can be documented here to provide a single source of complete information on the requirements for the new or changed service. Each requirement that has been analysed is documented using a standard template, such as that shown in Table 5.3.

Table 5.3 Requirements template

IT service	Author		Date	
Requirement ID	Requirement name			
Source	Owner	Priority	Business process	
Functional requirement description				
Management and operational and usability requirements	Description			
Justification				
Related documents				
Related requirements				
Comments				
Resolution				
Version no	Change history	Date	Change request	

The key entries in the template are as follows:

- **Requirement ID** This is a unique ID that never changes and is used for traceability – for example, to reference the requirement in design documents, test specifications or implemented code. This ensures that all requirements have been met and that all implemented functions are based on requirements.

- **Source** The business area or users who requested the requirement or the document where the requirement was raised. Recording the source of a requirement helps ensure that questions can be answered or the need can be re-assessed in the future if necessary.

- **Owner** The user who accepts ownership of the individual requirement will agree that it is worded and documented correctly, and will sign it off at acceptance testing when satisfied.

- **Priority** The level of importance and need for a requirement. Usually approaches such as MoSCoW are used, where the following interpretation of the mnemonic applies:
  - **Must have** – a key requirement without which the service has no value.
  - **Should have** – an important requirement that must be delivered but, where time is short, could be delayed for a future delivery. This should be a short-term delay, but the service would still have value without it.
  - **Could have** – a requirement that would be beneficial to include if it does not cost too much or take too long to deliver, but it is not central to the service.
  - **Won't have** (but would like in the future) – a requirement that will be needed in the future but is not required for this delivery. In a future service release, this requirement may be upgraded to a 'must have'.

- **Requirement description** A succinct description of the requirement. A useful approach is to describe the requirement using the following structure:
  - Actor (or user role)
  - Verb phrase
  - Object (noun or noun phrase).

- **Related documents** Where the requirement incorporates complex business rules or data validation, a decision table or decision tree may be more useful to define complex business rules, while data validation rules may be defined in a repository. If a supplementary technique is used to specify or model the requirement, there should be a cross-reference to the related document.

- **Business process** A simple phrase to group together requirements that support a specific activity, such as sales, inventory, customer service, and so on.

- **Justification** Not all requirements that are requested will be met. This may be due to time and budget constraints, or may be because one requirement is dropped in favour of a conflicting requirement. Often a requirement is not met because it adds little value to the business. The justification sets out the reasons for requesting a requirement.

- **Related requirements** Requirements may be related to each other for several reasons. Sometimes there is a link between the functionality required by the requirements or a high-level requirement is clarified by a series of more detailed requirements.

- **Change history** The entries in this section provide a record of all the changes that have affected the requirement. This is required for configuration management and traceability purposes.

Guidance on assigning priority in the requirements template

The following should be clearly agreed:

- Requirement priorities can and do change over the life of a service development project.
- 'Should have' requirements need to be carefully considered because, if they are not delivered within the initial design stage, they may be impossible to implement later.
- Requirements are invariably more difficult and more expensive to meet later in the service lifecycle.
- It is not just the functional requirements that can be 'must haves' – some of the management and operational requirements should be 'must haves'.

5.1.5.2 Full requirements documentation

Effective requirements documentation should comprise the following elements:

- A glossary of terms, to define each organizational term used within the requirements document. This will help manage the problem of local jargon and will clarify synonyms and homonyms for anyone using the document
- A scoping model, such as a system context diagram
- The requirements catalogue, ideally maintained as part of an overall service portfolio
- Supporting models, such as business process models, data flow diagrams or interaction diagrams.

Managing changes to the documentation

Changes may come about because:

- The scope of the new service has altered through budget constraints
- The service must comply with new regulations or legislation
- Changes in business priorities
- Stakeholders have understood a requirement better after some detailed analysis (for example, using scenarios or prototyping) and amended the original requirement accordingly.

There are a number of specialist support tools on the market to support requirements processes. These are sometimes called CARE (computer-aided requirements engineering) or CASE. Features include:

- Maintaining cross-references between requirements
- Storing requirements documentation
- Managing changes to the requirements documentation
- Managing versions of the requirements documentation
- Producing formatted requirements specification documents from the database
- Ensuring documents delivered by any solution project are suitable to enable support.

5.1.6 Requirements and outsourcing

The aim is to select standard packaged solutions wherever possible to meet service requirements. However, whether solutions to IT requirements are to be purchased off the shelf, developed in-house or outsourced, all the activities up to the production of a specification of business requirements are done in-house. Many IT service development contracts assume it is possible to know what the requirements are at the start, and that it is possible to produce a specification that unambiguously expresses the requirements. For all but the simplest services this is almost never true. Requirements analysis is an iterative process – the requirements will change during the period the application and service are being developed. It will require user involvement throughout the development process, as in the DSDM and other 'agile' approaches.

5.1.6.1 Typical requirements outsourcing scenarios

Typical approaches to a contract for the development of IT systems to be delivered in support of an IT service are as follows:

- **Low-level requirements specification** The boundary between 'customer' and provider is drawn between the detailed requirements specification and any design activities. All the requirements that have an impact on the user have been specified in detail, giving the provider a very clear and precise implementation target. However, there is increased specification effort, and the added value of the provider is restricted to the less difficult aspects of development.
- **High-level requirements specification** The customer/provider boundary is between the high-level requirements and all other phases. The provider contract covers everything below the line. The customer is responsible for testing the delivered service against the business requirements. As it is easier to specify high-level requirements, there is reduced effort to develop contract inputs. However, there may be significant problems of increased cost and risk for both customer and provider, together with increased room for mistakes, instability of requirements and increased difficulty in knowing what information systems are wanted.

5.2 MANAGEMENT OF DATA AND INFORMATION

Data is one of the critical asset types that need to be managed in order to develop, deliver and support IT services effectively. Data/information management is how an organization plans, collects, creates, organizes, uses, controls, disseminates and disposes of its data/information, both structured records and unstructured data. It also ensures that the value of that data/information is identified and exploited, both in support of its internal operations and in adding value to its customer-facing business processes.

A number of terms are common in this area, including 'data management', 'information management' and 'information resource management'. For the purposes of this publication, the term 'data management' is used as shorthand for all of the three above.

Key message

The role of data management is not just about managing raw data: it is about managing all the contextual metadata – additional 'data about the data' – that goes with it, and when added to the raw data gives 'information' or 'data in context'.

Data, as the basis for the organization's information, has all the necessary attributes to be treated as an asset (or resource). For example, it is essential for 'the achievement of business objectives and the successful daily workings of an organization'. In addition, it can be 'obtained and preserved by an organization, but only at a financial cost'. Finally it can, along with other resources/assets, be used to 'further the achievement of the aims of an organization'.

Key factors for successful data management are as follows:

- All users have ready access through a variety of channels to the information they need to do their jobs.
- Data assets are fully exploited, through data sharing within the organization and with other bodies.
- Data assets are adequately protected and secured in accordance with corporate and IT security policies.
- The quality of the organization's data is maintained at an acceptable level, and the information used in the business is accurate, reliable and consistent.

- Legal requirements for maintaining the privacy, security, confidentiality and integrity of data are observed.
- The organization achieves a high level of efficiency and effectiveness in its data and information-handling activities.
- An enterprise data model is used to define the most important entities and their relationships – this helps to avoid redundancies and to avoid the deterioration of the architecture as it is changed over the years.

5.2.1 Managing data assets

If data is not managed effectively:

- People maintain and collect data that is not needed.
- The organization may have historic information that is no longer used.
- The organization may hold a lot of data that is inaccessible to potential users.
- Information may be disseminated to more people than it should be, or not to those people to whom it should.
- The organization may use inefficient and out-of-date methods to collect, analyse, store and retrieve the data.
- The organization may fail to adhere to regulatory requirements such as data retention or security.
- The organization may fail to collect the data that it needs, reducing data quality, and data integrity is lost, for example, between related data sources.

In addition, whether or not information is derived from good-quality data is a difficult question to answer, because there are no measurements in place against which to compare it. For example, poor data quality often arises because of poor checks on input and/or updating procedures. Once inaccurate or incomplete data has been stored in the IT system, any reports produced using this data will reflect these inaccuracies or gaps. There may also be a lack of consistency between internally generated management information from the operational systems, and from other internal, locally used systems, created because the central data is not trusted.

One way of improving the quality of data is to use a data management process that establishes policies and standards, provides expertise and makes it easier to handle the data aspects of new services. This should then allow full data/information asset management to:

- Add value to the services delivered to customers
- Reduce risks in the business
- Reduce the costs of business processes
- Stimulate innovation in internal business processes.

5.2.2 Scope of data management

There are four areas of management included within the scope of data/information management:

- **Management of data resources** The governance of information in the organization must ensure that all these resources are known and that responsibilities have been assigned for their management, including ownership of data and metadata. This process is normally referred to as data administration and includes responsibility for:
  - Defining information needs
  - Constructing a data inventory and an enterprise data model
  - Identifying data duplication and deficiencies
  - Maintaining a catalogue/index of data/information content
  - Measuring the cost and value of the organization's data.
- **Management of data/information technology** The management of the IT that underpins the organization's information systems; this includes processes such as database design and database administration. This aspect is normally handled by specialists within one of the IT functions – see *ITIL Service Operation* for more details.
- **Management of information processes** Business processes will lead to IT services involving one or other of the data resources of the organization. The activities of creating, collecting, accessing, modifying, storing, deleting and archiving data – i.e. the data lifecycle – must be properly controlled, often jointly with the application management activities.
- **Management of data standards and policies** The organization will need to define standards and policies for its data management as an element of an IT strategy. Policies will govern the procedures and responsibilities for data management in the organization, as well as technical policies, architectures and standards

that will apply to the IT infrastructure that supports the organization's information systems.

The best-practices scope of data management activities includes managing non-structured data that is not held in conventional database systems – for example, using formats such as text, image and audio. It is also responsible for ensuring process quality at all stages of the data lifecycle, from requirements to retirement. The main focus in this publication will be on its role in the requirements, design and development phases of the asset and service lifecycle.

The team supporting data management activities may also provide a business information support service. In this case the team is able to answer questions about the meaning, format and availability of data internal to the organization because it manages the metadata. It is also able to understand and explain what external data might be needed in order to carry out necessary business processes and will take the necessary action to source this.

Critically, when creating or redesigning processes and supporting IT services, it is best practice to consider reusing data and metadata across different areas of the organization. The ability to do this may be supported by a corporate data model – sometimes known as a common information model – to help support reuse, often a major objective for data management.

5.2.3 Data management and the service lifecycle

It is recommended that a lifecycle approach be adopted in understanding the use of data in business processes. General issues include:

- What data is currently held and how can it be classified?
- What data needs to be collected or created by the business processes?
- How will the data be stored and maintained?
- How will the data be accessed, by whom and in what ways?
- How will the data be disposed of, and under whose authority?
- How will the quality of the data be maintained (accuracy, consistency, currency etc.)?

■ How can the data be made more accessible/ available?

5.2.4 Supporting the service lifecycle

During requirements and initial design, data management can assist design and development teams with service-specific data modelling and give advice on the use of various techniques to model data.

During detailed ('physical') design and development, the data management team (usually part of the technical management function) can provide technical expertise on database management systems and on how to convert initial 'logical' models of data into physical, product specific, implementations.

Many new services have failed because poor data quality has not been addressed during the development of the service, or because a particular development created its own data and metadata, without consultation with other service owners, or with data management.

5.2.5 Valuing data

Data is an asset and has value. Clearly in some organizations this is more obvious than in others. Organizations that are providers of data to others – for example, Yell, Dun & Bradstreet, and Reuters – can value data as an 'output' in terms of the price that they are charging external organizations to receive it. It is also possible to think of value in terms of what the internal data would be worth to another organization.

It is more common to value data in terms of what it is worth to the owner organization. A number of ways of doing this have been suggested:

■ **Valuing data by availability** One approach often used is to consider which business processes would not be possible if a particular piece of data was unavailable, and how much that non-availability of data would cost the business.
■ **Valuing lost data** Another approach is to think about the costs of obtaining some data if it were to be destroyed.
■ **Valuing data by considering the data lifecycle** This involves thinking about how data is created or obtained in the first place, how it is made available to people to use, and how data is retired, either through archiving or physical destruction. It may be that some data

is provided from an external source and then held internally, or it may be that data has to be created by the organization's internal systems. In these two cases, the lifecycle is different and the processes that take place for data capture will be entirely separate. In both cases the costs of redoing these stages can be evaluated.

The more highly valued the data, the more the effort that needs to be expended on ensuring its confidentiality, integrity and availability.

5.2.6 Classifying data

Data can be initially classified as operational, tactical or strategic:

■ **Operational data** This data is necessary for the ongoing functioning of an organization and can be regarded as the lowest, most specific, level.
■ **Tactical data** This data is usually needed by second-line management – or higher – and is typically concerned with summarized data and historical data, typically year-to-year data or quarterly data. Often the data that is used here appears in management information systems that require summary data from a number of operational systems in order to deal with an accounting requirement, for example.
■ **Strategic data** This data is often concerned with longer-term trends and comparison with the outside world. Therefore providing the necessary data for a strategic support system involves bringing together the operational and tactical data from many different areas with relevant external data. Much more data is required from external sources.

An alternative method is to use a security classification of data and documents. This is normally adopted as a corporate policy within an organization. An orthogonal classification distinguishes between organization-wide data, functional-area data and service-specific data:

■ Organization-wide data needs to be centrally managed.
■ The next level of data is functional-area data, which should be shared across a complete business function. This involves sharing data 'instances' (for example, individual customer records) and also ensuring that consistent metadata across that functional area, such as standard address formats, are being used.

- The final level is IT service-specific, where the data and metadata are valid for one IT service and do not need to be shared with other services.

5.2.7 Setting data standards

One of the critical aspects of data administration is to ensure that standards for metadata are in place – for example, what metadata is to be kept for different underlying 'data types'. Different details are kept about structured tabular data than for other areas. 'Ownership' is a critical item of this metadata, some sort of unique identifier is another, a description in business meaningful terms another, and a format might be another. The custodian or steward, someone in the IT organization who takes responsibility for the day-to-day management of the data, is also recorded.

Another benefit of a data management process would be in the field of reference data. Certain types of data, such as postcodes or names of countries, may be needed across a variety of systems and need to be consistent. It is part of the responsibility of data administration to manage reference data on behalf of the whole business, and to make sure that the same reference data is used by all systems in the organization.

> **Hints and tips**
>
> Standards for naming must be in place, so, for example, if a new type of data is requested in a new service, then there is a need to use names that meet these standards. An example standard might be 'all capitals, no underlining and no abbreviations'.

5.2.8 Data ownership

Data administration can assist the service developer by making sure responsibilities for data ownership are taken seriously by the business and by the IT department. One of the most successful ways of doing this is to get the business and the IT organization to sign up to a data charter – a set of procedural standards and guidance for the careful management of data in the organization, by adherence to corporately defined standards. Responsibilities of a data owner are often defined here and may include:

- Agreeing a business description and a purpose for the data

- Defining who can create, amend, read and delete occurrences of the data
- Authorizing changes in the way data is captured or derived
- Approving any format, domain and value ranges
- Approving the relevant level of security, including making sure that legal requirements and internal policies about data security are adhered to.

5.2.9 Data migration

Data migration is an issue where a new service is replacing one or more existing services, and it is necessary to carry across, into the new service, good-quality data from the existing systems and services. There are two types of data migration of interest to projects here: one is the data migration into data warehouses etc., for business intelligence/analytics purposes; the other is data migration to a new transactional, operational service. In both cases it will be beneficial if data migration standards, procedures and processes are laid down by data management. Data migration tools may have already been purchased on behalf of the organization by the data management team. Without this support, it is very easy to underestimate the amount of effort that is required, particularly if data consolidation and cleaning has to take place between multiple source systems, and the quality of the existing services' data is known to be questionable.

5.2.10 Data capture

It is also very important to work with data management on effective measures for data capture. The aim here is to capture data as quickly and accurately as possible. There is a need to ensure that the data capture processes require the minimum amount of keying, and exploit the advantages that graphical user interfaces provide in terms of minimizing the number of keystrokes needed, also decreasing the opportunity for errors during data capture. It is reasonable to expect that the data management process has standards for, and can provide expertise on, effective methods of data capture in various environments, including 'non-structured' data capture using mechanisms such as scanning.

5.2.11 Data storage

One area where technology has moved on very rapidly is in the area of storage of data. There is a need to consider different storage media (for example, optical storage) and to be aware of the size and cost implications associated with this. The main reason for understanding the developments in this area is that they make possible many types of data management that were considered too expensive before. For example, to store real-time video, which uses an enormous bandwidth, has, until the last two to three years, been regarded as too expensive. The same is true of the scanning of large numbers of paper documents, particularly where those documents are not text-based but contain detailed diagrams or pictures. Understanding technology developments with regard to electronic storage of data is critical to understanding the opportunities for the business to exploit the information resource effectively by making the best use of new technology.

5.2.12 Data retrieval and usage

Once the data has been captured and stored, the next aspect to consider is the retrieval of information from the data. Services to allow easy access to structured data via query tools of various levels of sophistication are needed by all organizations, and generate their own specific architectural demands.

The whole area of searching within scanned text and other non-structured data such as video, still images or sound is a major area of expansion. Techniques such as automatic indexing, and the use of search engines to give efficient access via keywords to relevant parts of a document, are essential technologies that have been widely implemented, particularly on the internet. Expertise in the use of data or content within websites should exist within the data management as well as content management – standards and procedures that are vital for websites.

5.2.13 Data integrity and related issues

When defining requirements for IT services, it is vital that management and operational requirements related to data are considered. In particular, the following areas must be addressed:

- Recovery of lost or corrupted data
- Controlled access to data

- Implementation of policies on archiving of data, including compliance with regulatory retention periods
- Periodic data integrity checks.

Data integrity is concerned with ensuring that the data is of high quality and uncorrupted. It is also about preventing uncontrolled data duplication, and hence avoiding any confusion about what is the valid version of the data. There are several approaches that may assist with this. Various technology devices such as 'database locking' are used to prevent multiple, inconsistent, updating of data. In addition, prevention of illegal updating may be achieved through access control mechanisms.

5.3 MANAGEMENT OF APPLICATIONS

Definition: application

An application is defined as software that provides functions which are required by an IT service. Each application may be part of more than one IT service. An application runs on one or more servers or clients.

Applications, along with data and infrastructure components such as hardware, the operating system and middleware, make up the technology components that are part of a service. The application itself is only one component, albeit an important one of the service. Therefore it is important that the application delivered matches the agreed requirements of the business. However, too many organizations spend too much time focusing on the functional requirements of the new service and application, and insufficient time is spent designing the management and operational requirements (non-functional requirements) of the service. This means that when the service becomes operational, it meets all of the functionality required, but totally fails to meet the expectation of the business and the customers in terms of its quality and performance; it therefore becomes unusable.

Two alternative approaches are necessary to fully implement management of applications. One approach employs an extended service development lifecycle (SDLC) to support the development of a service. SDLC is a systematic approach to problem solving and is composed of the following steps:

- Feasibility study
- Analysis
- Design
- Testing
- Implementation
- Evaluation
- Maintenance.

The other approach takes a global view of all services to ensure the ongoing maintainability and manageability of the applications:

- All applications are described in a consistent manner, via an application portfolio that is managed and maintained to enable alignment with dynamic business needs.
- Consistency of approach to development is enforced through a limited number of application frameworks and design patterns and through a 'reuse first' philosophy.
- Common software components, usually to meet management and operational requirements, are created or acquired at an 'organizational' level and used by individual systems as they are designed and built.

5.3.1 The application portfolio

This is simply a full record of all applications within the organization and is dynamic in its content. Table 5.4 presents examples of the attributes an organization may wish to capture in the

application portfolio for each application listed there.

5.3.2 Linking application and service portfolios

Some organizations maintain a separate application portfolio with separate attributes, while in other organizations the application portfolio is stored within the configuration management system (CMS), together with the appropriate relationships. Other organizations combine the application portfolio together with the service portfolio. It is for each organization to decide the most appropriate strategy for its own needs. What is clear is that there should be very close relationships and links between the applications and the services they support and the infrastructure components used.

5.3.3 Application frameworks

The concept of an application framework is a very powerful one. The application framework covers all management and operational aspects and actually provides solutions for all the management and operational requirements that surround an application.

Implied in the use of application frameworks is the concept of standardization. If an organization uses and has to maintain an application framework for every single application, there will not be many benefits of the use of an application framework.

Table 5.4 Examples of application portfolio attributes

Application name	IT operations owner	New development cost
Application identifier	IT development owner	Annual operational costs
Application description	Support contacts	Annual support cost
Business process supported	Database technologies	Annual maintenance costs
IT services supported	Dependent applications	Outsourced components
Executive sponsor	IT systems supported	Outsource partners
Geographies supported	User interfaces	Production metrics
Business criticality	IT architecture, including Network topology	OLA link
SLA link	Application technologies used	Support metrics
Business owner	Number of users	

An organization that wants to develop and maintain application frameworks, and to ensure the application frameworks comply with the needs of the application developers, must invest in doing so. It is essential that applications framework architectures are not developed in isolation, but are closely related and integrated with all other framework and architectural activities. The service, infrastructure, environment and data architectures must all be closely integrated with the application architecture and framework.

5.3.3.1 Architecture, application frameworks and standards

Architecture-related activities have to be planned and managed separately from individual system-based software projects. It is also important that architecture-related activities be performed for the benefit of more than just one application. Application developers should focus on a single application, while application framework developers should focus on more than one application, and on the common features of those applications in particular.

A common practice is to distinguish between various types of application. For instance, not every application can be built on top of a Microsoft® Windows operating system platform, connected to a UNIX server, using HTML, Java applets, JavaBeans and a relational database. The various types of application can be regarded as application families. All applications in the same family are based on the same application framework.

Utilizing the concept of an application framework, the first step of the application design phase is to identify the appropriate application framework. If the application framework is mature, a large number of the design decisions are given. If it is not mature, and all management and operational requirements cannot be met on top of an existing application framework, the preferred strategy is to collect and analyse the requirements that cannot be dealt with in the current version of the application framework. Based on the application requirements, new requirements can be defined for the application framework. Next, the application framework can be modified so that it can cope with the application requirements. In fact, the whole family of applications that corresponds to the application framework can then use the newly added or changed framework features.

Hints and tips

Developing and maintaining an application framework is a demanding task and, like all other design activities, should be performed by competent and experienced people. Alternatively, application frameworks can be acquired from third parties.

5.3.4 The need for CASE tools and repositories

One important aspect of that overall service design is the need to align applications with their underlying support structures. Application development environments traditionally have their own CASE tools that offer the means to specify requirements, draw design diagrams (according to particular modelling standards), or even generate complete applications, or nearly complete application skeletons, almost ready to be deployed. These environments also provide a central location for storing and managing all the elements that are created during application development, generally called a repository. Repository functionality includes version control and consistency checking across various models. The current approach is to use metaCASE tools to model domain-specific languages and use these to make the CASE-work more aligned to the needs of the business.

5.3.5 Design of specific applications

The requirements phase was addressed earlier in the requirements engineering section of this chapter. The design phase is one of the most important phases within the application lifecycle. It ensures that an application is conceived with operability and management of the application in mind. This phase takes the outputs from the requirements phase and turns them into the specification that will be used to develop the application.

The goal for designs should be satisfying the organization's requirements. Design includes the design of the application itself, and the design of the infrastructure and environment within which the application operates. Architectural considerations are the most important aspect of this phase, since they can impact on the structure and content of both application and operational model. Architectural considerations for the application (design of the application architecture) and architectural considerations for the environment (design of the IT architecture) are strongly related and need to be aligned. Application architecture and design should not be considered in isolation but should form an overall integrated component of service architecture and design. Ensuring that this overall integrated approach is used falls within the design coordination process.

Generally, in the design phase, the same models will be produced as have been delivered in the requirements phase, but during design many more details are added. New models include the architecture models, where the way in which the different functional components are mapped to the physical components (e.g. desktops, servers, databases and network) needs to be defined. The mapping, together with the estimated load of the system, should allow for the sizing of the infrastructure required.

Another important aspect of the architecture model is the embedding of the application in the existing environment. Which pieces of the existing infrastructure will be used to support the required new functions? Can existing servers or networks be used? With what impact? Are required functions available in existing applications that can be utilized? Do packages exist that offer the functionality needed or should the functions be built from scratch?

The design phase takes all requirements into consideration and starts assembling them into an initial design for the solution. Doing this not only gives developers a basis to begin working; it is also likely to bring up questions that need to be asked of the customers/users. If possible, application frameworks should be applied as a starting point.

It is not always possible to foresee every aspect of a solution's design ahead of time. As a solution is developed, new things will be learned about how to do things and also how not to.

The key is to create a flexible design, so that making a change does not send developers all the way back to the beginning of the design phase. There are a number of approaches that can minimize the chance of this happening, including:

- Designing for management and operational requirements

- Managing trade-offs
- Using application-independent design guidelines; using application frameworks
- Employing a structured design process/manageability checklist.

Design for management and operational requirements means giving management and operational requirements a level of importance similar to that for the functional requirements, and including them as a mandatory part of the design phase. This includes a number of management and operational requirements such as availability, capacity, maintainability, reliability, continuity and security. It is now inconceivable in modern application development projects that user interface design (usability requirements) would be omitted as a key design activity. However, many organizations ignore or forget manageability. Details of the necessary management and operational requirements are contained within the service design package (SDP) and service acceptance criteria (SAC) in Appendices A and B, respectively.

5.3.6 Managing trade-offs

Managing trade-off decisions focuses on balancing the relationship among resources, the project schedule, and those features that need to be included in the application for the sake of quality.

When development teams try to complete this balancing, it is often at the expense of the management and operational requirements. One way to avoid that is to include management and operational requirements in the application-independent design guidelines – for example, in the form of an application framework. Operability and manageability effectively become standard components of all design processes (for example, in the form of an application framework) and get embedded into the working practices and culture of the development organization.

5.3.7 Typical design outputs

The following are examples of the outputs from an applications design forming part of the overall service design:

- Input and output design, including forms and reports
- A usable user interface (human/computer interaction) design

- A suitable data/object model
- A process flow or workflow model
- Detailed specifications for update and read-only processes
- Mechanisms for achieving audit controls, security, confidentiality and privacy
- A technology specific 'physical' design
- Scripts for testing the systems design
- Interfaces and dependencies on other applications.

There are guidelines and frameworks that can be adopted to determine and define design outputs within application management, such as CMMI.

5.3.8 Design patterns

A design pattern is a general, repeatable solution to a commonly occurring problem in software design. Object-oriented design patterns typically show relationships and interactions between classes or objects, without specifying the final application classes or objects that are involved. Design patterns describe both a problem and a solution for common issues encountered during application development.

An important design principle used as the basis for a large number of the design patterns found in recent literature is that of separation of concerns (SoC). Separation of concerns will lead to applications divided into components, with a strong cohesion and minimal coupling between components. The advantage of such an application is that modification can be made to individual components with little or no impact on other components.

In typical application development projects, more than 70% of the effort is spent on designing and developing generic functions and on satisfying the management and operational requirements. That is because each individual application needs to provide a solution for such generic features as printing, error handling and security.

Among others, the Object Management Group (OMG, www.omg.com) defined a large number of services that are needed in every application. OMG's object management architecture clearly distinguishes between functional and management and operational aspects of an application. It builds on the concept of providing a run-time environment that offers all sorts of facilities to an application.

In this concept, the application covers the functional aspects, and the environment covers all management and operational aspects. Application developers should, by definition, focus on the functional aspects of an application, while others can focus on the creation of the environment that provides the necessary management and operational services. This means that the application developers focus on the requirements of the business, while the architecture developers or application framework developers focus on the requirements of the application developers.

5.3.9 Developing individual applications

Once the design phase is completed, the application development team will take the designs that have been produced and move on to developing the application. Both the application and the related environment are made ready for deployment. Application components are coded or acquired, integrated and tested.

To ensure that the application is developed with management at the core, the development team needs to focus on ensuring that the developing phase continues to correctly address the management and operational aspects of the design (e.g. responsiveness, availability, security). Application development must also be done with clear understanding of how the application fits into the overall service solution. All service requirements should be found in the SDP.

The development phase guidance covers the following topics:

- Consistent coding conventions
- Application-independent building guidelines
- Operability testing
- Management checklist for the building phase
- Organization of the build team roles.

5.3.9.1 Consistent coding conventions

The main reason for using a consistent set of design and coding conventions is to standardize the structure and coding style of an application so that everyone can easily read, understand and manage the application development process. Good design and coding conventions result in precise, readable and unambiguous source code that is consistent with the organizational coding and management standards and is as intuitive to follow as possible. Adding application operability into this convention ensures that all applications are built in a way that ensures that they can be fully managed all the way through their lifecycles.

A coding convention itself can be a significant aid to managing the application, as consistency allows the management tools to interact with the application in a known way. It is better to introduce a minimum set of conventions that everyone will follow rather than to create an overly complex set that encompasses every facet but is not followed or used consistently across the organization.

5.3.10 Templates and code generation

A number of development tools provide a variety of templates for creating common application components. Rather than creating all the pieces of an application from scratch, developers can customize an existing template. They can also reuse custom components in multiple applications by creating their own templates. Other development tools will generate large pieces of code (skeletons) based on the design models and coding conventions. The code could include hooks at the code pieces that need to be added.

In this respect, templates and application frameworks should be considered IT assets. These assets not only guide the developing of applications, but also incorporate the lessons learned or intellectual capital from previous application development efforts. The more that standard components are designed into the solution, the faster applications can be developed, against lower costs in the long term (not ignoring the fact that development of templates, code generators and application frameworks requires significant investment).

5.3.11 Embedded application instrumentation

The development phase deals with incorporating instrumentation into the fabric of the application. Developers need a consistent way to provide instrumentation for application drivers/middleware components (e.g. database drivers) and applications that is efficient and easy to implement. To keep application developers from trying to start from the beginning for every new application they develop, the computer industry provides methods and technologies to simplify and facilitate the instrumentation process.

These include:

- Application Response Measurement (ARMS)
- IBM Application Management Specification (AMS)
- Common Information Model (CIM) and Web-Based Enterprise Management (WBEM) from the Distributed Management Task Force (DMTF)
- Desktop Management Interface (DMI)
- Microsoft Windows© Management Instrumentation (WMI)
- Java Management Extension (JMX).

Each of these technologies provides a consistent and richly descriptive model of the configuration, status and operational aspects of applications and services. These are provided through programming application program interfaces (APIs) that the developer incorporates into an application, normally through the use of standard programming templates.

It is important to ensure that all applications are built to conform to some level of compliance for the application instrumentation. Ways to do this could include:

- Provide access to management data through the instrumentation API
- Publish management data to other management systems, again through the instrumentation API
- Provide applications event handling
- Provide a diagnostic hook.

5.3.11.1 Diagnostic hooks

Diagnostic hooks are of greatest value during testing and when an error has been discovered in the production service. They mainly provide the information necessary to solve problems and application errors rapidly and restore service. They can also be used to provide measurement and management information of applications.

The four main categories are:

- System-level information provided by the operating systems and hardware
- Software-level information provided by the application infrastructure components such as database, web server or messaging systems

- Custom information provided by the applications
- Information on component and service performance.

5.3.12 Major outputs from development

The major outputs from the development phase are:

- Scripts to be run before or after deployment
- Scripts to start or stop the application
- Scripts to check hardware and software configurations of target environments before deployment or installation
- Specification of metrics and events that can be retrieved from the application and that indicate the performance status of the application
- Customized scripts initiated by service operation staff to manage the application (including the handling of application upgrades)
- Specification of access control information for the system resources used by an application
- Specification of the details required to track an application's major transactions
- SLA targets and requirements
- Operational requirements and documentation
- Support requirements
- Application recovery and backups
- Other IT service management requirements and targets.

Organizing for
service design

6

6 Organizing for service design

This chapter describes the general concepts of organizing for service management in relation to service design and the related practices. It includes generic roles, responsibilities and competencies that apply across the service lifecycle and specific aspects for the processes described in this publication.

Section 2.2.3 describes the basic concepts of organization, function, group, team, department, division and role that are used in this chapter.

6.1 ORGANIZATIONAL DEVELOPMENT

There is no single best way to organize, and the best practices described in ITIL need to be tailored to suit individual organizations and situations. Any changes made will need to take into account resource constraints and the size, nature and needs of the business and customers. The starting point for organizational design is strategy. Organization development for service management is described in more detail in *ITIL Service Strategy*, Chapter 6.

6.2 FUNCTIONS

A function is a team or group of people and the tools or other resources they use to carry out one or more processes or activities. In larger organizations, a function may be broken out and performed by several departments, teams and groups, or it may be embodied within a single organizational unit (e.g. the service desk). In smaller organizations, one person or group can perform multiple functions – e.g. a technical management department could also incorporate the service desk function.

For service design to be successful, an organization will need to clearly define the roles and responsibilities required to undertake the processes and activities identified in Chapters 4 and 5. These roles will need to be assigned to individuals, and an appropriate organizational structure of teams, groups or functions established and managed.

ITIL Service Design does not define any specific functions of its own, but it does rely on the technical and application management functions described in *ITIL Service Operation*. Technical and application management provide the technical resources and expertise to manage the whole service lifecycle, and practitioner roles within service design may be performed by members of these functions.

An organization may already have one or both of the functions described in sections 6.2.1 and 6.2.2. If either or both of these functions exist, they will play a prominent role in service design activities.

6.2.1 Alignment with application development

While it is possible for an IT service provider to design, deploy, deliver and improve IT services without developing any applications in house, many if not most organizations perform some of their own software development. When this is the case, the organization will typically assign the work to a functional unit specializing in application development.

If an application development function exists, this team will focus on building functionality – that is, the utility – required by the business. Historically, what the application does is more important to this team than how the application is operated. This is why the input of application management, technical management, IT operations management and even the service desk should be sought during service design to ensure that the overall output of service design will meet all customer needs, not just those related to functionality.

Most application development work is performed as part of a project where the focus is on delivering specific units of work to specification, on time and within budget. Application development may, therefore, be overly focused on the narrow parameters of the project, particularly if they have little responsibility to support the application once the team has moved on to the next project. This problem can be compounded if the person(s) leading the overall service requirements definition are part of the application development function. In this situation they may be too focused on functionality of the most prominent application in the service and neglect the detailed requirements and design of manageability, training, documentation, marketing and other important elements needed for success in transition and ongoing service operation.

> **Hints and tips**
>
> While costs associated with application development may seem relatively easy to quantify, since they are frequently linked to carefully budgeted projects, time needed to diagnose and recover from application errors discovered in service operation should also be accounted for and budget reserved for these activities.

The application development function utilizes software development lifecycles to guide and provide formal structure to their work. This work must then, in turn, be integrated into the overall service lifecycle as the applications to be developed form a central part of the IT services provisioned by the IT service provider organization as a whole. As the various possible software development lifecycles that could be employed are well documented in other sources, they are not discussed here.

6.2.2 Alignment with project management

Another functional unit that may exist within the IT service provider organization is project management, sometimes called the project management office (PMO). The purpose of this team is to define and maintain the service provider's project management standards and to provide overall resources and management of IT projects. The project management function usually leverages the principles of project management as described in one or more of the recognized project management methodologies such as PROjects IN Controlled Environments (PRINCE2) from the Office of Government Commerce (OGC) or the Project Management Body of Knowledge (PMBOK) from the Project Management Institute (PMI).

If a project management function exists, they will be actively involved in the work of the service design as well as the service transition stages of the service lifecycle, as well as during any other temporary endeavour that would benefit from application of formal project management.

The project management function can provide value not only through the management of individual projects and through the propagation of consistent and repeatable project management methods, but also through providing project portfolio management. Project portfolio management interfaces with overall service portfolio management and ensures that resources are appropriately allocated across the complete set of projects being managed and maximizes project success.

For more information on how to establish, develop and maintain appropriate support structures for portfolios, programmes and projects, see *Portfolio, Programme and Project Offices* (OGC, 2008).

6.2.3 Example service design organization structures

The following example organization structures show how the various service design roles might be combined and structured. Each organization should consider all of the roles that they require and how these can be combined within their organizational constraints to create a structure that meets their needs.

6.2.3.1 Small organization

In the small organization illustrated in Figure 6.1, there is a service design manager who is the process owner, process manager and process practitioner for overall design coordination (see section 6.3.5), as well as serving as the process owner for the service level management process. This role may be fulfilled by a manager of the functional unit in which most of the responsibility for the design of new or changed services resides. In some organizations that may be the application development function or the department responsible for the infrastructure.

For each specific service design project, the activities that relate to service design under processes such as availability management, capacity management and IT service continuity management may be led by the project manager with regular involvement from the service owner, but the design of reliable and repeatable processes is still under the authority of the individual process owners and process managers. Practitioners are likely to be drawn as needed for each service design effort from the technical management, application management and application development functions.

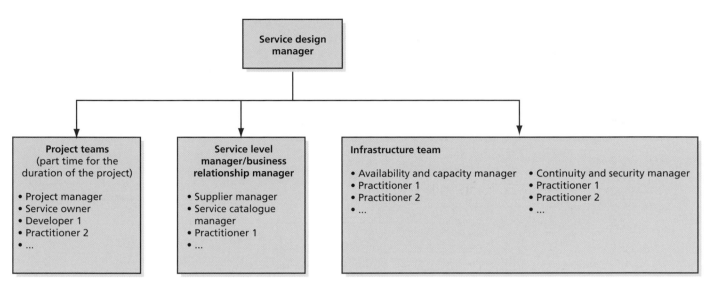

Figure 6.1 Example of a service design organization structure for a small organization

There may be a full-time service level manager who is the process manager for service level management and who also fills the role of process manager for the business relationship management process. In the small organization illustrated in Figure 6.1 most of the supplier management process is performed by the corporate procurement function, but the service level manager is the process owner from IT's perspective and a supplier manager ensures coordination and alignment with IT and business needs. A service catalogue manager reports to the service level manager who owns this process.

The roles of process owner and process manager in many instances are likely to be combined in a small organization, as well has having the same person fulfil several roles. For example, leadership of availability management and capacity management may be assigned to the same person, or leadership of IT service continuity management and information security management may be combined. Another possibility is the assignment of leadership of availability, capacity and IT service continuity management to the same person, although this is most likely in a very small organization. It is important, however, not to combine roles when there is a requirement for governance or compliance reasons to retain a separation. This may be to ensure checks and balances within a critical activity or process.

6.2.3.2 Larger organization

In the sample larger organization illustrated in Figure 6.2 there is a central headquarters (HQ) organization which includes all process owners, as well as a service design team to plan, coordinate and manage all service designs under the leadership of one or more service design managers or design coordination process managers. The HQ has a service management office (SMO) which oversees the adoption and deployment of service management methods, including guiding all process design and improvement. Obviously, this office will be active in all stages of the lifecycle, but is particularly critical to service design. There is also a project management office (PMO) which performs project/programme portfolio management and provides project management resources and capabilities. A global programmes group also resides in the HQ to lead programmes and projects of a global nature.

Each geographical region has its own process managers and practitioners for key processes such as service level management, change management, availability management and supplier management. (Note: Although the detailed discussion of change management resides in *ITIL Service Transition*, this process is very active in the service design stage, so it is mentioned in this example.)

Although clearly defined roles and responsibilities, as well as good communication, are critical to all organizations, these are particularly important in a large organization. Failure to clearly define the boundaries between what is done in the

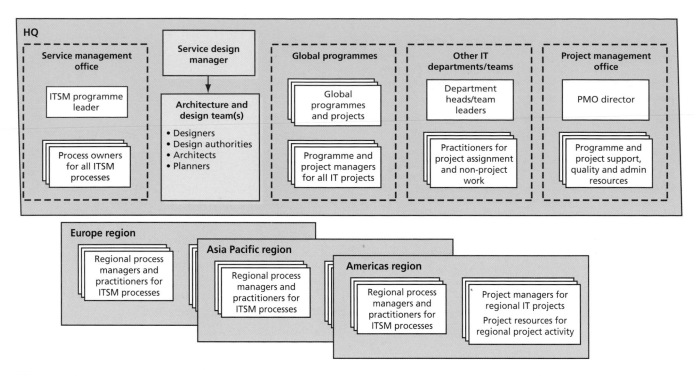

Figure 6.2 Example of a service design organization structure for a large organization

various individual locations versus what is done at the corporate level can lead to unfilled gaps, duplicated efforts, delays, rework and unsatisfactory results. Authority must be clearly delineated and regular lines of communication established and maintained.

6.3 ROLES

A number of roles need to be performed in support of service design. Please note that this section provides guidelines and examples of role descriptions. These are not exhaustive or prescriptive, and in many cases roles will need to be combined or separated. Organizations should take care to apply this guidance in a way that suits their own structures and objectives.

A role is a set of responsibilities, activities and authorities granted to a person or team. A role is defined in a process or function. One person or team may have multiple roles – for example, the roles of configuration manager and change manager may be carried out by a single person.

Roles are often confused with job titles, but it is important to realize that they are not the same. Each organization will define appropriate job titles and job descriptions that suit its needs, and individuals holding these job titles can perform one or more of the required roles.

It should also be recognized that a person may, as part of their job assignment, perform a single task that represents participation in more than one process. For example, a technical analyst who submits a request for change (RFC) to add memory to a server to resolve a performance problem is participating in activities of the change management process at the same time as taking part in activities of the capacity management and problem management processes.

Roles fall into two main categories – generic roles such as process manager and process owner, and specific roles that are involved within a particular lifecycle stage or process such as a service design manager or IT designer/architect. Roles can be combined or divided in a number of different ways, depending on the organizational context. For example, in many organizations there will be one person who fulfils both the service catalogue process owner and service catalogue process manager roles. In a small organization the availability manager role may be combined with process manager roles from capacity management or IT service continuity management. In larger organizations there may be many different people carrying out each of these roles, split by geography, technology or other criteria. The exceptions to this are that there must be only one process owner for each process and one service owner for each service.

Roles are accountable or responsible for an activity. They may also be consulted or informed about something: for example a service owner may be consulted about a change during an impact assessment activity. The RACI model, described in section 6.4, provides a useful way of defining and communicating roles and responsibilities.

ITIL does not describe all the roles that could possibly exist in an organization, but provides representative examples to aid in an organization's definition of their own roles.

> **What is a service manager?**
>
> Service manager is a generic term for any manager within the service provider. The term is commonly used to refer to a business relationship manager, a process manager or a senior manager with responsibility for IT services overall. A service manager is often assigned several roles such as business relationship management, service level management and continual service improvement.

6.3.1 Generic service owner role

To ensure that a service is managed with a business focus, the definition of a single point of accountability is absolutely essential to provide the level of attention and focus required for its delivery.

The service owner is accountable for the delivery of a specific IT service. The service owner is responsible to the customer for the initiation, transition and ongoing maintenance and support of a particular service and accountable to the IT director or service management director for the delivery of the service. The service owner's accountability for a specific service within an organization is independent of where the underpinning technology components, processes or professional capabilities reside.

Service ownership is as critical to service management as establishing ownership for processes which cross multiple vertical silos or departments. It is possible that a single person may fulfil the service owner role for more than one service.

The service owner has the following responsibilities:

- Ensuring that the ongoing service delivery and support meet agreed customer requirements
- Working with business relationship management to understand and translate customer requirements into activities, measures or service components that will ensure that the service provider can meet those requirements
- Ensuring consistent and appropriate communication with customer(s) for service-related enquiries and issues
- Assisting in defining service models and in assessing the impact of new services or changes to existing services through the service portfolio management process
- Identifying opportunities for service improvements, discussing these with the customer and raising RFCs as appropriate
- Liaising with the appropriate process owners throughout the service lifecycle
- Soliciting required data, statistics and reports for analysis and to facilitate effective service monitoring and performance
- Providing input in service attributes such as performance, availability etc.
- Representing the service across the organization
- Understanding the service (components etc.)
- Serving as the point of escalation (notification) for major incidents relating to the service
- Representing the service in change advisory board (CAB) meetings
- Participating in internal service review meetings (within IT)
- Participating in external service review meetings (with the business)
- Ensuring that the service entry in the service catalogue is accurate and is maintained
- Participating in negotiating service level agreements (SLAs) and operational level agreements (OLAs) relating to the service
- Identifying improvement opportunities for inclusion in the continual service improvement (CSI) register
- Working with the CSI manager to review and prioritize improvements in the CSI register
- Making improvements to the service.

The service owner is responsible for continual improvement and the management of change affecting the service under their care. The service owner is a primary stakeholder in all of the underlying IT processes which enable or support the service they own. For example:

- **Incident management** Is involved in (or perhaps chairs) the crisis management team for high-priority incidents impacting the service owned
- **Problem management** Plays a major role in establishing the root cause and proposed permanent fix for the service being evaluated
- **Release and deployment management** Is a key stakeholder in determining whether a new release affecting a service in production is ready for promotion
- **Change management** Participates in CAB decisions, authorizing changes to the services they own
- **Service asset and configuration management** Ensures that all groups which maintain the data and relationships for the service architecture they are responsible for have done so with the level of integrity required
- **Service level management** Acts as the single point of contact for a specific service and ensures that the service portfolio and service catalogue are accurate in relation to their service
- **Availability management and capacity management** Reviews technical monitoring data from a domain perspective to ensure that the needs of the overall service are being met
- **IT service continuity management** Understands and is responsible for ensuring that all elements required to restore their service are known and in place in the event of a crisis
- **Information security management** Ensures that the service conforms to information security management policies
- **Financial management for IT services** Assists in defining and tracking the cost models in relation to how their service is costed and recovered.

6.3.2 Generic process owner role

The process owner role is accountable for ensuring that a process is fit for purpose. This role is often assigned to the same person who carries out the process manager role, but the two roles may be separate in larger organizations. The process owner role is accountable for ensuring that their

process is performed according to the agreed and documented standard and meets the aims of the process definition.

The process owner's accountabilities include:

- Sponsoring, designing and change managing the process and its metrics
- Defining the process strategy
- Assisting with process design
- Ensuring that appropriate process documentation is available and current
- Defining appropriate policies and standards to be employed throughout the process
- Periodically auditing the process to ensure compliance to policy and standards
- Periodically reviewing the process strategy to ensure that it is still appropriate and change as required
- Communicating process information or changes as appropriate to ensure awareness
- Providing process resources to support activities required throughout the service lifecycle
- Ensuring that process technicians have the required knowledge and the required technical and business understanding to deliver the process, and understand their role in the process
- Reviewing opportunities for process enhancements and for improving the efficiency and effectiveness of the process
- Addressing issues with the running of the process
- Identifying improvement opportunities for inclusion in the CSI register
- Working with the CSI manager and process manager to review and prioritize improvements in the CSI register
- Making improvements to the process.

6.3.3 Generic process manager role

The process manager role is accountable for operational management of a process. There may be several process managers for one process, for example regional change managers or IT service continuity managers for each data centre. The process manager role is often assigned to the person who carries out the process owner role, but the two roles may be separate in larger organizations.

The process manager's accountabilities include:

- Working with the process owner to plan and coordinate all process activities
- Ensuring that all activities are carried out as required throughout the service lifecycle
- Appointing people to the required roles
- Managing resources assigned to the process
- Working with service owners and other process managers to ensure the smooth running of services
- Monitoring and reporting on process performance
- Identifying improvement opportunities for inclusion in the CSI register
- Working with the CSI manager and process owner to review and prioritize improvements in the CSI register
- Making improvements to the process implementation.

6.3.4 Generic process practitioner role

A process practitioner is responsible for carrying out one or more process activities.

In some organizations, and for some processes, the process practitioner role may be combined with the process manager role; in others there may be large numbers of practitioners carrying out different parts of the process.

The process practitioner's responsibilities typically include:

- Carrying out one or more activities of a process
- Understanding how their role contributes to the overall delivery of service and creation of value for the business
- Working with other stakeholders, such as their manager, co-workers, users and customers, to ensure that their contributions are effective
- Ensuring that inputs, outputs and interfaces for their activities are correct
- Creating or updating records to show that activities have been carried out correctly.

6.3.5 Design coordination roles

This section describes roles that need to be performed in support of the design coordination process. These roles are not job titles, and each organization will have to define appropriate job titles and job descriptions depending on its needs.

6.3.5.1 Design coordination process owner

The design coordination process owner's responsibilities typically include:

- Carrying out the generic process owner role for the design coordination process (see section 6.3.2 for more detail)
- Setting the scope and policies for service design
- Overseeing the overall design of all service design processes to ensure that they will work together to meet the needs of the business.

6.3.5.2 Design coordination process manager

The design coordination process manager's responsibilities typically include:

- Carrying out the generic process manager role for the design coordination process (see section 6.3.3 for more detail)
- Coordinating interfaces between design coordination and other processes
- Ensuring that overall service strategies are reflected in the service design practice
- Ensuring the consistent design of appropriate services, service management information systems, architectures, technology, processes, information and metrics to meet current and evolving business outcomes and requirements
- Coordinating all design activities across projects, changes, suppliers and support teams, and managing schedules, resources and conflicts where required
- Planning and coordinating the resources and capabilities required to design new or changed services
- Producing service design packages (SDPs) based on service charters and change requests
- Ensuring that appropriate service designs and/ or SDPs are produced and that they are handed over to service transition as agreed
- Managing the quality criteria, requirements and handover points between the service design stage and service strategy and service transition
- Ensuring that all service models and service solution designs conform to strategic, architectural, governance and other corporate requirements
- Improving the effectiveness and efficiency of service design activities and processes

- Ensuring that all parties adopt a common framework of standard, reusable design practices in the form of activities, processes and supporting systems, whenever appropriate.

The service design manager

Many organizations will have a person with the job title 'service design manager'. This job typically combines the roles of design coordination process owner and design coordination process manager. It may also include some degree of line management of the people involved in service design.

6.3.6 Service catalogue management roles

This section describes a number of roles that need to be performed in support of the service catalogue management process. These roles are not job titles, and each organization will have to define appropriate job titles and job descriptions depending on its needs.

6.3.6.1 Service catalogue management process owner

The service catalogue management process owner's responsibilities typically include:

- Carrying out the generic process owner role for the service catalogue management process (see section 6.3.2 for more detail)
- Working with other process owners to ensure there is an integrated approach to the design and implementation of service catalogue management, service portfolio management, service level management and business relationship management.

6.3.6.2 Service catalogue management process manager

The service catalogue management process manager's responsibilities typically include:

- Carrying out the generic process manager role for the service catalogue management process (see section 6.3.3 for more detail)
- Coordinating interfaces between service catalogue management and other processes, especially service asset and configuration management, and release and deployment management

- Ensuring that all operational services and all services being prepared for operational running are recorded within the service catalogue
- Ensuring that all the information within the service catalogue is accurate and up to date
- Ensuring that appropriate views of the service catalogue are maintained and made available to those for whom they are targeted
- Ensuring that all the information within the service catalogue is consistent with the information within the service portfolio
- Ensuring that the information within the service catalogue is adequately protected and backed up.

6.3.7 Service level management roles

This section describes a number of roles that need to be performed in support of the service level management process. These roles are not job titles, and each organization will have to define appropriate job titles and job descriptions depending on its needs.

6.3.7.1 Service level management process owner

The service level management process owner's responsibilities typically include:

- Carrying out the generic process owner role for the service level management process (see section 6.3.2 for more detail)
- Liaising with the business relationship management process owner to ensure proper coordination and communication between the two processes
- Working with other process owners to ensure there is an integrated approach to the design and implementation of service catalogue management, service portfolio management, service level management and business relationship management.

6.3.7.2 Service level management process manager

The service level management process manager's responsibilities typically include:

- Carrying out the generic process manager role for the service level management process (see section 6.3.3 for more detail)

- Coordinating interfaces between service level management and other processes, especially service catalogue management, service portfolio management, business relationship management and supplier management
- Keeping aware of changing business needs
- Ensuring that the current and future service level requirements (service warranty) of customers are identified, understood and documented in SLA and service level requirements (SLR) documents
- Negotiating and agreeing levels of service to be delivered with the customer (either internal or external); formally documenting these levels of service in SLAs
- Negotiating and agreeing OLAs and, in some cases, other SLAs and agreements that underpin the SLAs with the customers of the service
- Assisting with the production and maintenance of an accurate service portfolio, service catalogue, application portfolio and the corresponding maintenance procedures
- Ensuring that targets agreed within underpinning contracts are aligned with SLA and SLR targets
- Ensuring that service reports are produced for each customer service and that breaches of SLA targets are highlighted, investigated and actions taken to prevent their recurrence
- Ensuring that service performance reviews are scheduled, carried out with customers regularly and documented, with agreed actions progressed
- Ensuring that improvement initiatives identified in service reviews are acted on and progress reports are provided to customers
- Reviewing service scope, SLAs, OLAs and other agreements on a regular basis, ideally at least annually
- Ensuring that all changes are assessed for their impact on service levels, including SLAs, OLAs and underpinning contracts, including attendance at change advisory board (CAB) meetings if appropriate
- Identifying all customers and other key stakeholders to involve in SLR, SLA and OLA negotiations
- Developing relationships and communication with customers, key users and other stakeholders

- Defining and agreeing complaints and their recording, management, escalation (where necessary) and resolution
- Definition recording and communication of all complaints
- Measuring, recording, analysing and improving customer satisfaction.

These next two roles, while not strictly speaking service level management roles, typically play a large part in the successful execution of the process.

6.3.7.3 Service owner role in service level management

Persons assigned to the role of service owner participate in the service level management process by:

- Ensuring that the ongoing service delivery and support meet agreed customer requirements
- Ensuring consistent and appropriate communication with customer(s) for service-related enquiries and issues
- Providing input in service attributes such as performance and availability
- Participating in external service review meetings (with the business)
- Soliciting required data, statistics and reports for analysis and to facilitate effective service monitoring and performance
- Participating in negotiating SLAs and OLAs relating to the service.

6.3.7.4 Business relationship manager role in service level management

Persons assigned to the role of business relationship manager participate in the service level management process by:

- Ensuring high levels of customer satisfaction
- Establishing and maintaining a constructive relationship between the service provider and the customer at a strategic level
- Confirming customer high-level requirements
- Facilitating service level agreement negotiations by ensuring that the correct customer representatives participate
- Identifying opportunities for improvement.

6.3.8 Availability management roles

This section describes a number of roles that need to be performed in support of the availability management process. These roles are not job titles, and each organization will have to define appropriate job titles and job descriptions depending on its needs.

6.3.8.1 Availability management process owner

The availability management process owner's responsibilities typically include:

■ Carrying out the generic process owner role for the availability management process (see section 6.3.2 for more detail)

■ Working with managers of all functions to ensure acceptance of the availability management process as the single point of coordination for all availability-related issues, regardless of the specific technology involved

■ Working with other process owners to ensure there is an integrated approach to the design and implementation of availability management, service level management, capacity management, IT service continuity management and information security management.

6.3.8.2 Availability management process manager

The availability management process manager's responsibilities typically include:

■ Carrying out the generic process manager role for the availability management process (see section 6.3.3 for more detail)

■ Coordinating interfaces between availability management and other processes, especially service level management, capacity management, IT service continuity management and information security management

■ Ensuring that all existing services deliver the levels of availability agreed with the business in SLAs

■ Ensuring that all new services are designed to deliver the levels of availability required by the business, and validation of the final design to meet the minimum levels of availability as agreed by the business for IT services

■ Assisting with the investigation and diagnosis of all incidents and problems that cause availability issues or unavailability of services or components

■ Participating in the IT infrastructure design, including specifying the availability requirements for hardware and software

■ Specifying the requirements for new or enhanced event management systems for automatic monitoring of availability of IT components

■ Specifying the reliability, maintainability and serviceability requirements for components supplied by internal and external suppliers

■ Being responsible for monitoring actual IT availability achieved against SLA targets, and providing a range of IT availability reporting to ensure that agreed levels of availability, reliability and maintainability are measured and monitored on an ongoing basis

■ Proactively improving service availability wherever possible, and optimizing the availability of the IT infrastructure to deliver cost-effective improvements that deliver tangible benefits to the business

■ Creating, maintaining and regularly reviewing an availability management information system and a forward-looking availability plan, aimed at improving the overall availability of IT services and infrastructure components, to ensure that existing and future business availability requirements can be met

■ Ensuring that the availability management process, its associated techniques and methods are regularly reviewed and audited, and that all of these are subject to continual improvement and remain fit for purpose

■ Creating availability and recovery design criteria to be applied to new or enhanced infrastructure design

■ Working with financial management for IT services, ensuring the levels of IT availability required are cost-justified

■ Maintaining and completing an availability testing schedule for all availability mechanisms

■ Ensuring that all availability tests and plans are tested after every major business change

■ Assisting security and IT service continuity management with the assessment and management of risk

- Assessing changes for their impact on all aspects of availability, including overall service availability and the availability plan
- Attending CAB meetings when appropriate.

6.3.9 Capacity management roles

This section describes a number of roles that need to be performed in support of the capacity management process. These roles are not job titles, and each organization will have to define appropriate job titles and job descriptions depending on its needs.

6.3.9.1 Capacity management process owner

The capacity management process owner's responsibilities typically include:

- Carrying out the generic process owner role for the capacity management process (see section 6.3.2 for more detail)
- Working with managers of all functions to ensure acceptance of the capacity management process as the single point of coordination for all capacity and performance-related issues, regardless of the specific technology involved
- Working with other process owners to ensure there is an integrated approach to the design and implementation of capacity management, availability management, IT service continuity management and information security management.

6.3.9.2 Capacity management process manager

The capacity management process manager's responsibilities typically include:

- Carrying out the generic process manager role for the capacity management process (see section 6.3.3 for more detail)
- Coordinating interfaces between capacity management and other processes, especially service level management, availability management, IT service continuity management and information security management
- Ensuring that there is adequate IT capacity to meet required levels of service, and that senior IT management is correctly advised on how to match capacity and demand and to ensure that use of existing capacity is optimized

- Identifying, with the service level manager, capacity requirements through discussions with the business users
- Understanding the current usage of the infrastructure and IT services, and the maximum capacity of each component
- Performing sizing on all proposed new services and systems, possibly using modelling techniques, to ascertain capacity requirements
- Forecasting future capacity requirements based on business plans, usage trends, sizing of new services etc.
- Production, regular review and revision of the capacity plan, in line with the organization's business planning cycle, identifying current usage and forecast requirements during the period covered by the plan
- Ensuring that appropriate levels of monitoring of resources and system performance are set
- Analysis of usage and performance data, and reporting on performance against targets contained in SLAs
- Raising incidents and problems when breaches of capacity or performance thresholds are detected, and assisting with the investigation and diagnosis of capacity-related incidents and problems
- Identifying and initiating any tuning to be carried out to optimize and improve capacity or performance
- Identifying and implementing initiatives to improve resource usage – for example, demand management techniques
- Assessing new technology and its relevance to the organization in terms of performance and cost
- Being familiar with potential future demand for IT services and assessing this on performance service levels
- Ensuring that all changes are assessed for their impact on capacity and performance and attending CAB meetings when appropriate
- Producing regular management reports that include current usage of resources, trends and forecasts
- Sizing all proposed new services and systems to determine the computer and network resources required, to determine hardware utilization, performance service levels and cost implications

- Assessing new techniques and hardware and software products for use by capacity management that might improve the efficiency and effectiveness of the process
- Testing performance of new services and systems
- Preparing reports on service and component performance against targets contained in SLAs
- Maintaining a knowledge of future demand for IT services and predicting the effects of demand on performance service levels
- Determining performance service levels that are maintainable and cost-justified
- Recommending tuning of services and systems, and making recommendations to IT management on the design and use of systems to help ensure optimum use of all hardware and operating system software resources
- Acting as a focal point for all capacity and performance issues.

6.3.10 IT service continuity management roles

This section describes a number of roles that need to be performed in support of the IT service continuity management process. These roles are not job titles, and each organization will have to define appropriate job titles and job descriptions depending on their needs.

6.3.10.1 IT service continuity management process owner

The IT service continuity management process owner's responsibilities typically include:

- Carrying out the generic process owner role for the IT service continuity management process (see section 6.3.2 for more detail)
- Working with the business to ensure proper coordination and communication between business continuity management and IT service continuity management
- Working with managers of all functions to ensure acceptance of the IT service continuity management process as the single point of coordination for all IT service continuity-related issues, regardless of the specific technology involved
- Working with other process owners to ensure there is an integrated approach to the design and implementation of IT service

continuity management, information security management, availability management and business continuity management.

6.3.10.2 IT service continuity management process manager

The IT service continuity management process manager's responsibilities typically include:

- Carrying out the generic process manager role for the IT service continuity management process (see section 6.3.3 for more detail)
- Coordinating interfaces between IT service continuity management and other processes, especially service level management, information security management, availability management, capacity management and business continuity management
- Performing business impact analyses for all existing and new services
- Implementing and maintaining the IT service continuity management process, in accordance with the overall requirements of the organization's business continuity management process, and representing the IT services function within the business continuity management process
- Ensuring that all IT service continuity management plans, risks and activities underpin and align with all business continuity management plans, risks and activities, and are capable of meeting the agreed and documented targets under any circumstances
- Performing risk assessment and risk management to prevent disasters where cost-justifiable and where practical
- Developing and maintaining the organization's continuity strategy
- Assessing potential service continuity issues and invoking the service continuity plan if necessary
- Managing the service continuity plan while it is in operation, including fail-over to a secondary location and restoration to the primary location
- Performing post-mortem reviews of service continuity tests and invocations, and instigating corrective actions where required
- Developing and managing the IT service continuity management plans to ensure that, at all times, the recovery objectives of the business can be achieved

- Ensuring that all IT service areas are prepared and able to respond to an invocation of the continuity plans
- Maintaining a comprehensive IT testing schedule, including testing all continuity plans in line with business requirements and after every major business change
- Undertaking quality reviews of all procedures and ensuring that these are incorporated into the testing schedule
- Communicating and maintaining awareness of IT service continuity management objectives within the business areas supported and IT service areas
- Undertaking regular reviews, at least annually, of the continuity plans with the business areas to ensure that they accurately reflect the business needs
- Negotiating and managing contracts with providers of third-party recovery services
- Assessing changes for their impact on service continuity and continuity plans
- Attending CAB meetings when appropriate.

6.3.11 Information security management roles

This section describes a number of roles that need to be performed in support of the information security management process. These roles are not job titles, and each organization will have to define appropriate job titles and job descriptions depending on its needs.

6.3.11.1 Information security management process owner

The information security management process owner's responsibilities typically include:

- Carrying out the generic process owner role for the information security management process (see section 6.3.2 for more detail)
- Working with the business to ensure proper coordination and communication between organizational (business) security management and information security management
- Working with managers of all functions to ensure acceptance of the information security management process as the single point of coordination for all information security-related issues, regardless of the specific technology involved

- Working with other process owners to ensure there is an integrated approach to the design and implementation of information security management, availability management, IT service continuity management and organizational security management.

6.3.11.2 Information security management process manager

The information security management process manager's responsibilities typically include:

- Carrying out the generic process manager role for the information security management process (see section 6.3.3 for more detail)
- Coordinating interfaces between information security management and other processes, especially service level management, availability management, IT service continuity management and organizational security management
- Developing and maintaining the information security policy and a supporting set of specific policies, ensuring appropriate authorization, commitment and endorsement from senior IT and business management
- Communicating and publicizing the information security policy to all appropriate parties
- Ensuring that the information security policy is enforced and adhered to
- Identifying and classifying IT and information assets (configuration items) and the level of control and protection required
- Assisting with business impact analyses
- Performing security risk assessment and risk management in conjunction with availability and IT service continuity management
- Designing security controls and developing security plans
- Developing and documenting procedures for operating and maintaining security controls
- Monitoring and managing all security breaches and handling security incidents, taking remedial action to prevent recurrence wherever possible
- Reporting, analysing and reducing the impact and volumes of all security incidents in conjunction with problem management
- Promoting education and awareness of security
- Maintaining a set of security controls and documentation, and regularly reviewing and auditing all security controls and procedures

- Ensuring all changes are assessed for impact on all security aspects, including the information security policy and security controls, and attending CAB meetings when appropriate
- Ensuring security tests are performed as required
- Participating in any security reviews arising from security breaches and instigating remedial actions
- Ensuring that the confidentiality, integrity and availability of the services are maintained at the levels agreed in the SLAs and that they conform to all relevant statutory requirements
- Ensuring that all access to services by external partners and suppliers is subject to contractual agreements and responsibilities
- Acting as a focal point for all security issues.

6.3.12 Supplier management roles

This section describes a number of roles that need to be performed in support of the supplier management process. These roles are not job titles, and each organization will have to define appropriate job titles and job descriptions depending on its needs.

6.3.12.1 Supplier management process owner

The supplier management process owner's responsibilities typically include:

- Carrying out the generic process owner role for the supplier management process (see section 6.3.2 for more detail)
- Working with the business to ensure proper coordination and communication between corporate vendor management and/or procurement and supplier management
- Working with other process owners to ensure there is an integrated approach to the design and implementation of supplier management, service level management and corporate vendor management and/or procurement processes.

6.3.12.2 Supplier management process manager

The supplier management process manager's responsibilities typically include:

- Carrying out the generic process manager role for the supplier management process (see section 6.3.3 for more detail)

- Coordinating interfaces between supplier management and other processes, especially service level management and corporate vendor management and/or procurement processes
- Providing assistance in the development and review of SLAs, contracts, agreements or any other documents for third-party suppliers
- Ensuring that value for money is obtained from all IT suppliers and contracts
- Ensuring that all IT supplier processes are consistent and interface with all corporate supplier strategies, processes and standard terms and conditions
- Maintaining and reviewing a supplier and contract management information system
- Reviewing and making risk assessments of all suppliers and contracts on a regular basis
- Ensuring that any underpinning contracts, agreements or SLAs developed are aligned with those of the business
- Ensuring that all supporting services are scoped and documented and that interfaces and dependencies between suppliers, supporting services and supplier processes are agreed and documented
- Ensuring that all roles and relationships between lead and any sub-contracted suppliers are documented, maintained and subject to contractual agreement
- Reviewing lead suppliers' processes to ensure that any sub-contracted suppliers are meeting their contractual obligations
- Performing contract or SLA reviews at least annually, and ensuring that all contracts are consistent with organizational requirements and standard terms and conditions wherever possible
- Updating contracts or SLAs when required, ensuring that the change management process is followed
- Maintaining a process for dealing with contractual disputes, and ensuring that any disputes are dealt with in an efficient and effective manner
- Maintaining a process for dealing with the expected end, early end or transfer of a service
- Monitoring, reporting and regularly reviewing supplier performance against targets, identifying improvement actions as appropriate and ensuring these actions are implemented

- Ensuring changes are assessed for their impact on suppliers, supporting services and contracts and attending CAB meetings when appropriate
- Coordinating and supporting all individual IT supplier and contract managers, ensuring that each supplier/contract has a nominated owner within the service provider organization.

6.3.13 Other service design roles

This section describes a number of roles that may exist in an organization to support the service design stage of the service lifecycle. Some of these roles may also include responsibilities that associate with other service lifecycle stages. These roles are not job titles, and each organization will have to define appropriate job titles and job descriptions depending on its needs. Responsibilities described may also be reorganized into other roles based on the organization's needs and objectives.

6.3.13.1 IT planner

An IT planner is responsible for the production and coordination of IT plans. The main objectives of the role are as follows:

- Developing IT plans that meet and continue to meet the IT requirements of the business
- Coordinating, measuring and reviewing the implementation progress of all IT strategies and plans
- Producing and maintaining the overall set of IT standards, policies, plans and strategies, encompassing all aspects of IT required to support an organization's business strategy. IT planning includes participation in the creation of SLAs and the planning of all aspects of infrastructure – internal and external, public or private, internet and intranet – necessary to ensure that the provision of IT services satisfies business
- Assuming responsibility for all aspects of IT standards, policy and strategy implementation for IT as a whole and for significant projects or major new strategic applications
- Recommending policy for the effective use of IT throughout the organization and working with IT designers to ensure that overall plans and strategies are developed in conjunction with IT design for all areas of IT

- Reviewing IT costs against budgets and new developments, initiating proposals to change IT plans and strategies where appropriate, in conjunction with financial management for IT services
- Assuming full responsibility for the management, planning and coordination of IT systems and services, including investigation, analysis, specification, design, development, testing, maintenance, upgrade, transition and operation. It is essential that while performing these activities, the business, IT management and all the service management processes are kept up to date with the progress of projects
- Obtaining and evaluating proposals from suppliers of equipment, software, transmission services and other services, ensuring that all business and IT requirements are satisfied
- Identifying internal and external influencing factors, forecasting future needs and setting plans for the effective use of IT within the organization
- Sponsoring and monitoring research, development and long-term planning for the provision and use of IT architectures, products and services
- Reviewing IT performance with all other areas and initiating any improvements in organization to ensure that service levels and targets continue to be met in all areas
- Taking ultimate responsibility for prioritizing and scheduling the implementation of new or changed services within IT
- Working with senior management and other senior specialists and planners in formulating plans and making procurement decisions applicable to all areas of IT
- Recognizing the key business drivers and those areas of business need that are not adequately supported by current and planned IT services, developing the plans and IT response to the business requirements
- Identifying suitable applications, services and products, together with their environments, to meet business needs within the required planning timeframe
- Developing the initial plans for the implementation of authorized new IT services, applications and infrastructure support,

identifying budgetary, technical and staffing constraints, and clearly listing costs and expected benefits

- Monitoring the existing IT plans in relation to business needs and IT strategy to determine opportunities for improving business processes through the use of new technology, and to identify unforeseen risks to the achievement of forecast business benefits

- Investigating major options for providing IT services effectively and efficiently and recommending new innovative solutions, based on new approaches to processes, provision, recruitment and retention, and global supply contracts

- Producing feasibility studies, business models, IT models, business cases, statements of requirements (SoRs) and invitations to tender (ITTs) for recommended new IT systems, identifying the business impact, the probability of satisfying business needs, the anticipated business benefits and the risks and consequences of failure

- Overseeing and coordinating the programme of planned IT project implementations and changes, taking appropriate action to identify and overcome problems and resolve conflict

- Conducting post-implementation reviews in conjunction with change management of those information systems introduced in pursuit of the plans, to assess the extent to which expected business benefits were realized

- Liaising with strategy, transition and operations teams and processes to plan for their immediate and future needs

- Providing authoritative advice and guidance on relevant national and international standards, regulations, protocols and tariffs

- Documenting all work using required standards, methods and tools

- Ensuring that all IT planning processes, roles, responsibilities and documentation are regularly reviewed and audited for efficiency, effectiveness and compliance

- Maintaining a good overall knowledge of all IT product capabilities and the technical frameworks in which they operate

- Where required, assessing changes for their conformance to the design strategies, including attendance at CAB meetings if appropriate.

6.3.13.2 IT designer/architect

An IT designer/architect is responsible for the overall coordination and design of the required technology. Often designers and architects within large organizations specialize in one of the five aspects of design (see Chapter 3). However, an integrated approach to design should always be adopted; therefore designers and architects need to work together within a formal method and framework to ensure consistent and compatible designs are produced. In smaller organizations, some or all of the roles are usually combined, and this is less of an issue, although a formal approach should still be used. Whenever designs are produced, they should always adopt an integrated approach, covering all areas, and should be accepted and signed off by all areas. All designers need to understand how architectures, strategies, designs and plans fit together and understand all the main aspects of design.

The designer/architect should produce a detailed process map that documents all the processes and their high-level interfaces. This ensures that the overall structure is not unnecessarily complex, that the process's central interfaces are part of the design, and provides an overview to everyone on how the customer and all other stakeholders interact with the processes.

To perform the role of designer or architect, it is necessary for staff to have good knowledge and practical experience of design philosophies and planning, including programme, project and service management, methods and principles. The main objectives of the IT designer/architect are as follows:

- Producing and reviewing the designs of all new or changed services, SLAs, OLAs and contracts
- Producing a process map of all of the processes and their high-level interfaces, to ensure integration, consistency and continuity across all processes
- Designing secure and resilient technology architectures that meet all the current and anticipated future IT requirements of the organization
- Ensuring that the design of all processes, roles, responsibilities and documentation is regularly reviewed and audited for efficiency, effectiveness and compliance

- Designing an appropriate and suitable service portfolio, supporting all activities within the complete service lifecycle
- Designing measurement methods and metrics to support the continual improvement of service provision and all supporting processes
- Producing and keep up to date all IT design, architectural, policy and specification documentation
- Producing and maintaining all aspects of IT specification, including the overall designs, architectures, topologies and configurations of the infrastructure, environment, applications and data, and the design documentation of all IT systems. This should include not just the technology, but also the management systems, processes, information flows and external services
- Recommending proactive, innovative IT solutions for the improvement of IT design and operation whenever and wherever possible
- Translating logical designs into physical designs, taking account of business requirements, target environments, processes, performance requirements, existing systems and services, and any potential safety-related aspects
- Creating and maintaining IT design policies, philosophies and criteria, covering all areas including connectivity, capacity, interfaces, security, resilience, recovery, access and remote access, and ensuring that all new services meet their service levels and targets
- Working with capacity management and reviewing IT traffic volumes and requirements, identifying trends in traffic flows and levels of service
- Proposing design enhancements to IT infrastructure, capacity changes, continuity, backup and recovery arrangements, as required, and being aware of operational requirements, especially in terms of service levels, availability, response times, security and repair times. All these activities are performed in liaison with all of the service management processes
- Reviewing IT costs against external service providers, new developments and new services, initiating proposals to change IT design where appropriate cost reductions and benefits can be achieved, in consultation with financial management for IT services

- Providing advice and guidance to management on the design and planning phases of IT systems, to ensure that requirements (particularly capacity, recovery, performance and security needs) are reflected in the overall specifications
- Providing advice and guidance to all areas of IT and business management, analysts, planners, designers and developers on all aspects of IT design and technology
- Interfacing with designers and planners from external suppliers and service providers, ensuring all external IT services are designed to meet their agreed service levels and targets
- Playing a major role in the selection of any new IT infrastructure or technology solutions
- Assuming technical responsibility for IT standards, policy and design for all significant projects or major application areas, assisting with the impact assessment and evaluation of major new IT design options
- Providing technical advice and guidance on relevant national and international standards, regulations, protocols and tariffs
- Taking full responsibility for the design aspects of all stages of the lifecycle of IT systems, including investigation, analysis, specification, design, development, construction, testing, maintenance, upgrade, transition, operation and improvement
- Working with IT colleagues where appropriate, producing or updating IT and corporate design documentation and models
- Updating or providing input to cost benefit analyses, risk assessments, business cases, SoRs and ITTs and development plans, to take account of design decisions
- Obtaining and assisting with the evaluation and selection of proposals and solutions from suppliers of equipment, software and other IT service and product providers
- Constructing, interpreting and monitoring test plans to verify correct operation of completed systems against their design objectives
- Documenting all work using required standards, methods and tools
- Maintaining a good technical knowledge of all IT product capabilities and the technical frameworks in which they operate
- Where required, assessing changes for their conformance to the design principles, including attendance at CAB meetings if appropriate.

6.4 RESPONSIBILITY MODEL – RACI

Clear definitions of accountability and responsibility are essential for effective service management. To help with this task the RACI model or 'authority matrix' is often used within organizations to define the roles and responsibilities in relation to processes and activities. The RACI matrix provides a compact, concise, easy method of tracking who does what in each process and it enables decisions to be made with pace and confidence.

The RACI model is described in more detail in section 3.7.4.

6.5 COMPETENCE AND TRAINING

6.5.1 Competence and skills for service management

Delivering service successfully depends on personnel involved in service management having the appropriate education, training, skills and experience. People need to understand their role and how they contribute to the overall organization, services and processes to be effective and motivated. As changes are made, job requirements, roles, responsibilities and competencies should be updated if necessary.

Each service lifecycle stage depends on appropriate skills and experience of people and their knowledge to make key decisions. In many organizations, personnel will deliver tasks appropriate to more than one lifecycle stage. They may well find themselves allocated (fully or partially) from operational tasks to support a design exercise and then follow that service through service transition. They may then, via early life support activities, move into support of the new or changed services that they have been involved in designing and implementing into the live environment.

The specific roles within ITIL service management all require specific skills, attributes and competences from the people involved to enable them to work effectively and efficiently. However, whatever the role, it is imperative that the person carrying out that role has the following attributes:

- Awareness of the business priorities, objectives and business drivers
- Awareness of the role IT plays in enabling the business objectives to be met
- Customer service skills
- Awareness of what IT can deliver to the business, including latest capabilities
- The competence, knowledge and information necessary to complete their role
- The ability to use, understand and interpret the best practice, policies and procedures to ensure adherence.

The following are examples of attributes required in many of the roles, dependent on the organization and the specific roles assigned:

- Management skills – both from a person management perspective and from the overall control of process
- Ability to handle meetings – organizing, chairing, and documenting meetings and ensuring that actions are followed up
- Communication skills – an important element of all roles is raising awareness of the processes in place to ensure buy-in and conformance. An ability to communicate at all levels within the organization will be imperative
- Articulateness – both written (e.g. for reports) and verbal
- Negotiation skills are required for several aspects, such as procurement and contracts
- An analytical mind – to analyse metrics produced from the activity.

Many people working in service management are involved with continual service improvement. *ITIL Continual Service Improvement* provides specific guidance on the skill levels needed for CSI activities.

6.5.2 Competence and skills framework

Standardizing job titles, functions, roles and responsibilities can simplify service management and human resource management. Many service providers use a common framework of reference for competence and skills to support activities such as skill audits, planning future skill requirements, organizational development programmes and resource allocation. For example, resource and cost models are simpler and easier to use if jobs and roles are standard.

The Skills Framework for the Information Age (SFIA) is an example of a common reference model for the identification of the skills needed to develop effective IT services, information systems and technology. SFIA defines seven generic levels at which tasks can be performed, with the associated professional skills required for each level. A second dimension defines core competencies that can be combined with the professional skills. SFIA is used by many IT service providers to identify career development opportunities.

More information on SFIA can be found at www.sfia.org.uk

6.5.3 Training

Training in service management helps service providers to build and maintain their service management capability. Training needs must be matched to the requirements for competence and professional development.

The official ITIL qualification scheme enables organizations to develop the competence of their personnel through approved training courses. The courses help students to gain knowledge of ITIL best practices, develop their competencies and gain a recognized qualification. The scheme has four levels:

- Foundation level
- Intermediate level
- ITIL Expert
- ITIL Master.

More information on ITIL qualifications can be found at www.itil-officialsite.com

Technology considerations

7

7 Technology considerations

It is generally recognized that the use of service management tools is essential for the success of all but the very smallest process implementations. However, it is important that the tool being used supports the processes – not the other way around. As a general rule, do not modify processes to fit the tool. However, while striving to adhere to this principle, organizations need to be pragmatic and recognize that there may not be a tool that supports the designed process exactly – some degree of process re-design may be necessary.

Organizations should also not limit their tool requirements to functionality: consider the product's ability to perform, enlarge the size of the databases, recover from failure and maintain data integrity. Does the product conform to international standards? Is it efficient enough to enable you to meet your service management requirements?

Often organizations believe that by purchasing or developing a tool all their problems will be solved, and it is easy to forget that we are still dependent on the process, the function and, most importantly, the people. Remember:

'A fool with a tool is still a fool.'

7.1 SERVICE DESIGN TOOLS

There are many tools and techniques that can be used to assist with the design of services and their associated components. These tools and techniques enable:

- Hardware design
- Software design
- Environmental design
- Process design
- Data design.

The tools and techniques are many and varied, including both proprietary and non-proprietary, and are useful in:

- Speeding up the design process
- Ensuring that standards and conventions are followed
- Offering prototyping, modelling and simulation facilities

- Enabling 'What if?' scenarios to be examined
- Enabling interfaces and dependencies to be checked and correlated
- Validating designs before they are developed and implemented to ensure that they satisfy and fulfil their intended requirements.

Developing service designs can be simplified by the use of tools that provide graphical views of the service and its constituent components, from the business processes, through the service and service level agreement (SLA) to the infrastructure, environment, data and applications, processes, operational level agreements (OLAs), teams, contracts and suppliers. Some service asset and configuration management tools provide such facilities, and are sometimes part of an integrated ITSM tool. They can contain or be linked to 'auto-discovery' tools and mechanisms and allow the relationships between all of these elements to be graphically represented, providing the ability to drill down within each component and obtain detailed information if needed.

If these types of tool also contain financial information, and are then linked to a 'metrics tree' providing key performance indicators (KPIs) and metrics of the various aspects of the service, then the service can be monitored and managed through all stages of its lifecycle. Sharing this single, centralized set of service information allows everyone in the service provider organization and the business to access a single, consistent, 'real-world' view of the service and its performance, and provides a solid base for the development of good relationships and partnerships between the service provider and its customers.

These types of tool not only facilitate the design processes, but also greatly support and assist all ITSM methods and lifecycle stages, including:

- Management of all stages of the service lifecycle
- All aspects of the service and its performance
- Service achievement, SLA, OLA, contractual and supplier measurement, reporting and management

- Consolidated metrics and metrics trees, with views from management dashboards down to detailed component information, performance and fault analysis and identification
- Consistent and consolidated views across all processes, systems, technologies and groups
- Relationships and integration of the business and its processes with IT services, systems and processes
- A comprehensive set of search and reporting facilities, enabling accurate information and analysis for informed decision-making
- Management of service costs
- Management of relationships, interfaces and inter-dependencies
- Management of the service portfolio and service catalogue
- A configuration management system (CMS)
- A service knowledge management system (SKMS).

The following generic activities will be needed to implement such an approach:

- Establish the generic lifecycle for IT assets (requirements, design and develop, build, test, deploy, operate and optimize, dispose) and define the principal processes, policies, activities and technologies within each stage of the lifecycle for each type of asset
- Formalize the relationships between different types of IT asset, and the relationship between IT asset acquisition and management and other IT disciplines
- Define all roles and responsibilities involved in IT asset activities
- Establish measures for understanding the (total) cost of ownership of an IT service
- Establish policies for the reuse of IT assets across services – for example, at the corporate level
- Define a strategy for the acquisition and management of IT assets, including how it should be aligned with other IT and business strategies.

For the applications asset type, additionally:

- Document the role played by applications in the delivery of IT services to the business
- Ensure the generic IT asset lifecycle model is adapted to an applications lifecycle, tailored to different application types

- Set standards for the use of different approaches to developing applications, and recognize the role of development methodologies, including those based on 'reuse' (see section 3.11.3 for further discussion)
- Ensure that procedures are in place to consider all requirement types (such as operability, service performance, maintainability, security) in the early stages of application development
- Set standards for deciding on the optimal delivery of applications to the organization, such as the use of application service providers, customized developments, commercial off-the-shelf and package customization.

For the data/information asset type, additionally:

- Establish how the general principles of IT asset acquisition and management can help to manage the data/information resources of an organization.

Ensure that data designs are undertaken in the light of:

- The importance of standardized and reusable metadata
- The need for data quality
- The value of data to an organization
- The importance of legacy data and the need to carry data forward into new systems
- The need for data administration and database administration skills
- Understanding the 'corporate' (or common/cooperative) subject area and individual service ('system') views of data
- The need to manage data of non-traditional types such as text, scanned images, video and audio
- Awareness of the major storage, security and legal issues for data
- Specifying how the generic IT assets lifecycle model can be adapted to the data asset type.

For the IT infrastructure and environmental asset type, additionally:

- Establish standards for acquisition and management of the IT infrastructure and environmental equipment (including hardware, power, operating system software, database management system software, middleware and networks) and ensure they provide a stable yet adaptable foundation that underpins the provision of IT services to the business

- Establish how the generic IT assets lifecycle model should be adapted to a specific IT infrastructure lifecycle
- Establish activities to optimize the usage of IT infrastructure assets through their reuse
- Specify the need for tools and describe how their overall use and integration assists in the management of an effective IT infrastructure and related services
- Specify green IT/sustainability requirements in areas such as power consumption and recyclability of assets at the end of the asset lifecycle review.

For the skills (people, competencies), additionally:

- Formalize how the competencies of individuals responsible for the IT assets and related services can be regarded as an asset within the organization and are managed as such
- Specify how the IT asset lifecycle applies to people assets, particularly in terms of measurable competencies, such as skill, knowledge, understanding, qualifications, experience, attitude and behaviour
- Ensure the documentation of the competencies currently in place and specify how these can be reused or enhanced
- Ensure organization standards are compatible with existing standard competency frameworks for the IT sector, such as SFIA+ (Skills For The Information Age) skills, and competencies are incorporated into roles and responsibilities.

In addition, to establish effective interfaces and dependencies:

- Define the interfaces that IT asset acquisition and management has with IT-enabled business change, IT project management and IT security
- Formalize the interfaces that IT asset acquisition and management have with functions and processes outside IT
- Formalize measurement and reporting in this area by:
  - Identifying suitable metrics and the reports on IT assets for distribution throughout the organization as appropriate

- Formalizing quality control and measurement in the acquisition and management of IT assets.

7.2 SERVICE MANAGEMENT TOOLS

Tools will enable the service design processes to work more effectively. Tools will increase efficiency and effectiveness, and provide a wealth of management information, leading to the identification of weaknesses and opportunities for improvement. The longer-term benefits to be gained from the use of tools are cost savings and increased productivity, which in turn can lead to an increase in the quality of the IT service provision.

The use of tools will enable the centralization of key processes and the automation and integration of core service management processes. The raw data collected by the tools can be analysed, resulting in the identification of 'trends'. Preventive measures can then be implemented, again improving the quality of the IT service provision.

7.2.1 Defining tool requirements

Some points that organizations should consider when evaluating service management tools include:

- Data structure, data handling and integration
- Integration of multi-vendor infrastructure components, and the need to absorb new components in the future – these will place particular demands on the data-handling and modelling capabilities of the tool
- Conformity to international open standards
- Flexibility in implementation, usage and data sharing
- Usability – the ease of use permitted by the user interface
- Support for monitoring service levels
- Distributed clients with a centralized shared database (e.g. client server)
- Conversion requirements for previously tracked data
- Data backup, control and security
- Support options provided by the tool vendor
- Scalability at increasing of capacity (the number of users, volume of data and so on).

Consideration must be given to the exact requirements for the tool. What are the mandatory requirements and what are the desired requirements? Generally the tool should support the processes, not the other way round, so minimize modification of the processes to fit the tool. Where possible, it is better to purchase a fully integrated tool (although not at the expense of efficiency and effectiveness) to underpin many (if not all) service management processes. If this is not possible, consideration must be given to the interfaces between the various tools.

It is essential to have a statement of requirements (SoR) for use during the selection process – this statement can be used as a checklist. The tool requirements should be categorized using the MoSCoW analysis:

- M – **Must** have this
- S – **Should** have this if at all possible
- C – **Could** have this if it does not affect anything else
- W – **Won't** have this time but **would** like in the future.

For more information on the documentation of requirements, see section 5.1.5.

The tool must be adequately flexible to support your required access rights. You must be able to determine who is permitted to access what data and for what purpose – for example, read access to customers.

7.2.2 Tool selection

In the early stages, consideration must also be given to the platform on which the tool will be expected to operate – this may be on existing hardware and software or a new purchase. There may be restrictions laid down by IT strategy – for example, all new products may have to reside on specific servers. This might restrict which products could be included in the evaluation process. Make sure that the procurement fits within existing approved budgets.

Hints and tips

There are many service management tools available. Details can be found on the internet, in service management manuals, from asking other organizations, from asking consultants or by attending seminars and conferences to see what products are available.

During the early stages of the selection process, think about vendor and tool credibility. Are they still going to be supporting the purchase in a few months' or a year's time? Consider the past record of the supplier as well as that of the tool. Telephone the supplier's service desk to see how easy it is to get through, and ask some test questions to assess their technical competence. Ask the vendor to arrange a visit to a reference site to see what the experience is with the tool in practice – if possible without the vendor or supplier present. Make sure that the organization has similar requirements of the tool. See the tool in operation and speak to the users about their experiences, both initially and ongoing.

Assess the training needs of the organization and evaluate the capability of the supplier to provide the appropriate training. Also the ongoing training and tool update (upgrades and changes in user requirements) will need to be assessed to ascertain the support and training costs. In particular, consider training costs, training location, time required, and how soon after training the tool will be in use; and during the implementation project ensure that sufficient training is provided – think about how the new tool will impact both IT and customer. Also ensure that interfaces with other tools and telephony are functioning correctly. It is wise to identify whether the planned combination has been used (or tried) elsewhere and with what results. Consider periods of parallel running alongside existing solutions before finally going live.

When evaluating tools, a 100% fit to requirements should not be expected and will almost certainly not be found. The '80/20 rule' should be brought into effect instead. A tool is deemed to be fit for its purpose if it meets 80% or more of the business's operational requirements. Those operational requirements should be categorized as discussed earlier.

Any product should be rejected as unsuitable, however, if not all of the mandatory requirements ('must haves') are met. In some circumstances, it will be impossible to find an existing software product that will either meet all of the mandatory requirements or provide an 80% match. In this situation, the product offering the best functional design should be selected and the unsuitable elements re-written. This enhancement process should be done by the vendor if at all possible. In some cases, part of the enhancement costs may be met by the purchaser. Some products have been designed to include user hooks – this provides accessibility to site-written code at key procedural points, without the need for the package to be modified.

7.2.3 Implementation considerations

The work does not end when the product has been selected. In many ways this could be considered as only the beginning. The tool now has to be implemented. Once the hardware platform has been prepared and the software loaded, data population needs to be considered. What, where from, how and when? Timing is important to the testing, implementation and the go-live processes. Resources must be available to ensure success. In other words, do not schedule implementation during a known busy period, such as year-end processing.

> **Hints and tips**
>
> Today 'Software as a Service' (SaaS) products are available where hardware and software are not required (see *ITIL Service Strategy*, section C.2). These products give network-based access to and management of commercially available software. These types of product will still require planning and implementation, but this should simplify the process as no dedicated hardware is required.

Consideration should also be given to managed service providers and application service providers that may be able to provide the same functionality.

7.2.4 Evaluation process and criteria

Whatever tool or type of tool is chosen, the fulfilment of the requirements can be differentiated between:

- **Out of the box** The requirement is fulfilled.
- **Configuration** The tool can be configured with x days of effort to fulfil the requirement, and this will be preserved over product upgrades.
- **Customization** The tool must be reprogrammed with x days of effort to fulfil the requirement, and this may have to be repeated on every product upgrade.

Extensive customization of any product is always best avoided because of the high costs incurred at product upgrade. Vendors may be unwilling to support old releases, and purchasers may be unable to resource the necessary re-application of any bespoke customization. Customization may also release the vendor from much of its support obligations – this would be disastrous if, as a result, your service management system is unavailable for any length of time. Further costs would be incurred in providing the bespoke training that would be required. It would be impossible to take advantage of any cheap scheduled training courses being run by the software supplier.

The process of tool evaluation is shown in Figure 7.1.

Figure 7.1 shows the standard approach of identifying requirements before identifying products, but pragmatically there may be some element of overlap, where exploration of tools on the market opens one's eyes to new options that change the requirements. These stages are

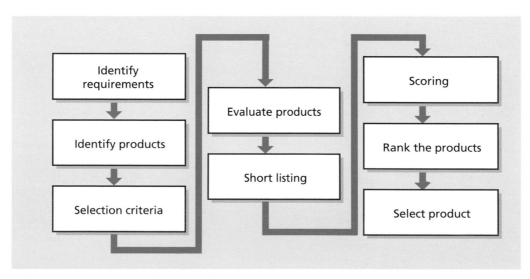

Figure 7.1 Service management tool evaluation process

targeted primarily at the evaluation of packaged software products, but a similar approach could also be used when evaluating custom-built software. Produce a clear SoR that identifies the business requirements together with the mandatory facilities and those features that it would be 'nice to have'. Also identify the site policies and standards to which the product must conform. Such standards may include it running under particular system software, or on specific hardware.

Remember the considerations about the supplier's suitability, and carry out a formal evaluation of the products under consideration.

If well-developed and appropriate tools are used to support the processes, the results achieved will be far greater and often the overall costs of service provision will be less. Selecting the right tool means paying attention to a number of issues:

- An 80% fit to all functional and technical requirements
- A meeting of all mandatory requirements
- Little (if any) product customization required
- Adherence of tool and supplier to service management best practice
- A sound data structure and handling
- Integration with other service management and operational management tools
- Support of open standards and interfaces
- Being business-driven not technology-driven
- Administration and maintenance costs within budget
- Acceptable levels of maintenance and release policies
- Security and integrity
- Availability of training and consultancy services
- Good report generation
- Scalability and growth.

Implementing
service design

8

8 Implementing service design

This chapter considers the task of implementing the service design processes and tackles issues such as:

- Where do we start?
- How do we improve?
- How do we know we are making progress?

The activities of implementing and improving service design need to be focused on the needs and desires of the customer and the business. Therefore these activities should be driven and prioritized by:

- Business needs and business impacts
- Risks to the services and processes.

The activities will be influenced significantly by the requirements outlined in the SLRs and by the agreements made in the SLAs.

8.1 BUSINESS IMPACT ANALYSIS

A valuable source of input when trying to ascertain the business needs, impacts and risks is the business impact analysis (BIA). The BIA is an essential element of the overall business continuity process (see section 4.6) and will dictate the strategy for risk reduction and disaster recovery. Its normal purpose is to identify the effect a disaster would have on the business. It will show which parts of the organization will be most affected by a major incident and what effect it will have on the company as a whole. It therefore enables the recognition of the most critical business functions to the company's survival and where this criticality differs depending on the time of the day, week, month or year. Additionally, experience has shown that the results from the BIA can be an extremely useful input for a number of other areas as well, and will give a far greater understanding of the service than would otherwise be the case.

The BIA could be divided into two areas:

- One by business management, which has to investigate the impact of the loss (or partial loss) of a business process or a business function. This includes the knowledge of manual workarounds and their costs.

- A second role located in service management is essential to break down the effects of service loss to the business. This element of the BIA shows the impact of service disruption to the business. The services can be managed and influenced by service management. Other aspects also covered in 'business BIA' cannot be influenced by service management.

As part of the design phase of a new or changed service, a BIA should be conducted to help define the business continuity strategy and to enable a greater understanding about the function and importance of the service. This will enable the organization to define:

- Which are the critical services, what constitutes a major incident on these services, and the subsequent impact and disruption caused to the business – important in deciding when and how to implement changes
- Acceptable levels and times of service outage levels – again important in the consideration of change and implementation schedules
- Critical business and service periods – important periods to avoid
- The cost of loss of service – important for financial management for IT services
- The potential security implications of a loss of service – important considerations in the management of risk.

8.2 SERVICE LEVEL REQUIREMENTS

As part of the service level management process (see Chapter 4), the service level requirements for all services will be ascertained and the ability to deliver against these requirements will be assessed and finally agreed in a formal service level agreement (SLA). For new services, the requirements must be ascertained at the start of the development process, not after completion. Building the service with service level requirements uppermost in mind is essential from a service design perspective.

8.3 RISKS TO THE SERVICES AND PROCESSES

When implementing the service design and IT service management processes, business-as-usual practices must not be adversely affected. This aspect must be considered during the production and selection of the preferred solution to ensure that disruption to operational services is minimized. This assessment of risk should then be considered in detail in the service transition activities as part of the implementation process.

8.4 IMPLEMENTING SERVICE DESIGN

The process, policy and architecture for the design of IT services outlined in this publication will need to be documented and utilized to ensure the appropriate innovative IT services can be designed and implemented to meet current and future agreed business requirements.

The IT service management processes outlined in Chapter 4 and in the other ITIL publications in this series will also need to be implemented to ensure service delivery that matches the requirements of the business.

8.4.1 Where do we start?

The question often asked is 'Which process shall I implement first?' The real answer is all of them, as the true value of implementing all of the service management processes is far greater than the sum of the individual processes. All the processes are interrelated, and in some cases are totally dependent on others. What is ultimately required is a single, integrated set of processes, providing management and control of a set of IT services throughout their entire lifecycle.

While recognizing that, to get the complete benefit of implementing IT service management, all of the processes need to be addressed, it is also recognized that organizations cannot do everything at once. It is therefore recommended that the areas of greatest need be addressed first. A detailed assessment needs to be undertaken to ascertain the strengths and weaknesses of IT service provision. This should be undertaken by performing customer satisfaction surveys, talking to customers, talking to IT staff and analysing the processes in action. If desired, process and organizational maturity can also be assessed

using established maturity scales. See section 8.4.2 and Appendix H for more information on maturity assessment. From the detailed assessment, short-, medium- and long-term strategies can be developed.

It may be that 'quick wins' need to be implemented in the short term to improve the current situation, but these improved processes may have to be discarded or amended as part of the medium- or long-term strategies. If 'quick wins' are implemented, it is important that they are not done at the expense of the long-term objectives, so these must be considered at all times. Every organization will have to start somewhere, and the starting point will be wherever the organization is now in terms of IT service management maturity. If the right 'quick wins' are selected, their achievement will not only improve the immediate situation, but will also build commitment to the adoption of a service management approach through demonstrated value of the principles in action.

Implementation priorities should be set against the goals of a service improvement plan (SIP). For example, if availability of IT services is a critical issue, focus on those processes aimed at maximizing availability (e.g. incident management, problem management, change management and availability management). Throughout the implementation process, key players must be involved in the decision-making process. These will include receivers as well as providers of the service. There can be a tendency, when analysing the areas of greatest need, to go straight for tools to improve the situation. Workshops or focus groups will be beneficial in understanding the requirements and the most suitable process for implementation that will include people, processes, products and partners.

8.4.2 How do we improve?

The first thing to do is to establish a formal process and method of implementation and improvement of service design, with the appropriate governance in place. This formal process should be based around the six-stage approach illustrated in Figure 8.1. More information can also be found on this approach in section 4.1.4.2 as well as in *ITIL Continual Service Improvement*.

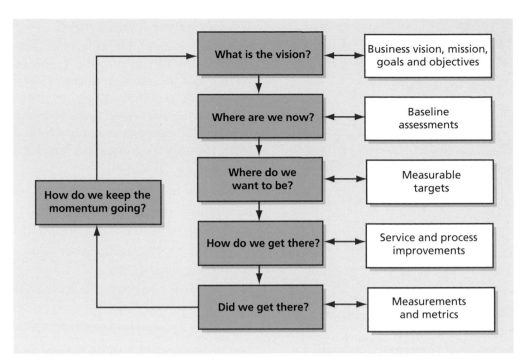

Figure 8.1 Implementation/continual service improvement approach

It is important that, when implementing or improving processes, a structured project management method is used. The improvement process can be summarized as:

■ First, understanding the vision by ascertaining the high-level business objectives. The 'vision-setting' should set and align business and IT strategies.

■ Second, assessing the current situation to identify strengths that can be built on and weaknesses that need to be addressed. So 'Where are we now?' is an analysis of the current position in terms of the business, organization, people and process.

■ Third, 'Where do we want to be?' is a development of the principles defined in the vision-setting, agreeing the priorities for improvement.

■ Fourth, detailing the SIP to achieve higher-quality service provision.

■ Next, measurements and metrics need to be put in place to show that the milestones have been achieved and that the business objectives and business priorities have been met.

■ Finally, the process should ensure that the momentum for quality improvement is maintained.

The implementation/continual service improvement approach is useful in checking the alignment between the business and IT, as shown in Figure 8.1.

The following are key elements for successful alignment of IT with business objectives:

■ Vision and leadership in setting and maintaining strategic direction, clear goals, and measurement of goal realization in terms of strategic direction

■ Acceptance of innovation and new ways of working

■ Thorough understanding of the business, its stakeholders and its environment

■ IT staff understanding the needs of the business

■ The business understanding the potential of IT

■ Information and communication available and accessible to everyone who needs it

■ Separately allocated/dedicated time to familiarize with the material about the business

■ Continuous tracking of technologies to identify opportunities for the business.

The implementation/continual service improvement approach may be used at any level – strategic, tactical or operational – depending on the focus of the implementation or improvement being addressed. In the following sections each step in the approach will be discussed in greater detail.

Further information on the continual service improvement approach can be found in Chapter 3 of *ITIL Continual Service Improvement*.

8.4.2.1 What is the vision?

The starting point for all of these activities is the culture and environment of the service provider organization. The people and the culture have to be appropriate and acceptable to improvement and change. Therefore, before attempting anything else, the culture within the service provider needs to be reviewed to ensure that it will accept and facilitate the implementation of the required changes and improvements. The following key steps need to be completed to achieve this stage of the cycle:

■ Establish a vision, aligned with the business vision and objectives
■ Establish the scope of the project/programme
■ Establish a set of high-level objectives
■ Establish governance, sponsorship and budget
■ Obtain senior management commitment
■ Establish a culture focused on:
  ● Quality
  ● Customer and business focus
  ● A learning environment
  ● Continual improvement
  ● Commitment to the 'improvement cycle'
  ● Ownership and accountability.

8.4.2.2 Where are we now?

Once the vision and high-level objectives have been defined, the service provider then needs to review the current situation, in terms of what processes are in place and the maturity of the organization. The activities that need to be completed here are a review, assessment or a more formal audit of the current situation, using a preferred technique such as:

■ Internal review or audit
■ Maturity assessment
■ External assessment or benchmark
■ ISO/IEC 20000 assessment or audit
■ Audit against COBIT
■ Strengths, weaknesses, opportunities and threats (SWOT) analysis
■ Risk assessment and management methodology.

The review should include people, processes, products and partners, as well as cultural and other factors:

■ The culture and maturity of the service provider organization
■ The processes in place and their capability, maturity and adoption
■ The skills and competence of the people
■ The services and technology
■ The suppliers, contracts and their capability
■ The quality of service and the current measurements, metrics and key performance indicators (KPIs)

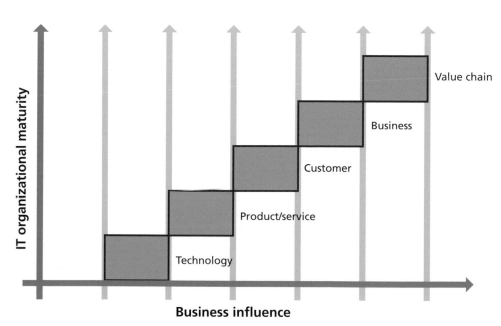

Figure 8.2 Cultural maturity assessment

- The alignment with business goals, objectives and business strategy
- A report summarizing the findings and recommendations.

Special attention should be paid to obtaining baseline measurements and metrics of the current state. These baselines will provide a valuable objectivity in assessing the best opportunities for improvement, inform the development of measurable targets for improvement, and provide a basis for later comparison after improvement efforts have been undertaken. It may be that the quality of the metrics available prior to improvement are of poor quality, with issues about accuracy and completeness, but any available metrics are better than none. Also, creating a baseline early will uncover measurement and reporting weaknesses for future improvement.

The review of the culture should include assessing it in terms of its capability and maturity within the IT service provider organization, as shown in Figure 8.2. This assessment should be based on the fact that each growth stage represents a transformation of the IT organization and as such will examine:

- Changes in people (skills and competencies)
- Processes and ways of working
- Technology and tools (to support and enable the people and processes)
- Steering (the visions, goals and results)
- Attitude (the values and beliefs)

- The appropriate level and degree of interaction with the business, customers, users and other stakeholders.

The assessment should also include a review of the capability and maturity of the service design processes, as shown in Figure 8.3. All aspects of the processes and their use should be examined, including:

- Vision: steering, objectives and plans
- Process maturity, functionality, usage, application, effectiveness and efficiency together with ownership, management and documentation
- People: the roles, responsibilities, skills and knowledge of the people
- Products, including the tools and technology used to automate the processes
- Culture: the focus, attitudes and beliefs.

The above framework can be used to provide consistency in process assessment. Assessing these two aspects will determine the current state of the organization and its service management capability and maturity. When starting out on the implementation or improvement of service design, or any set of processes, it is important to build on the strengths of the existing cultures and processes and rapidly identify and improve the weaknesses. A more detailed explanation of this framework is contained in Appendix H.

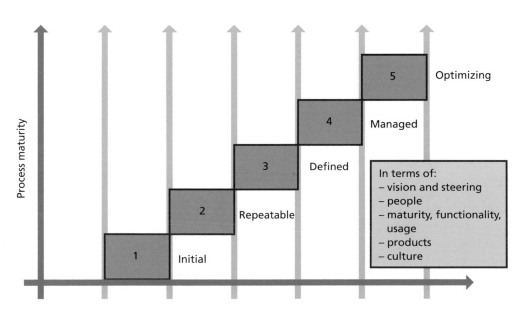

Figure 8.3 Process maturity framework

8.4.2.3 Where do we want to be?

Based on the current state assessment, and the vision and high-level objectives, a future desired state can be defined. This should be expressed in terms of planned outcomes, including some or all of:

- Improved IT service provision alignment with total business requirements
- Improved quality of service design
- Improvements in service levels and quality
- Increases in customer satisfaction
- Improvements in process performance.

The future desired state should be defined as specifically as possible to ensure success. The use of SMART objectives (specific, measurable, achievable, relevant and time-bound) is valuable in building clear and unambiguous expectations for the improvement.

8.4.2.4 How do we get there?

A set of improvements should then be identified to move forward from the current state to the agreed future state. A plan to implement these improvements should then be developed, incorporating service transition and service operation, and should include:

- The improvement actions
- The approach to be taken and the methods to be used
- Activities and timescales
- Risk assessment and management
- Resources and budgets
- Roles and responsibilities
- Monitoring, measurement and review.

Improvement plans should also take into consideration challenges, critical success factors and risks. See Chapter 9 for a discussion of these elements.

8.4.2.5 Did we get there?

Often organizations instigate improvement initiatives without considering or designing the measurement system from the outset. The success of the initiative cannot, therefore, be ascertained because we have no benchmark or baseline before, during or after the implementation. It is imperative that the measurements are designed before the implementation. A defined set of metrics needs to be utilized in order to ensure that the desired future state is achieved. This desired future state needs to be expressed in measurable terms (a central aspect of SMART objectives) such as:

- X% reduction in service design non-conformances
- X% increase in customer satisfaction
- X% increase in the service availability of critical services.

Thus once the improvement actions and plans have been completed, checks and reviews should be completed in order to determine:

- Did we achieve our desired new state and objectives?
- Are there any lessons learnt and could we do it better next time?
- Did we identify any other improvement actions?

For examples of specific metrics that might be used for process improvement, see the 'Critical success factors and key performance indicators' sections for each process in Chapter 4.

8.4.2.6 How do we keep the momentum going?

Having improved, the need is to consolidate and move on. The organization and the culture must recognize that they can always get better, and therefore must establish an environment of continual improvement. So, once they have achieved the new desired state, they must review the vision and objectives, identify more improvement actions, log them in the continual service improvement (CSI) register, and repeat the six-stage approach again. So this stage is all about:

- Developing a learning environment
- Establishing a desire to improve throughout the organization
- Recognizing and reinforcing the message that quality and improvement are everybody's job
- Maintaining the momentum on improvement and quality.

8.5 MEASUREMENT OF SERVICE DESIGN

The success of the service design and the success of the improvement to the processes around the service design must be measured, and the data must be analysed and reported on. Where the design or process does not meet the requirements of the business as a whole, changes to the process may be required and the results of those changes must also be measured. Continuous measurement, analysis and reporting are mandatory requirements for both the service design stage and the IT service management processes.

There are measurement methods available that enable the analysis of service improvement. The balanced scorecard is a method developed by Robert Kaplan and David Norton as a concept for measuring a company's activities in terms of its vision and strategies. It gives a comprehensive view of the performance of a business. The system forces managers to focus on the important performance metrics that drive success. It balances a financial perspective with customer, internal process, and learning and growth perspectives. More information can be found on the balanced scorecard method in *ITIL Continual Service Improvement*.

Six Sigma is a methodology developed by Bill Smith at Motorola Inc. in 1986, and was originally designed to manage process variations that cause defects, defined as unacceptable deviation from the mean or target, and to systematically work towards managing variation to eliminate those defects. Six Sigma has now grown beyond defect control and is often used to measure improvement in IT process execution. (Six Sigma is a registered service mark and trademark of Motorola Inc.)

Six Sigma (DMADV) is an improvement system used to develop new processes at Six Sigma quality levels and is defined as:

- **Define** Formally define the goals of the design activity that are consistent with customer demands and organization strategy
- **Measure** Identify critical success factors, capabilities, process capability and risk assessment
- **Analyse** Develop and design alternatives, create high-level design and evaluate design capability to select the best design
- **Design** Develop detailed design, optimize design and plan for design verification
- **Verify** Set up pilot runs, implement production process and hand over to process owners.

The Six Sigma (DMAIC) process (define, measure, analyse, improve, control) is an improvement system for existing processes falling below specification and looking for incremental improvement.

8.5.1 Prerequisites for success

Introducing and managing an effective and efficient measurement programme for service design is dependent upon:

- Clearly defined goals and objectives for the service design stage
- A strong understanding of the processes, procedures, functions, roles and responsibilities associated with successful service design
- A strong understanding of the interfaces and dependencies between service design elements and the rest of the service lifecycle
- A strong understanding of and alignment with the needs of the business
- Development of appropriate measurement and analysis technology, methods and techniques to enable plans to be realized
- Alignment of measurements with the required metrics to accurately evaluate the health of service design, identify and implement opportunities for improvement and validate improvement accomplishments
- Regular review of the measurement programme to ensure ongoing alignment with overall service and service management requirements.

It is important to long-term success that those activities necessary for successful measurement of service design be automated wherever possible to free up human resources for the critical tasks of analysing the metrics and determining the true meaning of the information uncovered.

Measurement of service design must lead to well-prioritized and efficient improvement of service design results without unnecessary expenditure of resources to obtain the metrics.

For further information on service improvement practices, see *ITIL Continual Service Improvement*.

Challenges, risks and critical success factors

9 Challenges, risks and critical success factors

9.1 CHALLENGES

With every undertaking there will be challenges or difficulties to face and to overcome. This will be especially true when attempting to design new services and processes that meet the requirements of all stakeholders within the business. Experience has shown that the following will help to overcome the challenges:

- Understanding the business requirements and the business priorities and ensuring that these are uppermost in mind when designing the processes and the services
- Understanding the people and the organizational culture
- Effective communication both for explaining what is happening and how individuals will be affected and for listening to the requirements and needs of the individuals. It is vitally important to communicate with people about concerns that relate to their daily job
- Involving as many people as possible in the design. Setting up focus groups or steering groups can be very effective in getting the right solution as well as gaining wider support
- Gaining commitment from senior management as well as from all levels of staff.

Some examples of challenges that may be faced are:

- Organizational resistance to change
- Difficulty with documentation and adherence to agreed practices and processes
- Unclear or changing requirements from the business. This may be unavoidable in some cases because business needs are likely to change. The important thing is to ensure that there is a very close relationship between the IT service provider organization and the business customer of the service, so that any changing requirements can be identified as quickly as possible
- A lack of awareness and knowledge of service and business targets and requirements
- Linked to the above point, it may be that certain facilities are not built into the design. Again, it is imperative that representatives of every user of the designed service or process are involved

throughout the process to reduce the chance of this happening. Details of service testing (an important element here) are contained within *ITIL Service Transition*

- A resistance to planning, or a lack of planning leading to unplanned initiatives and unplanned purchases
- Inefficient use of resources causing wasted time and money
- Lack of good knowledge and appreciation of the business impacts and priorities, as mentioned previously
- Poor relationships, communication or lack of cooperation between the IT service provider and the business may result in the design not achieving the business requirements
- Resistance to work within the agreed strategy
- Use of, and therefore the constraints of, old technology and legacy systems
- Required tools are too costly or too complex to implement or maintain with the current staff skills
- Lack of information, monitoring and measurements
- Unreasonable targets and timescales previously agreed in the SLAs and OLAs
- Over-commitment of available resources with an associated inability to deliver (e.g. projects always late or over budget)
- Poor supplier management and/or poor supplier performance
- Lack of focus on service availability
- The need to ensure alignment with current architectural directions, strategy and policies. An example of this may be that the procured infrastructure may have poor monitoring and control features
- The use of diverse and disparate technologies and applications
- Lack of awareness and adherence to the operational aspects of security policies and procedures
- Ensuring normal daily operation or business as usual is considered as part of the design
- Cost and budgetary constraints

- Difficulty ascertaining the return on investments and the realization of business benefit.

9.2 RISKS

There are a number of risks directly associated with the service design stage of the service lifecycle. These risks need to be identified to ensure that they are appropriately addressed. The risks include:

- If any of the CSFs for service design are not met, then the service design or service management process will not be successful.
- If maturity levels of one process are low, it will be impossible to achieve full maturity in other processes.
- Business requirements are not clear to IT staff.
- Business timescales are such that insufficient time is given for proper service design.
- Insufficient testing, resulting in poor design and therefore poor implementation.
- An incorrect balance is struck between innovation, risk and cost while seeking a competitive edge, where desired by the business.
- The fit between infrastructures, customers and partners is not sufficient to meet the overall business requirements.
- A coordinated interface is not provided between IT planners and business planners.
- The policies and strategies, especially the service management strategy, are not available from service strategy, or its content is not clearly understood.
- Over- or under-engineered processes. Processes with too little definition and control may not consistently meet the stated objectives. Processes with too much definition and control can become an impediment to efficiency and may actually produce a negative impact on business outcomes.
- There are insufficient resources and budget available for service design activities.
- Services being developed in isolation using their 'own' assets and infrastructure. This can appear to be cheaper in isolation, but can be much more costly in the long term because of the financial savings of corporate buying and the extra cost of supporting different architectures.

- Insufficient time given to the design stage, or insufficient training given to the staff tasked with the design.
- Insufficient engagement or commitment with the application's functional development, leading to insufficient attention to service design requirements.

9.3 CRITICAL SUCCESS FACTORS AND KEY PERFORMANCE INDICATORS

Critical success factor (CSF) is a term for an element that is necessary for an organization or project to achieve its mission. CSFs can be used as a means for identifying the important elements of success.

Key performance indicators (KPIs) are measures that quantify objectives and enable the measurement of performance. KPIs should be set and measured against the design and for each of the processes to ensure that the CSFs are met. Together, CSFs and KPIs establish the baseline and mechanisms for tracking performance. Achievement against KPIs should be monitored and used to identify opportunities for improvement, which should be logged in the CSI register for evaluation and possible implementation.

Hints and tips

It is recommended that each IT organization focuses on a small sub-set of CSFs and KPIs at any one time. The required CSFs and KPIs should be set at the beginning of any implementation or improvement activities.

It is important that CSFs are agreed during the design stage of a service and of the processes, and that KPIs are set, measured and reported on to indicate the quality of the service design and the service design processes. There is a requirement to be able to analyse how well the service infrastructure was designed. It is possible to arrive at a good design in a very resource-inefficient manner, and vice versa, so it is important to look at the quality as well as resources needed to achieve the required quality. KPIs around the success of delivery of the service indicate the effectiveness of the service design – for example, does the service meet the (defined) business requirements for availability, reliability, throughput, security, maintainability, serviceability, functionality etc.?

KPIs around the resource estimates, however, will show us how efficient the design is.

These should be defined as part of quality assurance (QA) planning and release acceptance. These KPIs could be supported by similar component metrics.

KPIs for the service design stage may include:

- Percentage of service design requirement specifications produced on time (and to budget)
- Percentage of service design plans produced on time
- Percentage of service design packs completed on time
- Percentage of QA and acceptance criteria plans produced on time
- Accuracy of service design – for example, was the correct infrastructure built to support the service?
- Percentage accuracy of the cost estimate of the whole service design stage
- Accuracy of service level agreement(s), operational level agreement(s) and contract(s) – do they really support the required level of service?

To judge service provision and ITSM process performance, clearly defined objectives with measurable targets should be set. Confirmation needs to be sought that these objectives and the milestones set in the continual service improvement (CSI) stage of the lifecycle have been reached and that the desired service quality or desired improvement in quality has been achieved. It is vital when designing services or processes that KPIs are designed from the outset and collected regularly and at important milestones. For example, at the completion of each significant stage of the programme, a post-implementation review (PIR) should be conducted to ensure the objectives have been met. The PIR will include a review of supporting documentation and the general awareness among staff of the refined processes.

A comparison is required of what has been achieved against the original goals set in the project. Once this has been confirmed, new improvement targets should be defined. To confirm that the milestones have been reached, KPIs need to be constantly monitored. These KPIs include customer satisfaction targets, so there will be a need to survey customers planned at various stages to confirm that changes made are improving the customer perception of the service quality. It is possible that the services have higher availability, that there are fewer incidents and that response times have improved, but at the same time the customer's perception of service quality has not improved. Clearly this is as important, and will need to be addressed by talking to customers to ascertain their concerns. Confirmation will need to be sought that improvements put in place are addressing the customer's primary needs.

Afterword

Afterword

Service design can be described as the design of appropriate and innovative IT services, including their architectures, processes, policies and documentation, to meet current and future agreed business requirements. This publication has explained that the better and more careful the design, the better the solution taken into live operation. It is also highly likely that the better the design, the less re-work time that will need to be undertaken during the transition and live stages of the service lifecycle.

Excellence in service design requires that the service provider moves beyond a focus on the purely technical aspects of a service and considers the non-technical aspects that can be just as critical to maximizing the value ultimately received by the customer. Proper service design does not merely allow for the activation of a new or changed service in the live environment, but also provides the basis for establishing effective use of the service by business users and customers and for effective and efficient service management, maintenance, support and ongoing improvement. As organizations move to adopt the principles of service management, the guidance in this publication will aid the evolution of their service design practices towards the holistic approach advocated in these pages.

Appendix A: The service design package

A

Appendix A: The service design package

A 'service design package' (SDP) should be produced during the design stage, for each new service, major change to a service or removal of a service or changes to the 'service design package' itself. This pack is then passed from service design to service transition and details all aspects of the service and its requirements through all of the subsequent stages of its lifecycle. The contents of the SDP are shown in Table A.1.

Table A.1 Contents of the service design package

	Sub-category	Description of what is in the SDP
Requirements	Business requirements	The initial agreed and documented business requirements
	Service applicability	This defines how and where the service would be used. This could reference business, customer and user requirements for internal services
	Service contacts	The business contacts, customer contacts and other stakeholders in the service
Service design	Service functional requirements	The changed functionality (utility) of the new or changed service, including its planned outcomes and deliverables, in a formally agreed statement of requirements (SoR)
	Service level requirements	The service level requirements (SLR), representing the desired warranty of the service for a new or changed service. Once specific service level targets have been agreed and validated, the revised or new service level agreement (SLA), including service and quality targets
	Service and operational management requirements	Management requirements to manage the new or changed service and its components, including all supporting services and agreements, control, operation, monitoring, measuring and reporting
	Service design and topology	The design, transition and subsequent implementation and operation of the service solution and its supporting components, including: ■ The service definition, service model, packaging and service options ■ All service components and infrastructure (including hardware, software, networks, environments, data, applications, technology, tools, documentation), including version numbers and relationships, preferably within the configuration management system (CMS) ■ All user, business, service, component, transition, support and operational documentation ■ Processes, procedures, measurements, metrics and reports ■ Supporting products, services, agreements and suppliers
Organizational readiness assessment	Organizational readiness assessment	'Organizational readiness assessment' report and plan, including: business benefit, financial assessment, technical assessment, resource assessment and organizational assessment, together with details of all new skills, competences, capabilities required of the service provider organization, its suppliers, supporting services and contracts

Table continues

Table A.1 continued

	Sub-category	Description of what is in the SDP
Service lifecycle plan	Service programme	An overall programme or plan covering all stages of the lifecycle of the service, including the timescales and phasing, for the transition, operation and subsequent improvement of the new service including: ■ Management, coordination and integration with any other projects, or new or changed activities, services or processes ■ Management of risks and issues ■ Scope, objectives and components of the service ■ Skills, competences, roles and responsibilities ■ Processes required ■ Interfaces and dependencies with other services ■ Management of teams, resources, tools, technology, budgets, facilities required ■ Management of suppliers and contracts ■ Progress reports, reviews and revision of the programme and plans ■ Communication plans and training plans ■ Timescales, deliverables, targets and quality targets for each stage

	Service transition plan	Overall transition strategy, objectives, policy, risk assessment and plans including:
		
		■ Build policy, plans and requirements, including service and component build plans, specifications, control and environments, technology, tools, processes, methods and mechanisms, including all platforms
		
		■ Testing policy, plans and requirements, including test environments, technology, tools, processes, methods and mechanisms
		
		■ Testing must include:
		
		  ● Functional testing
		
		  ● Component testing, including all suppliers, contracts and externally provided supporting products and services
		
		  ● User acceptance and usability testing
		
		  ● System compatibility and integration testing
		
		  ● Service and component performance and capacity testing
		
		  ● Resilience and continuity testing
		
		  ● Failure, alarm and event categorization, processing and testing
		
		  ● Service and component, security and integrity testing
		
		  ● Logistics, release and distribution testing
		
		  ● Management testing, including control, monitoring, measuring and reporting, together with backup, recovery and all batch scheduling and processing

	Sub-category	Description of what is in the SDP
	Service transition plan *continued*	■ Deployment policy, release policy, plans and requirements, including logistics, deployment, staging, deployment environments, cultural change, organizational change, technology, tools, processes, approach, methods and mechanisms, including all platforms, knowledge, skill and competence transfer and development, supplier and contract transition, data migration and conversion
	Service operational acceptance plan	Overall operational strategy, objectives, policy, risk assessment and plans including: ■ Interface and dependency management and planning ■ Events, reports, service issues, including all changes, releases, resolved incidents, problems and known errors, included within the service; and any errors, issues or non-conformances within the new service ■ Final service acceptance
	Service acceptance criteria	Development and use of service acceptance criteria for progression through each stage of the service lifecycle, including: ■ All environments ■ Guarantee and pilot criteria and periods

Appendix B: Service acceptance criteria

B

Appendix B: Service acceptance criteria

The service acceptance criteria (SAC) comprise a set of criteria used to ensure that a service meets its expected functionality and quality and that the service provider is ready to deliver the new service once it has been deployed. Table B.1 gives examples of such criteria.

Table B.1 Examples of service acceptance criteria

Criteria	Responsibility
Have the 'go-live' date and the guarantee period been agreed with all concerned parties, together with final acceptance criteria?	Change, service level
Have the deployment project and schedule been documented, agreed and made public to all affected personnel?	Change, incident
Has the service level agreement (SLA)/requirements (SLR) been reviewed, revised and agreed with all concerned parties?	Service level
Has the service been entered/updated in the service catalogue/service portfolio within the configuration management system (CMS) and appropriate relationships established for all supporting components?	Service level, configuration
Have all customers and other stakeholders been identified and recorded in the CMS?	Service level, business relationship
Have all operational risks associated with running the new service been assessed and mitigation actions completed where appropriate?	Business continuity, availability
Have contingency and fail-over measures been successfully tested and added to the overall resilience test schedule?	Business continuity, availability
Can all SLA/SLR targets be monitored, measured, reported and reviewed, including availability and performance?	Service level, availability
Have all users been identified/approved and their appropriate accounts created for them?	Account management
Can all workload characteristics, performance and capacity targets be measured and incorporated into capacity plans?	Capacity
Have all operational processes, schedules and procedures been agreed, tested, documented and accepted (e.g. site documentation, backups, housekeeping, archiving, retention)?	Operations, business continuity
Have all batch jobs and printing requirements been agreed, tested, documented and accepted?	Operations
Have all test plans been completed successfully?	Test manager
Have all security checks and tests been completed successfully?	Security compliance
Are appropriate monitoring and measurement tools and procedures in place to monitor the new service, together with an out-of-hours support rota?	Systems management
Have all ongoing operational workloads and costs been identified and approved?	Operations, IT finance
Are all service and component operational costs understood and incorporated into financial processes and the cost model?	IT finance
Have incident and problem categories and processes been reviewed and revised for the new service, together with any known errors and deficiencies?	Incident, problem reporting

Table continues

Table B.1 *continued*

Criteria	Responsibility
Have all new suppliers been identified and their associated contracts drawn up accordingly?	Contract and supplier management
Have all support arrangements been reviewed and revised – SLAs, SLRs, operational level agreements (OLAs) – and contracts agreed, with documentation accepted by all teams (including suppliers, support teams, supplier management, development teams and application support)?	Project manager
Has appropriate technical support documentation been provided and accepted by incident, problem and all IT support teams?	Incident, problem
Have all requests for change and release records been authorized and updated?	Change
Have all service, SLA, SLR, OLA and contract details, together with all applications and infrastructure component details, been entered on the CMS?	Project management, support teams configuration
Have appropriate software licences been purchased or reallocated licences used?	Configuration
Have all new hardware components been recorded in the CMS?	Configuration
Have all new software components been lodged in the definitive media library (DML) with details recorded in the CMS?	Configuration
Have all maintenance and upgrade plans been agreed, together with release policies, frequencies and mechanisms?	Release and deployment
Have all users been trained, and has user documentation been accepted and supplied to all users?	Project manager
Are all relationships, interfaces and dependencies with all other internal and external systems and services documented, agreed and supported?	Project manager
Have appropriate business managers signed off acceptance of the new service?	Project manager

Appendix C: Process documentation template

C

Appendix C: Process documentation template

C.1 PROCESS FRAMEWORK

When designing a new or revised process for any of the service management processes, it is recommended that a process specification or framework be produced. The specification should be kept at a fairly high level, but it needs to detail the scope and interfaces of the process. More detailed procedures and work instructions will also be needed to ensure consistency of the process and its application. The typical contents of a process framework or specification are:

- Process name, description and administration (documentation administration: version, change control, author etc.)
- Vision and mission statements
- Objectives
- Scope and terms of reference
- Process overview:
  - Description and overview
  - Inputs
  - Procedures
  - Activities
  - Outputs
  - Triggers
  - Tools and other deliverables
  - Communication and training
- Roles and responsibilities:
  - Operational responsibilities
  - Process owner
  - Process members
  - Process users
  - Other roles
- Associated documentation and references
- Interfaces and dependencies to:
  - Other service management processes
  - Other IT processes
  - Business processes
- Process measurements and metrics:
  - Critical success factors
  - Key performance indicators
  - Process reviews, assessments and audits

- Deliverables and reports produced by the process:
  - Frequency
  - Content
  - Distribution
- Glossary, abbreviations and references.

Appendix D: Design and planning documents and their contents

Appendix D: Design and planning documents and their contents

This appendix contains suggested details of the types of design documents, plans and standards documents that should be produced and maintained by IT, and also outlines the minimum contents of IT architectures and plans. However, it should be stressed again that all these documents should be frequently and regularly reviewed and revised and should be actively used within everyday IT processes and procedures.

They must also be maintained in alignment with all similar documents in use within the business and the overall organization.

D.1 DESIGN AND ARCHITECTURAL DOCUMENTS AND STANDARDS

The design documents and standards developed and maintained by IT should include:

- Design and planning standards, policies, processes and procedures
- Application architectures, design methods and standards
- Business requirements, business impact assessment and prioritization and business case methods and standards
- Functional requirements standards
- Statements of requirements (SoR) and invitations to tender (ITT) standards and methods for their evaluation
- IT technology architectures, design standards and policies, covering all areas of technology, including mainframe, server, desktop, laptop, hand-held and mobile devices, telephony systems, storage, backup, network and network addressing
- Operating systems, systems software, utilities and firmware architectures, design policies and standards
- Data, information and database architectures, design policies and standards, including information flows, knowledge management, information security and access, data management, data storage, data warehousing, data analysis and data mining

- Management systems, platforms, tools and agents and their architectures and design polices and standards, including functionality, domains, interfaces, management protocols, event and alarm handling and categorization, automation and escalation
- Cabling architectures, designs and standards
- Development standards, methods and policies
- Testing methods, polices and standards
- Handover, acceptance and sign-off standards and methods
- Partner, supplier and contract standards and policies
- Communications policies and standards
- Document and document library standards and policies
- Internet and intranet architectures, design standards and policies, including e-commerce and e-business
- Email and groupware architectures, design standards and policies
- Environmental requirements, design policies and standards
- IT security design policies and standards, including firewalling, virus checking, service and system access levels, methods and policies, remote access, user account and password management
- Procurement standards and policies
- Programme standards and policies, project methods and project planning and review policies and standards
- Quality standards and policies
- User interfaces and standards.

D.2 IT PLANS

IT should produce and maintain a number of plans in order to coordinate and manage the overall development and quality of IT services. These should include:

- **IT business plans** The business plans for the development of IT services

- **Strategic plans** Providing plans for the achievement of the long-term vision, mission and objectives of IT
- **Tactical plans** Providing plans for the achievement of the short- and medium-term vision, mission and objectives of ICT
- **Functional plans** Providing plans for the achievement of the vision, mission and objectives of key IT functions
- **Operational plans** Providing plans for the development and improvement of operational processes, procedures and methods
- **Project plans and programmes:**
  - IT and business programmes
  - IT projects
- **Processes plans and programmes:**
  - Objectives and targets
  - Process improvement
  - Roles and responsibilities
- **Transition plans:**
  - Build plans and schedules
  - Testing and release schedules
  - Development and test environments
  - Transition schedules
- **Service management plans:**
  - Service quality plan(s)
  - Service improvement plans and programmes
  - Financial plans and budgets
  - IT service continuity and recovery plans and business continuity plans
  - Capacity plan
  - Availability plan
  - Service support plans
  - Release plans and schedules
  - Service asset and configuration management plans
  - Change management plans and the change schedule
  - Service desk, incident management and problem management plans
  - Supplier and contract plans.

All IT plans should be developed, maintained and reviewed in line within the business and the overall organization. This should be achieved using the impact assessment process of a suitable change management system. Organizations should take the legal requirements for systems into consideration and also look into international and national standards and regulation and the need for corporate governance.

Appendix E: Environmental architectures and standards

Appendix E: Environmental architectures and standards

This appendix contains details of environmental architectures and standards. Every organization should produce an environmental policy for equipment location, with minimum agreed standards for particular concentrations of equipment. Additionally, minimum standards should be agreed for the protection of buildings containing equipment and equipment room shells.

Tables E.1–E.6 cover the major aspects that need to be considered, with example characteristics.

Note: This section is concerned with items that require attention in design. It is not intended to cover all the related concerns of the facilities management function, which is covered in Appendix E of *ITIL Service Operation*. However, a review of this related area may yield additional ideas for design.

Table E.1 Building/site

Access	Secure perimeters, secure entrances, audit trail
Building and site protection	Security fencing, video cameras, movement and intruder detectors, window and door alarms, lightning protectors, good working environment (standard)
Entry	Multiple controlled points of entry
External environment	Safeguards to minimize external risks such as floods, electrical storms or hurricanes
Services	Where possible and justifiable, alternative routes and suppliers for all essential services, including network services

Table E.2 Major equipment room

Access	Secure controlled entry, combination lock, swipe card, video camera (if business critical and unattended)
Location	First floor wherever possible, with no water, gas, chemical or fire hazards within the vicinity, above, below or adjacent
Temperature	Strict control, 22°C (± 3°C). Provide for up to 550 W/m². 6°C variation throughout the room and a maximum of 6°C per hour
Visibility	No signage, no external windows
Shell	External shell: waterproof, airtight, soundproofed, fire-resistant (0.5 hours to 4 hours depending on criticality)
Equipment delivery	Adequate provision should be made for the delivery and positioning of large delicate equipment
Internal floor	Sealed
Separate plant room	Uninterruptible power supply (UPS). Electrical supply and switching, air-handling units, dual units and rooms if business critical
Fire extinguishers	Sufficient electrical fire extinguishers with adequate signage and procedures
External	Generator for major data centres and business-critical systems

Table continues

Table E.3 Major data centres

Access	Secure controlled entry, combination lock, swipe card, video camera (if business critical and unattended)
Temperature	Strict control, 22°C (± 3°C). Provide for up to 550 W/m². 6°C variation throughout the room and a maximum of 6°C per hour
Humidity control	Strict control: 50% (± 10%)
Air quality	Positive pressure, filtered intake, low gaseous pollution (e.g. sulphur dioxide ≤ 0.14 ppm), dust levels for particles > 1 micron, less than 5 × 106 particles/m³. Auto shut-down on smoke or fire detection
Power	Power distribution unit (PDU), with three-phase supply to non-switched boxes, one per piece of equipment, with appropriate rated circuit-breakers for each supply. Alternatively, approved power distribution strips can be used. Balanced three-phase loadings. UPS (online or line interactive with simple network management protocol [SNMP] management) to ensure voltage supplied is within ± 5% of rating with minimal impulse, sags, surges and over/under voltage conditions
False floors	Antistatic, liftable floor tiles 600 × 600 mm on pedestals, with alternate pedestals screwed to the solid floor. Minimum of 600 mm clearance to solid floor. Floor loadings of up to 5 kN/m² with a recommended minimum of 3 m between false floor and ceiling
Internal walls	From false floor to ceiling, fire-resistant, but with air flow above and below floor level
Fire detection/ prevention	HSSD or VESDA multi-level alarm with auto FM200 (or alternative halon replacement) release on 'double-knock' detection
Environmental detectors	For smoke, temperature, power, humidity, water and intruder with automated alarm capability. Local alarm panels with repeater panels and also remote alarm capability
Lighting	Normal levels of ceiling lighting with emergency lighting on power failure
Power safety	Clean earth should be provided on the PDU and for all equipment. Clearly marked remote power-off buttons on each exit. Dirty power outlets, clearly marked, should also be supplied
Fire extinguishers	Sufficient electrical fire extinguishers with adequate signage and procedures
Vibration	Vibrations should be minimal within the complete area
Electromagnetic interference	Minimal interference should be present (1.5 V/m ambient field strength)
Installations	All equipment should be provided and installed by qualified suppliers and installers to appropriate electrical and health and safety standards
Network connections	The equipment space should be flood-wired with adequate capacity for reasonable growth. All cables should be positioned and secured to appropriate cable trays
Disaster recovery	Fully tested recovery plans should be developed for all major data centres including the use of stand-by sites and equipment

Table E.4 Regional data centres and major equipment centres

Access	Secure controlled entry, combination lock, swipe card, video camera (if business critical and unattended)
Temperature	Temperature control, 22°C (± 5°C), preferable
Humidity control	Strict control: 50% (± 10%) preferable
Air quality	Positive pressure, filtered intake, low gaseous pollution (e.g. sulphur dioxide ≤ 0.14 ppm), dust levels for particles > 1 micron, less than 5 × 106 particles/m³. Auto shut-down on smoke or fire detection
Power	PDU with three-phase supply to non-switched boxes, one per piece of equipment, with appropriate rated circuit-breakers for each supply. Alternatively, approved power distribution strips can be used. Balanced three-phase loadings. Room UPS to ensure voltage supplied is within ± 5% of rating with minimal impulse, sags, surges and over/under voltage conditions
False floors	Antistatic, liftable floor tiles 600 × 600 mm on pedestals, with alternate pedestals screwed to the solid floor. Minimum of 600 mm clearance to solid floor. Floor loadings of up to 5 kN/m² with a recommended minimum of 3 m between false floor and ceiling
Internal walls	From false floor to ceiling, fire-resistant, but with air flow above and below floor level
Fire detection/ prevention	Generally fire detection but not suppression, although HSSD or VESDA multi-level alarm with auto FM200 (or alternative halon replacement) release on 'double-knock' detection may be included if business-critical systems are contained
Environmental detectors	For smoke, temperature, power, humidity, water and intruder with automated alarm capability
Lighting	Normal levels of ceiling lighting with emergency lighting on power failure
Power safety	Clean earth should be provided on the PDU and for all equipment. Clearly marked remote power-off buttons on each exit. Dirty power outlets, clearly marked, should also be supplied
Fire extinguishers	Sufficient electrical fire extinguishers with adequate signage and procedures
Vibration	Vibrations should be minimal within the complete area
Electromagnetic interference	Minimal interference should be present (1.5 V/m ambient field strength)
Installations	All equipment should be provided and installed by qualified suppliers and installers to appropriate electrical and health and safety standards
Network connections	The equipment space should be flood-wired with adequate capacity for reasonable growth. All cables should be positioned and secured to appropriate cable trays
Disaster recovery	Fully tested recovery plans should be developed for all regional data centres, including the use of stand-by sites and equipment where appropriate

Table E.5 Server or network equipment rooms

Access	Secure controlled entry, by combination lock, swipe card or lock and key. In some cases equipment may be contained in open offices in locked racks or cabinets
Temperature	Normal office environment, but if in closed/locked rooms adequate ventilation should be provided
Humidity control	Normal office environment
Air quality	Normal office environment
Power	Clean power supply with a UPS-supplied power to the complete rack
False floors	Recommended minimum of 3 m between floor and ceiling with all cables secured in multi-compartment trunking
Internal walls	Wherever possible all walls should be fire-resistant
Fire detection/prevention	Normal office smoke/fire detection systems, unless major concentrations of equipment
Environmental detectors	For smoke, power, intruder with audible alarm capability
Lighting	Normal levels of ceiling lighting with emergency lighting on power failure
Power safety	Clean earth should be provided for all equipment, with clearly marked power-off buttons
Fire extinguishers	Sufficient electrical fire extinguishers, with adequate signage and procedures
Vibration	Vibrations should be minimal within the complete area
Electromagnetic interference	Minimal interference should be present (1.5 V/m ambient field strength)
Installations	All equipment should be provided and installed by qualified suppliers and installers to appropriate electrical and health and safety standards
Network connections	The equipment space should be flood-wired with adequate capacity for reasonable growth. All cables should be positioned and secured to appropriate cable trays
Disaster recovery	Fully tested recovery plans should be developed where appropriate

Table E.6 Office environments

Access	All offices should have the appropriate secure access depending on the business, the information and the equipment contained within them
Lighting, temperature, humidity and air quality	A normal clean, comfortable and tidy office environment, conforming to the organization's health, safety and environmental requirements
Power	Clean power supply for all computer equipment, with UPS facilities if appropriate
False floors	Preferred if possible, but all cables should be contained within appropriate trunking
Fire detection/ prevention and extinguishers	Normal office smoke/fire detection systems and intruder alerting systems, unless there are major concentrations of equipment. Sufficient fire extinguishers of the appropriate type, with adequate signage and procedures
Network connections	The office space should preferably be flood-wired with adequate capacity for reasonable growth. All cables should be positioned and secured to appropriate cable trays. All network equipment should be secured in secure cupboards or cabinets
Disaster recovery	Fully tested recovery plans should be developed where appropriate

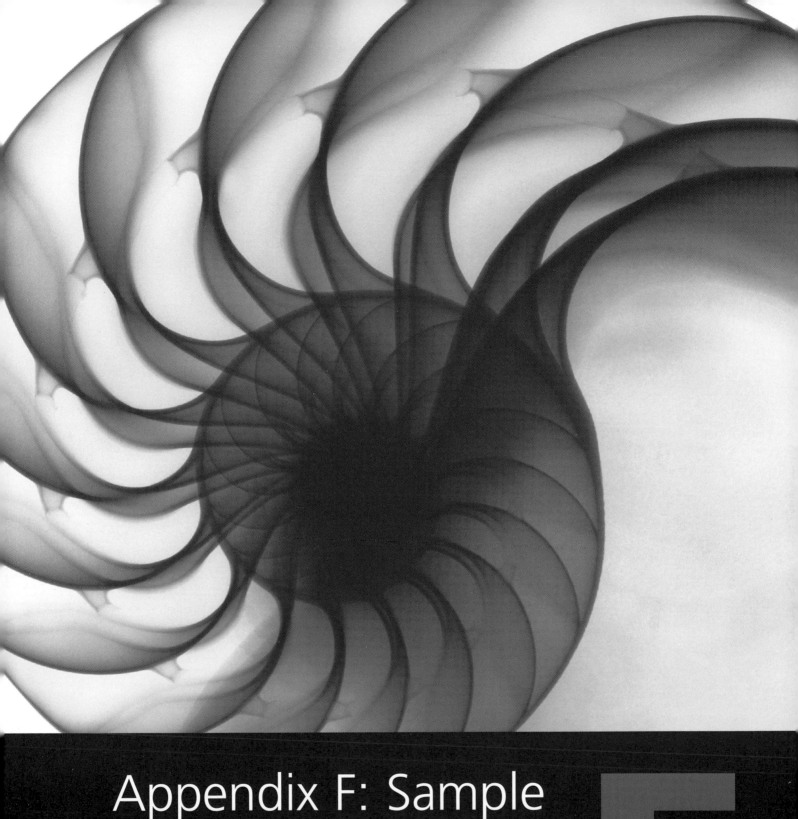

Appendix F: Sample service level agreement and operational level agreement

F

Appendix F: Sample service level agreement and operational level agreement

This appendix contains examples of a service level agreement (SLA) and an operational level agreement (OLA) and their contents. It is not recommended that every SLA or OLA should necessarily contain all of the sections listed within the following sample documents. It is suggested that these areas are considered when preparing document templates, but that they are only incorporated into the actual documents themselves where they are appropriate and relevant. So the following outlines should only be considered as guidelines or checklists.

F.1 SAMPLE SERVICE LEVEL AGREEMENT

This agreement is made between .... and ....

The agreement covers the provision and support of the ABC services which .... (brief service description).

This agreement remains valid for 12 months from (date) until (date). The agreement will be reviewed annually. Minor changes may be recorded on the form at the end of the agreement, provided they are mutually endorsed by the two parties and managed through the change management process.

Signatories:

Name .... Position .... Date ....

Name .... Position .... Date ....

Service description

The ABC service consists of .... (a fuller description to include key business functions, deliverables and all relevant information to describe the service and its scale, impact and priority for the business).

Scope of the agreement

What is covered within the agreement and what is excluded?

Service hours

A description of the hours that the customers can expect the service to be available (e.g. 7 × 24 × 365, 08:00 to 18:00, Monday to Friday).

Special conditions for exceptions (e.g. weekends, public holidays) and procedures for requesting service extensions (whom to contact – normally the service desk – and what notice periods are required).

This could include a service calendar or reference to a service calendar.

Details of any pre-agreed maintenance or housekeeping slots, if these impact on service hours, together with details of how any other potential outages must be negotiated and agreed – by whom and notice periods etc.

Procedures for requesting permanent changes to service hours.

Functionality (if appropriate)

Details of the minimal functionality to be provided and the number of errors of particular types that can be tolerated before the SLA is breached. Should include severity levels and the reporting period.

Service availability

The target availability levels that the IT service provider will seek to deliver within the agreed service hours. Availability targets within agreed service hours, normally expressed as percentages (e.g. 99.5%), measurement periods, method and calculations must be stipulated. This figure may be expressed for the overall service, supporting services and critical components or all three. However, it is difficult to relate such simplistic percentage availability figures to service quality, or to customer business activities. It is therefore often better to try to measure service unavailability in terms of the customer's inability to conduct its business activities. For example, 'sales are immediately affected by a failure of IT to provide an adequate Point of Sale (PoS) support service'. This strong link between the IT service and the customer's business processes is a sign of maturity in both the service level management and the availability management processes.

Agreed details of how and at what point this will be measured and reported, and over what agreed period, should also be documented.

Reliability

The maximum number of service breaks that can be tolerated within an agreed period (may be defined either as number of breaks (for example, four per annum) or as a mean time between failures (MTBFs) or mean time between service incidents (MTBSIs)).

Definition of what constitutes a 'break' and how these will be monitored and recorded.

Service performance

Details of the expected responsiveness of the IT service (such as target workstation response times for average, or maximum workstation response times, sometimes expressed as a percentile, e.g. 95% within two seconds), details of expected service throughput on which targets are based, and any thresholds that would invalidate the targets).

This should include indication of likely traffic volumes, throughput activity, constraints and dependencies (e.g. the number of transactions to be processed, number of concurrent users, and amount of data to be transmitted over the network). This is important so that performance issues that have been caused by excessive throughput outside the terms of the agreement may be identified.

Batch turnaround times

If appropriate, details of any batch turnaround times, completion times and key deliverables, including times for delivery of input and the time and place for delivery of output where appropriate.

Service continuity

Brief mention of and/or reference out to the organization's service continuity plans, together with details of how the SLA might be affected or reference to a separate continuity SLA, containing details of any diminished or amended service targets should a disaster situation occur. Details of any specific responsibilities on both sides (e.g. data backup, off-site storage). Also details of the invocation of plans and coverage of any security issues, particularly any customer responsibilities (e.g. coordination of business activities, business documentation, backup of freestanding PCs, password changes).

Security

Brief mention of and/or reference out to the organization's security policy (covering issues such as password controls, security violations, unauthorized software, viruses etc.). Details of any specific responsibilities on both sides (e.g. virus protection, firewalls).

Customer support

Details of how to contact the service desk, the hours it will be available, the hours support is available and what to do outside these hours to obtain assistance (e.g. on-call support, third-party assistance etc.) must be documented. The SLA may also include reference to internet/intranet self help and/or incident logging. Metrics and measurements should be included such as telephone call answer targets (number of rings, missed calls etc.)

Targets for incident response times (how long will it be before someone starts to assist the customer – may include travelling time etc.) should be provided. A definition is needed of 'response' (Is it a telephone call back to the customer or a site visit?) as appropriate.

Arrangements for requesting support extensions, including required notice periods (e.g. request must be made to the service desk by 12 noon for an evening extension, by 12 noon on Thursday for a weekend extension) should be specified. Note that:

- Both incident response and resolution times will be based on whatever incident impact/priority codes are used – details of the classification of incidents should also be included here.
- In some cases, it may be appropriate to reference out to third-party contacts and contracts and OLAs – but not as a way of diverting responsibility.

Contact points and escalation

Details of the contacts within each of the parties involved in the agreement and the escalation processes and contact points. This should also include the definition of a complaint and procedure for managing complaints.

Change management

Brief mention of and/or reference out to the organization's change management procedures that must be followed – just to reinforce compliance. Also targets for approving, handling and implementing requests for change, usually based on the category or urgency/priority of the change, should be included, as well as details of any known changes that will impact on the agreement, if any.

Printing

Details of any special conditions relating to printing or printers (e.g. print distribution details, notification of large centralized print runs, or handling of any special high-value stationery).

Responsibilities

Details of the responsibilities of the various parties involved within the service and their agreed responsibilities, including the service provider, the customer and the users.

Charging (if applicable)

Details of any charging formulas used, charging periods, or reference out to charging policy documents, together with invoicing procedures and payment conditions etc. must be included. This should also include details of any financial penalties or bonuses that will be paid if service targets do not meet expectations. What will the penalties/bonuses be and how will they be calculated, agreed and collected/paid (more appropriate for third-party situations)? If the SLA covers an outsourcing relationship, charges should be detailed in an appendix as they are often covered by commercial in-confidence provisions.

It should be noted that penalty clauses can create their own difficulties. They can prove a barrier to partnerships if unfairly invoked on a technicality and can also make service provider staff unwilling to admit to mistakes for fear of penalties being imposed. This can, unless used properly, be a barrier to developing effective relationships and problem solving.

Service reporting and reviewing

The content, frequency, timing and distribution of service reports, and the frequency of associated service review meetings. Also details of how and when SLAs and the associated service targets will be reviewed and possibly revised, including who will be involved and in what capacity.

Glossary

Explanation of any unavoidable abbreviations or terminology used, to assist customer understanding.

Amendment sheet

To include a record of any agreed amendments, with details of amendments, dates and signatories. It should also contain details of a complete change history of the document and its revisions.

It should be noted that the SLA contents given above are examples only. They should not be regarded as exhaustive or mandatory, but they provide a good starting point.

F.2   SAMPLE OPERATIONAL LEVEL AGREEMENT

This agreement is made between .... and ....

The agreement covers the provision of the support service providing .... (brief service description).

This agreement remains valid for 12 months from (date) until (date).

The agreement will be reviewed annually. Minor changes may be recorded on the form at the end of the agreement, provided they are mutually endorsed by the two parties and managed through the change management process.

Signatories:

Name .... Position .... Date ....

Name .... Position .... Date ....

Details of previous amendments

Support service description

Comprehensive explanation and details of the support service being provided.

Scope of the agreement

What is covered within the agreement and what is excluded.

Service hours

A description of the hours for which the support service is provided.

Service targets

The targets for the provision of the support service and the reporting and reviewing processes and frequency.

Contact points and escalation

Details of the contacts within each of the parties involved within the agreement, and the escalation processes and contact points.

Service desk and incident response times and responsibilities

The responsibilities and targets agreed for the progress and resolution of incidents and for support by the service desk.

Problem response times and responsibilities

The responsibilities and targets agreed for the progress and resolution of problems.

Change management

The responsibilities and targets agreed for the progress and implementation of changes.

Release and deployment management

The responsibilities and targets agreed for the progress and implementation of releases.

Service asset and configuration management

The responsibilities for the ownership, provision and maintenance of accurate service asset and configuration management information.

Information security management

The responsibilities and targets agreed for the support of the security policy(s) and the information security management process.

Availability management

Responsibility for ensuring that all components within their support domain are managed and supported to meet and continue to meet all of the service and component availability targets.

IT service continuity management

Responsibility for ensuring that all components within their support domain have up-to-date and tested recovery plans that support agreed and documented business requirements. This should include assistance with the technical assessment of risk and its subsequent management and mitigation.

Capacity management

Responsibility for supporting the needs of the capacity management process within the agreed scope of their technical domain.

Service level management

Assistance with the definition and agreement of appropriate targets within SLAs, service level requirements and OLAs, concerning components within the scope of their technical domain.

Supplier management

Assistance with the management of contracts and suppliers, again principally within the scope of their technical domain.

Provision of information

The provision and maintenance of accurate information, including financial data for all components within the agreed scope of their technical domain.

Glossary

Explanation of any unavoidable abbreviations or terminology used, to assist understanding of terms contained within the agreement.

Amendment sheet

To include a record of any agreed amendments, with details of amendments, dates and signatories. It should also contain details of a complete change history of the document and its revisions.

Appendix G: Service catalogue example

G

Appendix G: Service catalogue example

The service catalogue (Table G.1) is a key document containing valuable information on the complete set of services offered. It should preferably be stored as a set of 'service' configuration items within a configuration management system, maintained under change management. As it is such a valuable set of information, it should be available to anyone within the organization. Every new service should immediately be entered into the service catalogue once its initial definition of requirements has been documented and agreed. So as well as the information below, the service catalogue should record the status of every service, through the stages of its defined lifecycle.

Table G.1 Service catalogue example

Service name	Service description	Service type	Supporting services	Business owner(s)	Business unit(s)	Service owner(s)	Business impact	Business priority	Service level agreement	Service hours	Business contacts	Escalation contacts	Service reports	Service reviews	Security rating
Service 1															
Service 2															
Service 3															
Service 4															

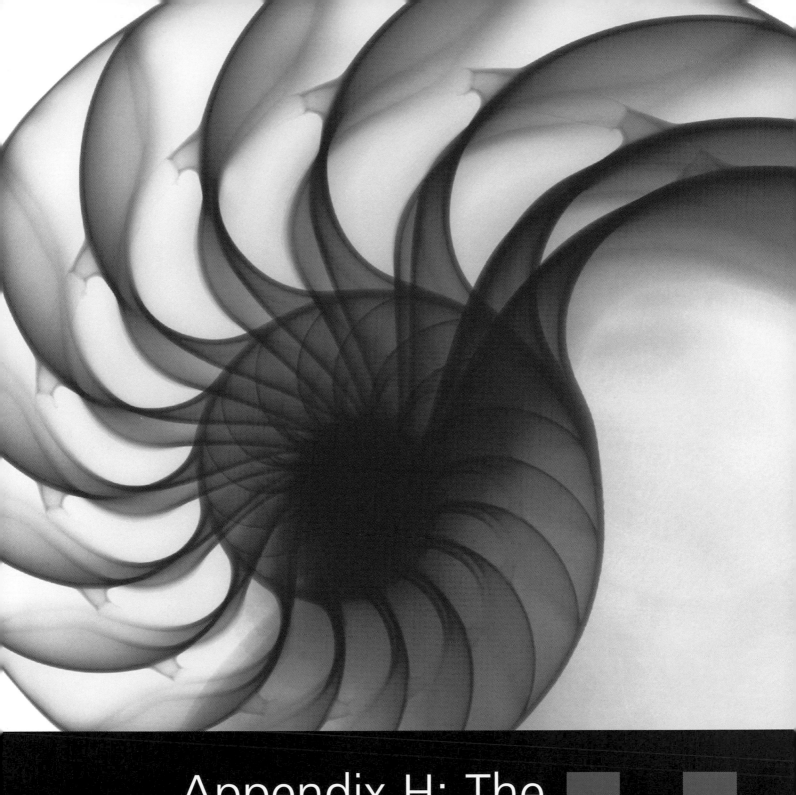

Appendix H: The service management process maturity framework

Appendix H: The service management process maturity framework

The process maturity framework (PMF) can be used either as a framework to assess the maturity of each of the service management processes individually, or to measure the maturity of the service management process as a whole. This is an approach that has been widely used in the IT industry for a number of years, with many proprietary models being used by a number of organizations. This particular PMF has been developed to bring a common, best-practice approach to the review and assessment of service management process maturity. This framework, which is shown in Figure 8.3, can be used by organizations to internally review their own service management processes as well as by third-party organizations brought in as external reviewers, assessors or auditors.

The use of the PMF in the assessment of service management processes relies on an appreciation of the IT organization growth model. The maturity of the service management processes is heavily dependent on the stage of growth of the IT organization as a whole. It is difficult, if not impossible, to develop the maturity of the service management processes beyond the maturity and capability of the overall IT organization. The maturity of the IT organization is not just dependent on the maturity of the service management processes. Each level requires a change of a combination of elements in order to be fully effective. Therefore a review of processes will require an assessment to be completed against the five areas of:

- Vision and steering
- Process
- People
- Technology
- Culture.

These are the five areas described within the PMF for assessing process maturity. The major characteristics of each level of the PMF are as follows.

H.1 INITIAL (LEVEL 1)

The process has been recognized but there is little or no process management activity and it is allocated no importance, resources or focus within the organization. This level can also be described as 'ad hoc' or occasionally even 'chaotic'. See Table H.1.

Table H.1 PMF level 1: initial

Vision and steering	Minimal funds and resources with little activity
	Results temporary, not retained
	Sporadic reports and reviews
Process	Loosely defined processes and procedures, used reactively when problems occur
	Totally reactive processes
	Irregular, unplanned activities
People	Loosely defined roles or responsibilities
Technology	Manual processes or a few specific, discrete tools (pockets/islands)
Culture	Tool and technology-based and driven with a strong activity focus

H.2 REPEATABLE (LEVEL 2)

The process has been recognized and is allocated little importance, resource or focus within the operation. Generally activities related to the process are uncoordinated, irregular, without direction and are directed towards process effectiveness. See Table H.2.

Table H.2 PMF Level 2: repeatable

Vision and steering	No clear objectives or formal targets
	Funds and resources available
	Irregular, unplanned activities, reporting and reviews
Process	Defined processes and procedures
	Largely reactive process
	Irregular, unplanned activities
People	Self-contained roles and responsibilities
Technology	Many discrete tools, but a lack of control
	Data stored in separate locations
Culture	Product- and service-based and driven

H.3 DEFINED (LEVEL 3)

The process has been recognized and is documented but there is no formal agreement, acceptance or recognition of its role within the IT operation as a whole. However, the process has a process owner, formal objectives and targets with allocated resources, and is focused on the efficiency as well as the effectiveness of the process. Reports and results are stored for future reference. See Table H.3.

Table H.3 PMF Level 3: defined

Vision and steering	Documented and agreed formal objectives and targets
	Formally published, monitored and reviewed plans
	Well-funded and appropriately resourced
	Regular, planned reporting and reviews
Process	Clearly defined and well-publicized processes and procedures
	Regular, planned activities
	Good documentation
	Occasionally proactive process
People	Clearly defined and agreed roles and responsibilities
	Formal objectives and targets
	Formalized process training plans
Technology	Continuous data collection with alarm and threshold monitoring
	Consolidated data retained and used for formal planning, forecasting and trending
Culture	Service- and customer-oriented with a formalized approach

H.4   MANAGED (LEVEL 4)

The process has now been fully recognized and accepted throughout IT. It is service-focused and has objectives and targets that are based on business objectives and goals. The process is fully defined, managed and has become proactive, with documented, established interfaces and dependencies with other IT process. See Table H.4.

Table H.4 PMF level 4: managed

Vision and steering	Clear direction with business goals, objectives and formal targets, measured progress
	Effective management reports actively used
	Integrated process plans linked to business and IT plans
	Regular improvements, planned and reviewed
Process	Well-defined processes, procedures and standards, included in all IT staff job descriptions
	Clearly defined process interfaces and dependencies
	Integrated service management and systems development processes
	Mainly proactive process
People	Inter- and intra-process team working
	Responsibilities clearly defined in all IT job descriptions
Technology	Continuous monitoring measurement, reporting and threshold alerting to a centralized set of integrated toolsets, databases and processes
Culture	Business-focused with an understanding of the wider issues

H.5   OPTIMIZING (LEVEL 5)

The process has now been fully recognized and has strategic objectives and goals aligned with overall strategic business and IT goals. These have now become 'institutionalized' as part of the everyday activity for everyone involved with the process. A self-contained continual process of improvement is established as part of the process, which is now developing a pre-emptive capability. See Table H.5.

Table H.5 PMF level 5: optimizing

Vision and steering	Integrated strategic plans inextricably linked with overall business plans, goals and objectives
	Continuous monitoring, measurement, reporting alerting and reviews linked to a continual process of improvement
	Regular reviews and/or audits for effectiveness, efficiency and compliance
Process	Well-defined processes and procedures part of corporate culture
	Proactive and pre-emptive process
People	Business aligned objectives and formal targets actively monitored as part of the everyday activity
	Roles and responsibilities part of an overall corporate culture
Technology	Well-documented overall tool architecture with complete integration in all areas of people, processes and technology
Culture	A continual improvement attitude, together with a strategic business focus. An understanding of the value of IT to the business and its role within the business value chain

This maturity framework is aligned with the Software Engineering Institute Capability Maturity Model® Integration (SEI CMMI) and its various maturity models including the evolving CMMI-SVC, which focuses on the delivery of services.

Appendix I: Example of the contents of a statement of requirements and/or invitation to tender

Appendix I: Example of the contents of a statement of requirements and/or invitation to tender

The following is an example of a minimum set of contents that should be included in an invitation to tender (ITT) or statement of requirements (SoR):

- A description of the services, products and/or components required
- All relevant technical specifications, details and requirements
- A service level requirement (SLR) where applicable
- Availability, reliability, maintainability and serviceability requirements
- Details of ownership of hardware, software, buildings, facilities etc.
- Details of performance criteria to be met by the equipment and the supplier(s)
- Details of all standards to be complied with (internal, external, national and international)
- Legal and regulatory requirements (industry, national, EU and international)
- Details of quality criteria
- Contractual timescales, details and requirements, terms and conditions
- All commercial considerations: costs, charges, bonus and penalty payments, and schedules
- Interfaces and contacts required
- Project management methods to be used
- Reporting, monitoring and reviewing procedures and criteria to be used during and after the implementation
- Supplier requirements and conditions
- Sub-contractor requirements
- Details of any relevant terms and conditions
- Description of the supplier response requirements:
  - Format
  - Criteria
  - Conditions
  - Timescales
  - Variances and omissions
  - Customer responsibilities and requirements
- Details of planned and possible growth
- Procedures for handling changes

Appendix J: Typical contents of a capacity plan J

Appendix J: Typical contents of a capacity plan

The typical contents of a capacity plan are as follows.

J.1 INTRODUCTION

This section briefly explains the background to this issue of the capacity plan, how it was produced and what it contains. For example:

- The current services, technology and resources
- The organization's current levels of capacity
- Problems being experienced or envisaged due to over- or under-capacity
- The degree to which service levels are being achieved
- What has changed since the last issue of the plan.

J.2 MANAGEMENT SUMMARY

Much of the capacity plan, by necessity, contains technical detail that is not of interest to all readers of the plan. The management summary should highlight the main issues, options, recommendations and costs. It may be necessary to produce a separate executive summary document that contains the main points from each of the sections of the main plan.

J.3 BUSINESS SCENARIOS

It is necessary to put the plan into the context of the current and envisaged business environment. For example, a British airline planned to move a large number of staff into its headquarters building. A ratio of 1.7 people per desktop terminal was forecast. Capacity management was alerted and was able to calculate the extra network traffic that would result.

It is important to mention explicitly all known business forecasts so that readers can determine what is within and what is outside the scope of the plan. It should include the anticipated growth in existing services, the potential new services and existing services scheduled for closure.

J.4 SCOPE AND TERMS OF REFERENCE OF THE PLAN

Ideally, the capacity plan should encompass all IT resources. This section should explicitly name those elements of the IT infrastructure that are included and those that are excluded, if any.

J.5 METHODS USED

The capacity plan uses information gathered by the sub-processes. This sub-section, therefore, should contain details of how and when this information was obtained – for example, business forecasts obtained from business plans, workload forecasts obtained from customers, service level forecasts obtained by the use of modelling tools.

J.6 ASSUMPTIONS MADE

It is important that any assumptions made, particularly those concerning the business drivers for IT capacity, are highlighted early on in the plan. If they are the cornerstones on which more detailed calculations are built, then it is vital that all concerned understand this.

J.7 SERVICE SUMMARY

The service summary section should include:

- **Current and recent service provision** For each service that is delivered, provide a service profile. This should include throughput rates and the resulting resource utilization, for example, of memory, storage space, transfer rates, processor usage and network usage. Short-, medium- and long-term trends should be presented here.
- **Service forecasts** The business plans should provide capacity management with details of the new services planned and the growth or contraction in the use of existing services. This sub-section should report on new services and the demise of legacy systems.

J.8   RESOURCE SUMMARY

The resource summary section should include:

- **Current and recent resource usage** This sub-section concentrates on the resulting resource usage by the services. It reports, again, on the short-, medium- and long-term trends in component usage, broken down by hardware platform. Information on component and other resource usage has been gathered and analysed by the sub-processes of service capacity management and component capacity management and so should be readily available.
- **Resource forecasts** This sub-section forecasts the likely resource usage resulting from the service forecasts. Each business scenario mentioned above should be addressed here. For example, a carpet wholesale business in the north of England could accurately predict what the peak and average processor usage would be before it decided to take over a rival business. It was proved that an upgrade would not be required. This was fed into the cost model, leading to a successful takeover.

J.9   OPTIONS FOR SERVICE IMPROVEMENT

Building on the results of the previous section, this section outlines the possible options for improving the effectiveness and efficiency of service delivery. It could contain options for merging different services on a single processor, upgrading the network to take advantage of technological advances, tuning the use of resource or service performance, rewriting legacy systems, purchasing new hardware or software etc.

J.10   COSTS FORECAST

The costs associated with these options should be documented here. In addition, the current and forecasted cost of providing IT services should be included. In practice, capacity management obtains much of this information from the financial management for IT services process and the IT financial plan.

J.11   RECOMMENDATIONS

The final section of the plan should contain a summary of the recommendations made in the previous plan and their status – for example, rejected, planned, implemented – and any variances from the plan. Any new recommendations should be made here, i.e. which of the options mentioned in the plan is preferred, and the implications if the plan and its recommendations are not implemented should also be included.

The recommendations should be quantified in terms of the:

- Business benefits to be expected
- Potential impact of carrying out the recommendations
- Risks involved
- Resources required
- Costs, both setup and ongoing.

Appendix K: Typical contents of a recovery plan

Appendix K: Typical contents of a recovery plan

The typical contents of an IT service continuity management recovery plan are as follows.

K.1 GENERIC RECOVERY PLAN

K.1.1 Document control

This document must be maintained to ensure that the systems, infrastructure and facilities included, appropriately support business recovery requirements.

K.1.1.1 Document distribution

Copy	Issued to	Date	Position
1.			
2.			
3.			
4.			

K.1.1.2 Document revision

This document will be reviewed every X months.

Current revision .... Date ....

Next revision .... Date ....

Revision date	Version no	Summary of changes

K.1.1.3 Document approval

This document must be approved by the following personnel:

Name	Title	Signature

K.1.1.4 Scope

The following describes what is in scope of this document and what is out of scope:

In scope of document:

Out of scope of document:

K.2 SUPPORTING INFORMATION

K.2.1 Introduction

This document details the instructions and procedures that are required to be followed to recover or continue the operation of systems, infrastructure, services or facilities to maintain service continuity to the level defined or agreed with the business.

K.2.2 Recovery strategy

The systems, infrastructure, services or facilities will be recovered to alternative systems, infrastructure, services or facilities.

It will take approximately X hours to recover the systems, infrastructure, services or facilities. The system will be recovered to the last known point of stability/data integrity, which is [point in day/timing].

The required recovery time for this system, infrastructure, service or facility is: ....

The recovery time and procedures for this system, infrastructure, service or facility was last tested on:

....

K.2.3 Invocation

The following personnel are authorized to invoke this plan:

1 ....

2 ....

K.2.4 Interfaces and dependencies on other plans

Details of the inter-relationships and references with all other continuity and recovery plans and how the interfaces are activated. Includes recovery prioritization between systems.

K.2.5 General guidance

All requests for information from the media or other sources should be referred to the company procedure.

When notifying personnel of a potential or actual disaster, follow the defined operational escalation procedures, and in particular:

- Be calm and avoid lengthy conversation
- Advise them of the need to refer information requests to escalation point
- Advise them of expectations and actions (avoid giving them details of the incident unless absolutely necessary)
- If the call is answered by somebody else:
  - Ask if the contact is available elsewhere
  - If they cannot be contacted, leave a message to contact you on a given number
  - Do not provide details of the incident
  - Always document call time details, responses and actions.

All activities and contact/escalation should be clearly and accurately recorded. To facilitate this, actions should be in a checklist format and there should be space to record the date and time the activity was started and completed, and who carried out the activity.

K.2.6 Dependencies

System, infrastructure, service, facility or interface dependencies should be documented (in priority order) so that related recovery plans or procedures that will need to be invoked in conjunction with this recovery plan can be identified and actioned. The person responsible for invocation should ensure recovery activities are coordinated with these other plans. Documented dependencies should include services/infrastructure dependent upon this system, and services/infrastructure that this system depends upon.

System	Document reference	Contact

K.2.7 Contact lists

Lists of all contact names, organizations and contact details and mechanisms:

Name	Organization/role	Title	Contact details

K.2.8 Recovery team

The following staff/functions are responsible for actioning these procedures or ensuring the procedures are actioned, and for recording any issues or problems encountered. Contact will be made via the normal escalation procedures.

Name	Title	Contact details

K.2.9 Recovery team checklist

To facilitate the execution of key activities in a timely manner, a checklist similar to the following should be used.

Task	Target completion	Actual completion
Confirm invocation		
Initiate call tree and escalation procedures		
Instigate and interface with any other recovery plans necessary (e.g. business continuity plan, crisis management, emergency response plan)		
Arrange for backup media and documentation to be shipped to recovery site(s)		
Establish recovery teams		
Initiate recovery actions		
Confirm progress reporting		
Inform recovery team of reporting requirements		
Confirm liaison requirements with all recovery teams		
Advise customers and management of estimated recovery completion		

K.3 RECOVERY PROCEDURE

Enter recovery instructions/procedures or references to all recovery procedures here.

Content/format should be in line with company standards for procedures. If there are none, guidance should be issued by the manager or team leader for the area responsible for the system, infrastructure, services or facility. The only guideline is that the instructions should be capable of being executed by an experienced professional without undue reliance on local knowledge.

Where necessary, references should be made to supporting documentation (and its location), diagrams and other information sources. This should include the document reference number (if it exists). It is the responsibility of the plan author to ensure that this information is maintained with this plan. If there is only a limited amount of supporting information, it may be easier for this to be included within the plan, providing this plan remains easy to read/follow and does not become too cumbersome.

Appendix L: Procurement documents

L

Appendix L: Procurement documents

Table L.1 lists the documents that are frequently utilized in the process of procuring services from an external supplier.

Table L.1 Procurement documents

Abbreviation	Document	Description
SoR	Statement of requirements	A document detailing all of the requirements for a product purchase, or a new or changed IT service
ToR	Terms of reference	A document specifying the requirements, scope, deliverables, resources and schedule for a project or activity
RFI	Request for information	A document sent to a broad base of potential suppliers soliciting responses for the purpose of gathering information supporting broad understanding. An RFI is frequently a preliminary for preparing for an RFP or RFQ, and can assist the requesting organization in developing a strategy and/or narrowing the field of potential suppliers
RFP	Request for proposal	A document inviting potential suppliers to submit a proposal on a specific commodity or service. An RFP describes the need of the requesting organization and specifies when and how responses are to be submitted and considered. Comparison of RFP responses can allow the requesting organization to evaluate different potential approaches to addressing their business need and further narrow the field of potential suppliers
RFQ	Request for quotation	A document sent to potential suppliers containing in exacting detail a list or description of all relevant parameters of an intended purchase and soliciting a competitive price. In contrast to an RFP, an RFQ provides information on the exact requirements of the requesting organization, allowing comparison of pricing across multiple suppliers
ITT	Invitation to tender	A document inviting short-listed suppliers to 'tender their services' through a formal, written document that is evaluated against specific criteria

Appendix M:
Risk assessment
and management

Appendix M: Risk assessment and management

This appendix contains basic information about several broadly known and used approaches to the assessment and management of risk. It is not intended to be a comprehensive study of the subject, but rather to provide an awareness of some of the methods in use.

M.1 DEFINITION OF RISK AND RISK MANAGEMENT

Risk may be defined as uncertainty of outcome, whether a positive opportunity or negative threat. It is the fact that there is uncertainty that creates the need for attention and formal management of risk. After all, if an organization were absolutely certain that a negative threat would materialize, there would be little difficulty in determining an appropriate course of action. Likewise, if an organization could be guaranteed that the positive opportunity would be realized, then its path would be clear. Managing risks requires the identification and control of the exposure to those risks which may have an impact on the achievement of an organization's business objectives.

Every organization manages its risk, but not always in a way that is visible, repeatable and consistently applied to support decision-making. The purpose of formal risk management is to enable better decision-making based on a sound understanding of risks and their likely impact on the achievement of objectives. An organization can gain this understanding by ensuring that it makes cost-effective use of a risk framework that has a series of well-defined steps. Decision-making should include determining any appropriate actions to take to manage the risks to a level deemed to be acceptable by the organization.

A number of different methodologies, standards and frameworks have been developed for risk management. Some focus more on generic techniques widely applicable to different levels and needs, while others are specifically concerned with risk management relating to important assets used by the organization in the pursuit of its objectives. Each organization should determine the approach to risk management that is best suited to its needs and circumstances, and it is possible that the approach adopted will leverage the ideas reflected in more than one of the recognized standards and/or frameworks.

In this appendix the following approaches to managing risks are briefly explained:

- Management of Risk (M_o_R)
- ISO 31000
- ISO/IEC 27001
- Risk IT.

M.2 MANAGEMENT OF RISK (M_o_R)

Management of Risk (M_o_R) is intended to help organizations put in place an effective framework for risk management. This will help them take informed decisions about the risks that affect their strategic, programme, project and operational objectives.

M_o_R provides a route map of risk management, bringing together principles, an approach, a process with a set of interrelated steps and pointers to more detailed sources of advice on risk management techniques and specialisms. It also provides advice on how these principles, approach and process should be embedded, reviewed and applied differently depending on the nature of the objectives at risk.

The M_o_R framework is illustrated in Figure M.1.

The M_o_R framework is based on four core concepts:

- **M_o_R principles** Principles are essential for the development and maintenance of good risk management practice. They are informed by corporate governance principles and the international standard for risk management, ISO 31000: 2009. They are high-level and universally applicable statements that provide guidance to organizations as they design an appropriate approach to risk management as part of their internal controls.

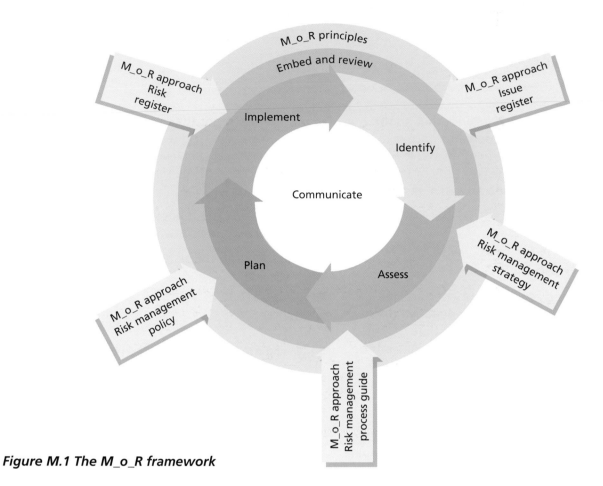

Figure M.1 The M_o_R framework

- **M_o_R approach** Principles need to be adapted and adopted to suit each individual organization. An organization's approach to the principles needs to be agreed and defined within a risk management policy, process guide and strategies.

- **M_o_R process** The process is divided into four main steps: identify, assess, plan and implement. Each step describes the inputs, outputs, tasks and techniques involved to ensure that the overall process is effective.

- **Embedding and reviewing M_o_R** Having put in place an approach and process that satisfy the principles, an organization should ensure that they are consistently applied across the organization and that their application undergoes continual improvement in order for them to be effective.

There are several common techniques which support risk management, including a summary risk profile. A summary risk profile is a graphical representation of information normally found in an existing risk register, and helps to increase the visibility of risks. For more information on summary risk profiles and other M_o_R techniques, see *Management of Risk: Guidance for Practitioners* (OGC, 2010).

M.3 ISO 31000

ISO 31000 was published in November 2009 and is the first set of international guidelines for risk management, intended to be applicable and adaptable for 'any public, private or community enterprise, association, group or individual.' ISO 31000 is a process-oriented rather than a control-oriented approach to risk management, and provides guidance on a broader, more conceptual basis, rather than specifying all aspects of an organization's risk assessment and management approach. For example, ISO 31000 does not define how an organization will create risk data or measure risk, nor does it ensure that an organization will include a review of all risk areas relevant to the achievement of their objectives. ISO 31000 was published as a standard without certification.

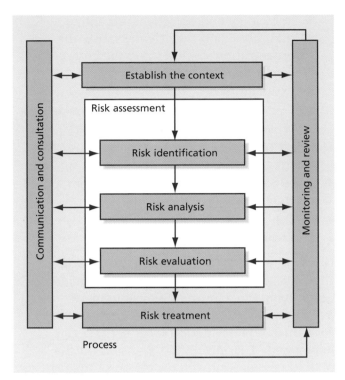

Figure M.2 ISO 31000 risk management process flow

ISO 31000 defines risk as 'the effect of uncertainty on objectives'. Risk management should be performed within a framework that provides the foundations and provisions which will embed the management of risk throughout all levels of the organization. ISO 31000 identifies the necessary components of such a framework as:

- Mandate and commitment
- Design of framework for managing risk
- Understanding the organization and its context
- Establishing risk management policy
- Accountability
- Integration into organizational processes
- Resources
- Establishing internal communication and reporting mechanisms
- Establishing external communication and reporting mechanisms
- Implementing risk management
- Monitoring and review of the framework
- Continual improvement of the framework.

Within this context the risk management process is seen at a high level in Figure M.2.

Once the framework has been established and the context understood, risk assessment is undertaken. This consists of three steps: risk identification, risk

analysis and risk evaluation. The risk identification step is intended to create a comprehensive list of risks based on those events that might create, enhance, prevent, degrade, accelerate or delay the achievement of the organization's objectives. Risk analysis involves developing a full understanding of the risks as an input to risk evaluation and the decisions regarding the plan for treating the risks. Risk evaluation is to make decisions about which risks require treatment and the relative priorities amongst them.

Risk treatment involves the modification of risks using one or more approaches. These approaches are not necessarily mutually exclusive and may include:

- Avoiding the risk by deciding not to start or continue with the activity that gives rise to the risk
- Taking or increasing the risk in order to pursue an opportunity
- Removing the risk source
- Changing the likelihood
- Changing the consequences
- Sharing the risk with another party or parties (including contracts and risk financing)
- Retaining the risk by informed decision.

The approach described in ISO 31000 provides broad scope for each organization to adopt the high-level principles and adapt them to their specific needs and circumstances.

M.4 ISO/IEC 27001

ISO/IEC 27001 was published in October 2005 and is an information security management system (ISMS) standard which formally specifies a management system that is intended to bring information security under explicit management control. While ISO/IEC 27001 is a security standard, not a risk management standard, it mandates specific requirements for security, including requirements relating to risk management. The risk management methods described in this context may be applied to general risk management activities as well.

ISO/IEC 27001 requires that management:

- Systematically examines the organization's information security risks, taking account of the threats, vulnerabilities and impacts

- Designs and implements a coherent and comprehensive suite of information security controls and/or other forms of risk treatment (such as risk avoidance or risk transfer) to address those risks that are deemed unacceptable
- Adopts an overarching management process to ensure that the information security controls continue to meet the organization's information security needs on an ongoing basis.

The key risk management-related steps described in ISO/IEC 27001 include:

- Define the risk assessment approach of the organization
- Identify a risk assessment methodology that is suited to the ISMS, and the identified business information security, legal and regulatory requirements
- Develop criteria for accepting risks and identify acceptable levels of risk
- Identify the risks
- Identify the assets within the scope of the ISMS, and the owners of these assets
- Identify the threats to these assets
- Identify the vulnerabilities that might be exploited by the threats
- Identify the impact that losses of confidentiality, integrity and availability may have on these assets
- Analyse and evaluate the risks
- Assess the business impacts on the organization that might result from security failures, taking into account the consequences of a loss of confidentiality, integrity or availability of the assets
- Assess the realistic likelihood of security failures occurring in the light of prevailing threats and vulnerabilities, and impacts associated with these assets, and the controls currently implemented
- Estimate the levels of risk
- Determine whether the risks are acceptable or require treatment using the previously established criteria for accepting risks
- Identify and evaluate options for the treatment of risks. Possible actions may include:
  - Applying appropriate controls

- Knowingly and objectively accepting risks, providing they clearly satisfy the organization's policies and the criteria for accepting risks
- Avoiding risks
- Transferring the associated business risks to other parties, e.g. insurers, suppliers
- Select control objectives and controls for the treatment of risks
- Obtain management approval of the proposed residual risks
- Obtain management authorization to implement and operate the ISMS.

During the implementation and operation of the ISMS, a plan for risk treatment is formulated (identifying the appropriate management action, resources, responsibilities and priorities for managing information security risks) and implemented. ISO/IEC 27001 also calls for the ongoing monitoring and reviewing of the risks and risk treatment and the formal maintenance of the ISMS to ensure that the organization's goals are met.

This approach is focused specifically on the assets involved in organizational information security, but the general principles can be applied to overall service provision.

M.5   RISK IT

Risk IT is part of the IT governance product portfolio of ISACA that provides a framework for effective governance and management of IT risk, based on a set of guiding principles. Risk IT is about IT risk, including business risk related to the use of IT. The publications in which Risk IT is documented include *The Risk IT Framework* (ISACA, 2009) and *The Risk IT Practitioner Guide* (ISACA, 2009) (available from www.isaca.org).

The key principles in Risk IT are that effective enterprise governance and management of IT risk:

- Always connect to the business objectives
- Align the management of IT-related business risk with overall enterprise risk management
- Balance the costs and benefits of managing IT risk
- Promote fair and open communication of IT risk

- Establish the right tone from the top while defining and enforcing personal accountability for operating within acceptable and well-defined tolerance levels
- Are continuous processes and part of daily activities.

The framework provides for three domains, each containing three processes, as shown in Figure M.3. *The Risk IT Framework* describes the key activities of each process, the responsibilities for the process, information flows between the processes and the performance management of each process.

Risk governance ensures that IT risk management practices are embedded in the enterprise, enabling it to secure optimal risk-adjusted return. Risk evaluation ensures that IT-related risks and opportunities are identified, analysed and presented in business terms. Risk response ensures that IT-related risk issues, opportunities and events are addressed in a cost-effective manner and in line with business priorities.

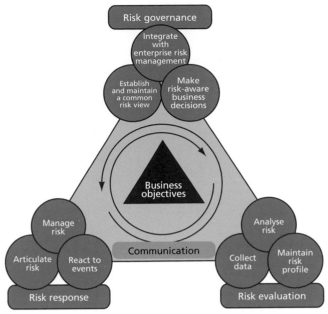

Figure M.3 ISACA Risk IT process framework

Appendix N:
Related guidance

Appendix N: Related guidance

This is a common appendix across the ITIL core publications. It includes frameworks, best practices, standards, models and quality systems that complement and have synergy with the ITIL service lifecycle.

Section 2.1.7 describes the role of best practices in the public domain and references some of the publications in this appendix. Each core publication references this appendix where relevant.

Related guidance may also be referenced within a single ITIL core publication where the topic is specific to that publication.

N.1   ITIL GUIDANCE AND WEB SERVICES

ITIL is part of the Best Management Practice (BMP) portfolio of best-practice guidance (see section 1.3). BMP products present flexible, practical and effective guidance, drawn from a range of the most successful global business experiences. Distilled to its essential elements, the guidance can then be applied to every type of business and organization.

The BMP website (www.best-management-practice.com) includes news, reviews, case studies and white papers on ITIL and all other BMP best-practice guidance.

The ITIL official website (www.itil-officialsite.com) contains reliable, up-to-date information on ITIL – including information on accreditation and the ITIL software scheme for the endorsement of ITIL-based tools.

Details of the core publications are as follows:

- Cabinet Office (2011). *ITIL Service Strategy*. TSO, London.
- Cabinet Office (2011). *ITIL Service Design*. TSO, London.
- Cabinet Office (2011). *ITIL Service Transition*. TSO, London.
- Cabinet Office (2011). *ITIL Service Operation*. TSO, London.
- Cabinet Office (2011). *ITIL Continual Service Improvement*. TSO, London.

The full ITIL glossary, in English and other languages, can be accessed through the ITIL official site at:

www.itil-officialsite.com/InternationalActivities/ITILGlossaries.aspx

The range of translated glossaries is always growing, so check this website for the most up-to-date list.

Details of derived and complementary publications can be found in the publications library of the Best Management Practice website at:

www.best-management-practice.com/Publications-Library/IT-Service-Management-ITIL/

N.2   QUALITY MANAGEMENT SYSTEM

Quality management focuses on product/service quality as well as the quality assurance and control of processes to achieve consistent quality. Total Quality Management (TQM) is a methodology for managing continual improvement by using a quality management system. TQM establishes a culture involving all people in the organization in a process of continual monitoring and improvement.

ISO 9000:2005 describes the fundamentals of quality management systems that are applicable to all organizations which need to demonstrate their ability to consistently provide products that meet customer and applicable statutory and regulatory requirements. ISO 9001:2008 specifies generic requirements for a quality management system.

Many process-based quality management systems use the methodology known as 'Plan-Do-Check-Act' (PDCA), often referred to as the Deming Cycle, or Shewhart Cycle, that can be applied to all processes. PDCA can be summarized as:

- **Plan** Establish the objectives and processes necessary to deliver results in accordance with customer requirements and the organization's policies.
- **Do** Implement the processes.
- **Check** Monitor and measure processes and product against policies, objectives and requirements for the product and report the results.

■ **Act** Take actions to continually improve process performance.

There are distinct advantages of tying an organization's ITSM processes, and service operation processes in particular, to its quality management system. If an organization has a formal quality management system that complies with ISO 9001, then this can be used to assess progress regularly and drive forward agreed service improvement initiatives through regular reviews and reporting.

Visit www.iso.org for information on ISO standards.

See www.deming.org for more information on the W. Edwards Deming Institute and the Deming Cycle for process improvement.

N.3   RISK MANAGEMENT

A number of different methodologies, standards and frameworks have been developed for the assessment and management of risk. Some focus more on generic techniques widely applicable to different levels and needs, while others are specifically concerned with risk management relating to important assets used by the organization in the pursuit of its objectives. Each organization should determine the approach to risk management that is best suited to its needs and circumstances. It is possible that the approach adopted will leverage the ideas reflected in more than one of the recognized standards and/or frameworks.

Appendix M gives more information on risk management. See also:

■ Office of Government Commerce (2010). *Management of Risk*: *Guidance for Practitioners*. TSO, London.
■ ISO 31000:2009 Risk management – principles and guidelines.
■ ISO/IEC 27001: 2005 Information technology – security techniques – information security management systems – requirements.
■ ISACA (2009). *The Risk IT Framework* (based on COBIT, see section N.5).

N.4   GOVERNANCE OF IT

Corporate governance refers to the rules, policies, processes (and in some cases, laws) by which businesses are operated, regulated and controlled. These are often defined by the board or shareholders, or the constitution of the organization; but they can also be defined by legislation, regulation or consumer groups.

ISO 9004 (Managing for the sustained success of an organization – a quality management approach) provides guidance on governance for the board and executive of an organization.

The standard for corporate governance of IT is ISO/IEC 38500. The purpose of this standard is to promote effective, efficient and acceptable use of IT in all organizations by:

■ Assuring stakeholders (including consumers, shareholders and employees) that, if the standard is followed, they can have confidence in the organization's corporate governance of IT
■ Informing and guiding directors in governing the use of IT in their organization
■ Providing a basis for objective evaluation of the corporate governance of IT.

Typical examples of regulations that impact IT include: financial, safety, data protection, privacy, software asset management, environment management and carbon emission targets.

Further details are available at www.iso.org

ITIL Service Strategy references the concepts of ISO/IEC 38500 and how the concepts can be applied.

N.5   COBIT

The Control OBjectives for Information and related Technology (COBIT) is a governance and control framework for IT management created by ISACA and the IT Governance Institute (ITGI).

COBIT is based on the analysis and harmonization of existing IT standards and good practices and conforms to generally accepted governance principles. It covers five key governance focus areas: strategic alignment, value delivery, resource management, risk management and performance management. COBIT is primarily aimed at internal and external stakeholders within an enterprise who wish to generate value from IT investments;

those who provide IT services; and those who have a control/risk responsibility.

COBIT and ITIL are not 'competitive', nor are they mutually exclusive – on the contrary, they can be used in conjunction as part of an organization's overall governance and management framework. COBIT is positioned at a high level, is driven by business requirements, covers the full range of IT activities, and concentrates on *what* should be achieved rather than *how* to achieve effective governance, management and control. ITIL provides an organization with best-practice guidance on *how* to manage and improve its processes to deliver high-quality, cost-effective IT services. The following COBIT guidance supports strategy management and continual service improvement (CSI):

■ COBIT maturity models can be used to benchmark and drive improvement.
■ Goals and metrics can be aligned to the business goals for IT and used to create an IT management dashboard.
■ The COBIT 'monitor and evaluate' (ME) process domain defines the processes needed to assess current IT performance, IT controls and regulatory compliance.

Further details are available at www.isaca.org and www.itgi.org

N.6 ISO/IEC 20000 SERVICE MANAGEMENT SERIES

ISO/IEC 20000 is an internationally recognized standard for ITSM covering service providers who manage and deliver IT-enabled services to internal or external customers. ISO/IEC 20000-1 is aligned with other ISO management systems standards such as ISO 9001 and ISO/IEC 27001.

One of the most common routes for an organization to achieve the requirements of ISO/IEC 20000 is by adopting ITIL best practices. ISO/IEC 20000-1 is based on a service management system (SMS). The SMS is defined as a management system to direct and control the service management activities of the service provider. ISO/IEC 20000 includes:

■ ISO/IEC 20000-1:2005 – Information technology – Service management – Part 1: Specification

■ ISO/IEC 20000-1:2011 – Information technology – Service management – Part 1: Requirements for a service management system (the most recent edition of the ISO/IEC 20000 standard)
■ ISO/IEC 20000-2:2005 – Information technology – Service management – Part 2: Code of practice (being updated to include guidance on the application of service management systems and to support ISO/IEC 20000-1:2011)
■ ISO/IEC 20000-3:2005 – Information technology – Service management – Part 3: Scope and applicability
■ ISO/IEC TR 20000-4 – Information technology – Service management – Part 4: Process reference model
■ ISO/IEC TR 20000-5:2010 – Information technology – Service management – Part 5: Exemplar implementation plan for ISO/IEC 20000-1.

A closely related publication that is under development is ISO/IEC TR 15504-8 – Process assessment model for IT service management.

Further details can be found at www.iso.org or www.isoiec20000certification.com

Organizations using ISO/IEC 20000-1: 2005 for certification audits will transfer to the new edition, ISO/IEC 20000-1: 2011.

ITIL guidance supports organizations that are implementing service management practices to achieve the requirements of ISO/IEC 20000-1: 2005 and the new edition ISO/IEC 20000-1: 2011.

Other references include:

■ Dugmore, J. and Lacy, S. (2011). *Introduction to ISO/IEC 20000 Series: IT Service Management*. British Standards Institution, London.
■ Dugmore, J. and Lacy, S. (2011). *BIP 0005: A Manager's Guide to Service Management* (6th edition). British Standards Institution, London.

N.7 ENVIRONMENTAL MANAGEMENT AND GREEN/SUSTAINABLE IT

The transition to a low-carbon economy is a global challenge. Many governments have set targets to reduce carbon emissions or achieve carbon neutrality. IT is an enabler for environmental and cultural change that will help governments to achieve their targets – for example, through enabling tele- and video-conferencing, and remote and home working. However, IT is also a major user of energy and natural resources. Green IT refers to environmentally sustainable computing where the use and disposal of computers and printers are carried out in sustainable ways that do not have a negative impact on the environment.

Appendix E includes further information on environmental architectures and standards. Appendix E in *ITIL Service Operation* also provides useful considerations for facilities management, including environmental aspects.

The ISO 14001 series of standards for an environment management system is designed to assure internal and external stakeholders that the organization is an environmentally responsible organization. It enables an organization of any size or type to:

- Identify and control the environmental impact of its activities, products or services
- Improve its environmental performance continually
- Implement a systematic approach to setting and achieving environmental objectives and targets, and then demonstrating that they have been achieved.

Further details are available at www.iso.org

N.8 ISO STANDARDS AND PUBLICATIONS FOR IT

ISO 9241 is a series of standards and guidance on the ergonomics of human system interaction that cover people working with computers. It covers aspects that impact the utility of a service (whether it is fit for purpose) such as:

- ISO 9241-11:1999 Guidance on usability
- ISO 9241-210:2010 Human-centred design for interactive systems
- ISO 9241-151:2008 Guidance on world wide web user interfaces.

ISO/IEC JTC1 is Joint Technical Committee 1 of ISO and the International Electrotechnical Commission (IEC). It deals with information technology standards and other publications.

SC27 is a subcommittee under ISO/IEC JTC1 that develops ISO/IEC 27000, the information security management system (ISMS) family of standards. For further details, Appendix M includes information

on ISO/IEC 27001. SC7 is a subcommittee under ISO/IEC JTC1 that covers the standardization of processes, supporting tools and supporting technologies for the engineering of systems, services and software. SC7 publications include:

- ISO/IEC 20000 Information technology – service management (see section N.6)
- ISO/IEC 19770-1 Information technology – software asset management processes. ISO/IEC 19770-2:2009 establishes specifications for tagging software to optimize its identification and management
- ISO/IEC 15288 Systems and software engineering – systems life cycle processes. The processes can be used as a basis for establishing business environments – e.g. methods, procedures, techniques, tools and trained personnel
- ISO/IEC 12207 Systems and software engineering – software life cycle processes
- ISO/IEC 15504 Process assessment series. Also known as SPICE (software process improvement and capability determination), it aims to ensure consistency and repeatability of the assessment ratings with evidence to substantiate the ratings. The series includes exemplar process assessment models (PAM), related to one or more conformant or compliant process reference model (PRM). ISO/IEC 15504-8 is an exemplar process assessment model for IT service management that is under development
- ISO/IEC 25000 series – provides guidance for the use of standards named Software product Quality Requirements and Evaluation (SQuaRE)
- ISO/IEC 42010 Systems and software engineering — recommended practice for architectural description of software-intensive systems.

SC7 is working on the harmonization of standards in the service management, software and IT systems domains. Further details are available at www.iso.org

N.9 ITIL AND THE OSI FRAMEWORK

At around the time that ITIL V1 was being written, the International Standards Organization launched an initiative that resulted in the Open Systems Interconnection (OSI) framework. Since this initiative covered many of the same areas as ITIL V1, it is not surprising that there was considerable overlap.

However, it is also not surprising that they classified their processes differently, used different terminology, or used the same terminology in different ways. To confuse matters even more, it is common for different groups in an organization to use terminology from both ITIL and the OSI framework.

The OSI framework made significant contributions to the definition and execution of ITSM programmes and projects around the world. It has also caused a great deal of debate between teams that do not realize the origins of the terminology that they are using. For example, some organizations have two change management departments – one following the ITIL change management process and the other using the OSI installation, moves, additions and changes (IMAC) model. Each department is convinced that it is completely different from the other, and that it is performing a different role. Closer examination will reveal that there are several areas of commonality.

In service operation, the management of known errors may be mapped to fault management. There is also a section related to operational capacity management, which can be related to the OSI concept of performance management.

Information on the set of ISO standards for the OSI framework is available at: www.iso.org

N.10 PROGRAMME AND PROJECT MANAGEMENT

Large, complex deliveries are often broken down into manageable, interrelated projects. For those managing this overall delivery, the principles of programme management are key to delivering on time and within budget. Best management practice in this area is found in *Managing Successful Programmes* (MSP).

Guidance on effective *portfolio, programme and project management is brought together in Portfolio, Programme and Project Offices (P3O), which* is aimed at helping organizations to establish and maintain appropriate business support structures with proven roles and responsibilities.

Structured project management methods, such as PRINCE2 (PRojects IN Controlled Environments) or the Project Management Body of Knowledge

(PMBOK) developed by the Project Management Institute (PMI), can be used when improving IT services. Not all improvements will require a structured project approach, but many will, due to the sheer scope and scale of the improvement. Project management is discussed in more detail in *ITIL Service Transition*.

Visit www.msp-officialsite.com for more information on MSP.

Visit www.p3o-officialsite.com for more information on P3O.

Visit www.prince-officialsite.com for more information on PRINCE2.

Visit www.pmi.org for more information on PMI and PMBOK.

See also the following publications:

- Cleland, David I. and Ireland, Lewis R. (2006). *Project Management: Strategic Design and Implementation* (5th edition). McGraw-Hill Professional.
- Haugan, Gregory T. (2006). *Project Management Fundamentals*. Management Concepts.
- Office of Government Commerce (2009). *Managing Successful Projects with PRINCE2*. TSO, London.
- Cabinet Office (2011). *Managing Successful Programmes*. TSO, London.
- Office of Government Commerce (2008). *Portfolio, Programme and Project Offices*. TSO, London.
- The Project Management Institute (2008). *A Guide to the Project Management Body of Knowledge* (PMBOK Guide) (4th edition). Project Management Institute.

N.11 ORGANIZATIONAL CHANGE

There is a wide range of publications that cover organizational change including the related guidance for programme and project management referred to in the previous section.

Chapter 5 in *ITIL Service Transition* covers aspects of organizational change elements that are an essential part of, or a strong contributor towards, service transition. *ITIL Service Transition* and *ITIL Continual Service Improvement* refer to Kotter's 'eight steps for organizational change'.

Visit www.johnkotter.com for more information. See also the following publications:

- Kotter, John P. (1996). *Leading Change*. Harvard Business School Press.
- Kotter, John P. (1999) *What Leaders Really Do*. Harvard Business School Press.
- Kotter, J. P. (2000). Leading change: why transformation efforts fail. *Harvard Business Review* January–February.
- Kotter, John P. and Cohen, Dan S. (2002) *The Heart of Change: Real-Life Stories of How People Change their Organizations*. Harvard Business School Press.
- Kotter, J. P. and Schlesinger, L. C. (1979). Choosing strategies for change. *Harvard Business Review* Vol. 57, No. 2, p.106.
- Kotter, John P., Rathgeber, Holger, Mueller, Peter and Johnson, Spenser (2006). *Our Iceberg Is Melting: Changing and Succeeding Under Any Conditions*. St. Martin's Press.

N.12 SKILLS FRAMEWORK FOR THE INFORMATION AGE

The Skills Framework for the Information Age (SFIA) enables employers of IT professionals to carry out a range of human resource activities against a common framework including a skills audit, planning future skill requirements, development programmes, standardization of job titles and functions, and resource allocation.

SFIA provides a standardized view of the wide range of professional skills needed by people working in IT. SFIA is constructed as a simple two-dimensional matrix consisting of areas of work on one axis and levels of responsibility on the other. It uses a common language and a sensible, logical structure that can be adapted to the training and development needs of a very wide range of businesses.

Visit www.sfia.org.uk for further details.

N.13 CARNEGIE MELLON: CMMI AND ESCM FRAMEWORK

The Capability Maturity Model Integration (CMMI) is a process improvement approach developed by the Software Engineering Institute (SEI) of Carnegie Mellon University. CMMI provides organizations with the essential elements of effective processes. It can be used to guide process improvement across a project, a division or an entire organization. CMMI helps integrate traditionally separate organizational functions, sets process improvement goals and priorities, provides guidance for quality processes, and suggests a point of reference for appraising current processes. There are several CMMI models covering different domains of application.

The eSourcing Capability Model for Service Providers (eSCM-SP) is a framework developed by ITSqc at Carnegie Mellon to improve the relationship between IT service providers and their customers.

Organizations can be assessed against CMMI models using SCAMPI (Standard CMMI Appraisal Method for Process Improvement).

For more information, see www.sei.cmu.edu/cmmi/

N.14 BALANCED SCORECARD

A new approach to strategic management was developed in the early 1990s by Drs Robert Kaplan (Harvard Business School) and David Norton. They named this system the 'balanced scorecard'. Recognizing some of the weaknesses and vagueness of previous management approaches, the balanced scorecard approach provides a clear prescription as to what companies should measure in order to 'balance' the financial perspective. The balanced scorecard suggests that the organization be viewed from four perspectives, and it is valuable to develop metrics, collect data and analyse the organization relative to each of these perspectives:

- The learning and growth perspective
- The business process perspective
- The customer perspective
- The financial perspective.

Some organizations may choose to use the balanced scorecard method as a way of assessing and reporting their IT quality performance in general and their service operation performance in particular.

Further details are available through the balanced scorecard user community at www.scorecardsupport.com

N.15 SIX SIGMA

Six Sigma is a data-driven process improvement approach that supports continual improvement. It is business-output-driven in relation to customer specification. The objective is to implement a measurement-oriented strategy focused on process improvement and defects reduction. A Six Sigma defect is defined as anything outside customer specifications.

Six Sigma focuses on dramatically reducing process variation using statistical process control (SPC) measures. The fundamental objective is to reduce errors to fewer than 3.4 defects per million executions (regardless of the process). Service providers must determine whether it is reasonable to expect delivery at a Six Sigma level given the wide variation in IT deliverables, roles and tasks within IT operational environments.

There are two primary sub-methodologies within Six Sigma: DMAIC (Define, Measure, Analyse, Improve, Control) and DMADV (Define, Measure, Analyse, Design, Verify). DMAIC is an improvement method for existing processes for which performance does not meet expectations, or for which incremental improvements are desired. DMADV focuses on the creation of new processes. For more information, see:

- George, Michael L. (2003). *Lean Six Sigma for Service: How to Use Lean Speed and Six Sigma Quality to Improve Services and Transactions*. McGraw-Hill.
- Pande, Pete and Holpp, Larry (2001) *What Is Six Sigma?* McGraw-Hill.
- Pande, Peter S., Neuman, Robert P. and Cavanagh, Roland R. (2000). *The Six Sigma Way: How GE, Motorola, and Other Top Companies are Honing their Performance*. McGraw-Hill.

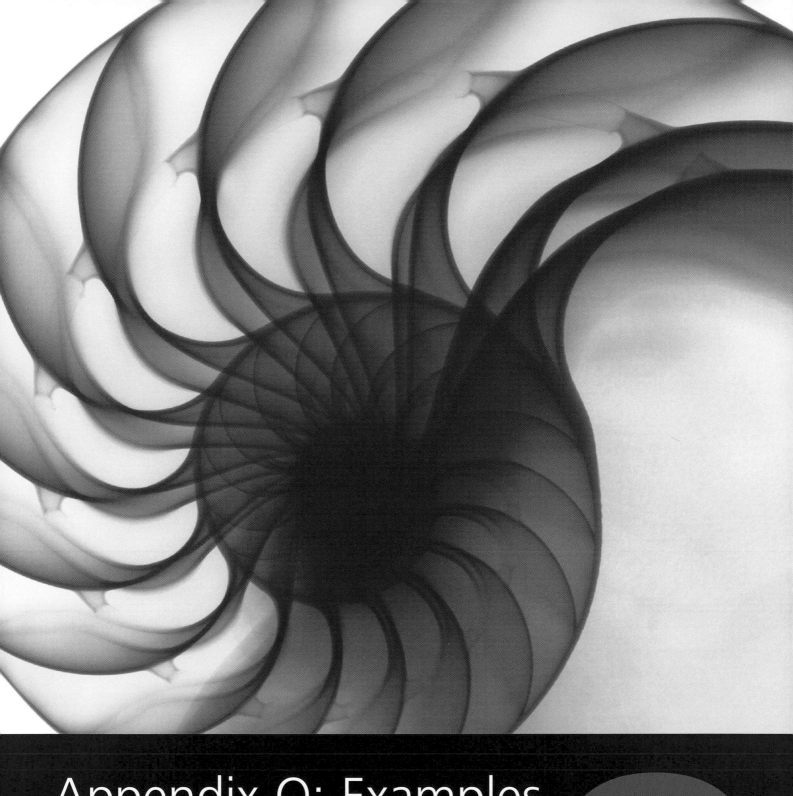

Appendix O: Examples of inputs and outputs across the service lifecycle

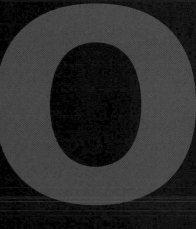

Appendix O: Examples of inputs and outputs across the service lifecycle

This appendix identifies some of the major inputs and outputs between each stage of the service lifecycle. This is not an exhaustive list and is designed to help understand how the different lifecycle stages interact. See Table 3.7 for more detail on the inputs and outputs of the service design stage.

Lifecycle stage	Examples of inputs from other service lifecycle stages	Examples of outputs to other service lifecycle stages
Service strategy	Information and feedback for business cases and service portfolio Requirements for strategies and plans Inputs and feedback on strategies and policies Financial reports, service reports, dashboards, and outputs of service review meetings Response to change proposals Service portfolio updates including the service catalogue Change schedule Knowledge and information in the service knowledge management system (SKMS)	Vision and mission Strategies, strategic plans and policies Financial information and budgets Service portfolio Change proposals Service charters including service packages, service models, and details of utility and warranty Patterns of business activity and demand forecasts Updated knowledge and information in the SKMS Achievements against metrics, KPIs and CSFs Feedback to other lifecycle stages Improvement opportunities logged in the CSI register
Service design	Vision and mission Strategies, strategic plans and policies Financial information and budgets Service portfolio Service charters including service packages, service models, and details of utility and warranty Feedback on all aspects of service design and service design packages Requests for change (RFCs) for designing changes and improvements Input to design requirements from other lifecycle stages Service reports, dashboards, and outputs of service review meetings Knowledge and information in the SKMS	Service portfolio updates including the service catalogue Service design packages, including: ■ Details of utility and warranty ■ Acceptance criteria ■ Updated service models ■ Designs and interface specifications ■ Transition plans ■ Operation plans and procedures Information security policies Designs for new or changed services, management information systems and tools, technology architectures, processes, measurement methods and metrics SLAs, OLAs and underpinning contracts RFCs to transition or deploy new or changed services Financial reports Updated knowledge and information in the SKMS Achievements against metrics, KPIs and CSFs Feedback to other lifecycle stages Improvement opportunities logged in the CSI register

Lifecycle stage	Examples of inputs from other service lifecycle stages	Examples of outputs to other service lifecycle stages
Service transition	Vision and mission Strategies, strategic plans and policies Financial information and budgets Service portfolio Change proposals, including utility and warranty requirements and expected timescales RFCs for implementing changes and improvements Service design packages, including: ■ Details of utility and warranty ■ Acceptance criteria ■ Service models ■ Designs and interface specifications ■ Transition plans ■ Operation plans and procedures Input to change evaluation and change advisory board (CAB) meetings Knowledge and information in the SKMS	New or changed services, management information systems and tools, technology architectures, processes, measurement methods and metrics Responses to change proposals and RFCs Change schedule Known errors Standard changes for use in request fulfilment Knowledge and information in the SKMS (including the configuration management system) Financial reports Updated knowledge and information in the SKMS Achievements against metrics, KPIs and CSFs Feedback to other lifecycle stages Improvement opportunities logged in the CSI register
Service operation	Vision and mission Strategies, strategic plans and policies Financial information and budgets Service portfolio Service reports, dashboards, and outputs of service review meetings Service design packages, including: ■ Details of utility and warranty ■ Operations plans and procedures ■ Recovery procedures Service level agreements (SLAs), operational level agreements (OLAs) and underpinning contracts Known errors Standard changes for use in request fulfilment Information security policies Change schedule Patterns of business activity and demand forecasts Knowledge and information in the SKMS	Achievement of agreed service levels to deliver value to the business Operational requirements Operational performance data and service records RFCs to resolve operational issues Financial reports Updated knowledge and information in the SKMS Achievements against metrics, KPIs and CSFs Feedback to other lifecycle stages Improvement opportunities logged in the CSI register
Continual service improvement	Vision and mission Strategies, strategic plans and policies Financial information and budgets Service portfolio Achievements against metrics, key performance indicators (KPIs) and critical success factors (CSFs) from each lifecycle stage Operational performance data and service records Improvement opportunities logged in the CSI register Knowledge and information in the SKMS	RFCs for implementing improvements across all lifecycle stages Business cases for significant improvements Updated CSI register Service improvement plans Results of customer and user satisfaction surveys Service reports, dashboards, and outputs of service review meetings Financial reports Updated knowledge and information in the SKMS Achievements against metrics, KPIs and CSFs Feedback to other lifecycle stages

Abbreviations and
glossary

Abbreviations

ACD	automatic call distribution	FTA	fault tree analysis
AM	availability management	IRR	internal rate of return
AMIS	availability management information system	ISG	IT steering group
		ISM	information security management
ASP	application service provider	ISMS	information security management system
AST	agreed service time		
BCM	business continuity management	ISO	International Organization for Standardization
BCP	business continuity plan		
BIA	business impact analysis	ISP	internet service provider
BMP	Best Management Practice	IT	information technology
BRM	business relationship manager	ITSCM	IT service continuity management
BSI	British Standards Institution	ITSM	IT service management
CAB	change advisory board	itSMF	IT Service Management Forum
CAPEX	capital expenditure	IVR	interactive voice response
CCM	component capacity management	KEDB	known error database
CFIA	component failure impact analysis	KPI	key performance indicator
CI	configuration item	LOS	line of service
CMDB	configuration management database	MIS	management information system
CMIS	capacity management information system	M_o_R	Management of Risk
		MTBF	mean time between failures
CMM	capability maturity model	MTBSI	mean time between service incidents
CMMI	Capability Maturity Model Integration	MTRS	mean time to restore service
CMS	configuration management system	MTTR	mean time to repair
COBIT	Control OBjectives for Information and related Technology	NPV	net present value
		OLA	operational level agreement
COTS	commercial off the shelf	OPEX	operational expenditure
CSF	critical success factor	PBA	pattern of business activity
CSI	continual service improvement	PDCA	Plan-Do-Check-Act
CTI	computer telephony integration	PFS	prerequisite for success
DIKW	Data-to-Information-to-Knowledge-to-Wisdom	PIR	post-implementation review
		PMBOK	Project Management Body of Knowledge
DML	definitive media library		
ECAB	emergency change advisory board	PMI	Project Management Institute
ELS	early life support	PMO	project management office
eSCM-CL	eSourcing Capability Model for Client Organizations	PRINCE2	PRojects IN Controlled Environments
		PSO	projected service outage
eSCM-SP	eSourcing Capability Model for Service Providers	QA	quality assurance
		QMS	quality management system

RACI	responsible, accountable, consulted and informed		UP	user profile
			VBF	vital business function
RCA	root cause analysis		VOI	value on investment
RFC	request for change		WIP	work in progress
ROA	return on assets			
ROI	return on investment			
RPO	recovery point objective			
RTO	recovery time objective			
SAC	service acceptance criteria			
SACM	service asset and configuration management			
SAM	software asset management			
SCM	service capacity management			
SCMIS	supplier and contract management information system			
SDP	service design package			
SFA	service failure analysis			
SIP	service improvement plan			
SKMS	service knowledge management system			
SLA	service level agreement			
SLM	service level management			
SLP	service level package			
SLR	service level requirement			
SMART	specific, measurable, achievable, relevant and time-bound			
SMIS	security management information system			
SMO	service maintenance objective			
SoC	separation of concerns			
SOP	standard operating procedure			
SOR	statement of requirements			
SOX	Sarbanes-Oxley (US law)			
SPI	service provider interface			
SPM	service portfolio management			
SPOF	single point of failure			
TCO	total cost of ownership			
TCU	total cost of utilization			
TO	technical observation			
TOR	terms of reference			
TQM	total quality management			
UC	underpinning contract			

Glossary

The core ITIL publications (*ITIL Service Strategy, ITIL Service Design, ITIL Service Operation, ITIL Service Transition, ITIL Continual Service Improvement*) referred to in parentheses at the beginning of a definition indicate where a reader can find more information. Terms without such a reference may either be used generically across all five core publications, or simply may not be explained in any greater detail elsewhere in the ITIL series. In other words, readers are only directed to other sources where they can expect to expand on their knowledge or to see a greater context.

acceptance

Formal agreement that an IT service, process, plan or other deliverable is complete, accurate, reliable and meets its specified requirements. Acceptance is usually preceded by change evaluation or testing and is often required before proceeding to the next stage of a project or process. *See also* service acceptance criteria.

access management

(*ITIL Service Operation*) The process responsible for allowing users to make use of IT services, data or other assets. Access management helps to protect the confidentiality, integrity and availability of assets by ensuring that only authorized users are able to access or modify them. Access management implements the policies of information security management and is sometimes referred to as rights management or identity management.

accounting

(*ITIL Service Strategy*) The process responsible for identifying the actual costs of delivering IT services, comparing these with budgeted costs, and managing variance from the budget.

accredited

Officially authorized to carry out a role. For example, an accredited body may be authorized to provide training or to conduct audits.

active monitoring

(*ITIL Service Operation*) Monitoring of a configuration item or an IT service that uses automated regular checks to discover the current status. *See also* passive monitoring.

activity

A set of actions designed to achieve a particular result. Activities are usually defined as part of processes or plans, and are documented in procedures.

agreed service time (AST)

(*ITIL Service Design*) A synonym for service hours, commonly used in formal calculations of availability. *See also* downtime.

agreement

A document that describes a formal understanding between two or more parties. An agreement is not legally binding, unless it forms part of a contract. *See also* operational level agreement; service level agreement.

alert

(*ITIL Service Operation*) A notification that a threshold has been reached, something has changed, or a failure has occurred. Alerts are often created and managed by system management tools and are managed by the event management process.

analytical modelling

(*ITIL Continual Service Improvement*) (*ITIL Service Design*) (*ITIL Service Strategy*) A technique that uses mathematical models to predict the behaviour of IT services or other configuration items. Analytical models are commonly used in capacity management and availability management. *See also* modelling; simulation modelling.

application

Software that provides functions which are required by an IT service. Each application may be part of more than one IT service. An application runs on one or more servers or clients. *See also* application management; application portfolio.

application management

(*ITIL Service Operation*) The function responsible for managing applications throughout their lifecycle.

application portfolio

(*ITIL Service Design*) A database or structured document used to manage applications throughout their lifecycle. The application portfolio contains key attributes of all applications. The application portfolio is sometimes implemented as part of the service portfolio, or as part of the configuration management system.

application service provider (ASP)

(*ITIL Service Design*) An external service provider that provides IT services using applications running at the service provider's premises. Users access the applications by network connections to the service provider.

application sizing

(*ITIL Service Design*) The activity responsible for understanding the resource requirements needed to support a new application, or a major change to an existing application. Application sizing helps to ensure that the IT service can meet its agreed service level targets for capacity and performance.

architecture

(*ITIL Service Design*) The structure of a system or IT service, including the relationships of components to each other and to the environment they are in. Architecture also includes the standards and guidelines that guide the design and evolution of the system.

assembly

(*ITIL Service Transition*) A configuration item that is made up of a number of other CIs. For example, a server CI may contain CIs for CPUs, disks, memory etc.; an IT service CI may contain many hardware, software and other CIs. *See also* build; component CI.

assessment

Inspection and analysis to check whether a standard or set of guidelines is being followed, that records are accurate, or that efficiency and effectiveness targets are being met. *See also* audit.

asset

(*ITIL Service Strategy*) Any resource or capability. The assets of a service provider include anything that could contribute to the delivery of a service. Assets can be one of the following types: management, organization, process, knowledge, people, information, applications, infrastructure or financial capital. *See also* customer asset; service asset; strategic asset.

asset management

(*ITIL Service Transition*) A generic activity or process responsible for tracking and reporting the value and ownership of assets throughout their lifecycle. *See also* service asset and configuration management; fixed asset management; software asset management.

attribute

(*ITIL Service Transition*) A piece of information about a configuration item. Examples are name, location, version number and cost. Attributes of CIs are recorded in a configuration management database (CMDB) and maintained as part of a configuration management system (CMS). *See also* relationship; configuration management system.

audit

Formal inspection and verification to check whether a standard or set of guidelines is being followed, that records are accurate, or that efficiency and effectiveness targets are being met. An audit may be carried out by internal or external groups. *See also* assessment; certification.

authority matrix

See RACI.

availability

(*ITIL Service Design*) Ability of an IT service or other configuration item to perform its agreed function when required. Availability is determined by reliability, maintainability, serviceability, performance and security. Availability is usually calculated as a percentage. This calculation is often based on agreed service time and downtime. It is best practice to calculate availability of an IT service using measurements of the business output.

availability management (AM)

(*ITIL Service Design*) The process responsible for ensuring that IT services meet the current and future availability needs of the business in a cost-effective and timely manner. Availability management defines, analyses, plans, measures and improves all aspects of the availability of IT services, and ensures that all IT infrastructures, processes, tools, roles etc. are appropriate for the agreed service level targets for availability. *See also* availability management information system.

availability management information system (AMIS)

(*ITIL Service Design*) A set of tools, data and information that is used to support availability management. *See also* service knowledge management system.

availability plan

(*ITIL Service Design*) A plan to ensure that existing and future availability requirements for IT services can be provided cost-effectively.

back-out

(*ITIL Service Transition*) An activity that restores a service or other configuration item to a previous baseline. Back-out is used as a form of remediation when a change or release is not successful.

backup

(*ITIL Service Design*) (*ITIL Service Operation*) Copying data to protect against loss of integrity or availability of the original.

balanced scorecard

(*ITIL Continual Service Improvement*) A management tool developed by Drs Robert Kaplan (Harvard Business School) and David Norton. A balanced scorecard enables a strategy to be broken down into key performance indicators. Performance against the KPIs is used to demonstrate how well the strategy is being achieved. A balanced scorecard has four major areas, each of which has a small number of KPIs. The same four areas are considered at different levels of detail throughout the organization.

baseline

(*ITIL Continual Service Improvement*) (*ITIL Service Transition*) A snapshot that is used as a reference point. Many snapshots may be taken and recorded over time but only some will be used as baselines. For example:

- An ITSM baseline can be used as a starting point to measure the effect of a service improvement plan
- A performance baseline can be used to measure changes in performance over the lifetime of an IT service
- A configuration baseline can be used as part of a back-out plan to enable the IT infrastructure to be restored to a known configuration if a change or release fails.

See also benchmark.

benchmark

(*ITIL Continual Service Improvement*) (*ITIL Service Transition*) A baseline that is used to compare related data sets as part of a benchmarking exercise. For example, a recent snapshot of a process can be compared to a previous baseline of that process, or a current baseline can be compared to industry data or best practice. *See also* benchmarking; baseline.

benchmarking

(*ITIL Continual Service Improvement*) The process responsible for comparing a benchmark with related data sets such as a more recent snapshot, industry data or best practice. The term is also used to mean creating a series of benchmarks over time, and comparing the results to measure progress or improvement. This process is not described in detail within the core ITIL publications.

Best Management Practice (BMP)

The Best Management Practice portfolio is owned by the Cabinet Office, part of HM Government. Formerly owned by CCTA and then OGC, the BMP functions moved to the Cabinet Office in June 2010. The BMP portfolio includes guidance on IT service management and project, programme, risk, portfolio and value management. There is also a management maturity model as well as related glossaries of terms.

best practice

Proven activities or processes that have been successfully used by multiple organizations. ITIL is an example of best practice.

billing

(*ITIL Service Strategy*) Part of the charging process. Billing is the activity responsible for producing an invoice or a bill and recovering the money from customers. *See also* pricing.

brainstorming

(*ITIL Service Design*) (*ITIL Service Operation*) A technique that helps a team to generate ideas. Ideas are not reviewed during the brainstorming session, but at a later stage. Brainstorming is often used by problem management to identify possible causes.

British Standards Institution (BSI)

The UK national standards body, responsible for creating and maintaining British standards. See www.bsi-global.com for more information. *See also* International Organization for Standardization.

budget

A list of all the money an organization or business unit plans to receive, and plans to pay out, over a specified period of time. *See also* budgeting; planning.

budgeting

The activity of predicting and controlling the spending of money. Budgeting consists of a periodic negotiation cycle to set future budgets (usually annual) and the day-to-day monitoring and adjusting of current budgets.

build

(*ITIL Service Transition*) The activity of assembling a number of configuration items to create part of an IT service. The term is also used to refer to a release that is authorized for distribution – for example, server build or laptop build. *See also* configuration baseline.

business

(*ITIL Service Strategy*) An overall corporate entity or organization formed of a number of business units. In the context of ITSM, the term includes public sector and not-for-profit organizations, as well as companies. An IT service provider provides IT services to a customer within a business. The IT service provider may be part of the same business as its customer (internal service provider), or part of another business (external service provider).

business capacity management

(*ITIL Continual Service Improvement*) (*ITIL Service Design*) In the context of ITSM, business capacity management is the sub-process of capacity management responsible for understanding future business requirements for use in the capacity plan. *See also* service capacity management; component capacity management.

business case

(*ITIL Service Strategy*) Justification for a significant item of expenditure. The business case includes information about costs, benefits, options, issues, risks and possible problems. *See also* cost benefit analysis.

business continuity management (BCM)

(*ITIL Service Design*) The business process responsible for managing risks that could seriously affect the business. Business continuity management safeguards the interests of key stakeholders, reputation, brand and value-creating activities. The process involves reducing risks to an acceptable level and planning for the recovery of business processes should a disruption to the business occur. Business continuity management sets the objectives, scope and requirements for IT service continuity management.

business continuity plan (BCP)

(*ITIL Service Design*) A plan defining the steps required to restore business processes following a disruption. The plan also identifies the triggers for invocation, people to be involved, communications etc. IT service continuity plans form a significant part of business continuity plans.

business customer

(*ITIL Service Strategy*) A recipient of a product or a service from the business. For example, if the business is a car manufacturer, then the business customer is someone who buys a car.

business impact analysis (BIA)

(*ITIL Service Strategy*) Business impact analysis is the activity in business continuity management that identifies vital business functions and their dependencies. These dependencies may include suppliers, people, other business processes, IT services etc. Business impact analysis defines the recovery requirements for IT services. These requirements include recovery time objectives, recovery point objectives and minimum service level targets for each IT service.

business objective

(*ITIL Service Strategy*) The objective of a business process, or of the business as a whole. Business objectives support the business vision, provide guidance for the IT strategy, and are often supported by IT services.

business operations

(*ITIL Service Strategy*) The day-to-day execution, monitoring and management of business processes.

business perspective

(*ITIL Continual Service Improvement*) An understanding of the service provider and IT services from the point of view of the business, and an understanding of the business from the point of view of the service provider.

business process

A process that is owned and carried out by the business. A business process contributes to the delivery of a product or service to a business customer. For example, a retailer may have a purchasing process that helps to deliver services to its business customers. Many business processes rely on IT services.

business relationship management

(*ITIL Service Strategy*) The process responsible for maintaining a positive relationship with customers. Business relationship management identifies customer needs and ensures that the service provider is able to meet these needs with an appropriate catalogue of services. This process has strong links with service level management.

business relationship manager (BRM)

(*ITIL Service Strategy*) A role responsible for maintaining the relationship with one or more customers. This role is often combined with the service level manager role.

business service

A service that is delivered to business customers by business units. For example, delivery of financial services to customers of a bank, or goods to the customers of a retail store. Successful delivery of business services often depends on one or more IT services. A business service may consist almost entirely of an IT service – for example, an online banking service or an external website where product orders can be placed by business customers. *See also* customer-facing service.

business service management

The management of business services delivered to business customers. Business service management is performed by business units.

business unit

(*ITIL Service Strategy*) A segment of the business that has its own plans, metrics, income and costs. Each business unit owns assets and uses these to create value for customers in the form of goods and services.

call

(*ITIL Service Operation*) A telephone call to the service desk from a user. A call could result in an incident or a service request being logged.

call centre

(*ITIL Service Operation*) An organization or business unit that handles large numbers of incoming and outgoing telephone calls. *See also* service desk.

capability

(*ITIL Service Strategy*) The ability of an organization, person, process, application, IT service or other configuration item to carry out an activity. Capabilities are intangible assets of an organization. *See also* resource.

Capability Maturity Model Integration (CMMI)

(*ITIL Continual Service Improvement*) A process improvement approach developed by the Software Engineering Institute (SEI) of Carnegie Mellon University, US. CMMI provides organizations with the essential elements of effective processes. It can be used to guide process improvement across a project, a division or an entire organization. CMMI helps integrate traditionally separate organizational functions, set process improvement goals and priorities, provide guidance for quality processes, and provide a point of reference for appraising current processes. See www.sei.cmu.edu/cmmi for more information. *See also* maturity.

capacity

(*ITIL Service Design*) The maximum throughput that a configuration item or IT service can deliver. For some types of CI, capacity may be the size or volume – for example, a disk drive.

capacity management

(*ITIL Continual Service Improvement*) (*ITIL Service Design*) The process responsible for ensuring that the capacity of IT services and the IT infrastructure is able to meet agreed capacity- and performance-related requirements in a cost-effective and timely manner. Capacity management considers all resources required to deliver an IT service, and is concerned with meeting both the current and future capacity and performance needs of the business. Capacity management includes three sub processes: business capacity management, service capacity management, and component capacity management. *See also* capacity management information system.

capacity management information system (CMIS)

(*ITIL Service Design*) A set of tools, data and information that is used to support capacity management. *See also* service knowledge management system.

capacity plan

(*ITIL Service Design*) A plan used to manage the resources required to deliver IT services. The plan contains details of current and historic usage of IT services and components, and any issues that need to be addressed (including related improvement activities). The plan also contains scenarios for different predictions of business demand and costed options to deliver the agreed service level targets.

capacity planning

(*ITIL Service Design*) The activity within capacity management responsible for creating a capacity plan.

capital expenditure (CAPEX)

See capital cost.

category

A named group of things that have something in common. Categories are used to group similar things together. For example, cost types are used to group similar types of cost. Incident categories are used to group similar types of incident, while CI types are used to group similar types of configuration item.

certification

Issuing a certificate to confirm compliance to a standard. Certification includes a formal audit by an independent and accredited body. The term is also used to mean awarding a certificate to provide evidence that a person has achieved a qualification.

change

(*ITIL Service Transition*) The addition, modification or removal of anything that could have an effect on IT services. The scope should include changes to all architectures, processes, tools, metrics and documentation, as well as changes to IT services and other configuration items.

change advisory board (CAB)

(*ITIL Service Transition*) A group of people that support the assessment, prioritization, authorization and scheduling of changes. A change advisory board is usually made up of representatives from: all areas within the IT service provider; the business; and third parties such as suppliers.

change evaluation

(*ITIL Service Transition*) The process responsible for formal assessment of a new or changed IT service to ensure that risks have been managed and to help determine whether to authorize the change.

change history

(*ITIL Service Transition*) Information about all changes made to a configuration item during its life. Change history consists of all those change records that apply to the CI.

change management

(*ITIL Service Transition*) The process responsible for controlling the lifecycle of all changes, enabling beneficial changes to be made with minimum disruption to IT services.

change model

(*ITIL Service Transition*) A repeatable way of dealing with a particular category of change. A change model defines specific agreed steps that will be followed for a change of this category. Change models may be very complex with many steps that require authorization (e.g. major software release) or may be very simple with no requirement for authorization (e.g. password reset). *See also* change advisory board; standard change.

change proposal

(*ITIL Service Strategy*) (*ITIL Service Transition*) A document that includes a high level description of a potential service introduction or significant change, along with a corresponding business case and an expected implementation schedule. Change proposals are normally created by the service portfolio management process and are passed to change management for authorization. Change management will review the potential impact on other services, on shared resources, and on the overall change schedule. Once the change proposal has been authorized, service portfolio management will charter the service.

change record

(*ITIL Service Transition*) A record containing the details of a change. Each change record documents the lifecycle of a single change. A change record is created for every request for change that is received, even those that are subsequently rejected. Change records should reference the configuration items that are affected by the change. Change records may be stored in the configuration management system, or elsewhere in the service knowledge management system.

change request

See request for change.

change schedule

(*ITIL Service Transition*) A document that lists all authorized changes and their planned implementation dates, as well as the estimated dates of longer-term changes. A change schedule is sometimes called a forward schedule of change, even though it also contains information about changes that have already been implemented.

change window

(*ITIL Service Transition*) A regular, agreed time when changes or releases may be implemented with minimal impact on services. Change windows are usually documented in service level agreements.

charging

(*ITIL Service Strategy*) Requiring payment for IT services. Charging for IT services is optional, and many organizations choose to treat their IT service provider as a cost centre. *See also* charging process; charging policy.

charging policy

(*ITIL Service Strategy*) A policy specifying the objective of the charging process and the way in which charges will be calculated. *See also* cost.

charging process

(*ITIL Service Strategy*) The process responsible for deciding how much customers should pay (pricing) and recovering money from them (billing). This process is not described in detail within the core ITIL publications.

charter

(*ITIL Service Strategy*) A document that contains details of a new service, a significant change or other significant project. Charters are typically authorized by service portfolio management or by a project management office. The term charter is also used to describe the act of authorizing the work required to complete the service change or project. *See also* change proposal; service charter; project portfolio.

classification

The act of assigning a category to something. Classification is used to ensure consistent management and reporting. Configuration items, incidents, problems, changes etc. are usually classified.

client

A generic term that means a customer, the business or a business customer. For example, client manager may be used as a synonym for business relationship manager. The term is also used to mean:

- A computer that is used directly by a user – for example, a PC, a handheld computer or a work station
- The part of a client server application that the user directly interfaces with – for example, an email client.

closed

(*ITIL Service Operation*) The final status in the lifecycle of an incident, problem, change etc. When the status is closed, no further action is taken.

closure

(*ITIL Service Operation*) The act of changing the status of an incident, problem, change etc. to closed.

COBIT

(*ITIL Continual Service Improvement*) Control OBjectives for Information and related Technology (COBIT) provides guidance and best practice for the management of IT processes. COBIT is published by ISACA in conjunction with the IT Governance Institute (ITGI). See www.isaca.org for more information.

code of practice

A guideline published by a public body or a standards organization, such as ISO or BSI. Many standards consist of a code of practice and a specification. The code of practice describes recommended best practice.

cold standby

See gradual recovery.

commercial off the shelf (COTS)

(*ITIL Service Design*) Pre-existing application software or middleware that can be purchased from a third party.

compliance

Ensuring that a standard or set of guidelines is followed, or that proper, consistent accounting or other practices are being employed.

component

A general term that is used to mean one part of something more complex. For example, a computer system may be a component of an IT service; an application may be a component of a release unit. Components that need to be managed should be configuration items.

component capacity management (CCM)

(*ITIL Continual Service Improvement*) (*ITIL Service Design*) The sub-process of capacity management responsible for understanding the capacity, utilization and performance of configuration items. Data is collected, recorded and analysed for use in the capacity plan. *See also* business capacity management; service capacity management.

component CI

(*ITIL Service Transition*) A configuration item that is part of an assembly. For example, a CPU or memory CI may be part of a server CI.

component failure impact analysis (CFIA)

(*ITIL Service Design*) A technique that helps to identify the impact of configuration item failure on IT services and the business. A matrix is created with IT services on one axis and CIs on the other. This enables the identification of critical CIs (that could cause the failure of multiple IT services) and fragile IT services (that have multiple single points of failure).

concurrency

A measure of the number of users engaged in the same operation at the same time.

confidentiality

(*ITIL Service Design*) A security principle that requires that data should only be accessed by authorized people.

configuration

(*ITIL Service Transition*) A generic term used to describe a group of configuration items that work together to deliver an IT service, or a recognizable part of an IT service. Configuration is also used to describe the parameter settings for one or more configuration items.

configuration baseline

(*ITIL Service Transition*) The baseline of a configuration that has been formally agreed and is managed through the change management process. A configuration baseline is used as a basis for future builds, releases and changes.

configuration item (CI)

(*ITIL Service Transition*) Any component or other service asset that needs to be managed in order to deliver an IT service. Information about each configuration item is recorded in a configuration record within the configuration management system and is maintained throughout its lifecycle by service asset and configuration management. Configuration items are under the control of change management. They typically include IT services, hardware, software, buildings, people and formal documentation such as process documentation and service level agreements.

configuration management

See service asset and configuration management.

configuration management database (CMDB)

(*ITIL Service Transition*) A database used to store configuration records throughout their lifecycle. The configuration management system maintains one or more configuration management databases, and each database stores attributes of configuration items, and relationships with other configuration items.

configuration management system (CMS)

(*ITIL Service Transition*) A set of tools, data and information that is used to support service asset and configuration management. The CMS is part of an overall service knowledge management system and includes tools for collecting, storing, managing, updating, analysing and presenting data about all configuration items and their relationships. The CMS may also include information about incidents, problems, known errors, changes and releases. The CMS is maintained by service asset and configuration management and is used by all IT service management processes. *See also* configuration management database.

continual service improvement (CSI)

(*ITIL Continual Service Improvement*) A stage in the lifecycle of a service. Continual service improvement ensures that services are aligned with changing business needs by identifying and implementing improvements to IT services that support business processes. The performance of the IT service provider is continually measured and improvements are made to processes, IT services and IT infrastructure in order to increase efficiency, effectiveness and cost effectiveness. Continual service improvement includes the seven-step improvement process. Although this process is associated with continual service improvement, most processes have activities that take place across multiple stages of the service lifecycle. *See also* Plan-Do-Check-Act.

continuous availability

(*ITIL Service Design*) An approach or design to achieve 100% availability. A continuously available IT service has no planned or unplanned downtime.

continuous operation

(*ITIL Service Design*) An approach or design to eliminate planned downtime of an IT service. Note that individual configuration items may be down even though the IT service is available.

contract

A legally binding agreement between two or more parties.

control

A means of managing a risk, ensuring that a business objective is achieved or that a process is followed. Examples of control include policies, procedures, roles, RAID, door locks etc. A control is sometimes called a countermeasure or safeguard. Control also means to manage the utilization or behaviour of a configuration item, system or IT service.

Control OBjectives for Information and related Technology

See COBIT.

control perspective

(*ITIL Service Strategy*) An approach to the management of IT services, processes, functions, assets etc. There can be several different control perspectives on the same IT service, process etc., allowing different individuals or teams to focus on what is important and relevant to their specific role. Examples of control perspective include reactive and proactive management within IT operations, or a lifecycle view for an application project team.

control processes

The ISO/IEC 20000 process group that includes change management and configuration management.

core service

(*ITIL Service Strategy*) A service that delivers the basic outcomes desired by one or more customers. A core service provides a specific level of utility and warranty. Customers may be offered a choice of utility and warranty through one or more service options. *See also* enabling service; enhancing service; IT service; service package.

cost

The amount of money spent on a specific activity, IT service or business unit. Costs consist of real cost (money), notional cost (such as people's time) and depreciation.

cost benefit analysis

An activity that analyses and compares the costs and the benefits involved in one or more alternative courses of action. *See also* business case; internal rate of return; net present value; return on investment; value on investment.

cost element

(*ITIL Service Strategy*) The middle level of category to which costs are assigned in budgeting and accounting. The highest-level category is cost type. For example, a cost type of 'people' could have cost elements of payroll, staff benefits, expenses, training, overtime etc. Cost elements can be further broken down to give cost units. For example, the cost element 'expenses' could include cost units of hotels, transport, meals etc.

cost model

(*ITIL Service Strategy*) A framework used in budgeting and accounting in which all known costs can be recorded, categorized and allocated to specific customers, business units or projects. *See also* cost type; cost element; cost unit.

cost type

(*ITIL Service Strategy*) The highest level of category to which costs are assigned in budgeting and accounting – for example, hardware, software, people, accommodation, external and transfer. *See also* cost element; cost unit.

cost unit

(*ITIL Service Strategy*) The lowest level of category to which costs are assigned, cost units are usually things that can be easily counted (e.g. staff numbers, software licences) or things easily measured (e.g. CPU usage, electricity consumed). Cost units are included within cost elements. For example, a cost element of 'expenses' could include cost units of hotels, transport, meals etc. *See also* cost type.

cost effectiveness

A measure of the balance between the effectiveness and cost of a service, process or activity. A cost-effective process is one that achieves its objectives at minimum cost. *See also* key performance indicator; return on investment; value for money.

countermeasure

Can be used to refer to any type of control. The term is most often used when referring to measures that increase resilience, fault tolerance or reliability of an IT service.

course corrections

Changes made to a plan or activity that has already started to ensure that it will meet its objectives. Course corrections are made as a result of monitoring progress.

crisis management

Crisis management is the process responsible for managing the wider implications of business continuity. A crisis management team is responsible for strategic issues such as managing media relations and shareholder confidence, and decides when to invoke business continuity plans.

critical success factor (CSF)

Something that must happen if an IT service, process, plan, project or other activity is to succeed. Key performance indicators are used to measure the achievement of each critical success factor. For example, a critical success factor of 'protect IT services when making changes' could be measured by key performance indicators such as 'percentage reduction of unsuccessful changes', 'percentage reduction in changes causing incidents' etc.

CSI register

(*ITIL Continual Service Improvement*) A database or structured document used to record and manage improvement opportunities throughout their lifecycle.

culture

A set of values that is shared by a group of people, including expectations about how people should behave, their ideas, beliefs and practices. *See also* vision.

customer

Someone who buys goods or services. The customer of an IT service provider is the person or group who defines and agrees the service level targets. The term is also sometimes used informally to mean user – for example, 'This is a customer-focused organization.'

customer asset

Any resource or capability of a customer. *See also* asset.

customer agreement portfolio

(*ITIL Service Strategy*) A database or structured document used to manage service contracts or agreements between an IT service provider and its customers. Each IT service delivered to a customer should have a contract or other agreement that is listed in the customer agreement portfolio. *See also* customer-facing service; service catalogue; service portfolio.

customer-facing service

(*ITIL Service Design*) An IT service that is visible to the customer. These are normally services that support the customer's business processes and facilitate one or more outcomes desired by the customer. All live customer-facing services, including those available for deployment, are recorded in the service catalogue along with customer-visible information about deliverables, prices, contact points, ordering and request processes. Other information such as relationships to supporting services and other CIs will also be recorded for internal use by the IT service provider.

dashboard

(*ITIL Service Operation*) A graphical representation of overall IT service performance and availability. Dashboard images may be updated in real time, and can also be included in management reports and web pages. Dashboards can be used to support service level management, event management and incident diagnosis.

Data-to-Information-to-Knowledge-to-Wisdom (DIKW)

(*ITIL Service Transition*) A way of understanding the relationships between data, information, knowledge and wisdom. DIKW shows how each of these builds on the others.

definitive media library (DML)

(*ITIL Service Transition*) One or more locations in which the definitive and authorized versions of all software configuration items are securely stored. The definitive media library may also contain associated configuration items such as licences and documentation. It is a single logical storage area even if there are multiple locations. The definitive media library is controlled by service asset and configuration management and is recorded in the configuration management system.

deliverable

Something that must be provided to meet a commitment in a service level agreement or a contract. It is also used in a more informal way to mean a planned output of any process.

demand management

(*ITIL Service Design*) (*ITIL Service Strategy*) The process responsible for understanding, anticipating and influencing customer demand for services. Demand management works with capacity management to ensure that the service provider has sufficient capacity to meet the required demand. At a strategic level, demand management can involve analysis of patterns of business activity and user profiles, while at a tactical level, it can involve the use of differential charging to encourage customers to use IT services at less busy times, or require short-term activities to respond to unexpected demand or the failure of a configuration item.

Deming Cycle

See Plan-Do-Check-Act.

dependency

The direct or indirect reliance of one process or activity on another.

deployment

(*ITIL Service Transition*) The activity responsible for movement of new or changed hardware, software, documentation, process etc. to the live environment. Deployment is part of the release and deployment management process.

design

(*ITIL Service Design*) An activity or process that identifies requirements and then defines a solution that is able to meet these requirements. *See also* service design.

design coordination

(*ITIL Service Design*) The process responsible for coordinating all service design activities, processes and resources. Design coordination ensures the consistent and effective design of new or changed IT services, service management information systems, architectures, technology, processes, information and metrics.

detection

(*ITIL Service Operation*) A stage in the expanded incident lifecycle. Detection results in the incident becoming known to the service provider. Detection can be automatic or the result of a user logging an incident.

development

(*ITIL Service Design*) The process responsible for creating or modifying an IT service or application ready for subsequent release and deployment. Development is also used to mean the role or function that carries out development work. This process is not described in detail within the core ITIL publications.

development environment

(*ITIL Service Design*) An environment used to create or modify IT services or applications. Development environments are not typically subjected to the same degree of control as test or live environments. *See also* development.

diagnosis

(*ITIL Service Operation*) A stage in the incident and problem lifecycles. The purpose of diagnosis is to identify a workaround for an incident or the root cause of a problem.

differential charging

A technique used to support demand management by charging different amounts for the same function of an IT service under different circumstances. For example, reduced charges outside peak times, or increased charges for users who exceed a bandwidth allocation.

document

Information in readable form. A document may be paper or electronic – for example, a policy statement, service level agreement, incident record or diagram of a computer room layout. *See also* record.

downtime

(*ITIL Service Design*) (*ITIL Service Operation*) The time when an IT service or other configuration item is not available during its agreed service time. The availability of an IT service is often calculated from agreed service time and downtime.

driver

Something that influences strategy, objectives or requirements – for example, new legislation or the actions of competitors.

early life support (ELS)

(*ITIL Service Transition*) A stage in the service lifecycle that occurs at the end of deployment and before the service is fully accepted into operation. During early life support, the service provider reviews key performance indicators, service levels and monitoring thresholds and may implement improvements to ensure that service targets can be met. The service provider may also provide additional resources for incident and problem management during this time.

economies of scale

(*ITIL Service Strategy*) The reduction in average cost that is possible from increasing the usage of an IT service or asset. *See also* economies of scope.

economies of scope

(*ITIL Service Strategy*) The reduction in cost that is allocated to an IT service by using an existing asset for an additional purpose. For example, delivering a new IT service from an existing IT infrastructure. *See also* economies of scale.

effectiveness

(*ITIL Continual Service Improvement*) A measure of whether the objectives of a process, service or activity have been achieved. An effective process or activity is one that achieves its agreed objectives. *See also* key performance indicator.

efficiency

(*ITIL Continual Service Improvement*) A measure of whether the right amount of resource has been used to deliver a process, service or activity. An efficient process achieves its objectives with the minimum amount of time, money, people or other resources. *See also* key performance indicator.

emergency change

(*ITIL Service Transition*) A change that must be introduced as soon as possible – for example, to resolve a major incident or implement a security patch. The change management process will normally have a specific procedure for handling emergency changes. *See also* emergency change advisory board.

emergency change advisory board (ECAB)

(*ITIL Service Transition*) A subgroup of the change advisory board that makes decisions about emergency changes. Membership may be decided at the time a meeting is called, and depends on the nature of the emergency change.

enabling service

(*ITIL Service Strategy*) A service that is needed in order to deliver a core service. Enabling services may or may not be visible to the customer, but they are not offered to customers in their own right. *See also* enhancing service.

enhancing service

(*ITIL Service Strategy*) A service that is added to a core service to make it more attractive to the customer. Enhancing services are not essential to the delivery of a core service but are used to encourage customers to use the core services or to differentiate the service provider from its competitors. *See also* enabling service; excitement factor.

enterprise financial management

(*ITIL Service Strategy*) The function and processes responsible for managing the overall organization's budgeting, accounting and charging requirements. Enterprise financial management is sometimes referred to as the 'corporate' financial department. *See also* financial management for IT services.

environment

(*ITIL Service Transition*) A subset of the IT infrastructure that is used for a particular purpose – for example, live environment, test environment, build environment. Also used in the term 'physical environment' to mean the accommodation, air conditioning, power system etc. Environment is used as a generic term to mean the external conditions that influence or affect something.

error

(*ITIL Service Operation*) A design flaw or malfunction that causes a failure of one or more IT services or other configuration items. A mistake made by a person or a faulty process that impacts a configuration item is also an error.

escalation

(*ITIL Service Operation*) An activity that obtains additional resources when these are needed to meet service level targets or customer expectations. Escalation may be needed within any IT service management process, but is most commonly associated with incident management, problem management and the management of customer complaints. There are two types of escalation: functional escalation and hierarchic escalation.

eSourcing Capability Model for Client Organizations (eSCM-CL)

(*ITIL Service Strategy*) A framework to help organizations in their analysis and decision-making on service sourcing models and strategies. It was developed by Carnegie Mellon University in the US. *See also* eSourcing Capability Model for Service Providers.

eSourcing Capability Model for Service Providers (eSCM-SP)

(*ITIL Service Strategy*) A framework to help IT service providers develop their IT service management capabilities from a service sourcing perspective. It was developed by Carnegie Mellon University in the US. *See also* eSourcing Capability Model for Client Organizations.

estimation

The use of experience to provide an approximate value for a metric or cost. Estimation is also used in capacity and availability management as the cheapest and least accurate modelling method.

event

(*ITIL Service Operation*) A change of state that has significance for the management of an IT service or other configuration item. The term is also used to mean an alert or notification created by any IT service, configuration item or monitoring tool. Events typically require IT operations personnel to take actions, and often lead to incidents being logged.

event management

(*ITIL Service Operation*) The process responsible for managing events throughout their lifecycle. Event management is one of the main activities of IT operations.

exception report

A document containing details of one or more key performance indicators or other important targets that have exceeded defined thresholds. Examples include service level agreement targets being missed or about to be missed, and a performance metric indicating a potential capacity problem.

excitement factor

(*ITIL Service Strategy*) An attribute added to something to make it more attractive or more exciting to the customer. For example, a restaurant may provide a free drink with every meal. *See also* enhancing service.

expanded incident lifecycle

(*ITIL Continual Service Improvement*) (*ITIL Service Design*) Detailed stages in the lifecycle of an incident. The stages are detection, diagnosis, repair, recovery and restoration. The expanded incident lifecycle is used to help understand all contributions to the impact of incidents and to plan for how these could be controlled or reduced.

external customer

A customer who works for a different business from the IT service provider. *See also* external service provider; internal customer.

external service provider

(*ITIL Service Strategy*) An IT service provider that is part of a different organization from its customer. An IT service provider may have both internal and external customers. *See also* outsourcing; Type III service provider.

facilities management

(*ITIL Service Operation*) The function responsible for managing the physical environment where the IT infrastructure is located. Facilities management includes all aspects of managing the physical environment – for example, power and cooling, building access management, and environmental monitoring.

failure

(*ITIL Service Operation*) Loss of ability to operate to specification, or to deliver the required output. The term may be used when referring to IT services, processes, activities, configuration items etc. A failure often causes an incident.

fast recovery

(*ITIL Service Design*) A recovery option that is also known as hot standby. Fast recovery normally uses a dedicated fixed facility with computer systems and software configured ready to run the IT services. Fast recovery typically takes up to 24 hours but may be quicker if there is no need to restore data from backups.

fault

See error.

fault tolerance

(*ITIL Service Design*) The ability of an IT service or other configuration item to continue to operate correctly after failure of a component part. *See also* countermeasure; resilience.

fault tree analysis (FTA)

(*ITIL Continual Service Improvement*) (*ITIL Service Design*) A technique that can be used to determine a chain of events that has caused an incident, or may cause an incident in the future. Fault tree analysis represents a chain of events using Boolean notation in a diagram.

financial management

(*ITIL Service Strategy*) A generic term used to describe the function and processes responsible for managing an organization's budgeting, accounting and charging requirements. Enterprise financial management is the specific term used to describe the function and processes from the perspective of the overall organization. Financial management for IT services is the specific term used to describe the function and processes from the perspective of the IT service provider.

financial management for IT services

(*ITIL Service Strategy*) The function and processes responsible for managing an IT service provider's budgeting, accounting and charging requirements. Financial management for IT services secures an appropriate level of funding to design, develop and deliver services that meet the strategy of the organization in a cost-effective manner. *See also* enterprise financial management.

fit for purpose

(*ITIL Service Strategy*) The ability to meet an agreed level of utility. Fit for purpose is also used informally to describe a process, configuration item, IT service etc. that is capable of meeting its objectives or service levels. Being fit for purpose requires suitable design, implementation, control and maintenance.

fit for use

(*ITIL Service Strategy*) The ability to meet an agreed level of warranty. Being fit for use requires suitable design, implementation, control and maintenance.

fixed asset management

(*ITIL Service Transition*) The process responsible for tracking and reporting the value and ownership of fixed assets throughout their lifecycle. Fixed asset management maintains the asset register and is usually carried out by the overall business, rather than by the IT organization. Fixed asset management is sometimes called financial asset management and is not described in detail within the core ITIL publications.

fixed cost

(*ITIL Service Strategy*) A cost that does not vary with IT service usage – for example, the cost of server hardware. *See also* variable cost.

fixed facility

(*ITIL Service Design*) A permanent building, available for use when needed by an IT service continuity plan. *See also* portable facility; recovery option.

fulfilment

Performing activities to meet a need or requirement – for example, by providing a new IT service, or meeting a service request.

function

A team or group of people and the tools or other resources they use to carry out one or more processes or activities – for example, the service desk. The term also has two other meanings:

- An intended purpose of a configuration item, person, team, process or IT service. For example, one function of an email service may be to store and forward outgoing mails, while the function of a business process may be to despatch goods to customers.
- To perform the intended purpose correctly, as in 'The computer is functioning.'

governance

Ensures that policies and strategy are actually implemented, and that required processes are correctly followed. Governance includes defining roles and responsibilities, measuring and reporting, and taking actions to resolve any issues identified.

gradual recovery

(*ITIL Service Design*) A recovery option that is also known as cold standby. Gradual recovery typically uses a portable or fixed facility that has environmental support and network cabling, but no computer systems. The hardware and software are installed as part of the IT service continuity plan. Gradual recovery typically takes more than three days, and may take significantly longer.

guideline

A document describing best practice, which recommends what should be done. Compliance with a guideline is not normally enforced. *See also* standard.

high availability

(*ITIL Service Design*) An approach or design that minimizes or hides the effects of configuration item failure from the users of an IT service. High availability solutions are designed to achieve an agreed level of availability and make use of techniques such as fault tolerance, resilience and fast recovery to reduce the number and impact of incidents.

hot standby

See fast recovery; immediate recovery.

immediate recovery

(*ITIL Service Design*) A recovery option that is also known as hot standby. Provision is made to recover the IT service with no significant loss of service to the customer. Immediate recovery typically uses mirroring, load balancing and split-site technologies.

impact

(*ITIL Service Operation*) (*ITIL Service Transition*) A measure of the effect of an incident, problem or change on business processes. Impact is often based on how service levels will be affected. Impact and urgency are used to assign priority.

incident

(*ITIL Service Operation*) An unplanned interruption to an IT service or reduction in the quality of an IT service. Failure of a configuration item that has not yet affected service is also an incident – for example, failure of one disk from a mirror set.

incident management

(*ITIL Service Operation*) The process responsible for managing the lifecycle of all incidents. Incident management ensures that normal service operation is restored as quickly as possible and the business impact is minimized.

incident record

(*ITIL Service Operation*) A record containing the details of an incident. Each incident record documents the lifecycle of a single incident.

indirect cost

(*ITIL Service Strategy*) The cost of providing an IT service which cannot be allocated in full to a specific customer – for example, the cost of providing shared servers or software licences. Also known as overhead. *See also* direct cost.

information security management (ISM)

(*ITIL Service Design*) The process responsible for ensuring that the confidentiality, integrity and availability of an organization's assets, information, data and IT services match the agreed needs of the business. Information security management supports business security and has a wider scope than that of the IT service provider, and includes handling of paper, building access, phone calls etc. for the entire organization. *See also* security management information system.

information security management system (ISMS)

(*ITIL Service Design*) The framework of policy, processes, functions, standards, guidelines and tools that ensures an organization can achieve its information security management objectives. *See also* security management information system.

information security policy

(*ITIL Service Design*) The policy that governs the organization's approach to information security management.

information system

See management information system.

information technology (IT)

The use of technology for the storage, communication or processing of information. The technology typically includes computers, telecommunications, applications and other software. The information may include business data, voice, images, video etc. Information technology is often used to support business processes through IT services.

infrastructure service

A type of supporting service that provides hardware, network or other data centre components. The term is also used as a synonym for supporting service.

insourcing

(*ITIL Service Strategy*) Using an internal service provider to manage IT services. The term insourcing is also used to describe the act of transferring the provision of an IT service from an external service provider to an internal service provider. *See also* service sourcing.

integrity

(*ITIL Service Design*) A security principle that ensures data and configuration items are modified only by authorized personnel and activities. Integrity considers all possible causes of modification, including software and hardware failure, environmental events, and human intervention.

intermediate recovery

(*ITIL Service Design*) A recovery option that is also known as warm standby. Intermediate recovery usually uses a shared portable or fixed facility that has computer systems and network components. The hardware and software will need to be configured, and data will need to be restored, as part of the IT service continuity plan. Typical recovery times for intermediate recovery are one to three days.

internal customer

A customer who works for the same business as the IT service provider. *See also* external customer; internal service provider.

internal rate of return (IRR)

(*ITIL Service Strategy*) A technique used to help make decisions about capital expenditure. It calculates a figure that allows two or more alternative investments to be compared. A larger internal rate of return indicates a better investment. *See also* net present value; return on investment.

internal service provider

(*ITIL Service Strategy*) An IT service provider that is part of the same organization as its customer. An IT service provider may have both internal and external customers. *See also* insourcing; Type I service provider; Type II service provider.

International Organization for Standardization (ISO)

The International Organization for Standardization (ISO) is the world's largest developer of standards. ISO is a non-governmental organization that is a network of the national standards institutes of 156 countries. See www.iso.org for further information about ISO.

International Standards Organization

See International Organization for Standardization.

invocation

(*ITIL Service Design*) Initiation of the steps defined in a plan – for example, initiating the IT service continuity plan for one or more IT services.

ISO 9000

A generic term that refers to a number of international standards and guidelines for quality management systems. See www.iso.org for more information. *See also* International Organization for Standardization.

ISO 9001

An international standard for quality management systems. *See also* ISO 9000; standard.

ISO/IEC 20000

An international standard for IT service management.

ISO/IEC 27001

(*ITIL Continual Service Improvement*) (*ITIL Service Design*) An international specification for information security management. The corresponding code of practice is ISO/IEC 27002. *See also* standard.

IT infrastructure

All of the hardware, software, networks, facilities etc. that are required to develop, test, deliver, monitor, control or support applications and IT services. The term includes all of the information technology but not the associated people, processes and documentation.

IT operations

(*ITIL Service Operation*) Activities carried out by IT operations control, including console management/operations bridge, job scheduling, backup and restore, and print and output management. IT operations is also used as a synonym for service operation.

IT operations control

(*ITIL Service Operation*) The function responsible for monitoring and control of the IT services and IT infrastructure. *See also* operations bridge.

IT operations management

(*ITIL Service Operation*) The function within an IT service provider that performs the daily activities needed to manage IT services and the supporting IT infrastructure. IT operations management includes IT operations control and facilities management.

IT service

A service provided by an IT service provider. An IT service is made up of a combination of information technology, people and processes. A customer-facing IT service directly supports the business processes of one or more customers and its service level targets should be defined in a service level agreement. Other IT services, called supporting services, are not directly used by the business but are required by the service provider to deliver customer-facing services. *See also* core service; enabling service; enhancing service; service; service package.

IT service continuity management (ITSCM)

(*ITIL Service Design*) The process responsible for managing risks that could seriously affect IT services. IT service continuity management ensures that the IT service provider can always provide minimum agreed service levels, by reducing the risk to an acceptable level and planning for the recovery of IT services. IT service continuity management supports business continuity management.

IT service continuity plan

(*ITIL Service Design*) A plan defining the steps required to recover one or more IT services. The plan also identifies the triggers for invocation, people to be involved, communications etc. The IT service continuity plan should be part of a business continuity plan.

IT service management (ITSM)

The implementation and management of quality IT services that meet the needs of the business. IT service management is performed by IT service providers through an appropriate mix of people, process and information technology. *See also* service management.

IT service provider

(*ITIL Service Strategy*) A service provider that provides IT services to internal or external customers.

IT steering group (ISG)

(*ITIL Service Design*) (*ITIL Service Strategy*) A formal group that is responsible for ensuring that business and IT service provider strategies and plans are closely aligned. An IT steering group includes senior representatives from the business and the IT service provider. Also known as IT strategy group or IT steering committee.

ITIL

A set of best-practice publications for IT service management. Owned by the Cabinet Office (part of HM Government), ITIL gives guidance on the provision of quality IT services and the processes, functions and other capabilities needed to support them. The ITIL framework is based on a service lifecycle and consists of five lifecycle stages (service strategy, service design, service transition, service operation and continual service improvement), each of which has its own supporting publication. There is also a set of complementary ITIL publications providing guidance specific to industry sectors, organization types, operating models and technology architectures. See www.itil-officialsite.com for more information.

job description

A document that defines the roles, responsibilities, skills and knowledge required by a particular person. One job description can include multiple roles – for example, the roles of configuration manager and change manager may be carried out by one person.

job scheduling

(*ITIL Service Operation*) Planning and managing the execution of software tasks that are required as part of an IT service. Job scheduling is carried out by IT operations management, and is often automated using software tools that run batch or online tasks at specific times of the day, week, month or year.

key performance indicator (KPI)

(*ITIL Continual Service Improvement*) (*ITIL Service Design*) A metric that is used to help manage an IT service, process, plan, project or other activity. Key performance indicators are used to measure the achievement of critical success factors. Many metrics may be measured, but only the most important of these are defined as key performance indicators and used to actively manage and report on the process, IT service or activity. They should be selected to ensure that efficiency, effectiveness and cost effectiveness are all managed.

knowledge base

(*ITIL Service Transition*) A logical database containing data and information used by the service knowledge management system.

knowledge management

(*ITIL Service Transition*) The process responsible for sharing perspectives, ideas, experience and information, and for ensuring that these are available in the right place and at the right time. The knowledge management process enables informed decisions, and improves efficiency by reducing the need to rediscover knowledge. *See also* Data-to-Information-to-Knowledge-to-Wisdom; service knowledge management system.

known error

(*ITIL Service Operation*) A problem that has a documented root cause and a workaround. Known errors are created and managed throughout their lifecycle by problem management. Known errors may also be identified by development or suppliers.

lifecycle

The various stages in the life of an IT service, configuration item, incident, problem, change etc. The lifecycle defines the categories for status and the status transitions that are permitted. For example:

- The lifecycle of an application includes requirements, design, build, deploy, operate, optimize

- The expanded incident lifecycle includes detection, diagnosis, repair, recovery and restoration

- The lifecycle of a server may include: ordered, received, in test, live, disposed etc.

line of service (LOS)

(*ITIL Service Strategy*) A core service or service package that has multiple service options. A line of service is managed by a service owner and each service option is designed to support a particular market segment.

live

(*ITIL Service Transition*) Refers to an IT service or other configuration item that is being used to deliver service to a customer.

live environment

(*ITIL Service Transition*) A controlled environment containing live configuration items used to deliver IT services to customers.

maintainability

(*ITIL Service Design*) A measure of how quickly and effectively an IT service or other configuration item can be restored to normal working after a failure. Maintainability is often measured and reported as MTRS. Maintainability is also used in the context of software or IT service development to mean ability to be changed or repaired easily.

major incident

(*ITIL Service Operation*) The highest category of impact for an incident. A major incident results in significant disruption to the business.

manageability

An informal measure of how easily and effectively an IT service or other component can be managed.

management information

Information that is used to support decision making by managers. Management information is often generated automatically by tools supporting the various IT service management processes. Management information often includes the values of key performance indicators, such as 'percentage of changes leading to incidents' or 'first-time fix rate'.

management information system (MIS)

(*ITIL Service Design*) A set of tools, data and information that is used to support a process or function. Examples include the availability management information system and the supplier and contract management information system. *See also* service knowledge management system.

Management of Risk (M_o_R)

M_o_R includes all the activities required to identify and control the exposure to risk, which may have an impact on the achievement of an organization's business objectives. See www.mor-officialsite.com for more details.

management system

The framework of policy, processes, functions, standards, guidelines and tools that ensures an organization or part of an organization can achieve its objectives. This term is also used with a smaller scope to support a specific process or activity – for example, an event management system or risk management system. *See also* system.

manual workaround

(*ITIL Continual Service Improvement*) A workaround that requires manual intervention. Manual workaround is also used as the name of a recovery option in which the business process operates without the use of IT services. This is a temporary measure and is usually combined with another recovery option.

market space

(*ITIL Service Strategy*) Opportunities that an IT service provider could exploit to meet the business needs of customers. Market spaces identify the possible IT services that an IT service provider may wish to consider delivering.

maturity

(*ITIL Continual Service Improvement*) A measure of the reliability, efficiency and effectiveness of a process, function, organization etc. The most mature processes and functions are formally aligned to business objectives and strategy, and are supported by a framework for continual improvement.

maturity level

A named level in a maturity model, such as the Carnegie Mellon Capability Maturity Model Integration.

mean time between failures (MTBF)

(*ITIL Service Design*) A metric for measuring and reporting reliability. MTBF is the average time that an IT service or other configuration item can perform its agreed function without interruption. This is measured from when the configuration item starts working, until it next fails.

mean time between service incidents (MTBSI)

(*ITIL Service Design*) A metric used for measuring and reporting reliability. It is the mean time from when a system or IT service fails, until it next fails. MTBSI is equal to MTBF plus MTRS.

mean time to repair (MTTR)

The average time taken to repair an IT service or other configuration item after a failure. MTTR is measured from when the configuration item fails until it is repaired. MTTR does not include the time required to recover or restore. It is sometimes incorrectly used instead of mean time to restore service.

mean time to restore service (MTRS)

The average time taken to restore an IT service or other configuration item after a failure. MTRS is measured from when the configuration item fails until it is fully restored and delivering its normal functionality. *See also* maintainability; mean time to repair.

metric

(*ITIL Continual Service Improvement*) Something that is measured and reported to help manage a process, IT service or activity. *See also* key performance indicator.

middleware

(*ITIL Service Design*) Software that connects two or more software components or applications. Middleware is usually purchased from a supplier, rather than developed within the IT service provider. *See also* commercial off the shelf.

mission

A short but complete description of the overall purpose and intentions of an organization. It states what is to be achieved, but not how this should be done. *See also* vision.

model

A representation of a system, process, IT service, configuration item etc. that is used to help understand or predict future behaviour.

modelling

A technique that is used to predict the future behaviour of a system, process, IT service, configuration item etc. Modelling is commonly used in financial management, capacity management and availability management.

monitoring

(*ITIL Service Operation*) Repeated observation of a configuration item, IT service or process to detect events and to ensure that the current status is known.

near-shore

(*ITIL Service Strategy*) Provision of services from a country near the country where the customer is based. This can be the provision of an IT service, or of supporting functions such as a service desk. *See also* offshore; onshore.

net present value (NPV)

(*ITIL Service Strategy*) A technique used to help make decisions about capital expenditure. It compares cash inflows with cash outflows. Positive net present value indicates that an investment is worthwhile. *See also* internal rate of return; return on investment.

objective

The outcomes required from a process, activity or organization in order to ensure that its purpose will be fulfilled. Objectives are usually expressed as measurable targets. The term is also informally used to mean a requirement.

off the shelf

See commercial off the shelf.

Office of Government Commerce (OGC)

OGC (former owner of Best Management Practice) and its functions have moved into the Cabinet Office as part of HM Government. See www.cabinetoffice.gov.uk

offshore

(*ITIL Service Strategy*) Provision of services from a location outside the country where the customer is based, often in a different continent. This can be the provision of an IT service, or of supporting functions such as a service desk. *See also* near-shore; onshore.

onshore

(*ITIL Service Strategy*) Provision of services from a location within the country where the customer is based. *See also* near-shore; offshore.

operate

To perform as expected. A process or configuration item is said to operate if it is delivering the required outputs. Operate also means to perform one or more operations. For example, to operate a computer is to do the day-to-day operations needed for it to perform as expected.

operation

(*ITIL Service Operation*) Day-to-day management of an IT service, system or other configuration item. Operation is also used to mean any predefined activity or transaction – for example, loading a magnetic tape, accepting money at a point of sale, or reading data from a disk drive.

operational

The lowest of three levels of planning and delivery (strategic, tactical, operational). Operational activities include the day-to-day or short-term planning or delivery of a business process or IT service management process. The term is also a synonym for live.

operational cost

The cost resulting from running the IT services, which often involves repeating payments – for example, staff costs, hardware maintenance and electricity (also known as current expenditure or revenue expenditure). *See also* capital expenditure.

operational level agreement (OLA)

(*ITIL Continual Service Improvement*) (*ITIL Service Design*) An agreement between an IT service provider and another part of the same organization. It supports the IT service provider's delivery of IT services to customers and defines the goods or services to be provided and the responsibilities of both parties. For example, there could be an operational level agreement:

■ Between the IT service provider and a procurement department to obtain hardware in agreed times
■ Between the service desk and a support group to provide incident resolution in agreed times.

See also service level agreement.

operations bridge

(*ITIL Service Operation*) A physical location where IT services and IT infrastructure are monitored and managed.

operations control

See IT operations control.

operations management

See IT operations management.

optimize

Review, plan and request changes, in order to obtain the maximum efficiency and effectiveness from a process, configuration item, application etc.

organization

A company, legal entity or other institution. The term is sometimes used to refer to any entity that has people, resources and budgets – for example, a project or business unit.

outcome

The result of carrying out an activity, following a process, or delivering an IT service etc. The term is used to refer to intended results as well as to actual results. *See also* objective.

outsourcing

(*ITIL Service Strategy*) Using an external service provider to manage IT services. *See also* service sourcing.

overhead

See indirect cost.

Pareto principle

(*ITIL Service Operation*) A technique used to prioritize activities. The Pareto principle says that 80% of the value of any activity is created with 20% of the effort. Pareto analysis is also used in problem management to prioritize possible problem causes for investigation.

partnership

A relationship between two organizations that involves working closely together for common goals or mutual benefit. The IT service provider should have a partnership with the business and with third parties who are critical to the delivery of IT services. *See also* value network.

passive monitoring

(*ITIL Service Operation*) Monitoring of a configuration item, an IT service or a process that relies on an alert or notification to discover the current status. *See also* active monitoring.

pattern of business activity (PBA)

(*ITIL Service Strategy*) A workload profile of one or more business activities. Patterns of business activity are used to help the IT service provider understand and plan for different levels of business activity. *See also* user profile.

percentage utilization

(*ITIL Service Design*) The amount of time that a component is busy over a given period of time. For example, if a CPU is busy for 1,800 seconds in a one-hour period, its utilization is 50%.

performance

A measure of what is achieved or delivered by a system, person, team, process or IT service.

performance management

Activities to ensure that something achieves its expected outcomes in an efficient and consistent manner.

pilot

(*ITIL Service Transition*) A limited deployment of an IT service, a release or a process to the live environment. A pilot is used to reduce risk and to gain user feedback and acceptance. *See also* change evaluation; test.

plan

A detailed proposal that describes the activities and resources needed to achieve an objective – for example, a plan to implement a new IT service or process. ISO/IEC 20000 requires a plan for the management of each IT service management process.

Plan-Do-Check-Act (PDCA)

(*ITIL Continual Service Improvement*) A four-stage cycle for process management, attributed to Edward Deming. Plan-Do-Check-Act is also called the Deming Cycle. **Plan** – design or revise processes that support the IT services; **Do** – implement the plan and manage the processes; **Check** – measure the processes and IT services, compare with objectives and produce reports; **Act** – plan and implement changes to improve the processes.

planned downtime

(*ITIL Service Design*) Agreed time when an IT service will not be available. Planned downtime is often used for maintenance, upgrades and testing. *See also* change window; downtime.

planning

An activity responsible for creating one or more plans – for example, capacity planning.

policy

Formally documented management expectations and intentions. Policies are used to direct decisions, and to ensure consistent and appropriate development and implementation of processes, standards, roles, activities, IT infrastructure etc.

portable facility

(*ITIL Service Design*) A prefabricated building, or a large vehicle, provided by a third party and moved to a site when needed according to an IT service continuity plan. *See also* fixed facility; recovery option.

post-implementation review (PIR)

A review that takes place after a change or a project has been implemented. It determines if the change or project was successful, and identifies opportunities for improvement.

practice

A way of working, or a way in which work must be done. Practices can include activities, processes, functions, standards and guidelines. *See also* best practice.

prerequisite for success (PFS)

An activity that needs to be completed, or a condition that needs to be met, to enable successful implementation of a plan or process. It is often an output from one process that is a required input to another process.

pricing

(*ITIL Service Strategy*) Pricing is the activity for establishing how much customers will be charged.

PRINCE2

See PRojects IN Controlled Environments.

priority

(*ITIL Service Operation*) (*ITIL Service Transition*) A category used to identify the relative importance of an incident, problem or change. Priority is based on impact and urgency, and is used to identify required times for actions to be taken. For example, the service level agreement may state that Priority 2 incidents must be resolved within 12 hours.

problem

(*ITIL Service Operation*) A cause of one or more incidents. The cause is not usually known at the time a problem record is created, and the problem management process is responsible for further investigation.

problem management

(*ITIL Service Operation*) The process responsible for managing the lifecycle of all problems. Problem management proactively prevents incidents from happening and minimizes the impact of incidents that cannot be prevented.

problem record

(*ITIL Service Operation*) A record containing the details of a problem. Each problem record documents the lifecycle of a single problem.

procedure

A document containing steps that specify how to achieve an activity. Procedures are defined as part of processes. *See also* work instruction.

process

A structured set of activities designed to accomplish a specific objective. A process takes one or more defined inputs and turns them into defined outputs. It may include any of the roles, responsibilities, tools and management controls required to reliably deliver the outputs. A process may define policies, standards, guidelines, activities and work instructions if they are needed.

process control

The activity of planning and regulating a process, with the objective of performing the process in an effective, efficient and consistent manner.

process manager

A role responsible for the operational management of a process. The process manager's responsibilities include planning and coordination of all activities required to carry out, monitor and report on the process. There may be several process managers for one process – for example, regional change managers or IT service continuity managers for each data centre. The process manager role is often assigned to the person who carries out the process owner role, but the two roles may be separate in larger organizations.

process owner

The person who is held accountable for ensuring that a process is fit for purpose. The process owner's responsibilities include sponsorship, design, change management and continual improvement of the process and its metrics. This role can be assigned to the same person who carries out the process manager role, but the two roles may be separate in larger organizations.

production environment

See live environment.

pro-forma

A template or example document containing sample data that will be replaced with real values when these are available.

programme

A number of projects and activities that are planned and managed together to achieve an overall set of related objectives and other outcomes.

project

A temporary organization, with people and other assets, that is required to achieve an objective or other outcome. Each project has a lifecycle that typically includes initiation, planning, execution, and closure. Projects are usually managed using a formal methodology such as PRojects IN Controlled Environments (PRINCE2) or the Project Management Body of Knowledge (PMBOK). *See also* charter; project management office; project portfolio.

Project Management Body of Knowledge (PMBOK)

A project management standard maintained and published by the Project Management Institute. See www.pmi.org for more information. *See also* PRojects IN Controlled Environments (PRINCE2).

Project Management Institute (PMI)

A membership association that advances the project management profession through globally recognized standards and certifications, collaborative communities, an extensive research programme, and professional development opportunities. PMI is a not-for-profit membership organization with representation in many countries around the world. PMI maintains and publishes the Project Management Body of Knowledge (PMBOK). See www.pmi.org for more information. *See also* PRojects IN Controlled Environments (PRINCE2).

project management office (PMO)

(*ITIL Service Design*) (*ITIL Service Strategy*) A function or group responsible for managing the lifecycle of projects. *See also* charter; project portfolio.

project portfolio

(*ITIL Service Design*) (*ITIL Service Strategy*) A database or structured document used to manage projects throughout their lifecycle. The project portfolio is used to coordinate projects and ensure that they meet their objectives in a cost-effective and timely manner. In larger organizations, the project portfolio is typically defined and maintained by a project management office. The project portfolio is important to service portfolio management as new services and significant changes are normally managed as projects. *See also* charter.

projected service outage (PSO)

(*ITIL Service Transition*) A document that identifies the effect of planned changes, maintenance activities and test plans on agreed service levels.

PRojects IN Controlled Environments (PRINCE2)

The standard UK government methodology for project management. See www.prince-officialsite. com for more information. *See also* Project Management Body of Knowledge (PMBOK).

qualification

(*ITIL Service Transition*) An activity that ensures that the IT infrastructure is appropriate and correctly configured to support an application or IT service. *See also* validation.

quality

The ability of a product, service or process to provide the intended value. For example, a hardware component can be considered to be of high quality if it performs as expected and delivers the required reliability. Process quality also requires an ability to monitor effectiveness and efficiency, and to improve them if necessary. *See also* quality management system.

quality assurance (QA)

(*ITIL Service Transition*) The process responsible for ensuring that the quality of a service, process or other service asset will provide its intended value. Quality assurance is also used to refer to a function or team that performs quality assurance. This process is not described in detail within the core ITIL publications. *See also* service validation and testing.

quality management system (QMS)

(*ITIL Continual Service Improvement*) The framework of policy, processes, functions, standards, guidelines and tools that ensures an organization is of a suitable quality to reliably meet business objectives or service levels. *See also* ISO 9000.

quick win

(*ITIL Continual Service Improvement*) An improvement activity that is expected to provide a return on investment in a short period of time with relatively small cost and effort. *See also* Pareto principle.

RACI

(*ITIL Service Design*) A model used to help define roles and responsibilities. RACI stands for responsible, accountable, consulted and informed.

reciprocal arrangement

(*ITIL Service Design*) A recovery option. An agreement between two organizations to share resources in an emergency – for example, high-speed printing facilities or computer room space.

record

A document containing the results or other output from a process or activity. Records are evidence of the fact that an activity took place and may be paper or electronic – for example, an audit report, an incident record or the minutes of a meeting.

recovery

(*ITIL Service Design*) (*ITIL Service Operation*) Returning a configuration item or an IT service to a working state. Recovery of an IT service often includes recovering data to a known consistent state. After recovery, further steps may be needed before the IT service can be made available to the users (restoration).

recovery option

(*ITIL Service Design*) A strategy for responding to an interruption to service. Commonly used strategies are manual workaround, reciprocal arrangement, gradual recovery, intermediate recovery, fast recovery, and immediate recovery. Recovery options may make use of dedicated facilities or third-party facilities shared by multiple businesses.

recovery point objective (RPO)

(*ITIL Service Design*) (*ITIL Service Operation*) The maximum amount of data that may be lost when service is restored after an interruption. The recovery point objective is expressed as a length of time before the failure. For example, a recovery point objective of one day may be supported by daily backups, and up to 24 hours of data may be lost. Recovery point objectives for each IT service should be negotiated, agreed and documented, and used as requirements for service design and IT service continuity plans.

recovery time objective (RTO)

(*ITIL Service Design*) (*ITIL Service Operation*) The maximum time allowed for the recovery of an IT service following an interruption. The service level to be provided may be less than normal service level targets. Recovery time objectives for each IT service should be negotiated, agreed and documented. *See also* business impact analysis.

redundancy

(*ITIL Service Design*) Use of one or more additional configuration items to provide fault tolerance. The term also has a generic meaning of obsolescence, or no longer needed.

relationship

A connection or interaction between two people or things. In business relationship management, it is the interaction between the IT service provider and the business. In service asset and configuration management, it is a link between two configuration items that identifies a dependency or connection between them. For example, applications may be linked to the servers they run on, and IT services have many links to all the configuration items that contribute to that IT service.

relationship processes

The ISO/IEC 20000 process group that includes business relationship management and supplier management.

release

(*ITIL Service Transition*) One or more changes to an IT service that are built, tested and deployed together. A single release may include changes to hardware, software, documentation, processes and other components.

release and deployment management

(*ITIL Service Transition*) The process responsible for planning, scheduling and controlling the build, test and deployment of releases, and for delivering new functionality required by the business while protecting the integrity of existing services.

release record

(*ITIL Service Transition*) A record that defines the content of a release. A release record has relationships with all configuration items that are affected by the release. Release records may be in the configuration management system or elsewhere in the service knowledge management system.

reliability

(*ITIL Continual Service Improvement*) (*ITIL Service Design*) A measure of how long an IT service or other configuration item can perform its agreed function without interruption. Usually measured as MTBF or MTBSI. The term can also be used to state how likely it is that a process, function etc. will deliver its required outputs. *See also* availability.

remediation

(*ITIL Service Transition*) Actions taken to recover after a failed change or release. Remediation may include back-out, invocation of service continuity plans, or other actions designed to enable the business process to continue.

repair

(*ITIL Service Operation*) The replacement or correction of a failed configuration item.

request for change (RFC)

(*ITIL Service Transition*) A formal proposal for a change to be made. It includes details of the proposed change, and may be recorded on paper or electronically. The term is often misused to mean a change record, or the change itself.

request fulfilment

(*ITIL Service Operation*) The process responsible for managing the lifecycle of all service requests.

requirement

(*ITIL Service Design*) A formal statement of what is needed – for example, a service level requirement, a project requirement or the required deliverables for a process. *See also* statement of requirements.

resilience

(*ITIL Service Design*) The ability of an IT service or other configuration item to resist failure or to recover in a timely manner following a failure. For example, an armoured cable will resist failure when put under stress. *See also* fault tolerance.

resolution

(*ITIL Service Operation*) Action taken to repair the root cause of an incident or problem, or to implement a workaround. In ISO/IEC 20000, resolution processes is the process group that includes incident and problem management.

resolution processes

The ISO/IEC 20000 process group that includes incident and problem management.

resource

(*ITIL Service Strategy*) A generic term that includes IT infrastructure, people, money or anything else that might help to deliver an IT service. Resources are considered to be assets of an organization. *See also* capability; service asset.

response time

A measure of the time taken to complete an operation or transaction. Used in capacity management as a measure of IT infrastructure performance, and in incident management as a measure of the time taken to answer the phone, or to start diagnosis.

responsiveness

A measurement of the time taken to respond to something. This could be response time of a transaction, or the speed with which an IT service provider responds to an incident or request for change etc.

restoration of service

See restore.

restore

(*ITIL Service Operation*) Taking action to return an IT service to the users after repair and recovery from an incident. This is the primary objective of incident management.

retire

(*ITIL Service Transition*) Permanent removal of an IT service, or other configuration item, from the live environment. Being retired is a stage in the lifecycle of many configuration items.

return on investment (ROI)

(*ITIL Continual Service Improvement*) (*ITIL Service Strategy*) A measurement of the expected benefit of an investment. In the simplest sense, it is the net profit of an investment divided by the net worth of the assets invested. *See also* net present value; value on investment.

return to normal

(*ITIL Service Design*) The phase of an IT service continuity plan during which full normal operations are resumed. For example, if an alternative data centre has been in use, then this phase will bring the primary data centre back into operation, and restore the ability to invoke IT service continuity plans again.

review

An evaluation of a change, problem, process, project etc. Reviews are typically carried out at predefined points in the lifecycle, and especially after closure. The purpose of a review is to ensure that all deliverables have been provided, and to identify opportunities for improvement. *See also* change evaluation; post-implementation review.

rights

(*ITIL Service Operation*) Entitlements, or permissions, granted to a user or role – for example, the right to modify particular data, or to authorize a change.

risk

A possible event that could cause harm or loss, or affect the ability to achieve objectives. A risk is measured by the probability of a threat, the vulnerability of the asset to that threat, and the impact it would have if it occurred. Risk can also be defined as uncertainty of outcome, and can be used in the context of measuring the probability of positive outcomes as well as negative outcomes.

risk assessment

The initial steps of risk management: analysing the value of assets to the business, identifying threats to those assets, and evaluating how vulnerable each asset is to those threats. Risk assessment can be quantitative (based on numerical data) or qualitative.

risk management

The process responsible for identifying, assessing and controlling risks. Risk management is also sometimes used to refer to the second part of the overall process after risks have been identified and assessed, as in 'risk assessment and management'. This process is not described in detail within the core ITIL publications. *See also* risk assessment.

role

A set of responsibilities, activities and authorities assigned to a person or team. A role is defined in a process or function. One person or team may have multiple roles – for example, the roles of configuration manager and change manager may be carried out by a single person. Role is also used to describe the purpose of something or what it is used for.

root cause

(*ITIL Service Operation*) The underlying or original cause of an incident or problem.

running costs

See operational costs.

scalability

The ability of an IT service, process, configuration item etc. to perform its agreed function when the workload or scope changes.

scope

The boundary or extent to which a process, procedure, certification, contract etc. applies. For example, the scope of change management may include all live IT services and related configuration items; the scope of an ISO/IEC 20000 certificate may include all IT services delivered out of a named data centre.

security

See information security management.

security management

See information security management.

security management information system (SMIS)

(*ITIL Service Design*) A set of tools, data and information that is used to support information security management. The security management information system is part of the information security management system. *See also* service knowledge management system.

security policy

See information security policy.

separation of concerns (SoC)

An approach to designing a solution or IT service that divides the problem into pieces that can be solved independently. This approach separates what is to be done from how it is to be done.

server

(*ITIL Service Operation*) A computer that is connected to a network and provides software functions that are used by other computers.

service

A means of delivering value to customers by facilitating outcomes customers want to achieve without the ownership of specific costs and risks. The term 'service' is sometimes used as a synonym for core service, IT service or service package. *See also* utility; warranty.

service acceptance criteria (SAC)

(*ITIL Service Transition*) A set of criteria used to ensure that an IT service meets its functionality and quality requirements and that the IT service provider is ready to operate the new IT service when it has been deployed. *See also* acceptance.

service asset

Any resource or capability of a service provider. *See also* asset.

service asset and configuration management (SACM)

(*ITIL Service Transition*) The process responsible for ensuring that the assets required to deliver services are properly controlled, and that accurate and reliable information about those assets is available when and where it is needed. This information includes details of how the assets have been configured and the relationships between assets. *See also* configuration management system.

service capacity management (SCM)

(*ITIL Continual Service Improvement*) (*ITIL Service Design*) The sub-process of capacity management responsible for understanding the performance and capacity of IT services. Information on the resources used by each IT service and the pattern of usage over time are collected, recorded and analysed for use in the capacity plan. *See also* business capacity management; component capacity management.

service catalogue

(*ITIL Service Design*) (*ITIL Service Strategy*) A database or structured document with information about all live IT services, including those available for deployment. The service catalogue is part of the service portfolio and contains information about two types of IT service: customer-facing services that are visible to the business; and supporting services required by the service provider to deliver customer-facing services. *See also* customer agreement portfolio; service catalogue management.

service catalogue management

(*ITIL Service Design*) The process responsible for providing and maintaining the service catalogue and for ensuring that it is available to those who are authorized to access it.

service change

See change.

service charter

(*ITIL Service Design*) (*ITIL Service Strategy*) A document that contains details of a new or changed service. New service introductions and significant service changes are documented in a charter and authorized by service portfolio management. Service charters are passed to the service design lifecycle stage where a new or modified service design package will be created. The term charter is also used to describe the act of authorizing the work required by each stage of the service lifecycle with respect to the new or changed service. *See also* change proposal; service portfolio; service catalogue.

service continuity management

See IT service continuity management.

service culture

A customer-oriented culture. The major objectives of a service culture are customer satisfaction and helping customers to achieve their business objectives.

service design

(*ITIL Service Design*) A stage in the lifecycle of a service. Service design includes the design of the services, governing practices, processes and policies required to realize the service provider's strategy and to facilitate the introduction of services into supported environments. Service design includes the following processes: design coordination, service catalogue management, service level management, availability management, capacity management, IT service continuity management, information security management, and supplier management. Although these processes are associated with service design, most processes have activities that take place across multiple stages of the service lifecycle. *See also* design.

service design package (SDP)

(*ITIL Service Design*) Document(s) defining all aspects of an IT service and its requirements through each stage of its lifecycle. A service design package is produced for each new IT service, major change or IT service retirement.

service desk

(*ITIL Service Operation*) The single point of contact between the service provider and the users. A typical service desk manages incidents and service requests, and also handles communication with the users.

service failure analysis (SFA)

(*ITIL Service Design*) A technique that identifies underlying causes of one or more IT service interruptions. Service failure analysis identifies opportunities to improve the IT service provider's processes and tools, and not just the IT infrastructure. It is a time-constrained, project-like activity, rather than an ongoing process of analysis.

service hours

(*ITIL Service Design*) An agreed time period when a particular IT service should be available. For example, 'Monday–Friday 08:00 to 17:00 except public holidays'. Service hours should be defined in a service level agreement.

service improvement plan (SIP)

(*ITIL Continual Service Improvement*) A formal plan to implement improvements to a process or IT service.

service knowledge management system (SKMS)

(*ITIL Service Transition*) A set of tools and databases that is used to manage knowledge, information and data. The service knowledge management system includes the configuration management system, as well as other databases and information systems. The service knowledge management system includes tools for collecting, storing, managing, updating, analysing and presenting all the knowledge, information and data that an IT service provider will need to manage the full lifecycle of IT services. *See also* knowledge management.

service level

Measured and reported achievement against one or more service level targets. The term is sometimes used informally to mean service level target.

service level agreement (SLA)

(*ITIL Continual Service Improvement*) (*ITIL Service Design*) An agreement between an IT service provider and a customer. A service level agreement describes the IT service, documents service level targets, and specifies the responsibilities of the IT service provider and the customer. A single agreement may cover multiple IT services or multiple customers. *See also* operational level agreement.

service level management (SLM)

(*ITIL Service Design*) The process responsible for negotiating achievable service level agreements and ensuring that these are met. It is responsible for ensuring that all IT service management processes, operational level agreements and underpinning contracts are appropriate for the agreed service level targets. Service level management monitors and reports on service levels, holds regular service reviews with customers, and identifies required improvements.

service level package (SLP)

See service option.

service level requirement (SLR)

(*ITIL Continual Service Improvement*) (*ITIL Service Design*) A customer requirement for an aspect of an IT service. Service level requirements are based on business objectives and used to negotiate agreed service level targets.

service level target

(*ITIL Continual Service Improvement*) (*ITIL Service Design*) A commitment that is documented in a service level agreement. Service level targets are based on service level requirements, and are needed to ensure that the IT service is able to meet business objectives. They should be SMART, and are usually based on key performance indicators.

service lifecycle

An approach to IT service management that emphasizes the importance of coordination and control across the various functions, processes and systems necessary to manage the full lifecycle of IT services. The service lifecycle approach considers the strategy, design, transition, operation and continual improvement of IT services. Also known as service management lifecycle.

service management

A set of specialized organizational capabilities for providing value to customers in the form of services.

service manager

A generic term for any manager within the service provider. Most commonly used to refer to a business relationship manager, a process manager or a senior manager with responsibility for IT services overall.

service model

(*ITIL Service Strategy*) A model that shows how service assets interact with customer assets to create value. Service models describe the structure of a service (how the configuration items fit together) and the dynamics of the service (activities, flow of resources and interactions). A service model can be used as a template or blueprint for multiple services.

service operation

(*ITIL Service Operation*) A stage in the lifecycle of a service. Service operation coordinates and carries out the activities and processes required to deliver and manage services at agreed levels to business users and customers. Service operation also manages the technology that is used to deliver and support services. Service operation includes the following processes: event management, incident management, request fulfilment, problem management, and access management. Service operation also includes the following functions: service desk, technical management, IT operations management, and application management. Although these processes and functions are associated with service operation, most processes and functions have activities that take place across multiple stages of the service lifecycle. *See also* operation.

service option

(*ITIL Service Design*) (*ITIL Service Strategy*) A choice of utility and warranty offered to customers by a core service or service package. Service options are sometimes referred to as service level packages.

service owner

(*ITIL Service Strategy*) A role responsible for managing one or more services throughout their entire lifecycle. Service owners are instrumental in the development of service strategy and are responsible for the content of the service portfolio. *See also* business relationship management.

service package

(*ITIL Service Strategy*) Two or more services that have been combined to offer a solution to a specific type of customer need or to underpin specific business outcomes. A service package can consist of a combination of core services, enabling services and enhancing services. A service package provides a specific level of utility and warranty. Customers may be offered a choice of utility and warranty through one or more service options. *See also* IT service.

service pipeline

(*ITIL Service Strategy*) A database or structured document listing all IT services that are under consideration or development, but are not yet available to customers. The service pipeline provides a business view of possible future IT services and is part of the service portfolio that is not normally published to customers.

service portfolio

(*ITIL Service Strategy*) The complete set of services that is managed by a service provider. The service portfolio is used to manage the entire lifecycle of all services, and includes three categories: service pipeline (proposed or in development), service catalogue (live or available for deployment), and retired services. *See also* customer agreement portfolio; service portfolio management.

service portfolio management (SPM)

(*ITIL Service Strategy*) The process responsible for managing the service portfolio. Service portfolio management ensures that the service provider has the right mix of services to meet required business outcomes at an appropriate level of investment. Service portfolio management considers services in terms of the business value that they provide.

service provider

(*ITIL Service Strategy*) An organization supplying services to one or more internal customers or external customers. Service provider is often used as an abbreviation for IT service provider. *See also* Type I service provider; Type II service provider; Type III service provider.

service reporting

(*ITIL Continual Service Improvement*) Activities that produce and deliver reports of achievement and trends against service levels. The format, content and frequency of reports should be agreed with customers.

service request

(*ITIL Service Operation*) A formal request from a user for something to be provided – for example, a request for information or advice; to reset a password; or to install a workstation for a new user. Service requests are managed by the request fulfilment process, usually in conjunction with the service desk. Service requests may be linked to a request for change as part of fulfilling the request.

service sourcing

(*ITIL Service Strategy*) The strategy and approach for deciding whether to provide a service internally, to outsource it to an external service provider, or to combine the two approaches. Service sourcing also means the execution of this strategy. *See also* insourcing; internal service provider; outsourcing.

service strategy

(*ITIL Service Strategy*) A stage in the lifecycle of a service. Service strategy defines the perspective, position, plans and patterns that a service provider needs to execute to meet an organization's business outcomes. Service strategy includes the following processes: strategy management for IT services, service portfolio management, financial management for IT services, demand management, and business relationship management. Although these processes are associated with service strategy, most processes have activities that take place across multiple stages of the service lifecycle.

service transition

(*ITIL Service Transition*) A stage in the lifecycle of a service. Service transition ensures that new, modified or retired services meet the expectations of the business as documented in the service strategy and service design stages of the lifecycle. Service transition includes the following processes: transition planning and support, change management, service asset and configuration management, release and deployment management, service validation and testing, change evaluation, and knowledge management. Although these processes are associated with service transition, most processes have activities that take place across multiple stages of the service lifecycle. *See also* transition.

service validation and testing

(*ITIL Service Transition*) The process responsible for validation and testing of a new or changed IT service. Service validation and testing ensures that the IT service matches its design specification and will meet the needs of the business.

serviceability

(*ITIL Continual Service Improvement*) (*ITIL Service Design*) The ability of a third-party supplier to meet the terms of its contract. This contract will include agreed levels of reliability, maintainability and availability for a configuration item.

seven-step improvement process

(*ITIL Continual Service Improvement*) The process responsible for defining and managing the steps needed to identify, define, gather, process, analyse, present and implement improvements. The performance of the IT service provider is continually measured by this process and improvements are made to processes, IT services and IT infrastructure in order to increase efficiency, effectiveness and cost effectiveness. Opportunities for improvement are recorded and managed in the CSI register.

shift

(*ITIL Service Operation*) A group or team of people who carry out a specific role for a fixed period of time. For example, there could be four shifts of IT operations control personnel to support an IT service that is used 24 hours a day.

simulation modelling

(*ITIL Continual Service Improvement*) (*ITIL Service Design*) A technique that creates a detailed model to predict the behaviour of an IT service or other configuration item. A simulation model is often created by using the actual configuration items that are being modelled with artificial workloads or transactions. They are used in capacity management when accurate results are important. A simulation model is sometimes called a performance benchmark. *See also* analytical modelling; modelling.

single point of contact

(*ITIL Service Operation*) Providing a single consistent way to communicate with an organization or business unit. For example, a single point of contact for an IT service provider is usually called a service desk.

single point of failure (SPOF)

(*ITIL Service Design*) Any configuration item that can cause an incident when it fails, and for which a countermeasure has not been implemented. A single point of failure may be a person or a step in a process or activity, as well as a component of the IT infrastructure. *See also* failure.

SLAM chart

(*ITIL Continual Service Improvement*) A service level agreement monitoring chart is used to help monitor and report achievements against service level targets. A SLAM chart is typically colour-coded to show whether each agreed service level target has been met, missed or nearly missed during each of the previous 12 months.

SMART

(*ITIL Continual Service Improvement*) (*ITIL Service Design*) An acronym for helping to remember that targets in service level agreements and project plans should be specific, measurable, achievable, relevant and time-bound.

software asset management (SAM)

(*ITIL Service Transition*) The process responsible for tracking and reporting the use and ownership of software assets throughout their lifecycle. Software asset management is part of an overall service asset and configuration management process. This process is not described in detail within the core ITIL publications.

source

See service sourcing.

specification

A formal definition of requirements. A specification may be used to define technical or operational requirements, and may be internal or external. Many public standards consist of a code of practice and a specification. The specification defines the standard against which an organization can be audited.

stakeholder

A person who has an interest in an organization, project, IT service etc. Stakeholders may be interested in the activities, targets, resources or deliverables. Stakeholders may include customers, partners, employees, shareholders, owners etc. *See also* RACI.

standard

A mandatory requirement. Examples include ISO/IEC 20000 (an international standard), an internal security standard for Unix configuration, or a government standard for how financial records should be maintained. The term is also used to refer to a code of practice or specification published by a standards organization such as ISO or BSI. *See also* guideline.

standard change

(*ITIL Service Transition*) A pre-authorized change that is low risk, relatively common and follows a procedure or work instruction – for example, a password reset or provision of standard equipment to a new employee. Requests for change are not required to implement a standard change, and they are logged and tracked using a different mechanism, such as a service request. *See also* change model.

standard operating procedures (SOP)

(*ITIL Service Operation*) Procedures used by IT operations management.

standby

(*ITIL Service Design*) Used to refer to resources that are not required to deliver the live IT services, but are available to support IT service continuity plans. For example, a standby data centre may be maintained to support hot standby, warm standby or cold standby arrangements.

statement of requirements (SOR)

(*ITIL Service Design*) A document containing all requirements for a product purchase, or a new or changed IT service. *See also* terms of reference.

status accounting

(*ITIL Service Transition*) The activity responsible for recording and reporting the lifecycle of each configuration item.

strategic

(*ITIL Service Strategy*) The highest of three levels of planning and delivery (strategic, tactical, operational). Strategic activities include objective setting and long-term planning to achieve the overall vision.

strategic asset

(*ITIL Service Strategy*) Any asset that provides the basis for core competence, distinctive performance or sustainable competitive advantage, or which allows a business unit to participate in business opportunities. Part of service strategy is to identify how IT can be viewed as a strategic asset rather than an internal administrative function.

strategy

(*ITIL Service Strategy*) A strategic plan designed to achieve defined objectives.

strategy management for IT services

(*ITIL Service Strategy*) The process responsible for defining and maintaining an organization's perspective, position, plans and patterns with regard to its services and the management of those services. Once the strategy has been defined, strategy management for IT services is also responsible for ensuring that it achieves its intended business outcomes.

supplier

(*ITIL Service Design*) (*ITIL Service Strategy*) A third party responsible for supplying goods or services that are required to deliver IT services. Examples of suppliers include commodity hardware and software vendors, network and telecom providers, and outsourcing organizations. *See also* supply chain; underpinning contract.

supplier and contract management information system (SCMIS)

(*ITIL Service Design*) A set of tools, data and information that is used to support supplier management. *See also* service knowledge management system.

supplier management

(*ITIL Service Design*) The process responsible for obtaining value for money from suppliers, ensuring that all contracts and agreements with suppliers support the needs of the business, and that all suppliers meet their contractual commitments. *See also* supplier and contract management information system.

supply chain

(*ITIL Service Strategy*) The activities in a value chain carried out by suppliers. A supply chain typically involves multiple suppliers, each adding value to the product or service. *See also* value network.

support group

(*ITIL Service Operation*) A group of people with technical skills. Support groups provide the technical support needed by all of the IT service management processes. *See also* technical management.

support hours

(*ITIL Service Design*) (*ITIL Service Operation*) The times or hours when support is available to the users. Typically these are the hours when the service desk is available. Support hours should be defined in a service level agreement, and may be different from service hours. For example, service hours may be 24 hours a day, but the support hours may be 07:00 to 19:00.

supporting service

(*ITIL Service Design*) An IT service that is not directly used by the business, but is required by the IT service provider to deliver customer-facing services (for example, a directory service or a backup service). Supporting services may also include IT services only used by the IT service provider. All live supporting services, including those available for deployment, are recorded in the service catalogue along with information about their relationships to customer-facing services and other CIs.

SWOT analysis

(*ITIL Continual Service Improvement*) A technique that reviews and analyses the internal strengths and weaknesses of an organization and the external opportunities and threats that it faces. SWOT stands for strengths, weaknesses, opportunities and threats.

system

A number of related things that work together to achieve an overall objective. For example:

- A computer system including hardware, software and applications
- A management system, including the framework of policy, processes, functions, standards, guidelines and tools that are planned and managed together – for example, a quality management system
- A database management system or operating system that includes many software modules which are designed to perform a set of related functions.

system management

The part of IT service management that focuses on the management of IT infrastructure rather than process.

tactical

The middle of three levels of planning and delivery (strategic, tactical, operational). Tactical activities include the medium-term plans required to achieve specific objectives, typically over a period of weeks to months.

technical management

(*ITIL Service Operation*) The function responsible for providing technical skills in support of IT services and management of the IT infrastructure. Technical management defines the roles of support groups, as well as the tools, processes and procedures required.

technical support

See technical management.

terms of reference (TOR)

(*ITIL Service Design*) A document specifying the requirements, scope, deliverables, resources and schedule for a project or activity.

test

(*ITIL Service Transition*) An activity that verifies that a configuration item, IT service, process etc. meets its specification or agreed requirements. *See also* acceptance; service validation and testing.

test environment

(*ITIL Service Transition*) A controlled environment used to test configuration items, releases, IT services, processes etc.

third party

A person, organization or other entity that is not part of the service provider's own organization and is not a customer – for example, a software supplier or a hardware maintenance company. Requirements for third parties are typically specified in contracts that underpin service level agreements. *See also* underpinning contract.

threat

A threat is anything that might exploit a vulnerability. Any potential cause of an incident can be considered a threat. For example, a fire is a threat that could exploit the vulnerability of flammable floor coverings. This term is commonly used in information security management and IT service continuity management, but also applies to other areas such as problem and availability management.

threshold

The value of a metric that should cause an alert to be generated or management action to be taken. For example, 'Priority 1 incident not solved within four hours', 'More than five soft disk errors in an hour', or 'More than 10 failed changes in a month'.

throughput

(*ITIL Service Design*) A measure of the number of transactions or other operations performed in a fixed time – for example, 5,000 e-mails sent per hour, or 200 disk I/Os per second.

total cost of ownership (TCO)

(*ITIL Service Strategy*) A methodology used to help make investment decisions. It assesses the full lifecycle cost of owning a configuration item, not just the initial cost or purchase price. *See also* total cost of utilization.

total cost of utilization (TCU)

(*ITIL Service Strategy*) A methodology used to help make investment and service sourcing decisions. Total cost of utilization assesses the full lifecycle cost to the customer of using an IT service. *See also* total cost of ownership.

total quality management (TQM)

(*ITIL Continual Service Improvement*) A methodology for managing continual improvement by using a quality management system. Total quality management establishes a culture involving all people in the organization in a process of continual monitoring and improvement.

transaction

A discrete function performed by an IT service – for example, transferring money from one bank account to another. A single transaction may involve numerous additions, deletions and modifications of data. Either all of these are completed successfully or none of them is carried out.

transition

(*ITIL Service Transition*) A change in state, corresponding to a movement of an IT service or other configuration item from one lifecycle status to the next.

transition planning and support

(*ITIL Service Transition*) The process responsible for planning all service transition processes and coordinating the resources that they require.

trend analysis

(*ITIL Continual Service Improvement*) Analysis of data to identify time-related patterns. Trend analysis is used in problem management to identify common failures or fragile configuration items, and in capacity management as a modelling tool to predict future behaviour. It is also used as a management tool for identifying deficiencies in IT service management processes.

tuning

The activity responsible for planning changes to make the most efficient use of resources. Tuning is most commonly used in the context of IT services and components. Tuning is part of capacity management, which also includes performance monitoring and implementation of the required changes. Tuning is also called optimization, particularly in the context of processes and other non-technical resources.

Type I service provider

(*ITIL Service Strategy*) An internal service provider that is embedded within a business unit. There may be several Type I service providers within an organization.

Type II service provider

(*ITIL Service Strategy*) An internal service provider that provides shared IT services to more than one business unit. Type II service providers are also known as shared service units.

Type III service provider

(*ITIL Service Strategy*) A service provider that provides IT services to external customers.

underpinning contract (UC)

(*ITIL Service Design*) A contract between an IT service provider and a third party. The third party provides goods or services that support delivery of an IT service to a customer. The underpinning contract defines targets and responsibilities that are required to meet agreed service level targets in one or more service level agreements.

urgency

(*ITIL Service Design*) (*ITIL Service Transition*) A measure of how long it will be until an incident, problem or change has a significant impact on the business. For example, a high-impact incident may have low urgency if the impact will not affect the business until the end of the financial year. Impact and urgency are used to assign priority.

usability

(*ITIL Service Design*) The ease with which an application, product or IT service can be used. Usability requirements are often included in a statement of requirements.

use case

(*ITIL Service Design*) A technique used to define required functionality and objectives, and to design tests. Use cases define realistic scenarios that describe interactions between users and an IT service or other system.

user

A person who uses the IT service on a day-to-day basis. Users are distinct from customers, as some customers do not use the IT service directly.

user profile (UP)

(*ITIL Service Strategy*) A pattern of user demand for IT services. Each user profile includes one or more patterns of business activity.

utility

(*ITIL Service Strategy*) The functionality offered by a product or service to meet a particular need. Utility can be summarized as 'what the service does', and can be used to determine whether a service is able to meet its required outcomes, or is 'fit for purpose'. The business value of an IT service is created by the combination of utility and warranty. *See also* service validation and testing.

validation

(*ITIL Service Transition*) An activity that ensures a new or changed IT service, process, plan or other deliverable meets the needs of the business. Validation ensures that business requirements are met even though these may have changed since the original design. *See also* acceptance; qualification; service validation and testing; verification.

value chain

(*ITIL Service Strategy*) A sequence of processes that creates a product or service that is of value to a customer. Each step of the sequence builds on the previous steps and contributes to the overall product or service. *See also* value network.

value for money

An informal measure of cost effectiveness. Value for money is often based on a comparison with the cost of alternatives. *See also* cost benefit analysis.

value network

(*ITIL Service Strategy*) A complex set of relationships between two or more groups or organizations. Value is generated through exchange of knowledge, information, goods or services. *See also* partnership; value chain.

value on investment (VOI)

(*ITIL Continual Service Improvement*) A measurement of the expected benefit of an investment. Value on investment considers both financial and intangible benefits. *See also* return on investment.

variable cost

(*ITIL Service Strategy*) A cost that depends on how much the IT service is used, how many products are produced, the number and type of users, or something else that cannot be fixed in advance.

variance

The difference between a planned value and the actual measured value. Commonly used in financial management, capacity management and service level management, but could apply in any area where plans are in place.

verification

(*ITIL Service Transition*) An activity that ensures that a new or changed IT service, process, plan or other deliverable is complete, accurate, reliable and matches its design specification. *See also* acceptance; validation; service validation and testing.

version

(*ITIL Service Transition*) A version is used to identify a specific baseline of a configuration item. Versions typically use a naming convention that enables the sequence or date of each baseline to be identified. For example, payroll application version 3 contains updated functionality from version 2.

vision

A description of what the organization intends to become in the future. A vision is created by senior management and is used to help influence culture and strategic planning. *See also* mission.

vital business function (VBF)

(*ITIL Service Design*) Part of a business process that is critical to the success of the business. Vital business functions are an important consideration of business continuity management, IT service continuity management and availability management.

vulnerability

A weakness that could be exploited by a threat – for example, an open firewall port, a password that is never changed, or a flammable carpet. A missing control is also considered to be a vulnerability.

warm standby

See intermediate recovery.

warranty

(*ITIL Service Strategy*) Assurance that a product or service will meet agreed requirements. This may be a formal agreement such as a service level agreement or contract, or it may be a marketing message or brand image. Warranty refers to the ability of a service to be available when needed, to provide the required capacity, and to provide the required reliability in terms of continuity and security. Warranty can be summarized as 'how the service is delivered', and can be used to determine whether a service is 'fit for use'. The business value of an IT service is created by the combination of utility and warranty. *See also* service validation and testing.

work instruction

A document containing detailed instructions that specify exactly what steps to follow to carry out an activity. A work instruction contains much more detail than a procedure and is only created if very detailed instructions are needed.

workaround

(*ITIL Service Operation*) Reducing or eliminating the impact of an incident or problem for which a full resolution is not yet available – for example, by restarting a failed configuration item. Workarounds for problems are documented in known error records. Workarounds for incidents that do not have associated problem records are documented in the incident record.

workload

The resources required to deliver an identifiable part of an IT service. Workloads may be categorized by users, groups of users, or functions within the IT service. This is used to assist in analysing and managing the capacity, performance and utilization of configuration items and IT services. The term is sometimes used as a synonym for throughput.

Index

Index